Exploring Developmental Psychology

Exploring Developmental Psychology

FROM INFANCY TO ADOLESCENCE

Edited by

DAVID MESSER
Professor of Psychology, University of Hertfordshire
and
STUART MILLAR
Professor of Psychology, London Guildhall University

A member of the Hodder Headline Group
LONDON • SYDNEY • AUCKLAND
Co-published in the United States of America by
Oxford University Press Inc., New York

First published in Great Britain in 1999 by
Arnold, a member of the Hodder Headline Group,
338 Euston Road, London NW1 3BH

http://www.arnoldpublishers.com

Co-published in the United States of America by
Oxford University Press Inc.,
198 Madison Avenue, New York, NY 10016

British Library Cataloguing in Publication Data
A catalogue entry for this book is available from the British Library

Library of Congress Cataloging-in-Publication Data
A catalog entry for this book is available from the Library of Congress

ISBN 0 340 67683 3 (hb)
ISBN 0 340 67682 5 (pb)

1 2 3 4 5 6 7 8 9 10

Production Editor: Rada Radojicic
Production Controller: Sarah Kett
Cover Design: Julie Delf

Typeset by J&L Composition Ltd, Filey, North Yorkshire
Printed and bound in Great Britain by The Bath Press, Bath

What do you think about this book? Or any other Arnold title?
Please send your comments to feedback.arnold@hodder.co.uk

Contents

List of contributors

The Editors

Professor David Messer, University of Hertfordshire, UK

Professor Stuart Millar, London Guildhall University, UK

The Contributors

Dr Mike Anderson, University of Western Australia, Australia

Professor J. Gavin Bremner, University of Lancaster, UK

Dr Charles K. Crook, University of Loughborough, UK

Professor Julie Dockrell, South Bank University, London, UK

Professor Dr Lutz H. Eckensberger, Deutsches Institut für Internationale Pädagogische Forschung, Germany

Dr Nicola Grove, City University, London, UK

Professor Leo B. Hendry, University of Aberdeen, UK and Norwegian University of Science and Technology, Norway

Professor Mark H. Johnson, Birkbeck College, University of London, UK

Dr Marion Kloep, Norwegian University of Science and Technology, Norway

Dr Mark Meerum Terwogt, Free University, Amsterdam, The Netherlands

Professor David Messer, University of Hertfordshire, UK

Professor Rod Nicolson, University of Sheffield, UK

Dr Ann Phoenix, Psychology Discipline, Faculty of Social Science, Open University, UK

Dr Alison Pike, University of Surrey, UK

Dr Karen Pine, University of Hertfordshire, UK

Professor Robert Plomin, Institute of Psychiatry, London, UK

Professor Stuart D. Powell, University of Hertfordshire, UK

Dr Carlo Schuengel, Leiden University, The Netherlands

Pamela M. Smith, University of Hertfordshire, UK

Katherine Stanford, University of Hertfordshire, UK

Dr Howard Steele, University College London, UK

Dr Miriam Steele, University College London and the Anna Freud Centre, UK

Dr Hedy Stegge, Free University, Amsterdam, The Netherlands

Professor Marinus H. van IJzendoorn, Leiden University, The Netherlands

Professor Dieter Wolke, University of Hertfordshire, UK

Professor Anne Woollett, University of East London, UK

Preface

University teaching in all disciplines is now receiving more intense scrutiny than ever before. This comes from both external monitoring of quality and from internal pressures as students, who increasingly have a financial stake in their own education, are more vocal in their demands. Furthermore, in some countries such as Great Britain, there has been a rapid expansion in student numbers which has not been accompanied by a corresponding increase in resources. Coupled with these pressures there is a more general concern within the whole of education that 'standards are slipping'.

These widespread changes make it particularly important that students have access to text books which enable them to go beyond a superficial examination of their subject. There is increasing emphasis given to the need for graduates to think in an independent and critical manner, and some would argue that these are the most important aspects of university education. These abilities are difficult to foster when using texts that over-simplify complex issues. In the past, for our own lecture courses, we have shied away from recommending text books as sources of additional information, despite demands from students. We did not recommend text books, despite their availability, because most did not provide the focus and level of detail that students require. The text books could not provide a backup and expansion to lecture material, or provide a basis for essay writing and exam revision. Rather than recommend text books we suggested sources which would take students beyond a cursory knowledge base to an appreciation of current research findings, to provide them with the material necessary to write about and discuss an issue. The recommended reading for our courses were review chapters and individual articles from academic journals. In recommending more specialist chapters and journals to students we have tried to help them not merely learn facts about a particular topic, but develop the ability to think about complex issues. This policy was not without difficulty as students usually have limited access to these sources, and for part-time students there is the added difficulty of simply gaining access to a library.

Consequently, the primary motivation for this volume was the wish to provide students with a Developmental Psychology text with a distinct and different content. We wanted students to be able to go to one source to obtain the information needed for the understanding of a wide range of current issues and perspectives in this subject. Our aim was to provide a knowledge base about developmental psychology and information about current research findings and perspectives. We also wanted to have a format which could help students think about these matters in a critical manner. We are confident that from such a base it will be possible for students to learn about developmental psychology, but appreciate its scope and at the same time advance their own thinking.

As our text could not hope to cover all the topics that are the concern of developmental psychology we were presented with the challenge of deciding which topics to include. Even with the comparative luxury of having 21 chapters this was still a difficult matter to resolve. In the end we chose one set of topics which are both well established within developmental psychology and continue to be a focus of research effort (e.g. infant cognition, language development, attachment, intelligence, moral development, family functioning, and adolescence). In other cases we selected issues which have recently attracted attention at conferences and in journals or been the focus of discussion among colleagues (these topics include behavioural genetics, developmental neuroscience, children's drawing, current psychoanalytic views, emotional development, bullying, cultural perspectives, and personal growth in a multicultural society). We also wanted to pay special attention to atypical development and development in special circumstances because of the importance and general interest of these matters. This concern is reflected in the content of many chapters, and by the inclusion of chapters which have specific concerns with dyslexia, sensory impairments, cognitive impairments, and autism.

The individual chapters are written by experts in their field. Consequently, one of the distinctive features of this text is that each contributor brings their own perspective. The benefits of this is that one can start to see developmental psychology from a number of different viewpoints and from different international perspectives. This approach has avoided the blandness of some single authored text books as it provides contributors with the opportunity to convey their enthusiasm about their area of interest and have a complete chapter to discuss their particular topic. Furthermore, we believe that an understanding of a range of perspectives can help students in a number of ways. It can result in a more comprehensive view that is based on an appreciation of the diversity of psychology processes involved in development. The exposure to these perspectives also provides students with different interpretations of the developmental process.

The book adopts a topic-based approach within a chronological framework. A topic-based approach has the advantage of allowing lecturers and students to select the issues which are relevant to their concerns, as it is not necessary to read the chapters in a particular order. The chapters are organized into five sections. The sequence is not a strictly chronological one, as such an order is difficult to maintain with a topic based approach. The first section concerns Life Processes and Infancy. The first two chapters of the section deal with fundamental issues about the biological basis of behaviour – genetics and neuroscience. The remaining chapters of the section are focused on issues directly connected with infancy – cognition, language and attachment. The second section is devoted to a major topic in Developmental Psychology, that of cognitive and representational growth. The chapters in this section provide: a general overview of major theories of development; an examination of children's drawing; a discussion of the topic of intelligence and finally an examination of the cognitive processes involved in reading. The next section considers Atypical Development and Development in Special Circumstances. There are three chapters exclusively concerned with this issue (many other chapters also make reference to the issue). The three chapters in this section deal with the subjects of sensory impairments, cognitive impairments and there is a specific chapter devoted to autism. The largest section of the book is devoted to Interpersonal Processes: Others and their Influence. Here there are a range of issues and perspectives which are considered; from the first chapter of the section, which is concerned with psychoanalytic perspectives about the consequences of relationships between infants and their mothers, to the last chapter of the section which contains arguments about the importance of taking account of wider cultural influences on development. The remaining chapters in the section review emotional development, socio-moral development, and families and their role. The final section of the book is concerned with issues about children's progress Towards Adulthood, and the influences on this process. There is first an examination of whether in today's society adolescence is an important life phase, then an examination of the risks and challenges of adolescence and finally a discussion of personal growth with a particular reference to racialized identities in multicultural societies.

We anticipate that this text book will be particularly useful to those courses in which students are expected to go beyond the lectures to access supplementary reading which consolidates and extends their understanding. For this reason, our textbook includes a number of devices designed to help independent study and to assist self-directed learning. Editorial prefaces draw attention to general connections with other chapters and specific links are made within the text of the chapter. This allows comparisons of different perspectives and enables students to broaden their understanding of a subject by pursuing more individual study plans. The chapters contain 'boxes' which provide additional information or material of special interest, along with figures and tables. The inclusion of discussion points within chapters are designed to encourage students to reflect on issues and to relate research findings to their own experiences, by reviewing what they have read, and by asking them to think about disagreements between investigators. Seminar questions at the end of the chapter serve a similar function, but in this case are designed to address broader issues in terms of the content of the chapter or provide examples of the types of questions which might occur in an exam. Recommendations for further reading are provided at the end of the chapter to enable students to pursue a self-directed course of independent study. This type of independent study can be complemented by consulting a companion volume which provides a set of original articles to extend study and revision – *Developmental Psychology: A Reader* edited by David Messer and Julie Dockrell (Arnold, 1998). The reader contains recommendations about study and revision strategies as well as introductory sections which set the individual papers in context.

Editing this book has been an exciting enterprise. And at this point, we need to mention our gratitude to all the contributors for their tolerance of our suggestions and for the hard work they have put into writing their chapters. Thanks also to Naomi Meredith who initiated this project and to Christina Wipf Perry and Elena Seymenliyska at our publishers, Edward Arnold, for their support and patience. Like most enterprises the editorial process has had its highs (and lows). The highpoints have been learning about new research findings and broadening and deepening our own knowledge about the range of perspectives in developmental psychology. There also has been satisfaction derived from assisting contributors to develop better ways to present information about their area of expertise. In addition, there has been the real reward of seeing the contents of the book grow in size and stature. We and the contributors have done our thinking for this text, now it's your turn.

David Messer
Stuart Millar

Introduction

The study of developmental psychology – issues and questions

Knowledge about the process of psychological development has many applications and it can touch many aspects of our lives. For example, educational and clinical psychologists work with children who have been identified as having some form of difficulty. Here the findings of developmental psychology can provide background information about typical development, provide information about the characteristics of certain syndromes, suggest methods of assessment and suggest methods of intervention. Developmental psychology can also be relevant to health professionals who need information about children and developmental processes to enable them to go beyond the medical concerns with illness. Developmental psychology is also of relevance to those who teach by providing a richer understanding of the process of learning and of the different influences on children's progress. And, of course, developmental psychology is relevant to parents, caregivers and those who come into regular contact with children by providing a source of knowledge about something that is usually a major part of their lives.

Many of us know about the broad features of human development from our own personal experience, but we usually need to be concerned about whether this knowledge can usefully be applied to all children. Most of us also have ideas about what factors influence development and some type of 'theory' about the mechanisms of these processes. However, such theories are usually based on fitting ideas to somewhat unsystematic observations. Developmental psychology seeks to remedy this situation by providing information about the growth of a whole range of abilities ranging from motor movements to language. In addition, it aims to construct theories about the way that growth takes place. Thus, developmental psychology can be characterized as asking two basic questions: does an ability change with age? and how do these changes come about?

Obtaining an answer to the first question usually involves describing the increase in abilities as individuals become older. Such descriptive information has often provided a basis for a more detailed understanding of why developments take place. As a result, although these two basic questions are logically separable, often they are both addressed in psychological investigations. It seems almost inevitable that a description of development raises questions about why this development takes place, and about what is the precise nature of the increase in abilities.

The second question concerning the reasons why this development takes place is a far more difficult one to answer. Indeed, some would maintain that we still do not have a very good understanding of the mechanisms of psychological development. Development involves the contradictory ideas of change and continuity. If there was no change then we would not consider development to have taken place. The changes from an egg to a caterpillar, to a chrysalis, and then to a butterfly are dramatic, but most of us are happy to accept this as continuous development – because we know that the same individual continues to go through all these changes and perhaps because we know that there are complex biological processes which enable these changes to take place. However, it is also the case that there is a marked discontinuity in the development from egg to butterfly. Thus, for someone interested in development there are questions of whether influences on the animal when it was a caterpillar also has consequences for the animal when it is a butterfly, and there are questions about whether the characteristics of one stage of development influence progress at later stages.

A further example may help to clarify these points. In the case of IQ scores there can be a change in ability; so that as a child becomes older she is able to correctly answer more items of an IQ test. However, there may (or may not) also be continuity in ability. Continuity would involve a child who has high IQ scores at one age and also has high scores at another age. Interestingly, it is unusual for psychological characteristics to be highly predictable from one age to another (IQ scores are one of the most predictable characteristics of children, *see* Chapter 8), and in this sense discontinuity rather than continuity is a feature of child development. The lack of high predictability across ages also suggests that there are many complex processes which influence development and suggests that often the course of the life path is not closely constrained by characteristics at one particular age.

Previous questions and debates about development

Many of the debates about development have been concerned, in some form or another, with whether development is the result of experience or the result of our inherited abilities. This is often known as the nature–nurture debate, or the opposition of empiricist and nativist. We have evidence from early civilizations that people were interested in the origins of abilities such as language. For example, it is reported that an Egyptian pharaoh isolated children from other people to try to discover what language they would speak, this may be one of the earliest examples of an investigation of child development.

Another related example, comes from the writings of St Augustine who discusses the way children are able to use information from the environment to understand the speech they hear:

> 'when they (my elders) named some object, and accordingly moved towards something, I saw this and I grasped that the thing was called by the sound they uttered when they meant to point it out. Their intention was shewn by their bodily movements, as it were the natural languages of all peoples: the expression of the face, the play of the eyes' (translated in Wittgenstein, 1958).

and these claims of St Augustine are still quoted in discussions about the way children acquire language.

Interestingly the philosophical discussions of nature and nurture during the 'age of enlightenment' provide examples of the more extreme positions in this debate. John Locke (1632–1704) believed that children's minds were a *tabula rasa* (Latin for a blank slate) on which experience would write and be the most powerful influence on development. Another significant figure in discussions about development is Roussou (1712–1778). He believed the essential goodness of children could be influenced by experience, and his ideas represented a move away from the extreme positions of empiricists and nativists. All these discussions were primarily of a theoretical nature, not involving empirical studies.

In contrast, some of the work of the nineteenth century provides examples of careful observations that were linked to theory. Charles Darwin's detailed observations of emotions in animals and humans provided a basis for his discussion about their development (*see* Chapter 14). The ideas of Freud also had a basis in data collection, but in this instance it involved case notes about the recollections of clinical patients (*see* Chapter 13). Freud's work drew attention to the importance of the experiences of childhood in the formation of adult characteristics while also proposing basic mechanisms of the mind that are common to the human race. Much of his theorizing was carried out without direct observations of children.

Another emphasis on data collection came from the work of Binet (1857–1911) who was responsible for the first intelligence test for children (*see* chapters 7 and 8). The test originated from concerns about identifying children who were not making good progress in French schools so that other provision could be made for them. At about the same time G Stanley Hall (1844–1924) was influential in drawing attention to the need for research into child development and as a result he is often seen as the founding father of modern developmental psychology. His contribution was to emphasize the scientific approach to data collection. This legacy has remained with us, although his theories have not provided such a lasting influence. Another important figure in the development of tests was Arnold Gesell (1856–1961) who wanted to chart the milestones of early infant development as a way of documenting the maturation of innate characteristics. Considerable effort was spent by him and his colleagues in testing and documenting the early capacities of children.

Between the 1930s and 1950s much of the theorizing in Great Britain and the USA was based on ideas concerning the way that reinforcement (i.e. a reward) is the basis for the learning of new abilities. Rewards increase the frequency of behaviour, whereas punishment decreases the frequency of behaviour. The ideas and approach of John B Watson (1878–1958) provided a foundation for behaviourism and for learning theory. Behaviourism focused on observable events (i.e. behaviour) and sought to eliminate descriptions of unobservable mental processes from psychological discussions. Learning theory was influenced by behaviourism and as a result concentrated on the relation between environmental stimuli and behavioural responses. By collecting data about observable behaviour, and by ignoring unobservable mental processes it was hoped to make psychology into a science similar to chemistry or physics.

BF Skinner was a leading exponent of learning theory and also applied these ideas to development. By shaping the responses of animals to produce complex behaviours (such as two pigeons 'playing' ping pong) Skinner indicated that reinforcement could be responsible for the learning of complex new skills. However, although learning theory can explain many of our activities, it does not provide a satisfactory explanation of many other developmental processes. This became apparent when Skinner tried to use the theoretical principles of learning theory to explain language acquisition.

Chomsky's (1959) dismissal of Skinner's account of the acquisition of language was a significant critique which was part of a general reaction against learning theory. Essentially Chomsky argued that the ability to use language is not the result of associations formed by reinforcement, but the result of acquiring grammatical rules. Furthermore, he argued that these grammatical rules were the result of innate predispositions (*see* Chapter 4). Another significant finding which fuelled the reaction against learning theory was the work of Harlow (1958) who showed that the attachment of infant monkeys was not based on the availability of the basic reinforcements such as food (*see* Chapter 5). Schaffer and Emerson (1964) extended this perspective when they reported that infants often develop attachment on the basis of play and interaction, rather than food and basic caregiving. From a different perspective, Bandura's (1973) findings about the effectiveness of observational learning also provided a further attack on human behaviour being the result of simple processes of reinforcement.

During this time researchers in Great Britain and the USA were also becoming better informed about the work of Piaget (1896–1980) and Vygotsky (1896–1934). Both theoreticians had already rejected learning theory, and these ideas found a receptive audience. As is discussed in chapters 3, 6 and 15 (among others), Piaget has had a lasting influence on developmental psychology by providing a comprehensive theoretical model of cognitive development and by carrying out observations to support this theory. His legacy is still with us, and although many of his ideas and observations are questioned he remains a pivotal figure in the growth of this subject. A strength of his approach was that he believed that children actively constructed their knowledge of the world, in contrast to learning theory which seemed to suggest children were passive recipients of information. Furthermore, educationalists found these ideas attractive as they provided arguments for more flexible, child-centred learning.

Another major theorist has been Vygotsky whose ideas still have a strong influence on current discussions (*see* chapters 6 and 18). Vygosky's socio-cultural theory has appealed to those who believe that social interaction and culture provide the basis for human learning and development. From this perspective, psychological development is not an individual struggle with facts and concepts. Instead development can be facilitated by adults or peers who help children develop new understanding. Particularly important is the idea of children learning through co-operative interactions which involve the support of other individuals. Such interactions help the child make new insights and construct new views about the world. In addition, Vygostky gave emphasis to the way that human culture provides tools to assist development. Consequently, the process of instructions by others enables cultural knowledge and adaptations to the environment to be transmitted from one generation to another. The most obvious of all such cultural tools is language, but we also have culturally defined systems for many aspects of our lives, such as counting and graphical representation (*see* chapters 7 and 18). For Vygotsky, language enabled the development of thinking while also reflecting aspects of the culture in which children grow up. This idea has been developed by those working in the 'cultural-context' framework who believe that biological and environmental influences are mediated by the particular culture in which a child is developing.

The theories of Piaget and Vygotsky are similar as they regarded children as being active rather than passive agents in their own development. According to this viewpoint children are not like a sponge, merely passively absorbing information from the environment. Instead they take in information and process it in relation to their existing cognitive structures, and in some circumstances these structures will change because of the information that is provided.

A related viewpoint is that children have an influence on those around them. A paper by Robert Bell (1968) drew attention to the misguided assumption present in much of developmental psychology at the time, the assumption that most of the influence between caregivers and children is from the caregiver to the child. Bell argued that children have a powerful influence on parents and their own own environment (*see* Chapter 1 for a more recent examination of this issue). These ideas have been taken further by Arnold Sameroff (1975; 1990) in his transaction model of development. This involves development being seen as a continuous process of mutual influence between child and environment. For example, the characteristics of a baby can influence her environment (if she cries a lot her parent may feel less like playing with her), but at the same time the characteristics of the environment can influence the baby (it might be an environment which makes the baby less likely to cry). Thus, these two sets of mutual influence affect the development of the baby and her environment (*see* Figure 1).

The last 20–30 years have seen a considerable expansion of research concerned with developmental psychology. Major conferences attract several thousand delegates who present and listen to research findings. This expansion has resulted in tensions between the need for general theories of development and specific explanations which can be used for the phenomena under investigation. Today there are no theories which dominate thinking about developmental processes as was the case with Piaget. Instead, each area uses theories and investigative procedures which suit the topic under investigation. After all there are many different levels of explanation of developmental phenomena ranging from genetic (Chapter 1), and neurophysiological (Chapter 2) to those that focus on cognitive or social processes (chapters 6 and 15), and to others which are concerned with the wider impact of society as a whole (Chapter 21).

The growth in research into child development has also raised questions about whether the whole of adult life should be seen from a developmental perspective. An influential figure who brought this issue to prominence was Erikson (1976) who proposed that there are eight stages of psychosocial development across the life-span. Another important figure has been Baltes (1999) who has emphasized the need for a 'life-span' developmental perspective. Such viewpoints also raise questions about whether increasing age always is accompanied by development. One example of this is the change in the elderly, where there may be a decline in some abilities, thereby suggesting that increasing age does not inevitably result in development.

Methods used in developmental psychology

The methodologies used in psychology range from observational case studies of individuals to the use of controlled experimental investigations.

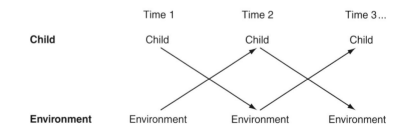

Figure 1 A summary of Sameroff's Transactional Model.

The important principle linking this range of techniques is that investigations should be able to be replicated so that there can be challenges to findings about which there is controversy and doubt. When considering the range of ways of investigating children's development it is useful to think about *when* individuals are studied, *where* they are studied, as well as considering *how* they are studied.

INVESTIGATIONS: WHEN, WHERE AND HOW

If one is examining age-related changes then the two most obvious ways of finding out about this are to either use a cross-sectional or a longitudinal design. A cross-sectional study design involves seeing different groups of children at different ages. Thus, an investigator might go into a school and collect information about how good children aged five, seven and nine years are at remembering information. A longitudinal design would involve collecting data when the children were five years old, going back to the school to see the same children when they were seven years old, and then seeing them again when they were nine years old.

DISCUSSION POINT

What do you think are the advantages and disadvantages (both practical and in terms of the conclusions that can be drawn) of cross-sectional and longitudinal study designs?

One feature of cross-sectional designs is that there can be *cohort effects* when there are relatively large differences in experience between the age groups. A cohort effect occurs when these differences are not attributable to age, but to the different life circumstances of two age groups, for example the two groups of children may have been taught in different ways. Cohort effects can be avoided by use of a longitudinal design, but with this type of study there is usually *subject loss*, as some people move away or are not willing to take part in the study. Often these individuals are not typical of the whole population and this can, over time, result in a change in the characteristics of the sample. A well-known example of these two effects is that IQ in cross-sectional studies is usually found to decline with age (probably due to cohort effects such as type of schooling or nutrition), whereas IQ tends to rise in longitudinal studies (probably due to the less motivated and less able participants leaving the study).

In relation to these issues it should be remembered that not all investigators of development have based their studies on large groups of children. There have been a number of important longitudinal case studies, often conducted by one of the parents of the child. Some of Piaget's work is a famous example of this. These case studies have been valuable in giving a detailed description of changes and in raising questions about the process of development. However, such studies need to be interpreted with caution as there is uncertainty about the generality of findings obtained from one child.

Another important dimension on which investigations differ is in whether an experimental or non-experimental design is employed. In experiments there is a group of children who have an experience, and another group which does not receive this experience. The crucial element of the experiment is that children are randomly allocated to these two groups so that any differences can be attributed to the differences in experience. Such studies may take a few minutes to conduct, or years. These studies can identify whether experience has an effect on the children (i.e. whether there is a difference between the two groups of children). However, it is often the case that, for ethical reasons, it is not possible to randomly assign children to conditions. For example, it would not be ethical to ask mothers to breast feed their infants according to whether the baby was a member of an experimental or control group in order to investigate the effect of this on sleeping or IQ. Consequently, many investigations adopt what is variously termed a 'natural experiment', a 'quasi-experimental' design or a 'correlational design'. In such studies comparisons are usually made between children who do and do not receive an experience of some sort. However, because the children are not randomly assigned to conditions it is always possible that any difference is the result of some association between the variables which are of concern to the study. For example, in the case of breast feeding, mothers who do this tend to be middle class and better educated, and these latter characteristics are associated with earlier progress on a number of developmental measures. Thus, when examining the effect of breast feeding on cognitive development it is important to rule out confounding factors, such as social class, which could bias the results. In other words, these investigations do not allow one to be certain that a particular experience influences the development of children. However, if a number of different studies using different methods point to similar findings then such causal relations begin to be accepted by investigators.

Another problem in trying to work out the factors that influence development is that children are not necessarily passive recipients of the experiences provided by carers (*see* page xvii). For example, there has been interest in whether simplifications in speech to young children can help language acquisition (*see* Chapter 6). But there has been difficulty in answering this question because it is always possible that parents who produce the most simple speech may be responding to some characteristic of their child. As a result, non-experimental studies often need to consider whether the independent variable that is the focus of attention (e.g. maternal speech), could be influenced by the dependent variable (e.g. the child's cognitive or communicative ability).

Studies also vary according to the place where they are conducted. Some studies are conducted in a child's home, street or school. Other studies are conducted in laboratories which at first will be unfamiliar to the participants. The advantage of more naturalistic settings is that children are likely to feel more secure and relaxed, the disadvantage is that there will be differences across children in their homes, schools and streets, and this could in some circumstances affect the findings of an investigation. The opposite set of criticisms can be directed at laboratory settings. Children may not behave in their normal manner in the atypical surroundings of a laboratory, but at least the context can be standardized. Nor should one imagine that the issue is as clear-cut as this. Children might feel 'at home' in a laboratory where they have been carefully introduced to the people and settings, alternatively, in their own homes children might feel uncomfortable when there is an intrusive and insensitive investigator.

The actual process of data collection from children also involves a whole range of techniques. Direct observations of their behaviour can be made or their behaviour can be video recorded and subsequently coded. Often, observational studies are time-consuming and may involve a degree of subjective judgement on the part of the observer. Consequently, it is important to make sure that good inter-observer reliability can be obtained (whether different observers can agree about the way to code behaviour). Observational studies are not limited to 'natural' situations such as children's homes, but can also take place in laboratories. The ethological approach to investigating animal and human behaviour emphasizes the benefits of detailed observations in naturally occurring situations. An extension to this method of data collection, which is based on very different principles, is ethnographic observations (*see* Chapter 21). Here, the observer attempts to become part of the group that is being observed and evidence about the processes being investigated is derived from samples of conversation, observations of events and so on.

In some circumstances parents can be enlisted to help provide descriptions of behaviours as diverse as children's language and sleeping. These can be useful as parents will know more about their children's behaviour than investigators, but there can be problems with parental responses being influenced by social desirability or by a lack of objective evaluation. Data can also be collected by interviewing or administering questionnaires to children, with the obvious limitations being their language and literacy. In addition, psychologists have found to their cost that children do not always provide answers which reflect what they think. Children, partly because of their reliance on non-verbal cues when interpreting speech pay more attention to the context than to the content of the speech they hear. In addition, because of the power relation which makes it more likely that adults are 'right', children often give answers that they think the adult wants to hear and may use non-verbal cues to help them guess what is the correct answer. However, questionnaire studies, can be usefully employed with adolescents to obtain valuable information about their beliefs and attitudes (*see* chapters 19 to 21).

Given the number of these dimensions it should be apparent that there are many different techniques for investigating child development. The important point to bear in mind is that there can be many permutations, so that an experimental study does not have to take place in a laboratory, it may take place in a child's home and involve detailed observations of behaviour. In contrast, a non-experimental study may take place in the standardized situation provided by a laboratory. All research methods have advantages and disadvantages, and as a result the choice of a particular technique will usually be a matter of compromise.

The structure of this book

Developmental psychology has become such a vast enterprise that it has been impossible in this book to cover every topic in the detail that we would wish. As a result, our aim has been to select topics in developmental psychology which continue to attract attention and interest, and for these topics to ask an expert in the area to review the literature. Consequently, we have tended to place emphasis on depth rather than breadth. Despite this, virtually every contributor has had to struggle (and sometimes there has been a struggle with them!) to keep chapters to the appropriate length.

The book is organized into five sections. The first section concerns 'Life processes and infancy' and begins with a chapter on 'Genetics and development'. Recent advances in both biological and psychological research have resulted in a renewed interest in the way that genetics and environmental processes contribute to development. This fundamental issue about development makes the position of this chapter at the beginning of the book an appropriate one. The second chapter of this section, 'Developmental cognitive neuroscience', reflects important links between psychological and biological processes. In many ways developmental psychologists have neglected issues connected with physiological processes, hopefully the opportunities provided by new techniques of data collection and of conceptualizing development will remedy this situation. The following chapter ('Cognitive development in infancy') provides a detailed discussion of research which has been generated by Piaget's ideas about the way children understand their world and Gavin Bremner argues that Piaget's ideas still have a relevance for present day discussions. Infancy is not only a period when children show remarkable growth in their understanding of the physical world, but it is also marked by important advances in the ability to communicate with others and the advent of language, this is the topic of the fourth chapter of the section. Here there is a description of the development of communication from birth to the pre-school years and this involves a return to discussions of nature and nurture. Another remarkable change in the early years is the beginning of attachment relationships at about eight months of age, a topic reviewed by the last chapter of the section. The development of children's attachment to caregivers continues to attract considerable attention from researchers and carers. The chapter discusses the important methodological advances that have been made in the assessment of attachment and how this has provided the basis for the many investigations into the causes and consequences of different patterns of attachment. Interestingly, research on attachment processes is not limited to young children, research on this topic has extended to adulthood.

Part 2 concerns 'Cognitive and representational growth'. The section begins with a chapter which sets the scene for many of the subsequent ones by providing a clearly explained overview of the major theories about cognitive development, that is the way children's thinking changes and the way that their cognitive structures become more advanced. Some of these theories are also discussed in the following chapter 'Development of graphical representations'. The chapter shows the way both general and specific theories are useful in helping us to understand children's ability to draw images. The chapter also shows that this seemingly innocent activity can provide insights about children's thinking and the way they represent their world. The next chapter, 'Intelligence', concerns a topic which involves a different perspective to the previous chapters of the section. Studies of general cognitive development are usually concerned with the way that 'average' children make progress and are less concerned with differences between children. In contrast, studies of intelligence are usually concerned with individual differences. Here, the interest is in the best way to assess this characteristic, in the developmental continuity of this capacity and in the underlying processes which result in differences in intelligence. The final chapter of Part 2 discusses reading, a skill that involves both cognitive processes and representation. In today's society reading is an essential skill and the teaching of reading is never far from public and political discussion. The chapter provides a wide-ranging examination of the topic bringing together issues about perceptual and cognitive processes, as well as considering the topic of dyslexia.

The main focus of Part 2 was the development of typical children (the 'average' child), even so all the chapters mention the development of children who have disabilities or developmental difficulties. These are often referred to as 'atypical' children, this avoids the use of terms such as 'abnormal' or 'mentally retarded' which carry many negative associations. 'Atypical development and development in special circumstances' is the subject of Part 3 of the book. It begins with an examination of the development of children who have the sensory impairments of vision or hearing, and the findings that are presented show the remarkable adaptability of children and carers to these special circumstances. This is followed by a chapter which emphasizes the need to use a developmental perspective to think about children with cognitive impairments. The chapter considers both the general effects of cognitive impairments and the more specific effects of particular syndromes. One particular syndrome, that of autism, is the subject of the next chapter. Autism has attracted considerable research interest partly because of the claim that children with autism lack a 'theory of mind' (the ability to appreciate that others can have different beliefs and thoughts to themselves) and this capacity now occupies a central place in discussions about early child development.

Part 4, 'Beyond the self: others and their influence', is concerned with the interactions that children have with other people and the wider context of their development. The section starts with an overview of recent psychoanalytic views, and here emphasis is given to the way that interaction with others provides a basis for development. The chapter also highlights important cross-fertilization between this tradition and developmental psychology. The second chapter of this section, 'Emotional development', takes a different perspective and is concerned with the way that children express emotions to others, and come to understand their own emotions, as well as those of others. The third chapter of the section is devoted to a consideration of socio-moral development, and involves a discussion of the development of cognitive capacities which are used to reason about the behaviour of the self and others; here we also see that recent research is taking account of family and cultural issues in relation to moral reasoning. Obviously, one of the most important of all social groups for children is the family. The next chapter in this section provides an examination of the behavioural and psychological processes in families with a discussion of the role of the mother and that of other family members. Another social context which figures prominently in the lives of children is the school and while there is much that is positive in the school environment there are also negative aspects of interactions among pupils. One of these negative processes, that of bullying, provides the subject for the penultimate chapter of the section. The section concludes with a discussion of children's use of the electronic media, 'The uses and significance of electronic media during development'. This chapter makes valuable general points about the way we should think about developmental processes and the type of research questions that we should ask.

The final part of the book considers the transition to adulthood. It begins with a consideration of the usual tasks that face individuals as they make progress from childhood to adulthood. This is followed by a chapter which develops some of these themes by discussing the way that the tasks facing adolescents can be challenges or risks. The chapter concludes with a discussion of educational methods that could be used to reduce these risks. The final chapter of Part 5, and of the book, deals with new ideas about the process of personal growth, an issue which covers all times of the life-cycle, but which is particularly relevant to the period of adolescence. Ann Phoenix argues for the need to see the growth in personal identity as a dynamic non-deterministic process which is influenced by broad-features of the society in which an individual lives.

It is worth bearing in mind that a useful general source of original articles is the *Reader in Developmental Psychology* which has been produced to complement the topics considered in this text (Messer and Dockrell, 1998). This Reader also contains suggestions about what to look for when reading articles as well as general writing and revision strategies.

David Messer
Stuart Millar

Part 1

LIFE PROCESSES AND INFANCY

Genetics and development

1

ALISON PIKE AND ROBERT PLOMIN

Editors' preface

There has been a revolution in our understanding of the biological basis of genetics. For example there is a massive research programme to map the human genome and be able to specify which genes determine which characteristics. In addition, it is now a relatively routine process to be able to identify a particular person from samples of their DNA. Research 'firsts' from biochemical investigations are often in the news, and in a similar manner findings from behavioural genetic studies often make media headlines. This suggests that not only psychologists but also the general public are interested whether our behaviour is the result of genetics or our environment (*see also* the Introduction and Chapter 4).

The revolution in biochemical research has been accompanied by a renewed interest in the way psychological processes are determined by genetics. A major factor in generating this interest has been several large-scale studies of heredibility. These studies have calculated the relative contribution of genetics and environment in relation to psychological characteristics such as IQ (*see* Chapter 8) or even autism (*see* Chapter 12). This has been possible either by studying the development of identical twins or the development of children who have been adopted away from their parents. As Dr Alison Pike and Professor Robert Plomin stress in their chapter, most studies indicate that there is often a roughly equal contribution from both genetics and environment. Often there are heated discussions about genetic and environmental influences on human characteristics. This chapter provides a very useful basis to understand and have an informed opinion about these discussions.

This chapter considers how nature (genes) work with nurture (environment) to affect children's development. The biological mechanism of genetic transmission will not be a focus of this chapter, however, a brief discussion of the biology of inheritance is provided in Box 1.1. To appreciate the significance of findings and recent developments concerning nature and nurture, however, an understanding of behavioural genetic theory and methods is required, therefore we begin with a brief explanation of these. Next, are considered behavioural genetic results from two major domains, cognitive abilities and psychopathology. The remainder of the chapter is devoted to two new advances in the field, the specification of nonshared environmental influences and molecular genetics.

BOX 1.1   The biology of genetics and heredity

What does it mean to say that someone has inherited some physical feature or behavioural trait? The answer lies in genetics, the biology of inheritance. The story begins with the chemistry of the human body and with the chromosomes contained within each of its cells. Most human cells contain 46 chromosomes, arranged in 23 matching pairs. These **chromosomes** are long, thin structures that are made up of thousands of genes. **Genes** are the biochemical units of heredity that govern the development of an individual by controlling the synthesis of protein. They are composed of **deoxyribonucleic acid (DNA)** – strands of sugar, phosphate and nitrogen-containing molecules twisted around each other in a double spiral. It is the particular order in which the molecules are arranged in the DNA that determines, through the production of ribonucleic acid (RNA), which protein each gene will produce. Protein molecules, in turn, form the physical structure of each cell and also direct the activity of the cell. Thus, as a function of DNA, the genes contain a coded message that provides a blueprint for constructing every aspect of a physical human being, including eye colour, height, blood type, inherited disorders, and the like – and all in a space smaller than the full stop that ends this sentence.

New cells are constantly being produced by the division of existing cells. Most of the body's cells divide through a process called **mitosis**, in which the cell's chromosomes duplicate themselves, so that each new cell contains copies of the 23 pairs of chromosomes in the original. A different kind of cell division occurs when a male's sperm cells and a female's egg cells (called ova) are formed. This process is called **meiosis**. In meiosis, the chromosome pairs are not copied. Instead, they are randomly split and rearranged, leaving each new sperm and egg cell with just one member of each chromosome pair, or 23 single chromosomes. No two of these special new cells are quite the same, and none contains an exact copy of the person who produced it. So, at conception, when a male's sperm cell penetrates, or fertilizes, the female's ovum, a truly new cell is formed. This fertilized cell, called a zygote, carries 23 pairs of chromosomes – half of each pair from the mother and half from the father. Thus, the **zygote** represents a unique heritage, a complete genetic code for a new person that combines randomly selected aspects from both parents. The zygote divides first into copies of itself and then into the billions of specialized cells that form a new human being.

Whether genes express themselves in the individual who carries them depends on whether they are dominant or recessive. **Dominant** genes are outwardly expressed whenever they are present; **recessive** genes are expressed only when they are paired with a similar gene from the other parent. For example, phenylketonuria (PKU), a disorder seen in about 1 in 10 000 newborns – is caused by a recessive gene. When inherited from both parents, this gene disrupts the body's ability to control phenylalanine, an amino acid in milk and other foods. As a result, this acid is converted into a toxic substance that can cause severe mental retardation. (Discovery of this genetic defect made it possible to prevent retardation in PKU children simply by making sure they did not consume foods high in phenylalanine.) PKU is an example of a single-gene disorder, but relatively few human characteristics are controlled by just one gene. Most characteristics are **polygenic**, meaning that they are controlled by many genes. Even a person's eye colour and height are affected by more than one gene.

The genes contained in the 46 chromosomes inherited from the parents make up an individual's **genotype**. Because identical twins develop from one fertilized egg cell, they are described as monozygotic; they have exactly the same genotype. So, why don't all identical twins look exactly alike? Because they do not have the same **phenotype**. An individual's phenotype is the set of observable characteristics that result from the interaction of heredity and environment. Thus, in twins and non-twins alike, the way people actually look and act is influenced by the combination of genes they carry as well as by environmental factors – in other words, by both nature and nurture.

What is behavioural genetics?

Behavioural genetics is the study of nature and nurture. The theory postulates that behavioural differences among individuals in a population are due to genetic differences between people, and differences in their environmental experiences. Specifically, behavioural geneticists explore the origins of individual differences (i.e. differences between people) in complex behaviours, such as reading. It is as important to point out what behavioural genetics does *not* address, as well as what it does. For example, researchers may be interested in how, generally, children learn to read. This is a question concerning normative development and is not addressed by behavioural genetics. Similarly, many researchers are concerned with group differences (e.g. differences between boys and girls in reading ability), and again, behavioural genetic methods cannot answer such questions. Instead, the focus is on individual differences. Continuing the example, behavioural geneticists would argue that an important question is why some children have difficulty in reading, whereas others read without any trouble. It is worth noting that individual differences, though often ignored in psychological research, or merely thought of as 'error', are often of far greater magnitude than group differences.

Behavioural genetic methods

By use of behavioural genetic methods, variability for any given trait may be divided into three sources, **heritability**, **shared environment**, and **nonshared environment**. **Heritability** is defined as the amount of total variation in scores of a given trait that can be explained by genetic differences between people. Therefore, the heritability of reading ability refers to the proportion of variation in scores of reading ability originating from differences in people's genetic make-up. **Shared environment** refers to environmental influences that are shared by siblings reared in the same family and lead to sibling similarity (e.g. neighbourhood, parental attitudes). On the other hand, **nonshared environment** refers to aspects of the environment that are not shared by siblings and lead to differences between them (e.g. siblings' different peer groups, birth order). Further discussion of heritability, shared environment, and nonshared environment can be found in Box 1.2.

BOX 1.2　Understanding heritability, shared environment, and nonshared environment

Behavioural genetic studies indicate the relative contributions of **heritability**, **shared environment** and **nonshared environment**, although the contributions of these three to a characteristic are not directly assessed. Therefore, we may find that heritability accounts for one-third of the differences seen between people for a given trait, but this does not tell us which specific genes are involved. Similarly, finding that shared environment accounts for one-third of the variation would indicate that experiences siblings in a family have in common are responsible, but we don't know *what* those experiences are. Finally, finding nonshared environmental influence indicates that siblings are turning out differently from one another because of different experiences, but this does not pinpoint what these differing experiences are.

Heritability
For a single individual, both genetics and environment are indispensable – a person would not exist without both genes and environment. For example, the heritability of height is about 90 per cent, but this does not mean that you grow to 90 per cent of your height for reasons of heredity and that the other inches were added by the environment.

What it means is that most of the height differences among individuals are due to the genetic differences between them. Heritability is a statistic that describes the contribution of genetic differences to observed differences among individuals in a particular population at a particular time. A related point is that heritability describes *what is* in a particular population at a particular time rather than *what could be*. Therefore, if environmental factors within a population change (e.g. changes in educational opportunity) then the relative impact of genes and environment will change. Even for a highly heritable trait such as height, changes in the environment *could* make a big difference, for example, if an epidemic struck or if children's diets were altered. Indeed, the huge increase in height during this century is almost certainly a consequence of improved diet.

Shared and nonshared environment
Shared environmental influences are those experiences that cause sibling similarity, and we can guess that these experiences may include socio-economic status, parental attitudes, or neighbourhood factors, but with traditional behavioural genetic designs, we cannot know for sure. On the other hand, nonshared environmental influences cause siblings to be different from one another, and might include different friendship experiences, or different experiences at school, but these are only speculations. The nonshared environment can also include events or circumstances that are objectively 'shared' by siblings, such as their neighbourhood context, but which are interpreted differently by siblings, therefore rendering them as non-shared experiences. For example, an objectively crime-ridden neighbourhood may be interpreted as a dangerous, frightening place by one sibling, but as a community of like-minded peers by another.

Although behavioural geneticists are beginning to identify specific genes that are associated with behaviour, the classic methods are indirect quasi-experimental methods, such as twin and adoption studies. These methods estimate the relative contributions of genetic, shared and nonshared environmental influence of a given trait or behaviour. Studies in which family members (e.g. parents, siblings) are assessed provide indications of familial resemblance, but cannot disentangle this resemblance into its genetic and shared environmental sources.

DISCUSSION POINT

Why are studies of the similarity among family members only of limited help to behavioural geneticists?

Twin and adoption studies compare the similarity of family members of varying genetic relatedness, and estimate genetic and environmental contributions to specific traits. The twin method involves the comparison of resemblance between monozygotic (MZ) twin pairs and dizygotic (DZ) twin pairs. MZ twins are 100 per cent genetically similar (they are 'identical' genetically like clones), whereas dizygotic twins, like regular siblings, are only 50 per cent similar. Therefore, if genetic influence is important for a trait, MZ twins will be more similar than DZ twins. To the extent that twin similarity cannot be attributed to genetic factors, the shared environment is implicated. Finally, the extent to which MZ twins differ within pairs is accounted for by nonshared environmental factors.

Because identical twins are identical genetically and fraternal twins are 50 per cent similar genetically, the difference in their correlations reflects half of the genetic effect and is doubled to estimate heritability. For example, MZ twins correlate about 0.90 for height, and DZ twins about 0.45. Doubling the difference between these correlations yields a heritability estimate of 0.90 (2(0.90–0.45) = 0.90), suggesting substantial heritability for height (*see* Box 1.1). Shared environmental influence can be indirectly estimated from twin correlations by subtracting the heritability estimate from the MZ twin correlation. In this case the estimate is 0.0 (0.90–0.90 = 0.0). Nonshared environmental influence is estimated by subtracting the MZ twin correlation from 1.0 – yielding 0.10 in this case (1.0–0.90 = 0.10).

The other classic quantitative genetic design is the adoption design. Because adoptive siblings are unrelated genetically to other siblings in their adoptive family, the degree of similarity between these siblings is a direct index of shared environmental influences. That is, adoptive siblings do not share genes any more than pairs of randomly selected individuals, and so they only resemble one another because of shared environmental reasons. Heritability can also be estimated using the adoption design. In this case, non-adoptive (biological) siblings share 50 per cent of their genes, whereas adoptive siblings share 0 per cent of their genes. The difference in correlations between biological siblings and adoptive siblings reflects half of the genetic effect and is doubled to estimate heritability. Biological siblings correlate about 0.45 for height, and adoptive siblings are uncorrelated, 0.00. Doubling the difference between these correlations yields a heritability estimate of 0.90 (2(0.45–0.00) = 0.90), again suggesting substantial heritability for height. Finally, in adoption studies, nonshared environment is estimated to be that which is 'left over' after heritability and shared environment have been accounted for, i.e. 1.0–0.90 (heritability) – 0.00 (shared environment) = 0.10. Each design has its strengths and weaknesses; therefore it is the overall picture of results emerging from different studies that is important.

Results from traditional behavioural genetic studies

Traditional behavioural genetic studies have concentrated on the domains of cognitive abilities, personality and psychopathology. Due to space limitations, cognitive abilities and psychopathology only are considered here.

GENERAL COGNITIVE ABILITY

There are hundreds of different tests of cognitive ability, based on several different theories (see Anderson, this volume). Nearly all of the genetic research is based on the psychometric model, that considers cognitive abilities to be organized hierarchically (Carroll, 1993). We limit this review to studies that assess general cognitive ability, or g which is often assessed by intelligence (IQ) tests rather than studies of specific abilities such as verbal and spatial abilities (see a recent review by Plomin and DeFries, 1998).

First-degree relatives living together are moderately correlated for g (about 0.45). This resemblance could be due to genetic or to environmental influences, because such relatives share both. For g the correlation between children adopted away and their 'genetic' parents is 0.24 (Bouchard and McGue, 1981). The correlation between genetically related siblings reared apart is also 0.24. Because first-degree relatives are only 50 per cent similar genetically, doubling these correlations gives a rough estimate of heritability of 48 per cent.

The twin method supports this conclusion. Identical twins are nearly as similar as the same persons tested twice. The average twin correlations are 0.86 for monozygotic twins and 0.60 for dizygotic twins (Bouchard and McGue, 1981). Doubling the difference between MZ and DZ correlations estimates heritability at 52 per cent. Although heritability could differ in different cultures, so far it appears that the level of heritability of g applies not only to American and Western European countries, where most studies have been conducted, but also to twin studies in Russia (Lipovechaja et al., 1978), former East Germany (Weiss, 1982), Japan (Lynn and Hattori, 1990), urban India (Nathwat and Puri, 1995), and rural India (Pal et al., 1997).

If half of the variance of g can be attributed to genetic factors, the other half is accounted for by the environment. Some of this environmental influence is shared by family members. Model-fitting estimates of the role of shared environment for g are about 20 per cent for parents and offspring, about 25 per cent for siblings, and about 40 per cent for twins (Chipuer et al., 1990). Obviously, parents and offspring will share some aspects of the environment (e.g. socio-economic status) but twins will have a much greater degree of sharing. The remaining variance is attributed to non-shared environment and errors of measurement, which accounts for about 10 per cent of the variance.

During the past decade, however, it has been discovered that these average results differ dramatically across development. Genetic factors become increasingly important for g throughout the life span (McCartney et al., 1990). There is high heritability even in twins over 80 years old (McClearn et al., 1997). For example, the longitudinal Colorado Adoption Project (CAP) (DeFries et al., 1994) provides parent–offspring correlations for general cognitive ability from infancy through adolescence. Correlations between parents and children for non-adoptive families increase from less than 0.20 in infancy to about 0.20 in middle childhood and to about 0.30 in adolescence. The correlations between biological mothers and their adopted-away children follow a similar pattern, thus indicating that parent–offspring resemblance for g is due to genetic factors. Parent–offspring correlations for adoptive parents and their adopted children hover around zero. This study suggests that the family environment shared by parents and offspring does not contribute importantly to parent–offspring resemblance for g. The most likely explanation for this increase in heritability during the life-span is that relatively small genetic effects early in life snowball during development, creating larger and larger behavioural effects.

DISCUSSION POINT

How might population-wide changes in education affect the heritability of cognitive ability in childhood?

Another important developmental finding is that the effects of shared environment appear to decrease. The most impressive evidence for this comes from a 10-year longitudinal follow-up study of more than 200 pairs of adoptive siblings. At the average age of eight years, the IQ correlation was 0.26. This is similar to other studies of young adoptive siblings and suggests that the shared environment makes an important contribution to IQ at this age. Ten years later, their IQ correlation was near zero (Loehlin et al., 1989). These results represent a dramatic example of the importance of genetic research for understanding the environment. Shared environment is important for g during childhood when children are living at home. However, its importance fades in adulthood as influences outside the family become more salient.

PSYCHOPATHOLOGY

Mental illness has been a particularly active area of genetic research in recent years, largely because of its social importance. Much of this research has been devoted to the three major areas of adult psychopathology: schizophrenia, mood disorders and anxiety disorders (see Plomin et al., 1997). We limit our review here, however, to two types of disorders usually first diagnosed in childhood: autism, and attention-deficit and disruptive behaviour disorders.

Autism

Autism was once thought to be a childhood version of schizophrenia but it is now known to be a distinct disorder marked by abnormalities in social relationships, communication deficits, and stereotyped behaviour (see Chapter 12). This is an extremely rare disorder. At first, autism was thought to be environmentally caused. Genetics did not seem to be important because there were no reported cases of an autistic child having an autistic parent, and because the risk to siblings was only about 3–6 per cent (Smalley et al., 1988). However, this rate of 0.03 to 0.06 is 100 times greater than the population rate of 0.0003, implying strong familial resemblance. In 1977, the first systematic twin study of autism began to change the view that autism was environmental in origin (Folstein and Rutter, 1977). Four of 11 pairs of identical twins were concordant for autism, whereas none of 10 pairs of fraternal twins were. These pairwise concordance rates of 35 per cent and 0 per cent rose to 82 per cent and 10 per cent when the diagnosis was broadened to include cognitive disabilities. These findings have now been replicated in other twin studies (e.g. Bailey et al., 1995). On the basis of these results, views regarding autism have changed radically. Instead of being seen as an environmentally caused disorder, it is now considered to be one of the most heritable mental disorders (Rutter et al., 1993).

DISCUSSION POINT

How might the behavioural genetic findings concerning autism affect the parents of an autistic child?

Attention-deficit and disruptive behaviour disorders

Attention-deficit hyperactivity disorder (ADHD) refers to children who are very restless and have a poor attention span, combined with impulsivity. Estimates of the prevalence of ADHD vary according to how broad a definition is used, peaking at about 4 per cent in North America. ADHD usually continues into adolescence and, in about a third of cases, continues through into adulthood (Klein and Mannuzza, 1991).

Twin studies have been quite consistent in showing a strong genetic effect on hyperactivity regardless of whether it is measured by questionnaire (Goodman and Stevenson, 1989) or by standardized and detailed interviewing (Eaves et al., 1996), and regardless of whether it is treated as a continuously distributed dimension (Thapar et al., 1995) or as a clinical diagnosis (Gillis et al., 1992). Putting the findings together, a heritability of about 70 per cent seems to be a reasonable estimate.

In contrast to ADHD, twin studies of juvenile delinquency yield concordance rates of 87 per cent for identical twins and 72 per cent for fraternal twins, suggesting only modest genetic influence (McGuffin and Gottesman, 1985). What is striking about these results is that they imply the strongest influence of shared environment found for any behavioural disorder. However, this overall heritability figure conceals more than it reveals, because antisocial behaviour is so heterogeneous. For example, it seems that antisocial behaviour that continues into adult life shows a substantially stronger genetic component than that which is confined to the childhood years (DiLalla & Gottesman, 1989).

Nonshared environment

IMPORTANCE OF NONSHARED ENVIRONMENTAL FACTORS

A surprise from genetic research has been the discovery that genetic factors are so important throughout psychology; however, this excitement should not overshadow the fact that environmental factors are at least as important. Heritability rarely exceeds 50 per cent and thus 'environmentality' is rarely less than 50 per cent. The environmental influence of primary importance is of the nonshared variety (Plomin and Daniels, 1987). That is, environmental factors that have the strongest effect are those that make siblings in the same family different from one another (Dunn and Plomin, 1990). It has been only in the past 15 years that the importance of this component of variance has been recognized (*see* Plomin et al., 1994, for a recent review). For the three major areas studied by behavioural geneticists – personality, cognitive ability and psychopathology – most of the environmental contribution is of the nonshared variety.

This finding of the importance of nonshared environment has broad implications. Many global family factors such as the marital relationship, parental personality, neighbourhood context and socio-economic status may not operate in the same way for all family members as has often been implied. To the extent that factors such as these are experienced in a similar manner by siblings in a family, they cannot affect the developmental outcomes of these children. Instead, such factors may affect children in the same family differently (*see* Box 1.1 earlier). For example, divorce is usually considered an event that is obviously shared by children in a family. However, the key issue might be each child's unique perception of, and reaction to, the divorce.

For a more detailed description of the findings concerning the importance of nonshared environment and its implications, as well as peer commentaries, see Plomin and Daniels (1987). It is remarkable that a finding with such far-reaching implications as the importance of nonshared environment has scarcely been challenged (cf Hoffman, 1991), but its interpretation and its implications for research have created a lively debate (see Plomin, 1994). Despite these arguments, siblings do, in fact, differ from one another quite substantially, and these differences and their causes are certainly worth examining.

PINPOINTING SPECIFIC ASPECTS OF THE NONSHARED ENVIRONMENT

Traditional behavioural genetic studies do not pinpoint *which* aspects of the environment are important (*see* Box 1.1 earlier), but do indicate that each child in a family should be considered separately, rather than the family being assessed as a unitary whole. Thus far, much of the work of trying to detect specific sources of nonshared environment has focused on differential parental treatment. That is, researchers have examined parents' distinct, or differing behaviour towards each of their children. Most of this work has used siblings rather than twins to detect differential treatment. For example, Dunn et al., (1990) found that older siblings receiving less affection from their mothers than their younger siblings also displayed more internalizing problems (e.g. depression, social withdrawal) than did their younger siblings. In addition, older siblings who were the recipients of more maternal control demonstrated more internalizing and externalizing problems (e.g. aggressiveness, delinquency) than their younger siblings.

Sibling studies such as this cannot, however, address the direction of effects. It is often assumed that it is the parental behaviour *causing* the differences in sibling behaviour, but it could be that the children's behaviour is in fact influencing parental behaviour. In the example outlined above, it might be more plausible that it is the problem behaviours of the children that are driving the differential maternal treatment, rather than the differential maternal treatment that is driving the children's problem behaviour. One specific mechanism whereby children may be affecting their parents' behaviour is via their genetically influenced traits.

Thus, as links between differential parental treatment and children's outcome have been found, it has become necessary to disentangle possible genetic sources of these associations. Because siblings differ genetically, relations between their environment and behavioural outcomes may be due to their genetic differences rather than to the differential parental treatment. Continuing the example above, it may be that *genetic* differences between siblings in families were the root of *both* the differential maternal treatment *and* the differences observed in the siblings' behaviour problems. In order to study such a possibility, family environment measures (such as parental treatment), as well as children's outcome measures, must both be included within a **genetically sensitive design**. A genetically sensitive design refers to a research design in which the similarity of relatives of differing genetic relatedness (e.g. MZ versus DZ twins) can be compared, yielding genetic and environmental estimates, as explained in Behavioural Genetic Methods earlier in this chapter.

The Non-shared Environment and Adolescent Development project (NEAD) (Reiss et al., 1994) was specifically designed to explore the family environment and children's outcomes within a behavioural genetic framework. As part of the NEAD project, parental treatment and its association with adolescent depressive symptoms and antisocial behaviour was examined by use of **bivariate genetic model-fitting techniques** (Pike et al.,

1996). Basic genetic analyses are univariate; they decompose observed variance of a single measure (i.e. the range of scores) into genetic and environmental components. Bivariate genetic analysis focuses on the correlation between traits, decomposed into its genetic and environmental components (Fig 1.1) and can, for example, tell us whether a link between parental treatment and adolescent adjustment is due to the non-shared environmental processes indicated by Dunn and colleagues (1990), i.e. differential parental treatment, or whether it is a common genetic component linking parental treatment and adolescent adjustment.

Four bivariate associations from the NEAD study were examined using this bivariate genetic model-fitting technique: maternal negativity and paternal negativity, both with depressive symptoms and antisocial behaviour. In line with non-genetic studies, the bivariate correlations were moderate for negativity and depressive symptoms (0.33–0.37) and substantial for negativity and antisocial behaviour (0.57–0.60). Bivariate model-fitting analyses then yielded the degree to which each of the correlations was due to genetic, shared environmental and nonshared environmental influences (*see* Fig 1.1).

Fig 1.2 contains the results from these analyses. Looking at the pie charts, there is a clear pattern of results for the parental negativity and adjustment associations. Although shared and nonshared environmental influences account for modest to moderate amounts of the variation, in all cases genetic influences account for the lion's share of the variation. Thus, this study indicates that parental treatment is linked to adolescent adjustment primarily because of a common genetic component. That is, an array of genes that influence children's adjustment also lead parents to treat their children in a more or less negative fashion. It seems that it is the children's

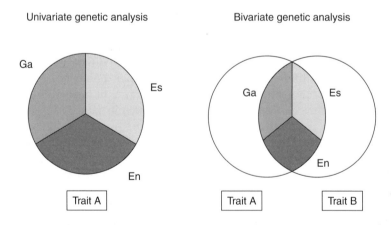

Univariate genetic analysis   Bivariate genetic analysis

Figure 1.1 Univariate genetic analysis decomposes the variance of one trait into its genetic (Ga), shared environmental (Es), and nonshared environmental (En) components. Bivariate genetic analysis decomposes the covariance between two traits into its genetic (Ga), shared environmental (Es), and nonshared environmental (En) components.

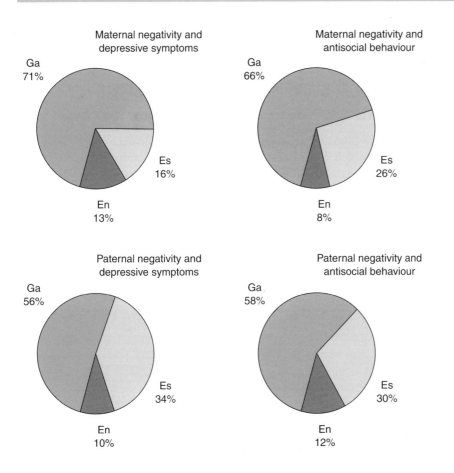

Figure 1.2 Genetic, shared environmental and nonshared environmental contributions to four parental negativity-adjustment associations. Ga, Es and En represent the genetic, shared environmental and nonshared environmental contributions, respectively.

behaviour that is driving the parental treatment, rather than the other way around.

These results require that non-genetic studies be interpreted with caution. Much of the developmental research relating parenting to children's adjustment is interpreted to mean that the parents' behaviour is *causing* the child's behaviour. The genetic findings suggest that this is not always the case. Instead, it is the children's genes that are reflected in both the parents' behaviour and in the adolescent's adjustment. In terms of process, it is quite plausible that an adolescent's genetic propensities that lead to adjustment difficulties would also lead to displays of negativity from parents. This presence of genetic influence is consistent with the idea that socialization is bi-directional. When parents interact with their children, this interaction is affected by the children's behaviour as well as that of the parents (Bell, 1968).

This study also indicated that the differential treatment of siblings by their parents is not the 'answer' to the nonshared environment puzzle. The results in no way discredit the importance of nonshared environment – both depressive symptoms and antisocial behaviour are influenced by nonshared environmental factors. However, only a small piece of the nonshared environmental influence was attributed to parental differential treatment. Most nonshared environmental influence remains anonymous.

EXTRA-FAMILIAL RELATIONSHIPS AS SOURCES OF NONSHARED ENVIRONMENT

In response to the findings described above, an NEAD sub-project was launched in which 32 of the original identical twin pairs (14 male and 18 female pairs) were interviewed about how and why they differed from their twins (Manke and Pike, 1997). Identical twins were examined because they are genetically identical and share the same rearing environment. Therefore, any differences between identical twins must be due to non-shared environmental sources. The goal of conducting these interviews was to identify fruitful areas of nonshared environmental experience for future research, and to guide the development of new measures of non-shared environment.

DISCUSSION POINT

Identify experiences that might be nonshared for siblings, perhaps drawing from your own experiences.

Data were collected during one-hour audiotaped interviews. Each twin was interviewed separately and questioned about perceived twin differences in seven domains (athletic competence, peers and sociability, self-esteem, scholastic achievement, depression, other behaviour problems and use of humour). Twins were asked the extent to which they differed from their co-twin. Next, if they did perceive a difference between themselves and their twin for a particular domain, they were asked how they thought those differences had come about (i.e. the nonshared environmental source of twin differences).

Transcripts were coded for each substantive domain. Sources of twin differences were noted, and grouped into categories of nonshared environmental experience. Table 1.1 lists these categories, as well as example quotes from the transcripts. Interestingly, most of the categories emanated from outside the family, suggesting that our quest to pinpoint specific nonshared environmental factors should focus less on the family and more on extra-familial factors.

It should come as no surprise that the twins pointed to relationships outside the home as being particularly important experiences. By the time children enter into adolescence, non-classroom time spent with peers exceeds that spent with family (Csikszentmihalyi and Larson, 1984). Adolescent friendships are qualitatively different from those of children (the quality rather than quantity of friends becomes the important predictor for well-being), and friends take on an increasingly important role in the lives of

Table 1.1 Categories of nonshared environmental experience

Source	Example quote from transcripts
Parental differential treatment	'It sometimes seems like they [parents] appreciate my sister more then me.'
Different familial roles/ expectations	'I guess I didn't feel like there was anything special about me because Teresa [co-twin] was the smart one, Kate was the popular one, and Tony had problems . . . so I felt left out.'
Different friends/experiences with friends	'I hang around friends that are funny and he hangs around people that are serious – 4.0 students and stuff like that.'
Different romantic experiences	'I have been dumped at least 10 times . . . he [co-twin] has never even asked a girl out on a date yet so he doesn't have as much hurt in his life.'
Different teachers/school-related experiences	'I had a good biology teacher that helped me and encouraged me . . . he [co-twin] just had a regular biology teacher.'
Different experiences with death	'Well, my grandpa's death is why she is more depressed because she was sick when he was in the hospital and she didn't get to see him and say good-bye. I did so I had a sense of closure and she didn't and she feels guilty.'
Different moving experiences	'We moved around a lot and every time I was eager to move and make new friends . . . he [co-twin] would get more emotionally attached to a specific place or people than I would so the moves were more difficult for him.'
Differential involvement in activities	'I would say we became different because of the different activities that we are involved in. I belong to Young Leaders in Action and they teach us leadership skills and the importance of grades.'
Different paid employment experiences	'The biggest reason we were different [in terms of scholastic achievement] was because in college I work 40 hours a week at my job and go to school full-time and she only has a part-time job.'
Different illness and accidents	'Yeah well I broke my leg and he hasn't had anything wrong with him yet. I had to take six months off [from playing sports] and he was able to get an edge on me.'

adolescents (Savin-Williams and Berndt, 1990; *see also* Chapter 20). Although parents remain influential over future educational and career aspirations, friends play a larger role in day-to-day decision making (Hartup, 1983).

To summarize this section, traditional behavioural genetic studies indicate that environmental factors affect children in a family *differently*, rather than in a uniform manner. That is, nonshared environmental influences are important and often substantial, whereas shared environmental influences are usually negligible. More recently efforts have been made to pinpoint specific aspects of the nonshared environment responsible for sibling differences in outcome. Initial attempts indicate that differential parental treatment is not an important nonshared environmental influence. Instead, adolescents themselves point to *extra*-familial relationships and activities as important reasons for sibling differences in behavioural outcome.

Molecular genetics

Behavioural genetic research is at the dawn of a new era in which molecular genetic tools can begin to be used to identify specific genes involved in complex dimensions and disorders (Plomin et al., 1994; *see* Box 1.3). The quest is to find not *the* gene for a trait, but the multiple genes that affect the trait in a probabilistic rather than predetermined manner. The breathtaking pace of molecular genetics leads us to predict that psychologists will routinely use DNA markers as a tool in their research to identify some of the relevant genetic differences among individuals.

BOX 1.3 How are specific genes identified?

Although 99.9 per cent of the 3.5 billion steps in the spiral staircase of DNA (that is, the DNA base pairs in the double helix) are the same for every human being, the remaining 0.1 per cent constitutes millions of DNA differences between people. Before 1980, only a few dozen genetic markers were available, these involved the products of genes rather than DNA itself. For example, a person's ABO blood system (which is coded by a gene at the tip of chromosome 9 with three forms, or alleles, called A, B and O) can be determined from blood products, rather than from DNA itself. The major advance making it possible to find genes associated with complex traits is a new type of DNA marker. These new markers identify differences between people in DNA itself. The new DNA markers can involve a single base pair that differs, or sets of base pairs that differ in the number of times they repeat.

The simplest way to show that a gene is linked to a trait, even if many other genes also affect the trait, is to show that the frequency of an **allele** (a particular form of a gene) for a DNA marker is correlated with the trait. For example, the best-documented association is between a gene called apolipoprotein E on chromosome 19 and the very common disorder of late-onset Alzheimer's disease. The frequency of a particular allele for this gene is 40 per cent in Alzheimer's patients but only 15 per cent in control samples. This gene is therefore a genetic risk factor for Alzheimer's disease. However, this gene does not determine that someone will succumb to Alzheimer's disease because over half of Alzheimer's patients do not have that allele. Other genes and environmental factors are responsible for the rest of the risk.

An example of things to come is the recent finding of a gene associated with the personality trait of novelty-seeking. This gene, dopamine D_4 receptor (DRD4), includes a 48-base pair repeat sequence that varies in the number of repeats for different individuals. The number of repeats affects this dopamine receptor's functioning. In three studies, individuals with more DRD4 repeats were found to have higher novelty-seeking scores (Benjamin et al., 1996; Ebstein et al., 1995). Moreover, on the basis of this finding, it was predicted and confirmed that hyperactive children, especially those driven by impulsivity rather than cognitive deficits, are more likely to have more DRD4 repeats (LaHoste et al., 1996), a finding that has been replicated in other studies (Sunohara et al., 1997; *see also* Plomin and Caspi, in press). Long DRD4 repeats have also been shown to be a risk factor for drug abuse in several studies (Ebstein and Belmaker, 1997).

Even though this genetic association involves only a small amount of variance in novelty seeking, DRD4 could be used as a handhold in the climb towards understanding the contribution of genetics to complex developmental disorders. For example, do children with more DRD4 repeats have more trouble forming friendships? Do they find friends who are risk takers or delinquents? Do parents respond to such children by attempting to damp down their propensity towards impulsivity? DRD4 is just the first shock wave from the explosion of molecular genetic research on behaviour.

Genes associated with other personality traits have also been reported (Hamer and Copeland, 1998) as well as other disorders and dimensions, such as reading disability, autism, smoking, general intelligence, mental retardation and mental illness. As more associations are found between specific genes and behaviour, genetic research on behavioural development will be revolutionized (Plomin and Rutter, 1998). To answer questions about how genes influence behaviour, nothing can be more important than identifying specific genes involved and characterizing the genes' products. As specific genes are found that begin to account for some of the widespread genetic influence in children's development, more precise questions can be asked, using measured genotypes. Do the effects of the genes change during development? Do the genetic effects interact or correlate with the environment? For example, consider a gene on chromosome 6 that has been reported to be associated with high general intelligence in children (Chorney et al., 1998). The quantitative genetic results we have reviewed show that genetic factors become increasingly important throughout the life span. It therefore makes sense to ask whether children with the high-IQ allele select or create environments (friends, television programmes, books) that foster their cognitive growth.

This new knowledge about specific genes may create new problems as well, such as problems of labelling and ensuing educational and employment discrimination. It also raises fears such as the use of DNA markers prenatally to select 'designer babies', and more generally, concerns about free will. However, the benefits of identifying genes seem likely to far outweigh the potential abuses (Rutter and Plomin, 1997). Although the benefits seem most likely for basic science such as understanding the pathways between genes and behaviour, it holds out the hope that environmental interventions, and especially preventions, can be developed that are especially effective for children who are at genetic risk. Despite the problems created by such advances in science, it would be a mistake, and futile as well, to try to cut off the flow of knowledge and its benefits in order to avoid having to confront new problems.

Conclusion

A summary of this chapter is given in Box 1.4.

BOX 1.4 Chapter summary

Behavioural genetic theory and methods
- Behavioural genetic theory proposes that variation seen among individuals in a population stem from individuals' genetic variability, and the variability of the environments that are experienced by individuals.
- By the use of behavioural genetic methods, variation for any given trait may be divided into three sources: heritability, shared environment and nonshared environment. The classic methods used to disentangle these influences are twin and adoption studies.

Results from traditional behavioural genetic studies
- About half of the variance for general cognitive ability is due to genetic factors. Of the half of the variance that is due to non-genetic factors, about half is accounted for by shared environmental factors, and the other half to nonshared environment and errors of measurement. Across development, genetic factors become increasingly important for general cognitive ability, and the effects of shared environment decrease.

- Autism was once thought to originate environmentally; however, twin studies have shown it to be one of the most heritable mental disorders. Twin studies are also consistent in showing a strong genetic effect on hyperactivity.

Nonshared environment
- Empirically, the environmental influence of primary importance is of the nonshared variety. Efforts to specify nonshared environmental effects have concentrated on differential parental treatment, however most nonshared environmental variance remains unspecified.
- Recent interviews with MZ twins indicate that extra-familial experiences may be important domains of nonshared environment.

Molecular genetics
- Molecular genetic tools are beginning to be used to identify specific genes influencing behaviour. Genetic research on development will be revolutionized as more associations are found between specific genes and dimensions and disorders.

Molecular genetics has already had a major impact on developmental psychology, however, much remains to be learned from quantitative genetic studies involving twins and adoptees, even in the major areas of research such as cognitive abilities, personality and psychopathology. For example, little is known about cognitive abilities in relation to measures of information processing. For personality, little is known about measures other than self-report questionnaires. For many other areas of development, hardly anything is known about the genetic and environmental origins of individual differences, such as attachment, language development, theory of mind, motor development, learning, health psychology and psychological aging. The main direction for research is to move beyond simply asking *whether* and *how* genetic factors affect a trait to asking questions about how *genes* and *environment* interact and correlate during development. Genetic research may make its most important contribution by helping us to understand how the environment works, as the example of the importance of nonshared environment shows.

Seminar questions

1. What problems might there be in drawing generalizable conclusions from twin and adoption studies?
2. Do the findings outlined in this chapter challenge traditional socialization and learning theories of children's development?
3. What ethical dilemmas surround the identification of genes associated with IQ?

Further reading

Plomin, R., DeFries, J.C., McClearn, G.E., Rutter, M. 1997. *Behavioural genetics*. New York: W.H. Freeman & Co. This textbook provides an overview of behavioural genetics, including further details on all of the issues considered in this chapter.

Loehlin, J.C. 1992. *Genes and environment in personality development*, Newbury Park, CA: Sage Publications. This short book reviews the behavioural genetic literature concerning personality development. In addition, the book contains basic behavioural genetic methodology, including model-fitting.

Plomin, R. 1994. *Genetics and experience: the interplay between nature and nurture*, Newbury Park, CA: Sage Publications. As the title suggests, this book explores what behavioural genetics can tell us about the environment. Included is information about the surprising finding that many so-called 'environmental' measures, such as parenting, demonstrate genetic influence.

Developmental cognitive neuroscience

RELATING BRAIN DEVELOPMENT TO COGNITIVE CHANGE

2

MARK H JOHNSON

Editors' preface

This chapter introduces you to the exciting and relatively new field of developmental research – developmental cognitive neuroscience. It is a rapidly emerging field. After decades of simply recognizing that there clearly is a relation between brain and behaviour, developmental cognitive neuroscience is transforming our understanding of the specificity of the relation. It was not until the late 1980s that the parent discipline – cognitive neuroscience, itself concerned with the relation between neural and cognitive activity began to bring together developmentalists and neuroscientists. This new subdiscipline is providing a valuable interface for understanding the developmental course of the neural underpinning of normal cognitive functioning. Professor Mark Johnson guides you through early brain development, the differentiation of the cerebral cortex, and the role of the prefrontal regions in relation to early cognitive development. This is followed by a speculative discussion of the child as an active participant in the development of its own brain which draws on recent work on the neural circuitry for preferential orienting and early face perception. Developmental cognitive neuroscience is still a comparatively new discipline and is often concerned with infants, however, it will become apparent that the techniques which are employed have the potential to be applied to a wide range of ages, to answer a wide range of questions.

Introduction

What is development? In my view, development may be defined as the constructive process through which genes interact with the environment at various levels resulting in complex biological structures such as the human brain and the mind it supports. Roughly speaking, as development proceeds higher orders of organization emerge from molecular to cellular to organismal. Traditionally, these various levels of biological organization tended to be studied by scientists from different disciplines who often use quite different methodologies. It should, however, be evident that a comprehensive study of development requires an interdisciplinary approach in which changes at different levels of biological organization can be examined simultaneously, including changes in mental functions. Generally speaking, over the past few decades the study of human cognitive and behavioural development has not been characterized by such an interdisciplinary approach. Although cognitive developmentalists commonly draw on concepts and data from adult cognitive psychology, until recently they rarely turned to information and ideas from neural development and other facets of biology. Indeed, on the few occasions when information from brain development has been brought to bear on issues in cognitive development, it has sometimes been declared to be irrelevant or misleading. This scepticism was fuelled by the lack of empirical methods and theoretical tools for studying the relation between brain and cognitive development. Within the past decade, however, advances in theoretical and methodological approaches has made a new interdisciplinary and integrative approach to psychological development possible: **Developmental Cognitive Neuroscience (DCN)**.

The recent emergence of the interdisciplinary science of DCN has been facilitated by theoretical advances along the lines of neural network and connectionist modelling. These computational models, based to some extent on the properties and structure of real brain networks, offer the hope of relating changes in detailed structure of the brain during post-natal development with changes in cognitive abilities (for review, see Elman et al., 1996; Plunkett et al., 1997) (see Box 2.1). Alongside these theoretical advances are new empirical methods, including new methods for imaging the working brain and for manipulating and analysing the genetic contribution to cognition. Finally, our knowledge of brain development has increased dramatically over the past decade.

BOX 2.1 Connectionist models of neural and cognitive development

Connectionist models are a form of computer modelling of the brain and mind which, to some extent, are inspired by real neural circuits in the brain. In general, these models involve nodes (which roughly approximate **neurons**), connections between nodes (which roughly approximate **dendrites** and **synapses**) and a learning rule which determines changes in the strength of links between the nodes. Different models use different learning rules, with some being more biologically plausible than others (*see* Elman et al., 1996). The effects of training (exposure to repeated inputs) in these network models are changes in the strength or weights of the links between nodes. Some networks use variations of a so-called 'Hebbian' learning rule in which links between nodes are strengthened when the nodes at either end of a link tend to be active simultaneously.

Representations of aspects of the input information form within these networks as particular patterns of strengths of links between nodes. This is analogous to the real brain where dendritic trees and synaptic structure are thought to be sensitive to input from sensory and motor experience. Connectionist models vary from those concerned to simulate many aspect of the real brain, such as the properties of certain neuron types, or the selective loss of synapses observed in the real brain, to those intended as abstract 'cognitive' models of psychological phenomena. At any level, these models may be more appropriate than other types of computer models for simulating and understanding developmental transitions for a variety of reasons, including that they are graded in nature allowing for the study of weak and partial representations (*see* Elman et al., 1996; Munakata et al., 1997).

It is important to stress that DCN is not a reductionist science. In other words, it does not seek to replace cognitive explanations with accounts that identify specific genes or regions of the brain as being maturationally 'turned on' at different ages. Rather, the goal is to arrive at plausible cognitive, or neurocomputational, explanations constrained by evidence from the brain as well as from behaviour. This may require us to entertain types of cognitive theories very different from those derived from analogies with digital computers.

This chapter reviews some basic findings about the pre-natal and post-natal development of the brain, before focusing on the development of the cerebral cortex in particular. It then describes a number of attempts that have been made to apply our knowledge of brain development to issues and findings in cognitive development before, finally, discussing future research directions and prospects for the field.

Building a brain

Brain development may be divided into that which occurs prior to birth, pre-natally and that which takes place after birth, post-natally. Although the same developmental processes can be traced from pre- to post-natal life, in post-natal development there is obviously more scope for influence from the world outside the infant. A striking feature of human brain development is the comparatively long phase of development post-natally and therefore the increased extent to which the later stages of brain development can be influenced by the environment of the child.

PRE-NATAL BRAIN DEVELOPMENT

The major stages of pre-natal brain development in humans correspond closely to those of other mammals. Shortly after conception a fertilized cell undergoes a rapid process of cell division, resulting in a cluster of proliferating cells (called the **blastocyst**) that resembles a bunch of grapes. Within a few days, the blastocyst differentiates into a three-layered structure, with each of these layers subsequently differentiating into major parts of the body. The outer layer (**ectoderm**) gives rise to the skin surface and the nervous system (including the eyes). The nervous system continues its development with a process known as **neurolation**. A portion of the ectoderm begins to fold in on itself to form a hollow cylinder called the **neural tube**.

The neural tube differentiates along three dimensions: length, circumference and radius. The length dimension gives rise to the major subdivisions of the central nervous system (CNS), with the forebrain and midbrain arising at one end and the spinal cord at the other. The end which will become the spinal cord differentiates into a series of repeated units or segments, whereas the front end of the neural tube organizes in a different way with a series of bulges and convolutions emerging. Approximately five weeks after conception these bulges can be identified as protoforms for major components of the mammalian brain. Within these bulges cells are born, travel from one place to another and develop into particular types. Most of the cells that will compose the brain are born in the so-called **proliferative zones**. These zones are close to the hollow of the neural tube (which subsequently becomes the ventricles of the brain).

Division of cells within the proliferative zone produces **clones** (clones are a group of cells which are produced by division of a single precursor cell). **Neuroblasts** produce neurons and **glioblasts** produce glial cells. Although glial cells are not thought to play a major role in computation in the brain, as will be seen later they are important for a variety of support functions in the brain. Each of the neuroblasts gives rise to a definite and limited number of neurons. In some cases particular neuroblasts also give rise to particular types of cell. After young neurones are born, they have to travel or **migrate** from the proliferative zone to the particular region where they will be employed in the mature brain. There are two forms of migration observed during brain development. The first and more common, is **passive cell displacement**. This occurs when cells that have been generated are simply pushed further away from the proliferative zone by more recently born cells. This form of migration gives rise to an outside-to-inside spatiotemporal gradient. That is, the oldest cells are pushed toward the surface of the brain, whereas the most recently produced cells are toward the inside. Passive migration gives rise to brain structures such as the thalamus, the dentate gyrus of the hippocampus and many regions of the brain stem. The second form of migration is more active and involves the young cell moving past previously generated cells to create an 'inside-out' gradient. This pattern is found in the cerebral cortex and in some subcortical areas that have a **laminar** (divided into parallel layers) structure.

The pre-natal development of the cerebral cortex, the region of the brain implicated in many cognitive, perceptual and motor functions, has been studied in some detail. In particular, Rakic (1988) has proposed a 'radial unit model' of cortical development in which the laminar organization of the cerebral cortex (*see* Fig 2.1) is determined by the fact that each cortical neuroblast gives rise to about 100 neurones. The progeny from each neuroblast all migrate up the same one of many radial glial fibres, with the latest to be born travelling past their older relatives. A radial glial fibre is a long process that stretches from top to bottom of the cortex and originates

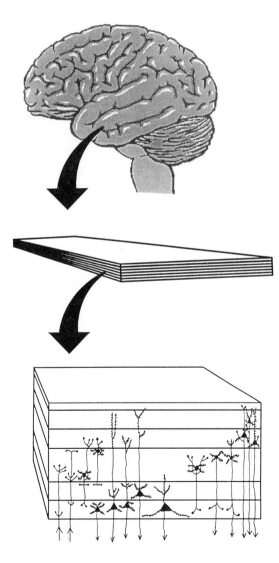

Figure 2.1 A simplified schematic diagram that illustrates that despite its convoluted surface appearance (top), the cerebral cortex is a thin sheet (middle) composed of six layers (bottom).

from a glial cell. These radial glial fibres act like a climbing rope to ensure that cells produced by a single neuroblast all contribute to one radial column of neurons within the cortex. Rakic's (1988) proposed method of migration is illustrated in Fig 2.2.

In the human brain by around the time of birth the vast majority of cells

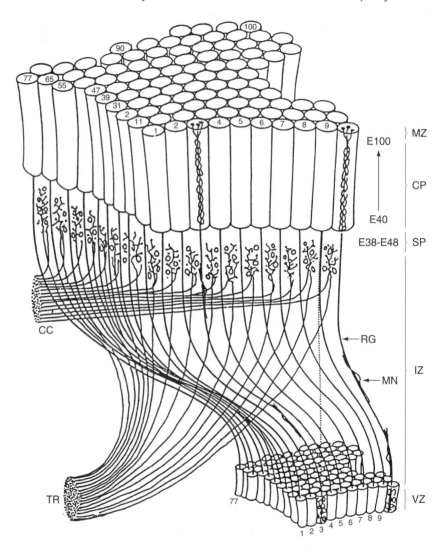

Figure 2.2 The radial unit model of Rakic (1987). Radial glial fibres span from the ventricular zone (VZ) to the cortical plate (CP) via a number of intermediate regions. RG indicates a radial glial fibre, and MN a migrating neuron. Each MN integrates with incoming fibres from the thalamus (TR) and from other cortical regions (CC). Once neurons reach the cortical plate they migrate past their predecessors to the top of the cortex (MZ). From Rakic P. Intrinsic and extrinsic determinants of neocortical parcellation: a radial unit model. *Neurobiology of Neocortex* by P. Rakic and W. Singer (eds). © John Wiley & Sons Limited. Reproduced with permission.

are in their appropriate adult locations and all of the major landmarks of the brain, such as the most distinctive patterns of folding of the cerebral cortex, are in place. However, as will be seen in the next section this does not mean that brain development is complete. Further, it is important to stress that pre-natal brain development does not consist simply of the unfolding of a rigid 'genetic plan'. Many of the architectural features of the human brain are the result of complex interactions at the cellular level, such as that between the radial glial fibres and the neurons they guide. For example, the detailed folding patterns of the cerebral cortex can vary considerably, even between identical twins (Bartley et al., 1997).

POST-NATAL BRAIN DEVELOPMENT

A number of lines of evidence indicate that there are substantive changes during post-natal development of the human brain. At the most gross level of analysis, the volume of the brain quadruples between birth and adulthood. This increase comes from a number of sources such as more extensive fibre bundles and nerve fibres becoming covered in a fatty myelin sheath which helps to conduct electrical signals. But perhaps the most obvious manifestation of post-natal neural development as viewed through a standard microscope is the increase in size and complexity of the dendritic tree of many neurons. This is illustrated in Fig 2.3 which shows drawings from microscope views of the human visual cortex from birth to six months of age. Whereas the extent and reach of a cell's dendritic tree may increase dramatically, it also often becomes more specific and specialized. Less apparent through standard microscopes, but more evident with electron microscopy, is a corresponding increase in density of functional contacts between neurons, **synapses**.

Huttenlocher (1990) and colleagues have reported a steady increase in the density of synapses in several regions of the human cerebral cortex. For example, in parts of the visual cortex, the generation of synapses (**synaptogenesis**) begins around the time of birth and reaches a peak around 150 per cent of adult levels toward the end of the first year. In the frontal cortex the peak of synaptic density occurs later, at around 24 months of age. Although there is variation in the timetable, in all regions of cortex studied so far synaptogenesis begins around the time of birth and increases to a peak level well above that observed in adults. Thus, the potential number of connections between neurons increases, the functional consequences of which we will return to later.

Somewhat surprisingly, regressive events are commonly observed during the development of nerve cells and their connections in the brain. For example, in the primary visual cortex the mean density of synapses per neuron starts to decrease at the end of the first year of life (e.g. Huttlenlocher, 1990). In humans, most cortical regions and pathways appear to undergo this 'rise and fall' in synaptic density.

The post-natal rise and fall developmental sequence can also be seen in other measures of brain physiology and anatomy. For example, positron

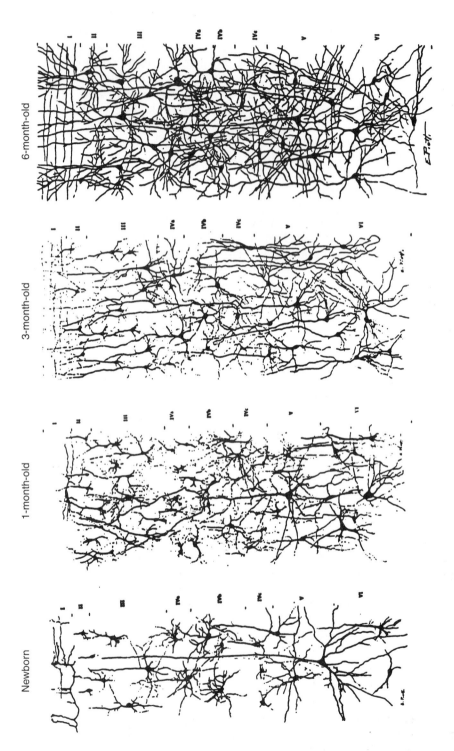

Figure 2.3 Drawing of the cellular structure of the human visual cortex from Conel (1939–1967). These drawings illustrate the laminar structure of the cortex, and the increasing extent of the dendritic trees of neurons over the first few months after birth. Reprinted by permission of the publisher from *Postnatal Development of the Human Cerebral Cortex*, volumes I–VIII, by JL Conel. Cambridge, MA: Harvard University Press. © 1939–1967 by the President and Fellows of Harvard College.

emission tomography (PET) studies of human infants can measure the glucose uptake of regions of the brain. Glucose uptake is necessary in regions of the brain that are active and since it is transported by the blood is also a measure of blood flow. Using this method, Chugani et al. (1987) observed an adult-like distribution of resting brain activity within and across brain regions by the end of the first year. However, the overall level of glucose uptake reaches a peak during early childhood which is much higher than that observed in adults. The rates return to adult levels after about nine years of age for some cortical regions. The extent to which these changes relate to those in synaptic density is currently the topic of further investigation.

Differentiation of the cerebral cortex

A controversial issue in developmental neuroscience concerns the extent to which the differentiation of the cerebral cortex into areas or regions with particular cognitive, perceptual or motor functions, can be shaped by postnatal interactions with the external world. This issue reflects the debate in cognitive development about whether infants are born with domain-specific 'modules' for particular cognitive functions such as language, or whether the formation of such modules is an experience-dependent process (*see* Karmiloff-Smith, 1992; Elman et al., 1996 for further discussion of this issue).

Brodmann (1912) was one of the first to propose a scheme for the division of cortex into structural areas assumed to have differing functional properties. Although a century of neuropsychology has taught us that the majority of normal adults tend to have similar functions within approximately the same regions of cortex, we cannot necessarily infer from this that this pattern of differentiation is intrinsically pre-specified ('prewired'), since most humans share very similar pre- and post-natal environments.

In developmental neurobiology this issue has focused on the relative importance or otherwise of neural activity for cortical differentiation, as opposed to molecular and genetic specification of cortical areas. Supporting the importance of the latter processes, Rakic (1988) proposed that the differentiation of the cortex into areas is due to a **protomap**. The hypothesized protomap either involves pre-specification of the proliferative zone, or intrinsic molecular markers that guide the division of cortex into particular areas. One mechanism for this would be through the radial glial fibre path from the proliferative zone to the cortex discussed earlier. By this view the differentiation of cortex is mainly due to the unfolding of a genetic plan implemented by molecular markers. The alternative viewpoint, advanced by O'Leary (1989) among others, is that genetic and molecular factors build an initially undifferentiated **protocortex**, but that the cortex then subsequently becomes divided into specialized areas as a result of activity within neural circuits. This activity within neural circuits need not be the result of input from the external world, but may result from intrinsic, spontaneous patterns of firing within sensory organs or subcortical structures that feed into cortex, or from activity within the cortex itself (Katz and Shatz, 1996).

Whereas the neurobiological evidence is complex, overall it tends to support the importance of neural activity dependent processes (*see* Johnson, 1997; Elman et al., 1996 for reviews). With several exceptions (such as primary sensory regions), it seems likely that activity-dependent processes contribute to the differentiation of functional areas of the cortex, especially those involved in higher cognitive functions. During pre-natal life this activity may largely be a spontaneous intrinsic process, whereas in post-natal life this neural activity is likely also to be influenced by sensory and motor experience. In humans, where post-natal development is considerably extended relative to other mammals, it is likely that the later stages of cortical specialization are influenced by experience. As just one example of this, PET studies of word recognition have identified a localized region of the left visual cortex as being involved in English word recognition, but not responding to other stimuli such as random letter strings (Peterson et al., 1988). Since it seems implausible to suggest that we are born with a region of cortex pre-specified for English word recognition, we are forced to conclude that at least some cortical functional specialization is experience-dependent. Other lines of evidence also support this conclusion. For example, studies of scalp recorded event-related potentials (*see* Box 2.2) in congenitally deaf subjects show that regions of the temporal lobe which are normally auditory, or multimodal, become dominated by visual input in this group (Neville, 1991). Despite these examples it is clear that there are also limits on the plasticity of cortex. Analysing normal and abnormal processes of post-natal cortical specialization will be one of the major challenges for DCN over the next decade or so.

BOX 2.2 Seeing a baby's brain at work

The task of relating brain development to changes in cognitive abilities in infants and children would be greatly facilitated by tools allowing us to directly study the infants' brain at work. Unfortunately, most of the forms of functional brain imaging used with adults, such as PET and functional MRI, are not suitable for use with infants and young children. However, one comparatively old method, electroencephalography (EEG), is viable for use with infants. In this method, the electrical activity of groups of neurons firing within the cortex is detected by means of electrodes placed on the scalp surface. These electrodes detect minute changes in electrical fields on the scalp. Clear changes in these electrical fields can be detected in relation to the presentation of a visual or auditory stimulus and are called 'event-related potentials', or ERPs for short.

Although ERPs enable the experimenter to investigate changes in brain activity that take place at the speed of thought (tens of milliseconds), the method has relatively poor spatial resolution. That is, it is hard to identify the exact brain regions which are active on the basis of recording from the scalp surface. This problem has partially been alleviated by the recent invention of the so-called geodesic sensor net in which a large number of electrodes (64 or 128) gently rest on the scalp sewn together in an elasticated net (*see* fig 2.4). The net is particularly useful with infants since it is quick to install and comfortable to wear.

Biological approaches to cognitive development

Over the past decade there have been an increasing number of attempts to relate the post-natal development of the brain to cognitive changes during infancy and childhood. Some of these approaches have entailed hypotheses about direct relations between performance in particular tasks and the development of specific brain regions. Others have been concerned to characterize the mechanisms of change at the cognitive level as being based on a process of developmental change at the neural level. Here, some examples of each of these approaches are discussed.

Piaget (1954) was the first to observe a striking type of error made by young infants. He found that infants younger than seven and a half months often fail to retrieve a hidden object after a short delay if the object's location is changed from where, on previous trials, it was retrieved successfully (*see* Chapter 3). Instead, infants of this age often reach towards the location

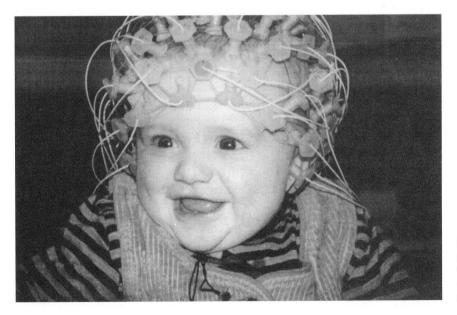

Figure 2.4   A six-month-old infant wearing the 64-channel geodesic sensor net.

where the object was found on the preceding trial. This characteristic pattern of error was cited by Piaget as evidence for the failure of infants to understand that objects retain their existence, or permanence, when moved from view. Between seven and a half and nine months, infants begin to succeed in the task at successively longer delays of 1–5 seconds (Diamond, 1985). However, their performance is unreliable and infants continue to make this error up to about 12 months of age if the delay between hiding and retrieval is increased as the infants age (Diamond, 1985).

In the view of Diamond (1991), the emergence of the ability to demonstrate knowledge about an object's permanence results from the maturation of pre-frontal regions of the cerebral cortex between the ages of five and 12 months. These regions are thought to subserve the infant's ability to carry out plans of action over temporal delays and to inhibit inappropriate responses. The evidence for this position is based on the fact that the failure of infants younger than seven and a half months to retrieve hidden objects is very similar to that of adult monkeys with damage to the prefrontal cortex. Extensive neuropsychological evidence from adult humans also implicates the pre-frontal cortex in spatial working memory performance and dissociations of this region frequently reveal patterns of behaviour in which the inhibition of inappropriate responses is impaired. Consequently, the functional state of the pre-frontal cortex is argued to be a critical factor in determining an infant's behaviour on delayed response tasks.

Although relating the development of the dorsolateral prefrontal cortex (DLPC) to changes in infant behaviour at the end of the first year of life is a good first step, many further questions remain. For example, since it is likely that all the DLPC neurons are in place shortly after birth, what aspect of anatomical or neurochemical change takes place in this region at the end of the first year? Further, to what extent are these changes open to influence by experiential factors? Whereas the answers to these and other questions are largely unknown, Munakata and colleagues (Munakata et al., 1997; Munakata, 1998) have devised connectionist neural network models (*see* Box 2.1) in which representations of objects become gradually strengthened following training with 'objects' that move behind occluders. As these networks learn, aspects of their detailed architecture, such as the strength of links between nodes, become modified. In this way simple representations of the objects emerge during training and can persist for some time even when the object is removed from view. During the early stages of training (taken to correspond to early infancy) the network has only developed weak and partial representations of the object. Thus, when the object is removed only very weak traces of it are retained by the network. These very weak representations may not be sufficiently strong to influence the 'behaviour' (output) of the network. Later on in training, when the representation of the object is stronger, it persists well even when the object is not visible. Thus, the fully trained network shows a form of object permanence associated with infants over eight months of age. To the extent that such simple connectionist models can be extended to the real brain, they suggest that detailed anatomical and neurochemical changes in regions of the brain may be partly the result of previous experiences, rather than due to maturation.

Other attempts have related the mechanisms of change at the neural level to those at the cognitive level. These have often centred on the post-natal loss of synapses and connections described earlier. For example, Changeux and Dehaene (1989) argued that synaptic loss is a process of selection from an initial set. They argued that connections between classes of cells are specified genetically, but initially these connections are labile. Synapses in their labile state may either become stabilized or die, depending on the total activity of the post-synaptic cell. The activity of the post-synaptic cell is, in turn, dependent upon its input. The critical concept here is that of *selective stabilization*. This involves learning proceeding by elimination, as opposed to growth of new links. Changeux and Dehaene (1989) suggest that an analogous mechanism might operate at the cognitive level. The initial step, the generation of options, is achieved, they suggest, by the presence of 'pre-representations'. Pre-representations are described as transient, dynamic, 'privileged' spontaneous activity states in neural circuits. The selection process is achieved by particular pre-representations from the set available 'resonating' with particular sensory inputs. This process probably takes place in seconds or less, whereas a more prolonged time course may be necessary for the process of attrition at the neural level.

One example of selectionist change in the performance of human infants comes from work on speech perception. Infants aged four to six months are sensitive to a variety of five phonetic differences that distinguish syllables in both their native and unfamiliar languages. However, by 10–12 months this sensitivity is restricted to those contrasts found in the native tongue to which they have been exposed (Werker and Tees, 1984). For example, Japanese infants would no longer be sensitive to the distinctions between 'r' and 'l'. Thus, although infants are initially sensitive to all the phonetic contrasts in human languages, through experience the subset relevant to their native tongue is stabilized while the others are lost.

Another hypothesis generated by selectionist views on development is that the initial over-connectivity of the cortex may mean that in the new-born sensory processing is not differentiated. That is, many of the same cortical circuits may be activated by a visual stimulus as by an auditory one (Maurer, 1993; Johnson and Vecera, 1995). Many mammals appear to have transient connections between different sensory cortices early in life. For example, Dehay et al. (1984, 1988) have reported transient connections between visual, auditory, somatosensory and motor cortices in the kitten. The subsequent selective loss of connections would presumably result in less cross-talk between sensory modalities at the level of primary sensory representations.

One line of evidence consistent with this hypothesis came from Wolff et al. (1974) who investigated the cortical evoked response of three- and four-day-old infants to somatosensory and auditory stimulation. They found that auditory input (white noise) had a modulating effect on the somatosensory evoked responses in these very young infants. However, when a similar experiment was run with adults, no effects of auditory input on somatosensory responses was found. One interpretation of these results is that there is less inter-sensory integration at this level in adults as a result of parcellation between the auditory and somatosensory modalities.

Although selectionist theories of developmental change may prove useful in relating neural to cognitive change, Quartz and Sejnowski (1997) argue that to focus only on selective loss ignores the importance of the earlier phase of synaptic and dendritic growth. Whereas selectionist accounts suggest that experience helps select from an initial 'overproduced' set, Quartz and Sejnowski hypothesize that there is also activity-dependent directed growth of dendrites and synapses. That is, the initial growth of the dendritic trees of neurons and their patterns of synaptic connectivity with other neurons, is also influenced by neural activity. In this way, input from the environment can not only sculpt the brain through selective loss, but also through directed growth. Currently, however, there is little direct neurobiological evidence from the brain of activity-induced directed growth.

DISCUSSION POINT

To what extent do you consider there is a danger that DCN will become reductionist?

Babies build brains: the child as an active participant in its own brain development

In previous sections we have discussed the effects of experience on the specialization of cortex during ontogeny. It is important to stress, however, that the brain is not a passive organ shaped by the outside world. Rather, through the behaviour of the infant, the brain seeks out the appropriate stimulation it requires for its own further development. One of the clearest examples of this point comes from research on the development of face recognition in infants.

Although there is a considerable literature on the development of face recognition in young infants, only recently has there been speculation about the neural basis of these abilities. Specifically, de Schonen and Mathivet (1989), Johnson and Morton (1991 and Morton and Johnson, 1991) hypothesized that preferential responses to faces seen in newborn infants may be mediated by primarily subcortical visual pathways, whereas later developing abilities to recognize individual faces (on the basis of internal features) are mediated by developing cortical visual pathways. Johnson and Morton (1991) discussed two apparently contradictory bodies of evidence from the existing literature: although the prevailing view and most of the evidence, supported the contention that it takes the infant about two or three months to learn about the arrangement of features that compose a face (for reviews *see* Maurer, 1985; Nelson and Ludemann, 1989), one study (Goren et al., 1975) suggested that newborns around 10 minutes old would track, by means of head and eye movements, a face-like pattern further than various 'scrambled' face patterns. This newborn study was replicated by Johnson et al. (1991) with minor changes to improve the methodology.

The newborn studies provided evidence in support of a nativistic account of infant face recognition, but many studies using more conventional infant testing methods, such as preferential looking, had indicated that a preference for face patterns over others was not found until two or three months after birth (for review *see* Maurer, 1985; Nelson and Ludemann, 1989). Clearly, these apparently contradictory findings raised a problem for existing theories of the development of face recognition which involved only one process. In order to shed some light on the issues, Johnson and Morton (1991) turned to evidence from two areas of biology: **ethology** and **brain development**.

The primary source of evidence from other species (ethology) that Johnson and Morton (1991) used to interpret the human infancy results concerned **filial imprinting** in the domestic chick. This area was chosen because it is very well-studied both in terms of the behaviour and in terms of its neural basis. Imprinting is the process by which young pre-cocial birds, such as chicks or ducklings, recognize and develop an attachment for the first conspicuous object that they see after hatching (Bolhuis, 1991).

The results of a series of experiments on the brain basis of imprinting led to the proposal that there are two independent neural systems that underlie filial preference in the chick (Horn, 1985; Johnson et al., 1985). First is a specific predisposition for the young chick to orient toward objects resembling others of its own species. This system appears to be specifically tuned to the correct spatial arrangement of elements of the head and neck region and is sufficient to pick out the mother hen from other objects the chick is likely to be exposed to in the first few days after hatching. The neural basis for this predisposition is currently unknown, but the optic tectum, the homologue of the mammalian superior colliculus, is a likely candidate. The second system acquires information about the objects to which the young chick attends and is supported by a particular part of the chick forebrain (similar to mammalian cortex). In the natural environment, it was argued, the first system ensures that the second system acquires information about the particular individual mother hen close by.

The other source of biological data which Johnson and Morton (1991) used to generate an account of human infant face recognition came from the post-natal development of the cerebral cortex. Both neuroanatomical and neurophysiological data indicate that visually guided behaviour in the newborn infant is largely mediated by subcortical structures such as the superior colliculus and pulvinar and that it is not until two or three months of age that cortical circuitry comes to dominate subcortical circuits.

Consistent with these arguments is the position that visually guided behaviour in human infants, like that in domestic chicks, is based on activity in at least two distinct brain systems. Since these systems have distinct developmental time courses, then they may differentially influence behaviour in infants of different ages.

These two sources of biological evidence led Johnson and Morton (1991 and Morton and Johnson, 1991) to propose a two-process theory of infant face preferences analogous to that in chicks. These authors argued that the first process consists of a system accessed via the subcortical visual pathway (but possibly also involving some cortical structures) and underlies the preferential tracking of faces in newborns. However, the influence of this system over behaviour declines (possibly due to inhibition) during the second month of life. This is reflected in the fact that infants no longer preferentially track faces by two months of age. The second process depends upon cortical maturity and exposure to faces over the first month or so and begins to influence infant orienting preferences from two to four months of age.

By extension with the evidence on chicks, Johnson and Morton (1991) argued that the newborn preferential orienting system biases the input set to developing cortical circuitry. This circuitry is configured in response to a certain range of input, before it gains control over motor output around the third month of life. Once this occurs, the cortical system has enough experience with faces to ensure that it continues to acquire further information about them. As in the chick, the proposal is that a specific, early developing brain circuit acts in concert with the species' typical environment to bias the input to later developing brain circuitry.

Thus, in this example at least three factors contribute to the specialization that emerges; first, the primitive tendency of newborns to orient toward face-like patterns, second, the presence of many faces in the normal environment of the young infant and third, the architecture of cerebral cortical circuits activated when faces are within the visual field. These three factors acting in concert ensure the inevitable outcome of a brain specialized for processing the biologically important stimulus of faces.

Conclusions and future prospects

Recent advances in neural network modelling and brain imaging technology have opened up new vistas for the study of cognitive development. Now we not only have some tools for studying the functional development of the brain directly but also a type of theoretical model suitable for interfacing brain and behavioural observations. As a result of these developments, it is likely that our view of the infant's mind will change radically over the next decade or so.

Evidence from developmental neurobiology tells us that at least some of the functional specializations seen in the adult cortex are not 'pre-wired', but rather emerge as a result of pre- and post-natal activity dependent processes. These neurobiological facts have implications for the types of cognitive theories we hold. So-called 'evolutionary psychology' theories which argue that the infant is born with cortical 'modules' pre-wired for higher cognitive functions, such as language (Pinker, 1994), are not consistent with these findings.

The activity-dependent specialization of higher cognitive functions within the cerebral cortex may also have implications for clinical and educational issues. The view of an infant as an active participant in shaping its own subsequent brain development means that an infant who starts life with abnormal interactions with the world may increasingly deviate from the normal patterns of development. Thus, some developmental disorders may involve different patterns of cortical and cognitive specialization, or a failure of the process of specialization itself. On the other hand, the fact that there are several different possible patterns of cortical specialization can be beneficial following early focal damage to the cortex (e.g. Stiles and Thal, 1993). In some of these cases recovery can be achieved by non-damaged regions of cortex acquiring the functions normally subserved by the damaged region. Further, for some types of developmental deficit, intensive training of particular cortical regions may bolster their function through inducing greater activity within the region. For example, Tallal and colleagues (1996) claim improvement in language-learning impaired children following a training regime designed to improve speech analysis in the auditory cortex.

Finally, it may be feasible to perform cognitive neuroscience studies of education in which patterns of cortical specialization resulting from, for example, learning to read, are studied. Understanding the mechanisms through which cortical circuits acquire their patterns of specialization may eventually facilitate the design of syllabi. Some of these avenues for future research will clearly require long term research programmes. Further, they will require a new kind of developmental scientist, trained in methods and findings in neuroscience and computational modelling, as well as in cognitive development.

DISCUSSION POINT

Can you think of other developmentally challenging conditions for which intensive training of specific cortical areas might have an ameliorative effect?

Chapter summary

The interdisciplinary science of DCN has been introduced, in which the aim is to integrate brain and cognitive processes of development. Some of the main landmarks and findings concerning pre- and post-natal brain development were reviewed and the importance of activity-dependent processes in the specification of cortical areas was highlighted. Some examples of the application of biological knowledge to cognitive change were presented, including development of the prefrontal cortex in relation to object permanence and an account of selectionist theories of development. The point was then made that the infant can itself contribute to its brain specialization through biases to attend to biologically relevant types of stimuli, such as faces. Finally, some conclusions and prospects for future research have been outlined.

Seminar questions

1. Why is it important for those interested in psychological development to consider information about the brain?
2. What can be learned from disorders of development about normal brain and cognitive development?
3. How could connectionist modelling and/or brain imaging be used to address questions about the extent to which cognitive functions are innate?
4. Why should we be cautious about claims that the infant is born with regions of cortex pre-wired for higher cognitive functions, such as language?

Further reading

Elman, J., Bates, E., Johnson, M.H., Karmiloff-Smith, A., Parisi, D., Plunkett, K. 1996. *Rethinking Innateness: a connectionist perspective on development*. Cambridge, MA: MIT Press. A theoretical introduction to the use of connectionist modelling for understanding cognitive development. It also presents a broader framework for integrating information from developmental neuroscience, connectionism and cognitive development.

Johnson, M.H. 1997. *Developmental Cognitive Neuroscience: an introduction*. Oxford: Blackwell. A comprehensive introduction to relations between brain and cognitive development. Summarizes much of the research to date and proposes directions for future research.

Johnson, M.H. (Ed.) 1993. *Brain Development and Cognition: a reader*. Oxford: Blackwell. A series of classic readings on aspects of brain and cognitive development with introductions to each section.

Spreen, O., Risser, A.T. Edgell, D. 1995. *Developmental Neuropsychology*. New York: Oxford. An excellent introductory review to developmental deficits.

Knowledge of the physical world in infancy

3

J GAVIN BREMNER

Editors' preface

The ability of infants to understand the world about them has fascinated parents and psychologists for many years. This fascination has been fuelled by uncertainty about what children are thinking – obviously infants cannot explain their thoughts to adults. It has also been fuelled by competing views about early development, whether it is the result of nature, inborn capacities possessed by infants, or a result of nurture, the experience of the world (*see* the *Introduction*).

Piaget has provided us with a much more sophisticated view of development than this crude juxtaposition between nature and nurture (*see also* chapters 1, 4, 6 and 8). He supposed that children are born with certain basic ways of processing information from the world, and by processing information they construct an understanding of their world. As you will see in this chapter, Piaget's ideas and observations have resulted in an important body of research which has demonstrated that infants process information in different ways to adults, some of this research was designed to support his ideas, others to discredit them. Particularly interesting have been several innovative techniques which have been used to investigate infant cognitive processes. These have revealed levels of cognitive sophistication that few, including Piaget, had anticipated. In this chapter Professor Gavin Bremner draws these two research traditions together and provides new ideas to resolve conflict between these different findings.

Introduction

Infant cognition is a broad area, covering topics such as understanding of causality, categorization of objects and problem-solving. In addition, other topics that might at first sight appear to belong in other areas have implications for infant cognition. For instance, the social phenomenon of imitation is widely interpreted as evidence for the presence of early mental representational processes. Additionally, recent research and theorizing about infant perception actually suggests that, contrary to traditional theory, representational processes are not necessary for objective perception of the world. A consequence of the growing influence of this argument is that the boundary between perception and cognition has to a large extent dissolved. Thus, it would take several chapters to provide a full description of what we currently know about infants' knowledge of the world. Here, the focus is on the body of work that bears directly on the development of mental representation, since this concept is at the root of cognition. We shall also be covering the largest related body of research on infants' knowledge of the physical world. A key focus of infancy research is to do with the origins of mental representation. Mental processes are undoubtedly a fundamental aspect of adult life and a crucial question for developmental psychology is about the origins of these processes. Are they innate in newborns, or do they develop later? And if the latter, what are the processes and the timescale concerning their emergence?

Piaget (1952, 1954) provided a compelling account of the development of mental representation, claiming that it emerged in full form only at the end of the second year; representation of the world of objects and people was constructed gradually through the activities of the infant in the world. However, more recent evidence provides a rather different picture. Although the phenomena on which Piaget based his account have been replicated, there is now a body of work indicating that, much earlier than Piaget would have recognized, infants are capable of representing absent objects and understanding the constraints on movement of one object relative to another. This research constitutes a major challenge to Piaget's account. However, the phenomena on which Piaget based his account remain and there have been recent moves to re-interpret these in the light of this recent evidence. In the end, the outcome may be a modification of the Piagetian account rather than a rejection of it.

Piaget's account of infant cognitive development

According to Piaget, infants enter the world without ability to know the world, but are born with a tendency to act on the world in specific ways which ensures progressive adaptation to it (Piaget, 1952). Although the infant's acts are initially limited to a set of reflexes such as grasping and sucking, this adaptation process ensures that through their use they are gradually altered and then combined to form more complex activities. These sensorimotor structures, or **schemes**, form the basis of intelligence during this period. The adaptive process through which they are developed consists of two components, **assimilation** being the process by which new objects or events are incorporated within the scope of existing schemes and **accommodation** being the process through which the scheme is modified to meet the resistance to straightforward assimilation that is always presented by a new object. This sensorimotor knowledge is very different from knowledge as we normally think of it, since it is not based on mental representational processes and is only identified in the structure of the relationships between action and perceived events. However, it is from this that mental representation finally emerges.

An example should help to clarify this process. Suppose a six-month-old infant, who is already used to reaching out and grasping objects, encounters a new object, rather larger than previous ones successfully grasped. If the infant successfully reaches out and grasps the new object, Piaget would say that the new object had been **assimilated** to the reach-and-grasp scheme. But in order to be successful, the grasp will have to be modified in some way. In this particular case, the infant will have to open his or her hand wider, otherwise the attempt will fail. Thus the new object requires a modification of the grasp scheme and this internal change Piaget calls **accommodation**. In infancy, these processes always occur together and the outcome is the generation of sensorimotor schemes that become more and more generalized, incorporating both the underlying pattern general to all reach-and-grasp sequences and the variations which the physical characteristics of individual objects demand.

Piaget describes the product of these processes in terms of six stages in the development of concepts of objects, space, causality and time. In actuality, these concepts are inseparably linked and much of his account of these different domains is really just another slant on the same set of general arguments. Thus, we are limited here to describing his account as it applies to the most thoroughly researched aspect of his work, the development of object permanence. Piaget claims that in the early months (the first two stages) infants have no concept of objects as independent entities existing in an external world. Instead, he believes that infants detect images or pictures from the sensation arising from objects and these images are effectively created by action; the act of looking creates the sensation. It is worth noting here that he is not making claims about the infant's perception being limited to retinal images; this is rather a different point arising from classical views of perceptual development. The main point of Piaget's claim is that the infant's concept of the world is profoundly egocentric in the sense that the only thing known in the world is the self and the sensations arising therein. Consequently, awareness of objects is inextricably linked to the actions involved in perceiving (*see also* Chapter 12 for other views about awareness of self and others).

A step away from this egocentric awareness is taken when, in stage III (4–8 months), infants begin to observe themselves in action. The resultant mapping between vision and the bodily sensations arising from action leads to a certain externalization of the world. This means that visible objects are now recognized as being external. But there is no evidence that infants at this stage are capable of representing the object mentally. Piaget showed that if an interesting object is hidden from an infant of less than eight months of age, no attempt is made to search for it.

At approximately eight months of age, infants begin to search for hidden objects. This marks their transition to stage IV and indicates that they are capable of co-ordinating separate schemes, as a result of which they can represent the absent object in its relationship to the cover. From this one might conclude that mental representation, the major goal of the sensori-motor period, has been achieved. However, as is typical of his approach, Piaget complicates the search task to gain a measure of the generality of this new ability. After hiding the object in one position (A) and letting the infant retrieve it a few times, he hides it at a new location. Despite the fact that the infant watches the act closely, he or she searches consistently back at the old location. This stage IV, or **A not B**, error is a striking phenomenon which has attracted a good deal of research. According to Piaget, although infants are now capable of relating object and cover and so are no longer in the grips of the notion that the object is created by action, there remains a remnant of the egocentric link to action, such that they conceive of the object as existing only in the place where search was previously successful (Fig 3.1).

Eventually, infants overcome this error, which marks their passage to stage V (12–18 months). They now search accurately wherever they see an object hidden. However, that is still not the end of the matter in Piaget's investigation. He discovers that in this stage infants still have difficulties if an object is moved while it is hidden. For instance, take the following task. An object is hidden under a cover and is transferred under it to a box where it is deposited. Then the cover is returned to its original position. In reality, there is no way of knowing whether the object is still under the cover or in the box and an adult would search at one place and then the other. However, infants in this stage initially search only under the cover. Later in the stage, they search at both places and so recover the object. However, if a second box is introduced and the invisible movement is directed to it, infants search only under the cover or in the old box. In other words, a version of the stage IV error appears when the object is invisibly displaced. It should be no real surprise that such a task poses a problem. Effectively, it is a form of mental reasoning task based on the logic that if the object is not in one place it must be in the other and solution of this problem by older infants in stage VI (18–24 months) is really quite a striking achievement. And it is only at this point that Piaget would agree that infants possess a mental representation of absent objects that is completely objective and independent of action.

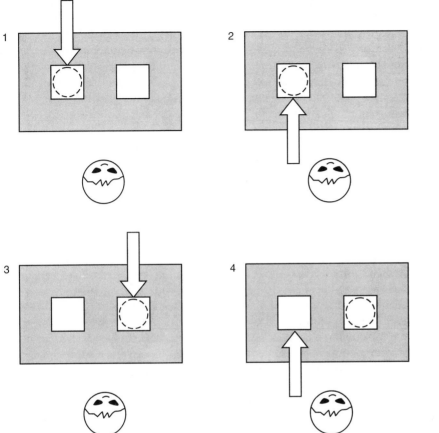

Figure 3.1 A typical experimental version of the Piagetian stage IV task. Downward arrows indicate position of hiding and upward arrows indicate typical position of search. The sequence indicates: (1) the object is hidden at A; (2) the infant searches correctly; (3) the object is hidden at B; (4) the infant errs by searching at A.

Research examining Piaget's phenomena

During the 1970s and to an extent the 1980s, a good deal of research was done on the basic Piagetian phenomena. Some of the work focused on search failure during stage III, but the major focus was on the stage IV search error. In this section I shall describe some of the main findings arising from this work and the alternative accounts that have been developed in the process.

SEARCH FAILURE

One obvious explanation of search failure is that infants lack the motor ability to remove whatever it is that conceals the object. In support of such a notion, Rader et al. (1979) found that infants would search for an object hidden under a small card but failed to do so when it was hidden under a larger cloth, concluding that search failure in the cloth condition was due to lack of manual dexterity. However, this is not a satisfactory explanation of search failure, because Bower and Wishart (1972) showed that infants who would not retrieve an object from an opaque cup would retrieve it from under a transparent cup. The motor component of both tasks was identical, but it was invisibility of the object that led to difficulty. And there is an alternative interpretation of the result obtained by Rader et al. (1979). Young infants engage in a good deal of non-directed arm movements and such movements are very much more likely to dislodge the card than remove the cloth.

So is object invisibility the sole problem? Bower and Wishart (1972) showed that infants who would not search under an opaque cup would reach out in the dark and retrieve an object which they had seen dangled in front of them before the lights went out. This study suffered from the same problem as the work of Rader et al. (1979), namely that random arm movements may have produced contact with the object, which was always at the midline. However, this problem was resolved in a study by Hood and Willatts (1986) in which the object was dangled to one side of midline and was removed once the lights were extinguished, to prevent fortuitous contact. Under these conditions, five-month-old infants showed clear evidence of reaching directed to the former location of the object. Thus it appears that not all forms of object invisibility create problems.

This conclusion is actually in keeping with Piaget's account. He noted that infants would reach for an object that had gone outside the visual field and claimed that search failure was due to lack of understanding of the relationship between object and occluder, in itself based on inability to co-ordinate cover lifting and object retrieval schemes. But Bower suggests that infants fail to understand specific object–occluder relationships that involve enclosure, as when, for instance, a cloth or cup occupies a location range that overlaps with that of the object. However, subsequent research (Dunst et al., 1982) cast doubt on the notion that enclosure relationships were particularly difficult and Neilson (1977) showed that the degree of separation in depth between object and occluder was important. It appears that perception of the distinct locations of object and occluder at the point of disappearance may be a determinant of search after disappearance and so the problem may be as much perceptual as conceptual.

Although the accounts of Bower and Piaget do not look too distant in respect of the infant's understanding of object–occluder relationships, it is important to note one fundamental disagreement. According to Bower (1982), infants understand object permanence from a very early age but have difficulties understanding certain relationships between objects. In contrast, Piaget believes that it is only through constructing the relationship between the object and occluder that the infant comes to understand object permanence. Solely on the basis of object search data, these alternative accounts are hard to dissociate and we shall have to wait till a later section to look for a resolution on this point.

DISCUSSION POINT

Consider whether you feel it is possible to understand the permanence of a hidden object without also understanding the spatial relationship between it and the thing that hides it.

THE A NOT B ERROR

Experimental work confirms that at around eight months of age infants begin to search for hidden objects, but that they make the error of searching only at the first place of concealment. In explaining this A not B or stage IV search error, Bower (1982) claims that even when infants begin to search for objects they do not understand the relationship between object and occluder, assuming that the object has been replaced by the occluder. Search is simply guided by a rule that when an object disappears manipulation of the replacement object will reveal it again. This is a direct extension of his explanation of search failure. However, this account has not been tested empirically. Other workers have investigated the A not B error in great detail and this is the work that is reviewed below. Although we may not yet have an entirely satisfactory explanation of the phenomenon, at least we have a good knowledge of the conditions under which it does and does not occur.

Manual activity

One of the early focuses of research on the stage IV error was on the role of manual activity. The question was whether the error was dependent on the infant having retrieved the object from the A location. Several investigators (Landers, 1971; Evans, 1973; Butterworth, 1974) performed studies in which infants searched on B trials after observational A trials in which they did not retrieve the object, and found that the error rate was much the same as usual. These results suggest that the error is not dependent on prior action at the A location and cast doubt on that aspect of Piaget's account. They also appear to indicate that the error is more than response repetition.

Memory interpretations

A second early focus was on the role of memory in the stage IV error. At first sight, it is tempting to guess that the error is due to forgetting the location of the object. However, the phenomenon cannot be due to global forgetting: that could explain search failure, but remember that on A trials infants are highly successful from the first trial. The problem to be tackled is why they should encode the object's location accurately on A trials but fail to do so on B trials. Harris (1973) suggested that this arose through memory interference: when the object is hidden at A, search is successful, but when the new location is used, interference takes place between memory for the past location and memory for the present location, such that infants often search back at the old location. In support of this account, Harris found that errors were infrequent when infants were allowed to search immediately on B trials. Gratch et al. (1974) found that a delay of only a second was sufficient to produce errors at the normal rate, but that delays above one second did nothing to increase error. So if interference is at the root of things, it has its effect very quickly. Gratch et al. (1974) interpret their results differently, suggesting that the lack of error with delays of less than a second is due to the maintenance of a postural orientation (and possibly a partial reach) towards the correct location. Infants are fortuitously correct because they simply continue an act that began when the object was in view.

Bjork and Cummings (1984) provide a rather different memory account, suggesting that infants make a rather imprecise coding of the object's position on B trials, so that they often make errors. Their evidence for this was that if infants were provided with more than two potential hiding places, errors on B trials were rarely to the original location, being more often directed to positions close to the B location.

There is, however, a major problem for all memory accounts. Piaget noted that the error would still occur when the object was visible at the new location. This finding has been replicated by Butterworth (1974) and Harris (1974) in versions of the task using transparent covers and by Bremner and Knowles (1984) who did not even cover the object on B trials. It is not clear how memory accounts can explain this, since there should be no need to hold the visible object in memory.

Spatial analyses

One possible explanation of the error is that infants have difficulty updating the spatial location of the object when it is moved from A to B. A number of workers have investigated the spatial demands of the stage IV task. Harris (1973) and later, Butterworth (1975) pointed out that when the object is moved from the A location to the B location, both its absolute position in space changes and its relative position changes, that is, it goes from, say, the left-hand to the right-hand container. By changing the position of the containers between A and B trials Butterworth (1975) made it possible to hide the object either in the same relative location but a different absolute position, or in the same absolute position but a different relative location. The finding was that a change in location according to either of these spatial reference systems led to error at about the same rate as if object location changed relative to both reference systems at once. So apparently infants use both ways of coding the position of the hidden object and have difficulty if its position changes relative to either.

Bremner and Bryant (1977) pointed out that because infants remained stationary throughout the task, it was impossible to tell if they were coding the object's position in absolute terms, or through self-reference, in relation

to their own body. However, the confound between these two types of coding is removed if the infant is moved to the opposite side of the table. On B
trials, following such a movement, infants searched at the same position
relative to self as before and hence at a different absolute position. This
happened despite the fact that the two locations lay on clearly different
backgrounds. However, Bremner (1978a) found that if differently coloured
covers were used, the effect was reversed: infants now searched at the same
absolute location after movement and hence at a different self-referent location. Thus it appears that absolute position coding is possible if the alternative locations are clearly distinguished.

  So what does this tell us about the basis for the stage IV error?
Butterworth et al. (1982) claim that knowledge of object identity is intimately linked to keeping track of the spatial history of the object. It is only
through linking the successive positions of an object that infants perceive
its identity over the move and it is because infants encounter difficulties in
doing this that search errors occur. But although this is a plausible account,
there may be reasons to doubt whether the data unambiguously support
such a conclusion. Box 3.1 expands on an alternative argument, namely
that these spatial analyses of the stage IV task tell us important things
about infants' spatial abilities but do not give us the key to the search error
itself. After you have read the material there, you may wish to think
through the possible relations between spatial coding and the A not B error.

BOX 3.1

I have already described how use of distinct covers led to a shift
from self-referent to absolute (**allocentric**) coding (Bremner, 1978a).
Instead of searching after movement at the same relative position as
previously, the infants searched under the same coloured cover as
before. However this did not eliminate search errors because if the
object was hidden at the absolute opposite location after movement,
they made errors by searching at the old absolute location. The conclusion was that these analyses do not provide the key to the error, but
rather use the error as a useful phenomenon through which infants'
spatial ability can be investigated. In a later study (Bremner, 1978b) a
modified technique was used in which the infant was moved to the
opposite side of the table while the object was hidden in its original
location (*see* fig 3.2). In this case no object shift was involved and very
much the same results emerged. That is, nine-month-old infants
coded the object's position relative to self (say to their left) and so
failed to find it after movement. But if differently coloured covers
were used, they escaped from this tendency and searched correctly.
This finding fits with similar work by Acredolo (1978) (*see* fig 3.2). In
her task, infants were trained to anticipate, on the sound of a buzzer,
the appearance of a human face at one of two windows in the side
walls of the room in which they were placed. Following training, they

were moved to the opposite side of the room, facing the opposite way, and direction of anticipative looking was measured following the sounding of the buzzer. This task was performed with the correct location either clearly marked by a surrounding star pattern, or unmarked. She found that six-month-olds responded to the same window relative to self and so anticipated wrongly, whereas 16-month-olds responded correctly. At the intermediate age of 11 months the results showed an effect of position marking: infants responded correctly when the correct window was clearly marked but incorrectly when it was unmarked. Although these infants are somewhat older than the nine-month-olds in my study, the position cuing effect is similar. It appears that during the period when infants are developing the ability to code positions in absolute terms, strong spatial cues support the emerging ability. And it is worth noting that this ability is emerging around the time that infants develop the ability to crawl. This may be no coincidence, since mobility makes fixed self-referent coding unreliable and there is growing evidence (Campos and Bertenthal, 1988) that there is a causal relationship between the development of locomotion and development of environment-centred (**allocentric**) coding of position.

Summary

Studies of the stage IV error in the period up to the mid-1980s eliminated a number of possible explanations. The error occurs without repeated manual action at A, so it does not appear to be due to response repetition. Errors occur when the object is visible at B, so memory-based accounts fail. Spatial analyses of the error may reveal more about infants' spatial coding than about the basis for the error. This state of affairs led to something of an impasse. Additionally, there was a growth in studies using promising alternative techniques to measure infants' object knowledge. The result was that research on the stage IV error almost died out. As we shall see, however, it later came back to centre stage and is currently being re-interpreted in the light of recent data and theory about the abilities for very young infants.

A challenge to the theory of sensorimotor development: direct realism and objective perception

One of the fundamental notions in Piaget's account of cognitive development is that infants' awareness of the world is initially subjective. The young infant is unaware of an independent objective world separate from self. And a major developmental task is the gradual objectification of the

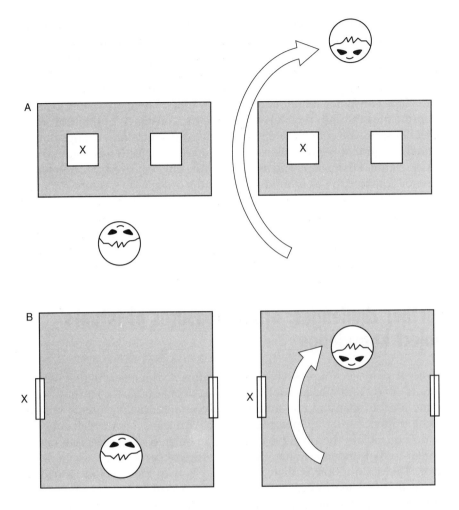

Figure 3.2 Tasks used (A) by Bremner (1978b) and (B) Acredolo (1978) to investigate self-reference versus absolute coding of position.

world through construction of sensorimotor intelligence and ultimately development of representation. A theoretical challenge to this view is presented by the **ecological**, or **direct realist** approach (Gibson, 1979). Contrary to traditional theories of perceptual development, this approach claims that the objective world is directly perceived without need for mediating representational processes. So according to this account, we are misguided in looking for evidence of construction of objective reality from subjective sensory data.

If this account is correct, we would expect to find evidence for objective perception very early in life: the claim is that objective perception is a fundamental of animal perceptual systems and is not dependent on the development of interpretative processes. And the application of a relatively simple technique has revealed evidence of impressive perceptual abilities very early in life. Infants are habituated to one stimulus (until looking declines to a set level) whereupon they are presented with a new stimulus, the question being whether looking recovers (dishabituation). The logic behind this **habituation–dishabituation** technique is that in order to dishabituate, infants must be able to discriminate the new from the old stimulus.

As well as revealing that newborn infants are capable of basic form perception (Slater et al. 1983), this type of investigation has shown that newborns exhibit the perceptual principles of size constancy (Slater et al. 1990) and shape constancy (Slater and Morison, 1985). These are the fundamental principles through which we perceive the constancy of the form of an object despite variations in viewing angle or distance and changes in the retinal image that result. This is the hallmark of objective perception and Piaget claimed that shape and size constancy only emerged through sensorimotor construction at around nine months of age. Thus recent data present a challenge to one of the fundamental notions embedded in the theory of sensorimotor development, namely that infants progressively construct an objective reality from subjective sense data. But, as the following section will indicate, probably even more telling challenges arise from recent work evaluating his claims about development of object permanence.

Further challenges: other measures of infants' object knowledge

In recent years, techniques have been developed which permit diagnosis of infants' object knowledge prior to the onset of object search. The basic technique used in many recent studies involves familiarizing infants with an event sequence and then presenting them with test events which either do or do not violate the physical principle under test. The principle here is similar to that underlying habituation studies of perception, with a difference. The assumption is that infants can be expected to look longer at events that violate physical principles. So increased looking at a new event sequence indicates more than surface discrimination: it indicates not just that something is different but that something is wrong with the new event. If this interpretation is appropriate, it is possible to diagnose the level of infants' awareness of object permanence or the rules by which one object moves relative to another, because if they note a violation they must at some level be aware of the principle that has been violated. One of the first studies to use this technique was carried out by Baillargeon et al. (1985). Five-month-old infants were familiarized with a repeated event in which a flap rotated from flat on the table through 180°. From the infant's perspective, this would look like the raising of a drawbridge, except that the rotation went through a full 180°. After familiarization, two types of test event were presented, in both of which a cube was placed in the path of the flap (*see* fig 3.3). In a 'possible' test event, the flap rotated but came to a stop on making contact with the cube, whereas in an 'impossible' test event, it rotated through 180° as usual, appearing to annihilate the cube in the process. Note that this comparison nicely creates an opposition between surface event similarity, in which the impossible event (full 180° rotation) is more similar to the familiarization event than the possible event is ($< 180°$ rotation) and event lawfulness, in which only the impossible event presents a violation of physical reality. Thus if infants were simply dishabituating on the basis of perceptual dissimilarity, we would expect most looking at the possible event where there is both a new object (the block) and a different rotation. However, they actually looked more at the impossible event. The conclusion was that infants of this age both understand object permanence and know that one object cannot move through another.

This initial finding was later replicated with infants as young as three and a half months (Baillargeon, 1987a). Additionally, Baillargeon (1987b) used the same technique to investigate the accuracy with which older infants could anticipate events of this sort. She found that seven-month-old infants had quite precise expectations about such collisions, expecting that the screen would stop rotating sooner if the cube was larger or closer to the screen, but expecting it to stop later if the object in its path was compressible.

Fig 3.4 illustrates another application of this approach (Baillargeon, 1986). Infants were familiarized with an event sequence in which a toy truck rolled down a ramp and passed behind a screen (prior to each trial the screen was raised, revealing nothing behind it and lowered again). After familiarization, infants saw one of two test events. In the possible event, a block was placed behind the screen, but behind the track so that it did not obstruct the path of the truck. In the impossible event, the block was placed behind the screen on the track, so that it presented an obstruction. In both cases, the screen was raised to reveal the block and lowered again, whereupon the truck rolled down the track and re-emerged from behind the screen as usual. Baillargeon (1986) found that 6–8-month-old

A Possible event

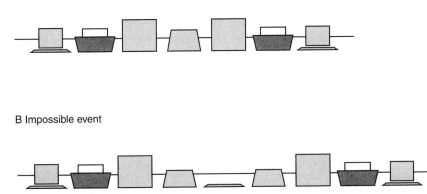

B Impossible event

Figure 3.3 The infant's view of the test events in the study by Baillargeon et al. (1985). For each event, the diagram indicates a coarse-grained sequence of the screen's rotation, from left to right. Note that for the possible event the sequence reverses at frame four (when it contacts the object), whereas for the impossible event, the sequence reverses at frame five, once it has rotated a full 180°.

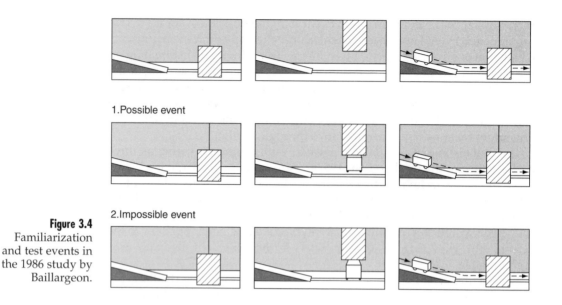

1. Possible event

2. Impossible event

Figure 3.4
Familiarization and test events in the 1986 study by Baillargeon.

infants looked longer at the impossible event, a finding replicated by Baillargeon and DeVos (1991). Apparently, infants not only appreciate the continued existence of the block but can use precise memory for its position to reach a conclusion about whether the truck event is possible.

Spelke et al. (1992) used modified versions of this task to test even younger infants. For instance, they familiarized infants aged two and a half months to an event in which a ball rolled behind a screen, whereupon the screen was lifted to show that the ball had come to rest against an end wall. On test trials, a box was placed in the path of the ball so that when the screen was lowered only the top part of the box was visible. Two events followed, a possible event, in which removal of the screen revealed the ball resting against the box having collided with it and an impossible event in which the object was revealed resting against the end wall, having apparently passed through the box to come to rest in its usual place. The infants looked longer at the impossible event, suggesting that at the age of two and a half months they can detect the position of the whole box from perception of a visible part and understand that one object cannot move through another in its path (*see* Box 3.2 for further applications of this general approach).

BOX 3.2

The approach described in this section can be used to investigate infants' understanding of a whole range of aspects of physical reality. As another example we can take a study by Baillargeon and DeVos (1991) which investigated infants' awareness of how the dimensions of an object affect its visibility as it passes behind a screen. These authors used the experimental setup shown in fig 3.5, first to familiarize infants with an event in which either a tall or a short carrot moved behind a screen, to re-emerge at the opposite side. Then test trials were carried out with a new screen with a window cut in it. The size of the window was such that the small carrot would not appear there, whereas in normal reality the top of the large carrot would appear. But neither the small nor the large carrot appeared at the window on these test trials, making the small carrot event sequence lawful and the large carrot event sequence unlawful. Infants aged three and a half months looked more at the unlawful test event, leading to the conclusion that they have a good awareness of the conditions under which one object will occlude another.

Secondly, Needham and Baillargeon (1993) have investigated infants' knowledge of the conditions under which they expect one object to provide support for another, by presenting events in which an object moved along a support to a point at which it either remain supported or would fall off (*see* fig 3.6). Their finding was that infants aged four and a half months appear to treat contact as sufficient for support, failing to identify the degree of support necessary. Baillargeon et al. (1992) showed that, in contrast, infants aged six and a half months had developed a more sophisticated understanding, recognizing when contact was insufficient to provide support.

Thirdly, Needham and Baillargeon (1997) have used this approach to investigate conditions under which infants detect objects as separate or interconnected. Their finding was that when two objects are in contact, infants aged eight months generally treat them as interconnected and so expect them to move together. However, a nice additional finding was that a prior demonstration that a blade could be passed between the objects at the point of contact led infants to expect them to move separately.

Habituation events

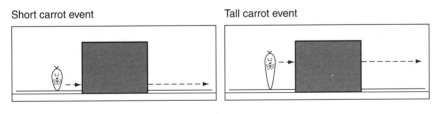

Test events

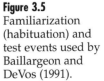

Figure 3.5
Familiarization (habituation) and test events used by Baillargeon and DeVos (1991).

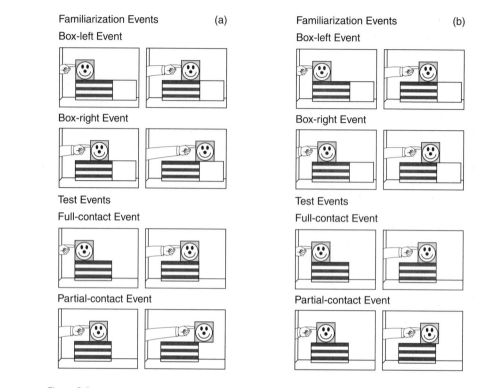

Figure 3.6 Familiarization and test events used by Baillargeon et al. (1992). On all trials, the box is pushed from left to right. On test events, the extended support is removed. The result is that in the 'box right' position, the left-hand partial contact event is inadequate for support, whereas the right-hand partial contact is adequate for support. Young infants treat both these cases as adequate, whereas those aged six and a half months treat only the right-hand case as adequate.

SUMMARY

The methodology developed by Baillargeon and Spelke has proved enormously fruitful, yielding exciting data about infants' awareness of the world. It seems that infants as young as three months have a quite sophisticated awareness of object permanence and the rules by which objects move relative to each other. But it would be wrong to conclude that their awareness matches that of adults. For instance, note the evidence in Box 3.2 that understanding of support relations is initially rather rudimentary and improves with age. Additionally Spelke and colleagues conclude that four-month-olds do not seem to understand the rules by which objects move under the influence of gravity, apparently not expecting an object to continue to fall until it hits a supporting surface (Spelke et al., 1992). Also, although young infants distinguish between object and background, they seem to be quite poor at treating two objects in close proximity as distinct units (*see* Box 3.2; also Prather and Spelke, 1982; Kestenbaum et al., 1987).

Search errors revisited

Although enthusiasm for what appeared to be better measures of infant cognition led to reduced interest in object search tasks, in the last few years there has been growing recognition of the need for a reconciliation between these two bodies of evidence. Search errors remain despite the research by Baillargeon and Spelke and they demand an explanation as never before. If infants aged six months perceive or understand object permanence, the fundamental question is why do they make errors in searching for hidden objects? Here I shall summarize accounts of the stage IV error that have attempted such a reconciliation.

ACTION PERSEVERATION

A recent interpretation revisits the notion that the error is due to action perseveration. Smith et al. (in press) obtained evidence that infants made search errors even when no objects were hidden. Instead of hiding an object at A and later at B, they simply attracted infants' attention to A (by waving and tapping the container lid) and later to B in the same way. They found that infants made 'search' errors with the same incidence as in the standard task and concluded that the phenomenon was due to establishment of a reaching habit and nothing to do with object permanence.

Although on face value this is a plausible possibility, the account is oversimple as I have stated it. We know from earlier work (Evans, 1973; Butterworth, 1974) that infants make search errors even if they have only seen the object hidden and revealed at the A location. So this account has to be modified to allow that repeated looking at the A location is sufficient to lead to reaching there later. However, the interpretation provided by Smith et al. (1995) also contains a logical flaw. If similar 'errors' occur when no object is hidden, it does not follow that the hiding of the object in the standard A not B task is irrelevant; superficially similar behaviours can have quite different bases. Munakata (1997) performed a study which makes this point. She compared infants' reaching in two tasks, one of which replicated that of Smith et al. (1995) in which no object was hidden on A or B trials and another in which no object was hidden on A trials, but an object was hidden on B trials. In the replication condition, just as Smith et al. (1995) found, infants made errors, but on the version in which the object was introduced and hidden on B trials, they did not make errors, despite the fact that up to that point the motor history of both groups was identical. The object had no prior history at A and they searched correctly when it was hidden for the first time at B. Munakata (1997) concludes that the hiding of an object has an effect and so is an important factor in the standard task.

DISCUSSION POINT

In what sense are infants making an error in the 'no object' task, indeed in what sense would we expect them to do anything other than stay with the A location? When no object is hidden, presumably the locations (possibly particularly the lids) become the foci of attention. If infants' attention has been drawn to the A container and their interest engaged in it, why should they shift their attention to an identical container at a new location?

LOCATIONS AS PLACES OF CONCEALMENT

Two things happen when an object is hidden: it disappears and a place takes on the function of container or place of concealment. Most previous accounts have assumed that object search phenomena tell us about object permanence. In contrast, Bremner (1985) developed an account based on knowledge of places as containers. During the early years, infants spend a good deal of time removing objects from containers (for instance taking toys from toy boxes) but, as parents know to their cost, they very rarely put them back. It is thus plausible that they have semi-magical notions about containers as sources of objects, notions which are based more on finding objects there than on seeing them go there. Admittedly, seeing an object disappear at a place must be a sufficient cue to lead to search at that place, otherwise infants would never search for an object on the first trial. And even the perceptual features of the container may cue its function. But my hypothesis was that object retrieval or revelation is a much more potent cue to a place as a container. Thus, once an object has been retrieved (or has been revealed) at A, that place is firmly established as a container where an object will be found. When the object is hidden at B, there is a conflict between object disappearance at B and the newly established function of A as a container and the greater salience of the latter normally wins that day.

This account does not make assumptions about limited object representation as the basis of error, an advantage given the evidence that object knowledge is well developed in the early months. It might also explain 'errors' when no object is hidden; by attracting infants' attention to the A container, Smith et al. (in press) may have prompted them to its potential (if not actual) containment function. However, the specifics of this containment model have not yet been tested.

A NEUROPHYSIOLOGICAL ACCOUNT

Diamond (1988) has suggested that the error can be explained by the fact that the frontal cortex becomes fully functional only rather late in infancy, an account that is based in part on the finding that rhesus monkeys with lesions of frontal cortex perform poorly on the stage IV task (Diamond, 1990). She proposes that a primary function of frontal cortex is the integration of two capacities, the maintenance of an object representation in memory and inhibition of incorrect responses, and her claim is that although infants are capable of these singly, they are incapable of integrating the two. There is some evidence that there is a link between error and frontal cortex development. For instance, Bell and Fox (1992) showed that infants who did not make the stage IV error showed more developed frontal EEG patterns than those who erred. We must note, however, that this is correlational evidence which does not allow us to assume a direct causal link.

In effect, this account suggests that the infant's problem is one of co-ordinating object memory and action. By presenting a multi-factor explanation, this is probably an advance over previous accounts that have tried to explain the error in terms of a single factor. However, there is reason to doubt the detail of the argument. It does not appear that failure to inhibit a previous response can explain the error, either alone or in conjunction with a memory factor. Remember that early studies (Landers, 1971; Evans, 1973; Butterworth, 1974) obtained errors after observational trials. In this case, no prior response had been established. And the problem for the memory side of Diamond's account is that it cannot explain why errors occur even when the object is visible under a transparent cover (Butterworth, 1977), or not even covered on B trials (Bremner and Knowles, 1984). In other words, errors still occur under conditions in which only one of Diamond's two factors are present, conditions under which errors should not occur.

Conclusion: a reconceptualization of cognitive development in infancy

Recent research based on looking duration provides convincing evidence that infants aged less than six months detect a great deal about the physical world of objects, including object permanence and the rules that constrain the movement of one object relative to another. Nonetheless, there is also abundant evidence that at least to the end of their first year, infants do not appear able to reflect this awareness in their manual action. In particular, the A not B search error has eluded a satisfactory single factor explanation. Lack of object permanence does not appear to explain the phenomenon. And results of a recent study further weaken the notion that representation of the hidden object's location is a primary factor. Wilcox et al. (1996) presented infants aged between two and a half and six and a half months with event sequences in which an object disappeared at one of two locations and after a delay either reappeared in the opposite location (impossible event) or in the same location (possible event). All age groups looked reliably longer at the impossible event, suggesting that they were capable of holding the location of the hidden object in memory and noting a violation when it reappeared in the wrong place. If such young infants have well developed location memory, it seems unlikely that this would be a major aspect of the problem six or seven months later.

It also appears that neither response habit nor memory defect can be at the root of the error. However, it may be that the Diamond's account is going in the right direction by suggesting that the reasons for the error lie in the relationship between representation and action. Elsewhere (Bremner, 1997) it has been suggested that although quite young infants are aware of objective properties of the world including object constancies and object permanence, they are not automatically able to bring this awareness to bear on their actions. In this respect, we may consider the awareness detected in looking duration studies as **implicit** knowledge which only becomes **explicit** once it can be used to guide action. The distinction is applied here with respect to the guidance of action rather than with respect to incorporation in mental activities (Karmiloff-Smith, 1992). But the basic principles are similar.

This model has a good deal in common with Diamond's account. But rather than assuming that the problem in the link to action is simply to do with suppression of previous actions, my more global suggestion is that infants need to learn how to guide action on the basis of implicit knowledge. They have to learn what sort of act to use in a particular situation and also where to direct this act. Of course, response suppression may be a part of this, but selection of an appropriate response is at least equally important. It may be assumed that this knowledge develops quite directly in the case of actions towards visible objects, but lags behind in the case of invisible objects, because part of the process involves converting a perceptually based implicit awareness of permanence to explicit sensorimotor knowledge of the relationship between object and occluder that carries with it knowledge of how to sequence acts to obtain the hidden object.

But why the A not B error? If infants already search for objects, does this not mean that they have successfully formed a link between object permanence and action? My suggestion is that by nine months of age they are not yet at that point. Instead it may be that they are developing pragmatic knowledge of where to act to obtain objects. Previously it has been proposed (Bremner, 1985) that the stage IV error arises because infants are in the process of forming knowledge about where objects can be found rather than knowledge of the objects themselves. An extension of this would be to suggest that this is a stopgap that allows them to use action more or less successfully and that it is the continued use of action on hidden objects that leads eventually to development of action guided by explicit knowledge of the relationship between hidden object and occluder. The reader will identify a distinct similarity to Piaget's account here and it is in this respect that I argued at the beginning of this chapter that the way forward was to seek common ground between accounts rather than to replace one entirely with another.

Seminar questions

1. Given that recent evidence based on measures of looking time indicates that infants of less than six months of age are aware of object permanence, why do they fail to show this awareness in their manual search?
2. Can we infer knowledge of the principles of the physical world from evidence that infants look longer at events that violate these principles?
3. In the light of current knowledge, evaluate Piaget's account of the development of object permanence.

Further reading

Bremner, J.G. 1994. *Infancy* (second edition). Oxford: Blackwell; Chapter 4. A fuller coverage of cognitive development in infancy.

Bremner, J.G. 1997. From perception to cognition. In Bremner, G., Slater A, Butterworth G. (eds) *Infant development: recent advances*. Hove: Psychology Press. At the beginning of the chapter, it was suggested that ecological direct perception theorists claim that much or all of infants' ability can be explained without recourse to the concept of mental representation; this text offers a review and evaluation of this position.

Slater, A. 1997. Visual perception and its organisation in early infancy. In Bremner, G., Slater A., Butterworth G. (eds) *Infant Development: recent advances*. Hove: Psychology Press. For a fuller review of evidence for objective perception from birth onwards.

Hopkins, B., Butterworth, G. 1997. Dynamical systems approaches to the development of action. In Bremner, G., Slater, A., Butterworth G. (eds) *Infant Development: recent advances*. Hove: Psychology Press. Another approach to infant development which, taken in conjunction with the direct perception approach, has potential to replace Piaget's account is the **dynamical systems** approach. This has much in common with Piaget's account in terms of emphasis on action as a developmental driving force, but it shares with the direct perception approach the rejection of the concept of mental representation; this text offers a review.

4

The development of communication and language

DAVID MESSER

Editors' preface

The human use of communication and language is often seen as the ability which makes us very different from other animals. According to the way these terms are used by psychologists and linguists, animals are able to communicate as they send information to other members of their species or even different species (e.g. a dog wagging its tail), but language is usually seen as a form of communication which only humans possess. This is because language involves a set of complicated grammatical rules, some of which involve correspondence between different elements of language (e.g. the 'agreement' between verbs and nouns depending on whether the noun is singular or plural). This factor alone would justify the intensive study of language.

In addition, language can be seen as one of the most important skills in relation to children's development. Without the use of language for socialization and learning children would have a very much more difficult time acquiring the skills of their culture. It is perhaps no coincidence that children who are deaf and fail to learn sign language tend to have more developmental delays in skills involving reading and mathematics (*see* Chapter 10). Moreover very different cognitive abilities are present after children can use language (*see* chapters 3 and 6). In this chapter the early development of communication during the first two years of life is described and this provides a context for a discussion of why children are able to acquire language.

Introduction

In this chapter some of the major features of the development of communication in the first few years of life are outlined. This includes a description of the more obvious milestones in development and of the process of interaction between adults and infants. Next is a consideration of the process of language acquisition, with special attention being paid to theories about the development of children's grammatical abilities.

Communication before language

NON-VERBAL INTERACTION IN THE FIRST YEAR

Infants come into the world with predispositions to attend to human beings. They find human faces interesting, they show preferences for listening to speech and older infants show a preference for human movements (*see* Box 4.1). More surprisingly, newborn babies prefer their mother's voice in comparison to that of other females, prefer to look at their mother's face to that of other females and within 10 days prefer the odour of their mother. Consequently, infants are already attuned to the person who is likely to be the most important provider of care and communication. Whether these capacities are the result of inborn preferences for specific human-like stimuli, or an inborn preference for certain general forms of stimuli that humans possess continues to be a topic of controversy (*see* Kleiner, 1987; Johnson and Morton, 1987).

BOX 4.1 The investigation of early preference for human stimuli

Preferences have been identified for :
Human faces – newborns   Goren et al. 1975
Human speech – newborns   Cooper and Aslin, 1990
Mother's face – newborns   Bushnell et al., 1989
Mother's speech – newborns   DeCasper and Fifer, 1980
Mother's odour – 7–10 days   Balough and Porter, 1986
Human movement – 3–4 months   Bertenthal et al. 1987

During the first four or five months, interaction in Western and many other cultures usually revolves around the activities of the baby and carer. There may be body games and long periods of mutual gaze, caregivers often comment on the baby's facial expression or how the baby might be feeling. A striking feature of interactions with young children is the fact that they usually break the rules of adult-to-adult interaction, there can be long periods of mutual gaze, close physical activity, the use of exaggerated facial expressions and the use of a sing song voice (Stern et al, 1982; Messer and

Vietze, 1988). Many of these features fit in with the attentional preferences of young babies, so that they help capture and sustain their interest (Fernald, 1991; Stern et al. 1982).

Some theorists, such as Kaye (1982), regard this as a time of mutual adjustment between baby and adult. He believes that adults fit their behaviour around that of the baby to give the appearance of adult conversation. A good example of this is vocal turn-taking. If you listen to a mother and child it often sounds like an adult conversation with the baby making a sound and the adult answering. However, careful analysis of these patterns suggest that it is adults fitting in their speech among the vocalizations of children which gives the appearance of a turn-taking conversation (Davis, 1978). It has even been suggested that it is not until 2–3 years of age before children time their own vocalizations to avoid speaking at the same time as another person (Rutter and Durkin, 1987).

Another important component of interaction is eye gaze. Infant eye gaze suggests that the baby is interested in something, and a lack of gaze suggests a lack of interest. Furthermore mutual eye gaze between carers and infants is often treated as something special by the adult. Mothers speak about the way it seems to indicate that the baby 'knows them'. Analyses suggest that mothers tend to promote periods of mutual gaze, by returning the infants' gaze if they are already looking at them, and sustaining their gaze when mutual gaze is occurring (Stern, 1974). Infants do not show the same strong patterns in their behaviour and this suggests that what is occurring is mothers structuring their behaviour around their infants (Messer and Vietze, 1988).

There also has been interest in whether early interaction sets up rhythms which are utilized in later verbal conversations (e.g. vocal turn-taking leading to turn-taking in speech). Certainly a strong case can be made for this on logical grounds, but empirical evidence is less convincing (Kaye, 1982).

Not everyone thinks that young infants are passive partners in social interaction. Some believe that they have a rudimentary understanding that they are involved in communication. Trevarthen (1979a) has for a long time claimed that infants show a desire to influence others and make their own feelings apparent to another person. He calls this ability **intersubjectivity**. He argues that the way infants move their limbs when excited indicates that they are trying to influence others. He has also observed what he terms 'pre-speech' mouth movements where young babies will move their lips and tongue in an apparent attempt to communicate something.

The views of Kaye and Trevarthen illustrate opposite interpretations of infants' behaviour. One claim is that infants learn to communicate through apprenticeship with their more expert caregivers. However, a difficulty with this view is that it is not clear how infants change from merely taking part in the social process to understanding that they are playing an active part in it. A similar issue is how the apprenticeship allows infants to become aware that they are communicating with things that move, have intentions and respond to communication. A provocative view about this has been made by Meltzoff and Gopnik (1993). They claim that infants are, perhaps even at birth, able to appreciate that people are not just a collection of interesting stimuli, but are animate beings similar to themselves. Their idea of infants being able to appreciate that people are 'like me' draws on the idea of **direct perception**, the ability to categorize or recognize something without having to think about the issues, one simply 'knows' (for example, usually without thinking we immediately know whether the *face* of a person is male or female). In a similar way infants may directly perceive other people not as a collection of stimuli, but as something that is animate and something that they can respond to in a social way (*see also* Chapter 12).

There are various forms of evidence to support the idea of intersubjectivity. Some comes from the studies of imitation by Meltzoff and his colleagues (Meltzoff and Moore, 1992). If young infants can imitate the actions of adults then one explanation (among others) is that they do so because they can relate the actions of others to their own self. Another source of evidence is the way that young infants respond to emotion and the way children with autism fail to make these responses (Hobson, 1986; *but see* Baron-Cohen, 1995; *see also* Chapter 12). However, it should be acknowledged that none of this evidence is conclusive. One cannot be certain of whether an infant is responding in an intersubjective or mechanistic way and as a result there continues to be debate about such issues.

The first five or six months can be characterized as a period when caregiver and infant interact with one another and largely ignore the wider physical world. Such a period may be important in allowing mutual knowledge to develop and for infants to start to become attuned to their particular caregiver and the characteristics of their culture. For example, even by three months of age there are differences between the social interaction of American and Japanese mother–infant pairs which appear to reflect differences in these cultures (Fogel et al., 1988). In addition, it is important to bear in mind that these early interactions may be part of attachment formation (*see* Chapter 5).

At about five or six months of age there seems to be a change in social interaction. This involves a greater interest in physical aspects of the environment (e.g. objects). Several investigations have documented these changes (e.g. Sylvester-Bradley and Trevarthen, 1978; Penman et al., 1983; Rabain-Jamin and Sabeau-Jouannet, 1989) such as adult speech involving more references to objects. At around nine months of age a further change in the nature of social interaction can be identified. For one thing, children are developing attachments to particular people. It is perhaps no coincidence that at around this age children start to show **social referencing**, they will check to see the reactions of familiar adults to unusual or threatening events and will of course be monitoring these adults to check where they are and what they are doing. Children also start to produce conventional **gestures**, such as pointing and start to use communication as a means of achieving certain objectives (Murphy and Messer, 1977; Bates et al., 1987; Butterworth and Jarrett, 1991). Although the development of gestures is clearly a significant advance it is still not entirely clear what are the reasons for the development of this ability.

THE BEGINNINGS OF SPEECH

Information about the development of speech has been provided by detailed diary records of researchers who are the parents. The descriptions and insights have been of great value, but there is a difficulty of knowing how typical any one child is. A recent innovation has been the MacArthur Communicative Development Inventories (CDI) which is a standardized check list that parents use to describe the words their children understand and produce (Fenson et al., 1993). This has allowed extensive data collection and has revealed considerable variability in children's speech. For example the range in the number of different words that were produced by children at 12 months was between 0 and 52 words, at 16 months between 0 and 347 and at 30 months between 208 and 675 (Bates et al., 1994). It is also striking that until children have a vocabulary of more than 200 words most of their words are common nouns.

Observations have revealed that adult speech is usually about an object that the infant is looking at, or which the adult or child are handling. In addition, children often hear a series of utterances about the same referent. The series tends to be marked by a longer than usual pause, by the manipulation of a new object and by the naming of the object. Thus, the immediate structure of social interaction provides very useful cues that can help children identify the physical referent of speech (Messer, 1994). Interestingly, a different pattern of behaviour is associated with verbs. Verbs tends to be said before the relevant event or after it has occurred (Tomasello and Kruger, 1992). Experimental studies confirm that these links between speech and visual attention provides a basis for the development of vocabulary (e.g. Tomasello and Farrar, 1986). It is also possible that social routines, such as the exchange of objects or games like peek-a-boo, help children to understand words within a well-learned format. Furthermore, as children become older so they seem to become more able to utilize contextual information to help them understand the meaning of a word.

A remarkable feature of early speech is that for a comparatively long time children only produce one-word utterances, this lasts until around 18–20 months of age. However, there are considerable changes in the way that words are used. It is often difficult to know whether a nine-month-old is merely imitating a sound, in contrast, an 18-month-old appears to use one-word utterances for a whole range of different purposes. When children first produce words they are often closely tied to a specific context. A child might only say 'chuff-chuff' with his train in the living room (Barrett, 1995). However, with experience the expression is applied to other trains in other circumstances. Such observations suggest that initially infants do not use words in exactly the same way as adults. There have been claims that one-word utterances stand for complete sentences of several words, at the other extreme it has been argued that these utterances are not language but a more primitive form of communication.

Attempts to classify the intent and pragmatic aspects of communication have encountered problems. This coding has to employ detective work in order to be able to classify a word on the basis of the context in which it occurs. Such issues illustrate the serious problems when investigating this period of development and should make us aware of the difficulties and pitfalls of too ready an interpretation of what a young child is saying.

It has become apparent that using and understanding words involves much more than associating a word with its referent. Even if a referent can be identified there is usually uncertainty about the precise link between word and object; does the word refer to the whole object, the colour of the object, or what the object is doing (Quine, 1960; 1969)? An associated problem concerns categorizing the world in a way that allows a child to use words appropriately. A category is a group of things (or more formally entities) which share something in common and which can be distinguished from other entities (e.g. 'birds' are a category of living things). To form a category infants needs to notice a similarity which is common to all members of the category and disregard any features which are dissimilar. They need to notice that dogs bark and wag their tails, but they vary in size, colour and shape. It has been pointed out that given the number of dimensions on which things can be similar and dissimilar the task of forming categories would seem to be almost impossible (Murphy and Medin, 1985).

Prototype theory is one way of explaining the early development of categories. Rosch and Mervis (1975) supposed that to form a prototype a child notices the characteristics of a set of things and by some process of averaging forms a prototype which contains many of the characteristics of these things and few characteristics of related categories. So a prototype of a bird might be something like a robin after seeing a sparrow, a crow, a thrush and so on, but is unlikely to look like a penguin or ostrich. There is support for the idea that children's categories are based on prototypes from studies which have asked them to pick out a referent from a range of similar objects. The children tend to pick out the referent which is central to the category and is therefore likely to be similar to any prototype (Rosch and Mervis, 1975). However, one difficulty with prototype theory is that it is not clear how any 'averaging' process occurs and given the range of things that children encounter it is difficult to understand how they achieve this complex computational process.

Another type of explanation about the acquisition of words is that children have a set of constraints and assumptions (Clark, 1991; Gelman and Byrnes, 1991; *but see* Nelson, 1988; Gathercole, 1987). The result of this is that they only consider one or a limited number of meanings of a word. The advantage of such proposals is that they explain how children are able to acquire the meaning of words when there are so many uncertainties about the referent. One of the most widely discussed proposals is the **whole object assumption**, which results in children treating a word as referring to the whole object rather than part of the object or some attribute of it (Clark, 1991). An example of this is a child using 'hot' to refer to an oven, probably as a result of having been told 'it's hot'. Constraints account for the apparent ease of acquiring new words. However, it is unclear whether these (and other) assumptions are the result of some innate predisposition (Behrend, 1990), or a result of experience of social interaction (Nelson, 1988). Experimental investigations indicate that children do not always use the whole object assumption, sometimes they will interpret a word as referring to the substance of an object, rather than the object itself. In addition, there is a difficulty in explaining how children acquire verbs if they are using the whole object assumption.

An interesting idea is that there are differences between children in the way they use speech. Nelson (1973) suggested that **referential** infants have a vocabulary that is predominantly composed of object names, they are early talkers and interaction with adults often involves objects. In contrast, **social expressive** infants have fewer object names in their vocabulary, having instead words which regulate interaction (e.g. bye-bye, ta, etc.) and they use formulas (words which tend to occur together, e.g. all-gone). Referential children tend to have mothers who produced more utterances per event, more descriptions and fewer directives. The referential style of maternal speech appears to be prevalent amongst first borns (DellaCorte et al., 1983; Goldfield, 1985; Pappas-Jones and Adamson, 1987). Subsequently, there has been criticism of these ideas because children sometimes use object words in a functional way (e.g. the referential word 'drink' when asking for some liquid). This highlights a problem of the classification of infant speech which is partly based on the way adults use words, not the children's intentions and so the same word could be used for both social and referential purposes (*see* McShane, 1980; Pine, 1992).

A noticeable feature of one word speech is the **vocabulary burst** when there is a rapid expansion of children's vocabularies at about 18–20 months of age (Bates et al., 1987). The change is from a vocabulary of 30–50 words to several hundred words in a few weeks, with an increase in the number and proportion of verbs, adjectives and adverbs. Several researchers have suggested that the vocabulary burst is a product of more advanced understanding about the nature of words and signals their use in an adult-like way (McShane, 1980; Meltzoff and Gopnik, 1989). It has been argued that this involves a 'nominal' insight that all concepts have a relevant word and all words refer to a concept (Dore, 1978). There is also evidence that a 50–100 word vocabulary is associated with the beginning of two-word speech. It may be that some 'critical mass' is necessary for two-word utterance (Marchman and Bates 1994). There have, however, been questions raised about the vocabulary burst. For one thing not all children appear to go through a vocabulary burst, some seem to show a gradual increase (Goldfield and Reznick, 1990). It has also been suggested by Bates et al. (1994) that the vocabulary burst is nothing more than the steepest part of the exponential curve that describes vocabulary growth.

TWO-WORD AND MULTI-WORD UTTERANCES

There are several months, usually towards the end of the second year, when children's speech mostly consists of two-word utterances. This speech can fulfil communicative functions such as those shown in Table 4.1. These functions were identified in a classic study by Brown (1973) and seem to generalise fairly well across a range of languages. This and similar schemes rely on contextual information to identify the semantic role of the words, a problem already discussed in relation to one word speech.

One way to explain the beginning of two-word speech is that a general cognitive advance allows children to combine different ideas in a single utterance. Interestingly at about this age there are other important cognitive changes including the start of pretend play, the ability to sort objects into different groups and the development of various imitative abilities. With such a flurry of cognitive developments it is not that surprising that there are developments in speech.

When discussing language it is necessary to define what we mean by the term. There is confusion in everyday speech between the words **communication** and **language**. Animals like bees, dolphins or monkeys often are said to use language. Psycholinguists use the word language to describe a form of communication in which different elements can be identified and in which the arrangement of these elements influences the meaning of the message. Most forms of animal communication do not meet these criteria (e.g. the growl of a dog conveys a threat, but the arrangement of the sounds do not convey different messages). If we wanted to be more strict in our definition and thereby exclude many of the remaining forms of animal communication then language could be restricted to communication which involves *structural dependency*, that is a set of relations between different elements (e.g. between the subject and a verb of a sentence). It is important to recognize that although there is a reasonable consensus about what is language, there can be disagreements over the fine detail and arguments over the fine details can be important in deciding whether or not we consider a particular form of communication as language.

Children's early multi-word utterances do not contain certain words, such as pronouns, articles and auxillary verbs, because of this such utterances are sometimes referred to as telegraphic speech. Telegraphic speech appears to be used at around two years, just before what is generally

Agent	+ Action	John kick
Action	+ Object	Kick ball
Agent	+ Object	John ball
Action	+ Location	Kick there
Entity	+ Location	John there
Possessor	+ Possessed	Adam ball
Entity	+ Attribute	Ball fast
Demonstrative	+ Entity	That ball

Table 4.1 Meaning in two-word utterances

agreed to be a proper language. There are a number of descriptive systems which capture this transition.

A classification of early multi-word speech which has been popular was constructed by Cazden (1968) and Brown (1973). The classification is based on the type of morphemes that are used (morphemes are considered to be the smallest meaningful elements in speech, so 'climb' and '-ed' are both morphemes) and the **mean length of utterances** (MLU). The first morphemes are acquired between 21 and 34 months and the sixth morpheme by 23–38 months (*see* Table 4.2). Both verbal and non-verbal information is used to establish not only that children produce a morpheme, but whether a particular morpheme should have been used (e.g. 'my doll' is appropriate if there is only one doll, but the use of this expression when there are several dolls reveals that the child was not using the morpheme '-s', needed for most plural nouns). The MLU is calculated from the mean number of morphemes in a sample of 100 utterances of a child. Because morphemes are counted instead of words it is possible for there to be more morphemes than words in an utterance (e.g. 'he kick-ed ball' consists of four morphemes). Although MLU is a widely used measure it has some deficiencies. The MLU may depend on the language being acquired, in some languages it seems easier to develop a long MLU at an early age. Another problem is that 100 utterances is a small sample to assess a child's language development, particularly when one considers the way that the context influences speech (*see* Table 4.2).

A copula involves the use of the verb 'to be' as the *main* verb of an utterance, it can be used either in the uncontracted (full) form (e.g. 'she *is* good') or in the contracted form (e.g. 'she's good'). An auxiliary verb is not the main verb of an utterance and it is used in the presence of another verb e.g. 'she *is* talking'. It can be used in its uncontracted form, or in a contracted form (e.g. 'she's talking').

It is important to be aware that English is a language in which word order is particularly important and the use of inflections is not so important. The language of the Greenlandic Inuit involves the use of a complex

1.	Present progressive verb	+ -ing
2/3.	Prepositions	in/on
4.	Plurals	noun + -s
5.	Irregular past tense	went, swam
6.	Possessive	hers
7.	Uncontracted copula (verb to be)	she was good
8.	Articles	the, a
9.	Regular past tense	looked, talked
10.	Third person present tense irregular	she has
11.	Third person present tense regular	she talks
12.	Uncontracted auxiliary (verb to be)	she was talking
13.	Contracted copula	she's good
14.	Contracted auxiliary	she's talking

Table 4.2 The sequence of acquisition of 14 morphemes investigated by Roger Brown

morphological system where a word may have a large number of affixes (word endings), up to eight morphemes can accompany a word. One observation of an Inuit two-year-old child by Fortescue (1984/5) revealed that in half an hour 40 separate inflections were produced, with the longest single word utterances containing several elements of meaning. Thus, the rate of language acquisition is clearly influenced by the structure of the language being acquired. Slobin (1985) has suggested semantic and syntactic complexity influences the age a morpheme will be acquired.

The acquisition of language

This section concentrates on the way that children acquire language as a system of morpho-syntactic rules (syntax concerns the rules of a language about word order; so morpho-syntax refers to what in everyday speech we call 'grammar'). Virtually all experts agree that humans would not be able to use complex grammatical rules if we did not possess certain innate cognitive abilities. However, there are major disagreements about two inter-related issues, the precise form of our inherited ability and whether environmental experiences assist language acquisition. Before addressing these questions we will briefly consider an issue which is often ignored in child language research, the way children can break into the language code.

DISCUSSION POINT

How do you think children acquire the ability to use language?

THE CHANGE FROM NON-LINGUISTIC TO LINGUISTIC COMMUNICATION

How do children identify the grammatical classes of words (nouns, verbs etc.) when these are not clearly marked in the speech they hear? For example, in English, there does not seem to be any consistent linguistic clue which will enable children to identify nouns. A noun can appear at various positions in an utterance and there is no word ending which only identifies nouns – the plural for nouns is '-s', but '-s' is also an ending for some verbs and adjectives. Several proposals about the way meaning (i.e. semantics) provides a basis for this process were made in the early 1980s. Pinker's (1987) ideas about semantic bootstrapping, is one of the most detailed and widely known. He suggested that the meaning of words is acquired from hearing them used in particular settings and that children understand the meaning of an utterance from the context and the meaning of individual words. He supposed that working out the meaning of words provides the first step in being able to work out the grammar of a language. He also suggested that identifying grammatical classes of words is helped because children instinctively know that the meaning of some words is related to their grammatical function, for example, names for concrete objects and people are universally nouns. Pinker also suggested that once children identify the way that a grammatical group of words is used, then if an unknown word is used in a similar way, children will apply their existing grammatical knowledge to the unknown word. This explains how children are able to produce an appropriate plural when given an unknown word like 'wug' and asked about two of these objects, even though they have never heard the word 'wugs' (Berko, 1958).

Pinker (1984; 1989) admits there are problems with the semantic bootstrapping idea such as: not all links between meaning and grammar are universal; the speech to children may include a number of complex utterances which would make semantic bootstrapping much more difficult; the incorrect interpretation of contextual information may produce grammatical errors; and no account is taken of individual differences. Pinker's later proposals (1989; 1991) include other types of information that provide clues about grammar, such as sound pattern and word order. In addition, he favours a process which involves both a top-down (working with given assumptions about language structure) and bottom-up (working with the elements of language and trying to work out the overall pattern of rules) processing of information, to explain how children make progress with this very difficult problem.

IMITATION

Imitation might seem a likely candidate in explaining how children acquire language, however, there are a number of reports of the difficulty of teaching children language by asking them to imitate. The following is a famous example of this.

Child.	Nobody don't like me.
Mother.	No, say 'Nobody likes me.'
Child.	Nobody don't like me.

This sequence was repeated eight times.

| Mother. | Now listen carefully, say 'NOBODY LIKES ME.' |
| Child. | Oh! Nobody don't like$S$ me. (McNeil, 1966). |

Examples such as this have been used to discredit the idea that imitation provides a basis for the acquisition of language. The next sections discuss other views about the role of the speech that children hear.

GRAMMATICAL RULES AS AN INHERITED CAPACITY

Chomsky has influenced the theoretical agenda for research in child language over the last 40 years. One important feature of his argument is that language is a rule-governed behaviour which involves the capacity to use a finite number of elements (i.e. morphemes) to produce an infinite number of messages, this is achieved by using different combinations of the elements. Furthermore, Chomsky supposes that language acquisition is possible because children have inherited knowledge about all the grammars of all human languages. His views produced a move away from environmental explanations of language learning in favour of innate processes which required little in the way of special help from adults and from ignoring children's internal cognitive processes to putting these at the centre of theory.

Chomsky's (1965) early proposals were that children possess a **language acquisition device** (LAD) which enables them to identify the grammatical rules that are in the speech they hear. The LAD was not described in any detail, however, fundamental to its operation was having access to the grammatical rules of all human languages, this was termed the access to a **universal grammar**. Consequently, the difficulty children face in acquiring language was not in working out the grammatical rules from scratch, but in identifying which set of rules were in the language they hear. These proposals were put forward because the grammars of language were seen as so complex that it would be impossible for children to work these out when they do not seem to receive any tuition or teaching.

The proposals about a LAD generated interest and investigations. Gradually problems became apparent. As a result, a new theory was developed which has been termed **government and binding theory** (from a book title by Chomsky published in 1981) or **principles and parameters theory** (PPT, from the terms in the theory). This theory still claims that children possess inherited abilities, but provides more details about the mechanism of language acquisition. The new theory assumes that some features of language are universal across the world, these are supposed to be represented by a set of linguistic **principles** (e.g. it is thought that all languages contain nouns). Whereas other features of languages differ in terms of their morpho-syntactic rules. Such differences are termed **parametric variation**. According to PPT, acquiring language involves identifying the correct parameter from a range of innately specified possibilities. This process was at first seen to be similar to setting a switch to one of several positions, much as you might switch a light on or off. In other words, children are supposed to match the language they hear with grammatical structures of speech they already possess. Discovering a match allows children to start to use the grammatical rule. This process is termed **parameter setting**. As there are a large number of dimensions on which languages vary it has been supposed that a number of parameters are set. It is also claimed that setting a parameter can affect other parts of the language system, so other characteristics which are associated with the parameter may start to be used by children.

The fact that early speech is not grammatically correct and the fact that their language develops over time has resulted in proposals about two different mechanisms of parameter setting. In one case it is supposed that all the principles and parameters are available from the very beginning, but peripheral problems (such as identifying parts of speech and memory limitations) prevent children from utilizing this knowledge. As a result, when these peripheral problems are overcome children's speech develops (Clahsen, 1992). This is sometimes known as the **continuity hypothesis**. An alternative is that children do not initially have access to all their inherited linguistic knowledge, but this becomes available as children become older (Felix, 1992). This has been termed the **maturation hypothesis**. The predictions from both these models are very similar, however, they are based on quite different mechanisms. An example of this type of research is given in Box 4.2. We also need to note that Chomsky has discussed further modifications to his ideas. The newer ideas suggests that grammatical rules are stored with information about individual words rather than as an independent grammatical system, but the implications of this for language acquisition are not fully worked out.

BOX 4.2 Explanations about telegraphic speech

The telegraphic speech of English-speaking children usually does not contain the subject of the utterance (e.g. 'want milk' is said rather than '*I* want milk'). In other languages 'want milk' is an acceptable form of adult speech (e.g. in Italian). Hyams (1986; 1992) uses the ideas of PPT to propose that when English-speaking children start to speak they assume that their mother tongue is like Italian. This was coupled with claims that if children cannot yet make a decision about which parameter setting should be used then they will employ a 'default' parameter. Thus, the use of a default parameter in English-speaking children would result in telegraphic speech which is similar in grammatical structure to Italian. Subsequent research has, however, shown that matters are more complex, particularly as Italian has word endings which indicate the subject of an utterance (Hyams, 1992; Meisel, 1995). In addition, although utterances with a subject are rare in English children, they occur and occur more often than in Italian children (Valian, 1990; 1993). Thus, although the idea of a default parameter is an interesting idea, subsequent research findings have not provided convincing support.

An alternative view about telegraphic speech has been put forward by Radford (1995). He supposes that the telegraphic speech of young children is because only a limited number of parameters are set at this time. The blossoming of language between two and two and a half years is because maturation allows more parameters to be set at these ages.

There are several areas of difficulty for PPT. One is to explain the acquisition of sign languages. Sign languages contain grammatical rules, (*see* Chapter 10). Thus, PPT has to suppose that children can identify the linguistic structure in both speech and in hand movements and relate this to a set of universal grammatical principles. Although this is logically possible, it does seem to considerably increase the amount of information which has to be genetically coded. There is also an issue about the way bilingual children are able to acquire two or more languages and whether the same parameter can be set in different positions for two different languages.

PPT has been very influential, but opinions about PPT have tended to be polarized. Advocates of the theory see it as providing a framework for understanding language acquisition and as providing a direction for research. They argue that it gives a coherent theory about the acquisition of grammatical rules which is lacking in most other approaches. Furthermore, it makes sense that humans have a set of cognitive operations which allow them to acquire any human language. However, I like others, worry about the plausibility of PPT, in biological and physiological terms. It is difficult to think of a realistic biological model that operates in the brain for a process which involves a considerable amount of innate information and that can be set in operation merely by hearing the speech of others. Furthermore, it is possible that children may be provided with more help than the parameter setting account supposes and as a result perhaps such a powerful innate device is unnecessary. This issue is considered in the next sections.

DISCUSSION POINT

Think about the way you would speak to a young child. List the differences between this speech and speech to your friends.

SPEECH TO CHILDREN

Numerous investigations have documented the way speech to young children is simplified when compared to adult-to-adult speech. The general findings are summarized in Table 4.3. All the characteristics of child directed speech (CDS) should make the grammar less complex and the processing of the speech much easier.

There is disagreement about whether these modifications help language acquisition. Studies have been conducted to discover if mothers who make more simplifications to their speech have children whose language is more advanced. The research has produced mixed findings, some studies reporting positive effects of simplified speech, others have reported few if any positive effects (Furrow and Nelson, 1986; Barnes et al., 1983; Scarborough and Wyckoff, 1986; Murray et al., 1990). In addition, because these studies were not true experiments it is difficult to draw any firm

Table 4.3 The characteristics of adult speech to young children		
	Shorter utterances	three- or four-word utterances common in CDS (Snow, 1973)
	Restricted vocabulary	smaller range of words and these often refer to common objects, activities or actions, fewer adjectives and adverbs (Snow, 1973)
	Pauses at end of sentences	the structure of CDS is more clearly marked by pauses than adult-to-adult speech (Broen, 1972)
	Slower	speech to children is about half as fast as speech among adults (Broen, 1972)
	Repetitions	about a fifth of speech to young children involves repetitions of previous utterances (Snow, 1995)
	Emphasis of words	words which are important for meaning are emphasized (Messer, 1981)
	Verbs usually in the present tense	morphosyntax is less complex as past and future events are rarely talked about in CDS (Snow, 1973)
	Fewer conjunctions (e.g. 'and', 'with')	Lack of conjunctions makes speech less complex (Remick, 1976)

conclusions about positive findings, for example, it is possible that the mother's speech is a consequence rather than a cause of the child being advanced (*see* Schwartz and Camarata, 1985).

One form of evidence which suggests that merely hearing speech is insufficient for language acquisition comes from reports of children whose main source of speech is television, either because their parents are deaf or because they watch the programmes from a different country. In these cases the children make little or no progress with the language they hear on television (Sachs and Johnson, 1976; Snow, 1977). However, the lack of progress may be as much due to this speech not occurring during an active social exchange, as to the speech not being simplified.

Questions have been raised about the universality of CDS. Studies by Ochs and Schieffelin (1984) suggest that there are people who do not use CDS as we do in the West. For example the Kaluli of Papua New Guinea are described as talking for their young infant rather than treating the child as a conversational partner. A typical interaction involves a baby facing outwards on the mother's lap, the mother speaks to other people as if she is the infant. In this way the infant is treated as establishing social relationships with other people. Furthermore, the mother's speech is not related to the infant's activities as it is in most Western families. Later, when a child starts to use the words for 'mother' and 'breast', they are formally taught elements of the language, this involves the adult saying a model utterance and the child being told to repeat it. The important point about these observations is that the same types of simplification seen in Western families do not always seem to be present in other cultures. However, the conclusion that children do not need a modified environment in which to acquire language is not accepted without question. CDS is found in many language groups (ranging from Apache to Arabic; Ferguson, 1964) and even four-year-olds use CDS with an infant (Shatz and Gelman, 1973). It would also seem that CDS is very well adapted to infant capacities, infants prefer to listen to CDS than other speech (Fernald and Mazzi, 1991). Furthermore, there have been concerns with the accuracy of cross-cultural studies involving translators and whether infants might receive CDS from, for example, other children (Harris, 1992).

ERRORS AND FEEDBACK

One of the assumptions of PPT is that children are supplied with examples of language, but not given feedback, or as it is sometimes termed **negative evidence**, about their mistakes. It is argued that this makes it impossible to acquire language without the possession of extra innate information. The reason being that a child might choose an incorrect grammatical rule and as they would not be told that this is incorrect, they would never change their grammar (it is reasoned mere exposure to correct forms would not be sufficient to cause a change).

A study by Brown and Hanlon (1970) examined the reactions of adults to children's ungrammatical speech. They found overt correction of errors was extremely rare, if a child said 'he goed', adults were likely to accept this and not reply 'that's incorrect, you should say he went'. Adults were much more likely to provide overt corrections to semantic errors (e.g. the use of a wrong name). Thus, the study appeared to confirm that childen's grammatical errors are not usually corrected and this supported arguments about a need for innate knowledge.

Studies in the 1980s confirmed the findings of Brown and Hanlon (1970), but also indicated that adults make different replies to children's grammatically correct and incorrect utterances (Hirsh-Pasek et al., 1984; Demetras et al., 1986; Penner, 1987; Bohannon and Stanowicz, 1988; Bohannon et al., 1990). In general, if children made a grammatical mistake then the adult was likely to follow this with a question or an expansion which usually supplied the correct form of the utterance. On the other hand if the utterance was grammatically correct adults were more likely to continue the topic of conversation. It was argued that these different reactions provide an important source of feedback and that the interruption of the flow of conversation, by asking questions and expanding on the child's speech, might put pressure on children to produce utterances which allow conversation to proceed smoothly.

The idea that such feedback aids language acquisition has been rejected by some investigators (Morgan and Travis, 1989; Pinker, 1989). These authors argue that the probabilistic nature of the feedback means that children can not be sure from an adult's reply whether a particular utterance is grammatically correct and that it is unlikely children can store their own utterances together with adults' reactions to make full use of the information that is provided.

Some investigations, however, have found that children are more likely to repeat an adult expansion than other utterances; this indicates that children are processing the information in the expansion (Farrer, 1992). More convincing support for the benefit of expansions comes from Saxton (1997). In an experiment using nonsense words, five-year-olds were better able to learn grammatical rules from expansions than from just hearing utterances giving examples of the rules. He argues that children learn from expansions because they recognize the difference (a 'contrast') between their own speech and the 'correct' adult utterance. Thus, the expansions provide mini-learning sessions for the child.

CONNECTIONIST NETWORKS

PPT involves the idea that there are special cognitive operations which are specific to language. A contrasting viewpoint involves **connectionist networks**, **neural networks**, and **parallel distributed processes** (the terms are often used interchangeably) and attempts to discover whether language acquisition involves general learning processes (*see* Plunkett, 1995). Connectionist networks consist of computer programs which are designed to mimic the information-processing in the brain. As a result, there are many inter-connections between an input message and some form of output. In studies of language acquisition computers are usually given speech which concerns a specific aspect of grammar (e.g. they might be given verbs in the present tense and have to learn to produce the past tense form). The computer is given speech which is converted to a numeric form. At first the computer makes random 'guesses' at which response is correct. After a guess the computer usually is given information about whether its response was correct or incorrect. Typically, if the response is correct the tendency to produce that response (and related ones) is strengthened, if the response is incorrect the tendency is weakened (this process is known as **backpropogation**). Computers are 'trained' by being repeatedly provided with feedback about their responses to the input. Such training has enabled computers to learn various features of language, such as the past tense of verbs. It should be noted that few people claim the computer programs exactly imitate children's language acquisition, rather this work concerns whether language acquisition occurs by learning and whether CDS contains information which allows this learning to occur.

Rumelhart and McClelland (1986) developed one of the first connectionist models of language this involved learning the past tense of verbs. The computer was given examples of the present tense of English verbs, for each verb that was presented the computer selected which of various various past tense verbs was correct. The computer was then given information about whether its choice was indeed correct or incorrect. The computer program did not form a direct association between the present and past tense of the same verb, as most previous models of learning.

Rather, the computation of the associations was a much more complex process involving a network of associations, so a number of parallel connections were modified as the result of feedback (*see* fig 4.1). At the time it was thought that the computer's learning followed the development of the past tense by children and like children it was able to produce the correct past tense of verbs which it had not been given before.

This and other work has resulted in a more careful analysis of children's speech. It would seem that there is an initial error-free period when children are able to produce regular verbs (e.g. start*ed*, finish*ed*) and irregular verbs (e.g. went, was) with very few errors. This is followed by intermittent errors which involve the **overregularization** of irregular verbs (e.g. 'go-*ed*'), the verbs which are overregularized tend to be the low frequency irregular verbs. More recent connectionist models of the past tense have been able to mimic this pattern of development and this seems to have been possible because, although irregular verbs do not follow general rules and would be expected to be more difficult to learn, they are much more common in CDS (think how often we say 'went' rather than 'started'). In other words, connectionist networks (and possibly children) are able to learn irregular verbs because they are so common in CDS and this learning occurs despite the fact that children also abstract a general principle of adding '-ed' to regular verbs. The single connectionist system is able to cope with both forms of learning. There are indications that this abstraction of a general principle occurs when vocabularies reach a critical size.

This and other research has challenged PPT in several ways (see Plunkett, 1995). First, the learning mechanisms are not specialized for language, these are general learning processes that can be used to model linguistic and non-linguistic cognitive processes. Second, the computer does not contain any linguistic rules (all the learning is in terms of mathematical adjustments which govern the choice of output), yet the computer behaves as if it was governed by rules. Third, there is no specific

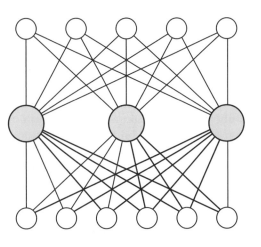

Output layer
(e.g. past tense
forms of verbs)

Hidden units
(these adjust the strength
of connections
between input and output)

Input layer
(e.g. present tense
forms of verbs)

Figure 4.1 A diagram of a simple connectionist network.

innate knowledge of the rules of grammar supplied to the computer. Thus, it would seem that non-specialized but sophisticated learning systems can acquire rules in a very different way to PPT. The more recent connectionist research has emphasized that language emerges as a product of innate capacities to process information which is coupled with particular frequencies of grammatical forms in the child's environment (Plunkett *et al.*, 1997).

However, two serious issues need to be resolved before connectionist accounts can provide a convincing account of language acquisition. The first is that most connectionist networks are given feedback about the correctness of every single response that they make, as we have seen this does not occur with children. One idea that goes some way to overcoming this objection supposes that children, as they listen to speech, make predictions about what will come next. In this way they are given the correct version of language in relation to their predictions. However, as yet we have no evidence that children actually do this. The other issue is that most connectionist modelling involves a single linguistic form (e.g. past tense) and speech used by the computer is usually selected to only contain these forms. Children, on the other hand, seem to learn a number of linguistic forms at the same time (e.g. tense, plurals, word order, etc.). It remains to be established whether connectionist systems can be devised to deal with a much higher level of complexity in the input and output.

Summary

Although I have reviewed important explanations of language acquisition, none is entirely satisfactory. The strength of the parameter setting approach is that it specifies innate capacities that might enable language acquisition to take place. Further, it is consistent with the idea that there is something special about language which makes it different from many other of our thought processes. However, the setting of parameters seems to be a crude and biologically unlikely processes. Furthermore, the theory is very difficult to test and it does not provide particularly clear suggestions for intervention. Explanations which stress the way that children's social environment can assist language acquisition capture an important aspect of caregiving. This research is able to account for the growth of semantic and pragmatic communication skills, but has some difficulty in explaining the way grammar is acquired. In addition, it has been surprisingly difficult to show that adults who more frequently employ particular features of speech help children to acquire language at an earlier age. I also suspect that language can be acquired by a variety of routes and sources, so that an absence of one type of information does not necessarily result in delays. The connectionist approach provides an interesting alternative to parameter setting. In some ways it can provide a compromise between extreme claims from nature and nurture. The approach provides what is equivalent to an innately specified set of cognitive operations, which processes information from the environment. However, it is still unclear how much we can learn from the use of connectionist models, they can show computer programs will learn to produce grammar from speech input, but it is going to be difficult to know whether children process information in the same way.

Seminar questions

1. What are the main features of the development of communication and speech during the first three years of life?
2. In what ways might adult–child social interaction help language acquisition?
3. Compare PPT and connectionist accounts of language acquisition.

Further reading

Bishop, D. 1997. *Uncommon understanding: development and disorders of language*. Hove: Psychology Press. A useful and comprehensive examination of language difficulties and their causes.

Dockrell, J., Messer, D. 1999. *Children's language and communication difficulties: understanding identification and intervention*. London: Cassell. An accessible overview of children's language difficulties.

Messer, D. 1994. *The development of communication*. Chichester: Wiley. An advanced text which considers in more detail many of the issues discussed in this chapter.

5

The development of attachment relationships

INFANCY AND BEYOND

MARINUS H VAN IJZENDOORN AND CARLO SCHUENGEL

Editors' preface

A child's 'love' for their caregiver is such a natural and seemingly automatic process that it is easy to forget that there are important issues to be explained and investigated. A little more thought quickly leads to the following questions: why does this attachment occur? are there differences between children in their attachments? and if there are differences, what are their consequences? The attempts to answer these questions have resulted in this subject area having a central place in developmental psychology and in psychoanalysis (*see* Chapter 13).

Here, Professor Marinus van IJzendoorn and Dr Carlo Schuengel show that the question about 'why does attachment occur?' can be answered on at least two levels, the evolutionary and the inter-personal (*see also* Chapter 1). Today it is generally accepted, following the work of John Bowlby, that attachments to caregivers take place because of innate dispositions which are the result of the process of evolution. It is also generally accepted that certain characteristics of interaction between caregivers and infants promote the development of attachment to specific people.

The authors also discuss the work of Mary Ainsworth which provided a methodological breakthrough in research into attachment. She realized that attachment should be characterized not as a continuous variable like the scale on a thermometer, but that it was more appropriate to see children as having distinct forms of attachment to their caregivers. This has had a profound effect on research and has provided a basis for hundreds of studies. As the following chapter describes the findings from these studies are providing indications that childhood attachment processes may have, in some circumstances, effects not only into adulthood, but also possibly across generations.

The emergence of attachment in the first year

This chapter is about the **attachment** relationship between young children and their parents and about the roots of this relationship in the parents' own attachment experiences. What is attachment? For the moment, we will speak about children as being attached, if they have a tendency to seek proximity to and contact with a specific caregiver in times of distress, illness and tiredness (Bowlby, 1984). The emergence of attachments in the first year of life will be described, as well as the determinants of individual differences in attachment. The consequences of infant attachments will be discussed in relation to longitudinal attachment studies from infancy to adulthood. Attachment is a major developmental milestone in the child's life and it will remain an important issue throughout the life-span.

HISTORICAL BACKGROUND OF ATTACHMENT THEORY

The Second World War caused the separation of parents and their children on a massive scale. Families were torn apart because of the bombardments of civilian targets, the insatiable need for the army to draft new men and the threat from Germany. In London, the psychotherapists Dorothy Burlingham and Anna Freud – the daughter of the famous Viennese psychiatrist Sigmund Freud – set up the so-called Hampstead Nurseries: several shelters for children between age zero and age ten who had lost their parents because of the war – either temporarily or for good. Burlingham and Freud poignantly describe the sufferings of these young children, who often pined away from grief for the loss of the attachment relationship with their parents, despite the fact that they received high quality care. Take, for example, Dell, an active little girl aged two and a half years. When first brought by her mother, she soon started playing and did not really notice her mother leaving. However, half an hour later Dell suddenly realized what had happened and walked around the house in despair to find her mother. Her bright cheer and activity disappeared and she became a different child. She was not able to connect to one of the professional caregivers and after a couple of weeks she treated her parents as any other visitors (Freud and Burlingham, 1974, p. 36ff).

By analysing these and similar observations John Bowlby, the British child psychiatrist and founder of attachment theory, discovered three phases in the reaction of young children on the breaking of the bond with their parents. In the starting phase of **protest**, the child panics and tries to undo the separation with all means available: crying being obviously the most important strategic weapon. Caregivers other than their own parents are rejected. After a few days, the phase of **despair** follows in which the child is still fixated on the absent parents but has also fallen into passivity. Finally, after a couple of weeks or months the phase of **detachment** sets in: the child again starts to be a bit more interested in the environment and is ready to interact with other caregivers. If the parents return, however, the attachment relationship appears to have been broken. The parents are not or only barely greeted and sometimes the child even actively rejects them. The child may be distracted and apathetic, often much to the despair of the parents.

Despite the paucity of systematic research in the 1950s, Bowlby soon came to the conclusion that attachment plays a key role in the nurturing and development of young children. On the basis of clinical case reports and his own observations he noticed that adolescents and adults who had been separated from their parents at an early age ran an increased risk of a disturbed development. In his famous report of 1951 for the World Health Organization Bowlby somewhat rhetorically compared attachment to be as important for psychological development as proteins and vitamins are for physical development. With this metaphor Bowlby placed the 'bias' of children to become attached among other primary needs such as feeding. This view contrasted with the then current psychoanalytical and behaviouristic way of thinking, which explained the bond between children and their parents by the fact that the parents provide food and physical care: according to these traditional views the way to an infant's heart is through the stomach.

Towards the end of the 1950s results from **ethological studies** became available that challenged the traditional views. Ethology is the science of animal and human behaviour. Harlow (1958) did historically important experiments with young rhesus monkeys that had been separated from their biological parents at birth. Instead of their real parents the monkeys were provided with 'surrogate' mothers made from wire mesh. Some surrogate mothers were covered with soft furry cloth; others remained somewhat macabre wire skeletons (fig 5.1). The young monkeys were fed through a bottle that could be mounted on both 'mothers'. In one of the experiments eight monkeys grew up with two kinds of surrogate mothers. Four monkeys were fed by the wire mesh mother and four by the furry cloth mother. The amount of time spent on each of the surrogate mothers was measured. The results were startling. In both groups the infant monkeys spent about 15 hours on the furry cloth mothers and no more than two hours on the bare wire mesh mothers, irrespective of which mother gave milk. In one other experiment monkeys were placed in a stressful situation. Monkeys that had been raised by non-feeding, furry cloth 'mothers' sought out and found support from their surrogate mother. The group feeding from non-furry mothers remained frightened.

Bowlby (1973; 1984; 1985) used these and many other ethological research findings as illustrations in favour of the hypothesis that the need to become attached to a protective adult is one of the primary needs in

Figure 5.1 The surrogate mothers of Harlow. Harlow Primate Laboratory, University of Wisconsin. Reprinted with permission.

the human species. Attachment theory is built upon the assumption that children come to this world with an inborn inclination to show behaviours leading to the formation of an attachment relationship – and this inclination would have had survival value in the environment in which human evolution originally took place. This explanation uses **evolutionary biology** (the study of the evolution of species, based on the evolution theory of Charles Darwin), but it is not at first obvious what the benefits are for caregivers to respond to the infants' signals. An answer to this question is provided by Porter and Laney (1980) and Lamb et al. (1985) who point to trends in modern evolutionary biology that stress the importance of the maximization of '**inclusive fitness**': the genes that remain in a population are the genes that make individuals act in the best interest of these genes – increasing the genes' chances of survival and multiplication. This theory is a strand of thinking in sociobiology and evolutionary biology that puts the ('selfish') genes central as a theoretical entity, instead of the organism or the species. An implication of this theory is that the efforts of parents to respond to their infant should not impair their overall reproductive success: parents have to distribute their attention over all their offspring. Furthermore, the reproductive success of the child is enhanced when the parent is able to direct some attention to siblings (Trivers, 1974). Thus, an evolutionary adaptation may be that children are able to deal with some insensitivity from the part of the parent (Lamb et al., 1985, p. 47 f; *see also* Hinde, 1982). Avoidant or ambivalent attachment may in some cases enable a child to survive in a (temporary) insensitive environment (*see below*).

DISCUSSION POINT

What is your own view or experience? What instinctive behaviours of newborn infants may lead to the forming of an attachment relationship?

DISCUSSION POINT

Do you also believe that caregiving by parents is an 'instinctive' behaviour?

THE DEVELOPMENT OF ATTACHMENT

The development of attachment can be described in two ways. First, a global description can be given of the phases in which attachment develops as a species-specific phenomenon. Second, attachment can be described by looking at individual differences within this species-specific development.

The development of attachment in young children is most often sub-divided into four phases (Ainsworth et al. 1978; Bowlby, 1984; Lamb et al., 1985). These phases should not be taken in classical sense as 'stages' and they are constantly challenged when new empirical evidence becomes available that often shows that infants are capable of much more than was previously assumed.

In *phase one* – indiscriminately orienting and signalling to people – the baby seems 'tuned' to certain wavelengths of signals from the environment. These signals are mostly of human origin (e.g. the sound of voices), but it is still unclear how much the saliency of the human voice has to do with the conspicuous and intrusive character of this type of social stimuli (Messer, 1994). However, fairly soon the baby is able to fixate the eyes of caregivers and crying, smiling and grasping appear as precursors of attachment. Until about 8–12 weeks of age, the baby does seem to have a preference for a familiar caregiver, but anybody can satisfy the baby's needs (Messer, 1994).

Probably first by smell and then by sight the baby develops preference for one or a few caregivers – the phase of orienting and signalling. During this *second phase*, the baby adapts to a limited number of caregivers (and vice versa of course) to which attachment behaviour is preferentially directed. Attachment behaviour such as crying can also be more easily stopped by these specific caregivers. Nevertheless, the preference for the regular caregivers is limited. In principle, with sufficient effort everybody should be able to take the role of the preferred caregiver.

Phase three, at about 6–8 months of age, involves the infant showing active attachment behaviour (e.g. actively seeking proximity to and following the specific attachment figure). The infant is able to remain aware of the existence of a person even if this person is out of hearing or sight – 'person-permanence'. There is some debate about whether 'person-permanence' as the social equivalent of object-permanence is really pre-conditional to this phase. Bell (1970) found empirical support for the idea, but Levitt et al. (1984) could not replicate her results. Attachment behaviour is now organized as a system in a goal-corrected fashion. The set-goal here is 'proximity' or 'felt security'. To arrive at this global goal different means are employed, depending on the distance. At this phase separation and loss cause the very intense separation anxiety mentioned earlier, which is expressed in protest and anger, followed by despair and apathy and finally leading to a somewhat shakier trust in new attachment relationships.

In phase three it is difficult to delay gratification of the infant's need for security and proximity; infants are still too **'egocentric'** in the Piagetian sense to be aware of the fact that their caregivers may have other plans, plans that do not necessarily involve them. Children enter the phase of the **goal-corrected partnership** when they can imagine plans and perceptions in the caregiver and fit their own plans and activities according to these (Marvin et al., 1977). This *fourth phase* has been less heavily researched, but there is the notion that from about three years of age (much earlier accord-ing to Main et al., 1985) children develop a so-called **working model**, a mental representation of their attachment relationships that influences attachment behaviour in an abstract way. Attachment behaviour has undergone transformation from primitive crying to the verbal communica-tion of relatively complex affective messages. Bowlby (1973) hypothesized that the working model stemming from this phase could influence later attachment relationships (*see below*).

BOX 5.1 The secure base phenomenon

Infants have a strong tendency to move away from their caregivers to explore. At first glance, attachment and exploration may seem anti-thetical, but Ainsworth discovered the **'secure base phenomenon'**: the smooth alteration of exploration with occasional proximity seek-ing (Ainsworth, 1973). This has become one of the cornerstones of attachment theory. She built upon the work of the British investigator J.W. Anderson. Entirely within the ethological tradition of studying behaviour in its natural context Anderson went to the London parks to secretly observe mothers and young children (Anderson, 1972). He recorded his comments on a portable tape-recorder. Children did stray across the park when they came with their mothers, but they also fre-quently returned. Often there was no obvious event that caused a return. It would appear that children used their caregiver as a secure base from which to explore, but they also frequently returned to re-establish contact and proximity. Ainsworth et al. (1978) found that the smoothest balance between exploration and proximity could be observed among children whose mothers had been sensitive and responsive during infancy.

INDIVIDUAL DIFFERENCES: THE STRANGE SITUATION

Until now we have discussed the development of attachment relationships without taking into account individual differences among children and parents in the type and the quality of attachment relationships. These differences have been, however, the focus of most research into attachment: describing and characterizing these differences, explaining them and determining their consequences. The many differences in the type and the quality of attachment relationships could originate in differences in the co-ordination or the smoothness of caregiver – infant interaction during the first year. This hypothesis resulted from the most important study in the history of attachment research, the Baltimore study by Mary Ainsworth and her colleagues (Ainsworth et al., 1978).

In this longitudinal study during the first year of life 26 mother–infant pairs were observed at home for four hours per three weeks. In order to make sense out of this enormous amount of data, these observations had to be compared to an external criterion measure. Ainsworth and Wittig (1969) had the brilliant idea of observing all children with their mothers in a standardized stressful separation procedure, to assess the amount of trust the children had in the accessibility of their attachment figures. This artificial separation procedure was created in the form of the now world-famous '**Strange Situation**' procedure (*see* Box 5.2) and it was hoped that the children's behaviour would indicate the degree of security in the relationship with the attachment figure.

BOX 5.2 Strange Situation procedure

The procedure comprises eight episodes of which the last seven ideally take three minutes. However, each episode can be curtailed at the request of the caregiver, and the experimenter may also shorten an episode, for instance if the infant seems very distressed.

- *Episode One* begins when the experimenter leads the caregiver and child into an unfamiliar room and gives some last instructions. The observations start when, on the request of the experimenter, the caregiver brings the infant towards a pile of toys.
- *Episode Two* is spent by the caregiver together with the child in the playroom.
- In *Episode Three* an unfamiliar adult (the 'stranger') enters the room, sits and reads and after a while starts to play with the infant (fig 5.2).

- *Episode Four* starts when the caregiver departs, and the infant is left with the stranger (fig 5.3).
- In *Episode Five* the caregiver returns (fig 5.4).
- *Episode Six* starts when the caregiver leaves again: the infant is alone in the room (fig 5.5).
- In *Episode Seven* the stranger returns (fig 5.6).
- In *Episode Eight* caregiver and infant are reunited once again (fig 5.7).

The focus of the procedure seems to be very much on the child, but the reaction of the child to the situation and of the caregiver is used to measure characteristics of the caregiver – child *dyad*. The behaviour of the child is rated by use of six rating scales, which contain detailed descriptions of the frequency, duration and latency of several behaviours. These are used to establish the final attachment classification or 'pattern of attachment'. Ainsworth et al. (1978) proposed three main categories and eight subcategories: secure, insecure–avoidant and insecure–ambivalent attachment.

In the Strange Situation procedure infants between 12 and 24 months of age are confronted with three stressful components: a strange environment, interaction with a stranger and two short separations from their caregiver. This stressful situation elicits attachment behaviour and on the basis of infants' reactions to the reunion with the parent or other caregiver three patterns of attachment can be distinguished. Infants who actively seek proximity to their caregivers upon reunion, communicate their feelings of

Figure 5.2 Episode Three: Stranger (left) sitting with mother (middle) and baby (right).

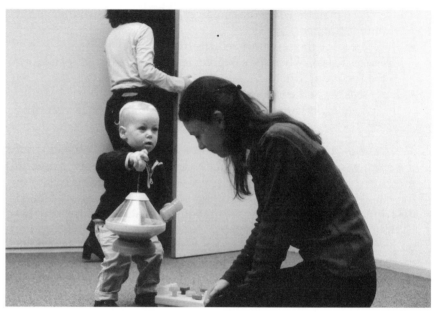

Figure 5.3 Episode Four: Mother leaving baby with stranger.

Figure 5.4 Episode Five: Mother returning.

stress and distress openly and then readily return to exploration are classified as **secure** (B) in their attachment to that caregiver. Infants who do not seem distressed and ignore or avoid the caregiver following reunion (although physiological research shows that their arousal during separation is similar to other infants, see Spangler and Grossmann, 1993), are classified as **insecure–avoidant** (A). Infants who combine strong proximity-seeking and contact-maintaining with contact resistance, or remain

Figure 5.5 Episode Six: Mother leaving, baby alone.

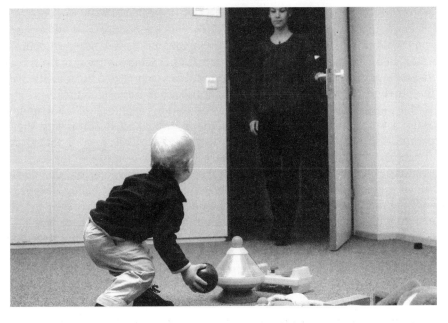

Figure 5.6 Episode Seven: Stranger returning.

inconsolable, without being able to return to play and explore the environment, are classified as **insecure–ambivalent** (C) (sometimes called insecure–resistant).

An overview of all American studies with non-clinical samples (21 samples with a total of 1584 infants, studies conducted in the years 1977–1990) shows that approximately 67 per cent of the infants are classified as secure, 21 per cent are classified as insecure–avoidant and 12 per cent are classified

Figure 5.7 Episode Eight: Reunion of mother and baby. *Note.* Thanks to Boris and Juliette Walma van der Molen and Julia van Os.

as insecure–ambivalent (*see* fig 5.8; van IJzendoorn et al., 1992). An overview of cross-cultural studies (van IJzendoorn and Kroonenberg, 1988) found somewhat fluctuating percentages: in Japan and Israel more insecure–ambivalent attachment relationships were found, whereas in Germany more insecure–avoidant attachment were found. However, it also turned out that the fluctuations were greater *within* countries than *between* countries.

Main and Solomon (1986) constructed a new category of attachment when several studies showed that some infants – often abused by their parents – showed behaviour that was antithetical to their overall pattern of attachment behaviour, or incomprehensible in the context of the overall classification. They developed a coding system for this kind of behaviour, which they called '**disorganized/disoriented**' attachment behaviour. This coding system is used in addition to the traditional classification system, so attachment relationships can be classified, for example, as secure, but also as disorganized/secure. The same goes for the avoidant and the resistant classifications.

Determinants of individual differences in attachment: parental attachment, sensitivity and constitutional factors

SENSITIVITY

Mary Ainsworth and her co-workers originally defined parental **sensitivity** as the ability to perceive and interpret children's attachment signals correctly and to respond to these signals promptly and adequately (Ainsworth et al., 1978). They suggested that early differences in parental sensitivity would lead to individual differences in attachment relationships later in the first year of life. Lack of responsiveness or inconsistent sensitivity was suggested to pave the way for feelings of insecurity in children, whereas consistent sensitive responsiveness would foster secure bonds of the children with their parents. Bowlby (1973, p. 367) and Ainsworth (1967) also speculated that the parents' own childhood attachment experiences would shape their ability or willingness to respond sensitively to their own infant signals. Parents who as children had been neglected or rejected would as parents run a greater risk of becoming neglectful or rejecting of their own children. Ainsworth's studies in Uganda (1967) and in Baltimore (Ainsworth et al., 1978) seemed to support the idea that parental sensitivity was a key factor in the emergence of attachment. Both studies, however, were conducted on rather small samples and were considered pioneering and promising explorations into the roots of early differences in attachment (Ainsworth and Bell, 1977). During the past few decades, several studies on larger samples have tried to confirm or falsify the original claim of a causal relation between parental sensitivity and attachment security. The speculations of Bowlby and Ainsworth about the role of parents' childhood attachment experiences remained unnoticed and untested until Mary Main and her co-workers were able to develop the **Adult Attachment Interview** (AAI) (George et al., 1985). This assessment of parental representations of past attachment experiences led to a series of explorative and confirmatory studies in the 1990s. In the next sections, we report on the outcome of investigations. First, we examine whether the sensitivity of the caregivers affects attachment. Then the role of temperament is discussed. This is followed by a consideration of intergenerational transmission of attachment.

Meta-analyses of caregiver sensitivity

The causal role of parental sensitivity in the formation of attachment security is now a firmly established fact – although it took some decades of painstaking and time-consuming efforts on the part of several hundred researchers to reach this conclusion. Three **meta-analyses** can be cited to support this rather bold statement. A meta-analysis is a review of empirical studies on a certain subject in which the results are summarized statistically. De Wolff and van IJzendoorn (1997) performed a meta-analysis of 66 studies in more than 4000 families on the association between parenting and attachment security. The 66 studies focused on different dimensions of parenting, of which one was 'sensitivity', defined as the appropriate and prompt response to the infant's attachment signals. The correlation between sensitivity and attachment was 0.24.

Is a correlation of 0.24 for sensitivity and attachment security large, or is it disappointingly small? The association is certainly much less impressive than the estimated correlation of 0.78 in the Baltimore study (De Wolff and van IJzendoorn, 1997). Nevertheless, the relation between sensitivity and attachment can be considered remarkably strong and theoretically as well as practically of great significance. In medical science and in medical practice, for example, drugs are prescribed to prevent important diseases such as heart attacks on the basis of effect sizes much smaller than the 0.24.

Intervention studies of caregiver sensitivity

Now let us look at the second reason for believing that the relation between sensitivity and attachment security is of a causal nature and of great significance. In the past few years quite a few intervention studies on attachment have been published. Several interventions were directed at parental sensitivity at the behavioural level. Other interventions have also focused on the parents' representation of attachment, in order to pave the way for subsequent behavioural changes. The behaviourally oriented interventions are often short-term and focused. The representational interventions often are long-term and broadband therapeutic interventions. These two types of intervention – the behavioural and the representational approach – are quite different in design. An example of the first approach is the study of Anisfeld et al. (1990). They provided mothers from deprived immigrant families with soft baby carriers to carry their babies during the first months. The idea was to promote close physical contact between parent and infant. Carrying the baby was supposed to lead to prompt responses to attachment signals such as crying behaviour. Carrying the baby in a sling would thereby stimulate feelings of security in the infant. They included a control group of mothers who were asked to use plastic baby seats. The outcome was dramatic: in the experimental group 83 per cent of the infants appeared to be securely attached at one year of age, whereas in the control group only 38 per cent of the children were secure. Experimental mothers received higher ratings on the sensitivity scale but the difference was not significant.

The second approach is often inspired by Fraiberg's infant–mother psychotherapy (Fraiberg et al., 1975) in which a parent discusses her 'ghosts' of the past, that is, her childhood experiences with insecure attachments and their influence on the interactions with her child. The intervention study of Lieberman et al. (1991) is an example of this approach. The intervenors provided support and therapy for the mothers from deprived immigrant families during a year, with the goal of enhancing their empathy for the affective and developmental needs of their children. Insecure dyads were randomly assigned to intervention and control groups. The intervention started immediately after the Strange Situation assessment and continued throughout the second year of life with unstructured home visits taking place weekly. After a year, security of attachment was assessed again. During a free-play session, maternal empathic responsiveness was rated. Experimental mothers appeared to have higher scores on empathic responsiveness, whereas there were no group differences in attachment security.

Across all intervention studies, it appears to be easier to enhance parental sensitivity than to enhance infant attachment security. In a meta-analysis on 12 studies on more than 800 families, it was shown that the impact of intervention on infant attachment security was significant, but small compared to the effect on maternal sensitivity. It was also found that short-term behaviourally oriented interventions were much more effective than long-term therapeutically based interventions (van IJzendoorn et al., 1995). In sum, the correlational studies on parental sensitivity and infant attachment security showed a consistent association indicating that the more sensitive parents have more secure children. The intervention studies support this correlational evidence in showing that enhancing parental sensitivity leads to more secure children.

Studies in non-Western cultures (Gusii, Kung San and Efe in Africa, Japan and Indonesia in Asia) generally support that caregiver sensitivity leads to secure attachment. Sometimes 'culture' is invoked as an explanation when a study fails to find the link between sensitivity and attachment (e.g., the Sapporo study in Japan; Takahashi, 1990). However, a single study is not enough evidence. In Japan, another study did find the link (the Tokyo study; Vereijken, 1996), thus the universality of the theory could not be disconfirmed. Differences between methods and samples may account for these discrepancies. Fathers and other caregivers have been studied much less often than mothers. In reviewing the studies on sensitivity and attachment with fathers, we found that the majority of the children develop a secure bond with their father. Mechanisms leading up to this secure bond are, however, less well understood: the association between sensitivity and security of attachment was weaker among fathers than generally found among mothers (van IJzendoorn and DeWolff, 1997).

TEMPERAMENT

In his book, *The Nature of the Child*, Kagan (1984) was one of the first authors to discuss a temperamental interpretation of the main attachment classifications. The child's temperamental vulnerability to becoming anxious is, according to Kagan, an obvious factor in the measurement of the attachment relationship with the parent, especially in the case of the Strange Situation procedure (p. 58ff). Temperament seems to be associated with attachment behaviours in the Strange Situation procedure, as proneness to distress will result in more fussing and crying in stressful situations (Belsky and Rovine, 1987). The Strange Situation is a novel and stressful procedure for young children and if temperament is defined as reactivity to stress and novelty, there will be overlap between temperament assessments and children's behaviour in the Strange Situation. Indeed, rather strong associations have been found between negative reactivity and crying in the Strange Situation. Even on the level of attachment classifications, associations with temperament have been documented. In particular, infants with border zone insecure–avoidant and secure attachment classifications differ rather strongly from infants with border zone secure and insecure–ambivalent classifications. Children at the 'avoidant' side are less irritable and reactive and more open to novel experiences than children at the 'resistant/ambivalent' side. There is no dispute about these findings or about the interpretations. The crucial issue is, of course, whether temperament is (causally) related to the main attachment classifications (A, B, C). After two decades of research, the empirical evidence remains conflicting.

If temperament is a causal factor in the development of attachment the same child should develop similar attachments to both father and mother. In 1991, Fox and co-workers reported a strong relation between infant–mother and infant–father attachment security, amounting to a correlation of 0.31 (Fox et al., 1991). This finding has been often used to demonstrate the temperamental basis of attachment. If attachment is a characteristic of the *relationship* and emerges from unique interactions with a specific caregiver, it should show only weak associations across relationships. Otherwise, the child's temperament or other constitutional factors may be the cause of the similarity of the infant's attachments with his two parents and other caregivers. Recently, van IJzendoorn and De Wolff (1997) replicated and extended the meta-analysis on infant–mother/infant–father attachment. In 14 studies on approximately 950 families a correlation of 0.17 between infant–mother and infant–father attachment was found. That is, infant–mother and infant–father attachment shared only 2 per cent common variance. Furthermore, there is a simple and elegant explanation for some common variance between infant–mother and infant–father attachment security. In fig 5.9, the results of four different meta-analyses have been summarized in a hypothetical model. From this model it can be derived that marital partners share attachment security or insecurity to a certain extent. Mothers with secure representations of their past attachment experiences appear more often to marry secure partners. Birds of a feather seem to flock together. Assortative mating or the therapeutic influence of a partner may be the cause for the similarity in attachment between father and mother within the same family. This correspondence may easily be translated into some correspondence on the level of the child's attachment with his mother and father in that same family. The temperament interpretation is more speculative and less economic.

PARENTAL ATTACHMENT REPRESENTATIONS AND INTERGENERATIONAL TRANSMISSION OF ATTACHMENT

Parents' childhood attachment experiences may affect their attachment relationship with their children. Insensitive parents may have experienced insensitive parenting themselves and they may have been unable to change the child-rearing model that they experienced in their childhood years. The potential pervasive influence of parental attachment experiences is a widespread and popular belief and a major theme in literature. Although the idea of **intergenerational transmission of attachment** is popular, it has been rather difficult to prove scientifically. Only longitudinal research can establish connections between past events and current relationships with

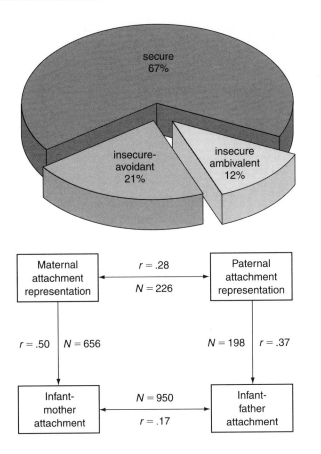

Figure 5.8 The distribution of the attachment classifications in normal North American samples (van IJzendoorn et al., 1992).

Figure 5.9 A data-based model of the family attachment network. Note. Copyright 1997 by the Society for Research in Child Development. Reprinted with permission.

some degree of plausibility, but longitudinal data are scarce and extremely difficult to collect. More importantly, parents may not be completely determined by their own childhood attachment experiences even if those experiences were disappointing. The current mental representation of past attachment experiences may well be different from what exactly happened in childhood because our autobiographical memory is the continuous reconstruction of the past on the basis of the present (Wagenaar, 1986). Positive experiences with friends, partners or therapists may change one's view of the past (Bowlby, 1988). The Adult Attachment Interview mentioned earlier (AAI) (George et al., 1985; Main and Goldwyn, in press) was developed in order to assess the current mental representation of childhood attachment experiences. This avoided the problem of distortions in retrospective accounts of early experiences by focusing on the structure instead of the content of the autobiographical story.

The Adult Attachment Interview

The Adult Attachment Interview (AAI) is a semistructured, hour-long interview with 15 open-ended questions that revolve around issues of attachment, separation and loss during childhood and adulthood. The content of the autobiographical story is not as important as the way in which the story is told. That is, the interview is considered a discourse task: the respondents are supposed to stick to some basic rules governing all our discourses, for example the requirement to be coherent and not contradictory. The British philosopher J.L. Austin provided the definition of coherence as it is applied in the AAI coding system. He differentiated between *quality* (only say what you are able to defend as true), *quantity* (do not provide too many or too few arguments), *relevance* (arguments should be related to the statements that are being defended) and *manner* (make yourself understandable in plain language). In fact, the interview constitutes a dual task (Hesse, 1999): on the one hand the participants must focus on their attachment experiences – which in the case of bad experiences may sometimes be very uncomfortable. On the other hand, contemplating their past the participants should keep focused on the discourse and remain in touch with the interviewer and the interview context. For many people this dual task is very stressful and even insolvable (Dozier and Kobak, 1992). In particular, insecure adults are not able to complete this dual task successfully. They remain too much focused either on the discourse context or on the past experiences. Only secure adults are able to keep a balance between focus on the present discourse and the past experiences, even when they were treated badly in their childhood. It is the discourse style – and not the attachment experiences *per se* – that determine the coding of the security of attachment representations.

The AAI can be considered a stressful situation and the balance between discourse context and autobiographical content runs parallel to the balance children have to strike between their focus on the attachment figure and the playroom in the Strange Situation. In fact, Main and co-workers developed the AAI coding system with the assumption that for every Strange Situation classification a corresponding AAI classification should be found. In subsequent independent replication studies this assumption has been confirmed. Interviews are coded into one of four classifications, indicating four types of attachment representations: **insecure–dismissing**, **autonomous/secure**, **insecure–preoccupied** and **unresolved** attachment.

- *Insecure–dismissing* adults often present a very positive global evaluation of their attachment experiences, without being able to illustrate it with concrete events. They often tell the interviewer that they are unable to remember much of their childhood experiences. When they acknowledge negative aspects of their childhood they insist to have remained untouched or even to have profited from those experiences. Insecure-dismissing subjects seem to minimize or de-activate their attachment concerns. An example is the following small extract: 'Very happy childhood . . . that is absolutely true. With much more luxury than many other children.' 'I think it was just very harmonious, because I cannot remember much about it; everything must have been very happy, otherwise you would remember more.'

- *Autonomous or secure* adults are able to describe attachment-related experiences coherently, whether these experiences were negative or positive. They present a coherent and balanced picture without idealizations and other contradictions.
- *Insecure–preoccupied* adults are still overwhelmed by their past attachment experiences, they feel mistreated by their parents and are not able to tell a coherent story. They express involved anger when they discuss the past and present relationship with their parents. They are said to maximize or hyper-activate their attachment concerns (Kobak and Sceery, 1988; Main, 1990).
- *Unresolved* adults discuss experiences of loss or other potential trauma in a disorientated way, and from their speech it seems as if they are still struggling with the loss or trauma. For example, vivid descriptions of the deceased attachment figure in the present tense may indicate that the adult thinks this person is still alive. Unresolved loss or trauma can be assigned on top of a classification as Dismissing, Secure or Preoccupied.

Correspondence between parental attachment and infant attachment

Intergenerational transmission of attachment suggests an analogy of adult and infant strategies to cope with negative emotions, that is, dismissing parents would develop avoidant attachments with their children, preoccupied parents would be inclined to have ambivalent children and secure parents would relate in a secure way to their children. The correspondence between parental attachment and infant attachment has been examined in at least 18 studies. In most studies, the AAI was administered to mothers; four studies, however, also concerned fathers. On these 18 studies (in total 854 parent–child dyads) three meta-analyses were performed and the effect sizes for the association between the parent and infant attachment were computed. Fig 5.9 shows that the infant and parent attachment classifications are strongly associated. Even when the mother is interviewed before the birth of her infant, her attachment security is highly predictive of the infants' security more than a year later (Fonagy et al., 1991). In about 75 per cent of the families the parents determine their infants' attachment security on the basis of their own attachment representations. We do not yet know exactly what the transmission mechanisms are. The first possibility that comes to mind is of course parental sensitivity. Sensitivity is causally related to attachment (De Wolff and van IJzendoorn, 1997) and it is also associated with parents' attachment representations (van IJzendoorn, 1995). Nevertheless, a transmission gap remains (van IJzendoorn, 1995). Transmission of genes may be involved. Suomi (1995) recently found that transmission of attachment also exists in non-human primates – even independent of the genetic link between the adult and infant monkey. Behaviour genetic studies (*see* Chapter 1) should replicate this outcome in humans.

From infancy to adulthood

The AAI has provided an opportunity for longitudinal attachment studies. For the first time it became possible to investigate the continuity and discontinuity of attachment from infancy to adulthood. In the past few years, at least seven longitudinal attachment studies have been reported, most of them starting in the first few years of life and following the same participants up into adolescence or early adulthood. In attachment theory, a high degree of continuity would not be expected. Infancy is not regarded as the 'critical period', in which the environment is imprinted upon the individual. The development of attachment should be regarded as 'environmentally labile' (Bowlby, 1973, p. 414). Bowlby (1973, p. 411 ff) compared the development of attachment to a railway system that starts with a single main route which leaves the city in a certain direction but soon forks into a range of distinct routes, some of which diverge from the main route while others take a convergent course. At any point, critical junctions may show up at which the lines fork; but once a train is on any particular line it has a tendency to stay on that line. Bowlby (1973) also insisted that at any stage during the years of immaturity – infancy, childhood and adolescence – changes in childrearing arrangements and life events such as rejections, separations and losses and later on even a supportive spouse or being in therapy may provoke a change in the course of attachment development.

What are the findings of the exciting longitudinal studies that have become available recently? In 50 stable, middle class families stability across 20 years was high: 70 per cent of the adults who were secure or insecure on the AAI had been secure or insecure as infants in the Strange Situation (Waters et al., 1995). Discontinuity was associated with negative events such as loss of a parent or parental divorce. Hamilton (1994), in a smaller sample, similarly found high stability across 17 years (77 per cent). Two German studies (Zimmermann et al., 1995; Becker-Stoll et al., 1996) and two American studies (Carlson, in press; Lewis et al., 1997) found low stability. Thus it seems that the relevant question to ask is not 'is there stability?' or 'how high is the stability?', but 'what are the circumstances under which stability is high or low?'

DISCUSSION POINT

Parental divorce or loss can be important experiences that may change the attachment representation. What other experiences can you imagine?

Strictly, the current wave of longitudinal studies does not address the issue of intergenerational transmission of attachment. These studies document the (dis-)continuity of attachment within the same individual across the first two decades of life. Intergenerational transmission of attachment in the strict sense, however, means that the parent as an infant in the past would have had the same attachment classification as his or her own infant at present. In the near future, studies will become available in which participants whose parents completed the AAI around their birth have become young parents themselves. This exciting prospect may lead to deeper insight not only into the continuity of attachment within one generation but also into the transmission of attachment across several generations.

Chapter summary

Attachment theory has its origins in Great Britain, in the period during and shortly after World War Two. It was developed by John Bowlby. At the heart of attachment theory is the assumption that attachment is a basic human need and that from very early on babies actively participate in the formation of attachment relationships. Attachment relationships can be secure or insecure and a laboratory paradigm, called the Strange Situation, is used to measure individual differences in quality of attachment. The sensitivity of the behaviour of the caregivers is regarded as the most important determinant of these differences. At the background are the caregivers' attachment representations of their own experiences, as is evident from research using the Adult Attachment Interview. Theory predicts that the stability of the attachment patterns from infancy to adulthood is limited by intervening events or changing life circumstances.

Seminar questions

1. Is it still fruitful to see attachment and caregiving as genetically determined phenomena in a world that seems so different from prehistoric times? How do you compare the initial experience of the world by a 'modern' baby to the experience by a 'prehistoric' baby?
2. According to operant conditioning theory, giving attention to crying infants will spoil them, turning them eventually into 'little tyrants' over their families. Attachment theory, however, stresses the importance of sensitive responsiveness: children have to feel that their needs are attended to, that they are not vulnerable, alone and unsafe. What advice should be given to prospective parents?
3. Much attachment research is focused on intergenerational transmission of attachment patterns. Some feel that everybody always blames the mothers. Would you say attachment theory gives parents a somewhat pessimistic orientation, compared to, say, a theory that put central the temperamental characteristics with which babies are born?

Further reading

Ainsworth, M.D.S., Bowlby, J. 1991. An ethological approach to personality development. *American Psychologist* **46**, 333–41.

This article is especially interesting from a human interest point of view. Who were Mary Ainsworth and John Bowlby? How did they become interested in studying attachment? How did their careers progress? They give it to you first-hand and they give you a sketch of the development of attachment theory.

Bowlby, J. 1969/1984. *Attachment and loss: Vol. 1. Attachment (second edition)*. London: Penguin.

The first volume of Bowlby's trilogy, *Attachment and loss*, describes the underpinnings of his theory, differences from the traditional (Freudian, behaviouristic) views of social development and the roots in ethology, cybernetics and also psychoanalysis. The development of attachment behaviour in children is described in great detail. This book won Bowlby's standing among leading theoreticians in developmental psychology.

Byng-Hall, J. 1995. *Rewriting family scripts: improvisation and systems change*. New York: Guilford Press.

John Byng-Hall was Bowlby's successor at the Tavistock Clinic. He has an original and influential approach to family therapy that is rooted in attachment theory. His work is informed by the latest findings with respect to attachment representation and intergenerational transmission. Excellent if one wants to know about a practical application of current attachment theory.

Main, M. 1990. Cross-cultural studies of attachment organization: recent studies, changing methodologies and the concept of conditional strategies. *Human Development* **33**, 48–61.

Currently one of the most important theoreticians as well as researchers, Mary Main gives an insightful account of the similarities between what she calls the 'attachment strategies' of children and adults. She also addresses questions about the maladaptive or adaptive nature of the secure and the insecure attachment strategies.

Sroufe, L.A. 1988. The role of infant–caregiver attachment in development. In Belsky, J. and Nezworkski, T. (eds) *Clinical implications of attachment*. Hillsdale, NJ: Lawrence Erlbaum Associates, 18–38.

Alan Sroufe is one of the leading specialists in the field of the social and emotional development of young children. In this influential article he describes implications of attachment theory for understanding development, but also draws the boundaries of attachment theory. He outlines some puzzles for attachment research and the preliminary answers that can be given on the basis of the research that has been done.

Part

COGNITIVE AND REPRESENTATIONAL GROWTH

Theories of cognitive development

6

KAREN PINE

Editors' preface

Almost all chapters in this book consider some aspect of cognitive development, the way that children's thinking develops. This chapter by Dr Karen Pine provides a summary of several of the most important perspectives about cognitive development.

The chapter starts with a consideration of the work of Piaget. We have already seen in the chapter by Gavin Bremner that Piaget's ideas continue to have an impact on discussions about cognitive processes in infancy, even though not everyone would now accept the validity of the ideas. Karen Pine provides an overview of Piaget's ideas about the later stages of development. This description is helpful in providing a background to other processes such as moral development (*see* Chapter 15), the investigation of intelligence (*see* Chapter 8), and the discussion of disabilities (chapters 10 and 12).

Karen Pine also pays attention to ideas and theories which have to a large extent supplanted those of Piaget. Piaget proposed that each stage of development involved children processing information in certain general ways, and this had ramifications to all aspects of their psychological functioning. More recently this idea has been challenged by the idea that children's (and adults') minds contain 'modules' which involve cognitive processes which are largely independent of other thinking. Thus, there could be a language module which enables us to carry out the complex grammatical operations without involving other aspects of thinking; such modules do not utilize conscious knowledge or depend on conscious control of the process (*see also* chapters 4 and 8). Another reason for the move away from the idea of general stages of development is research findings which indicate that cognition develops because children can process information more efficiently, and the extra resources available from the efficiency gains enable new levels of functioning. More recently, there also has been interest in the way connectionist modelling can provide ways of testing whether general ways of learning provide the basis for quite complex cognitive processes. An important theory which provides something of a middle position amongst all these different ideas is the Representational Redescription model of Karmiloff-Smith. This model also is important in capturing another aspect of development, the change from unconscious, unverbalizable procedures, to conscious understanding that can be expressed in words. There are many new ideas about the process of cognitive development, but there still are many questions awaiting answers.

Introduction

What do we mean by *cognitive development*? Cognition is concerned with thinking and development is about change over time so, putting it simply, cognitive development is about how children's thinking changes over time. It also encompasses learning and intelligence. Although there has been a science of psychology for over a century now, theories about cognitive development have only attracted attention relatively recently. You will see in this chapter that this is because, earlier this century, the fact that children's thinking could develop was not always acknowledged. Children were often thought of being less intelligent, and knowing less, than adults. A major shift in thinking about cognitive development came with the move from this quantitative belief to more qualitative approaches. The idea that children's thinking differed qualitatively from adults' and changed over time came with the work of Piaget, from whose ideas many theories of cognitive development have sprung. Consequently, this chapter contains quite a lot about the work of Piaget. It also looks at some post-Piagetian and information processing approaches to cognitive development, as well as the contribution which computer simulation has made to our understanding of how we think. Although the theories discussed here may all appear quite different they do at times overlap so, wherever possible, we will highlight links between them. Sometimes the theories may appear to diverge from each other because they are trying to answer different questions about development. In an effort to clarify what the main issues are for each theory the relevant sections will be headed with a question about cognitive development which that particular theory might be seen to be addressing.

'What can the child be taught?' the behaviourist approach

Throughout the early part of this century **behaviourism** was the dominant force in investigative psychology. The behaviourists believed that psychology should only be concerned with what could be directly seen or observed. Any ideas about the internal workings of the mind were rejected, since these were not overt or measurable. John Watson (1878–1958), for example, believed that children's behaviour could be explained in terms of learning theories along the lines of those proposed by Pavlov or Skinner. He is said to have induced a phobia in a child called Little Albert by making a loud noise whenever a pet rat was presented, until the child associated the two and feared the pet (Watson and Rayner, 1920). From experiments such as these, Watson concluded that much of children's learning could be explained by Pavlovian classical conditioning. Behaviourists like Watson held a quantitative view of development. This assumes that the young child's behaviour is simply less complex than that of adults and, whilst it becomes more complex as the child grows up, it is still the same kind of behaviour as it was earlier.

Learning theories of development have not altogether lost their appeal in later years. In the 1970s Patterson claimed operant conditioning accounted for children's learning, whereas Bandura argued that children learned by observing and imitating others. Although many would disagree with these approaches today, what these later theorists have in common with the earlier behaviourists is an assumption that the child is shaped by the external environment. They are concerned with how the child can be made to behave in a certain way. The child's own thinking processes were seen to play a much lesser role and you could say that cognitive development was not even part of the picture.

'How much does the child know?' intellectual power approaches

This tendency to neglect the role of the child's own thinking processes also characterized earlier intellectual power approaches. These tended to focus on how individual children differed in the amount of intelligence they had. At the turn of the century intelligence tests were widely used to measure individual differences in children. Again, the emphasis was less on the development of cognitive skills or processes and more on measuring how much intelligence a given child had.

In 1905 Alfred Binet was asked by the French government to develop a test which would measure the intelligence quotient (IQ) of children, with the aim of identifying those who had learning disabilities. The test Binet and his co-worker, Theodore Simon, developed asked children to make a series of judgements and compared their answers with others of the same chronological age. It was whilst working with Simon on an intelligence test in 1920 that Jean Piaget first became interested in how young children think. Indeed, it was his observations at that time which were to have a profound influence on the whole field of developmental psychology in the future.

'What is different about children's thinking?' Jean Piaget

The task of the IQ tester was to count the number of correct answers the children gave. This must have been rather boring for a man like Piaget who was a great thinker and who, by the age of 24, had already written 20 scientific papers and a philosophical novel. During the IQ testing Piaget became intrigued by the wrong answers the children gave and noticed something which to him seemed crucially significant. What he observed was that many children of the same age gave the same wrong answers to questions. Piaget decided this must be due to **qualitative** differences in the nature of children's thinking at different ages. It was not that the younger children knew **less** but that they thought **differently**. Furthermore, it suggested to him that the child's thinking was not just shaped by the environment (as the behaviourists had believed) but could be influenced by internal mental processes which changed as the child grew.

By shifting the emphasis from how much children knew (the quantitative) to the different ways in which they understood their world (the qualitative) Piaget was to mark a breakthrough in our understanding of cognitive development.

Subsequently, Piaget devoted himself to identifying these changes in the quality of children's thinking and the ages when these seemed to occur. Piaget argued that at each age the child has a particular logic for making sense of the world, which he believed was determined by their 'cognitive structures'. These cognitive structures could not be directly observed (thus going against the behaviourists' principles) but were inferred from various behaviours which Piaget measured, or observed, in children.

As well as identifying a sequence of cognitive developmental stages which, he claimed, all children go through, Piaget also proposed a number of processes which enable these changes to occur. Influenced by his early training as a biologist he believed the child, like any living organism, has to adapt to its environment. By a process of assimilation, Piaget claimed, new situations or problems are dealt with using the existing mental structures or schemas. Changing these schemas when existing ones were unsatisfactory he referred to as accommodation. These ongoing processes mean that thinking is an active process for the child who does not just passively receive information from the environment but is constantly undergoing mental reorganization so as to achieve a balanced, coherent state which Piaget called **equilibrium**.

There are many excellent text books which give a full account of the stages proposed by Piaget (*see* the Further Reading) so in this chapter a sample of the main characteristics of each stage (summarized in Box 6.1) are discussed.

BOX 6.1 Piaget's stages of cognitive development

Age	Stage	Characteristics
0–2 years	Sensorimotor	Understanding the world through the senses. Object concept acquired.
2–6 years	Pre-operational	Beginning of thought and language but from an ego-centric perspective.
6–12 years	Concrete operational	Mental manipulation possible but tied to the concrete. Conservation achieved.
12 years +	Formal operational	Manipulation of abstract ideas, logical systematic thinking, reflective thought.

THE SENSORIMOTOR STAGE

Piaget conducted extensive observations of young infants, including his own, when they were at the **sensorimotor** stage. He concluded that babies are born with a set of basic strategies, such as sucking, looking and grasping, which provide the starting points for the development of thinking in the second year. An important development concerns how the infant deals with hidden objects and the development of what Piaget called the object concept (*see* Chapter 3).

PRE-OPERATIONAL AND CONCRETE OPERATIONAL THOUGHT

Perhaps the essence of Piaget's ingenuity lay in the experiments he designed to support his theories of cognitive development. Two of these, investigating perspective taking and conservation, are explored in more detail below and characterize the difference between pre-operational and concrete operational thought.

Perspective taking and the pre-operational stage

Piaget argued that one feature of the **pre-operational** child's thinking is egocentrism. This means that very young children are unaware that there are ways of looking at things which differ from their own. If trying to play hide and seek, for example, a two-year-old 'hides' by covering her eyes only, unaware that the rest of her body is totally visible! This, according to Piaget, is due to the child's egocentrism which enables her only to entertain one viewpoint, her own. Piaget also showed how the young child is unable to take another's perspective, in a perceptual sense, with his Three Mountains Experiment (Box 6.2).

BOX 6.2   Piaget's Three Mountains experiment

In this experiment Piaget placed a papier-mâché model of three mountains on a table in front of the child. The three mountains differed slightly, one had a cross on top, one was covered in grass and another was snow-topped.

Piaget asked the child to describe what they saw, a task they could perform without difficulty from about four years old onwards. Next, a doll was placed on the opposite side of the table and Piaget asked the child to describe what the doll saw. Children under about seven years of age thought the doll's view was the same as their own.

The child was also shown drawings of the view of the three mountains from different perspectives, but again, it was not until about eight years of age that children realized that the three mountains looked different depending on the viewpoint of the observer.

Piaget saw this as an important development in the child's thinking, the ability to de-centre from their own position and attend to several aspects of a situation at once. This second skill also became evident when the child was at the concrete operations stage and was able to understand conservation, as the next section describes.

Conservation and concrete operations

Piaget noticed that children at the pre-operational stage made errors in his conservation experiments, which **concrete operational stage** children did not. He concluded that the child's thinking becomes more logical at around seven years of age and this could be demonstrated by the ability to conserve. Imagine placing a row of four sweets in front of a child and asking the child to make another row alongside it containing the same number. If asked if the two rows contained the same amount a child, from about four years onwards, would reply 'yes'. If you then rearranged one row, moving the sweets closer together and so shortening the line, the answer to the question 'Are they the same now?' would differ according to the age of the child. A child of around six or seven years would logically realize that nothing had been added or taken away and reply, 'Yes, of course they are still the same' but a younger child would not. The pre-operational child would be misled by the appearance of the two rows into believing that the longer one contained more sweets, even though he had previously agreed that they contained the same amount (*see* fig 6.1).

DISCUSSION POINT

Have you encountered, or can you think of examples of young children's ability to conserve in everyday life? Sometimes cutting a child's sausage into several pieces convinces them that they have more!

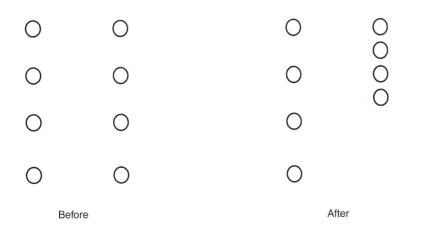

Before   After

Figure 6.1 The arrays of sweets before and after transformation in an experiment to demonstrate conservation of number.

Piaget referred to these as experiments in 'conservation' because they require the child to conserve, or hold constant, the number of items despite changes in the appearance of the array. The child needs now to attend to two aspects of the situation simultaneously which, Piaget said, had been the difficulty for children at the pre-operational stage. However, conservation of number was only one of Piaget's experiments. He also demonstrated children's understanding of conservation of volume (described below) and weight. Interestingly, not all conservation problems are mastered at once, with conservation of mass acquired first, then weight, with volume generally considered the hardest of the three (*see* Box 6.3).

BOX 6.3 Piaget's experiments on conservation of volume

In this experiment three containers are placed in front of the child on a table. The adult fills the first one with milk from a jug and asks the child to pour the same amount into the second, identical, container. The child does this and agrees that the two containers have the same amount of milk in them. The adult then produces a third container which is taller and thinner than the other two. The child then has to pour the milk from the second container into this taller one. The adult then asks the child if this third container contains the same amount of milk as the first one. Once again, a perceptual transformation has occurred which affects the pre-operational child but not the child who has reached concrete operations. The younger child will assert that the taller container now contains more than the original one, whereas the older child will tell the experimenter, 'Of course, they are still the same'. The younger child attends only to one feature of the containers, the height, and believes that taller must mean more. The older child, however, can appreciate two features, understanding that there is more height but less width, and that the amount in the container remains unchanged. He can also, mentally, reverse the operation and return the milk to the original container in his mind to understand that, logically, they must still be the same.

CONCRETE OPERATIONS AND EARLY EDUCATION

This ability to attend to more than one feature of a situation and perform the mental operation of reversibility, Piaget saw as crucial indicators that the child had reached the concrete operations stage. The development of these abilities at around age six or seven also coincided with the introduction of more formal schooling for the child and Piaget regarded them as prerequisites for understanding number and performing mathematical transformations. For example, to understand that:

if six add four equal ten, *then* ten minus four must equal six

the child needs to be able to perform the mental operation of reversibility. There have been a number of efforts to translate Piaget's theory into classroom practice, although not all of these have met with success. Piaget alerted educationalists to the notion that a particular concept cannot be taught unless the child has the appropriate cognitive structures in place and is ready to acquire it . However, teachers sometimes have overlooked Piaget's emphasis on the child as playing an active role in the construction of his thinking processes and may inadvertently have believed that the child could be forced along the sequence. It is also too easy to forget where the initial impetus for Piaget's theories came from, that is from looking at the child's wrong answers and trying to understand what they reveal about the child's logic. There is a danger that the current trend in the UK towards testing children at younger and younger ages will lead to an over pre-occupation with 'rightness'.

FORMAL OPERATIONAL STAGE AND LOGICAL THINKING

Although the acquisition of concrete operational logic was seen as a milestone in the child's cognitive development, the final stage proposed by Piaget was **formal operations** (*see* Box 6.4). Starting at age 12 and continuing through adolescence, this more sophisticated set of cognitive structures meant the young person could think not only in concrete terms (i.e. about objects) but in more abstract ways too (i.e. about ideas). It is during this stage of adolescence that strong opinions on issues such as world peace or vegetarianism emerge, because more abstract ideas and hypotheses can be entertained. Formal operations free the individual from reliance on direct experience and he is able to think logically about things of which he may have no experience. By this stage the young person is also capable, Piaget said, of reflective abstraction. That is, of being aware of his own thoughts and the strategies he uses in problem solving, increasing his ability to solve problems in a more systematic manner.

BOX 6.4 Formal operations and the pendulum task

Piaget demonstrated this by presenting adolescents with a number of physics tasks, one of which concerned the swing of a pendulum. The problem was to find out which variable (force of push, length of string, weight of object or height of push) determined the amount of time it takes a pendulum to complete one swing.

Younger children have been found to test these different variables in an unsystematic manner, sometimes changing two variables at a time so no firm conclusion about one could be drawn. An adolescent tends to try a more scientific approach, testing just one variable at a time while holding all the others constant. He might, for example, try a short string with a light object, a medium object and a heavy object to ascertain the effect of weight of object (in fact, only the string length affects the period of the pendulum swing).

The formal operational stage of development has had less attention focused on it than the earlier stages, although it has been suggested that not all adolescents, or indeed adults, reach this stage of mature intellectual functioning.

DISCUSSION POINT

Review the tasks used by Piaget to understand children's thinking. Do you think they were valid experiments to test his ideas? To what extent do you think his findings were influenced by the type of questions or materials he used?

'Was Piaget right?' Post-Piagetian research

Piaget's contributions to developmental psychology were so profound, and his many experiments both simple and ingenious, that much of the research that followed was aimed at testing his ideas and at identifying the mechanisms which might explain what he found. Extensive work has been carried out to find out, for example, whether the stages he proposed really did hold true. The generally accepted view now is that children's development is probably more gradual than stage-like (Flavell, 1963) and, more importantly, that the idea of over-arching changes occurring in all the child's thinking at a certain age is inaccurate. Piaget argued that the child's cognitive structures at a certain age would have a pervasive effect on all her thinking, i.e. a pre-operational child would think in a pre-operational way about all tasks and topics. However, it has been found that a child can exhibit pre-operational thought on one task but be at the concrete operations stage on another. Therefore, the child's type of thinking may not be as general as Piaget prescribed. More recent theorists (e.g. Chomsky, 1968; Fodor, 1983) have suggested that the mind may be more compartmentalized, or modular, and that instead of one set of cognitive structures driving all thinking, the different domains such as language, mathematics and perception may each have their own set of guiding principles. It has also been found that when Piaget's tasks are made more relevant to children they can reach many developmental milestones, like the ability to conserve, at an earlier age than Piaget discovered they could (Donaldson, 1978). New methods for testing infants have also produced results which challenge many of Piaget's findings. The work of Baillargeon, for example, has demonstrated object permanence in infants as young as five-months (Baillargeon, 1986).

'What is the child innately equipped with?' the Nativist view

The findings that infants are more cognitively capable than Piaget thought prompted later work aimed at specifying the type of mind that the infant is born with and identifying the role of innate and environmental influences on cognitive development. Piaget believed the newborn infant's cognitive system consisted only of some fundamental organizing principles, assimilation and accommodation, with cognitive structures developing as the child matured and interacted with its environment. This is often referred to as a **constructivist theory** of development. Conversely, nativists like Chomsky or Fodor claim that the newborn mind is equipped with much more. Indeed, as methods of testing infants have improved it has been possible to show that Piaget under-estimated infants' early ability to form representations. Also, some kinds of learning just seem to come more naturally to children than others. Language is one example and this led Chomsky to conclude that there must be some innate structures which help the child. However, there still remains a lot of work to be done to fully understand what the newborn infant brings with it to the world. Methodological advances in this area promise to yield a better understanding of how cognitive development occurs and particularly what the role of innate and environmental factors may be (*see* Spelke, 1994).

How important is the social world? Vygotsky's sociocultural theory

One significant challenge to Piaget's ideas comes from those who place emphasis on the child's social world as a major contributor to development. This emphasis stems largely from the work of a Russian psychologist, Vygotsky, who died in 1934 but whose writings were translated and adopted in the West in the 1960s and 1970s. Vygotsky rejected the reductionist model of cognition proclaimed by the behaviourists and, like Piaget, believed the child was an **active constructor** of its own knowledge. However there the similarity between the two theorists ends, since the core of Vygotsky's theory was founded on the belief that we can only understand children's mental growth if we take account of the social context in which they develop. Not only were the significant others around the child, its parents, teachers and friends, seen by Vygotsky as key players in the process of development, but he also acknowledged the wider influences of art, language and culture. For him there existed a complex yet inextricable link between the individual, interpersonal and social domains that Piaget's focus on internal mental structures had largely ignored.

Although Piaget recognized that the environment in which the child is raised is important, he attached more significance to the child's physical world than the social world. This is quite surprising given that the human infant is dependent upon others during the first two years of life, which Piaget termed the sensorimotor period. Many now feel that Piaget underplayed the importance of others in the child's development and that Vygotsky's theories redress this imbalance. Also, with the advent of more innovative techniques for testing infants, a lot more is known now about early social development than was known at the time of Piaget's writing. Research has shown that children are social beings from birth, with an innate attraction to human faces and, by just two days old, a preference for their own mother's face. Imitation of others has also been found to be a powerful learning mechanism and an important precursor to communication (Meltzoff and Moore, 1977). This knowledge about early social development may explain the decline in popularity of Piaget's individualistic account of development and a resurgence of interest in Vygotsky's theory. After all, if the infant is tuned in to other people from birth it is likely that he will continue to use others as an important source of learning throughout childhood.

According to Vygotsky's sociocultural theory children learn mainly with the help of other people and a major feature of this process is the **zone of proximal development**. This refers to the distance between the level of development a child can reach under adult guidance, and the level at which the child functions without help. Vygotsky saw the adult's role as introducing the child to a level of thinking that challenges them, but which is not too far beyond their current level. He believed that the child internalized the knowledge learned in a social context and eventually decontextualized it and took over responsibility from the adult. In this way the adult enables the child to achieve their full intellectual potential and reach a level of understanding which could not be attained by working independently. Not surprisingly, these ideas attracted a lot of interest from educators since they focused attention on the ways in which adults can guide and support children's learning. Since the 1970s there has been an upsurge in research into which forms of adult intervention may best help children to progress. One such form, derived from Vygotskian theory, is a type of instruction called **scaffolding** (Wood et al., 1976; Rogoff, 1990), where the amount and form of guidance given to a child is adjusted according to his level of development and eventually reduced until the child works independently. The scaffolding from the adult provides a temporary support for the child (as it does in a more literal sense for the building worker during construction) which can be removed once the child is able to work at the higher level without support. Parents and teachers tend to scaffold children's learning of a new skill in this way, offering more support early on and gradually withdrawing as the child improves.

Even today many current educational applications owe much to Vygotsky's writings, but his views about the adult as instructor and the child as a learner have undergone modification and the relationship is now seen as less of a one-way process. The current view is that the child is an active partner when working with an adult, contributing to and even structuring the interaction. Also, Vygotsky saw the adult as the best person to instruct the child and scaffolding, too, has been thought to be more effectively provided by adults rather than by other children. Yet this does not mean that children cannot learn from each other, merely that the processes may differ. Educators now believe that group learning or peer tutoring can offer an effective environment for guiding a child through their zone of proximal development (*see* Richards and Light, 1986). This may be because these settings encourage children to use language, to provide explanations, work co-operatively or competitively, all of which have been thought to bring about cognitive change. The fact that language figures largely in these learning environments also reinforces Vygotsky's conviction that talking to others, or to oneself ('inner speech'), is essential to cognitive development.

'How is knowledge processed?' information processing theories

A major force in developmental psychology which grew out of, and in some way was a reaction to, Piaget's theory was the information processing approach. This approach examines more closely the way in which major components of the mind, such as memory and attention, come into play when the child deals with particular tasks or problems. One assumption of this approach is that as children grow they develop better strategies for remembering and organizing knowledge and for encoding (or noticing) more aspects of a problem. The child thus becomes a better information processor. These theories also aim to identify the ways in which the child's knowledge is stored and the particular codes or representations used. This means that the final representation of a piece of information, after it has been processed by the child's cognitive system, may be quite different from the environmental input. This approach can also inform us further about the differences which appear both between individuals and between children of different ages.

INFORMATION PROCESSING: DO CHILDREN SIMPLY GET BETTER AT USING WHAT THEY HAVE?

A lot of this research has looked at basic perceptual or memory processes, to try and find out how these develop in the child and how they affect the way in which information is handled. One idea put forward is that these processes are innate but that, as the child grows, better strategies for using them are developed. The work of Flavell demonstrated this by giving children of different ages lists of items (presented as pictures) to remember. Before being tested on recall the majority of 8–10 year olds could be seen mouthing the list, a strategy called rehearsal. Just as you or I would repeat a telephone number to ourselves between seeing it and having to dial the number. What Flavell found, though, was that five-year-olds did not use this strategy and therefore remembered far fewer items than the older children. One explanation for Flavell's results could be that older children simply have better memories than younger ones. However, the important finding was that the younger children could be taught the rehearsal strategy and would then remember as many items as the older children (Keeney et al., 1967). Therefore, they had just as good a memory but were not so proficient at using it. Much of this type of work on memory from the information processing theorists has found that as children grow they acquire more and more powerful strategies for remembering. They also use them more efficiently and apply them to more and more different kinds of problems.

The work of one researcher, Chi (1978), suggests that it is not just that younger children's memory strategies are less developed but that lack of experience may also account for developmental differences. A study which demonstrated this involved showing 10-year-old children and adults a chess board with an organized arrangement of chess pieces on it for just 10 seconds. The task for the participants was to try and reproduce the previously seen arrangement of pieces on a new board. The children performed much better than the adults and remembered far more. This is surprising since adults usually out-perform children on memory tasks. However, all the children taking part were skilled chess players whilst the adults were novices. The children had had more experience of noticing arrangements of chess pieces on a board and hence did better than the adults. However, when the same participants were given a simple digit-span memory task the adults performed better than the children. Chi (1978) attributed this to the adult's greater familiarity with digits, not to their having better memories. This demonstrated that there may be fewer age-related constraints on children's learning than previously thought and that given the knowledge and experience they can do just as well as adults.

Thus, some information processing approaches regard cognitive development as the child making better and more efficient use of the processes required to organize and encode information, without any global reorganization of the cognitive system envisaged by Piaget. Whereas Flavell demonstrated that better strategy use can explain developmental differences, and Chi claimed experience was what counted, there is also considerable evidence that the child's mental capacity, e.g. its working memory, increases as it grows (Case, 1985).

SIEGLER'S WORK ON THE BALANCE SCALE – WHAT RULES DO CHILDREN DEVELOP?

Robert Siegler's work typifies the information processing approach. His studies led him to conclude that children's cognitive development can be characterized by the acquisition of increasingly complex rules for solving problems (Siegler, 1976; Klahr and Siegler, 1978). Siegler focused on children's performance on many Piagetian-type tasks, one of which was a balance scale. This consisted of a central fulcrum and arms with pegs spaced at equal distances from it, onto which could be placed one or more weights (*see* fig 6.2).

The task for the child was to predict, after the experimenter had set weights upon some of the pegs, whether the balance scale would remain balanced, or tip left or right if a lever that kept the scale from moving was removed. Siegler found that children are able to begin solving problems in a rule-governed way at around five years old. At this age they respond on the basis of a single feature and are likely to adopt unidimensional rules such as, 'If one end has more weight, that end of the balance scale will tip down', regardless of the distance of the weights from the fulcrum. His work led him to devise a four rule hierarchy where different performance patterns on the balance scale are the result of the rule the child is using. These are summarized in Box 6.5.

BOX 6.5 Siegler's classification of rule-use on the balance scale

Rule I: • Children consider only the number of weights on each side of the fulcrum. If they are the same for the two sides, children predict the scale will balance; otherwise they predict that the side with the greater weight will go down.

Rule II: • Children base their judgments solely on weight, if the two sides have different amounts of weight. If their weights are equal they also consider the distances of the weights from the fulcrum.

Rule III: • Children consider the amount of weight and the distance from the fulcrum. They answer correctly when the weights, distances or both are equal on both sides of the fulcrum. If one side has more weight and the other side more distance,

---

they do not have a consistent rule and muddle through, or guess.

Rule IV: • Children consider both weight and distance dimensions, use the sum of cross products formula when one side has more weight and the other side more distance and therefore answer all problem types consistently correctly. (from Siegler, 1976)

Siegler found that to discover the appropriate set of rules for the balance scale (the Law of Torque) the child had to encode and combine appropriately the relevant features of the problem, that is both weight and distance. Although younger children, between five and eight years old, focused on only one dimension of the problem (which side had more weight) he showed that feedback and training help them progress from one rule to the next (Siegler, 1984). Developmental differences, he claimed, have much to do with the way older and younger children encode problems. If trained to notice the relevant features younger children can do as well as older ones although he found, like Flavell, that they may not do so without being prompted.

Siegler's work also exemplifies an important feature of information processing theories. His rule-assessment account made specific predictions about the representations underlying children's errors. That is, he demonstrated how a particular representation (in this case a rule about the balance scale) could underlie both the child's right and wrong answers. McShane (1991) says that a theory of cognitive development is only complete if both correct and incorrect responses alike are predictable and explained by the child's representation of the task. Siegler's work satisfies this criterion, although the question of how the child progresses from using one rule to using a better one is not so well explained by his work. He goes some way towards addressing this issue by arguing that younger children prefer rules based on just one feature of a problem because they have had less experience which would disconfirm these rules. New rules are formed as the child becomes better at monitoring more features and encoding them (Siegler, 1984).

With the information processing theorists a more rigorous methodology for studying cognitive development was employed. Unlike Piaget's theory, Siegler's rule-based model has the advantage of being precisely specified and testable. Many years earlier Piaget, too, had used a balance scale in his

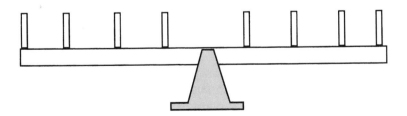

Figure 6.2   A balance scale similar to that used by Siegler (1976).

investigations with children (Inhelder and Piaget, 1958) but these yielded data which were far more anecdotal and no statistical procedures were applied. Siegler, on the other hand, adopted a rigorous, systematic approach and subjected the data to statistical analysis thus placing his work on a firmer scientific footing.

This system of analysing specific tasks and identifying the mental representations underlying children's performance on them has proved to be a very fruitful one. What has emerged from this is evidence for a sequence in children's acquisition of new strategies, but without advocating the overarching changes in thinking which Piaget had proposed. However, it is wrong to assume that a child either has or does not have a particular strategy in its repertoire in some all-or-none fashion. Siegler has also shown that children, when learning an addition strategy in mathematics, can be quite inconsistent in their strategy use (Siegler, 1989). What this body of research has shown is that a child may use a new strategy in a few situations but may forget to use it all the time or fail to see that it can be applied to new problems. As children develop they not only acquire new and more powerful ways of handling information but also become better at knowing where and when to use their new techniques.

DISCUSSION POINT

The next theory deals with how knowledge is represented in the mind. Before reading this section it will be useful to understand that not all knowledge is stored in a linguistic form. Try to think of examples of:

- Something which you know how to do but you would find hard to describe to someone else.
- Something which you can picture in your mind but cannot put into words.
- Something which you know how to do and would find easy to describe to someone else.

'How do the contents of the child's mind change?' Karmiloff-Smith's RR model

Information processing accounts have attached considerable importance to the child's representations of the world. More recently the work of Karmiloff-Smith (1992) has also focused on the child's representations and the way in which these may change. She sees development as involving the child's representations changing from implicit to explicit, through a number of levels. Implicit knowledge involves knowledge of how to do things without being able to express this process in words. For example, we produce perfectly grammatical speech every day of our lives without being able to explain the rules of grammar and syntax which underlie that speech. Explicit knowledge, on the other hand, means we have access to the representation of how we do something and can therefore verbalize it without any trouble. Not only can we find our way from home to work, but could also give another person explicit instructions of how to do so if required.

Karmiloff-Smith claims that children can go from having implicit knowledge of a task to having explicit knowledge about it. Moreover, she claims that there are levels in between implicit and explicit. After the implicit level there is level E1, then E2 and the final, fully explicit level is called E3.

We have seen earlier how balance problems have often been the testing ground for theories of cognitive development and the following account shows how Karmiloff-Smith applies her Representational Redescription model to children's behaviour on another sort of balance problem. The task involves the child placing some wooden beams upon a support so that they remain balanced upon it (*see* fig 6.3). The beams vary in shape but fall into two categories: symmetrical beams, typically a thin, wooden bar which balances in the centre, and asymmetrical beams, which are similar but have a wooden block (or sometimes two) glued to one end, which means that it balances off-centre.

Children aged 4–5 years old are successful at balancing all types of wooden beam by simply using trial and error, but cannot explain how they do it. Karmiloff-Smith says this is because their representations are at the implicit level and are not consciously accessible.

Older children at around 6–7 years, Karmiloff-Smith claims, have developed a 'things-balance-in-the-middle' or 'centre theory' (Karmiloff-Smith, 1988). They place all beams onto the support at their mid-point, even the unevenly weighted beams. When these fall they may replace them at the same point but eventually dismiss them as being 'impossible to balance'. Consequently they can only balance symmetrical beams. This is due to their having level E1 representations. At level E1 the child's behaviour is driven not by information from the environment but by the internal mental representation, and external information may be ignored. This can still

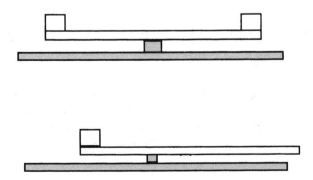

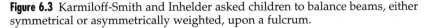

Figure 6.3 Karmiloff-Smith and Inhelder asked children to balance beams, either symmetrical or asymmetrically weighted, upon a fulcrum.

all go on outside of the child's conscious awareness, without the child being able to talk about what they 'know'.

At the next level, level E2, Karmiloff-Smith says the knowledge becomes available for conscious access but still cannot be expressed verbally. She does not offer any evidence for this from the balancing studies, although the notion of being aware of something but not being able to express it in words is probably familiar to us all. Pine and Messer (1995) found that some children could make predictions about whether beams could be balanced, without being able to verbally justify those predictions, which may be evidence for level E2 knowledge.

When children are about eight or nine years old they are able to balance all types of beam and can explain how they do it. Karmiloff-Smith says this is because they have developed E3 representations. Although the successful behaviour of these children is similar to that of the 4–5 year-olds, the underlying representations are very different. Their knowledge is now explicit as opposed to implicit and they can understand and talk about how the beams balance, and transfer that knowledge to other similar problems if necessary.

Thus, the work of Karmiloff-Smith breaks new ground by showing that doing and knowing can take two different paths developmentally. Earlier approaches which focused on children's successes and failures may not have given us the whole developmental picture. In common with other theorists, Karmiloff-Smith has tried to specify what type of cognitive architecture would support this form of development. Fodor's notion that the brain is innately made up of separate modules each with their own set of operating principles is rejected by Karmiloff-Smith, who adopts a more nativist–constructivist position. She argues that modules are constructed during the course of development rather than being there from the start. Furthermore, she claims that the process for transforming representations from one code for another (RR) can occur in all domains, but not necessarily all at the same time. This accounts for how children can be far more advanced in one domain than in another, as with Chi's young chess experts.

'Can computers simulate cognitive development?' connectionism

Researchers working in the field of cognitive development nowadays have one additional tool at their disposal which Piaget and earlier theorists did not – the computer. Although experimental techniques have long been used to demonstrate how the child thinks, they inevitably involve some degree of inference on the part of the experimenter. The developmental psychologist cannot examine the child's thought processes directly, since we cannot take out the brain and look at it. But computers offer a useful analogy for the workings of the brain and computer simulation of cognitive processes has been used to test theories of cognitive development in an 'uncontaminated' environment. When psychologists conduct experiments with human participants they have to have a large sample so that any individual differences or random effects will be minimized, allowing examination of the cognitive process with the minimum of extraneous noise. By use of a computer simulation it is possible to isolate the process they are interested in, without the need for a large sample and without any other interference. Therefore methodologically computer simulation appears to offer an alternative to, or to complement, existing methods for studying cognitive processes.

The first computer models processed information in a step-like, or serial, manner but later systems employ a more parallel process. This is sometimes called parallel distributed processing (PDP) and it involves networks which emulate more closely the neural structure of the brain. PDP systems consist of a number of neural-like units which either inhibit or excite each other, just as brain cells do. Each of the units in the network handles just a tiny fragment of the information and the connection strength between the units changes as learning occurs. A piece of information then comes to be represented as an overall pattern of connectivity between the units. As it concerns the way that neurons are connected together this approach is referred to as **connectionism**.

Rumelhart and McClelland (1986) used a connectionist system to model how children learn the past tense of verbs. The model appeared to 'behave' just like a child does, in that after having received a lot of linguistic input it began to over-regularize (by adding the -ed ending to irregular verbs to produce words like 'drinked' and 'runned'). Thus, the system appeared to have 'learnt' something about English past tenses. Whether this truly simulates how children learn is still under debate since the input to the model (hundreds of words, all of which were verbs) does not equate with the input which children receive when they hear spoken language. Thus, by isolating whatever process they are interested in these researchers also remove the context which constitutes a part of the child's rich learning environment. Nonetheless, connectionist models have provided us with some insightful simulations of how concepts may be formed (McClelland and Rumelhart, 1986), the nature of memory (*see* McShane, 1991) and shown that infants may be capable of creating representations from birth, contrary to what Piaget had concluded from his own observations. But despite these advances, there still remains a lot of cognitive development to be explained. Clark and Karmiloff-Smith (1993), for example, argue that whilst a connectionist system can simulate a child's initial learning in a domain it is not so good at modelling how that knowledge is transformed into explicit knowledge. A connectionist model can only use the knowledge for the specific purpose it was designed for, whereas children create more abstract knowledge which is transferable to other tasks and situations. It appears that, at present, connectionist systems are good at modelling cognitive *processes* but not so good at modelling *cognitive development*. Nonetheless, connectionism offers great promise for advancing our understanding of the potential architectural foundations for cognition and will no doubt continue to offer new insights into how children think for many years to come.

Chapter summary

This chapter has outlined some of the major views about children's cognitive development and the ways in which ideas about development have changed over the years. Piaget's theory represented a major shift away from quantitative approaches to a more qualitative explanation of why children at different ages think differently. Although many of his descriptions of children's behaviour still hold true today, his idea that overarching changes occur at specific points in development is now largely refuted. By contrast information processing accounts emphasized how a number of components (e.g. memory, encoding, interpretation) contribute to a child's success or failure on a task. This led to claims that how children make use of these processing components and strategies could explain developmental differences.

Although Piaget's observations have stood the test of time and accuracy, his approach has been accused of being too abstract and general. In contrast the information processing accounts, aiming for the specification of rules within single-task domains, have been criticized for the sterility which such systematicity inevitably brings. However, rule systems lend themselves more to computer simulation than abstract principles and the advent of connectionist systems has extended our understanding of how children acquire some types of knowledge. Recent developments have also occurred in methodological techniques for testing infant capabilities. These have produced evidence to suggest that the newborn mind is more sophisticated than previously established wisdom would have suggested. They also lend support to the Nativist proposals that the infant is biologically prepared for very specific types of learning (e.g. language) leading some to claim that the mind is composed of encapsulated, highly domain-specific, modules (e.g. Fodor). The task for psychologists now is to explain how subsequent development builds upon earlier domain specific competencies and, ultimately, how the system as a whole operates.

Seminar questions

1. Compare Vygotsky's and Piaget's approaches to cognitive development. Although very different, could they both be right?
2. In what ways do you think Karmiloff-Smith's theory of cognitive development might enhance our understanding of how knowledge is represented in the adult mind?
3. Why did the information processing theorists believe it is important to

focus on specific processes in the mind? What does this approach contribute to our understanding of cognitive development?

4. Discuss the advantages and disadvantages of being able to model a cognitive process on a computer.

Further reading

Anderson, J.R. 1990. *Cognitive psychology and its implications*. New York: W.H. Freeman.

McShane, J. 1991. *Cognitive development: an information processing approach*. Oxford: Blackwell.

Siegler, R.S. 1998. *Children's thinking* (third edition). New Jersey: Prentice Hall.

7 The development of pictorial representation

PAMELA M SMITH

Editors' preface

As has been emphasized in other chapters it is difficult to be sure about the way that children represent their world. Part of the reason for this is that they often have limited understanding of language and are liable to be influenced by the context of questions (*see* chapters 4 and 6). This may be one factor in the long and continuing interest in the way that children create graphical representations when they make images in their drawings.

Drawing has some similarities to language (*see* Chapter 4) in that both are involved in representing the world, both do not need to be formally taught, and drawing like language is an ability which humans take to higher levels of competence than other species. Archaeological evidence indicates that drawing has been a feature of our species for a considerable time.

In this chapter, Pamela Smith has provided an overview of four of the most important theories which attempt to describe or explain aspects of children's use of graphical representations. She also briefly considers the way that the levels of achievement shown in graphical representations can be very different from children's other abilities. This relates to current concerns about the relation between different areas of functioning, whether there are dissociated modules or whether cognition is a more integrated process (*see* chapters 4, 6 and 8). Thus, the seemingly simple process of drawing can provide us with a number of significant insights into children's cognitive processes.

Introduction

Anyone wishing to reduce a group of Western adults to giggling embarass-
ment has only to ask them to draw something they have not drawn before:
say a galloping horse; a jumbo jet; a train crossing a landscape; a famous
person. Their efforts are unlikely to satisfy them and may well be indistin-
guishable from the drawings of nine to ten-year-old children. The clumsiness of drawings by adults without specialized tuition tells us that
pictorial representation does not come easily to our species. Moreover,
even a cursory survey of art of different times and places demonstrates
there is no specific universal adult model of the activity. An evolutionary
perspective suggests that drawing is going to be the result of cobbling
together parts of systems and processes that have evolved for other functions. We should therefore expect that the development of drawing is going
to be a story of individual and cultural problem solving. In this chapter we
will outline the developmental course for Western children, review four
theoretical frameworks for the development of drawing: Luquet's (1927)
stage-like description, adapted by Piaget (1956); Arnheim's (1974) aestheti-
cally based invention approach; Willats' (1997) application of the concepts
of Marr's (1982) computational approach to visual perception and
Karmiloff-Smith's (1990) model of representational redescription. We also
look at some of those who have focused on the processes of drawing and
on experimental manipulations of drawing tasks and will briefly review
research on drawing in developmentally abnormal populations: gifted,
blind, autistic and individuals with Williams' syndrome. The chapter closes
with a comment on cross-cultural issues.

DISCUSSION POINT

Before reading further, draw something from memory and then draw
something that is present. Are your drawings good representations?
Try to identify what you found difficult in these two tasks.

Course of development

Children with access to drawing materials will begin to make marks on
surfaces some time in their second or third year. These marks are likely to
include dots made by stabbing movements, single lines, multiple lines
made by moving the marker backwards and forwards in a left–right arc,
or pushing the marker away and pulling it towards the child, without
breaking contact and spirals made by continuous circular movements.
These early drawings may or may not be representational but by the
fourth or fifth year the child will be making drawings that are clearly

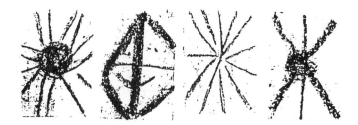

Figure 7.1 Four pastel drawings by Tom, aged five. He reported that three represented 'Jesus' goodness shining through the world' and one representing 'The Devil and his evil in the world'. They were so strongly representational that he insisted on the one depicting the Devil being banned from his home.

representational in intent because the child names them before drawing. The representation may not always be apparent to an observer because the child often uses idiosyncratic forms or fails to provide a coherent spatial organization. An example of representational drawings that are unlikely to be seen as such are the drawings of Jesus and the Devil shown in Figure 7.1.

However some interpretable common forms do appear at age three to five years: for instance the 'tadpole' human figures shown in Box 7.1. From about age three to about seven years children may use the same basic form for several objects as seen in Figure 7.2 .

The term 'schematic drawings' is often applied to this extension of one drawing form to other objects but the term is also applied to the repetitive drawing of a single object that is commonly observed in children in middle childhood. Children below about eight years may deny that they can draw

Figure 7.2 Schematic drawing by a girl aged four of family and pets: (a) Mummy; (b) her brother; (c) a cat; and (d) a dog.

BOX 7.1 Drawings of human figures by four-year-old children

'Tadpole' drawings such as these are typical of three to five-year-old children. Careful experimentation has established that they are not due to defective body image (Brittain and Chien (1983); Cox and Batra, cited in Cox (1993)), nor to the child's inability to hold all the parts in memory while drawing (Cox and Parkin, 1886). Persistent training is needed to persuade such artists to draw a conventional figure (Cox, 1992) and they tend to choose tadpole drawings as better than conventional drawings (Cox and Stone, cited in Cox (1992)). 'Tadpole' figures can, however, be used flexibly by some young children to depict relative size (Silk and Thomas, 1988), age and gender (Sitton and Light, 1992), motion (Smith, 1993) and a person with two heads (Zhi et al, 1997). 'Tadpoles' may also be produced by developmentally normal adults with no previous experience of drawing (Cox and Bayraktar, 1989, cited in Cox, (1993)). The evidence suggests that tadpole figures result from early graphic development and not from any general mental representation of people.

Drawings of human figures by four-year-old children.

something which they have not drawn before and for which they have not developed a drawing form. This protestation shows both a level of awareness (the child 'knows' she cannot draw the requested item) and the limitations of their awareness, since if the request is repeated the child will often proceed to produce the required representation. It is as if the child is often not aware that she has general drawing strategies at her disposal.

Between the ages of five and twelve years the child's repertoire expands and free drawing is likely to include scenic drawings full of action (particularly common among boys) as well as single figures or objects, with reasonable proportionality of elements and at least some of the devices that signal depth: occlusion, foreshortening, elevation on the page and diminishing size with distance. Perhaps the greatest variety both between children of the same age and among concurrent drawings by the same child is in the devices used to portray rectangular objects and their spatial locations relative to other objects and/or to the viewer. The variety of such devices can be plausibly classified into systems (*see* Willats, 1997 and below) and an approximate developmental sequence can be identified. The cultural norm for post-Renaissance Western art, linear perspective, appears late if at all.

A visit to any elementary school where drawings are displayed will demonstrate that children pick up graphic devices from each other in the absence of specific tuition, since you will see one common way of portraying, say, noses among one group of children and a different way among another. A particular child may be known as the class expert on drawing particular items and her style copied. Wilson (1985) links a specific feature, mounting arms on the back outline of a figure in profile, shown by children in a Californian school in the 1920s to an influx of Italian immigrants since this rare feature was common in a 1880s Italian sample (Ricci, 1887). But this social aspect should not be over-estimated since variety among children is also very common: van Sommers (1984), for example, found 23 types of tree drawn in a single session in an Australian primary school class. Although there have been short term training studies on particular aspects of drawing (e.g. Phillips et al., 1985) I do not know of any recent long term study of the effects of drawing tuition on the depictions produced by young children. For most people in Western cultures in the twentieth century, development of drawing skills does not progress beyond early adolescence.

Theoretical frameworks

Theories of drawing development have to address questions of what the child is trying to depict at a given time and why the nature of their depictions change in an age-related fashion. How they address these questions depends upon whether drawing is being considered as just one aspect of cognitive development or is being considered largely in isolation from other aspects of development. Piaget's adaptation of Luquet's theory and Karmiloff-Smith's theory belong to the first category; Arnheim and Willats to the second. The first two theories treat drawings as providing evidence of types of mental representation, whereas the latter two theories emphasize the relationship with visual perception, aesthetic values and the development of drawing strategies.

LUQUET'S STAGE-LIKE DESCRIPTION, ADAPTED BY PIAGET

Luquet (1927) insisted that in order to understand children's drawings you had to be present during the drawing process. It was from his 'natural history' observations that he derived a stage-like description of drawing in children aged from about eighteen months to twelve years. He argued that young children are representing some aspect of the world when they draw (not symbolizing it in an arbitrary fashion) and hence the word 'realism' is part of each 'stage' in his account. I have termed his descriptions 'stage-like' because he emphasized that he was describing tendencies, not a rigid, age-related progression.

At the very beginning, according to Luquet, the infant who has access to drawing materials will simply be making marks and enjoying the action and the traces on the paper, but then they recognize in their drawing a likeness to something in the world. If the child says the name of the object, the observer witnesses their discovery. This stage Luquet called 'fortuitous realism'. A example of fortuitous realism that then enables the child to transcend his usual drawings is shown in Figure 7.3.

According to his mother, this three-year-old was only drawing enclosed circular shapes to which he added marks. But on this occasion the child, having drawn an enclosed shape then said, very excitedly: 'It's a parrot!' and went on to add the eye and legs to what he had recognized as an outline of a bird.

In Luquet's theory this type of discovery leads the child into intending to represent something but because his skills are inadequate to actually produce a likeness, Luquet terms this stage 'failed realism'. He also used the term 'synthetic incapacity' because the child may make marks representing various parts of an object but fail to place the marks in correct spatial relationships.

The first stage of successful intentional representation Luquet calls 'intellectual realism'. He argues that the child is drawing from an internal model

Figure 7.3 An instance of 'fortuitous realism'. Kevin, aged three, whose typical drawings were merely enclosed shapes, paused after drawing the outline and said, very excitedly: 'It's a parrot!' He then added the eye, legs and feet.

of an object even if the object happens to be present. That internal model is not the list of words a child might use about something but a 'visual concept' which encapsulates appearance and other knowledge: 'everything that is there' (Luquet, 1927). For example, a cup would be drawn with a handle even if the child was faced with a cup with its handle hidden. Luquet recognized a tension between such a representation and representing the appearance of an object or scene from a single particular viewpoint. He pointed out that many pictorial representations by both children and adults contain elements of both types of representation. However, his observations led him to the conclusion that from middle childhood the attempt to portray a single viewpoint dominated with the child striving for what he termed 'visual realism'.

The shift from this subtle description to the cliché 'the child draws what he knows, rather than what he sees' (Freeman, 1980, p. 27) owes much to Piaget's incorporation of Luquet's work into his general cognitive developmental framework (Piaget and Inhelder, 1948/1956; Piaget et al., 1960). For Piaget, drawing was not a special domain of development but merely a window onto the child's general cognitive development. Piaget argued that drawing performance expressed the child's cognitive competence. Until the child was capable of reversible mental operations (the concrete operational stage) she was tied to an egocentric mental model of the world (*see* Chapter 3). Unable to reflect on different viewpoints, the child could only represent mentally an object, not a view of an object. Moreover, the perceptual knowledge of space gained during the sensorimotor period of infancy was of no use to her in drawing. At the beginning of the pre-operational stage the child was conceptually limited to simple topological notions of nearness, touching and enclosure and hence these are the only spatial relations to appear in her early drawings. Fig 7.4 shows a drawing of a house in which topological relations are preserved: furniture is enclosed within the house, items near each other in reality are near in the picture and an item such as the light switch is shown touching the wall. When the child developed concepts of spatial order among items and of parallelism and perpendicularity these concepts could only be applied locally within a drawing. This is also illustrated in fig 7.4 in the room on the left where the bed is placed at right angles to the boundary line which thus serves as both wall of the first room and floor of the second room.

According to Piaget, only when the child enters fully into the stage of concrete operations can she combine concepts of perpendicularity, parallelism, seriation and proportion with her new ability to discriminate different viewpoints and selecting a viewpoint to depict, produce visually realistic drawings. The child is now able to attempt an entire drawing in a coherent set of visually faithful co-ordinates, producing the first linear perspectival depictions by the end of childhood.

Criticism of Piaget's stage framework of cognitive development in the 1970s and 1980s lead to a body of experimental work on drawing seeking to refine the notion of stages by establishing the role of task variables in children's drawings. Useful reviews of this movement are Freeman (1980),

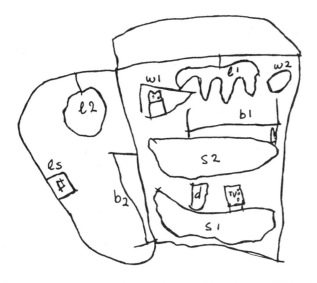

Figure 7.4 Drawing of his home by Marlon, aged four. The right-hand side of the picture was completed first but then he wanted to depict his own bedroom and added the left side of the picture. The following are depicted: s1 and s2 are stairs; d is the door, and near to that the TV set; b1 and b2 are beds (b1 with a pillow drawn underneath); w1 and w2 are windows (w1 with a cat looking out); l1 and l2 are lights and ls a light switch.

Freeman and Cox (1985) and Thomas and Silk (1990). The focus was on a dichotomy between intellectual realism (representing the child's knowledge about an object) and visual realism (representing a possible viewpoint of an object) and both single objects and arrays of two objects were used in the investigations.

A series of studies on cups produced evidence supporting an age-related intellectual to visual realism shift as well as flexible responses by children to task manipulations. A cup is a familiar object with clear functionality. If children are drawing what they know, they will draw a cup as a container with a handle, whatever the view of the model cup they are given to draw. Examples of intellectually realistic drawings produced by young children were obtained by Taylor and Bacharach (1982). They presented five- and eight-year-old children with one of three conditions: a cup and a separate flower stick-on side by side; a cup with the stick-on inside the cup but visible and a cup with the stick-on on the front surface of the cup. Children in the first condition had no difficulty in reproducing the cup and flower; children in the second condition drew the flower within the cup outlines. The eight-year-old children in the third condition drew the flower on the front surface of the cup but the five-year-old children drew either the cup or the flower. If the younger children were drawing an intellectually realistic depiction of the cup as a container then this is what one would predict because they know the stick-on is not *inside* the cup and therefore they cannot draw it within their simple outline.

Davis (1985) in a series of studies showed that children aged under eight would draw a cup with a handle even though the cup was presented to them with the handle out of sight. However, in some circumstances children would not draw the invisible handle. For example, if a cup with a handle hidden was paired with a cup with the handle visible, even five-year-old children would depict this difference. Moreover, if they were presented with this task first and then asked to draw a single cup which had the handle hidden, they were more likely to leave the handle out of their drawing. They appeared to be able to make a flexible choice of intellectually realistic or visually realistic drawings depending on their interpretation of what was required. Bremner and Moore (1984) showed that handling or naming an object before drawing it, increased the tendency for five- and six-year-old children to include features hidden from their view at the time of drawing. These drawings would be classified as intellectually realistic. Interpret along the lines of Luquet, one could say that certain task conditions elicit a mental model that the child cannot inhibit. An alternative interpretation is that these conditions lead children to think the experimenter wishes them to depict a stereotypical object displaying its functionality.

Studies on two objects, one placed behind the other, focused on whether children would draw an occlusion or partial occlusion to depict what was seen or whether they would depict both the objects in their entirety. Again a similar story to that with single objects emerges: when children are presented with one object behind another, there is an age-related trend from drawing both objects in their entirety (intellectually realistic), so that the objects are separated first horizontally and later diagonally or vertically, to then drawing partial or total occlusion (visually realistic). However, the trend is again responsive to task variables: instructions, the nature of the array, a communicative rationale for depicting the view, all affect the age at which visually realistic drawings are produced. Even four- and five-year-olds will draw partial occlusions in some circumstances (Cox, 1985; Light, 1985).

Inspection of the reported data in most of the studies on intellectual compared with visual realism show that it is not easy to place the drawings into these two mutually exclusive categories. Apart from the truly unclassifiable drawings (scribbles or objects other than those requested) there are drawings that show the compromise to which Luquet referred, drawings that include aspects of both conceptual knowledge and viewpoint information. It is instructive to look at the data from Light and Humphreys' 1981 study of children's drawings of an array of two pigs which is illustrated in Box 7.2.

The dichotomy between intellectual and visual realism has proved very fruitful in stimulating ingenious experimental investigations but in essence has established only some of the conditions under which one or other type of depiction will dominate. They can tell little about why particular marks and graphic forms are used by children to construct their depictions.

BOX 7.2

Light and Humphreys (1981) wished to establish whether young children would give priority to view-specific information (visual realism) or array-specific information (intellectual realism) when these were in conflict. They presented 35 five-year-old, 32 six-year-old and 30 seven-year-old children with two sets of stimuli (a red and a green block; a red and a green pig) at eye level and each in four orientations.

In the two **control conditions** the stimuli were arrayed laterally, to the left and to the right, in front of the child such that the child could depict what they saw and preserve the relationship within the array (e.g. the red pig following the green pig). These were drawn without difficulty by everyone, e.g.

In the two **experimental conditions** the stimuli were arranged in a file going towards and away from the child. In these conditions the child could not depict what she saw and preserve the spatial relationship. View-specific drawings would be occlusions or partial occlusions, e.g.

These accounted for 17 per cent at age five, 22 per cent at age six and 52 per cent at age seven.

Array-specific drawings would show two complete animals in the correct sequence, e.g.

 Two items drawn horizontally separated accounted for 41 per cent at age five; 34 per cent at age six and 8 per cent at age seven.

Drawings mixing view-specific and array-specific information: a third of the drawings at all ages showed two complete items separated vertically, e.g.

Ninety-two per cent of these depicted the further object higher on the page, using the convention for something seen further away and 20 per cent of them depicted two end-on views, e.g.

Moreover, 20 per cent of the horizontally separated drawings showed two end-on views, e.g.

A sizeable proportion of the children at all ages chose to depict a mixture of intellectual realism and visual realism in this task.

ARNHEIM'S AND KELLOGG'S GESTALTIST APPROACH

Piaget and the research inspired by him investigated childen's drawing performance in contexts determined by the experimenter. Arnheim (1974) and Kellogg (1970; 1979) concentrated on children's spontaneous drawings. Both drew on Gestalt perceptual theory to interpret what they observed.

Kellogg (1970; 1979) collected thousands of pictures produced by children aged under eight years in the USA and Europe and analysed them in terms of common graphic elements. She identified types of scribbles and patterns of placement on the drawing page in the youngest children; followed by graphic units such as crosses and closed forms (circles and rectangles) and then, by age four to five years combinations of these simple forms. Three classes of combinations she termed 'Suns' (closed circular or rectangular forms with short lines crossing the circumference at right angles), 'radials' (lines radiating from a central point) and 'mandalas' (combinations of forms that preserved symmetry on orthogonal axes). Fig 7.1 shows forms that would be classified as radials and mandalas drawn by a boy aged five. Kellogg argued that early pictures are non-representational; they are driven by the pleasure produced by the motor activity and the visual stimulus produced. That specific forms are produced is related to Gestalt principles of 'good form'. This rather elusive concept gives priority to 'the best, simplest and most stable shape' (Koffka, 1935 p. 138). Aesthetic pleasure is particularly elicited by symmetry and hence symmetrical forms of all kinds are common in the children's drawings. Kellogg linked this strong element to the religious significance attributed to mandala forms in many cultures. In her examination of children's pictures when they do become representational Kellogg stresses the perseveration of the early non-representational graphic units and the continued importance of aesthetic principles such as balance, pleasing visual shapes and implied contours around the entire figure providing a subjective 'good form' overall.

The work of Kellogg is very interesting and a good counterbalance to the emphasis placed by experimental studies on what information is being depicted in children's drawings, but her preoccupations may have lead her to miss what it is the child is depicting. It is easy to demonstrate that Kellogg was wrong to claim that very young children do not produce representational drawings: Matthews, for example, shows children as young as two years old depicting both form and action in drawings (Matthews, 1984); *see also* fig 7.5 showing three-year-old children representing movement in the case of the butterfly and sound in the case of the train.

In considering children's pictures Kellogg stresses throughout the aesthetic/decorative aspect and sees a tension between that and adults' emphasis on visual likeness to real world objects. This is echoed by Winner (1996) who suggests a child is more likely to be recognized as 'gifted' in visual arts if she demonstrates precocious visual likenesses rather than outstanding decorative effects. It seems a pity if Kellogg's rather dogmatic

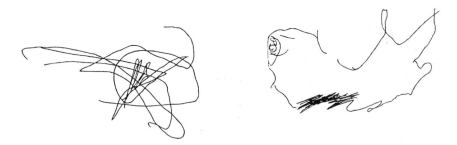

Figure 7.5 Two representational drawings by three-year-olds. Ann announced she wanted to draw a butterfly and then drew the picture on the left while moving her bent arms in and out like the beating of wings. Fred said he was going to draw a funny train and then drew the picture on the right. Having completed the outline and face he then said, 'and puffing noises' and, saying, 'puff, puff', he made heavy, pushing strokes at the bottom.

statements should lead readers to an under-estimation of the part played by aesthetic considerations in children's drawings.

Arnheim (1974) also applies Gestalt notions to children's drawings but he has been more interested in the developmental dimension. Arnheim does give a special place to the 'primordial circle' as a Gestalt 'good form' but he describes the child's development in drawing as the progressive production of graphic forms, either invented or taught, by which the child tries to realize her intention for that particular picture. Thus the emphasis is on drawing as a problem-solving domain in its own right, with development being charted not by age but from the time the person started drawing. This focus makes sense of the rare data from adults who have not drawn before and who produce drawings very similar to those produced by very young children (Cox and Bayrakar, cited in Cox (1993)).

For Arnheim (1974) children do draw what they see but 'Unquestionably children see more than they draw' (p. 168). He argues that the story of the development of drawing is one of progressive differentiation. Hence a child starts with a circle-like mark that is used as a neutral form to represent many objects in their entirety and then she gradually invents or learns graphic forms to represent more of what she sees: 'straightness', 'angularity', 'containment' and so on. Only when the child has several graphic forms at her disposal will circles come to represent roundness. These graphic patterns may be used to represent different objects with a similar underlying structure producing schematic depictions. An example of this can be seen in fig 7.2 where the similarity in underlying structure of animals and humans as rounded forms with heads and limbs attached leads to similar drawings. Arnheim (1974) recognizes the rigid appearance of schematic drawings but sees them as necessary steps towards more complex depictions rather than as deficient representations. In any case accuracy of details may be violated to preserve aesthetic properties, particularly of symmetry. Progression is by subdivision, integration of the elements thus constructed, then further subdivion and so on. Modifications such as bending of a body part are developed. Mental and motor maturity enables the child to move from necessarily constructing her drawing element by element towards being able to fuse the contours to produce a continuous outline of a complex figure. As the child gains control of an expanding repertoire of graphic forms she can deploy them for various functions. Smith (1993) shows children aged four to ten years using an increasing number of graphic elements to depict the difference between a person standing still and a person walking fast. For Arnheim (1974) whether the goal for an older child is linear perspective or decorative patterning or some other mode of expression depends on her purpose and her culture.

Willatts' application of Marr's theory of visual perception

The greatest contribution of Willats (1997) is to provide two frameworks for classifying depictions from which developmental predictions can be derived. The reader is referred to Willats (1997) for details of these frameworks which can only be introduced here. Willatts turned to Marr's (1982) theory of visual perception to inform his interpretation of children's drawing development. Marr attempted to provide a computational framework for visual perception, identifying sequences of processing and suggesting plausible algorithms for the transformations required in each sequence. He demonstrated how visual information that begins at the retina as describing what a person sees at any instant can be transformed into an object-centred representation of items and their relative locations, unaffected by the moment to moment changes of view. This enables a person to recognize an object even though the person and the object may be moving. Essential aspects of the object-centred representation is the representation of the main axes of the object and the degree to which the object extends in different dimensions. Marr refined this idea most for smooth rounded objects such as people and animals where the object can be represented as a construction of cylinders at different scales with specific features represented as modifications. Fig 7.6 gives an idea of how this would work.

If one accepts Marr's interpretation of the visual system, then these three-dimensional mental representations of objects are well-adapted for letting us recognize objects under different circumstances, but are not helpful when we wish to construct a drawing of the object on a two-dimensional surface. These mental representations are particularly unhelpful if we wish to recreate a specific view of an object, since that is not part of the mental representation. Willats took this as his starting point: that novice artists are working from an object-centred mental representation and need to find solutions to the problems of translating that representation into something that makes visual sense on the page. He surveyed adult art of different cultures as well as children's drawings to determine if there are any commonalities to these solutions. As a result he has devised two frameworks for analysing drawings; denotation systems and drawing systems. Denotation systems spell out the relationship between a mark on the

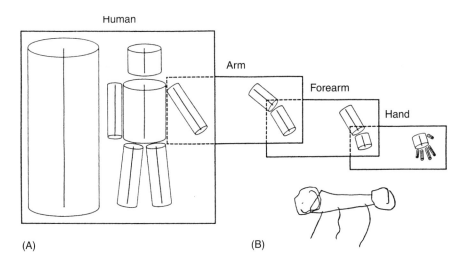

Figure 7.6 (A) The organization of shape information in a three-dimensional object-centred description, laid out in a viewer-centred format for clarity. From Marr, D., Nishihara, H.K., 'Representation and recognition of the spatial organisation of three-dimensional shapes'. *Proceedings of The Royal Society of London B 200*, 269–94. (Reproduced with permission.) (B) Drawing of a kitten by Tamsin, aged four, seems to preserve this type of mental description.

page and the aspect of an object it is denoting, e.g. a line may denote extension along an axis or an occluding contour or the boundary of a surface. Drawing systems locate objects in three-dimensional space, e.g. linear perspective is one drawing system. Taking these together and applying them to Western children's drawings one can chart developmental sequences in drawing both smooth objects and rectangular objects. For an example of how this might apply to the drawing of a cube see fig 7.7.

Applying these frameworks is not without difficulties. In many children's drawings you would need additional information to know what denotation system was being used. For example, Moore (1986) asked children to draw a cube, which had a different colour on each face, using a pencil only. Some children drew a single enclosed shape. Moore then provided them with coloured crayons. Of those childen who had produced a single enclosed form, the younger children, aged seven, proceeded to use the six relevant colours to colour in their drawing demonstrating that their form denoted the entire volume of the cube. The older children, aged nine, used only the colour of the front face, showing that their form denoted a surface only. If you look again at fig 7.4 you can see a further problem: that the child's intention may change during drawing. There appear to be two *regions* (or three if you count the roof) denoting *volumes* with their contents. But at the time the child drew window two he clearly thought in terms of the *region* denoting a *surface* because he depicts the cat partially occluded by a front wall. In applying drawing systems there is a different problem: some children's drawings, even of a single object, will show a mixture of

Figure 7.7 Analyses of the drawing and denotation systems in children's drawings of cubes, and their possible derivations in terms of actual mental processes. o-c = derived from object-centred internal descriptions; v-c = derived from viewer-centred internal descriptions. * Regions in class 5 have been distorted. Adapted with permission from Willats, J. 1997. *Art and representation: new principles in the analysis of pictures.* Princeton, N.J.: Princeton University Press, p. 177.

Class		Mean age	Drawing system	Denotation system	
1	 ⬡	4.0	Enclosure	(a) Region ➝ Volume (o-c) (b) Region ➝ Face (o-c) (c) Region ➝ Face (v-c) (d) Region ➝ Region (v-c)	
2	□	6.7	Orthogonal	(a) Region ➝ Volume (o-c) (b) Region ➝ Face (o-c) (c) Region ➝ Face (v-c)	
3	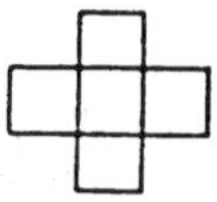 ✛	8.2	Fold-out	(a) Regions ➝ Faces (o-c)	
4	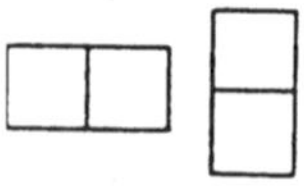	8.6	Horizontal or vertical oblique	(a) Regions ➝ Faces (o-c) (b) Regions ➝ Faces (v-c)	
5	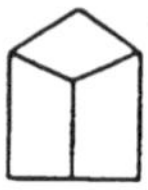	9.9	Near-oblique	(a) Regions* ➝ Faces (o-c)	
6	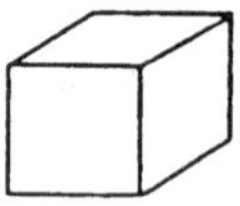	12.2	Oblique	(a) Lines ➝ Edges (o-c) (b) Lines ➝ Edges and contours (v-c)	

systems. Nevertheless it is possible to trace a broad developmental pathway through both systems.

Willats, then, like Arnheim sees drawing as a problem solving domain in which development resides in inventing or being taught solutions to particular problems. Whereas Arnheim sees progressive differentiation of generalized forms, driven largely by aesthetic considerations, Willats sees successive efforts to map object-centred mental representations onto graphic forms that provide the appropriate visual input to elicit satisfying object recognition. It is, perhaps, a difficult concept to understand but it provides insight into why visually realistic drawing is hard to achieve.

KARMILOFF-SMITH'S REPRESENTATIONAL REDESCRIPTION MODEL OF DRAWING

Karmiloff-Smith (1990) also sees drawing as a specific domain but one subject to the universal processes of her representational redescription (RR) model of cognitive development (*see* Chapter 6). In this model perception and action in a domain at first produce mental representations that are not coherently organized and are not available for flexible use or conscious reflection. At this point an artist can only 'run off' a habitual drawing of an object. Children she tested when asked to draw 'a person with two heads' tended to draw two heads and then continue to two completed bodies. However, at the next level of development in the drawing domain, endogenously driven processes create new, coherently organized mental representations which can be used flexibly. From then, with varying degrees of conscious reflection, drawings can include reordered elements or combinations of elements from different objects. Children can then produce non-habitual drawings such as a person with two heads without difficulty.

Later, Karmiloff-Smith (1992), suggested drawing was not a good domain in which to see RR at work because the act of drawing produces a visible trace on the paper and hence even when the child is operating from implicit mental representations, the act of drawing can be interrupted and restarted. However, empirical work by Zhi et al. (1997) suggests that the RR model may indeed be applicable to drawing. In two studies with four to five-year-old children these authors carefully established that the children had understood the instructions to draw a man with two heads and were willing to draw a novel object, but still about half of the children drew two complete figures. This needs explanation. In a third study three to four-year-old children were asked for three drawings: a postman and Father Christmas in one session and the man with two heads in a second session. The order in which the children drew parts of the figures was recorded. Half the children were shown a line drawing of a woman with two heads and half were given only the instructions. Only those shown the line drawing had any success in drawing a man with two heads. Of the 11 successful children, 10 added the second head at the beginning of the drawing. The five unsuccessful children all added the second head at the end of their drawing of the first figure and they then went on to draw a complete second figure. Examination of the order of drawing for all three drawings (disregarding the second head) by all 32 children in the study showed the majority had used the same sequence for each of their drawings. This stability of sequence and its relation to failure by some children to draw a man with two heads suggests that Karmiloff-Smith's level of implicit, procedural representation might well be involved in the drawing development of young children. The high rate of success in the study by Zhi et al. (1997), however, shows evidence for flexibility in some very young children.

A different explanation for stability in drawing is proposed by van Sommers (1984). Working with five to six-year-old children he identified a 'conservative' effect whereby if an object is drawn once, subsequent drawings tend to be very similar even though there has been further experience of the object. However, although Karmiloff-Smith identifies the constraints as arising from an implicit representation largely procedural in nature, van Sommers rules out such procedural constraints. He recorded the drawing process while five to six-year-old children drew objects outside their usual repertoire over several sessions. He found that for any one child, the drawings combined visual similarity with variability in action sequences. He locates much of this 'conservative' effect in the artist's visual memory for the overall drawing she produced last time and for the specific graphic forms she had invented to represent elements.

Application of the four frameworks

It might be useful to pause here to look at an aspect of drawing development and consider what type of explanation would be proposed within each of the four theoretical frameworks we have considered. Repetitious, schematic, depictions appear frequently in the drawings of typical children between the ages of approximately four to twelve years. Two related types of schematic drawings need explanation: those in which a very similar form is used by an artist for different objects (*see* fig 7.2) and those similar forms that appear in many artists' drawings (*see* Box 7.1). Luquet (1927) argues that the child's mental model of the object leads to a stable graphic form until the child's intention becomes that of realizing the visual appearance of the object, whereas Piaget and co-workers (1956; 1960) add to that idea restrictions in what the child can draw because of deficiency in the child's understanding of geometries of space. Arnheim (1974) and Kellogg (1970; 1979) stress that pleasure in balanced and particularly symmetrical drawings will tend to produce repetitions of pleasing drawings, whereas Arnheim (1974) adds the idea that simple schematic depictions are a necessary stage in developing more differentiated graphic forms. Willats (1997) places the cause of conservatism in the universal difficulties of trying to transform object-centred mental representations into appropriate visual stimuli. Karmiloff-Smith (1990; 1992) argues that early drawings are based on implicit mental representations which do not allow the child to reflect on their drawing and choose to vary it. Van Sommers (1984) suggests that each new object requires the invention of graphic forms which, once invented, become part of the child's visual memory of her drawing which in turn guides subsequent drawings.

DISCUSSION POINT

Can you apply each of these ideas to the drawings in Box 7.1 and fig 7.2? How might you set up experiments to test these ideas?

What all these frameworks have in common is the notion that drawing is a complex activity that requires considerable developmental time to mature. It is therefore instructive to look at cases which seem to contravene this requirement.

Drawing by developmentally special populations

By looking at the development of drawing in special populations, we may get some idea of the relationship of drawing to other cognitive abilities and also see what evidence there is for a common developmental pathway.

GIFTED

Golomb (1995) describes a child, Eitan, who appears to go through a typical developmental sequence but abnormally quickly. At two years of age he was drawing schematic tadpole figures that usually appear a year or so later and by three he was producing complex, richly detailed, drawings in projection systems that are not usually seen before nine or ten. As Golomb writes: 'By the time Eitan was four years old, he had mastered horizontal and vertical oblique projection systems, divergent and isometric projection and began to experiment with convergent perspective' (p. 172) (*see* fig 7.7 for examples of some of these). This achievement seems to have been driven by his own desire to depict objects and how they work and move as well as he could: his family apparently encouraged his drawing but did not provide direct teaching. His interest in drawing was intense and particularly focused on vehicles but his repertoire was always wide and he did not draw to the exclusion of other activities. He appears to be someone who progressed astonishingly rapidly through the graphic problem solving that most people do not attain by adulthood without instruction, if then. His progress seems to suggest that given talent and motivation the development of drawing skills may be independent of general intellectual development.

AUTISTIC

In contrast is Nadia, described by Selfe (1977; 1995). According to her family this child, who had very limited language, lacked pretend play and social skills and had poor gross motor skills, started at age three and a half to produce drawings in a visually realistic form, using perspective, occlusion and foreshortening and showing very good fine motor skills. Although usually based on pictures she had seen previously, her drawings involved changes, including changes in orientation and were thus not mere read-outs of remembered images. These drawings of early childhood astounded the developmental psychologists who saw them and led to an intensive investigation. However, in middle childhood Nadia's interest in drawing diminished and she produced fewer drawings, with ordinary schematic drawings alongside drawings showing her exceptional skill. By adolescence she was no longer taking an interest in drawing. In her case there appear to have been two separate trajectories of drawing: the visually realistic which started very early and showed no developmental progression and the schematic which appeared much later and co-existed with the very different visually realistic drawings. There may be similar dichotomies in the drawings of adults with brain damage (*see* MH reported in Franklin et al., 1992). Nadia and another exceptional artist, Stephen (Selfe, 1995) show signs of autism but exceptional drawing is not common among autistic individuals (Charman and Baron-Cole, 1993).

WILLIAMS' SYNDROME

A population where abnormal drawing may be an aspect of the syndrome is individuals with Williams' syndrome. In this case the drawing ability is poor. Individuals with Williams' syndrome show an uneven profile of abil-- ities, performing much better on language tests than on tests of conceptual understanding, Piagetian conservation skills or of spatial–motor skills, such as assembling blocks to copy a model (Bellugi et al., 1993). The adolescent individuals tested by Bellugi et al. (1993), were unable to copy simple geometric figures and could not produce coherent depictions of objects although they could verbally describe them in detail. A study by Bertrand and Mervis (1997) of 18 nine to 10-year-olds with Williams' syndrome confirmed the general finding that they performed badly specifically in integrating parts of geometric figures and objects (a flower, a house and an elephant drawn with and without a model) but found an unexpected range in drawing ability with some individuals producing drawings comparable to their mental age-matched peers and others unable to produce any recognizable drawings.

CONGENITALLY BLIND

Intact processes of spatial representation seem to be a prerequisite for the development of normal drawings, but visual input is not itself necessary as demonstrated by the drawings produced by congenitally blind individuals using a medium where a pen produces raised lines (Kennedy, 1993). These drawings, by congenitally blind adults as well as children, often show similar features to the drawings of very young children (features of the object in incorrect spatial locations) and of children in middle childhood (a drinking glass, for example, drawn as a circle forming the top side of a rectangle). Drawings of human figures resemble the conventional drawings of seven to nine-year-olds with head, torso and correctly proportioned and located limbs, complete with facial features and clothes. Drawings of tables produced orthogonal and vertical oblique depictions as well as fold-outs (*see* fig 7.7 for examples of these types of depiction). Only two of the individuals studied, who were both very interested in discussions of drawing, attempted to depict viewpoint information. One very interesting drawing by one of these showed a railway track with a dot representing a person in the middle, with the lines converging both 'in front of' and 'behind' the figure: presumably the artist had heard descriptions of lines converging to depict distance.

From this brief survey of some special populations it can be seen that development of drawing can be dissociated from the development of other abilities, that visual experience is not necessary and that there is in Nadia the tantalizing possibility that drawings can be produced by two very different mental routes.

Cross-cultural issues

It is unfortunate that all the developmental literature referred to so far has been based on Western children. It is not possible to consider in any depth the relationship between the development of drawing and the cultural context of the child. Wilson (1984) suggests cultural influences on children's drawings will be found at several levels: multi-regional effects of global media; multi-regional effects of religious and social beliefs, such as Islam; regional effects, such as Japanese comic culture, and local effects of an influential adult or child role model. He suggests that wherever there is an absence of strong adult graphic models children's drawing development will be limited to simple forms and a few graphic devices, such as avoiding overlap and a bias towards relating items perpendicularly. An interesting question is what happens to the developmental pathway of children exposed to more than one very different adult style. Cox (1993) includes in her discussion of cross-cultural comparisons of human figure drawing, some examples of drawings by Australian aboriginal children where the highly stylized traditional symbols are mixed with items depicted in a visually realistic style. It would be interesting to compare the ease with which different styles are mastered.

Chapter summary

A consideration of the development of drawing in normal and special populations shows it to be a complex activity. Explanations draw on theories of visual perception and cognitive development as well as on domain-specific factors. Although research on drawing has expanded in the last 20 years, this has not lead to a unifying theoretical framework but it has involved more recognition of the variation in the phenomena to be explained.

Seminar questions

1. Collect examples of spontaneous drawings by children and discuss them using each of the four theoretical frameworks in turn.
2. Ask four to eight-year-old children to draw a large dice (the dots will help you interpret what they draw). Can you classify these according to the table shown in fig 7.7?

3. Why do you think representational drawing skills do not develop much beyond twelve years of age for most people in the West?

Further reading

Cox, M. 1992. *Children's drawings*. London: Penguin.

Thomas, G.V., and Silk, A.M.J. 1990. *An introduction to the psychology of children's drawings*. New York: Harvester Wheatsheaf.

Willats, J. 1997. *Art and representation: new principles in the analysis of pictures*. PRinceton, N.J.: Princeton University Press.

Intelligence

MIKE ANDERSON

Editors' preface

We can find references in the writings of Homer, Plato and Aristotle which focus on the nature of individual differences in 'quickness of wit' or what we would better understand as intelligence. However, it was the psychometric movement with its roots in the ideas of Galton on how human faculty might be measured and the pragmatism of Simon and Binet in developing an instrument to measure intelligence which defined the area. The study and measurement of intelligence flourished for decades only to be followed by a period of questioning about the value of psychometric assessment in general, controversies over the use of the intelligence quotient (IQ) to determine individual differences in ability, and the issue of heritability of intellect (*see* Chapter 1). Many considered the psychometrics movement and the study of intelligence to be irreparably damaged by such arguments. The importance of this chapter is that it demonstrates that the study of the development and individual differences in intellectual functioning can be fruitful and constructive. It connects with the discussion of cognitive development (*see* Chapter 6) and with the issue of learning disabilities (*see* Chapter 11).

Dr Mike Anderson provides a speculative and integrative approach to defining the essential cognitive architectural elements which provide and explanation of both the developmental aspects and individual differences in intellectual performance. In addition, with the idea of a 'minimum cognitive architecture' he is able to consider the implications of these proposals for atypical functioning.

Introduction

How do we come to know what we know? Why do some people seem to know more than others? What processes underlie the human capacity for reasoning, rationality and logic? Can babies think? Why are older children more cognitively capable than younger children? All these questions can be subsumed under the general topic of the origins and development of intelligence. The last 20 years has seen a considerable shift in our understanding after many years of stagnation. Although there are still many different views on what we mean by intelligence, there are signs of convergence as more pieces of the puzzle fit together.

Some theorists have argued that intelligence is best thought of as a single global process (Spearman, 1904; Jensen, 1982) and others that intelligence is an umbrella term for a number of different abilities (Thurstone, 1939; Gardner, 1983). Some have argued that intelligence and developmental change in intelligence is a property of our underlying biology and probably largely genetically determined (Fodor, 1983; Chomsky, 1988; Eysenck, 1988; Bouchard et al., 1990, Deary and Caryl, 1997), whereas others argue that intelligence is inextricably linked to experience and culture (Howe, 1990; Ceci, 1990; Gardner, 1983). Some argue that differences in intelligence can be located in the simplest levels of information processing (Jensen, 1982; Nettelbeck, 1987; Anderson, 1992; Deary and Stough, 1996) and others that such differences are negligible compared with differences in higher level cognitive processes such as constructing and selecting problem solving strategies (Hunt, 1986; Sternberg, 1983). In terms of development some have viewed intelligence as a progression through qualitatively different cognitive stages, whereas others argue for common processes of change that can apply across all sorts of intellectual domains (Karmiloff-Smith, 1992). Some have viewed the process of developmental change as being driven by a single global factor such as speed of processing (Kail, 1988; Hale, 1990) or cognitive capacity (Pascual-Leone, 1970; Case, 1985; Halford, 1993) or, on the contrary, as a process of increased cognitive competence due to the maturation of modular competences (Anderson, 1992) or increased modularization of specific intellectual skills (Karmiloff-Smith, 1992). To see why, despite the diversity, progress has been made we need to begin at the beginning – when intelligence first became a scientific construct.

The psychometrics of intelligence

THE LEGACIES OF GALTON AND BINET

There are two great historical figures responsible for the current span in theories of intelligence – Francis Galton and Alfred Binet. At base they were interested in different aspects of intelligence – individual differences in adult intelligence in the case of Galton and developmental change in the case of Binet.

Francis Galton can be credited with the first systematic scientific attempt to both understand and measure human intelligence. Galton's essential idea was that differences in intelligence were to be found in differences in the efficiency of operation of simple neural processes. That is, he considered intelligence to be a low-level, inherited property of our nervous system. In his Kensington laboratory in the late nineteenth century he attempted to measure intelligence by relating the speed of simple sensory-motor processes (considered simple examples of neural circuitry) to 'estimates' of an individual's intellectual prowess (subjective judgements being necessary, of course, as there were no intelligence tests). However, Galton's own empirical efforts met with no success. Subsequently, Spearman (1904) developed Galton's view with his theory of general intelligence, or g, which he regarded as a unitary, biological and inherited determinant of measurable intellectual differences and likened to mental energy.

By contrast, Alfred Binet believed that intelligence was to be found in the higher faculties of the mind including knowledge, logic, reasoning and, particularly, judgement (Binet and Simon, 1905). When charged by the Parisian authorities in 1904 to develop tests that would identify children in need of special education, Binet decided his tests would have to tap these higher mental processes. He set about finding a method that would allow him to construct tests with objectively verifiable scales of difficulty. Binet's technique for constructing the first test relied on an important observation – whatever intelligence is we can be sure that it develops. Consequently, the first intelligence test was based on the central idea that the age that the average child can succeed at a particular problem is an indication of the difficulty of that problem. In turn, Binet turned this relationship on its head to derive a child's **mental age** – a radically new concept.

A child scoring better on intelligence tests than the average child of their age would have a higher mental age (MA) than chronological age (CA) and a child scoring lower than average would have a lower mental age than chronological age. It took one short step, by Stern (1912), to derive an index of differences in intelligence within ages. The resulting intelligence quotient, or IQ, was calculated by use of the classical formula: IQ = (MA/CA)* 100. The calculation of IQ gave birth to the idea that individual differences in intelligence could be expressed by a single score. This formulation helped to drive a wedge between the two different approaches to studying intelligence – the individual differences method (whose concern was IQ differences among peers) and the developmental method (whose concern was changes in mental age with chronological age). And this wedge finally split these different research approaches apart through the work of one of Binet's research workers – Jean Piaget.

Piaget's genius was to realize that errors on intelligence test items might be even more informative than the total test score used in Binet's calculations of mental age. Piaget's approach was to take more interest in the kinds of errors made by children of different ages (subsequently thought of as different stages of cognitive development) as indicators of underlying cognitive structure. Ever since Piaget, the psychometric approach to studying individual differences and research in cognitive development unfortunately have had very little to do with each other. In the remainder of this chapter we look at the separated strands of research in individual differences and cognitive development and the ways in which they contribute to the same story. We will look at theories of the relationship between individual differences in general and specific abilities. We will look at parallel ideas of domain general and domain specific cognitive development. Finally, we will consider an issue fundamental to both – the nature/nurture question. Threaded throughout will be a consideration of the one research domain where the individual differences and developmental approaches have always remained in contact – the study of the nature of intellectual disabilities[1].

General intelligence and specific abilities

Nearly 100 years on what is the status of Spearman's *g*? There are two separable aspects to this question: (1) what is the status of the *g* factor as a psychometric construct? (2) what is the status of general intelligence as a low-level biological property of the nervous system?

FACTOR ANALYSIS

If a range of different cognitive tests are given to a random sample of the population, performance on these tests will correlate. For example, individuals who are better than average on tests of vocabulary will be better than average on tests of mechanical reasoning. They will also be better at solving analogies, better at making inferences, better at arithmetical calculations, know more general information, be faster at substituting digits for other symbols and so forth. The fact that all these abilities are positively correlated indicates that these apparently very different tests may well tap similar underlying factors or traits.

Factor analysis is the statistical technique that can be used to 'extract' underlying factors that can account for patterns of correlations. The problem, as Gould (1996) has pointed out, is that there are different methods of factor analysis and each method generates a different list of underlying factors. This ranges from a method that produces a large general factor consistent with Spearman's *g,* to a method that generates a number of

---

1 Over the history of psychology many technical terms have been coined to refer to individuals of 'low intelligence' some of which have entered the popular vernacular and carry an unwanted stigma (for example, *cretin, imbecile, moron* and *idiot* began as labels for different low IQ-bands). There are still a number of different terms in use today in the scientific literature including *learning disability, intellectual disabilities, mental handicap* and *mental deficiency.* The term 'intellectual disability' is used as a theory-neutral technical term referring to individuals who would typically score below IQ 70 and who also demonstrate consequent social and functional impairment.

relatively independent abilities consistent with Thurstone's notion of a number of primary mental abilities (Thurstone, 1938). The point is that both account for the data equally well. So, mathematically there is no good reason to choose one solution rather than another. Hence the belief that general intelligence, or *g*, is the product of arbitrary statistical machinations and ultimately mythical. This state of affairs was seized upon by Gould to denounce the construct of *g* as a unitary factor:

> 'Thurstone dethroned *g* not by being right with his alternate system – but by being equally wrong and thus exposing the methodological errors of the entire enterprise' (Gould, 1996, p. 340).

Things are not quite so ambiguous as Gould would have us believe and the current psychometric consensus is that **hierarchical** models with a unitary *g* factor at the apex of the hierarchy fit the data better than any model without such a *g* factor (Gustafson, 1984; Carroll, 1993). Yet the central criticism of psychometric theories is valid: the issue of data interpretation is unresolvable within a purely psychometric framework. What we need is some kind of external validation of the contested psychometric constructs and this has been long recognized by those who believe that general intelligence is 'real' (Jensen, 1982). One of the main ways in which the construct of *g* has been validated is to look for non-psychometric correlates, particularly from measures of speed of processing.

g AS SPEED OF PROCESSING

In the 1970s Arthur Jensen began a research programme investigating the possibility that psychometric *g* may have its basis in speed of information processing. To measure speed of processing Jensen used a very simple decision time procedure where subjects have to respond quickly to the onset of light (*see* fig 8.1). Jensen found that individuals with higher IQs respond faster and their response times are less variable. Jensen claims that these studies show that the basis of individual differences in intelligence is to be found in the speed of processing a single bit of information and has conjectured that this may rest on the rate of oscillation of excitatory and inhibitory phases of neuronal firing (Jensen, 1982).

BOX 8.1 Measuring speed of processing

In Jensen's reaction time task subjects hold down a home key until one of the surrounding lights is illuminated (*see* fig 8.2). They must then move their finger from the 'home' button to press a button immediately below the light. In such a procedure there are two principal measures. Decision time (DT) is the length of time between the onset of the stimulus light and the time at which the subjects lift their finger off the home button. Movement time is the time from the offset of the home button to the press of the button below the stimulus light.

Jensen argues that this task is so simple that the instructions are easily understood by people of even mentally retarded ranges of IQ. Twenty years ago few psychologists would have predicted that intelligence would be correlated with performance on such a simple task: but it is. Individuals with higher IQs respond faster and are less variable. Importantly, movement time is uncorrelated with IQ suggesting that the relationship is specific to the time it takes to make a decision rather than the time it takes to move. Although Jensen's interpretation of reaction time data is not unchallenged (Longstreth, 1984) the speed of processing hypothesis has received support from a quite different task.

In an **inspection time** (IT) task a subject is required to make a perceptual discrimination at different exposure durations of a stimulus (see fig 8.3). For example, in a visual IT task, a test stimulus, usually two lines of markedly different length which are joined at the top with a short horizontal bar, is presented for a varying duration before the onset of a following masking stimulus that prevents any further processing of the test stimulus. The subject is required to make a discriminative judgement (is the longer line on the left or the right?) and their accuracy is recorded at different stimulus-mask onset asyncronies. At longer exposures (greater than 500 ms) performance is virtually error free. Inspection time is the stimulus exposure duration that a subject requires to maintain a given level of accuracy. In considered reviews of many studies, both Nettelbeck (1987) and Kranzler and Jensen (1989) came to the conclusion that IT and IQ correlate, negatively, at about –0.5. Higher IQ subjects have shorter ITs suggesting that they process information faster. When reviewing the IT data, Longstreth declared himself to be a 'Doubting Thomas no more' (Longstreth et al., 1986, p. 648). Deary and Stough (1996) argue that IT is the single best measure of speed of processing because it does not have some of the disadvantages of reaction time tasks, such as speed–accuracy trade-offs, that can contaminate the measure with strategic differences between subjects.

In an **inspection time** task a subject is required to make a perceptual discrimination at different exposure durations of a stimulus (*see* fig 8.2). Subjects with higher IQs can make the discrimination at shorter exposure durations of the stimulus – they have shorter inspection times. In considered reviews of many studies, both Nettelbeck (1987) and Kranzler and Jensen (1989) came to the conclusion that inspection time and IQ correlate, negatively, at about 0.5. In other words, the speed of processing a 'simple' unit of information predicts about 25 per cent of the variance in knowledge-rich performance measured by a typical intelligence test.

In sum, it seems that the hypothesis that a biological variable, speed of information processing, might be the basis of general intelligence has received increasing support from reaction time and inspection time studies and from some more recent attempts to measure the activity of the nervous

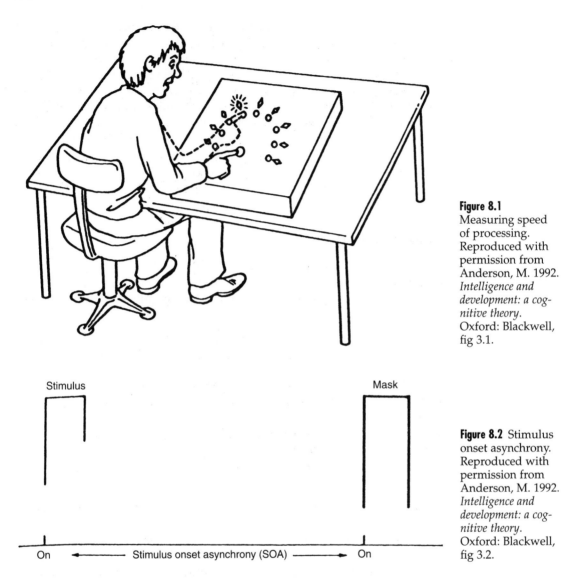

Figure 8.1
Measuring speed
of processing.
Reproduced with
permission from
Anderson, M. 1992.
*Intelligence and
development: a cog-
nitive theory.*
Oxford: Blackwell,
fig 3.1.

Stimulus

Mask

On ◄──── Stimulus onset asynchrony (SOA) ────► On

Figure 8.2 Stimulus
onset asynchrony.
Reproduced with
permission from
Anderson, M. 1992.
*Intelligence and
development: a cog-
nitive theory.*
Oxford: Blackwell,
fig 3.2.

system itself (using, for example, measures of the speed of neural conduc-
tion and properties of cortical evoked potentials; *see* Deary and Caryl,
(1997) for a review). As we shall see below the speed of processing hypothesis has also featured in new research on the causal basis of cognitive
development.

SPECIFIC ABILITIES AND THE MODULARITY OF MIND

Ever since Thurstone (1939) there have been a long series of challenges to
Spearman's unitary conception of intelligence. The most recent and most
comprehensive has been that of Gardner (1983). His theory of **multiple
intelligences** claims that there are a number of autonomous abilities –

linguistic, musical, logical–mathematical, spatial, bodily–kinaesthetic and personal. These candidate intelligences were identified from a diverse body of evidence including: evidence of the selective damage of abilities through brain damage; the existence of savants displaying extreme ability in one intelligence; extreme examples of excellence in one domain; and the constraint that the ability should be culturally valued and have a plausible evolutionary and developmental history. The idea that there is more to intelligence than g is now accepted by all. The real challenge from multiple intelligences theory is the argument that there is no evidence for, nor is there any theoretical requirement served by, the notion of general intelligence. So let us consider a cornerstone of multiple intelligences theory to examine critically this anti-g position.

SAVANT SYNDROME

Gardner (1983) takes the occurrence of savant abilities as crucial evidence of autonomous intelligences. **Savants** are individuals with low IQs who, nevertheless, display a single and exceptional cognitive ability. Examples are:

- Calculating what day of the week any calender date falls on (O'Connor and Hermelin, 1984; Hermelin and O'Connor, 1986; Howe and Smith, 1988).
- High musical ability (Sloboda et al., 1985; Hermelin et al., 1989).
- Artistic talent (Hermelin and O'Connor, 1990; O'Connor and Hermelin, 1990).
- The ability to learn foreign languages (O'Connor and Hermelin, 1991; Smith and Tsimpli, 1995).
- The ability to factorize numbers (Hermelin and O'Connor, 1990; Horowitz et al., 1965).

Gardner's point is, how are such feats possible if there is such a thing as general intelligence?

The central issue for determining whether savants represent a paradox for theories of general intelligence, is whether their talents are the product of *thinking* or whether they rely on rote-memory. It is only if savant abilities appear to require intelligent thought that they should be regarded as presenting a challenge to the notion of g.

In recent reviews of the savant literature Nettelbeck has argued that most savant skills can be explained in terms of an extensive and generative memory for domain relevant material (Nettelbeck, 1999; Nettelbeck and Young, in press, 1996; Young and Nettelbeck, 1994). For example, Norris (1990) has shown that a **connectionist** system, if exposed to days and dates under conditions that might replicate plausible real-world conditions available to savants, can learn to associate days and dates and to demonstrate a knowledge of day–date combinations that they would not have come across (*see* Box 8.2 for a more complex case). Such an ability does not rely on intelligent thought but on particular conditions of practice that allow the establishment of a memory for dates. Nettelbeck concludes that savant abilities do not overlap with different kinds of thinking skills. Rather the strongest evidence is that most abilities are based on extensive memory for (but no 'understanding' of) particular kinds of knowledge gained through frequent exposure to the material and practice of the skill. Consequently, Nettelbeck argues, *contra* Gardner, that rather than savants telling us what intelligence is composed of, savants tell us what intelligence is *not*. In other words, automatic skills based on highly specific memory stores (no matter how elaborate), acquired through extensive practice, coupled with the absence of 'understanding' or the ability to generalize to other knowledge domains, do not challenge the concept of g as a property of intelligent thought.

If savants are exceptions that prove the rule then what can we learn from those who obey the rule – those individuals with intellectual disabilities who show no exceptional cognitive abilities?

Many studies have shown that individuals with intellectual disabilities have slow speed of processing as measured by both reaction time and inspection time (Jensen et al., 1981, Nettelbeck and Brewer, 1981), as would be predicted from their low general intelligence. Yet even these individuals have remarkable cognitive abilities. For example, the capacity to extract speech from an auditory input and subsequently to interpret the signal as language is a process of staggering computational complexity. Such abilities are indeed remarkable when compared to the inability to solve, for example, simple arithmetic problems. How can we explain this paradox? To do so we will now consider a theory that will allow us to integrate the phenomena we have encountered so far.

THE THEORY OF THE MINIMAL COGNITIVE ARCHITECTURE UNDERLYING INTELLIGENCE AND DEVELOPMENT

The theory of the minimal cognitive architecture underlying intelligence and development (Anderson, 1992) argues that intelligence tests measure intelligence through assessing knowledge but that knowledge itself is acquired through two different routes (fig 8.3).

The first route is through **thought**. Thought is considered to be the implementation of a knowledge acquisition algorithm generated by one of two specific processors. Each specific processor, while capable of solving any computational problem, is better suited to one of two particular classes of knowledge – verbal/propositional on the one hand and spatial/analogue on the other. In other words, thoughtful problem solving can be done either by verbalizing a problem (using language-like propositions to think) or by visualizing it (using visuo–spatial representations to think). Individuals differ in their abilities to think in these ways because of the latent 'ability' of each specific processor – that is the *potential* power of each processor. The specific processors are, then, the source of individual differences in specific abilities.

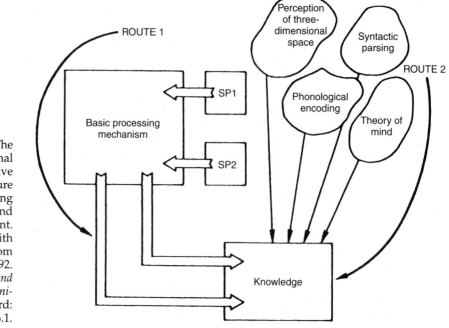

Figure 8.3 The theory of minimal cognitive architecture underlying intelligence and development. Reproduced with permission from Anderson, M. 1992. *Intelligence and development: a cognitive theory.* Oxford: Blackwell, fig 6.1.

The latent ability of each specific processor is normally distributed in the population and uncorrelated in the population – that is to say they are independent of each other (in theory, someone could be very good at spatial thinking and very bad at propositional thinking). However, in practice, the observed ability served by a specific processor is constrained by the speed of a basic processing mechanism – at slow speed only the simplest kinds of thoughts of either kind can be implemented (the speed of the basic processing mechanism can be measured by use of tasks such as inspection time and reaction time (*see* Box 8.1)). It is this constraint that is the basis of general intelligence and the reason why manifest specific abilities are correlated (giving rise to the *g* factor).

A particular feature of this processing route is that as speed of processing increases and the constraint on the specific processors decreases then manifest specific abilities will become less correlated. This predicts the differentiation of abilities (greater independence and importance of specific abilities) at higher levels of IQ (*see* Detterman and Daniel, 1989) and the complement – the pervasiveness and importance of difference in 'general intelligence' at lower levels of IQ.

The second route for acquiring the knowledge that will influence intelligence test performance is through dedicated information processing **modules** (*see* fig 8.3), fashioned after the theory of modularity developed by Fodor (1983 and *see section on* modularity and development *below*). These modules have evolved to provide information about the environment that could not be provided by central processes of thought (route 1, knowledge acquisition) in an ecologically useful time frame. Examples of modules are:

devices to construct three-dimensional visual representations from two-dimensional retinal information; various language acquisition devices; and the core computational procedures involved in acquiring a theory of mind (Leslie, 1987). In addition, modular processes can be acquired through extensive practice. The common features of both the acquired and the 'innate' modules are that they operate automatically and independently of thought and are consequently unconstrained by the speed of the basic processing mechanism.

The maturation and acquisition of modules is the prime cause of developmental change. Because modules function independently of variations in the speed of the basic processing mechanism their operation is independent of differences in IQ. This means that individual differences and cognitive development represent two independent dimensions of intelligence. It also means that these complex cognitive functions are available to non brain-damaged individuals with intellectual disabilities.

I have attempted to show how this architecture can make sense of both specific cognitive deficits (such as dyslexia) that are accompanied by normal levels of general intelligence and also some savant abilities (Anderson, 1992; see also Box 8.2). In the main they are explained respectively by the selective damage and sparing of processing modules. In the case of savants the modules may be of the innate kind (e.g. music, language, art) or acquired through practice (e.g. calendrical calculation). Because savant abilities are modular there is no paradox with their low-IQ which is a property of route 1 processing.

BOX 8.2 A prime number calculator

Michael is a young man with an extraordinary talent. He can recognize when a number is a prime number (an integer that can only be divided by itself and one with no remainder). He has this ability despite major communication and intellectual difficulties. As a young child he did not talk or attempt to engage in any kind of communication. He still cannot speak but has learned to copy numbers and letters, though only very poorly. Yet he could solve complex jigsaw puzzles, even with the pieces face down. He is good with money, time, maps and calendars and he is able to add, subtract, multiply, divide and factorize numbers.

Michael's abilities have been studied extensively (Hermelin and O'Connor, 1990). His performance on the *Peabody Picture Vocabulary Test* is unscorable and his non-verbal IQ on the *Columbia Mental Maturity Scale* is 74. However, his standard *Raven's Progressive Matrices* performance, thought to measure general intelligence, is anomalous being accurate and fast. He made only one careless error (raw score = 59), putting him in the top per centile of adult performance and giving him an IQ equivalent on this test of about 140. Not only is his accuracy excellent, O'Connor and Hermelin (personal communication) found that he completed the Matrices at high speed, rhythmically turning the pages one by one pointing almost immediately to the correct solution.

Michael's performance when factorizing numbers is remarkable. He accurately factorized 70 per cent of numbers greater than 10 000 in an average time of 38.2 sec (compared with 40 per cent accuracy and average time of 48 sec in a mathematically trained control subject). Although by comparison, his ability to recognize a prime number was poorer for numbers greater than 10 000, his performance for numbers less than 10 000 was outstanding (85 per cent accuracy). In a series of experimental studies his reaction times to report whether a number was, or was not prime, was compared with a number of 'control' subjects, including mathematics students and computer simulations (Anderson et al., in press) (*see* fig 8.4).

These data demonstrated that Michael was employing a calculating strategy first suggested by Eratosthenes, a Greek astronomer and mathematician, to detect a prime number, namely, dividing a target number by all primes up to the square root of the target number and testing for a remainder. Such an ability seems to require intelligence, making Michael an anomaly for theories that take general intelligence seriously. However, he also has an estimated inspection time (*see* Box 8.1) of about 30–50 ms which is in the range expected from individuals with average or above average IQs. Anderson et al. (in press) offer two explanations for his ability. Either he has a mathematical talent perhaps based on enhanced visuo–spatial processing and such talent is normally independent of IQ, or it might be that he has the potential for high general intelligence (which would explain his inspection time) and his low IQ is caused by the devastating long term effect of having no language.

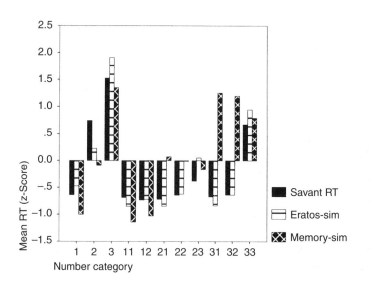

Figure 8.4 A prime number calculator.

Let us return to our second paradox that represents the complement of savant syndrome – the ability of people with intellectual disabilities to perform well at 'everyday' yet computationally complex activities.

As we have seen, modules would allow individuals with intellectual disabilities to access knowledge that otherwise would be unavailable to them. New evidence in support of this idea comes from two recent studies. Moore et al. (1995) have shown that individuals with intellectual disabilities may be as capable of executing the complex perceptual processes underlying person perception and some aspects of object perception, as individuals of normal IQ. In contrast, performance on a simple (but thoughtful) perceptual discrimination that is required by a standard inspection time task, is impaired in this group relative to normal IQ participants. Similarly Anderson and Miller (1998), using face processing as an example of a modular process, showed that if an inspection time judgement is presented as a discrimination between lengths of noses then this has a quite different relationship to intelligence than a task involving an identical judgement but in the context of a non-modular stimulus condition (where the face features are presented in a 'scrambled' configuration to prevent the operation of the face module).

We see, then, that this cognitive theory of intelligence can make compatible what seemed incompatible – the reality of general intelligence (caused by biologically based differences in speed of information processing) and the ability of some low IQ individuals to master some very specific cognitive feats.

We can now summarize our conclusions about the nature of individual differences in intelligence:

- There appears to be a general intelligence factor (g).
- g is caused by a low-level, biological property of the nervous system, possibly speed of information processing.
- There is more to intelligence than g, evinced by the existence of exceptional abilities of savants on the one hand and the existence of everyday, yet computationally complex abilities, available to all – even those with intellectual disabilities.

Now that we have considered individual differences, it is time to turn to the developmental dimension of intelligence.

Developmental change in intelligence

The distinction between general and specific abilities that has proved influential in the study of individual differences and useful for understanding intellectual disabilities appears again where we look for explanations for developmental change. In this context the major alternatives are that developmental change is caused by some single global factor or that developmental change is better characterized as changes in specific domains or abilities.

THE SINGLE GLOBAL HYPOTHESIS

The single global hypothesis of developmental change proposes that the ability of children to solve increasingly difficult problems as they age (and the corollary – the decreasing abilities of the elderly) can be attributed to a single factor. Rather than there being a number of specific abilities that undergo their own development the idea is that there is one common factor responsible for developmental change over a whole host of processing domains. On this view development represents quantitative rather than qualitative changes in cognition. This single global hypothesis can be likened to the *g* hypothesis for individual differences and, indeed, the same processing basis has been suggested – a change in speed of processing (Salthouse, 1985; Kail, 1988, 1992; Hale, 1990).

The evidence for the single global hypothesis stems from a number of related techniques. The essential idea behind all these techniques is that if we look at the performance of children of different ages on a number of speeded information processing tasks then we can predict the processing times of any age group on any battery of tasks from the processing times of any other age group on the same battery of tasks. For each task condition we can plot the reaction times for two age groups, with the x-co-ordinate being the reaction time of the older group on that condition and the y-co-ordinate being the reaction time of the younger group. When we do this it turns out that we almost invariably have plotted a straight line and the slope of the line measures the degree to which younger children process information more slowly than older children. The slope is steeper the greater the age difference between the children. In other words, the difference between age groups can be attributed to a simple multiplicative constant and this constant changes with age (Kail, 1988, 1992; Hale, 1990). This leads to a parsimonious hypothesis that changes in speed of processing can account for developmental change in the same way that differences in speed of processing have been hypothesized to account for differences in IQ.

There are a number of other theories that can be located within the single global camp but are somewhat closer to the position that argues there are also qualitative changes in intelligence with development. This tradition began with the M-capacity theory of Pasual-Leone (1970) and continued with the work of Case in the 1970s and 1980s (*see* Case, 1985). Perhaps the best articulated contemporary theory is the capacity theory of Halford (1982, 1993).

Halford argues that increasing problem solving ability can be understood as the increase in the complexity of relations that a child can process. The complexity of relations is determined by the number of arguments or dimensions that they require. An **unary** relation has one argument or dimension (for example, an attribute 'big' – big dog, big house, etc.), a **binary** relation has two dimension (for example, 'bigger-than' – Jack is bigger than Rosie; Rosie is smarter than Jack), a **ternary** relation has three dimensions (for example, arithmetical addition and multiplication: $5 = 3 + 2$; $6 = 3 \times 2$) and **quaternary** relations have four dimensions (for example, the four-way comparisons involved in relating proportions: $10/5 = 6/3$). Since most tasks that measure human reasoning (e.g. transitive inference, analogical reasoning) can be described in terms of the relational processing they require then it can be argued that the processing of relations is fundamental to intelligence.

The ability to process unary relations develops on average at about one year, binary relations at about two years, ternary relations between ages five and six and quaternary relations at about 11 or 12 years. Since older children can process more relations than younger children this means that they can handle problems of qualitatively different levels of complexity. In this sense Halford's theory is Piagetian. However, a central proposition of the theory is that problems with more dimensions require more cognitive capacity (seen as a non-computational **resource**). On the basis of a series of experiments in the 1980s using a dual-task procedure to measure available processing capacity in children, Halford claimed that available capacity predicted the number of dimensions that a child could handle (e.g. Halford et al.,). Since this change in capacity can be regarded as a quantitative shift in available resources this makes the theory neo-Piagetian and puts the reason for developmental change in the single-global hypothesis camp.

There are other theories that put an important stress on a single factor that might explain developmental change, for example resistance to interference (Dempster, 1991) or inhibition (Bjorklund and Harnishfeger, 1990). However, by way of contrast we will now consider another class of theory that proposes that developmental changes in intelligence take place across a number of different and autonomous abilities.

MODULARITY AND DEVELOPMENT

Fodor (1983) has argued that the architecture of the mind can be divided into two different systems. **Input systems** are responsible for constructing representations of the world from sensory information, which are then offered for evaluation by **central systems** of thought. The major claim is that input systems are modular. Modular systems are among other things, innate, fast, domain-specific and informationally encapsulated. In short they are dedicated, complex but reflexive, processing devices that have evolved to serve a single processing function when presented with the relevant stimulus information. Central systems of thought, by contrast, are slow and domain general.

We have already considered my theory of the minimal cognitive architecture in the context of individual differences. The developmental part of this theory argues that modules mature at different points in development and these modules increase the representational and computational capacity of children. The key hypothesis is that these modules mature on a biological programme and their development is independent of an individual's intelligence. Major modules underlie sensory motor development, language development and the development of a theory of mind (Leslie, 1987; Frith, 1989). In addition, information processing capacities such as the ability to inhibit and control the flow of information are considered to be modular (*see* Davis and Anderson, 1999). New modules can be acquired through extensive practice – effectively processing can become 'automatic' and occur outwith central processes of thought (Anderson, 1998). In contrast to the single global hypothesis this theory proposes that developmental change is qualitative and represents an independent dimension of intelligence to that of individual differences.

Karmiloff-Smith (1992) has reworked the whole idea of modularity in development, radically altering the notion of module from Fodor's original conception. She argues that there are a number of broad classes of knowledge domains that are served by developing modules. These allow us to characterize the child in a number of roles – the child as a linguist, a physicist, a mathematician, a notator (writing and drawing) and a psychologist (theory of mind). There are two key components to Karmiloff-Smith's theory.

The first is that modules are grounded in innate predispositions to process particular classes of environmental input. But this is an extremely primitive level of innate specification. An important role is given to environmental input in a developmental process of modularization. This view represents a compromise between the nativism of Chomsky and Fodor and the constructivism of Piaget. Modularity is the endstate of development rather than the pre-specified beginning.

The second component of the theory is representational redescription (RR). This is a process where representations are transformed by central processes and that leads, in turn, to a development of the modules themselves. RR theory argues that rather than development proceeding in a stage-like manner across all knowledge domains, different domains are characterized by different representational phases. The first phase involves achieving success on a task at a procedural level where the representation underlying performance is essentially implicit. In the second phase an explicit representation is formed which replaces external stimulation as the focus of the child's attention – in effect developing a mini-theory of task performance. The third phase involves reconciling a host of representations with external data and revising mini-theories about the knowledge domain. Development then consists of an interactive process (between experience and representations of the world) that results in the increased modularization of knowledge domains.

The single global hypothesis and the modularity theses offer radically different explanations of developmental changes in intelligence – the former arguing for quantitative changes in intellectual capacity and the latter qualitative. We see these alternatives expressed again when we consider the effect of low IQ on cognitive development.

DEVELOPMENT AND INTELLECTUAL DISABILITIES

Research on the development of intelligence in individuals with intellectual disabilities has been dominated by the classical debate between the **developmental** and the **difference** view (Zigler, 1969).

The developmental view, although acknowledging that low-IQ children as a group were handicapped with respect to their same age peers, argues that low-IQ children simply develop more slowly than children with normal levels of IQ but go through the same stages (Piagetian) of cognitive development, albeit with a lower ultimate level of cognitive competence.[2] The difference view, on the other hand, is that there is a fundamental deficit associated with intellectual disabilities that precludes cognitive equivalence between a person with intellectual disabilities and a normal-IQ person (Spitz, 1982). These views lead to a crucial test based on predictions about cognitive performance in individuals matched for mental age.

Mental age is an index of cognitive achievement or level. Equal mental ages can be achieved by children of varying IQs. Children with intellectual disabilities will be older when they attain the same mental age as a higher IQ child but they will have achieved the same cognitive 'level'. The developmental view predicts that if matched for mental age, low-IQ and normal-IQ groups would show cognitive equivalence. The difference view on the other hand predicts that because children with intellectual disabilities have an unchanging and fundamental cognitive deficit then cognitive equivalence can never be achieved.

In most studies comparing normal and low-IQ subjects matched for mental age on a large array of different cognitive tasks it has been found that the low IQ groups usually perform worse than the (much younger) normal-IQ children (Weiss et al., 1986). This phenomenon became known as mental age lag (Spitz, 1982).

Zigler and colleagues explained mental age lag by appealing to additional non-cognitive factors that might cause additional problems for a low-IQ group. Primarily these were motivational factors such as learned helplessness or the generalized effects of institutionalization on learning. Spitz has challenged this interpretation and pointed out that the size of the mental age lag on any cognitive test was predictable from the test's g loading. In other words the fundamental deficit was in g and equivalent mental ages were achieved by the low-IQ group only on tests where their greater experience could compensate for their lower g.

In the 1980s a series of meta-analyses by Wiesz and colleagues (*see* Weiss et al., 1986) offered a compromise position. They split the developmental proposition into two components – **cognitive stage** defined within a Piagetian framework and **cognitive structure** as defined by an information processing analysis. It turns out that there is no good evidence that children with intellectual disabilities go through a different sequence of cognitive stages. When matched with normal-IQ children of the same mental age they perform at equivalent levels on Piagetian measures of cognitive development, such as conservation or class-inclusion. However, when their

---

2 In the following section 'low-IQ children' and 'children with intellectual disabilities' is used to refer to children with IQs below 70. These children would be designated as mentally retarded in the major classificatory systems but mental retardation has an inappropriate theoretical connotation in this context.

performance on basic information processing tasks are compared the children with intellectual disabilities again lag behind their mental-age matched controls. The general picture is one where the more global and universal cognitive transitions in cognitive development described by Piaget occur in the same order but much later for children with intellectual disabilities. However, within any stage the process that underlies the differences in problem solving abilities of children at the same stage of cognitive development will still be deficient in low-IQ children.

It seems then that both the developmental and the difference theorists were right. Children with intellectual disabilities go through the same kinds of knowledge restructuring as described by Piaget but do so more slowly than normal-IQ children. However, the low-IQ children will always suffer a fundamental deficit in intelligent information processing even when compared with mental age peers. Low IQ has a pervasive and enduring effect that is not ameliorated through cognitive development.

There is one more important body of literature that touches on issues of continuity or qualitative change in development – the prediction of later IQ differences from measures in infancy.

INFANT PREDICTORS OF LATER IQ DIFFERENCES

It is only recently that measures in infancy have been found that correlate with later differences in IQ. Fagan and McGrath (1981) reported that measures of **novelty preference** (the amount of time babies look at a novel stimulus in preference to a familiar one) in young babies was correlated with later IQ measured at four and seven years. The correlations indicated that it is the babies that show a greater preference for novelty that subsequently have higher IQ scores. Similarly, features of **habituation**, where a stimulus is presented repeatedly until the baby's interest in the stimulus wanes (habituates), is also correlated with IQ (Rose et al., 1986). The explanation for these correlations have centred on the view that measures of infant attention share a common processing basis with IQ differences (*see* Bornstein and Sigman, 1986).

The two major features of infant attention from the habituation procedure that predict later IQ are: (1) first-look duration (the amount of time an infant will spend looking on the first trial they are presented with the stimulus); and (2) peak-look duration (the duration of the trial where the infant spends the longest time looking at the stimulus). Since these correlations are negative, i.e. it is the infants who look for the shortest time that turn out to have the higher IQs, this led to the hypothesis that the common process was speed of processing (Colombo, 1993). We have seen that speed of processing has been advanced as a likely basis for differences in general intelligence. An alternative to this hypothesis is that it may be infants who later have higher IQs are better at inhibiting processing, which means that they are less likely to be 'captured' by a stimulus (predicting shorter looking times) and this allows them switch attention from familiar to novel stimuli (McCall, 1994). It is not as clear how this process is related to later IQ differences but it is clear that the infancy research will open up new possibilities for understanding intelligence.

The nature/nurture question

Finally, we turn to the last major question – to what extent is the development of intelligence controlled by genetic and by experiential factors? To some extent of course the answer to this question will be influenced by views taken on the other two major issues presented in this chapter. Is intelligence best characterized as predominantly a single global factor underlying individual differences and developmental change, or must we look for more specific individual differences and modular-based developmental change? The single global factor view of intelligence has been largely associated with the genetic inheritance view. Equally, however, many modular-based developmental theories are avowedly nativist. And here we see a distinction that is rarely acknowledged and can lead to confusion – there are two quite different senses of 'genetic'.

NATIVISM

The first sense of 'genetic' refers to innateness or **nativism** – the proposition that cognitive abilities and developmental change cannot be explained without recourse to inborn genetic predispositions. Nativism is contrasted with **empiricism** or the view that the child comes into the world with a mind like a *tabula rasa* waiting to be etched by experience. There is a crucial difference between innate and heritable.

Down's syndrome and Fragile-X syndrome are two groups of low-IQ individuals where their low IQ is indisputably genetically caused. In 95 per cent of cases Down's syndrome is caused by an extra chromosome (trisomony 21) yet Down's syndrome is not heritable (i.e. passed on through the germ-line of parents). It is an innate disorder (children are born with Down's syndrome) caused by an early abnormality in embryonic cell division. Fragile-X on the other hand is inherited from parents through a weakness on the X-chromosome. Because of the genetic architecture it will be expressed in boys and carried by females. Both disorders are genetic conditions but one is heritable and one is not.

Although the role of experience is a basic concern of theories of development, it is the influence of the environment on individual differences in IQ that has received the most detailed and quasi-experimental study. The heritability of individual differences is the second, more controversial and quite different sense of 'genetic'.

Heritability of IQ differences

Estimates of the heritability of IQ differences vary between 50 per cent (Plomin et al., 1977) and 80 per cent (Bouchard et al., 1990) (*see also*

Chapter 1, *Genetics and development*, to see how different environmental and genetic sources of IQ differences can be estimated from twin and adoption studies).

Hence, even the more conservative estimates argue that the influence of genetic differences in populations is not trivial – they are at least as important as environmental differences and probably more so. The study of Bouchard et al. (1990) is particularly important because they measured a number of variables that potentially can confound twin studies and attempts were made to determine their influence on the estimate of heritability. For example, they measured the length of time the twins are together before they are separated and how similar the environments were for any twin pair (correlated placement reduces the estimates of the effect of the environment) and used these measures to adjust their estimates of heritability. It turns out that these effects are minor (contributing at most 3 per cent of the higher estimate of 70–80 per cent heritability).

Development data

The data from the Colorado adoption project suggest that the **common or shared environment** (*see* Chapter 1) is most influential early in development. The correlation between adopted children and their biologically unrelated siblings is about 0.2–0.3 during their early years. However, over the lifespan it seems that the most important environmental differences are those that are unique (or not shared amongst members of the same family). So rather than the major socio-economic variables (a large part of the shared, or common, environmental variance) being the principal environmental contributor to difference in intelligence, it is unique life events that happen to individuals that make up the major environmental contribution. Indeed, Scarr (1992) in a review of adoption and twin studies has estimated that the contribution of the shared environment to differences in IQ is approximately zero by adulthood. Consistent with this is the finding that the heritability of *g* increases throughout development as the effect of the shared environment decreases (McGue et al., 1993).

The Louisville longitudinal study of twins has shown that genes influence developmental change itself (Wilson, 1983). Comparing the cognitive abilities of twins from birth to 15 years this study has shown a striking similarity in 'growth spurts' of cognitive abilities in monozygotic (identical) twins compared with dizygotic twins. Not only do MZ twins become more similar over development and DZ twins if anything less similar but the spurts and lags individuals show are genetically influenced.

The influence of genes on development is not just through the changes in gene expression but through the indirect influence a genotype has on their environment – an effect called **gene-environment** (GE) correlation (Plomin et al., 1977; Scarr 1992). This correlation comes in three forms. **Passive** GE correlation is due to the fact that children inherit both genes and environments that can nurture those genes from their parents. For example, if musical ability is in part genetic then it is likely that the offspring of someone with high musical ability would inherit some of the genetic predisposition and an environment rich in musical stimulation. **Evocative** GE correlation is where children evoke reactions from others based on their own genetic propensities. Genes that lead to musical appreciation are likely to evoke musical interactions with others, again enriching the musical environment of the child. Finally, **Active** GE correlation is where the child seeks out the environments that mesh with their genetic predispositions. So the child might seek others interested in music, buy records, take lessons, go to concerts and so forth. The general image is of environments reinforcing genetic predispositions. Of course this can also work against the child whose genotype might poorly equip them for learning – with low ability children gravitating towards intellectually less stimulating environments.

Chapter summary

We have surveyed a number of research approaches to intelligence in this chapter. We have seen how the long running dispute between those who believe in a general factor of intelligence and those who argue for a number of independent 'intelligences' can be resolved within a common theory. In particular, general intelligence does not appear to be the invention of intelligence testers and rather is the consequence of a biological constraint on cognition, possibly speed of information processing. In a similar vein we have contrasted a single process and a multiple modular process to understanding developmental change in intelligence. This contrast is still hotly contested in the current research literature. We have also seen that studies of the changes in intelligence in children with intellectual disabilities broadly supports the idea that some aspects of developmental change are relatively independent of IQ differences. On the other hand we have also seen that low IQ represents a life-long pervasive deficit in intellectual functioning. Finally, there is evidence that both IQ differences and the development of intelligence is influenced substantially by genes. They are also influenced by non-shared (individual specific) environmental differences rather than the shared or common environment.

The study of intelligence is making great progress. Now that few dispute whether there is such a 'thing' as general intelligence, the goal is to understand the relationship between general and specific abilities. Theories of developmental change may once again be reintroduced to their empirical roots in intelligence testing by their application to understanding abnormal as well as normal cognitive development. Finally, the growing influence of behaviour genetics will illuminate the age-old questions about nature and nurture. These are exciting times.

Seminar questions

1. Can intellectual disabilities be 'cured'?
2. Are savants 'intelligent'?
3. How important is experience for the development of intelligence?

Further reading

Anderson, M. 1992. *Intelligence and development: a cognitive theory*. Oxford: Blackwell. All the issues pointed to in this chapter are dealt with in detail in this book.

Gardner, H., Kornhaber, M.L., and Wake, W.K. 1996. *Intelligence: multiple perspectives*. Fort Worth, TX: Harcourt Brace. Provides a counter point to Anderson (1992). This is a comprehensive textbook on intelligence that gives space to many different views but presents the general case for the multiple intelligences perspective.

Karmiloff-Smith, A. 1992. *Beyond modularity: a developmental perspective on cognitive science*. Cambridge, MA: MIT Press. This book provides an important treatment of modularity and cognitive development. A must for the serious student interested in the developmental perspective.

Reading skill and dyslexia

ROD NICOLSON

Editors' preface

Although there have been debates about whether other species are able to produce language (*see* Chapter 4) and whether other species can produce graphical representations (*see* Chapter 7), there is little dispute that the ability to read is a uniquely human accomplishment. However, it is only in the last 100 years or so, following the introduction of mass compulsory education, that reading has become such a widespread human ability. It is also worth remembering that reading, unlike language and drawing, is usually acquired through formal teaching.

In this chapter Professor Rod Nicolson summarizes the major perspectives about reading to provide you with an understanding of significant research traditions and controversies. He starts with an examination of the eye movements involved in the physical process of reading and next examines the way that the brain makes use of this information. He then considers ideas about the way children learn to read, and this is followed by a discussion of the difficulties children with dyslexia have with the reading process. Rod Nicolson's own work on reading and dyslexia has led him to the viewpoint that psychological knowledge about general skill acquisition can be used to augment current approaches to reading. In the final section of the chapter recommendations are made about the way to help children learn to read, there are similarities between these recommendations and those presented in Chapter 11 which deals with the more general issue of children with learning disabilities. The final section of the chapter also contains a discussion of the relation between the different research perspectives which are relevant to understanding the development of reading.

Introduction

Most books on cognitive psychology have a chapter on reading. As they should. After all, you are reading this chapter – reading is an important skill and an interesting one, a skill that is becoming increasingly crucial to full participation in the information society. In this chapter we try to get you to think about how psychology can help with reading. After reading this chapter it is hoped you will be mentally richer in the following ways:

- You will have an overview of why reading is so important – to psychologists, to educationalists, to politicians and to you.
- You will have participated in a discussion of the important aspects of reading, from the perspectives of cognitive psychology, of developmental psychology and of education.
- You will have been acquainted with a number of controversies about reading that make reading research such an exciting and infuriating domain.
- You will understand the perspective of reading as a learned skill, a perspective that helps provide answers to most of the controversies.
- You will have had a glimpse of a group of 'special' readers – dyslexic children who learn to read much less easily than normal youngsters.
- You will have had some fun, done some reading and some thinking and will have signposts to how you can continue an interest in reading.

We all know what reading is – it is a method of taking in information visually via written words (and perhaps pictures). The words may be isolated, as in a company logo or a shop sign, or connected prose as in a novel. We move our eyes along, fixating a word or two at a time, read the fixated words, work out their meanings, say them (if reading aloud), connect them with the words read just before, piece together the meaning and move on to the next words on the line. Easy.

Well it is not easy. It is more like miraculous. Indeed, until modern times anyone who had worked out how to read was considered close to a genius. This chapter presents an overview of the important aspects of reading – what skilled reading is, how children learn to read and how they can be helped to learn to read. Reading is of central importance in almost all disciplines of psychology – developmental psychologists try to construct theories of how reading develops and how this affects intellectual performance; discussions about how best reading should be taught provide a major current focus of educational psychology; cognitive psychologists try to model the processes involved in skilled reading, in the hope that these analyses will shed light on the way that concepts are represented and processed in the brain; cognitive scientists attempt to model reading in terms of connectionist models; and so on. Because the different disciplines had different languages, different approaches and different preoccupations, there has been no coherent attempt at an integrative rapprochement of these different aspects of reading. It is like the old Hindu tale, much loved by psychologists, of the four blindfolded men examining an elephant. One, feeling the trunk, said 'it's a snake'. Another, examining a leg said, 'it's a tree'. The third, examining the tail said 'it's a rope'. The fourth, examining the body, said 'it's a house'. They were all a bit right but a lot wrong.

My task here is to attempt to draw for you the whole elephant, sketching it from each perspective and then attempting to integrate these different viewpoints as best I can. Consequently, we will now take a look at reading from a number of important perspectives. The intention is to try to paint a broad picture by means of a few bold brush-strokes. Further material will be provided for those who wish to pursue particular themes to a greater depth.

Reading as a skill

FUNDAMENTALS

During reading, the eyes engage in saccadic movements, in which they jump abruptly from one point of fixation (typically the middle of a word) to the next point of fixation (typically the next word, or maybe two or three words further on). Usually, the eye jumps roughly every 200 ms (five times per second) from one fixation to the next. A jump is called a saccade and it is generally considered that information is extracted from the text only when the eye is at rest (in practice this is not a serious limitation because saccades are very brief, say 10–20 ms in duration, so five saccades in a second will take up only 50–100 ms of that second, that is only 5-10 per cent of the total time). An example of eye movements during reading a text is given in figure 9.1.

Readers of English normally proceed along one line at a time, fixating at various points in a left-to-right fashion. For difficult text most readers would fixate each word once or maybe twice and might have regressions (fixations to a point earlier on the line). Even with simple text it is rare to saccade more than two or three words to the right.

DISCUSSION POINT

Consider your own eye movements reading this line of text. Which words are you fixating? Now read it much faster. Which words are you fixating?

The first time, probably, you painstakingly fixated each word in turn (and were consciously aware of doing so) and the second time you were not sure which words you fixated. This is the way with most 'automatic' skills – we outgrow the need for conscious control of the subprocesses by developing subconscious routines and subsequently attempts to consciously control them may actually slow us down (*see also* Chapter 6).

As society has become progressively more complex, psychology has								
•	•	•	•		•	|	•	•	•
1	2	3	4		5	|	6	8	9
						7			
234	310	188	216		242	188	144	177	159

assumed an increasingly important role in solving human problems							
•	•		•	•	• •	• •	•
|	10	12	13	14	15	|	16	18
11						17		
244	206	317	229	269	196	277	144	202

Figure 9.1 The pattern of fixations while reading a passage. Reproduced with permission from Rayner, K. (1986). Eye movements and the perceptual span: Evidence for dyslexic typology. In Pavlidis, G. Th. and D.F. Fisher (Eds.). *Dyslexia, Its Neuropsychology and Treatment*. pp. 111–130. Chichester: Wiley. © John Wiley & Sons Limited.

The chart shows the fixations made by a reader while she is reading two lines starting:

'As society has become progressively more complex, psychology has . . .'

The figure indicates that the reader makes her first fixation on the 'c' of 'society'. This is labelled by a 1 under the 'c'. Her eyes rest there for 234 ms, then saccade (essentially instantaneously) to around the middle letter of most of the following words: 'has', 'become', 'progressively', and 'more'. The next fixation overshoots and focuses on the comma after 'complex'. This results in back-tracking to the letter 'p' and is indicated by the code 'I'. The following eye movements in the line mostly are the standard saccades to the middle of words.

The saccade to the start of the next line (10) does not go quite far enough, resulting in another regression (11).

Overall, the reader is showing the standard pattern of steady steps moving consistently across the page. A dyslexic reader might well show many more regressions.

So, that is the general plan for eye movements. Our eyes move along the text in a series of saccades. Typical saccades are 7–9 character spaces to the right, characterized by a short jump of about 20 ms followed by a longer fixation (200–1000 ms). As we get more skilled and read faster, how does this happen? There are three obvious ways that we might do this:

1. We could take in information during a saccade.
2. We could make bigger saccades, presumably taking in more information per fixation.
3. We could make shorter fixations, thereby making more saccades per second.

There has been very extensive work on these issues over the past 20 years, using eye movement tracking equipment. It turns out that (1) will not work. Saccades are 'ballistic', that is, pre-programmed and fast, so there is no stable pattern on the retina during a saccade and most researchers consider that there is little scope for visual information processing during a saccade (Rayner and Pollatsek, 1989).

It turns out also that (2) cannot be a complete solution. The amount of information taken in during a single fixation is very interesting. It was studied extensively by McConkie and Rayner in the 1970s using a computer linked to an eye movement measuring system. Each time the user made a fixation, the computer rearranged the words on the screen so that although a central 'window' around the point of fixation had the correct text, the information outside the window was garbled. The researchers varied the size of the window, arguing that if the subjects' reading was not affected by the procedure, then they could not be making any use of the information outside the window. By this means they established that readers cannot use information from more than about 10 characters each side of the fixation point. In later work they established that there is an asymmetry, with hardly any information left of the fixation point (four characters) being used, whereas up to 14 characters right of the fixation point might be used. One of the other interesting findings of the window studies was that the size of text was not that critical. Making the letters larger did not significantly decrease the maximum window size, so it looks as though it is more the number of characters than the position on the retina that counts. This is an interesting finding showing how psychologists can exploit careful experimentation to establish where the bottleneck lies – in this case deeper in the brain's information processing system rather than being merely a retinal limitation.

DISCUSSION POINT

You can have a try yourself (roughly) using fig 9.2 overleaf (do not turn the page yet!). The figure consists of a line of words with a boxed X in the middle. You have to fixate immediately on the X (without looking at any of the other letters). Now, while still fixating the X, try and see how many letters you can identify to the left. Then to the right. Remember, do not move your eyes!

DISCUSSION POINT

It is pretty obvious that if you do fixate only on the X, you cannot read more than one word away either to left or right. You do get something of a feel for the pattern of word shapes and spaces though. I think I can tell that there are four or five short words to the right of the fixation. This information could be all that is needed to guide the next fixation.

The above studies suggest that perceptual span cannot be increased beyond three words or so and so cannot be the complete answer to increasing reading speed. Finally, therefore, we turn to alternative (3), that is spend less time per fixation, reading the fixated word(s) more rapidly. This is indeed the normal way that readers speed up.

When considering how we could speed up processing per fixation, it is useful to distinguish between decoding a word (i.e. matching up the word to its underlying representation (the spoken form, at least in the early stages of reading)) and comprehending the word – identifying its meaning and fitting it in with the words already read. It gets very much harder to work out how long it takes to decode words because there is nothing external to measure. One therefore needs to develop a model of the process and to design experiments to try to test the model. In the following section we

ONE HOP SILK BUT EYE NOW ☒ How far away can you see?

Figure 9.2 A test of your span of conscious perception. Adapted from Foss and Hakes (1978).

consider the critical question of modelling the decoding and comprehension aspects of skilled reading.

Cognitive processes in word recognition

We have seen that typical adult reading rates are around 300-400 words per minute, about three times as fast as one can comfortably speak and around twice as fast as one can listen (and understand). It is clear therefore that reading is an efficient way of taking in information. Nonetheless, simple calculations suggest that it could in principle be very much more efficient. Assuming that we can see 18 letters – say three words – per fixation (four to the left, 14 to the right) and we can make five fixations per second, we should be able to read $3 \times 5 \times 60$ that is, 900 words per minute. Presumably, therefore, the upper limit on normal reading rate is that one cannot understand the three fixated words in 200 ms – one needs maybe 500 ms. The limits are therefore cognitive rather than sensory or motor.

READING AS TEXT COMPREHENSION

Interestingly, though there is no space to develop the theme here, for adult readers comprehension abilities do seem to be an important determinant of reading skill (Sticht, 1972). It would appear therefore that, except for special groups of readers such as dyslexic children, many adult reading difficulties may reflect comprehension difficulties. Consider the various factors known to be involved in text comprehension. First, we use our knowledge of the general syntactic and semantic patterns of the language to translate from words to meaning. Second, our general knowledge of the conventions of communication, such as the 'given-new contract' (Clark and Haviland, 1977) where speakers or writers attempt not to repeat information that the listener/reader knows, but make sure that new information is properly introduced, helps us to relate new information to old. Finally, general knowledge of the methods of communication and of text structure, with specific knowledge of the topic being discussed and the style of the speaker or writer, all help us to perceive the structure of the communication and to identify those aspects that are the most important.

Indeed, the goal of efficient communication is to extract the gist of what is being communicated. The rest of the message is just packaging to make the communication clearer. Consequently, it would be terribly inefficient to remember communications verbatim, all one needs is the gist. Interestingly, this is just what we do. Sachs (1967) found that even 25 seconds after reading a sentence, adults could not distinguish between the original sentence and another sentence with the same meaning but slightly changed syntax, whereas they could easily distinguish it from one with a different meaning. In other words, we try to remember the gist and dump the irrelevant information.

It is important to realize that there is more to reading than just reading speed and accuracy. There is considerable evidence that for many children and adults the learning of comprehension strategies may prove very beneficial for overall reading performance. Beck et al. (1982) trained children on semantic memory for a specific set of words that involved an attempt to increase the richness of the meanings of the words together with an attempt to improve the speed of mental access to the words. They demonstrated that this training programme led to substantial and lasting benefits not just for the words trained but also for reading and memory in general. We have also established that this type of training is effective even for dyslexic children (Fawcett and Nicolson, 1991). Emphasis on comprehension strategies should be an important component (but not the sole component!) of a reading support programme.

BOX 9.1 Different types of reading

There is no space here to pursue this theme, but from a self-help perspective it is critical to note that there is no substitute for good understanding of the *strategic* factors in reading. Study skills manuals emphasize the importance of using different types of reading for different purposes – **scanning** (up to 10 000 words per minute) to search for specific items of information in a text; **skimming** (800–1500 words per minute) to extract the main points of the text; normal reading (300–400 words per minute); and word-by-word reading of difficult text (say 150 words per minute). An effective reader may use all these strategies in reading a given passage. The PQ4R method (Thomas and Robinson, 1972) suggests that a student reading a textbook should use six phases: **Preview** (surveying the chapter to get an overview of the general topics and whether relevant) – skimming; **Questions** (deciding what information you intend to find out from the text); **Read** (reading carefully, trying to find out the questions you have asked yourself); **Reflect** (trying to understand the text as you read it, putting it into your own words, thinking of your own examples); **Recite** (after finishing the text, self-assess what you remember of it, especially those points relevant to your questions) – you might quickly scan the passage for points you were not sure of; and **Review** (recall the main points).

DECODING PROCESSES IN READING

The above sections have concentrated on the reading process and its components. We established that one of the difficulties in finding out why we do not read faster than 300–400 words per minute is that it is hard to measure what is happening in one's brain when reading. Attempts to solve this question have been of paramount importance for many cognitive psychologists and there has been considerable progress of late. We start with a classic 'model' of the processes involved in skilled reading. I think it is more of a description than a model myself, in that most of the details are missing. Nonetheless, getting a good description is the starting point of any scientific analysis.

THE DUAL- AND TRIPLE-ROUTE MODEL OF READING

One day a mib fell into the feg. He was so sup and tid that he cried. He said 'Chig'. Then he ran back to his dom. She said 'Oh stid' and gave him a reb lim drack.

Consider the above 'Jabberwock' type passage (taken from Fawcett and Nicolson, 1996), consisting of real words and nonsense words. Most of the words are familiar, but some are nonsense. There is general agreement about how words such as 'One' are read. The word is familiar (even though not a regular spelling). It will therefore have an entry in the reader's '**lexicon**' (this is a much used but poorly defined theoretical term intended to capture the fact that we must somehow have a 'store' of the words we know, with their spoken input representation (in terms of sounds); their spoken output representation (in terms of phonemes or even articulatory code); and presumably some indication of their semantics). Consequently, for a familiar word, its spoken output form can be accessed and it can then be pronounced and processed as though it had been spoken by someone else.

This lexical access route cannot work for nonsense words such as 'mib' because they have no entry in the lexicon. Nonetheless, even though a reasonably experienced reader has not seen 'mib' before, they should nonetheless be able to pronounce it. In order to do this, one must somehow translate the visual information (the graphemes) into articulatory information. This process is known as grapheme–phoneme translation (strictly, a phoneme is defined as the smallest unit of sound in the given language). Clearly, therefore, there must be at least two routes for speaking a written word, a lexical route (labelled Route 1 in fig 9.3) and a 'sub-lexical' letter-to-sound (grapheme–phoneme) route (labelled Route 2). This analysis (Rubenstein et al., 1971) was the underpinning for the celebrated 'dual route' model of reading (e.g. Coltheart et al., 1977). Finally, evidence from cognitive neuropsychology suggests that there are patients (with brain damage) who can pronounce familiar words, but cannot tell you their meaning. Furthermore, they cannot pronounce nonsense words and so their word pronunciation appears not to be via the sublexical route (Route 3). Consequently, it seems necessary to provide a triple route model, as shown in fig 9.3.

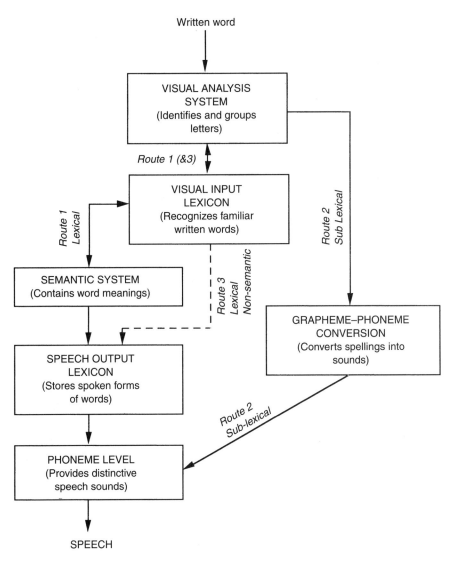

Figure 9.3 The dual- and triple-route models for reading aloud (after Ellis and Young, 1988).

CONNECTIONIST MODELLING OF PRINT-TO-SPEECH PROCESSES

There are several obvious limitations of the dual- and triple-route models. The main three limitations are, first, that it is descriptive rather quantitative, so it is difficult to test directly. Second, there is strong evidence that the lexical and sub-lexical routes are not independent. Consider the non-word 'yead'. This can be pronounced to rhyme with 'head' or 'bead'. Kay and Marcel (1981) showed that the way it is pronounced is affected by presentation of a previous word (e.g. bead). More surprisingly, Rosson (1983) primed a non-word by a word semantically related to the alternative pronunciation. For instance, 'louch' could be primed by 'feel' (cf. 'touch') or by 'sofa' (cf. 'couch'). Again, priming effects were found, confirming that the sub-lexical route is indeed affected by the current state of lexical processing. Third, there is no learning mechanism involved. Consequently, it is very hard to see quite how this architecture develops. It is also rather difficult to see why we should go to the trouble of building up an enormous set of letter–sound rules to cover the pronunciation of nonsense words when we already have the ability to pronounce all the words in our lexicon. Where do these rules come from?

One model that gets round all these difficulties with great elegance is the Seidenberg and McClelland (1989) distributed processing print-to-speech model. The system is a connectionist one with 400 orthographic (letter-string) units for input, 460 phonological (sound) units for output and 200 intervening (hidden) units. Words to be read are split into letter triples (for instance the word MAKE is split into the triples {_MA MAK AKE and KE_}, where _ is a beginning- or end-of-word marker) and presented to the orthographic units as input. The network processes the input and produces a sequence of phonological triples for output (for instance, the correct pronunciation for the input MAKE is /mAk/ and so the correct phonological (output) triples are {_mA, mAk and Ak} where A refers to the phoneme a in gave, etc.

Initially the network computes random pronunciations for letter strings presented to the orthographic units. However, the network can be 'trained' by presenting a succession of letter strings (input to the orthographic units), each followed by its correct pronunciation (to be compared with the output from the phonological units, thereby giving an 'error signal'). This error signal is then used to adjust automatically (via the backpropagation rule) the strengths of the links between units in the three layers so as to steadily increase the accuracy of pronunciation. Following training, the network is then found to make a reasonable job of pronouncing both words and non-words. In fact, following around 150 000 trials training on all 2897 uninflected monosyllabic English words with three or more letters, it resulted in very accurate pronunciation of words, with about 50-65 per cent correct non-words, which is good but not spectacular performance.

There has subsequently been a lively discussion of merits and demerits of rule-based modelling and connectionist modelling (e.g. Besner et al., 1990; Coltheart et al., 1993 criticize the Seidenberg and McClelland model and Plaut and McClelland (*see* Plaut et al., 1996) have developed a connectionist model that gives very much better reading of non-words and answers many of the points made by their critics). My feeling is that much of this is an artificial debate. Once a connectionist system has been trained, its performance can be reasonably well approximated as a collection of rather fuzzy rules. If one wishes to find the rules of the orthography (the traditional preoccupation of linguists), a rule-based representation is the appropriate one. If one wishes to understand how the representations are built from experience, the connectionist models seem the best way forward. (*See* Chapter 4 for a related discussion of connectionist models and language.) The connectionist models are not the last word on reading, in that there appears to be little correspondence between the specific training required for the models and the methods that children actually learn to read. Nonetheless, the overwhelming advantage of the connectionist models is that they have a learning method, make quantitative predictions and account for both routes within the same architecture.

Learning to read

This of course is the focus of intense interest in Western societies. There are league tables within cities, within countries and internationally of who is doing best. Tens of millions of pounds are spent on trying to improve children's reading.

There are a number of theories of the way that children learn to read. We only have space here to cover two of them, both classics of their kind and both highly influential for both psychologists and educationalists. The two theories to be considered are Frith's stage theory of reading and writing and Bryant and Goswami's causal model of reading development.

FRITH'S STAGE THEORY OF READING DEVELOPMENT

One of the standard methods of scientific enquiry is to attempt to split a long process into a set of stages, with clear transitions between the stages. Piaget's stage theory of child development (*see* Chapter 6) provides a classic example of the power of the approach and also of its limitations. Frith (1985) has provided a very plausible model of the stages of learning to read and spell and how they interact with each other.

The traditional developmental approach (*see* the Introduction) is based primarily on longitudinal (following a child's progress for several years) and cross-sectional (checking a group of children at one time) analyses of children's performance at various stages in learning to read. A key early study by Bradley and Bryant (1983) demonstrated that children who were not sensitive to rhyme and other phonological characteristics of words subsequently had difficulty in learning to read. Furthermore, if such children were given training in phonological awareness skills such as rhyme, they learned to read reasonably normally. Following this demonstration of the key role of phonological skills in subsequent reading acquisition, Frith (1985) proposed a three-stage model which consisted of the following three stages: logographic, alphabetic and orthographic.

- In the '**logographic**' stage children learn to read a few words as gestalten (i.e. as a single unit, a sight word).
- The next stage is the **alphabetic** stage, in which they learn the skills for decoding a word into single letters, which can then be combined into the appropriate sound using grapheme–phoneme conversion rules.
- Finally there is the **orthographic** stage, in which the child need not break down the word into single letters but need only break it down into a few orthographically standard chunks (letter sequences) which may be

spoken via letter-sequence to syllable–sound rules. Orthography refers to the rules of written English, including the use of prefixes, suffixes and morphemes (*see* Chapter 4).

For example, in the logographic stage, a child learns words such as 'the', their own name and words from their reading book (e.g. Sam, fat, pig etc.) by sight, maybe not even knowing the sounds of the individual letters making up the word. In order to get started, everyone has to have a basic vocabulary of sight words and many reading schemes attempt to build up a sight vocabulary of around 50 words by frequent repetition. Soon, however, it becomes necessary to learn the alphabetic principles – ways of reading a word that one does not already know. Here the traditional approach is to teach the single letter shapes (graphemes) and their sounds (phonemes) and to get the child to read them aloud one at a time: 'cat' to /c/ /a/ /t/ and then to blend the series of phonemes (cuh – ah – tuh) into a single sound /cat/. This involves considerable mental gymnastics!

More recent approaches (e.g. Goswami and Bryant, 1990) suggest that it is easier for the child to concentrate on the 'onset' and 'rime' of words. The onset of a syllable is the set of consonants before the first vowel (the onset of 'cat' is 'c'; the onset of 'train' is 'tr') and the rime is the rest of the syllable ('at' and 'ain' respectively). The advantage of using onsets and rimes is that one can learn rimes separately (e.g. by focusing on the word family 'at' – bat cat fat hat mat etc) and for simple words it is then easier to blend the resulting phonemes /c/ and /at/ go to /cat/ etc. These simple alphabetic principles do not scale up well to longer words, for which the principles of orthography are needed. Frith suggests that in the orthographic stage, children (and adults) are able to analyse words 'into orthographic units without phonological conversion', by recognizing strings of letters which 'can be used to create by recombination an almost unlimited number of words.' In other words, children move from a letter-by-letter approach to a letter-string-by-letter-string approach. The latter is clearly much more efficient and could also account for our ability to develop the sub-lexical route in the dual route models above. Finally (although not discussed by Frith) an adult reader might well develop essentially a logographic approach, in which their sight vocabulary might well expand to include almost all their reading vocabulary.

Frith also discusses spelling. She notes the surprising fact that some children are able to spell some words that they cannot read. Presumably the word in question (typically a simple word such as 'mat') is not in their logographic reading vocabulary, but can be constructed using alphabetic principles. This suggests that spelling (rather than reading) might be the causal skill underpinning the acquisition of the alphabetic stage. This led to the development of her 'six step' model for reading and spelling (fig 9.4). Note how spelling scaffolds the acquisition of alphabetic reading (2a to 2b), whereas reading scaffolds the acquisition of orthographic spelling (3a to 3b).

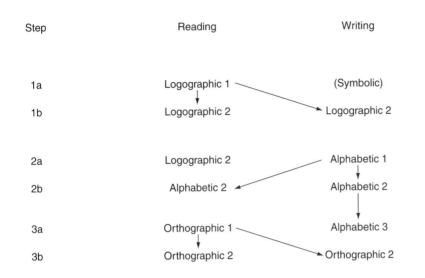

Figure 9.4 Frith's six-step model (Frith, 1985). Note: '1' signifies a very basic level of skill; '2' a more advanced level; and so on. Arrows have been added to indicate the way that reading and writing are thought to facilitate steps from one stage to another.

GOSWAMI AND BRYANT'S CAUSAL MODEL

On the basis of subsequent research, Goswami and Bryant (1990) argue that rather than progressing through a series of stages, much of a child's development involves just getting better at strategies that the child used right from the start. Furthermore, they consider it is more fruitful to look for causes for progression between stages rather than merely describing each stage and identified three hypothetical causal factors that facilitate progress.

- Pre-school phonological skills (such as rhyme and alliteration) provide the initial word attack skills and inference strategies that underlie the apparent transition from the logographic stage to the alphabetic stage and provide the basis for categorizing words by orthographic features (especially rime), as discussed above in Frith's model.
- The learning of the alphabetic script provides the basis for the skill of analysing the sounds of a word into phonemes that underlies the ability to spell words alphabetically. For instance, knowing that 'cat' is spelled 'c' 'a' 't' helps the child to analyse the sound /cat/ into its constituent phonemes /c/, /a/ and /t/. This skill only later transfers to the analogous reading skill and at this stage reading and spelling are relatively independent skills.
- Reading and spelling skills come together to provide mutual support for learning the many orthographic components of language. Later on in reading development, knowledge of orthographic rules such as 'ise' is pronounced with a long 'i', 'ate' is pronounced with a long 'a' and so on, allow the child to reason by analogy how to pronounce 'ite', 'ile', 'ate' words and consequently, by analogy, the entire set of 'silent e' pronunciation rules, thereby significantly enhancing the coverage of

their orthographic rules. Goswami (1993) has further developed their idea of the use of analogies.

A significant advantage of the Goswami/Bryant theory is that it does attempt to model not only what the stages are, but also what the causal factors are in allowing a child to move from one stage to the next. Their theory therefore goes beyond mere description towards a pedagogical theory. We argue below that the Bryant/Goswami theory provides an important integration of developmental and pedagogical approaches to reading, but that for completeness it needs to be augmented with the important concept of automaticity of the component skills. As we will see, one of the key requirements to effective learning of a complex skill is that the component skills are sufficiently fluent to allow them to be combined. Before this we will consider a special group of poor readers for whom phonological, alphabetical and automatic skills seem to be particularly difficult.

DISCUSSION POINT

What are the main differences between the models of Frith and of Goswami and Bryant?

Dyslexia and reading

Developmental dyslexia is defined as 'a disorder in children who, despite conventional classroom experience, fail to attain the language skills of reading, writing and spelling commensurate with their intellectual abilities' (World Federation of Neurology, 1968). In other words, children of average or above average ability, who for no obvious reason, write and spell very poorly. A typical estimate of the prevalence of dyslexia in Western school populations is five per cent, with roughly four times as many boys as girls being diagnosed. Dyslexia is therefore by far the most common of the development disorders. It has been assumed that the problems of children with dyslexia derive from impairment of some skill or cognitive component largely specific to the reading process and the consensus view (e.g. Snowling, 1987; Stanovich, 1988) is that the deficits are attributable to some disorder of phonological processing (e.g. the ability to split words up into their constituent sounds). Training in phonological skills (such as knowing about rhymes and ways of building up words from their sounds) is certainly one of the key requirements in helping dyslexic children learn to read better. In terms of Frith's model (see earlier), it would appear that dyslexic children cope pretty well with the logographic (whole word) stage of reading and spelling, but they have great difficulties acquiring the alphabetic principle (letter–sound regularities), probably because of lack of phonological skill. Consequently, they persist too long trying to learn words verbatim and cannot generalize to the orthographic rules.

It is established that if appropriate support is given at an early age, dyslexic children do seem to be able to learn to read reasonably well. One of the most frustrating aspects of dyslexia is that, given that dyslexia is currently defined in terms of reading deficit, for a formal diagnosis it is necessary to wait until a child is at least 18 months behind in reading. This consigns a dyslexic child to at least 18 months of failure in initial schooling, a traumatic experience that cannot help but leave serious emotional scars.

In any scientific analysis it is important to distinguish between cause, symptom and treatment. Phonological processing difficulties are an important symptom of dyslexia and phonological training is a valuable component of any remediation of the reading problems. However, it is possible that the phonological problems are not the underlying cause – they may be just one symptom of a deeper underlying cause. In a long-standing research programme, Angela Fawcett and I have been investigating the role of learning in dyslexia. Given the importance of automatization in acquisition of any skill and its known importance in reading, it seemed possible that difficulties in skill automatization might be involved. We tested dyslexic and matched control children on motor skills – skills with no phonological component and therefore a key discriminator between the theories. Clear deficits were found, even when the dyslexic children just had to stand still without wobbling. Interestingly, the difficulties showed up primarily under dual task conditions (for instance, when they had to count as well as balance), exactly as predicted by automatization deficit (Nicolson and Fawcett, 1990).

Our subsequent research has focused on two issues: first, attempting to identify the cause(s) underlying the difficulties in automatization and phonological skills; and, second, attempting to develop a screening test which can establish which children are at risk of dyslexia when they first go to school, thereby giving them immediate access to the extra support needed to help them to read. Research is still ongoing, but very promising results have been obtained. First, it appears that the underlying deficit may well be attributable, at least in part, to the cerebellum – the 'hind brain'. This structure is known to be involved in balance and motor skill and their automatization. Furthermore, recent evidence suggests that it is also centrally involved in development of a range of linguistic skills. Our recent research (Fawcett et al., 1996) indicates that many dyslexic children show the classic signs of cerebellar difficulty – problems in co-ordination and balance. A valuable applied product of this theoretical work is that, using phonological and naming tests known to cause problems for dyslexic children, together with tests of motor skill, we were able to develop the 'Dyslexia Early Screening Test' (DEST). The DEST is a simple 30-minute test which can be administered by a child's teacher when the child first starts school and will indicate whether the child is at risk of reading failure. This allows immediate support to be given (Nicolson and Fawcett, 1996).

Skill acquisition and reading

Consider the previous four sections – models of skilled reading, models of word recognition, theories of reading development and analyses of special readers. What do they have in common? Hardly anything! They are all looking at reading from a different perspective. Unfortunately, rather than seeing these perspectives as all legitimate viewpoints on a common problem, there is a tendency for theorists to dismiss other approaches to 'their' problem and to argue that theirs is the only fruitful approach. Let us conclude this chapter on a more positive note, attempting to integrate many of these perspectives within a more general framework, namely that of skill acquisition.

Humans have an innate predisposition to walk, to speak and to understand speech (this does not mean that such skills are 'hard-wired' and will emerge regardless of experience, but more that the combination of genetic endowment and learning abilities with a 'normal' environment for a human infant will lead to the emergence of these skills given sufficient time). (*See* chapters 1 and 4 for further discussion of innateness.) By contrast the ability to read is not innate, though presumably the ability to learn to read is. Consequently one might expect that study of skilled performance and skill acquisition would be of central relevance to the study of reading. Astonishingly, reading researchers have disregarded this approach. To their cost.

CHARACTERISTICS OF EXPERT PERFORMANCE

The influential cognitive psychologist Donald Norman, whose textbooks inspired a generation of psychology students in the 1970s, attempted to capture the characteristics of expert performance across a range of tasks. Consider the task of learning to drive. As one starts off, everything seems difficult. It is difficult to change gear at all, then it is difficult both to change gear and watch for traffic, we do not like to be asked a question when changing gear and so on. Later on the processes involved become automatic to the extent that one can even go on 'auto pilot', not being aware of having driven for a minute or two. On the basis of this sort of analysis Norman (1982) characterized expert performance as *smooth* – an expert performs with apparent ease, in an unhurried approach which is deceptively fast; *automatic* – an expert performs a task without having to think about it; *easy* – an expert needs to expend very little mental effort on the task and seems not to need to monitor their performance very carefully; and *routine* – for an expert the task just becomes routine – we just 'drive' in same way as we just 'walk'. It is no longer remarkable in any way.

We shall see later that this economy of effort through automatic processing is the hallmark of skilled performance in both motor skills and cognitive skills. We start with an influential characterization of the stages in learning a skill.

THE THREE STAGES OF SKILL LEARNING

My daughter Ellen has just learned to tie her shoe laces. The stages she went through are nicely described by Paul Fitts' analysis of the three stages in learning a simple motor skill (Fitts and Posner, 1967). The early or 'cognitive' stage involves initially understanding what the task is about and what to attend to and then using one's general skills making the first efforts to carry it out. For shoe laces this involves noting the initial and final arrangements, probably watching a parent do the operation, then using one's 'string handling' skills to attempt to do each operation in turn. The intermediate or 'associative' stage involves working out a method for actually doing the task. Here, Ellen goes through all the actions herself, learning more efficient ways of moving from one action to the next. Her performance is initially slow and error-prone and the final bows are loose. Nonetheless, the task is done. With further practice, her performance becomes faster and errors are eliminated. The late or 'autonomous' stage occurs after extensive practice and involves the escape from the need to attend consciously to the task – it has become automatic. At this stage one often loses conscious awareness of how the task is done. Do you end up pulling the right hand lace with your left hand or right hand? The only way to find out is either to imagine it or do it! This three-stage analysis has proved a reasonable description of the acquisition of a wide range of skills, including cognitive skills (Anderson, 1983). Fitts and Posner (1967) applied it to learning to fly an aeroplane and to learning telegraphy skills. When learning to fly the cognitive stage takes around 10 hours, but after that there are few major errors and performance gets gradually quicker and more automatic.

It may be seen that this three-stage model for skill learning tallies quite well with one's intuitions and it also fits in well with Norman's characterization of skilled performance. The idea of automaticity is at the heart of the development of expertise and the idea of somehow downloading the necessary calculations to some low level process independent of the need for conscious monitoring is clearly involved in the development of automaticity.

Learning complex skills such as reading

Most everyday skills, such as reading, or tennis, or car-driving are complex, in that the complete skill depends upon a range of sub-skills. It is clear that for fluent performance of the complete skill the sub-skills should be automatized, but one important question is whether each sub-skill should be automatized individually, in isolation (which is easier), or whether all the sub-skills need to be automatized in the context of performing the complete skill. Shea and Morgan (1979) provided a clear answer to this issue. Essentially the answer is that it is important *not* to train the sub-skills purely in isolation. If this happens there is a danger that the automatic method that the subject develops for the sub-skill might require some resources that are needed for performance of one of the other sub-skills and so, when one attempts to blend the sub-skills into the complete skill, there is interference between the sub-skills, preventing the complete skill from being performed efficiently. Therefore, in order to make sure that this interference will not arise, it is important to interleave sessions of the complete skill with automatization training on the sub-skills, so that the sub-skills are learned in a compatible fashion. This issue is known as that of 'part–whole' task training.

In summary, therefore, theoretical studies have suggested that we are able to automatize the components of *any* skill, as long as the training regime is appropriate. In particular, the training should be carefully designed such that it is consistent; the complete skill is interleaved with the individual components; and bad habits are not acquired. Automatization of the component skills allows more attentional resources to be deployed in the execution of the complete task, thereby allowing better and more adaptive performance (*see* Nicolson, 1998 for a review).

BOX 9.2 Motivation, enjoyment and feedback

Motivation holds the key to most human learning. It is common to distinguish between *intrinsic motivation,* in which the topic is interesting in its own right and *extrinsic motivation,* in which the motivation derives from some external source (e.g. a school requirement). Sometimes a change in focus can have marked effects upon motivation. A good example derives from children's recreational reading – quite frequently crazes sweep a school in which say World Cup cards providing dossiers on the various teams and their various players can be collected. These cards are a mine of written information and I estimate that my children spent well in excess of 200 hours collecting these cards and poring over the statistics therein recounted. At one stage my sons could not only tell me the names of all the players in each team in the UK Premier (soccer) League, but also also their height, weight, previous transfer fee and so on. Much (all right, some) of this activity was valuable reading practice that they would never undertake in a school context. This example demonstrates the power of 'ownership', that is, making a problem relevant to one's own interests. If the learner has a personal interest in a topic, motivation and success follow naturally. By contrast, if the learner cannot perceive the point of a topic, it is very difficult to make much headway. Furthermore, studies of failure (e.g. Holt, 1984) have often revealed a vicious circle, in which following repeated failures, a learner either adopts a passive learning strategy, or maybe some coping strategy which downplays learning at the expense of some more attainable goal (sport, disruption, truancy etc.).

There is also the concept of fun (Lepper and Cordova, 1992). Children (and adults) learn better if they are enjoying themselves. I'm

> afraid this critical insight seems to have been lost in most walks of life. If learning can be made fun, people will try harder, do better, come back for more and generally do better all round.

Review

We have now been all round the elephant, outlining five very different approaches to reading and summarizing their strengths and weaknesses. We now get to the difficult bit, where we try to integrate the different perspectives. I will use the multidisciplinary perspectives to address arguably the important issue in the reading and one that we have not yet discussed directly.

HELPING CHILDREN LEARN TO READ

There has been impassioned debate about the 'best' methods for teaching children to read. The collision between proponents of 'real books' and 'phonics' approach has been dubbed 'The Great Debate' in the US (Chall, 1967, *see also* Adams, 1990). This debate is misplaced. Reading is a complex skill and learning to read takes thousands of hours over many years. The real debate is how can we best help a child at a given stage of reading development to make progress. It is crucial for a child moving from the logographic stage to the alphabetic stage to have good support in phonics principles. It is crucial later on to give the child experience of real books, otherwise they will get so stultified by the didactic nature of phonics instruction that they just will not get the 'miles under the belt' to fully develop their word recognition modules. The debate is akin to saying: should we teach the child the backhand or the forehand? You need both to play a good game of tennis!

The limitations of both entrenched approaches to the reading debate does not mean that one should be indifferent to teaching method, that anything goes. Quite the reverse. Any reading support programme needs the following components.

Reading analysis

If a child is struggling (or even if not) we need a systematic method of getting a 'profile' of their performance (including performance fluency) on the key sub-skills. For the beginning reader a good procedure is described by Reason and Boote (1994), who identify three dimensions of skill, namely meaning, phonics and fluency and specify four stages for each of these three dimensions (*see* Table 9.1). Only when a performance profile is in place are we able to make an informed judgement of the appropriate reading objectives and thus the appropriate support programme. Consequently it is necessary for the cognitive, developmental and educational psycho-

Table 9.1 Four stages in learning to read (Reason and Boote, 1994, p. 32)

	Meaning	Phonics	Fluency
Stage 1 Early Development	Enjoys and joins in reading and discussion of stories Understands vocabulary of reading and writing	Recognizes rhymes and rhyming words Blends words into sounds Can play 'I-Spy'	Matches words by sight Matches letters by sight Identifies some words by sight
Stage 2 Beginning to read and write independently	Expects own reading to make sense Uses context and initial letters in working out meaning	Can read and write: single letter sounds words such as it, at, hat, sun, dog, lid, net, cup, red, bus	Reads some 100 words fluently from initial books
Stage 3 Becoming competent	Uses context to understand and predict meaning and to help with more complex phonics	Can read and write words with consonant blends (h*i*n*t*, *sp*lit), consonant digraphs (*sh*ip, *th*in), vowel digraphs (p*oo*l, r*ai*n), silent 'e' (b*a*k*e*, b*i*t*e*)	Extensive and increasing sight vocabulary from books that are read
Stage 4 Basic competences achieved	Context and phonological cues are used automatically in combination Selects books suitable to interests and needs	Reads and writes words with more advanced phonics: silent letters, longer word endings, polysyllabic words	Reads and writes all commonly used words with ease

logists to keep on trying to develop a full and systematic description of the processes involved in reading, the stages involved and the methods of facilitating progress from one stage to another.

Early diagnosis and support

Regardless of the adequacy of the support programme, early diagnosis of likely reading difficulty is crucial. In reading, as in most skills, 'a stitch in time saves nine'.

Reading as a skill

There are general rules for acquiring fluency in complex skills such as reading, as discussed above. Reading programmes ignore these at their peril. Key concepts are:

- *Automatization*. Sub-skills must be highly overlearned before they can provide solid building blocks for the next stages. Automatization is generally achieved only under consistent conditions and long practice with few mistakes. Nonetheless, practising sub-skills must not be undertaken in isolation, it is crucial to practise them in the context of the skill as a whole. One can only develop automaticity by doing it oneself, not by being told what to do. It may be worth emphasizing that automatization is important, but not an end in itself. Stultifying drills that destroy motivation to read do more harm than good – the key is to find methods of automatizing sub-skills while encouraging enjoyable reading.

- *Fun*. Skills acquired with fun are learned for free. Fun can be introduced externally by using a game format and immediate feedback on progress. It can also be internally generated by letting children play the reading game. Good readers really do enjoy reading. Get a good book at the right level and most children will enjoy it.

- *Ownership*. There is a world of difference between reading because one wants to and reading because the teacher wants one to. Ownership over the reading process can make the difference between perseverance and avoidance, between success and failure (*see* Box 9.2).

- *Importance of the teacher*. Different teachers have different methods of teaching reading. Most children will learn to read reasonably well almost regardless of the quality of the teaching. Those children who are at risk (for whatever reason) need sympathetic, targeted support from the teacher or Special Educational Needs co-ordinator.

- *Importance of the child's family*. Irrespective of the quality of teaching at school, it is known that the literacy of the child's home and the expectations and support given by the parents, are major determinants of whether or not an 'at risk' child will succeed or fail (Hannon, 1995). As Papert (1980) noted, children immersed in a culture will pick it up automatically – he argued that we need a 'Mathland' in which children could be immersed in order to learn mathematics. Equally, a child brought up in 'Bookland' where books are freely available and frequently used, has an enormous advantage over the same child brought up in a bookfree home. Unfortunately, the greater and greater hold of television (a medium inimical to literacy) makes Bookland homes rarer and rarer.

- *Importance of the child*. Over and above all the other factors, it is important to tailor the reading programme to each individual child, especially if they are at risk of failure. An individual approach allows the child's strengths and weaknesses, likes and dislikes, enthusiasms and hates, to be taken into account. Furthermore, if a child is dyslexic, a very much more systematic learning programme needs to be set in place.

We cannot conclude this section without a brief mention of the well-intentioned 'Literacy Hour' approach recently (1998) introduced to infant schools and junior schools throughout the UK. The basic requirement on every school is to provide, for every child, one hour per day of dedicated literacy support. This Literacy Hour is undertaken as a whole class activity, typically with the teacher using a 'big book' to explain various aspects of the reading process. This approach contrives to violate many of the above principles.

Chapter summary

In this chapter we have taken the strong line that it is necessary when considering a complex skill like reading to look at it from all angles. Theoretical psychology has a good deal to offer to apparently applied problems such as learning to read. Inevitably, we have not been able to offer definitive solutions to the problems either of how people read, how people learn to read, or how people can be helped to learn to read. This is an honest assessment of the current state of the art (and not just in reading!). It is one of the attractions of psychology that one is able to address some of the most important issues in education and society, providing new perspectives on old issues and suggesting new ways to tackle existing problems. It is hoped this short overview will motivate many readers to think deeply about reading and maybe to take up some of the references in the further reading because they want to find out more about it and perhaps make contributions to the further development of this crucial field.

Seminar questions

1. 'A skilled reader doesn't bother with phonological decoding, so all this stuff about learning the phonological skills is a complete waste of time. You are teaching children skills that actively obstruct skilled reading.' Criticize this statement.
2. 'I took a speedreading course and read *War and Peace* in two minutes. It's about Russia.' (Woody Allen.) Do you think it should be possible to read at 1000 words per minute and remember what you read? (Note: opinion is divided on the feasibility of speed reading at 1000+ words per minute.)
3. 'Reading and writing are just the visual forms of spoken language and so to understand reading you must first understand language.' Do you agree with this statement?

Further reading

READING AND EDUCATION

Funnell, E., Stuart, M. 1995. *Learning to read: psychology in the classroom.* Oxford: Blackwell. This includes a collection of accessible yet authoritative chapters giving the current UK education perspective.

READING AND COGNITIVE PSYCHOLOGY

Underwood, G., Batt, V. 1996. *Reading and understanding. An introduction to the psychology of reading*. Oxford: Blackwell. This provides a comprehensive overview of cognitive factors in reading and comprehension.

READING AND DYSLEXIA

Fawcett, A.J., Nicolson, R.I. (eds) 1994. *Dyslexia in children: multidisciplinary perspectives*. Hemel Hempstead: Harvester Press. This includes chapters written by experts in the field on phonological, visual and learning approaches to dyslexia.

READING AND SKILL ACQUISITION

Mackintosh, N.J., Colman, A.M. 1995. *Learning and skills*. London: Longman. This provides an accessible introduction to skill acquisition.

Part  3

ATYPICAL DEVELOPMENT AND DEVELOPMENT IN SPECIAL CIRCUMSTANCES

Growing and learning with sensory impairments

10

JULIE DOCKRELL AND NICOLA GROVE

Editors' preface

Up to now the chapters of this book have concentrated on the way that development occurs in typical children. However, in almost all these chapters there also has been a consideration of development which is not typical because of the characteristics of the children or of their environment. This reflects a theme that is often present in discussions of children's development, the way that the study of typical development can provide an important starting point for the study of atypical development, and the way that the study of atypical children can provide important information which is relevant to the study of typical development.

As you will discover in this chapter, the investigation of children with visual and hearing impairments can help us understand not only the ways in which the lack of these forms of sensory input affects development but also indicate the importance of these forms of sensory input to children's development. In this respect the chapter has a relevance to language development (*see* Chapter 4), cognitive development (*see* Chapter 6) and socio-emotional development (*see* Chapters 5 and 14). However, an important message from the chapter is that the study of these children is not the same as conducting a controlled study which deprives children of such inputs and keeps all other variables constant. It is emphasized that child development needs to be seen in a wider context where both caregivers and individuals make adaptations to new circumstances. In this chapter we see that the adaptations made by both families and the children themselves can, in some circumstances, bring about positive outcomes.

Introduction

Can you imagine what effect loss of sight or hearing might have on a child's experiences? In this chapter we consider the impact of such disabilities on cognitive skills, language development and social development. Children who experience sensory problems may develop in ways that are atypical. Their rate of development may be slow, or because different processes are used to achieve success on tasks their performance may differ from their hearing and seeing peers. Psychology has an important role to play in providing reliable and valid descriptions of developmental paths and in identifying the mechanisms which underlie different developmental trajectories.

Charting developmental progress is a complex endeavour. We cannot assume that simply because a child has a hearing problem or a visual impairment that they will develop in a similar fashion to other children with hearing or visual impairments. Individual functioning is the product of an interaction among a variety of biological, social and personal factors. Data from these children are useful in testing the extent to which theories and conclusions from typical situations are valid in more extreme circumstances (Burack, 1997). Such information is vital in the construction of adequate models of development. If, for example, we find that congenitally blind children acquired vocabulary at the same speed and in the same way as sighted children we would need to reconsider the central role given to joint visual attention in the acquisition of language. It is important to realise that, unlike the situation with learning disabilities (*see* Chapter 11) where cognitive processes are compromised, the effects of sensory impairment(s) may be indirect. To understand developmental paths our review pays attention to the developmental implications of:

- Variation in performance across different skills.
- Variation in performance across children.
- Variation in performance across levels of sensory loss.

Many children experience sensory losses. In most cases these losses are mild and have little direct effect on the children. However, a minority of children experience impairments with either vision or hearing that severely restrict their experiences.

Hearing impairments

Children who experience a hearing loss are not a unitary group. The children vary on a range of different dimensions. Moreover, we cannot predict the language or psychoeducational performance on the basis of hearing levels **alone**. In the discussion that follows, the term 'hearing impaired' will be used to refer to the population as a whole, whereas the term 'deaf' will be used when findings pertain more specifically to children with severe/profound hearing impairments. Other distinctions, for example between conductive and sensorineural losses, will be drawn where relevant.

BOX 10.1 Types of hearing loss and effects of these on perception

Types of loss

DISEASES OR OBSTRUCTIONS IN THE OUTER OR MIDDLE EAR CAUSE CONDUCTIVE HEARING LOSS

The passage of sound is impeded; the result being similar to putting cotton wool in your ears. Many kinds of conductive losses are amenable to medical or surgical treatment to improve or restore the hearing. Otitis media is a common form of conductive loss, in which the transmission of sound across the middle ear is impeded because the ear drum and ossicles are prevented by fluid from vibrating freely. One of the complicating factors about middle ear problems is that they can be fluctuating, so at one point a child appears to hear perfectly normally and at another does not respond.

SENSORINEURAL LOSSES

These are caused by damage of the hair cells or nerves in the inner ear; in these cases sounds are distorted rather than dampened.

MIXED

Mixed hearing losses occur when a child experiences a combination of a sensorineural loss and a conductive loss.

CENTRAL

Central hearing losses occur when there is damage to the areas which process sound in the central nervous system. In this case, the peripheral mechanisms may not be damaged, but individuals will not be able to make sense of what is heard.

Levels of loss

Regardless of the type of hearing loss a child's hearing test results are plotted on an audiogram which measures both the **intensity** and **frequency** of the child's loss. (*See* Table 10.1 and Figure 10.1).

Table 10.1 Levels of hearing loss (categories based on Webster, 1986)

Category	Loss (dB)	Impact
Normal	up to 25 dB	Minimal in adults
Mild	26–40 dB	Difficulties listening in noisy situations such as classrooms
Moderate	41–55 dB	Difficulties with normal conversation in quiet environments
Severe	59–90 dB	Need for amplification to process speech
Profound	> 90 dB	Limited and distorted speech sounds even with hearing aids

There are four key dimensions of hearing loss that need to be considered.

The type and degree of hearing loss

Box 10.1 describes the four types of loss that need to be distinguished. The extent of a loss refers to the intensity of sound required to elicit a response. Losses vary from mild to profound and are measured in decibels (dB). The decibel scale is logarithmic, this means that the actual difference between 100 dB and 120 dB is much greater than the difference between 20 dB and 40 dB.

Hearing loss is also measured in frequency; most vowels are low-frequency sounds, whereas consonants are usually high-frequency sounds. Since children can have different levels of loss across the frequencies, they can miss parts of words as well as whole words. Conductive losses tend to affect all frequencies or may be worse for low frequencies, whereas sensorineural losses vary across the frequency range. A child with a high-frequency loss would have difficulties hearing the beginnings and endings of words (for example, consonants such as **t** and **f**). A low-frequency loss would affect the processing of the sounds in the middle of words, which are often vowels.

Figure 10.1 Four audiograms reflecting differing levels of hearing. Reproduced with permission of J. Fossey, Somerset Education Authority.

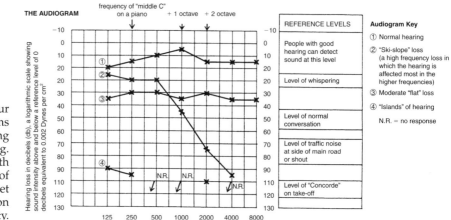

Associated factors

Hearing impairment is often associated with and caused by other problems, especially neurological problems. The presence of such additional problems makes assessment more complicated and calls into question research conclusions that are made from heterogeneous (i.e. mixed) populations. Generalizations about the sole effect of hearing loss cannot be made if the child also has a learning difficulty or a visual impairment.

The age of onset and identification of the hearing loss

The age at which a child experiences a hearing loss is critical for the development of later oral (i.e. spoken) language. Children who are born deaf (described as congenitally or prelingually deaf) never experience full oral language, and this affects their later language learning. In contrast children whose deafness occurs after they have started to master the oral language system (post-lingually deaf) will possess linguistic representations that can support their later language learning.

The child's language learning environment

Because they are unable to hear speech, these children tend to receive less linguistic information and are highly dependent on visual information. Hearing adults frequently have difficulty attuning themselves to the particular needs of young deaf children in social interaction (Wood et al., 1986).

PREVALENCE

Difficulties in definition and sampling mean that there is variation in the numbers of recorded cases of hearing impairment. Hall (1996) suggests that 1.3 children per 1000 experience a congenital sensorineural or mixed hearing impairment of > 40 dB, averaged over frequencies, in the better ear. About 90 per cent of children with congenital or early onset deafness are born into families in which both parents are hearing. A further 7 per cent of such children have one deaf parent and about 3 per cent have two deaf parents.

Conductive problems are more common than sensorineural losses. It has been estimated that at least 30 per cent of children suffer from some conductive loss in the first few years of life with a peak occurrence between 6 and 18 months of age. Children with other difficulties such as Down's syndrome and cleft palate are more prone to such problems. Approximately one in five children will have a mild hearing impairment at some point in their school career.

Cognitive skills and hearing impairments

There is a long history of assuming that deaf children are intellectually impaired. No sound evidence exists to support this contention for children with hearing impairments and no additional disabilities. Early studies continually placed deaf children's cognitive skills around two years behind their age-matched peers. For example, studies of cognition from a Piagetian perspective indicated that the hearing-impaired children showed marked delays in conservation and classification. However, many of these studies have been criticized on methodological grounds. They tend to rely on language comprehension thereby disadvantaging the hearing-impaired child even before the content of the task is encountered.

Recently researchers have asked whether hearing-impaired children have a different constellation of cognitive skills. Marschark (1993) has argued that because hearing-impaired children focus on the visuo–spatial channel they may have improved visual perceptual abilities, but poorer sequential memory. The evidence to support this is contradictory (Todman and Seedhouse, 1994; Das and Ojile, 1995). However, short term memory performance is inversely related to the extent of hearing loss: the larger the loss, the poorer children are on these tasks. As with hearing children, less successful performance on memory tasks is also linked to the use of meta-memory and the executive strategies used in planning, monitoring and evaluating (Rodda et al., 1993). It is important to consider the ways in which children with different developmental experiences solve tasks that are presented in appropriate formats.

When establishing whether hearing-impaired children lag behind or follow different cognitive pathways it is important to consider the child's learning environment. Even when deaf and hearing children have equivalent non-verbal IQs, hearing-impaired children still lag behind their peers on academic-related tasks. To some extent this can be explained by their poorer language skills (see below), but it is also important to consider the key role of environmental and educational factors (*see* Nunes and Moreno, 1998). The strongest data in support of the role of environmental factors comes from studies of deaf children with deaf parents. Deaf children of deaf parents have virtually equivalent developmental patterns, apart from oral language, to their hearing peers. These results highlight the importance of contextual factors and the availability of appropriate modes of communication to support the child's development (Zweibel, 1987 Marschark, 1993).

Language development in children with hearing impairments

Sign is the natural medium of language for deaf people, but until the 1970s it was viewed as essentially gestural and pictorial, and hence not an appropriate medium for education. However, since then research has established that sign languages are linguistically structured, with a vocabulary and a distinctive grammar, organized on visuo–spatial rather than auditory–vocal principles (Kyle and Woll, 1985). There is increasing recognition that pupils with hearing impairments need to develop their skills in the modalities of both sign and speech and that sign language is best learned from adults who are fluent users (Marschark, 1997).

DISCUSSION POINT

Consider why a child with a hearing impairment might need to develop skills in sign and speech.

Studies of language development in children with hearing impairments have been undertaken with various groups: children with conductive or sensorineural losses acquiring oral language; children acquiring sign language, either from deaf parents who are native signers, or from hearing parents who are novice signers. The first set of studies we will consider are those which focus on early communicative exchanges between carers and children with hearing impairments. We then go on to discuss speech development, and sign development.

EARLY COMMUNICATION

Communicative exchanges with children who have sensorineural losses tend to differ from those with hearing children. They often receive less linguistic information simply because they are unable to hear all the speech directed to themselves and other people. Mothers seem to speak less to their hearing-impaired children and use atypical intonation patterns so that the quality of these children's language experiences is different to that of their hearing peers. For example, in the early years carers may talk through or ignore early babbling; in later years there may be 'vocal clashes' when parent and child speak simultaneously (Gregory and Mogford, 1981). These different interactional styles have been described as dominating and controlling by some researchers. Alternatively, some strategies may be constructive adaptations to the child's impairment – for example, it may be necessary to use direct imperatives rather than descriptions and explanations to get clear messages about safety across to children whose understanding of speech is poor. These studies suggest that children specifically need language experiences that involve interaction (*see also* Chapter 4). Children with conductive losses also experience different communication exchanges. Wallace et al. (1996) investigated children with chronic otitis media. They found that children who experienced more directives and fewer enquiries from their parents, scored more poorly on measures of expressive language than similar children whose parents used more interactive styles of communication.

SPOKEN LANGUAGE (ORAL) AND PHONOLOGY

In children with moderate to severe hearing impairments, oral language skills are highly variable. Although many do benefit from intensive speech training, a large number fail to develop intelligible oral communication, or effective literacy skills (Quigley and Paul, 1987). Children with severely impaired hearing have a delay in oral language onset and they learn auditory–vocal language slowly. Their language can be 2–3 years behind that of typically developing children, with smaller vocabularies, delayed syntax and delayed articulation, even after substantial oral training (Meadow-Orleans, 1987). Yet degree of hearing loss does not appear to correlate very precisely with oral language skills. For example, in the study by Levitt et al. (1988) there was a slight reduction in language skills as the loss increased from 40 dB to 80 dB, and above the level of 115 dB, there is a ceiling effect but age of intervention was the best predictor of later language skills. However, severity of hearing loss is associated with one aspect of language, the level of speech intelligibility.

Conductive losses vary in severity and duration and it is difficult to be precise about the effects on oral language. Moreover, conductive losses are associated with other measures of disadvantage, such as poor housing, which are in turn associated with slower development of language and poorer academic achievement. This makes the interpretation of the studies difficult. Current evidence suggests that when there is early onset of otitis media, and the problems are severe and recurrent, delays in spontaneous speech and the development of articulation may occur. Children also tend to display a reduced number of consonants and a predominance of vowels. Language scores may still fall within the average range but they will be depressed in comparison to the norm (Friel-Patti and Finitzo, 1990). The pattern of development is complex and may contribute to developmental language disorders (Friel-Patti, 1992) especially if there are other factors such as peri-natal hazard (Bishop and Edmundson, 1986) and multiple episodes of middle ear infection in the first year of life (Friel-Patti et al., 1982).

For children with sensori-neural losses, the situation is both more complex and more severe. The onset of vocal babbling in hearing-impaired children is delayed in comparison to hearing infants. The vocalizations sound similar in the early stages, but by 10 months there is clear evidence of an effect of auditory deprivation. Congenitally deaf children find it difficult to perceive and produce speech, and to monitor their output, and their speech is often hard to understand (Bench, 1992). The problems include omissions, substitutions and mis-articulations of consonants, insertion of extraneous sounds, and particular difficulties with vowel production. Pitch, intonation and the co-ordination of breathing and speaking are also likely to be affected. These problems can also affect the speech of children whose deafness is post-lingually acquired (Oster, 1995; Parker and Rose, 1990).

Careful studies have shown that severely and profoundly hearing-impaired children can build up representations of speech sounds, although the acquisition process is slow. The actual processes of phonological development appear broadly similar to the norm (Mosford, 1988). The significant difficulties hearing-impaired children have with speech intelligibility and in reading appears to reflect the late acquisition of phonological representations, rather than a total absence of such representations (Hanson et al., 1983). Intelligibility of speech is linked not only to the extent of the hearing loss, but the use the child makes of residual hearing, the effectiveness of speech amplification and the availability of visual cues to the formation of speech sounds, on which the deaf child is highly dependent (Oster, 1995).

Vocabulary

On the whole the receptive **oral** vocabulary scores for of deaf children are significantly reduced in comparison to their hearing peers. Even children with the mildest delays can experience a 1–3 year gap in comparison to their age-matched peers (Davis et al., 1986). Hearing-impaired children use fewer words across all different form classes such as verbs, nouns, prepositions and so forth. There is some evidence that the children's vocabulary is not simply delayed but seems to differ in certain features, e.g. there are specific problems with terms for *time* and *quantity*. It is not yet clear whether these problems result from a lack of experience, the type of lexical input, a difficulty with forming adequate phonological representations of the lexicon, or difficulties grasping the relationship between word and referent. Gilbertson and Kahmi (1995) examined the ability of 20 hearing-impaired youngsters to learn novel words. They found that degree of hearing loss was not related to word learning ability, indicating that the problems were not specific to grasping the relationship between word and referent. Further support for this conclusion comes from studies which show that vocabularies are successfully acquired in sign by severely and profoundly deaf youngsters. The problem appears to be specific to **spoken** words.

Syntax

Deaf children develop similar syntactic structures in spoken language to hearing children, but more slowly. Performance varies considerably, but children tend to have difficulties in the use of grammatical morphemes such as auxiliaries (e.g. can, should, will) and past tense markers ('park' instead of 'parked'). Children may also fail to respond to negatives. These difficulties may be related to a failure to perceive words. For example the statement 'Matthew is not happy' may be perceived as 'Matthew is happy'. There are suggestions that such difficulties lead to adaptations, which in turn affect the child's response. Bishop (1983) analysed the performance of prelingually profoundly deaf children on the *Test of Reception of Grammar* (TROG) and found that the children were generally delayed. However, she also found that they adopted systematic strategies for decoding sentences that are not present in hearing children. For example, some children attended only to the content words, which could be an adaptive way of dealing with imprecise speech information. This strategy resulted in significant difficulties when meaning depended on subtler aspects of the language system.

ACQUISITION OF SIGN LANGUAGE

There is compelling evidence that deaf children, born to deaf parents who are fluent sign language users, fully develop their linguistic potential to sign (Bonvillian, 1999; Volterra and Erting, 1990). However, the majority of deaf children are born to non-signing hearing parents, and even among those born to deaf parents, a significant number will not be receiving totally fluent sign language. This is because so many deaf people received an oral education, learned signs relatively late in life, and never have fully mastered its complexities. Nowadays there is a recognition of the need to provide sign input as early as possible for children whose hearing impairments are severe enough to prevent adequate perception of speech. Oral language can be provided in parallel, or can be taught as a second language once the primary language (sign) is secure.

Most children of deaf parents learn to sign with their parents, who provide linguistic and communicative role models for their children. They make more use of facial expression in communication, a visual cue that is readily picked up (Meadow-Orleans et al., 1987). Deaf mothers are also skilled at managing the problem of divided attention (Wood et al., 1986). Whereas the hearing child can simultaneously look at an object and listen to their mother speaking, the deaf child has to shift visual attention from the object to their mother's signing to perceive the linguistic input. A variety of strategies are used to help the child perceive sign language, for example by moving signs into the child's visual field, or signing on the child's body. Hearing mothers are less successful with these strategies, with the result that their child often misses what is being communicated - (Harris et al., 1989).

In general, the major milestones of sign language seem to emerge at a similar time to those of spoken language (Meier and Newport, 1990). First signs appear slightly earlier than first words, but sign combinations, like word combinations, appear during the second year. Complex grammatical structures such as the acquisition of verb agreement, semantic relations and inflectional or derivational morphology emerge during the pre-school years, but full mastery of linguistic structures, with sign as with spoken language, is not complete until early adolescence. The evidence from the signing skills of deaf youngsters therefore supports the view that the children have an intact grammatical system.

For children who are acquiring sign from non-native users (i.e. those parents, whether deaf or hearing, who have limited skills in signing) the picture is complicated. Swisher (1984) found that many mothers provided only partial language input in sign, whereas Spencer (1993) found that the sign production rate of children was related to that of their mothers. Bilingual programmes, where fluent sign language input is provided by a skilled deaf person, and English is taught as a second language, appear to result in higher levels of linguistic and academic achievement (Gregory and Hindley, 1996).

Learning to sign early has important consequences for later signing competence. By school age, if children have not developed good signing skills, there is evidence that their acquisition of both sign vocabulary and syntax is likely to be delayed, compared to that of native sign users, or hearing children using spoken language (Kyle, 1990, quoted in Gregory and Hindley, 1996). Furthermore, the age children start to sign has a lasting effect. Mayberry and Eichen (1991) studied a group of individuals who had been signing for over 20 years. The group was subdivided into three – early acquisition, teenage acquisition and adult acquisition. Those in the group who had been signing since early childhood were more competent in syntax, semantics and morphology than those in the other two groups.

WRITTEN LANGUAGE

A large proportion of young people with severe or profound hearing impairments never read well enough to obtain information from textbooks, newspapers or instruction manuals, and their writing skills are also severely limited (Quigley and Paul, 1984; Harris and Beech, 1992). Reading demands the ability to link the sounds of words with their written representations, and deaf children unsurprisingly have difficulty in this area. Assessment of literacy skills inevitably involves assessment of English, so that the children are doubly disadvantaged. Some apparent errors in written English which are seen as resulting from deafness may in fact be evidence of interference from one language (sign) to another (English) (Maxwell, 1990; Gregory, 1997). Deaf children are likely to need different teaching strategies to hearing children if they are to develop good levels of literacy (Hirsch Pasek 1987; von Tetzchner et al. 1997).

The social and emotional development of deaf children

The socio-emotional difficulties that are experienced by children with hearing impairments can be understood in two rather different ways. It used to be thought that deafness was inherently associated with immature patterns of social interaction. Recent research, however, suggests that the fundamental problem is not the hearing loss *per se*, but the resulting communication difficulties that profoundly affect the quality of social experiences for the child with a hearing impairment. There is a considerable body of research to demonstrate that, in general, deaf children and deaf adults are less emotionally mature, more impulsive and more likely to have behavioural difficulties than their hearing peers (Marschark, 1993; Vostanis et al., 1997). However, most of the research has been carried out with deaf children of hearing parents: deaf children who are native signers appear better adjusted emotionally (Montanini-Manfredi, 1993), irrespective of their level of hearing loss (Preisler et al., 1997). Montanini-Manfredi and Fruggeri (1978) found that the level of psycho-social adjustment in children was related to maternal acceptance of deaf-ness, and the extent to which parents employed flexible and reciprocal communication strategies. For adults, difficulties are often compounded by the frustrations they face in the workplace and social contexts, where bullying can be rife, opportunities for interaction limited, and the jobs likely to be unstimulating and unsuited to their abilities (Gregory et al., 1995).

ATTACHMENT

Early attachment between parents and infants is likely to be severely affected by hearing loss. One important reason is that deaf children fail to pick up associations between facial expressions and vocal tones that carry affective meaning (Spelke and Cortelyou, 1981). Several researchers have suggested that deaf children are less likely than hearing children to develop secure attachments to their mothers (e.g. Schlesinger and Meadow, 1972; *see* Chapter 5). However, Marschark (1993) suggests that disrupted patterns of attachment are due to difficulties in early communication rather than a failure to bond.

EMOTIONAL DEVELOPMENT

Deaf babies produce a range of facial expressions similar to hearing babies by 12 months of age. However, Odom et al. (1973) found that deaf children aged between seven and eight years found it difficult to match facial expressions with the appropriate situation in a picture identification task. This may be because the young deaf child will not have experienced the same effortless association between an emotion and its verbal correlates. Explanations offered to deaf children by non-signing adults are inevitably simple and concrete, making it hard for them to grasp the connection between an event and its antecedents or consequences, as the following quotation from a parent makes clear:

> I mean, you can't say, like when Janet (his sister) gets older, we'll say 'Now you won't touch the fire because it will burn. Nasty. Hurts'. But all you say to Stephen is say 'No' and that's it. You just can't explain why. It's horrible. (Gregory, 1995).

The result is that deaf children have far less experience of developing their understanding of the effects of their own and others' behaviour through discussions and negotiations. Parents of deaf children are more likely than those of hearing children to be dominant and intrusive in interactions (Marschark, 1993), and to use physical punishment rather than other sanctions (Gregory, 1995), with possible negative consequences for the development of autonomy and self-esteem. It is unsurprising therefore that deaf children may show delays and difficulties in taking roles (Kusche and Greenberg, 1983) and moral reasoning (Couch, 1985). The fact that deaf children and adults tend to be impulsive, show frustration and lack internal 'loci of control' (Hindley, 1997) can be attributed both to long-standing problems in understanding events and interactions, and to a lack of the continuous experience of verbal mediation, in schools, homes and playgrounds, that contributes to a hearing child's dawning understanding of the complex relationships between intentions, behaviour and sequelae (Denmark, 1994). However, it appears that appropriate intervention may help to remediate these difficulties. Greenberg and Kusche (1997) report the success of a programme designed to teach problem solving, self-control and empathy to deaf children. The increased use of signing as a first language for deaf children may also preclude the development of many emotional problems (Marschark, 1997).

FRIENDSHIP

Again, most studies on the friendship patterns of deaf children and teenagers have been carried out with children of hearing parents, who have limited experience of sign. There is evidence to suggest that young deaf children spend less time than hearing children in co-operative play with peers, perhaps because of the difficulty of dividing attention between the environment and each other, and perhaps because of reduced knowledge of the skills of social interaction (Lederberg, 1993). Young deaf children seem to show similar patterns of peer interaction to hearing children, using a variety of non-verbal strategies to communicate (Gregory, 1995). However, by school age, the difference between children with high and low language levels (whether oral or sign) is increasingly apparent.

As children get older, their play becomes more dependent on language – for example, imaginative play or rule based games. Even deaf children with good linguistic skills use less language in play than hearing children (Lederberg, 1993). Children whose programmes are exclusively oral (and by implication, whose language is delayed) tend to be more disruptive and aggressive in play, whereas those who sign and have higher language levels show more co-operative play with peers. Deaf children tend to be left out of games with hearing children (Gregory, 1995), and this may be exacerbated by the natural protectiveness of their parents, which restricts their freedom to meet friends in locations other than the home or school. Lederberg et al. (1987) studied patterns of friendship in school age children and concluded that although they formed both temporary and long-term friendships, as did hearing children, the relationships of deaf children were more fragile and tended to lack stability.

The most detailed information about deaf adolescents comes from the series of interviews of 90 deaf young people carried out by Gregory et al. (1995). There was wide variation in the backgrounds, cognitive and linguistic ability of the youngsters, but the findings again indicated that deaf children with significant hearing loss who had only been exposed to oral input suffered socially by comparison with signers. Those with less effective communication skills in either modality were the most isolated. Amongst those with good communication, the pattern of relationships varied. Some young people identified and interacted predominantly with deaf people, others used speech and had mostly hearing friends. Others were able to relate to both groups. Interestingly, in view of the research quoted above by Lederberg and colleagues, parents tended to perceive their children's friendships as unstable, whereas the perception by the young people of their own relationships was much more positive.

The inescapable conclusion from a review of the literature on the socio-emotional development of deaf children is the cardinal importance of establishing good language and communication skills, in both sign and speech. Most of the families interviewed in Gregory's study saw sign language as important, and wished that they had learned about it earlier, if necessary by overruling professionals who had counselled against it. Both the young people and their families also regarded speech as important. This suggests that a bilingual approach, which seeks to develop both languages in parallel (Knight, 1997) may be the option most likely to result in a favourable outcome for the deaf child.

DISCUSSION POINT

Before reading the next section list the ways in which experiencing a visual impairment for a child may differ from the problems experienced with a hearing impairment.

Visual impairments

Problems with vision can be subdivided into two categories (a) serious defects likely to cause a disabling impairment of vision ranging from partial sight to complete blindness and (b) more common and usually less incapacitating problems including squint, colour blindness and so forth. In this section, we are concerned with the first of these two groups. In general the term 'blind' is used for children who have no vision or only limited light perception, whereas the term 'severely visually impaired' is used when the child has a minimal amount of vision, e.g. the ability to distinguish contours and colours. Visual impairment is rare, with an incidence of between 2–5 per 10,000 (DHSS, 1988). Visual impairments have some similarities with hearing impairments. First, both lie on a continuum; no sharp delineation can be drawn between a visual loss, which is disabling and one that is not. Second, the age of onset varies and even a few months of visual experience can make an important difference to a child. Furthermore, even some residual vision can provide significant additional information.

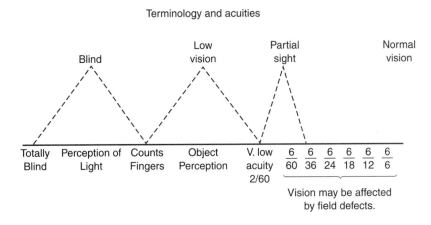

Figure 10.2 Levels of visual functioning of pupils with impaired sight.

Visual impairments are measured by acuity and field defects (Figure 10.2). Acuity involves both the sharpness and clarity of vision, it indicates how well a person is able to separate adjacent visual stimuli. The size of the field of vision represents the area that a child can see when looking straight ahead. Box 10.2 describes some common visual problems and their implications for the child's perception.

BOX 10.2 Impacts of visual impairment

Visual problem	Impact
Myopia – shortsightedness	Problems with distance vision
Hypermetropia – longsightedness	Blurred near vision
Astigmatism	Blurred vision, possible confusion of letters and numbers

---

Both within-child and situational factors will influence a child's use of sight. These factors include the child's experiences, motivation, needs and the expectations that are placed upon them (Barraga, 1976). Thus, children with comparable levels of visual acuity may use their sight differently. Yet the child's current level of visual functioning is also an important factor in how he or she responds to their environment and the ways in which intervention and support can be managed.

A wide range of problems can affect a child's visual status. Many of these causes are associated with other difficulties. In an RNIB survey (1994) more than half of the children were found to have one or more additional disability, including impaired hearing, specific language problems, physical disabilities and learning difficulties. The survey also suggested that those children with poorer sight were more likely to have additional impairments, especially in the areas of communication, and cognitive functioning. These additional problems make it difficult to draw conclusions from research where children's profiles are not clearly specified conclusions (*see*

Lewis and Collis, 1997). Furthermore, given the rarity of visual impairment, studies are often compromised by small samples, differing levels of visual acuity, other confounding disabilities and the complicating factor of prematurity.

Cognitive skills and visual impairments

The seminal work of Fraiberg (1977) alerted investigators to the experiences of blind children and the ways in which these might have an effect on developmental trajectories. Some authors have argued that infants who are born blind must necessarily follow a different developmental route yet others have argued that the absence of vision does not dramatically reduce the child's capabilities (Fogel 1997; Landau, 1997). The question of whether there are fundamental cognitive differences or simple delays still remains (Andersen et al., 1993; Dunlea, 1989). The absence of vision does not appear to dramatically reduce cognitive capabilities. When children with associated difficulties are excluded, children with visual impairments reflect the general range of intellectual abilities. The data that do exist indicates that on the whole children with some visual function are at an advantage in their cognitive development to those who are completely blind (Warren, 1994) apart from assessments of digit span (Hull and Mason, 1995). It appears that congenitally blind children have a particular advantage with digit span tasks, though even a small amount of sight removes the advantage. This advantage may well be associated with the children's enhanced skills at dealing with sequential information.

There is, however, little doubt that there are subtle differences resulting from the lack of experience with visual stimuli. It is precisely because vision offers continuity and detailed information about the child's surroundings that it can be seen as a potent force in early learning. Visual information provides an important incentive for the child's early explorations of the world. Without the immediacy of vision the child must search out information and the information that is received is sequential in nature, rather than simultaneous. Much of the work investigating the impact of visual impairments has focused on the child's ability to develop representations and form concepts and the ways in which these processes may affect language development. For example, observational studies have demonstrated that visually impaired children experience difficulties in sorting objects into groups. Landau (1983) argues that if children do not have the relevant experiences to develop concepts this restriction in conceptual structure will limit the acquisition of the relevant vocabulary.

Much of the empirical work on cognitive skills has used a Piagetian framework (Warren, 1994) and particular attention has been paid to children's difficulties in establishing object permanence (Dunlea, 1989; Bigelow, 1996). In general, blind children are delayed in their acquisition of object permanence. In many ways this is not surprising. Visually impaired children are deprived of a range of experiences that contribute to the acquisition of the object concept. Representations of objects or space achieved through the sensory modalities other than vision may be less detailed, accurate, precise or continuous and may make greater demands on recall, e.g. objects that emit sounds (such as the bell on a microwave oven or a TV set) are not always graspable and explorable. Fraiberg points out that the children in her sample experienced delays 'in the evolving forms of mental representation, the concepts of time and causality, and in self-representation and in the construction of the world of permanent objects' (1977: 254). Rather than indicating any inherent conceptual limitation in children with visual impairments, the delays in object concept acquisition and other Piagetian milestones highlight the salience of visual experience for the abilities under investigation (Webster and Roe, 1998). Reduced opportunities to explore the surrounding environment result in a reduced knowledge base to support further cognitive and linguistic development. However, when there are appropriately designed training and assessment procedures for Piagetian tasks, lack of visual experience is not a barrier to successful performance (Stephens and Grube, 1982).

Studies of memory, attention and cognitive strategies in the visually impaired have not received much direct attention from research. To date no inherent differences in capabilities have been detected, rather preferred strategies seem to develop as a result of the typical ways that children gain their primary information. For example, in the development of spatial cognition, if visual impairment leads children to neglect external cues, they will learn less and know less about the directional connections between external cues. This, in turn may strengthen the preference for strategies derived from the remaining modalities (Millar, 1994).

There is a clear need for more systematic study of the patterns of cognitive performance of blind children. Much of the work to date emphasizes the role of the environment in affording opportunities to learn about the world (see Fogel, 1997). If these data were complemented with analyses of the children's systematic search strategies for exploration through touch, it would enhance our understanding of the children's skills and allow an analysis of more general cognitive processes across modalities.

Language development in blind children

Blind children may be particularly sensitive to the language input they receive since they are so reliant on it. For a sighted child, oral input is only one of several sources of information they receive. There are differences of opinion concerning the impact of visual impairment on patterns of language development. It is not clear from research to date whether language follows normal, delayed or different pathways (Webster and Roe, 1998). The conflicting findings may be due to a number of factors: the inclusion in early studies of children who had associated learning difficulties; a lack of distinction between the initial stages of acquisition and later stages, and a reliance on single standardized measures which fail to capture subtle differences in language development, creating the impression that language is similar to that of typically developing children.

EARLY COMMUNICATION

A number of studies have documented how signals provided by the severely visually impaired child to carers may differ from those provided by sighted children. The children are described as having a limited repertoire of communicative behaviours, bland facial expressions and an absence of expressive behaviours. Blind babies do not use the communicative gestures such as pointing, or referential eye gaze that are so important in signalling the intentions of sighted babies (Preisler, 1997). Instead, they may use idiosyncratic tiny movements, such as head shifts, which are difficult for adults to pick up. In addition, a behaviour described as 'stilling' is reported. 'Stilling' refers to cases where a child actually stops what they are doing completely. Stilling can be interpreted by carers as a lack of interest. In fact, it may be a strategy to increase attention to auditory stimuli, and thus an indicator of interest. Such behaviours are thought to have implications for carers' responsivity. Research by Baird and colleagues (1997) confirm this conclusion. The visually impaired infants in their study displayed few behaviours that mothers considered meaningful. Furthermore, their results indicated that even those behaviours that were displayed by the blind infants provided the mothers with fewer messages. So not only were the babies emitting fewer signals, but even those signals they were emitting appeared to be interpreted in restricted ways.

The response of carers to blind infants also appears to differ in subtle ways from the norm. When carers talk to sighted children, comments and questions are used to follow up the naming of objects, people and events and introduce new information. By contrast, parents of blind children seem to concentrate on the labels themselves ('that's a dog: say dog'), and do not elaborate on the topic. This may make it difficult for the child (a) to build up representations of the concept, lacking all the visual contextual cues, and (b) to continue the conversation. It appears that carers often fail to sustain interactions with visually impaired children. Fewer interactions will result in limited opportunities to engage in conversation and thereby limit the children's opportunities to develop the necessary discourse skills. Researchers have observed differences in the conversational patterns and responses of blind and sighted children. Specifically:

- Blind children contribute fewer utterances to the overall conversational exchanges.
- Parents and teachers tend to be directive, using imperatives, and asking questions that test knowledge or understanding, rather than developing the conversation.
- Parents are less likely to respond contingently to the child's utterances. (Andersen et al., 1993; Kekelis and Prinz, 1996; Webster and Roe, 1998)

It does not necessarily follow that because patterns of interaction are different, they are necessarily deficient. Caretakers do often establish a successful framework for language development by combining sound, touch, rhythm and movement to support verbal interactions (Fraiberg, 1977). Further, some researchers have argued that mothers predict the children's language levels and respond to these by pacing their language input and providing repetitions and rephrasings. These data emphasize the role of the context in mediating the development of communicative competence and highlight the importance of a careful analysis of the carers' input in relation to the needs of the child.

EXPRESSIVE LANGUAGE AND PHONOLOGY

Since blind children can hear everything that is said to them, it is not immediately apparent why they should have difficulties in developing spoken language. However, there are a number of studies that suggest that subtle differences and delays do occur, particularly early in development. For example, Preisler (1997) discusses a longitudinal study of the development of ten congenitally blind children, the majority of whom were delayed in their acquisition of first words, word combinations and conversational language. For most children with visual impairments, these early language difficulties have resolved themselves by around the age of five years (Webster and Roe, 1998), but some difficulties may persist, and it is not clear what the long-term implications are for learning and social interaction.

Mills (1988) carried out a detailed study of the development of phonological skills of a number of visually impaired youngsters. The children's development appears slower, and follows a slightly different pattern than that of sighted children. Her careful analysis suggests that the children make more errors in production with sounds that have a visible articulation, such as *m* or *p*. However, there appear to be no long-lasting effects on the visually impaired child's ability to communicate.

VOCABULARY

Several researchers have investigated the vocabulary development of visually impaired children. Again, we find a number of contradictory reports. If we consider the data from a comparatively large sample (McConachie and Moore, 1994) there is evidence of a delay in the initial use of vocabulary. However, once started, the children seem on the whole to make rapid progress.

Vocabulary acquisition provides a good example of the subtler aspects of development. First, the content of blind children's vocabulary is different. Blind children seem to use more terms for social interaction, (sorry, excuse me) and words referring to their own actions, and fewer adjectives than typically developing children (Bigelow, 1987). There are also specific differences in the way that they acquire word meanings. The children use fewer general nominals, such as 'dog', but many more specific nominals, such as a particular dog's name. They may use words in idio-syncratic ways, such as action words to refer to themselves only (Dunlea, 1989). Terms that derive from visual experiences, such as 'look' and 'see', may be used to denote tactile exploration (Landau and Gleitman, 1985). Unlike sighted children, blind children tend not to over-extend their vocabulary, and under-extend words for a longer time. Dunlea and colleagues (Dunlea, 1989; Andersen et al., 1993) suggest that this indicates that the process of word learning is different for these children, with the features used to categorize meaning reflecting the child's reliance on the proximal senses of touch and smell. For example, 'cookie' was used for eating a biscuit, and for feeling rough surfaces (Dunlea, 1989). One explanation might be that the children's limited visual experience means that they have fewer opportunities for experiencing different exemplars, and thus tend not to construct a general hypothesis about categories. Other researchers have taken a different approach to the problem. Norgate (1998) argues that a focus on the development of object terms in blind children seriously under-estimates their skills, and that it is unreasonable to expect the child to be able to over-extend terms. She proposes that the focus of vocabulary investigations should be on action terms, where the visually impaired child is more competent. Landau (1997) argues that evidence to support these different views is lacking. She suggests blind children's access to the world and their ability to establish joint reference occurs through their fingertips. Their ability to learn a vocabulary is grounded in their ability to use the grammar of the language to guide and constrain their hypotheses. The reasons why a child might not extend a word are more to do with their not receiving information that 'invites additional usage' than a problem with categorization skills.

Grammar

Studies of the children's acquisition of syntax have failed to reveal significant differences. The onset of some syntactic constructions can be slightly delayed but rapid advances are made by the time the child is three years of age (Landau and Gleitman, 1985). Delays have also been noted in the children's appropriate use of pronouns and spatial deictic terms such as 'this' and 'that'. In both cases these language differences have been explained in terms of the children's difficulties in recognizing shifting roles and thereby change perspectives.

In contrast to the difficulties with deixis there is evidence that children are precocious in their grammaticalization of time. Severely visually impaired children tend to refer to past events in contrast to the sighted child's preference to refer to the here and now. Sighted children tend to develop spatial reference before time reference, whereas visually impaired children follow the opposite pattern. The children's focus on the sequential nature of events may sensitize them to the time dimension as opposed to spatial dimensions. Thus the different pattern of development reflects their experience with language and the world.

Pragmatics

The data discussed earlier about carer–infant interactions suggests that the visually impaired infant has fewer opportunities to learn and understand the rules of interpersonal communication. This is corroborated further by evidence that severely visually impaired children can have difficulty using language appropriately in communicative contexts. Their language can be perceived as self-centred and irrelevant to ongoing conversations – they may not readily initiate, or change a topic of conversation without signalling their intention to do so (Andersen et al., 1993). This maybe because they are unable to take advantage of the subtle visual cues that regulate conversational turns, such as eye gaze and body language. Studies have also noted over-use of routine phrases, a tendency to echo what is said, and flat intonation. However, routine phrases and imitations are also used by typically developing children, apparently as a way of acquiring units of language that are larger than individual words (Pine and Lieven, 1993). A single-case study by Perez-Pereira and Castro (1992) indicates that this may be a reflection of a particular strategy rather than of deviant language development. Studies of older children suggest that they are able to take on the perspectives of others, although they may take longer to do so than sighted children (Andersen et al., 1993).

Social and emotional development of children with visual impairments

We have seen that early interactions are problematic for blind children. Children who are visually impaired seem to suffer the greatest trauma in the early years of life, and it is at this time that it is hardest of all to get a window on their feelings, thoughts and inner world (Corley and Pring, 1996). Many of the children show evidence of autistic-like features, such as stereotypy, ritualistic behaviours, echolalia, difficulty with pronominal reversals and delayed symbolic play (Hobson et al., 1997; Brown et al., 1998). These authors suggest that the source of the problem may lie with the blind child's reduced ability to perceive the emotions and perspectives of others, given the significance of joint visual attention for the development of 'theory of mind' (*see* Chapter 12).

Visual impairment does not necessarily cause severe and long-term social and emotional difficulties, *provided* children have no additional disabilities, and are growing up in environments that are supportive and sensitive to their needs. For example, a longitudinal study by Freeman and colleagues (1989; 1991) found that in general, adult functioning was adequate, with around half the sample involved in a close relationship with a partner. Stereotypic behaviours that had been apparent in childhood were generally absent by the follow-up. Studies of self-concept and locus of control in childhood and adolescence similarly seem to show that development follows a slow but essentially typical course (Land and Vineberg, 1965).

These findings suggest that the effects of visual impairments may be less marked in their impact on social development when compared to hearing or learning difficulties (*see* Chapter 10). However, as yet relatively few long-term research studies have been undertaken. Warren (1994), in an extensive review of the development of blind children, stresses the importance of parental adaptation to the child's impairment, and points out that many studies that show equivalent functioning of blind and sighted children used subjects who had received high-quality intervention. The picture of social interaction in children with visual impairments is fairly consistent in suggesting that problems do exist. For example, the symbolic play of blind children may be delayed, they may engage less with other children than their sighted peers may, and they show passive tendencies (Troster & Brambring, 1994). In school, blind children can find it difficult to locate toys, and ongoing events, and to join in with other children, leading to isolation, or dependence on adults (Kekelis and Sacks, 1992; Preisler, 1997). Preisler's longitudinal studies (1997) showed that even by ten years of age, blind children were lacking in friendships and the experiences of their sighted peers. Wolffe and Sacks (1997) used interviews and time diary studies to compare the lives of adolescents with low vision or functional blindness, to those of sighted fellow students. The students with visual impairments had a narrower range of employment opportunities, needed more support from adults, and had fewer social interactions than the sighted group. They were more likely to interact with friends who also had visual impairments than sighted friends, and their social and leisure activities tended to be passive and solitary or of a moderate intensity, such as talking to friends on the phone.

Because of the relative paucity of research findings in this area, we should avoid the complacent assumption that children with visual impairments will grow out of their early difficulties. Webster and Roe's research in nurseries (1998) suggests that adults can actively influence the social integration and play of blind children by scaffolding interactions, describing what other children are doing and facilitating inclusion; providing consistent social and play groupings; organizing the layout of activities and toys so that children gain more independence. This kind of proactive support will be needed from families, professionals and society to reduce the risk of social isolation, unemployment and dependence of children with visual impairments.

Chapter summary

In this chapter we have explored the development of children with sensory impairments. Much of the data has highlighted the ways in which children's performance is affected both by the skills and knowledge they bring to tasks and situations and the wider context in which they are growing and developing. Interpretations of atypical development needs to be based on two premises – a theory-driven model of development and an understanding of development in context. Consider the development of deaf children as an example. On the whole deaf children are delayed in the development of their literacy skills. Yet when they are functioning in an environment which allows and supports the use of sign language their progress is much quicker. Thus although the absence of auditory input (the child-based factor) plays a significant role, the wider political and educational context affects the children's functioning, in terms of whether it allows alternative routes to development. Similarly, we have seen how visual impairments reduce the children's exposure to a range of experiences. Rather than indicating an inherent predisposition or limitation such data may reflect the lack of appropriately designed and organized environments for the children. A transactional (or constructivist) view in which the child and the environment are intricately linked at multiple levels can allow for an analysis of how the wider social system impacts on individuals and affords particular types of opportunities (Sameroff, 1990). Such an analysis is crucial if we are to develop appropriate descriptions and models of atypical development and by implication appropriate interventions.

Seminar questions

1. What difficulties can you identify in assessing the cognitive and language skills of visually impaired and hearing-impaired children? How might these problems be overcome?
2. Compare and contrast the effect of visual impairments and hearing impairments on the development of language and communication.
3. What can studies of children with sensory impairments tell us about typical development?

Further reading

Lewis, V. and Collis, G.M. (eds) 1997. *Blindness and psychological development in young children*. Leicester: British Psychological Society.
Marschark, M. 1993. *Psychological development of deaf children*. Oxford: Oxford University Press.
Marschark, M., and Clark, M.D. (eds) 1993. *Psychological perspectives on deafness*. Hillsdale, NJ: Lawrence Erlbaum Associates.
Warren, D. 1994. *Blindness and children: an individual differences approach*. Cambridge: Cambridge University Press.
Webster, A., and Roe, J. 1998. *Children with visual impairments: social interaction, language and learning*. London: Routledge.

11 Growing and learning with cognitive impairments

NICOLA GROVE AND JULIE DOCKRELL

Editors' preface

The previous chapter examined the impact of sensory disabilities on children's development. This chapter (by the same authors) considers children with a different form of difficulty, that of learning and cognitive impairments. Useful background to this topic is provided by chapters 6 and 8. Intelligence testing has been an important process in the assessment of children with learning and cognitive impairments, as intellectual functioning is an important aspect of decisions that are made about children's educational and wider needs. In addition, theories about typical development provide an important first step in attempts to understand the difficulties of children with learning and cognitive impairments.

In this chapter Julie Dockrell and Nicola Grove address the difficult issue of the definition of learning disabilities, a topic which has been a controversial one. This leads on to a consideration of cognitive skills (*see* Chapter 6), language development (*see* Chapter 4) and socio-emotional development (*see* chapters 5 and 14). In each of these attention is paid to the general profile of abilities of children with learning disabilities and to the characteristics of children with different forms of learning disability. An important theme running through the chapter is the way that diagnostic and classification systems can be of help in anticipating the abilities and needs of children, but that this needs to be accompanied by the realization that the great range in their abilities makes it essential for professionals to carefully consider the particular requirements and skills of individual children.

Introduction

Understanding the difficulties and strengths of children with learning disabilities is not a new endeavour. A range of terms is used to label this population, including *learning disabilities or difficulties, intellectual impairments, pervasive developmental disorder, mental retardation* and *mental handicap*.[1] It was around the end of the nineteenth century that scientists such as Galton and Cattell argued that high intelligence was associated with faster processing, and general superiority. 'Mental retardation' began to be both explained and described by an individual's performance on standardized tests of intelligence. Empirical investigations of 'retardation', as it was then called, continued throughout the early part of the century (*see* Witkin, 1964). From a Piagetian orientation, Inhelder (1943/1968) noted both similarities and differences between children with and without 'retardation'. Vygotsky, in contrast, was concerned with how the child's entire personality structure was structured in relation to a particular disability (Rieber and Carton, 1993; *see* Chapter 6). Vygotsky's notion of mediated learning and the role of the zone of proximal development still play a major role today in our understanding of learning disabilities and in designing effective interventions.

In the late 1960s Zigler developed a formal developmental approach which supposed that all forms of learning disability were linked to general developmental processes (Zigler, 1984; *see* Chapter 8). He highlighted three key issues which are still of central concern today. (Box 11.1)

BOX 11.1 Disability and development

1. Similar sequence – children with learning disabilities pass through the same sequence of stages as typically developing children. If typically developing children always achieve skill **A** before skill **B** then the same should be true of children with learning disabilities.
2. When children are matched for mental age they should show similar levels of functioning across tasks. No major discrepancies should occur either within a group of children, e.g. Down's syndrome or across groups of children.
3. The experiences of children with learning disabilities are different to their typically developing peers. These different experiences will affect the ways in which these children respond to the world. This implies that we have a good understanding of the ways in which children with disabilities are treated by their parents, peers and teachers if we are to understand developmental trajectories.

---

[1] In the American literature the term *learning disabilities* only denotes mild problems and is never used in the context of moderate, severe, or profound learning disabilities.

Studies which explore the range and variation of typical patterns of language acquisition are particularly important tests of Zigler's first point. The second assertion assumes that children with learning disabilities will have no particular areas of deficit relative to their other abilities. To assess this it is important to know about relationships between skills in typically developing groups of children. Zigler's third point is an important one, and one that is often ignored. It draws attention to the development of children in a broader context rather than concentrating solely on cognitive limitations. As we shall see, both current understandings of cognition (Pinker, 1993) and current research on atypical development indicate that the story is not as clear cut as Zigler assumed (Broman and Grafman, 1994).

In Britain several years ago, children with learning disabilities were often rejected by their families and consigned to residential institutions where they spent their lives. It is not surprising that their communication and cognitive skills showed many of the effects of social and environmental deprivation such as limited vocabulary (Mein and O'Connor, 1960) and reduced interactions (Lyle, 1959). Nowadays, although prejudice still remains, and not all provision is ideal, there is more acceptance of the principle that people with learning disabilities have a role in society, and this has brought increased opportunities in education, leisure and the workplace. Such opportunities have a 'knock-on' effect on language and cognition. If you are having to plan and cook your own meals, there is an immediate reason and purpose to memorizing related vocabulary, listening to instructions and interacting with the people who are going to sell you your food. The ability to count becomes important in carrying out shopping and the use of mnemonics helpful in remembering sequences and items. Language is always easier to acquire in context, and when it is functional for the person concerned. Thus, both models of cognitive functioning, and an understanding of the impact of the wider social systems on individuals are necessary to understand learning disabilities (Sameroff, 1990).

Another contribution to the lives of people with disabilities, which may have a direct effect on language and learning, is the quality of intervention. Improvements in early diagnosis mean that many impairments can be identified in infancy, and interventions can begin from an early stage. As indicated in Box 11.2 this may minimize some of the secondary effects of a disability such as disturbed parent–child interactions.

BOX 11.2 Children with Down's syndrome

Speech and language therapists now routinely work with the parents of babies with Down's syndrome to stimulate language development. Because so many of these children have hearing impairments, manual sign may be introduced to provide them with understanding and expression of vocabulary. One of the children studied by Le Prevost (1983), Meg, is now a teenager. At the beginning of the programme her performance IQ indicated that she had moderate learning difficulties, placing her within the typical range of ability for children with Down's syndrome. Currently, studies of her language show fluent sentence construction and good conversational skills, which is unusual and advanced for these children (Rondal and Edwards, 1997). Higher expectations are also contributory factors. Buckley and Bird (1993) initiated a programme of research and teaching to develop the literacy skills of children with Down's syndrome. Their results demonstrate that a combination of opportunity and appropriate methodology can allow individuals with learning difficulties to realize their potential in ways that were unforeseen in the days of mass institutionalization.

DISCUSSION POINT

In this chapter we consider the ways in which learning disabilities affect the whole child and by corollary the ways in which the child's atypical development may impact on the experiences they receive and the lives of those around them. As you read ask the following questions:

1. Is it the case that similar levels of functioning occur across tasks?
2. If there is variation what factors might account for these differences?
3. How do environmental influences support or constrain an individual's development?

What are learning disabilities?

DEFINITION AND IQ

When individuals are diagnosed as having a learning disability this does not mean they all experience the same type or degree of problem. Nor is a learning disability an illness or a disease. Illnesses or diseases, such as meningitis, however, may cause learning disabilities, and learning disabilities are often accompanied by other problems such as sensory impairments. When individuals have a learning disability they have some difficulty in acquiring and using information. Learning disabilities are usually distinguished by the level of their severity as measured by developmental or intelligence tests. In some cases, problems experienced with the demands of daily living also are assessed.

CLINICAL CLASSIFICATION

The two most influential classification schemes (that of the AAMD and DSM-IV (American Psychiatric Association)) are based on IQ scores. Figure 11.1 presents the subscale used at different ages to compute a general conceptual ability (GCA) and the additional diagnostic scales in the most recent version of the British Abilities Scale. The computation of a GCA results in a standard score with a mean of 100 and a SD of 15 just like the conventional IQ score. The use of standardized IQ assessments which indicate the extent of deviation from the norm can be useful, particularly in

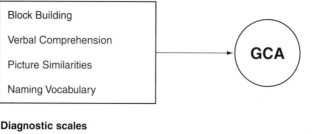

Core scales

| Block Building |
| Verbal Comprehension |
| Picture Similarities |
| Naming Vocabulary |

→ **GCA**

Diagnostic scales

| Recall of Digits Forward |
| Recognition of Pictures |

(a) Cognitive battery for ages 2.6–3.5 years

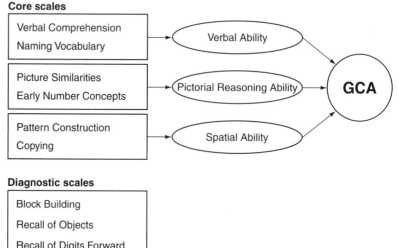

Core scales

| Verbal Comprehension |
| Naming Vocabulary |

→ Verbal Ability

| Picture Similarities |
| Early Number Concepts |

→ Pictorial Reasoning Ability → **GCA**

| Pattern Construction |
| Copying |

→ Spatial Ability

Figure 11.1 Sub-tests in the original British Abilities Scale. BAS II © Colin D. Elliott, 1996. Reproduced by permission of the Publishers, NFER-NELSON, Darville House, 2 Oxford Road East, Windsor SL4 1DF, England. All rights reserved.

Diagnostic scales

| Block Building |
| Recall of Objects |
| Recall of Digits Forward |
| Matching Letter-Like Forms |
| Recognition of Pictures |
| Recall of Digits Backward |

(b) Cognitive battery for ages 3.6–5.11 years

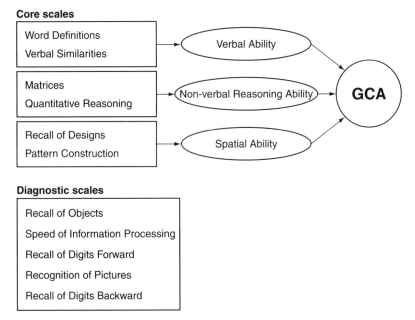

Core scales

Word Definitions
Verbal Similarities

→ Verbal Ability

Matrices
Quantitative Reasoning

→ Non-verbal Reasoning Ability →

Recall of Designs
Pattern Construction

→ Spatial Ability

GCA

Diagnostic scales

Recall of Objects
Speed of Information Processing
Recall of Digits Forward
Recognition of Pictures
Recall of Digits Backward

(c) Cognitive battery for ages 6.0–17.11 years

cases where a child's ability is under-estimated because of functional performance, or preconceptions, but as Box 11.3 indicates there are limitations
in the use of IQ tests. Individuals with an IQ score below 70 are usually
classified as experiencing a learning disability. This does not mean that
these individuals behave in a qualitatively different way from individuals
with scores above 70 as the division point is motivated by statistical rather
than behavioural or psychological reasons. The International Classification
of Diseases (ICD-10) defines an IQ between 50 and 70 as mild mental
retardation, between 35–49 as moderate mental retardation, between 20–34
as severe mental retardation and below 20 as profound. The 1992 definition
of 'mental retardation' departs from earlier categories. Levels of 'mental
retardation' have been eliminated and replaced with intensity of needed
supports to facilitate an individual's functioning across environments
(intermittent, limited, extensive, pervasive). An upper IQ point of 75 is
established and two of ten specified adaptive skill areas must be limited.

BOX 11.3   Problems with interpreting the results of intelligence tests

1. The tests are rarely developed for use with children with disabilities. Fuchs et al. (1987) carried out an analysis of user manuals
   and technical supplements of 27 widely-used intelligence and
   achievement tests to determine the inclusion of children with learning disabilities in item development, normative data, internal and
   test–retest reliability, and concurrent and predictive validity. With

the exception of two tests that had been specifically designed for the hearing impaired or visually impaired populations, the test either did not include children with disabilities or did not state that they were included.

2. IQ scores are not exact. The standard error of measurement on the WISC (Weschler Intelligence Scale) means that an IQ score of 70 would represent a zone of about 66–74.

3. IQ scores can change. Reports of increases and decreases in level of functioning across ages have been recorded.

4. The functional performance of children with similar IQs can vary markedly. Intelligence scores do not tell us which cognitive mechanism is affecting an individual's performance nor do they address what adaptive problems may be experienced.

Adaptive functioning

The observation that many academically disadvantaged individuals functioned adequately in society after their school years led clinicians in the 1960s to move away from the use of IQ as the sole criterion of disability and to take account of social and practical as well as academic functioning. Thus learning disabilities are now viewed as a significant impairment in the ability both to learn *and* to adapt to the demands of society (the President's Committee on Mental Retardation, 1973). There is considerable debate about what makes up adaptive behaviour and whether it is a valid concept (*see* Coulter and Morrow, 1978). Two elements in most definitions of adaptive behaviour are personal independence and social responsibility. Identifying appropriate measuring devices for such skills is difficult and will change across development. What is an adaptive skill for a four-year-old will not necessarily be adaptive for an 18-year-old. Adaptive behaviour is rarely used as a criterion by researchers for identification of groups or in the diagnostic process by clinicians. This is partly a result of the uncertainty surrounding reliability and validity. However, assessments of adaptability can play a central role in considering the likelihood of successful integration into mainstream school or in community living. In this context it is more important to know whether individuals can maintain themselves in the community and abide by socially acceptable standards of behaviour than to know their IQ score. The latter neither provides the descriptive information necessary for decisions about appropriate community support, nor provides enough information about learning to support academic achievement. IQ scores may guide practitioners, but they need detailed analyses of profiles of skills, educational needs, and context to understand the child's learning experience and performance.

PREVALENCE, AETIOLOGY AND CLASSIFICATION

The estimate of children with IQs of <70 in the general population is somewhere between 2 per cent and 2.5 per cent. Surprisingly, these prevalence rates have remained relatively constant over the last 50 years, despite medical advances. Increased longevity has offset the reduction in incidence of learning disabilities due to improved pre-natal care and screening.

A distinction is frequently drawn between individuals whose difficulties are of organic origin and those whose difficulties are of unknown aetiology. In 1983 Grossman reported there were 200 identified causes of 'mental retardation', whereas Dykens (1995) cites about 1000. Over the last 30 years advances in biomedical research have greatly increased our ability to identify causes of general learning disabilities. Organic insults are generally of three kinds: those occurring before birth, such as genetic abnormalities or problems *in utero*; those occurring at the time of birth, such as anoxia; those occurring post-natally, such as childhood encephalitis. Studies of severely learning disabled individuals indicate that more than a third have some known genetic abnormality, about one in five have multiple congenital anomalies and the majority of the remainder have some clear evidence of organic brain dysfunction at birth but without a known cause. Obstetric and perinatal complications are more frequent in the histories of learning disabled children (Rao, 1990). Moreover, there may be a greater association between obstetric complications and mild learning disabilities than was originally assumed (Simonoff et al., 1996).

The pattern of development will vary according to the severity of learning disabilities. Milder problems may result in a child being described as a 'slow learner' and falling behind their peers at school. In contrast children with moderate and severe difficulties often are delayed in the development of mobility and motor co-ordination. In these children there is no major area that is unaffected, but the pervasive abnormalities of development vary in severity. The most severely learning disabled may not be able to sit unsupported, or stand, walk, feed or toilet themselves. Many of these children also experience secondary sensory or physical impairments. This does not mean that there is no awareness of other people, no preferences for the people they know, or that they cannot learn (Remington, 1996). Identifying the existence of the more severe learning problems is relatively clear-cut and this generally occurs in the first year of life. In contrast identification of milder problems often only happens in the pre-school years or at school.

In the past it was often maintained that *mild* learning disabilities were part of normal variation in the distribution of intelligence. More recently Simonoff et al. (1996) have argued that the equating of severe learning disabilities with pathology and mild disabilities with normal variation is a misleading oversimplification. Within the milder range of learning difficulties, there may be some underlying neurological problems such as epilepsy or cerebral palsy, but their more diffuse character can make it difficult to specify precisely the mechanisms which contribute to the learning difficulty (Rondal and Edwards, 1997). However, reduced performance on intelligence and ability tests should not automatically be equated with neurological dysfunction.

The emphasis on organic causes of learning disabilities should not allow us to disregard the role of other factors. The mapping between genotypic variation and phenotypic behaviours is extremely complex. Major environmental variations affect cognitive performance in children from psychosocial high-risk backgrounds (Rutter, 1991). There is, for example, significant variation in the extent to which low intelligence is accompanied by social deficits. Mild learning disabilities occur more frequently in severely socially disadvantaged families. Simonoff at al. (1996) suggest that environmental influences have a larger influence on low intelligence than they do in the distribution of intelligence. It is important to describe and understand the ways in which the wider social and educational context can affect opportunities to learn and ability to utilize the opportunities that are presented. For example, it is likely that children with learning disabilities elicit different responses from their parents, teachers and peers. Such differences may influence their own later development. People from ethnic communities may face particular difficulties, such as racial discrimination, in addition to prejudice about disability. They may benefit from a strong cultural identity and close family ties but also have to deal with problems such as services which do not accommodate their traditions (Azmi et al., 1997). Cultural and linguistic background should always be taken into consideration for people with learning disabilities.

Cognitive skills and learning disabilities

To understand children's cognitive skills we need to discover the representations, processes, and strategies that are used in performing tasks. To do this it is important to reconsider the issues raised by Zigler's developmental framework.

DISCUSSION POINT

Consider in what ways the skills of children with learning disabilities are similar to their typically developing peers and in what ways if any, do patterns of deficits exist?

In the past, investigations were usually concerned with the level of intellectual functioning rather than aetiology. Intelligence was conceived as a general ability operating as a common factor in a wide variety of learning processes. Researchers compared children who had mild to moderate learning difficulties with typical children of a similar mental age (MA) or chronological age (CA), little attempt was made to consider how difficulties might vary among different aetiologies. Box 11.4 considers some of the issues in considering MA comparisons. Historically, we can trace three different approaches. Initially, studies focused on the children's development of Piagetian stages, this was followed by an interest in their information processing capacities and more recently studies have considered the

---

BOX 11.4 Interpreting the results of age-matched comparisons

We need to be very careful when we draw conclusions from age equivalent matches. Although in theory such a control allows a comparison between similar levels of linguistic or cognitive skills, there can be problems in interpreting the results.

First, the larger the chronological age gap between children and their age-matched comparisons, the more difficult it is to draw conclusions. A child of 16 with a mental age equivalent score of four years has 12 more years of additional experience (both positive and negative) to influence performance on tasks (Scroufe and Rutter, 1984). When there are large gaps it can not simply be assumed that the two individuals are comparable.

Second, some tests produce age-equivalent scores on the basis of summing over a number of subscales. This is particularly true of intelligence tests, although the precise number and combination varies according to the test. In these cases two individuals can have exactly the same age-equivalent score but for completely different reasons.

Third, general scores may over- or under-emphasize levels of functioning specifically related to the task at hand. The complexities in interpreting age-equivalent scores have led some researchers to argue that such scores should not be used.

---

extent to which differential patterns of performance reflect the modular structure of the mind. At each point questions arose as to whether the children's pattern of skills reflected differences or delays in development.

PIAGETIAN STUDIES

Research from the Piagetian perspective supported Zigler's similar sequence hypothesis regardless of children's aetiology (with the possible exception of severe seizure disorders), both across stages and within the substages (Weisz and Zigler, 1979; Weisz and Yeates, 1981). The children were found to progress through the Piagetian stages at a slower rate and with a lower ceiling. However, these studies failed to consider the ways in which a child's performance could vary across tasks. As we shall see, this is central to our understanding of both the architecture of the mind and variation according to aetiological considerations.

INFORMATION PROCESSING PARADIGM

Within the information processing framework the sequence of learning is analysed in order to identify critical processes in cognitive functioning. This allows specific areas of strengths and weakness to be pinpointed (Simon, 1976; Sternberg, 1988). Relevant research began at least 30 years ago with cognitive psychologists attempting to identify where problems in the learning system might occur, such as attention (Zeaman and House, 1963); short term memory (Ellis, 1963); or cross-modal coding (O'Connor and Hermelin, 1963). General learning difficulties were accounted for by identifying specific deficits and cognitive development was thought to be different for these children.

Of course it is possible that children with learning disabilities acquire skills more slowly and therefore they are unable to build up the knowledge and strategies needed to perform a task successfully. This might give the appearance of a different cognitive structure which in fact is the result of a delay in development. For example, children with mild to moderate general learning difficulties are more helpless in problem solving situations (Weisz, 1978) and therefore there is a danger of interpreting such passivity as indicating a different cognitive structure when it does not necessarily do so.

To date, more similarities than differences have appeared when children with learning disabilities have been compared with children matched for mental age on such cognitive tasks. A few cognitive impairments appear common across all types of learning disability, including problems with attention and short term memory, weakness in sequential information processing and poor academic achievement in arithmetic as compared to reading. Other areas of cognitive skill show a more diverse pattern. Children with mild, moderate, and severe learning difficulties are a heterogeneous group, and individuals show relative strengths and weaknesses in specific cognitive abilities. In such cases it is important to decide what is an acceptable variation in processing, and what is truly exceptional, since there is a wide range of abilities in the normal population.

DIFFERENTIAL PERFORMANCE ACROSS SUBGROUPS

In the past researchers investigating learning disabilities have been criticized for failing to consider differences in underlying cause, which is frequently associated with significant variations in neurological and cognitive functioning (Burack et al., 1988). More recently there has been growing interest in the characteristics of genetic syndromes (Hodapp et al., 1992). Although acknowledging that even within single gene or chromosome disorders there is marked variability in the range in IQ scores there appears to be a greater amount of similarity in profiles of skills than was initially envisaged. Some researchers have argued that this reflects modular differences in the cognitive system.

Studies of syndromes only account for a proportion of children with learning disabilities, but they can provide important information about both the similarities and differences in cognitive skills. However, generalization may be extremely difficult given the small and often select nature of the populations under investigation.[2] Moreover, there is suggestive evi-

2 Experiments where children and young people with learning disabilities participate are generally small (*but see* Romans et al., 1997). Although there are clear methodological reasons for this, data must be regarded with due caution.

dence that syndrome-specific differences may not hold when the learning difficulties are severe (Simon et al., 1995). These authors cautioned against generalizing cognitive profiles to all IQ levels of a specific genetic syndrome. Syndrome specificity and the variability in the manifestation of particular problems needs to be explained (Bregman and Hodapp, 1990).

Table 11.1 lists four of the common genetic disorders associated with learning disabilities. Three points are striking about the data documented in the table. First, there is tremendous variation in the recorded intelligence quotients of the children within specific groups. As an example, consider Fragile X syndrome, where the genetic mutation involved can cause a spectrum of learning disabilities ranging from the mild to the severe. No direct mapping between genotype and intelligence quotient exists, although problems with social use of language and the rhythm of speech seem to occur in all cases of Fragile X syndrome, irrespective of performance on IQ measures (Rondal and Edwards, 1997). Second, when we examine the significant factors column we can see that in some cases, e.g. Down's syndrome, it is important to consider both the child's environment and their approach to tasks. The learning strategies of young children with Down's syndrome may be affected by poor motivation on easy tasks, with avoidance strategies occurring with difficult tasks (Wishart, 1993). For example, children with Down's syndrome were as capable on a matching task as their MA and CA peers, but behaved differently with 'impossible shapes'. They adopted switching out strategies, misusing their social skills or producing 'party tricks' (*but see* Hasan and Messer, 1997). Third, there appear to be dissassociations between sets of cognitive skills, with some groups of children showing strengths in one particular area. For example, children with Williams' syndrome are often reported to have good verbal and poor non-verbal abilities (*see* Table 11.1). Children with Down's syndrome are thought to have specific difficulties with auditory–vocal processing and relatively good non-verbal skills (Kernan and Sabsay, 1996). However, recent research has qualified both sets of findings (Greer et al., 1997; Mundy et al., 1995). Jarrold et al. (1998) have suggested that it is oversimplistic to consider some skills as spared and others as impaired. Rather they suggest that verbal and non-verbal skills develop at different rates and that it is only in the more able that the stereotypical disassociation is evident.

IMPLICATIONS

In sum, while there is general agreement about certain core areas that are problematic for children with learning disabilities, there is accumulating evidence that there may be specific profiles of cognitive skill associated with specific genetic problems. Nonetheless even in these areas there are important, and often unanswered questions about the generality of the patterns found, the causes of the child's profile of skills and the ways in which these factors interact with the opportunities in the environment.

Table 11.1 The match between geneotype and cognitive and behavioural phenotype

Syndrome	Occurrence	Chromosomal involvement	IQ performance	Specific strengths	Specific weaknesses	Significant factors
Down's Syndrome	30% of moderate or severe LD. Most common genetic cause of learning disability.	95% trisomy 21 + translocations and mosaicism.	Varies across the range.	Visuo-spatial skills and visuo-spatial integration (Bellugi, Bihrle, Neville, Ternigan & Doherty 1992); proficiency in use of hand movements (Hodapp et al. 1992).	Language skills (Kernan & Sabasy 1996); auditory sequential memory (Varnhagen, Das, Vernhagen 1987); learning strategies (Wishart, 1993).	1. More favourable educational and social environments significantly enhance the children's development resulting in increased performance in a number of areas (Buckley 1985; Champion & Lawson 1996) 2. There are also consistent findings that the IQs of children with Down's Syndrome are correlated with the IQs of their parents.
Fragile X	Most common cause of inherited LD. Girls are usually less affected than boys.	Abnormal gene on X chromosome.	Wide spectrum from completely unaffected cognitively to severe learning disability (Hagerman 1991).	Vocabulary, visual memory (Hagerman 1996).	Sequential processing, mathematics and hyperactivity (Dykens, Hodapp & Leckmann 1989).	1. Slow in development in their teen years. 2. Patterns of strengths and deficits not characteristic of other groups (Dykens, Hodapp & Leckmann 1989).
Williams' Syndrome	1 in 25,000 live births; equal sex ratio.	Microdeletion of chromosome 7.	Ranges from low average to moderate learning disabilities (Arnold, Yule & Martin 1985).	Verbal skills (Bellugi, Wang & Jerrigan 1994); visual recall and face perception (Bellugi, Wang & Jerrigan 1994; Udwin & Yule 1991).	Integration of visual perceptual tasks and construction tasks (Bellugi, Wang & Jerrigan 1994); higher rates of emotional and behavioural disturbance, including poor attention and attention seeking behaviour (Udwin & Martin 1987).	1. Vocabulary scores are often impressive but semantics may appear aberrant (Tyler et al 1997 and see discussion below).
Turner's Syndrome	1:2,000 live births; occurs only in girls.	Second X chromosome abnormal or deleted (Saenger 1996).	Minor affect on general intellectual functioning.		Visuo-spatial and attention skills; social adjustment problems (Skuse et al. 1997).	1. Poor performance on items on intelligence tests is not in dispute although the nature of the deficit is (Romans, Roeltgen, Kushner & Ross 1997; Temple, Carney & Mullarkey 1996).

Language development and learning disabilities

In general terms, it is accepted that the overwhelming majority of children with intellectual impairments follow the normal course of language development, but with a later onset, a slower rate and a lower final level of achievement (Rosenberg and Abbeduto, 1993). Language is likely to be more severely affected, the greater the degree of intellectual impairment (Jarrold et al., 1998). Most researchers now conclude that (a) the differences between the language of people with mild, moderate and severe learning difficulties are quantitative rather than qualitative and (b) that language patterns are delayed rather than different. Rondal and Edwards (1997) argue strongly for a developmental perspective suggesting that even children with profound learning disabilities show patterns of communication which are typical of early child development. Yet, it is not possible to predict *patterns* of language development from a knowledge of a person's global, or non-verbal IQ. This is because the picture is complicated by the factors, such as aetiology, life experiences and quality of intervention, which affect the impact of a learning disability. In this section we are specifically concerned with the nature of language and its development.

There is increasing evidence that the different aspects of language are affected in different ways by impairments. In brief, there appear to be disassociations between the formal aspects (*phonology* and *grammar*) the conceptual aspects (*vocabulary*) and the functional aspects (*use*, or *pragmatics*). This means that one of these aspects may be relatively more preserved than another, and that different patterns may be associated with particular syndromes.

VOCABULARY

In general, people with learning disabilities have vocabularies that are appropriate to their mental ages, and which are organized in a similar way to those of non-disabled people (Tager-Flusberg, 1985; Rosenberg and Abbeduto, 1993). However, memory limitations affect the efficiency with which words are recalled in this population (Elliot, 1978; Davies et al., 1981). Although they find symbolic and abstract language difficult to understand, complex concepts can be acquired if they are relevant. For example, concepts such as 'empowerment' and 'civil rights' may be acquired successfully in work settings which emphasize self-advocacy. The vocabularies of older children and adults with learning difficulties are often larger than those of non-disabled children matched for mental age, because of increased life experiences (Chapman et al., 1991).

GRAMMAR

As a generalization, grammar and phonology appear to be more severely delayed in people with learning disabilities than would be predicted from their mental ages, and pose particular difficulties for people with Down's syndrome (Rondal and Edwards, 1997). This may be because the grammatical aspects of language tend to be encoded in small function words which are unstressed and may be reduced in speech (parts of verbs like 'is', 'have'; prepositions like 'of', 'by'; pronouns like 'it'; 'that'; 'we') and inflections or additions to words (-s for plurals, possessives and copula – be). This makes them more difficult to perceive and to produce. These elements may be omitted or further reduced in the speech of people with learning disabilities. However, there seem to be no problems with producing correct word order, and although they rarely produce complex sentences with multiple clauses (like this one!), development seems to follow that of typically developing children. Many people, particularly at the more severe end of the spectrum, will typically communicate in utterances of only one or two words at a time.

SPEECH SOUNDS

Reports suggest that between 70 and 90 per cent of the population of people with moderate and severe learning disabilities have problems with speech (Spradlin, 1963). This is unsurprising, given that intellectual impairments often co-exist with other impairments which will affect the production and perception of speech. These include hearing loss, structural abnormalities of the mouth and tongue, and muscular weakness or incoordination. Articulation can be unclear, particularly for long, polysyllabic words and connected speech. Voice quality and rate of speech are often affected – people may speak gruffly, or nasally; too quietly or too loudly; too fast or too slowly. This is because of difficulties in co-ordinating the muscle groups involved in breathing, voicing and sound production. Intelligibility is therefore a major problem for many people with learning disabilities; for example, Buckley and Sacks (1987) in a survey of teenagers with Down's syndrome found that over half the girls and 80 per cent of the boys were rated by their parents as unintelligible to strangers.

Since it is easier to interpret single word responses to direct questions, conversation partners are likely to find themselves taking the initiative, directing the conversation and repeating what a person has said (Leudar, 1987). Such compensatory techniques unfortunately reinforce learned passivity and limited use of vocabulary and syntax.

LANGUAGE USE

Studies of language use in people with learning disabilities are compromised to some extent, because so many have been carried out in institutional settings. A low staff–client ratio, predictable routines and lack of stimulating experiences will inevitably reduce the opportunities for conversations. Several research studies have shown that people in these settings participate less in conversations, and tend to respond rather than initiate (Beveridge and Hurrell, 1980). However, in contexts which are more stimulating, such as family homes or small group units, comparisons between groups with and without intellectual impairments, matched for mental age, show few differences in the range of purposes for which language is used (Abbeduto and Rosenberg, 1980; Owens and Macdonald, 1982). People with learning difficulties can take turns in conversations (Abbeduto and Rosenberg, 1992), but they may have problems in communicating information clearly and unambiguously, in ways which take into account what the listener does and does not know (Kernan and Sabsay, 1987; Hemphill et al., 1991). Pragmatics is an area in which there may be some progress with age, as people take on different roles and responsibilities. For example, the narratives of older teenagers with Down's syndrome are more complete and competent compared to younger children (Chapman, 1995). One reason why so many studies have shown difficulties in initiation is that people with learning disabilities may take longer to process and generate responses than non-disabled people. For example, infants with Down's syndrome seem to take a long time to respond to their mothers, and do not pause to allow the mothers to contribute, as do typically developing infants (Jones, 1977).

Pragmatics is an area of language that is particularly difficult for individuals on the autistic continuum (*see* Chapter 12). Interestingly, it has been suggested that children with Williams' syndrome, who are relatively advanced on measures of vocabulary and grammar, may have some high level pragmatic problems, making irrelevant comments, failing to sustain eye contact, or take listener perspectives into consideration (Arnold et al., 1985).

LANGUAGE COMPREHENSION

The normal development of comprehension in children shows that early on, understanding is highly dependent on contextual cues, tones of voice and familiar routines (Bishop, 1997). For example, up to the age of about four years, children who are asked to respond to unpredictable commands (such as 'make the cart push the horse') will use their real-world knowledge, rather than their linguistic knowledge, and fail to carry out the instruction correctly (Bridges and Smith, 1984). With increasing age, children rely less on context, and build up their ability to understand complex and abstract language. Hence it is not surprising that individuals with learning disabilities need support for language which is appropriate to their mental age, and respond better to simple sentences, backed up by contextual cues (Comblain, 1994). Appropriate responses occur at MAs below six years. However, at higher MA levels performance often falls below what would be expected from cognitive abilities. At this level of complexity, there are demands on memory as well as the decoding of meaning, which may account for the increased difficulty (Naigles et al., 1991).

In general, comprehension is at the same level, or slightly in advance of language production for people with learning disabilities; however, there are some cases where people can produce deceptively fluent language, which masks a lower level of comprehension. This reverse discrepancy has been observed in some children with hydrocephalus (Fletcher et al., 1992) and Williams' syndrome (Jarrold et al., 1998).

AUGMENTATIVE AND ALTERNATIVE COMMUNICATION (AAC)

This is a term that denotes all systems of communication that do not employ speech, including manual signs and graphic representations (Figure 11.2). For those who find speech relatively difficult to perceive and produce, the use of alternative modalities, which can complement vocalization, has proved effective.

Manual signs

Studies show that people with intellectual impairments whose speech is unclear, can learn to communicate effectively through manual signs (von Tetzchner and Martinsen, 1990). Some people, whose speech is unintelligible, rely almost entirely on signs to communicate, whereas others will use them as a back up to clarify their speech. It is important to sign to people, as well as expecting them to use signs to you, since signing can help comprehension. The advantages of signing are that it builds on existing skills of gesture and facial expression, it is quick, and new terms can be generalized, e.g. RED-APPLE for 'tomato' and DOCTOR-SHOP for 'hospital'. The disadvantages of signing are that people need to be taught signs; the signs have to be recalled from memory, and some individuals sign quite inaccurately. In Great Britain, the most commonly used system of signing with this population is the Makaton vocabulary (Grove and Walker, 1990).

Graphic representations

Graphic representations include pictures, photographs or line drawings, symbols or written words. A selection is made to reflect the abilities, needs and interests of individuals, and these are then displayed in books, charts or communication aids with speech output. Using these devices the person finds the symbol on the display, and points to it to indicate the topic of conversation. They are used to promote literacy as well as communication. There are several different symbol systems available in the UK (von Tetzchner and Martinsen, 1992). The advantages of graphic representations are that they are easy to recognize, since the printed word is nearly always provided, and that the availability of the display reduces demands on memory. The disadvantages of books and charts are that they are cumbersome to use, time-consuming to prepare and easy to mislay.

Objects of reference

For people with profound and multiple disabilities, or with dual sensory impairments, objects of reference are increasingly used to provide in-

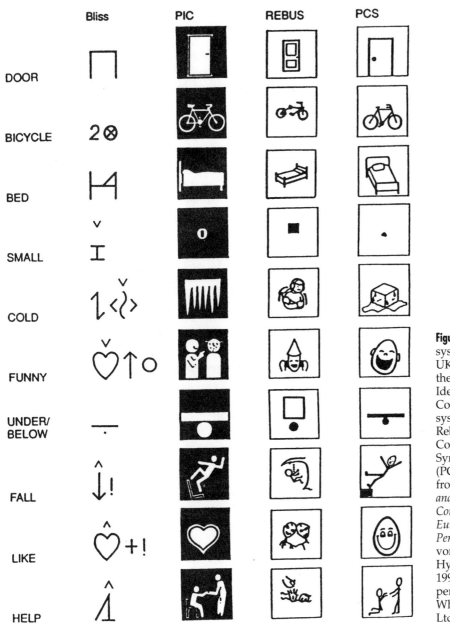

Figure 11.2 Graphics systems used in the UK: Blissymbols; the Picture Ideogram Communication system (PIC); Rebus; and Picture Communication Symbols (PCS). Reproduced from *Augmentative and Alternative Communication: European Perspectives*, von Tetzchner and Hygum Jensen 1996 with permission of Whurr Publishers Ltd.

formation about events, and a system of choices (Park, 1997). An associated object is handed to the person immediately prior to an event, for example, an armband to indicate swimming, or a spoon to indicate dinner. This helps to build up anticipation and recall, and to reduce uncertainty. For choice making, objects may be displayed on a board. The individual can touch the object to indicate a preference for an activity.

Implications

This overview of language and communication in people with learning disabilities suggests that in general terms, the pattern is one of delay rather than difference. The formal aspects of language – sentence construction and comprehension, and the perception and production of speech sounds – are likely to be more severely affected than the conceptual and social aspects (vocabulary and pragmatics). However, particular syndromes or patterns of neurological damage may have different effects, and life experiences will also offer different opportunities for language development and use. Studies show that there is considerable individual variation in achievement, even within groups which have been carefully matched for aetiology and ability. The availability of augmentative and alternative communication systems means that individuals need not be debarred from communication because of speech production problems. Although previously, these systems were considered as alternatives to speech, and to each other, current approaches are more flexible, and promote the combination of all modes of communication that are useful to the person. When people can use speech, sign and books with symbols and pictures, the possibility of a successful interaction may be increased, if not guaranteed.

Socio-emotional development and learning disabilities

Young children have made an impressive start on interpreting the feelings of themselves and other people, by the time they start school (*see* Chapter 14). However, understanding the complexities of emotional relationships is a skill which we continue to develop throughout our lives. There is evidence from the literature on typical development that children learn about emotions within social interactions, and that sensitivity to one's own feelings and those of others can be effectively scaffolded through discussion, modelling and explanation (*see* chapters 6 and 18).

In contrast to the rich research literature on typical emotional development, it is only comparatively recently that attention has been directed to the way in which people with learning disabilities perceive and express feelings. The findings suggest that, when matched for mental age, individuals with learning difficulties are not specifically impaired in the capacity to recognize feeling states from pictures or video displays (Weisman and Brosgole, 1994; *but* note the special case of autism, Chapter 12). When the task involves making inferences about emotions in more language based tasks, such as listening to and telling stories, IQ is predictive of performance (Reilly et al., 1990; Tager-Flusberg and Sullivan, 1995). As with typical development, the easiest emotions to decode are happiness and sadness. Happiness is also the emotion most reliably identified in people with learning disabilities. One difficulty is that displays of emotion may not be caused by affect, particularly in people with multiple disabilities, epilepsy or severe physical disabilities (Green and Reid, 1996; Lancioni et al., 1996). For example, people with cerebral palsy may display a rictus lip spread which has the appearance of a smile, in the absence of any positive event. Interpretations about the feelings of people who can only communicate non-verbally need to be validated by collecting information from multiple sources of evidence over time, and in different situations (Grove et al., submitted).

CHALLENGING BEHAVIOUR

Behaviour problems occur relatively frequently in people with severe disabilities. When these present a risk to the individual or those who care for them, or interfere significantly with participation in daily life, these problems present a challenge to services. They include a variety of behaviours, such as aggression, self-injury, and withdrawal. Prevalence estimates in the largest recent study are between 1 and 2 per cent (Qureshi and Alborz, 1992; Kiernan and Qureshi, 1993; Emerson and Bromley, 1995). Problem behaviours are more likely to occur in institutional settings, and when there are additional problems such as sensory impairments. They are the product of a complex set of interactions between organic, psychiatric, environmental, ecological and historical factors (Emerson et al., 1994). Currently, assessment and intervention focuses on the ecology of challenging behaviour, attempting to understand the factors that provoke or maintain it in context (Hastings, 1995; Toogood and Timlin, 1996). Generally, interventions which seek to improve quality of life appear to have a more positive outcome than interventions aimed purely at extinguishing the behaviours (Goldiamond, 1974).

SOCIAL INTERACTIONS

Social interactions have been studied within families and between peers. Research on interactions between infants with intellectual impairments and their parents has been somewhat contradictory (Rosenberg and Abbeduto, 1993). Some research studies suggest that parents are overly directive in their communications, resulting in fewer opportunities for the child to initiate and control, and possibly leading to passivity and learned helplessness (Hanzlik and Stevenson, 1986). Other research indicates that there are few qualitative differences in parental communication styles between disabled and non-disabled children; and that such differences as exist emerge as a consequence of the parent's adaptation to the communication style of the child (Rondal, 1978; Maurer and Sherrod, 1987). It seems likely that, once again, it is individual characteristics which determine the level of interaction – the baby who appears alert and responsive is likely to elicit more positive communication from caregivers than the passive, withdrawn, or difficult baby. Rosenberg and Abbeduto (1993) point out that although on average parents do appear to be more directive with children who have disabilities, the long-term consequences of this tendency are unknown, and may actually be beneficial.

Peer relationships have been studied in both integrated and segregated settings. In integrated settings, children with learning disabilities may adapt their behaviour positively in line with the models provided by peers, but equally they may experience problems with peer interactions. When non-disabled children interact with children with disabilities they are likely to either take over and dominate, or withdraw, particularly if the child with an intellectual impairment cannot communicate effectively (Siperstein et al., 1996). The quality of interactions can be improved by teaching relevant skills to both sets of children. In segregated settings, the balance of power may be more equal for children with intellectual impairments (Bayliss, 1992). Certainly, friendships are made and sustained in special schools, though it may be difficult to maintain them during holidays and into adulthood, because of a combination of the limited autonomy of individuals, and the fact that these pupils may live too far from each other to permit easy socialization.

As they grow older, non-disabled children become more independent and peer relationships assume increasing importance, especially in adolescence. However, young people with intellectual impairments can find it more difficult to make and sustain friendships outside the setting of schools or day centres (Griffiths, 1994). Richardson and Ritchie (1989) interviewed a group of young adults with learning disabilities, and found that they had fewer opportunities to go out and socialize, and that parents tended to be over-protective because of their concern about potential risks. This situation can lead to loneliness and isolation (Margalit, 1991). In recent years there has been more awareness of the need for friendship amongst people with learning disabilities, and befriending schemes have had some degree of success (Atkinson and Ward, 1987).

CLOSE RELATIONSHIPS

Intimacy is as important to people with learning disabilities as to anyone else. Nowadays there is an increasing acceptance that people will have normal sexual desires, and are entitled to support and advice to fulfil them (Atkinson and Ward, 1987; Craft, 1987; van Dyck et al., 1996). However, sexual relationships are complicated by numerous factors, including:

- Existing taboos and conventions which affect us all.
- The difficulty of clearly explaining all the implications of actions.
- The complexities of managing contraception.
- The continuing vulnerability to abuse of people with learning disabilities.
- The lack of inhibition in some individuals, leading to inappropriate displays of sexual feelings.

Training and support will be needed, not just for people with intellectual impairments, but for staff and parents (Craft and Downs, 1997). When the opportunities are provided, people with learning disabilities have the capacity to develop warm and loving relationships with partners, friends and families as the rest of the population, although they may be complicated or masked by difficulties in cognition and communication.

Chapter summary

In this chapter we have reviewed the current understanding of the difficulties experienced by children with learning disabilities. We have argued that increased understanding of the genetics and neurodevelopmental patterns of development have resulted in a clearer specification of language and cognitive profiles. Yet in all cases genetic markers result in phenotypic variation, which has yet to be fully explained. The contexts in which the children live and develop have important implications for current performance and later development. This should have a direct impact on the ways in which the children's needs are profiled and met. Categorization is important for research but the categorization that is used to meet the children's needs should be made using different criteria.

Seminar questions

1. Identify two measures of disadvantage which could affect a child's ability to learn in school.
2. Consider the ways in which a child with a learning disability may be compared to a typically developing peer. To what extent does the literature support a delay model of development?
3. Is there evidence from the language skills of children with learning disabilities to support a modular account of language?
4. Imagine that you had to design a study investigating the ability of children with learning disabilities to empathize. What measures would you take and why? What control group would you use to assess whether the children were following a typical course of development?

Further reading

Dockrell, J.E., McShane, J. 1993. *Children's learning difficulties: a cognitive approach.* Oxford: Basil Blackwell.

Luthar, S., Burack, J., Ciccheti, D., Weisz, J. (eds) 1997. *Developmental psychopathology: perspectives on adjustment, risk and disorder.* Cambridge; Cambridge University Press.

Rondal, J., Perera, J., Nadel, L., A. Comblan (eds) 1996. *Down's syndrome: psychological, psychobiological and socio-educational perspectives.* London: Whurr.

Stiles-Davis, J., Kritchevsky, M., U. Bellugi (eds) 1988. *Spatial cognition: brain bases and development*. Hillsdale NJ: Erlbaum.

Tager-Flusberg, H. (ed.) 1994. *Constraints on language acquisition: studies of atypical children*. Hillsdale, NJ: Erlbaum.

Autism

12

STUART D POWELL

Editors' preface

Autism is a comparatively rare condition. Despite this the syndrome has attracted considerable research and even media interest. A major reason for this seems to be that the asocial behaviour of children with autism is so very different from that of other children (*see* Box 12.1), and there still is the deep puzzle about what causes the children to behave in this way. Another reason for this interest has been the relation between research into autism and research into children's theory of mind, which involves the understanding that other people can have different thoughts and perspectives from oneself.

Piaget noted that in the late pre-school years children became less 'egocentric', by this he meant that they were able to understand the perspective of other people, for example what another person would see if they were viewing a model of some mountains from a different position (*see* Chapter 6). Over the last decade, great interest has been generated from findings that children below four years of age do not have a 'theory of mind'. These children seem simply to use what they know themselves, to predict what another person will think. The finding that many children with autism also fail on theory of mind tasks has linked these two research traditions with an ensuing deluge of investigations.

However, the theory of mind explanation of autism has not been accepted uncritically. There have been questions as to whether children aged below four years lack an understanding of others minds, for example, it is argued that they may have some form of intersubjectivity (*see* Chapter 4), and there are questions as to whether a lack of theory of mind provides a convincing explanation of autism. Professor Stuart Powell provides, in his chapter, an overview of this important subject of research, which also includes a description of more recent views about the cause of autism.

Introduction

Both Stephen and Rachel have been diagnosed as autistic. The brief description in Box 12.1 gives an initial indication of some, though clearly not all, of the features of autism and of the complexity and paradoxical nature of the condition.

BOX 12.1 Examples: behaviour of children with autism

Stephen met me at the School gate as I walked from the car park. 'Is your car red?' he asked. I replied that it was. He then proceeded to ask me about its make, the size of its engine and its top speed. I answered his questions. He then questioned me regarding details of the cars that I have had over the past few years and which I have used to visit the school, starting with: 'Was your last car blue?' All his questions required me simply to confirm his information. I asked him how he was, he did not reply. I asked him what he had been doing during the day. He hesitated and then said, 'he had assembly'. He did not look at me at all during this episode. Another visitor came up behind me. Stephen approached her and began asking questions about her car and then about other cars she had owned.

Rachel, the girl I had come to work with, was in the playground. She was 13 years old, used no spoken language and was walking round the playground, seemingly oblivious to the other children, making guttural noises, shaking her head and making jerky movements with her hands. Her forearms were sore from where she had scratched herself. She made no sign of recognition though she 'knows' me well. She came with me without any sign of resistance or pleasure.

DECEPTIVE APPEARANCES

At one level it might seem that Stephen is interested in cars, has a good memory, appropriate vocabulary, reasonable conversational skills and an outgoing manner. But all of these appearances are deceptive. His interest in cars is obsessional, certainly he can remember unusual amounts of detail within his range of interest (i.e. cars), but cannot remember simple things that have just happened to him. His recall of 'assembly' proved false, he had in fact arrived late in his taxi. It seems he is unable to recall recent personal events and had used his semantic memory of what typically happens (i.e. assembly takes place) to answer my question. Also, he misused the personal pronoun (saying 'he had assembly' rather than 'I'). Although Stephen's vocabulary is adequate he does not use it to communicate or converse in the true sense of the word; his conversational skills are extremely poor. His 'asking' and 'conversing' about the car is in fact just a ritual confirmation of what he can see (i.e. colour) or already knows (i.e. engine size). When encountering someone new he embarks on his ritual series of questions; the other person being fodder for his line of questioning rather than a partner in an interchange of ideas (which is what would constitute a conversation). His apparently outgoing manner is, then, a matter of him trying to find new people to ask his same questions with a lack of social flexibility. In short, Stephen's behaviours and abilities are not what they may seem.

Although Rachel appears to be unconcerned about others and what is happening to her it is also clear that she engages in 'self-injurious' behaviour. Rachel tends to injure herself when in social situations which put pressure on her. So, although she may seem disconnected from the social world around her she is, in fact, sensitive to the social context. If situations confuse or frighten her it would seem that she has no recourse to strategies for coping, other than to scratch her own arms, which tends to gain her the attention of others and at the same time stops whatever else is happening.

DISCUSSION POINT

Though both Stephen and Rachel have been diagnosed as autistic there are significant differences between them. List the differences and similarities.

RANGE OF INDIVIDUAL DIFFERENCES

In spite of differences both children have social and communicative difficulties and both exhibit behaviours indicating an inflexible and unimaginative approach to life. So, while individuals with autism share certain characteristics there are also likely to be significant individual differences.

THE PROBLEM OF UNDERSTANDING AUTISM

To understand autism one needs to use the very things (i.e. imagination and empathy) that are impaired in autism and this requires a complete re-evaluation of the reasons behind 'normal' social behaviour. What makes both Stephen and Rachel 'odd' is not just a number of personal characteristics which fall outside of what one normally expects and what might in other children be described as eccentricities, but rather their oddity seems to be caused by a fundamentally different way of operating in the world. They are not flouting convention but are outside of it; they are not unsociable or anti-social but rather they are asocial. The process of development that normally leads to an ability to engage with the social world and so learn within it breaks down in autism. Considering Stephen and Rachel and how they are able to operate, forces us to contemplate a kind of development that is fundamentally asocial and that therefore necessarily deviates from the normal developmental pathway.

The underlying premise of this chapter therefore, is that autism is both a pervasive and a developmental disorder. The chapter is structured so as to justify this case firstly by taking an historical perspective, then by considering current concerns about diagnosis and finally by reviewing ideas about the way in which the typical developmental process breaks down in autism.

Historical development of the concept of autism

ORIGINS OF THE CONCEPT

It is commonly accepted that autism as a distinct, identifiable syndrome was first noted by Kanner (1943) who used the term 'early infantile autism' (*autos* is the Greek word meaning self) to describe individuals who shared an 'aloneness', which involved the disregarding, ignoring or shutting out the world and living in an isolated, essentially asocial state. These individuals were limited in language and obsessive about the need for sameness in particular aspects of their environment. Kanner speculated that individuals with autism fall within the average range of intelligence and that any poor learning performance results from their [autistic] difficulties with the social aspects of learning (subsequent research has shown this claim to be incorrect).

Writing at the same period, in Austria, Asperger (1944) also noted a distinct group. He was working with an older age group and his observations were different in some details but nevertheless overlapped with those of Kanner. He also made use of the term 'autistic'. There is continuing debate over whether autism and Asperger syndrome are:

- Both expressions of the same condition.
- Both part of an autistic spectrum involving a range of characteristics, the individuals with high levels of intelligence being defined as a distinct sub-group (i.e. with Asperger syndrome).
- Separate conditions entirely.

The debate has not been resolved, however, it seems that autism and Asperger syndrome are not mutually exclusive syndromes and that those with Asperger syndrome do, in fact, have a particular form of autism. This debate illustrates the developmental diversity of autism noted in the description of Stephen and Rachel. Constraints on space in this present chapter preclude a fuller discussion of this issue, but the arguments are well rehearsed in Frith (1991).

PSYCHOANALYSIS

Early understandings of autism took place in an intellectual climate influenced by the legacy of Freud and psychoanalysis (*see* Chapter 13). Whereas

Kanner had suggested that autism had a genetic component, he also suggested that autism was in part a product of 'cold', unemotional parenting. The early history of autism supposed that it was a product of emotional harm inflicted unknowingly by parents and specifically by the mother. Such views were clearly very damaging for parents who were faced with both the difficulties of caring for the child and their own guilt.

DeMyer carried out studies (DeMyer, 1975; 1979) which failed to find evidence of abnormal parenting practices as part of the causation of autism. The prevailing current view is that the behaviour of parents does not initiate or in any way provoke autism. Retrospective analyses of the early years of a child's life (using video for example) may show that parents behaved differently with their child with autism, but such behaviours are more likely a product of the autism rather than a cause. Early interactions require two partners responding to each other; it is impossible to develop naturally what has been called the 'dance' of early social exchanges if a child is unresponsive.

LATER REVISIONS TO EARLIER THEORIES

The original conceptions of autism focused on the failure to develop social relations and to develop language. Later, ritualistic and compulsive dimensions were identified as being a crucial part of autism, thus forming the notion of a triad of impairments (social relations, language and rigidity of thought; Wing, 1988). Also Kanner's earlier assumptions about intelligence being at normal levels, was revised in the light of findings from the epidemiological study of Wing and Gould (1979) which revealed that learning disabilities (an IQ below 70; see Chapter 8) were clearly associated with the triad; 90 per cent of children who were described as having 'full' typical autism had an IQ of between 20 and 69. The relationship between intelligence, ways of testing and autism is complex and is detailed in several publications (see Frith, 1989; Jordan and Powell, 1995; Peeters, 1997).

Current concerns

DIAGNOSIS

As a consequence of the Wing and Gould studies, it became clear that there is a wide spectrum of autistic disorders of which 'Kanner's autism' is only a part. Wing and Gould (1979) reported a prevalence of 20 per 10,000 children who had autistic spectrum disorders and mental retardation. This cluster of features was recognized as the syndrome of autism in 1980 in DSM III which was subsequently revised (DSM-IV, American Psychiatric Association, 1994; see Box 12.2). Autism is also recognized by the World Health Organization (1990) within ICD-10. There is now considerable agreement on features central to autism with a convergence in the DSM-IV and ICD-10 definitions; yet significant issues remain, notably the simplification of methods for screening and epidemiological research as well as a need for alternative approaches to diagnosis using genetics (*see* Volkmar, 1996, for a review of diagnostic issues, and Waterhouse et al., 1996, for a useful comparison of different diagnostic procedures and a reflection on sub-groups).

INCIDENCE AND CLASSIFICATION

Although initial surveys put the prevalence of autism at 4–5/10 000, more recent estimates typically suggest a much higher incidence (e.g. Wing and Gould (1979), as noted above, and more recently Wing (1997) where an incidence is suggested of nine in every 1000 children falling within the diagnostic criteria for 'autistic spectrum disorders'). This change may reflect changes in diagnostic criteria as well as a wider recognition of autism in more capable individuals; but it also is possible that this change is the result of a rising prevalence of autism, an issue that is addressed by Fombonne (1996). A review of epidemiological issues in autism can be found in Bryson (1996).

GENETICS

Smalley and Collins (1996) have reviewed family and twin studies and suggest an important role of genetic influences on the development of autism. There is a significant familial clustering in autism which by itself could indicate either a common genetic or environmental influence. Twin studies provide additional support for a genetic influence (e.g. Bailey et al., 1995; *see* Chapter 1) and from studies of abilities and inabilities in parents of children with autism (e.g. Landa et al., 1991) where the suggestion is made that parents of children with autism have more difficulty in producing coherent spontaneous narratives than do parents of non-autistic children. The next challenge for geneticists will be to identify the gene(s) responsible for autism (the complexity of the challenge is illustrated in Lander and Schork (1994)).

BOX 12.2

Reciprocal and social interaction

- Marked impairment in the use of non-verbal behaviours.
- Failure to develop peer relationships appropriate to mental level.
- Lack of spontaneous seeking to share enjoyment, interests or achievement with other people.
- Lack of social or emotional reciprocity.

Communication

- Delay in or total lack of development of spoken language (not accompanied by compensation).
- In individuals with adequate speech, marked impairment in the ability to initiate or sustain a conversation.

- Stereotyped and repetitive use of language or idiosyncratic language.
- Lack of varied, spontaneous make believe play or social initiative play relative to developmental level.

Restricted repetitive and stereotyped behaviours, interests and activities
- Encompassing preoccupation with stereotyped and restricted patterns of interest that is abnormal in either intensity or focus.
- Inflexible adherence to specific, non-functional routines or rituals.
- Stereotyped and repetitive motor mannerisms.
- Persistent preoccupation with parts of objects. (NB. for a description of how these criteria may be employed diagnostically readers should refer to American Psychiatric Association, 1994.)

EARLY DETECTION

The diagnosis of autism relies on observation of behaviour and detailed analysis of reports from those close to the child; a developmental history is required. A diagnosis also needs to take account of chronological and mental age (*see* Chapter 10) because, there are some behaviours which will not occur below a certain mental age. Autism is often described as difficult to diagnose in 'borderline cases' and certainly high functioning children can confuse the diagnostician by not conforming to the typical pattern of autistic responses. Also, parents can become very adept at dealing with their autistic child and a child may seem 'less autistic' when with an experienced adult or peer. Added to all of this is the fact that within the range of developmental disabilities there may be 'autistic features' present, but this does not necessarily mean that a diagnosis of autism is appropriate. After all, if the features of autism are listed then it is clear that we all exhibit signs of these features at some point in our lives (we are all obsessive at some times and rigid in our thinking at others); what is unique in autism is the constant presence of the accepted features at a profound level. What is also clear is that autism is a developmental disorder. As a result, autism is often only recognized when children are several years old. Baron-Cohen et al. (1996) have designed an instrument, based on abilities to engage in joint referencing and pretend play (as aspects of the development of Theory of Mind, *see below*), that appears to be able to screen for autism at the age of 18 months. This is important because it enables early intervention, which, most educationists and psychologists would agree, is potentially beneficial to the child (*see* Rogers, 1996 for a review).

ADULTHOOD

It is very difficult to predict how individuals with autism will develop during adulthood. The way in which society treats them, specifically the educational, medical and care services, will affect levels of independence, behaviours and abilities. From a developmental perspective, interpersonal relationships may improve as children get older and many children with autism do become more socially appreciative and seem to take pleasure, for example, in the affection and approval of others (Newson, 1984). However, experience has shown that individuals who do not produce spoken language in the first few years of life are unlikely to do so in adulthood.

A follow-up study of 64 patients, who were then aged between 15 and 29 years, was conducted by Rutter (1970). He found that approximately half were in long-term care facilities and less than a fifth were in any kind of employment, only one of the ex-patients was described by Rutter as leading a 'normal' life. One might expect that more recent improvements in provision and understanding would result in better outcomes, nevertheless it is clear that for many individuals with autism difficulties will persist through adulthood. Some individuals will become more sociably able and a few will be able to develop friendships. However, many will remain socially naive and apparently unaware of the feelings of others and will not develop spoken language. Most who have the opportunity will self-select leisure activities that are unusually narrow, seemingly all-engrossing and typically involving repetition or systematic engagement. Collection of unusual items and memorization of things such as timetables or obscure numbers (e.g. railway carriage identification numbers) is common. The prognosis in the widest social sense is usually related to the level of intellectual functioning, with those with high levels being more likely to make progress in terms of social awareness and other social indicators such as employment. For a full discussion of autism in adulthood *see* Meldrum (1990) and Tantam (1991); for consideration of a particular approach *see* Van Bourgondien and Mesibov (1989); and for a brief review *see* Schroeder et al. (1996).

Interpersonal difficulties

Having briefly reviewed the history of autism, attention can now be focused on explanations about the syndrome. This starts with a consideration of the ideas of Hobson (1993), subsequent sections examine other explanations.

Hobson focuses on the way that inter-subjectivity provides a foundation for many of our cognitive and social processes. Inter-subjectivity involves being aware that other people are not simply collections of mechanistic responses but that they have motivations, minds and thoughts and that these thoughts and motivations may not be the same as one's own. Hobson believes that typical infants are able to directly perceive the emotions of others, in other words when an infant sees someone smile they know that person is in a positive mood, much in the same way that they know certain objects are big (*see also* Chapter 4). He also believes that typical infants start to notice that other people have different reactions to events than their own and this provides the basis for the development of symbolic capacities where children can hold different representations of a situation. Thus, pretend play (knowing I hold a banana, but pretending it is a telephone) develops out of these inter-personal capacities. Eventually typical children understand that there can be accurate and inaccurate representations about the world and that people can have different ideas from oneself (*see* 'theory of mind' below). Hobson argues that children with autism are unable to directly perceive the emotions of others and, as a result, they do not develop an inter-subjective awareness of others and fail to develop subsequent cognitive abilities such as pretend play.

AUTISM AND THE SELF

The importance of a lack of inter-subjective understanding can be seen in relation to several capacities involving the self. To better understand how the self operates in individuals with autism three sets of findings are considered:

- Knowing oneself in relation to others.
- The development of perception and conception of oneself.
- Agency and reflective self-awareness.

Knowing oneself in relation to others

Hobson focuses attention on what happens between a child with autism and others, rather than on what happens or fails to happen to the child as a single entity. This focusing is useful in that it highlights that autism is not simply a developmental problem within children, but rather that it arises from what happens or does not happen between them and the rest of the social world. This involves a lack of what Hobson terms 'mental co-ordination' (Hobson, 1993, p. 14) between children and others in relation to a shared understanding of the external world.

Self-perception and self-conception

A child with autism may remove a mark from their face following sighting in a mirror (Dawson and McKissick, 1984) – an act which is often taken as an indication of self-awareness as the child recognizes the mark as being on their own face rather than on the mirror image. Yet the fact that they do not appear to show the same signs of embarrassment or coyness as do non-autistic children suggests that while they know themselves at one level they remain unaware that they are in the minds of others (Hobson, 1993).

Rachel, provides an example of this, she would use public conveniences according to the clothes she wore. This indicates that she recognized the signs of a person wearing a skirt or trousers, but her choice was influenced by whether she was wearing a skirt or trousers at the time. It seems, therefore, that she could identify herself at a visual level and successfully relate that identification to a categorization. Although she had awareness of gender differences (albeit in a rather simplistic and ultimately misleading way), she was unaware of herself as being female and regarded by others as being female. When taught she could learn to list male and female characteristics, but found it difficult to relate this to a sense of her own self-hood. The learning that she was able to achieve was of a mechanistic kind, not mediated by any natural perceptions of the relations between genders.

Sense of agency and reflective self-awareness

The difficulties that children with autism have in developing a sense of self are apparent in many of their developmental characteristics. The way in which Stephen misappropriated the personal pronoun ('he had assembly') and the occasional echolalic speech in autism (repeating what others say sometimes after a period of time) indicates that sense of self is different from that of non-autistic individuals. In addition, there are longer than expected delays in using words about mental states such as 'think, believe and know' and the discussion of emotion topics is usually achieved by referring to behavioural actions. There also are difficulties in answering questions about differences between the mental and the physical worlds.

Understanding the minds of others

Baron-Cohen (1995) offers another perspective on lack of understanding about others' minds in autism. He points to the importance for typical development of the ability to 'read minds' (i.e. understand what others are thinking) and the difficulties when that ability is in any way impaired. Baron-Cohen suggests that those with autism are exceptional in that they fail to do this, or more properly that they fail to develop the capacity to attribute mental states to others. Clearly, such failure will have significant effects on communication where making sense of the intentions of the speaker (or writer) enables the listener to understand what is being said. In these terms his ideas are similar to those of Hobson.

In Baron-Cohen's (1995) view there are four mechanisms which under-pin the typical development of mind reading and which occur in a phase-like way between birth to about four years of age.

THE INTENTIONALITY DETECTOR

Baron-Cohen supposes that at about nine months an intentionality detector allows infants to distinguish examples of agency (at a primitive level anything that is self-propelled) from non-agency. Children with autism appear to be able to function at this level, for example there is evidence that they can distinguish animacy and understand that a person's emotional state can be caused by their desire for something.

THE EYE-DIRECTION DETECTOR

This cognitive mechanism enables individuals to detect the presence of eyes, work out whether those eyes are directed to itself or towards something else and infer what the eyes are looking towards. So, whereas the intentionality detector operates at the level of mental states the eye-direction detector operates on inferences about what an agent sees. Here again, it may be that children with autism can operate at least at a basic level in that they can interpret the eye-direction of another as that person 'seeing something' and can work out what that person is looking at (although it is a moot point as to whether this 'working out' is of the same kind as in non-autistic children).

SHARED-ATTENTION MECHANISM

This mechanism enables what Baron-Cohen terms 'triadic representations' to develop. That is, the child is able to form a mental representation such as 'you and I see that we are looking at the same object' (Baron-Cohen, 1995, p. 45); here the child is identifying the relationship between agent, self and object. It is possible to imagine this mechanism developing in a non-visual modality (with a visually impaired individual for example), but Baron-Cohen argues for the visual modality being easily the most efficient and therefore that the development of the ability to share attention is dependent to a large degree on the mechanism of eye-direction detection.

This third mechanism acts as a link between the first two mechanisms in that it enables eye-direction to be interpreted in terms of mental states such as desire and goal. So, when given a goal detection task 'which chocolate will Charlie take?' (using four chocolates and a face looking at one of them) normally developing young children will use eye-direction in achieving an answer (i.e. they tend to choose the chocolate that Charlie is looking at, even if an arrow pointing at a different chocolate is used as a distractor).

According to Baron-Cohen's model, it is at this third level that children with autism fail to develop the usual behaviours which relate to seeking and maintaining joint attention. They do not monitor the gaze of others, nor do they use the gesture of pointing in a protodeclarative way to direct the attention of others, nor do they use other gestures to show things to people. A typical child may point to a biscuit tin on a shelf, a child with autism is likely, at best, to lead the adult by the hand and push them in the direction of the tin. Where non-autistic children can operate successfully within social scenario because they can understand that attention can be shared, the child with autism is developmentally constrained because they lack this understanding.

THE THEORY OF MIND MECHANISM (ToMM)

In normal development ability to pretend, recognise the pretence of others and understand that people can have false as well as true beliefs are significant developmental advances. Normally developing children become involved in pretence for their pleasure and can do this in an effortless kind of way. In as much as children can use their understanding of mental states to explain and eventually predict the behaviour of others then Baron-Cohen would claim that they have a 'theory of mind' (Leslie, 1994) which they can use to understand social scenarios and the thinking of others.

The ToMM functions in such a way as to form (i) representations of mental states such as pretending and knowing and (ii) understandings of the relationships between these states and actions. Clearly, for the child to operate a theory of mind in this way they would need to detect what another person intends and the focus of their intention. Baron-Cohen supposes that in autism, because of the breakdown in the development of the mechanism that enables the child to operate on the basis of shared attention, the ToMM is dysfunctional. The child with autism, then, fails to come to know about the minds of others because they cannot operate in a social scenario through the sharing of attention with another person.

To test a child's awareness that another person is thinking about things in a different way to their own (which is the basis of the theory of mind ability) one can ask them about the beliefs of the other person which are false. In this way one can distinguish between the child simply repeating what they know in their own mind (i.e. the true state of affairs) and their ability to understand that what they know is not shared by another person. Perhaps the most famous experiment that seeks to investigate whether or not children can detect false belief in others is the 'Sally-Anne test' (Box 12.3).

BOX 12.3 The 'Sally-Anne test'

In a scenario acted out with puppets, Sally puts a marble in a particular place. Later, while Sally is away, Anne puts the marble somewhere else. Sally then returns and the child is asked 'where will Sally look for the marble?' Baron-Cohen et al. (1985) found that the majority of normally developing children and those with Down's syndrome passed this test, whereas only a small minority of children with autism did so. The children with autism tended to indicate where the marble really was; in other words they failed to distinguish between their own (true) belief and the (false) belief of Sally.

The conclusion drawn from this study and others is that children with autism have difficulty with understanding the mental state of belief. The findings are robust, however, a minority of children with autism (between 20 per cent and 35 per cent) pass these tests. Although some children with autism can pass theory of mind tests that are at the level of normally developing 3–4-year-olds, almost all have difficulty with the more complex tasks that involve beliefs about beliefs (nested belief questions) that typical 6–7-year-olds can pass.

There is considerable debate about what the theory of mind tests tell us about children's abilities. Simplifications of the tests have enabled children younger than 3–4 years of age to pass them (Lewis and Osborne, 1990; Lewis et al., 1994) and this suggests that the capacity may be present at an earlier age than previously supposed. There also have been arguments that inter-subjectivity involves a capacity to understand the minds of others and this capacity is even present during infancy. Other suggestions concern implicit and explicit understanding of theory of mind (*see also* Chapter 6), by monitoring the gaze of normally developing children aged younger than four years it is clear that they may look in the 'right' place when Sally enters the room but nevertheless give the wrong answer to the question when asked (i.e. revert to a description of reality), indicating that they may know at an implicit level where the marble is but not be able to make that knowledge explicit. The gap between the development of implicit and explicit knowledge may be greater in the autistic than the non-autistic population.

DIFFICULTIES ARISING FROM DSYFUNCTIONAL THEORY OF MIND

In a sense the child with autism is doubly handicapped by their inability to read minds. The subsequent stages of social learning, for example learning about how people can be deceived deliberately or inadvertently, will be impaired because this essential building block of social development is not in place. But also the usefulness of those social scenarios in which deception are employed (e.g. hide and seek games) for other kinds of learning will be impaired. So, to try to teach reading using a book which retells the story of Little Red Riding Hood is a meaningful experience for a child without autism (because they can understand the motives of the characters and the way in which Red Riding Hood is deceived by the disguise of the wolf) as well as being an exercise in decoding text. But for the child with autism the experience remains at the level of text decoding without the attendant [social] meaning.

Of course, this example makes all sorts of assumptions about the ability of the child with autism. One would need to recognize that sitting down to 'read a story together' involves sharing attention and this in itself, as we have already noted, is problematic in autism. Indeed, even before the stage of sharing attention there is the need to engage in the act of sitting together. If the child with autism does not recognize the intentions of the carer that this is what is desired of them then they will not be inclined to respond. Motivation to join in any shared social event (which is what is involved in most acts of teaching and learning) requires the child to recognize the intentions and hence motivations of the other. In the normal sense of the term then, the child with autism remains unmotivated because they fail to pick up social signals of intentionality and motivation. In another sense, of course, they have motivations which relate to their own needs and which are not mediated by any social influence and therefore remain idiosyncratic. In short, cognitive difficulties in autism have both social consequences and, because human learning is predominantly socially driven and socially constrained, consequences for further cognitive development. Whether the developmental pattern of autism is primarily a cognitive difficulty with metarepresentation (Leslie, 1994) or an emotion perception difficulty of engagement with others at an intersubjective level (Hobson, 1993) is a point of contrast in theoretical positions.

One important aspect of social development is the ability to understand the emotions of others. When normally developing children learn to theorize about the minds of others they learn that beliefs can influence emotion; in short, they come to understand that believing something can lead to a person becoming happy or sad independently of the situation (if you believe yourself to be treated well by your host you will be happy regardless of the actual treatment – if you believe your host has ulterior (and hostile) motives for treating you well you may be unhappy despite the fact that the treatment you are receiving is 'good'). Individuals with autism may be able to judge another person's emotional state in as much as it derives from a physical situation (the boy eating the ice cream is happy) but will have much more difficulty with tasks which require judgements about the effect of beliefs on the other person's emotions (the boy was happy because he thought he was going to go swimming). Again, here, the developmental nature of the difficulty in autism is apparent: the child can get so far but the crucial element of understanding beliefs and of course false beliefs is denied and this makes the later stages of development problematic.

DISCUSSION POINT

Discuss Baron-Cohen's four mechanisms which he suggests underpin the typical development of mind reading ability – how significant are they in developmental terms? What do 'Theory of Mind' tests tell us about children's abilities?

Central coherence theory

BEYOND MINDREADING

The evidence from the work of Baron-Cohen, Hobson and others that children with autism have a difficulty in mentalizing. This does not explain, however, all of the difficulties that are evident in autism (e.g. restricted range of interests, obsessive need for sameness, preoccupation with parts of the whole), nor does it address some of the apparent strengths that occur in at least some individuals with autism (e.g. Stephen's excellent rote memory, individuals' occasional islets of ability such as drawing) and their apparent abilities in experimental situations requiring, for example, memory for word strings (Hermelin and O'Connor, 1967) and unrelated items (Tager-Flusberg, 1991). (For a longer list of experimental studies indicating unusual strengths in autism *see* Happé, 1994, p. 116.)

Frith (1989) sought to resolve some of the unanswered questions that arise from the above by postulating that the strengths and weaknesses in autism have a single origin which can be found at a cognitive level involving the way in which information is integrated. Frith and Happé (Frith, 1989; Frith and Happé, 1994) argued that autism is, in part at least, a result of 'a weak drive for central coherence'. Where non-autistic individuals tend to process information at a global level they suggest that individuals with autism tend to process similar information at a local level in a 'bottom-up' way. Non-autistic thinking is typified by its tendency to operate on the basis of an impression of the whole rather than an analysis of the detail. This tendency enables, for example, the disambiguating of ambiguous words in discourse. Frith and Snowling (1983) and Happé (1994) showed that even autistic children who were able to complete theory of mind tasks, were unable to use the context of sentences to disambiguate homographs (words which contain the same letters but have different meanings, e.g. tear – meaning tearful or torn).

It is notable that even where individuals with autism pass experimental theory of mind tasks they invariably seem to have difficulties in real-life situations in which the operation of such theorising is necessary. Central coherence offers an explanation for this as when the mentalizing takes place in naturalistic situations then the theorizing requires the extraction of information from context (Happé, 1994). The operation of a theory without regard to context would lead to inappropriate actions and the kind of rigid, dogmatic behaviours that are typical of autism. Knowing the theory of how other minds work is simply not enough if that knowledge does not take account of context and in the social world context is all important, ever-changing and often implicit.

A PARTICULAR THINKING STYLE

Some individuals with autism are able to produce outstanding drawings which represent whole objects to a high degree of accuracy. Yet an analysis by Mottron and Belleville (1993) showed that the drawings are formed from detail to whole, rather than vice versa (as was the case with typical children). Certainly, artists with autism such as Steven Wiltshire are renowned for their attention to detail. It seems that artistic and other exceptional abilities in autism may relate to the idiosyncratic way in which individuals process information rather than to an enhanced ability of the kind 'normally' employed.

The tendency to process at a local level will be a benefit when tasks require an analytical approach and where global processing can be distracting (e.g. on tasks involving embedded figures as used by Shah and Frith (1983) where an object is 'hidden' by the rest of the picture). Individuals with autism are able, then, to perform well (sometimes better than children of a similar mental age) where tasks require a focusing on separate, constituent parts of a figure or design rather than on the whole and where attention to detail is required. The tendency also explains the ability often displayed in everyday life of locating fine detail and identifying slight changes to familiar layouts which go unnoticed by others.

The suggestion is not that a lack of central coherence is a primary deficit in autism and a precursor to theory of mind difficulties, but rather that it describes a particular thinking style. The question of whether or not a weakness in terms of central coherence is specific to autism has been investigated by Jarrold and Russell (1997). They examined the difference between children with autism, those with moderate learning difficulties and typical control subjects on a counting task in which the ability to interpret information at a global level was potentially advantageous. The results indicate that those with autism were biased towards a processing of information at an analytical rather than a global level (i.e. consistent with a weak drive for central coherence). However, there was no significant difference between them and the children with moderate learning, indicating that a failure to count 'globally' was not wholly specific to autism. So, a low drive for central coherence may not be entirely specific to autism, even so, there remains convincing evidence that this thinking style is pervasive in autism.

DISCUSSION POINT

To what extent do you think that 'Central Coherence Theory' explains the range of difficulties that are evident in autism (e.g. restricted range of interests, obsessive need for sameness, preoccupation with parts of the whole)?

Executive functioning

Executive functioning is defined as the ability to 'maintain an appropriate problem-solving set for the attainment of a future goal' (Ozonoff et al., 1991, p. 1083) and encompasses areas in which individuals with autism appear to be impaired such as: planning their own behaviours, controlling impulsive behaviours and searching for information in an organized way. The deficit was first identified in relation to brain damage of frontal lobes.

Individuals with autism are defined, in part at least, by the rigidity of their thinking; they tend to develop ritualistic behaviour patterns and may become distressed by changes to their immediate environment which interfere with these patterns; they do not plan ahead well and often seem unable to anticipate consequences of actions; they have difficulty in monitoring and reflecting on their own actions and they often behave in impulsive ways. All of these features may be seen as pointing to some level of impairment in executive functioning capacity.

Rumsey and Hamburger (1988) found evidence of executive function deficits in autistic adults (on tasks such as the Wisconsin Card Sorting Test) which contrasted with language and memory (both only mildly affected) and visuospatial and sensory-perceptual abilities (both entirely unaffected). Subsequently, Ozonoff et al. (1991) presented findings from studies using high-functioning individuals with autism which suggest selective deficits in executive function. Further, their studies indicate a universality of such deficits among autistic individuals which would suggest them to be primary to autism. This contrasts with their findings (presented in the same paper) which offered less convincing evidence for the universality of deficits in theory of mind (at least at first-order level; for further discussion, *see* Bishop, 1993).

This and other evidence have resulted in the suggestion that some features of autism are due to executive function deficits. Indeed, Ozonnof et al. (1991) suggest that there may be an underlying deficit in 'prefrontal function' (p. 1101) primary to autism. This argument enables explanation of the different patterns of difficulty in autism when compared to other groups who have similar problems with tasks in the different domains.

Whatever the case concerning particular impairments and specific brain systems it does seem that executive function problems are a feature of autism, but it is harder to be clear about the causal role of such problems in a developmental sense. It is not so much a matter of what abilities exist in an individual at a later stage of development, but rather what abilities exist at the earlier stages of development. To return to one of the main points underlying this chapter – autism needs to be seen as a developmental disorder.

Chapter summary

There is a wide spectrum of autistic disorders with the common feature of three areas of impairment: social interaction, communication and imagination. This triad exists in combination with levels of intellectual ability varying from profound mental retardation to high functioning. The disorders are developmental in nature, relate to physical abnormalities in the brain and have a complex of causes which may in part be genetic. Estimates of incidence vary considerably according to the authority cited but an approximate indication might be that nine in every 1000 children from across the range of intellectual abilities fall within the current diagnostic criteria for autistic spectrum disorders (Wing, 1997). There is no known 'cure' though there have been significant advances in recent years in terms of education and care in autism. These advances have been achieved within a context in which individuals with autism are respected in terms of their rights and the value of the contribution they can make to the lives of others. Psychological understandings have influenced the education and care of individuals with autism, for example through the notion that there is a pervasive need to develop the individual's repertoire of planning and organizational strategies and to teach them to use feedback in a reflective way and that this development requires overt and continuing structure typically using visual representation. What are normally accepted as 'givens' in education (e.g. the transfer of knowledge from the learned context to new situations and the ability to infer intent from teachers' actions) cannot be assumed in autism; a high level of situational analysis is therefore required.

It is important to note in conclusion that much of what has been written in this chapter concerns the way in which those with autism fail to develop a sense of self through subjective experiences with others, their difficulty in understanding the minds of others and their problems therefore in establishing empathetic understanding. Not withstanding all of this, those with autism remain individuals and there is a need on the part of the non-autistic to respect not only their difficulties but also the inordinate amounts of courage and effort that such individuals often expend in trying to learn about the world and their place in it. Their successes in this respect may be tenuous but will invariably be hard won.

Seminar questions

1. Discuss the way in which understanding of autism has developed over recent times and the implications of changing views of, for example: diagnosis, incidence and causation.
2. In what sense, if any, is the notion of autism as a developmental disorder likely to be important when considering approaches to the diagnosis, education and care of individuals with autism?
3. In what sense is autism a truly 'pervasive' disorder?
4. Using the brief description in Box 1, discuss the relationship between autism and self.
5. Do you think it likely that executive functioning difficulties are a cause or an effect of autism?
6. What particular ethical and human rights issues are likely to arise for professionals when working with individuals with autism?

Further reading

Baron-Cohen, S. 1995. *Mindblindness: an essay on autism and theory of mind*. Cambridge, MA: MIT Press.

Frith, U. (Ed.) 1991. *Autism and Aspenger syndrome*. Cambridge: Cambridge University Press.

Happé, F. 1994. *Autism: an introduction to psychology theory*. London: UCL Press.

Hobson, R.P. 1993. *Autism and the development of mind*. Hove: Lawrence Erlbaum Associates.

Part 

INTERPERSONAL PROCESSES: OTHERS AND THEIR INFLUENCE

Psychoanalytic views about development

HOWARD STEELE AND MIRIAM STEELE

Editors' preface

Most books on developmental psychology contain few if any references to pyschoanalytic perspectives. Furthermore, those references that are made often refer to 'classic' psychoanalytic ideas and work that is many decades old, while references to current perspectives and theorizing are usually absent. Psychology and psychoanalysis both focus on human behaviour and thinking, but as often is the case between related but different disciplines the relation has not always been a harmonious one. One of us can still remember, on a psychology course nearly 30 years ago, the first and only lecture about the views of Freud ending up as a tirade about the worthlessness of psychiatrists!

In this chapter Drs Howard and Miriam Steele show that current psychoanalytic perspectives seek to integrate knowledge about social interaction and social relationships to provide a fuller picture of human development than is usually available in pyschological descriptions. In the present chapter we see the way that many different ideas are drawn together to achieve this integration and the way that psychoanalysis places interpersonal processes at the centre of human development. It is useful to read this chapter in relation to the following one which concerns emotions (Chapter 14) and with the chapter about attachment processes (Chapter 5) so as to compare different perspectives about similar topics. In addition, the concern of psychoanalysts with personal growth also is related to the subject matter of Chapter 21. Thus, the present chapter provides a valuable summary of the way that current psychoanalytic views can provide insights and a different perspective about the process of development.

Introduction

This chapter provides a contemporary psychoanalytic perspective on three domains of development of concern and interest to psychoanalysts and developmental psychologists alike. These three domains make up the main sections of this chapter:

- Self, social relations, and emotion-regulation.
- Psychosexual and gender development.
- The long-term influence of early family experiences upon personality development and functioning.

Throughout the chapter, reference is made to the ways in which developmental research provides confirmation of some psychoanalytic assumptions concerning development (e.g. the widely shared view that the mind is inherently interpersonal), and refutation of other assumptions (e.g. the suggestion that human newborns are normally overwhelmed with confusion, fear and aggression). The chapter aims to provide a 'feel' for the history, continuing evolution, and contemporary value of the psychoanalytic approach to development which places the consideration of emotions, interpersonal and intrapersonal relations, and unconscious influences upon behaviour, at the top of the agenda.

DISCUSSION POINT

A discussion point relevant to this chapter's relation to the wider text concerns similarities and differences between psychoanalytic and psychological views about development. Box 13.1 provides a summary of some basic features to both views of development, where our interest is in highlighting points of differences, and underlining the specific value of a psychoanalytic approach.

BOX 13.1 Five contrasts between psychological and psychoanalytic approaches to development

Some features of the *psychological* approach	Some feature of the *psychoanalytic* approach
Focus on observable behaviour and the extent to which it may be reliably observed in the laboratory or naturalistic setting	Focus on internal organization of emotional and mental processes and mechanisms underlying observable behaviour

Primary focus is on age-related group differences as detailed in standard developmental texts	Focus on age-appropriate stages of development always in relation to individual differences
Unconscious influences upon behaviour doubted	Unconscious influences upon behaviour assumed
Adherence to the scientific method dictates caution concerning generalizations and value-judgements about the goals of development	Adherence to Freud's value-laden suggestion that the goal of development is psychological health defined as being able to love well, and work well
Understanding normal development	Understanding deviations from, and promoting a return to, normal 'healthy' development

It is important to hold in mind that psychoanalytic theories are clinical theories aimed at understanding the whole person and promoting their psychological health. In line with this, the psychoanalyst does not shy away from making value-judgements about development linked to beliefs in what constitutes health, usually conceived as loving well, playing well, and working well. By contrast, a developmental psychologist is often not a clinician, and is frequently satisfied with understanding in detail some specific aspect of normal child development (e.g. object permanence) and linking it to a biological, evolutionary and/or cognitive account of development. In sum, the value of the psychoanalytic view lies in a determination to understand the mind as a 'whole', a belief that social interactions fundamentally influence emotional and cognitive growth, a preparedness to make value judgements about developmental experiences, and a basic concern with development in relation to psychopathology.

Notwithstanding these over-arching shared characteristics of psychoanalytic approaches to development, there are some marked differences of opinion concerning the origins and direction of development within the psychoanalytic literature. The chapter continues by looking at the important distinction between classical and contemporary psychoanalytic views concerning development of the self.

SELF, SOCIAL RELATIONS, AND EMOTION-REGULATION

The term 'self' refers to that part of the mind which is both 'I' and 'me', both the one who senses and perceives the world, as well as the one who feels and knows things about one's place in the world (*see* Chapter 21). Psychoanalysis, in both its classical and contemporary forms, assumes that the self develops in the context of social relations. But out of what beginnings does the self develop? The contemporary psychoanalytic answer is rather different from the traditional Freudian one. Let us first consider the classical theory of Freud, before contrasting it with contemporary psycho-analytic thinking concerning child development.

DISCUSSION POINT

What are the main features of the classical Freudian approach to development?

Box 13.2, below provides a summary of the Freudian view in terms of three stages of early psychological development covering the first three stages of development (Freud, 1905, 1914, 1920, 1923, 1926). Notably, Box 13.2 does not specify ages at which these developments occur. The first phase refers to the early months of life, whereas the second phase begins as soon as parents take steps to deliberately limit their baby's behaviour (e.g. saying 'no'), and the third phase applies to the child with organized language skills, and at least a first-order theory of mind (*see* Chapter 12) in the preschool period. Box 13.2 underlines how the newborn baby in the classic Freudian view is nihilistic or without morals or awareness of other people. Satisfying personal desires not pleasure in social relations for their own sake is the primary or first goal of the newborn.

BOX 13.2 Three stages of development according to Freud

Descriptive features of the classic Freudian view of development summarized as three phases

Explanatory concepts invoked to anchor these descriptions in a theory of normal development

1. Life begins in a state of inward focus where the infant has no sense of an individual self, is driven by the wish to secure pleasure and avoid pain, and in turn loves those who satisfy their desires, and hates those who deny satisfaction.

Life begins in a state of 'primary narcissim' where 'id' (sexual/aggressive instinctual drives) and 'ego' (cognitive capacities) exist as as a single matrix, and life is governed by the 'pleasure principle' (what feels good, is good!)

2. Parents inevitably and in gradually increasing measure frustrate the baby, who slowly develops an increasing capacity to delay gratification. Parents' demands conflict with children's wishes, and child protests or tantrums may follow.

Ego becomes gradually different-iated from id; ego begins to deploy psychological defenses (e.g. denial) which help the individual work toward compromises between 'id' demands and parental (external world) demands.

3. Children become increasingly

Parents' love and demands become

able to negotiate with parents over goals, and intense emotional outbursts are less frequent. Moral behaviour becomes reliably observable, and behavioural evidence of sexual and aggressive interests is much less obvious. Peer relations and adaptation to the demands of school and society follow more or less naturally.

internally represented as the 'superego' which provides the child with a mental guide for how to behave (what the superego approves of is good!); 'pleasure principle' still governs in 'id' but 'reality principle' governs in ego and superego. What were previously external conflicts are now internal ones.

The more recent approach to development within psychoanalysis has moved away from classical Freudian views in three main respects. First, there is now a central focus on interpersonal relationships and the way these develop in the context of broader physiological and cognitive changes. Second, contemporary psychoanalytic views of development are searching for accounts of human motivation that are not limited to, or defined by, the Freudian belief in an eternal battle between life and death instincts. His view involved the ego or self in a perpetual struggle to defend itself against the ominous forces of sex and aggression. This was presumed to be achieved more or less successfully by the ego deploying strategies or mechanisms of defence that would diffuse the power of these impulses, and yet also permit their partial or transformed expression and satisfaction (Freud, 1920, 1926; *see also* Box 13.3 below for suggestions about the contemporary relevance of this view). Further, many classical psychoanalytic views of what was assumed to be normal development in *all* children are now appreciated mainly as accounts of development in only *some* children, namely children whose development is following atypical or psychopathological pathways (*see* Lyons-Ruth, 1991; Steele and Steele, 1998).

ORIGINS OF THE CONTEMPORARY PSYCHOANALYTIC APPROACH TO CHILD DEVELOPMENT

The Freudian view of early psychological development may be forgiven for being so out of touch with the concerns of contemporary psychoanalytic understandings of development as only the latter is based on reliably collected empirical observations of infants. Additionally, Freud's thinking about child development was primarily based on looking backward at what was presumed to have been the childhood experiences of his adult patients. The contemporary psychoanalytic view owes much to its reliance on data deriving from prospective longitudinal investigations of childhood, and, importantly, to the development of video-film. James and Joyce Robertson's (1952) film 'A two-year old goes to hospital', collected in consultation with the psychoanalyst John Bowlby, represents a hallmark in the emergence of the contemporary psychoanalytic approach to development which acknowledges the presence of complex social-emotional reactions in babies, including separation-anxieties and grief responses, indicative of an inborn propensity to search out meaningful social relations (*see also* Chapter 5).

Evidence of both the persistence of the classical perspective, and the powerful emergence of a contemporary psychoanalytic perspective, may be found in the work of Mahler who based her thinking in part on video-filmed observations (Mahler et al., 1975). Yet, within ten years of the book about her theory being published, the classical elements to the theory no longer had much credence owing to their incompatibility with research findings. Mahler's theorizing leaned very heavily upon Freud's (1914) suggestion that the psychological self or ego is initially a bodily ego, not yet aware of itself as having an existence separate from mother. She correspondingly framed her understanding of development as a move from 'normal autism' (*see* Chapter 12) and 'symbiosis' toward increasing measures of separation and individuation from the mother to whom we are initially biologically (and psychologically) fused. From a contemporary psychoanalytic perspective, Mahler's view of development seems to overvalue the human propensity for independence and correspondingly undervalues the equally important human need for social relations.

Mahler's conceptualization of early self-development as autistic-like is inconsistent with contemporary infancy research. This research suggests that newborn infants are able to recognize boundaries between themselves and their mothers, contrasting with Freud's (1914) notion of 'primary narcissism' and Mahler et al.'s (1975) concepts of 'normal autism' and 'normal symbiosis'. However, we may be less inclined to dismiss these clinical speculations when we consider the following two points:

- Laboratory-based infancy research is based largely upon observations of young babies in their most alert and responsive moments; and significant amounts of data from babies are lost because many are often too sleepy or inattentive.
- We should ask what are human newborns doing when they are not displaying their impressive organization of perceptual capacities? They are asleep as much as 75 per cent of the day.

Further, approximately 50 per cent of the human newborn's sleep is active-REM or dream-sleep. Thus, we should not forget to ask what is the baby dreaming about? Perhaps it is of some boundary-less state of being as Pine (1985), one of Mahler's co-authors, suggests in a poetic defence of her ideas. Pine points out that no phase of development is intended to describe all the child's experiences at that age. All that is intended by Mahler's phase-concept, Pine maintains, is a description of what comprise the high-intensity, affectively significant moments of a child's day:

the post-nursing moments of falling asleep at the mother's breast or in her arms against her body, especially since they follow and powerfully contrast with the moments of distress and confusion during crying and hunger, are moments . . . that are likely to be psychological high points of the infant's day and thus to become organizing nodes for other experiences. These moments (which look from the *outside* as though they could be accompanied by merging, melting, boundary-less experiences in the infant) are among the justifications for referring to this period as the normal symbiotic phase – or better, as the period of formative impact of experiences of boundarylessness. (Pine, 1985, p. 41)

Notably, this contemporary attempt to preserve some of the essential insights of Mahler's classical theorizing does *not* seek to replace Freud's instinctual-drive theory. Pine (1985) suggests that infants' positive interactions with their mothers activate libidinal/sexual/loving drives while negative experiences activate frustration and aggressive drives – both drives having been prominently included in classical psychoanalytic theories.

By contrast, contemporary object-relations approaches to self-development (e.g. Stern, 1985) consider the relational needs of the infant as the primary motivating force underlying development of the self, without recourse to the assumption of there being inborn aggressive or sexual drives (e.g. Greenberg and Mitchell, 1983). Further, the contemporary approach assumes that children's positive or negative emotions crucially depend on the extent to which infant's emotional needs are sensitively and responsively met by mother and others in the caregiving environment. This in turn lays the foundation for enduring mental resprespentations of the self and others.

The current object-relations perspective is consistent with much of the research into early human development over the last few decades which has helped to demonstrate the alertness and keen social interests of the human newborn (e.g. via preferential looking, EEG and brain scanning). Contributing to, and greatly influenced by, this new research have been a number of psychoanalysts (e.g. Robert Emde and Daniel Stern) who have made it their priority to observe infant development systematically. Most importantly, Emde (e.g. 1988) and Stern (e.g. 1985) are representative of a powerful contemporary voice in psychoanalysis. This voice describes infant behaviour without resort to classical psychoanalytic assumptions about the developmental roots of psychopathology in older children or adults on the one hand, or assumptions about quantities of unconscious sexual or aggressive instinctual energies seeking release through behaviour. Instead, the newborn human infant is seen as governed by self-organizing processes and an inborn propensity for social relations. Regulation of social interactions and psychophysiological states advance in line with identifiable underlying developmental shifts in the organization and functioning of brain processes (e.g. Emde, 1981). These shifts involve significant developments in neurobiological functions and lead to the reorganization of behaviours and abilities.

Stern's (e.g. 1985) thinking about the development of the self reads rather like a considered meditation on the recent infancy research, particularly the meaning of cross-modal perception. The basic finding seems to be that what adults take for granted – namely the capacity for linking and mentally representing information received from various senses, e.g. connecting-up what we are seeing with what we are hearing, with what we are feeling and so on – is not unique to older children and adults. Infants, from shortly after birth if not before, are engaged in something very similar. For example, three-week-old infants given one of two pacifiers with distinctive protruding nubs subsequently looked longer at the shape of the nipple they just sucked as opposed to an unfamiliar shape (Meltzoff and Borton, 1979). This is one piece of the evidence for trans-modal or inter-modal perception being a feature of the innate design of our perceptual system. In other words, it appears that the self does not need to learn to take in information from one modality and transfer it to another, we do this naturally. Stern (1985) comments on how this capacity leads not simply to the encoding of information but to the building up of a representation which can then be recognized and/or applied in more than one sensory modality and more than one context. Against this background, Stern sketches a likely progression as increasingly complex bits of information about the social, emotional and moral world are encoded, represented and utilised by distinct layers or strata of the self, including a core self, an emergent self, and a verbal self.

Contemporary psychoanalytic perspectives differ from their earlier classical forms most markedly in terms of their reinterpretation (or rejection) of Freud's instinctual drive theory. For Freud, the quality of the person's relations with objects (animate and inanimate) in the external world were understood as the expression of the individual's sexual and aggressive longings. Even for Freud, this was not invariably the case and thus he declared in one of his most often-cited phrases: 'some times a cigar is *just* a cigar'. Freud needed to make this point because in the thinking of classical psychoanalysis, anything and everything could become the target or 'object' of an instinctual drive. By contrast, contemporary psychoanaltyic theories share a belief that the 'objects' of primary interest are people, the primary 'object' is ordinarily the mother, and the primary longing determining the child's tie to the object is a wish to be cared for and loved.

Contemporary psychoanalytic perspectives thus share with mainstream developmental psychological thinking that human newborns' inclination to participate in social interactions and develop autonomous self-regulatory (ego) skills must be cultivated by one or more caregivers (usually but not necessarily mother and father). Ordinarily, caregivers during social interaction often experience a sense of joy, and promote a similar sense in the infant (*after* Bowlby, 1951). When there are significant deficits in the caregiving environment as when infants are physically abused, child development, at both the neurobiological and social–cognitive levels, is significantly compromised with potentially long-term deleterious consequences (Perry, 1997).

THE INTERPERSONAL ASSUMPTION, 'OBJECT-RELATIONS' THEORIES AND EMOTIONS

Thus infancy research appears to be increasingly demonstrating how self-development flourishes in an appropriate, sensitive and responsive, interpersonal context. As already suggested above, an interpersonal assumption is basic to many contemporary psychoanalytic approaches known as 'object-relations theories'. This is a term which denotes the fundamental importance of social relations to self-development. At the same time, retention of the word 'object' from classical psychoanalysis underlines the assumption that the self constructs, stores in memory and is influenced by representations or fantasies concerning what it *feels like* to participate in social relations. Clearly, there are times when feelings of pain and frustration are aroused by social interactions, just as at other times the self resounds with joy and satisfaction. In this section of the chapter, we aim to show how these ideas about social interaction and their mental representation provide a basis for understanding fundamental issues about the regulation of emotion. A focus upon the affect-regulatory function of self-development is shared by object-relations approaches, is implicit in the ideas of classical Freudian, Kleinian, and Mahlerian thinking, and is explicit in the ideas of contemporary psychoanalytic approaches (e.g. Emde, 1988; Stern, 1985).

Initially, in the first three months of life, infants are obviously unable to comfort themselves; the capacity for autonomous self-soothing or self-regulation develops only slowly as a result of the way infants' distress has been responded to by caregivers. The extent to which self-development may be regarded as a transition from complete dependence on the caregiver in order to achieve a balanced internal regulation of affect to relative independence in this domain was well captured by Anna Freud (e.g. A. Freud, 1965). Although drawing attention to the many different age-specific tasks that development of the self (or ego) involves, she argued that the object-relationship line of development determines to a large extent the child's progress on all other lines (e.g. from the body – to play – to work; from immaturity – to maturity – in body management). This object-relationship line begins with biological unity to the mother (*in utero*), then a prolonged period of dependence upon the mother for the satisfaction of urgent needs. The goal or normal end-point of this line was conceived by Anna Freud as 'emotional self-reliance'.

A central requirement of optimal self development in the object-relations frame of reference is the capacity to successfully handle *more or less on one's own* feelings of love and hate, normally felt with great intensity toward one's parents (e.g. Bowlby, 1956/1979). As Bowlby suggested, the extent to which individual children will be able to regulate these feelings within themselves will depend crucially upon how such feelings are handled *between* parents and their children. Do the parents prohibit all expressions of aggression toward them? Or do they (hopefully) create an emotional climate conducive to the expression of both negative and positive affect, where family members share the confidence that divergent feelings can be connected-up and resolved between and within people.

One early and enduring object-relations approach that addresses the aggression and frustration felt by young children, and indeed all people, is that model elaborated by Klein. According to Klein (1946) infants have an immense suspicion and fear of their mothers who are experienced as alternately fully satisfying and then ominously frustrating, even alien. In Klein's view, this leads to mental splits in young children's inner experience with parts of their mothers becoming represented as loving/lovable and yet other parts as frightening/feared *distinct* figures. Fear gives way to depression as normal development brings the awareness of whole individuals being both the source and target of diverse, often contradictory feelings. Achieving and maintaining an integrated sense of self and others becomes the challenge for the developing self, and the focus of therapy, from the Kleinian perspective.

Perhaps in order to underline her belief that psychopathology exists on the same continuum as mental health, Klein suggested that human life begins in a 'paranoid–schizoid' position. This involves the mind being haunted by fantasies of being isolated and under attack from the 'bad' breast (or frustrating mother) who is split off from the 'good' breast (or satisfying mother) with whom the infant wishes to merge. Healthy development, for Klein, involves passing into a 'depressive position' as she called it, around three months of age, which gives rise to an increasingly realistic appreciation for the whole mother in both her bad (frustrating) and good (available) elements. She believed that the paranoid–schizoid position is never fully left behind and life is thereafter experienced in terms of a complex array of negative feeling states (e.g. greed, envy, rage) and positive emotions (e.g. joy, gratitude and hope). Thus, every phase of development involves the risk of falling into the position of re-experiencing one of the two original emotional orientations to the world, fear or despair. Klein spoke of shifting 'positions' occupied by the self rather than a sequence of developmental 'phases' or 'stages'. This is because the latter terms assume the possibility of successfully passing into the next phase/stage by leaving behind or resolving the conflicts of the previous phase/stage (this idea of progress can be seen in Freud's theory of psychosexual stages or Erikson's theory of psychosocial stages, *see* Box 13.3 *below*). Klein was not so optimistic (*see* Grosskurth, 1985). With the term 'position', then, Klein meant modes of mental functioning, seeking to highlight the likelihood that throughout the life course, people may shift – often quite suddenly – from one position or mode to another in their thinking and feeling about the self and the social world. Thus, Klein's object-relations theory of self-development makes rather negative assumptions about the probable contents of the infant's inner emotional experience and is perhaps only directly relevant, as we have previously argued (Steele and Steele, 1998), to infants growing up in extremely frightening contexts.

DISCUSSION POINT

Do you think Klein accurately captures the way parent–child relations can be both intensely positive and negative? Do you think the model describes an important aspect of relationships?

A different psychoanalytically based approach to self-development which takes positive and non-frightening contexts to be the norm is Bowlby's (1969) attachment theory. According to attachment theory, the primary influence upon the child's developing sense of self is the quality of care provided by their caregivers. To the extent that the caregivers are sensitive, responsive and stimulating in the right measure, the child is expected to develop a secure sense of self, and trust in others (*see* Chapter 5). This inner sense of self and other is assumed to be stored in a largely unconscious mental structure known as the 'internal working model'. The internal working model stores mental representations of the feelings and thoughts that have been elicited by the child's interactions with caregivers. Providing these feelings and thoughts are neither overwhelming nor frightening, a coherent or integrated mental model of self, others and the world should develop. In normal development, this is a tolerably accurate model of experience.

The effects of negative experiences on development are still seen by psychoanalysts as influenced by both conscious and unconscious processes. One of the lasting insights of Freud was the discussion of how unconscious processes both represent and influence observable behaviour, and this insight remains a central part of contemporary psychoanalytic thinking. For example, multiple incoherent mental models are expected to follow from terrifying experiences where pressure is placed upon the child by the caregiver to represent negative experiences as benign or positive. Out of a wish to please the caregiver and/or protect the self, the result is a distortion of reality, with some typical non-specific representation of actually traumatic events being kept at a conscious level rather than a representation of the overwhelmingly negative details of the events themselves. At an unconscious level – outside of immediate awareness – the actually negative, perhaps terrifying, events and interactions are represented and stored (Bowlby, 1979). The unconscious (but accurate) mental model exerts a disruptive influence on the conscious (inaccurate) mental model and the rest of the mind. This inhibits the accurate processing of information and causes severe emotional distress. As a result, self-development is seriously compromised for the child who suffers early abusive experiences – a view of self-development entirely consistent with Freud's theorizing in the 1880s and early 1890s (*see* Sandler et al., 1972). For traumatized individuals, restoration to the path of normal self-development is usually thought to require the conscious acknowledgement of the repressed memories of the trauma and the reworking of these memories and associated feelings into a coherent narrative. Such re-working can only take place in the context of new, benign and supportive relationships.

SUMMARY

Contemporary psychoanalytic perspectives on development are known as object-relations theories and should be distinguished from the classical Freudian account of development framed in terms of instinctual drive theory. The contemporary perspective regards the primary motivation in human development as the inborn wish to form and maintain meaningful social relationships. A crucial function of these early relationships with caregivers is the model they provide to the infant for the regulation of emotional states. These aspects of contemporary psychoanalytic theory are highly consistent with mainstream developmental research on social and emotional development. However, psychoanalytic views, in both their classical and contemporary forms, tend to go further than those of psychologists by discussing broad features of the internal workings of the mind, by being more speculative, by trying to focus on features of development which play a central role in our emotional life, and by being concerned with the way psychopathology can emerge out of the interaction between the internal workings of the mind and the external environment to which the individual belongs.

Psychosexual and gender development

PSYCHOSEXUAL DEVELOPMENT

A core feature of the psychoanalytic perspective concerns the way that early social experiences often acquire multiple conscious and unconscious layers of meanings, and that individuals seek out certain kinds of interactions to confirm expectations and wishes of the self (*see* Sandler and Sandler, 1998). This became a central feature of psychoanalysis following Freud's observation that the profound emotional distress and anxiety symptoms of his abused patients often remained despite the disclosure of their past traumatic experiences. This was of crucial importance to the psychoanalytic theory of development as it set Freud upon the path of charting the domain of the inner world. He was led to a number of important discoveries, including the central place of sexual interests and pleasures in human development from birth onwards (Freud, 1905), the relentless phenomenon of unconscious guilt (Freud, 1907), and the closely related human capacity for violence (Freud, 1920). From the evidence he compiled in his consulting room, Freud wrote at length about the roles of sexuality and aggression in development and the mind's attempts to harness these powerful forces and arrive at compromise positions that permit the pursuit of both self-interest and social good (Freud, 1912).

This section is based on the view that understanding children's sense of self, gender and relations with others is enhanced by following what was long understood to be the cornerstone of personality development, the psychosexual stages (Freud, 1905, *see* Box 13.3). The term 'sexual' was intended by Freud (1940) to mean something rather more like what is conventionally understood by the term 'sensual'. However, by extending the term 'sexual' as Freud did he was led to regard children as 'polymorphously perverse' in so far as they seek sensual pleasures from all sort of activities far removed from the goal, or possibility of, reproduction.

BOX 13.3 An overview of psychosexual and psychosocial stages of development (after Freud, 1905, Erikson, 1950 A. Freud, 1936)

Age	Freud's psycho-sexual stages	Characteristic mode of ego defence/ functioning	Erikson's psychosocial stages	Characteristic psychosocial/ behavioural imperatives
Birth – one year	Oral	Incorporation	Basic trust versus mistrust	Trust mother and in turn self and others
1–3 years	Anal	Projection Displacement	Autonomy versus shame/doubt	Be self-sufficient and follow social rules
3–6 years	Phallic/Oedipal	Reaction formation Identification	Initiative versus guilt	Develop peer relations and internalize social rules
7–11 years	Latency	Sublimation Humour	Industry versus inferiority	Master cognitive and social skills at school
12–18 years	Genital	Intellectualiza-tion Asceticism	Identity versus role confusion	Develop a sense of personal direction re future and awareness re past
Early adulthood	–	–	Intimacy versus isolation	Achieve love and companion-ship beyond the family
Adulthood	–	–	Generativity versus stagnation	Raise and/or care for children; be productive at work
Maturity/ old age	–	–	Ego integrity versus despair	Reflect on life as being productive and satisfying

Freud's initial theorizing about these phases of development came from reconstructions of childhood based on his treatment of emotionally troubled adult patients. Many of his ideas were subsequently confirmed by later psychoanalysts who based their thinking about psychosexual development on extensive observations of normal and atypical children (e.g. Edgecumbe and Burgner, 1975). Freud's theorizing resulted in a conceptualization of human development as maturation through a series of psychosexual phases before eventual establishment and maintenance of the self in the genital phase some time after puberty. His interest was in the operation of the mind as a result of different experiences that in turn influence well-being and development.

The terms sensual and/or sexual to describe the strong motivational force informing much of children's behaviour can be seen to be relevant to observations of the profoundly passionate devotion underlying the behaviour of a hungry feeding infant, a toddler refusing to leave somewhere they like, or a defiantly proud schoolchild insistent on playing rough-and-tumble games at a high pitch of intensity without interruption. Further, the high prevalence of sexual perversions and violence in adult life involving other adults or children serves to further underline the diverse ways in which the sexual and the genital/reproductive 'often fail to coincide' (Freud, 1940, p. 151).

Box 13.3 provides an overview of both Freud's (1905) psychosexual stages of development, the characteristic modes of mental functioning or defence to cope with inner conflicts (*after* Freud, 1926; A. Freud, 1936), and the corresponding social challenges accompanying each phase of life according to Erikson (1950). Thus, Box 13.3 pulls together psychoanalytic thinking developed over the first half of the twentieth century that has enduring relevance to a broad understanding of human development. These views suggest that the child's progression through each phase may be viewed not only as a change in the child's focus of bodily interest, frustration and satisfaction but also, more fundamentally, as a developmental step forward in the child's social, emotional, cognitive and self-development.

A contemporary psychoanalytic understanding of the oral phase (the first year) involves foremost consideration of the way infants/caregivers are challenged to develop/promote a trusting as opposed to mistrusting orientation to the world; this is also a time when the infant's behaviour appears to be frequently governed by the question 'Will this go in my mouth?' and thus the characteristic ego defence to challenges is incorporation. Incorporation refers to the infant mentally representing, *taking inside* a sense, or schema, of what it feels like to be with mother/father/others (*after* Stern, 1985). At the anal phase, toddlers are faced with the challenge of arriving at an autonomous and proud attitude despite the imposition of social rules which could lead to a dependent and self-doubting orientation to the world. This can be avoided by a judicious combination on the parent's part of limit-setting and love. This is followed by the phallic/oedipal phase (at fourth, fifth and sixth years) of development which involves the challenges of demonstrating initiative and containing one's naturally evolving sense of guilt. Guilt is seen as a self-evaluative emotion, which evolves along side the internalized images of mother/father/others. These images of caregivers provide the social rules and ideals the child will strive toward. What follows is latency when the instinctual drives were assumed by Freud to be well-harnessed in the unconscious (7–11 years). This phase of childhood was, for Erikson, linked with the dilemma of industry versus inferiority, where there is a need to consolidate one's cognitive and social skills (peer relations) in the school setting and other contexts. These are tasks that are helped by the mind's increased capacity for transforming (or sublimating) intense emotional urges into culturally valued activities, e.g. music, art, sports, school work, theatre (including tragedy and comedy). With puberty comes adolescence and the dilemma of identity versus confusion as the teenager struggles to adjust to rapid bodily changes and achieve a direction *vis-à-vis* the future with a revised understanding of the past, particularly one's relationship to one's parents (*see* chapters 19 and 21). Typical modes of psychological defence in these years are intellectualization (engaging with vigor in newly achieved capacities for abstract thought) and/or ascetisim (denying bodily/sexual needs in the pursuit of a non-physical, political or spiritual truth). The years of early adulthood that follow carry the challenge of achieving meaningful long-term relationships involving love and companionship; achieving intimacy and preventing a gloomy sense of isolation is thought to be assisted by having successfully resolved the identity issues of adolescence. Beyond this await the dilemmas characteristic of middle adulthood: generativity (having a productive and fulfilling life) versus stagnation, and old age: integrity (a sense of satisfaction from one's life achievements) versus despair. Erikson's lifespan approach depended strongly on the view that the way in which the individual approaches psychosocial dilemmas in later childhood and adulthood is powerfully influenced by the way in which psychosocial dilemmas in earliest childhood were faced and resolved or not resolved.

Freud's account of development in terms of psychosexual stages is frequently cited in developmental textbooks and then quickly followed up, as the this chapter has done, with reference to Erikson's psychosocial stages. Somewhat unique to Box 13.3 is the inclusion of a list of psychological defences, which are the instruments deployed by the mind (or ego) in its ongoing attempts to satisfy one's own impulses (the id), the ideals stored in one's conscience (superego), and the rules imposed by the external world (*see* Box 13.1). Thus, while the first section of the chapter highlighted differences between classical and contemporary psychoanalytic views of development, this second section assumes there is value in distilling from classical psychoanalytic writings those contents which may be seen to link up with contemporary developmental observations and theorising. The result is an integrated overview of 'life-span' development including motivational, cognitive and social components, that draws attention to aspects of the life path which are central to adult functioning.

GENDER DEVELOPMENT

Freud's account of psychosexual development, tied as it was to the whole of personality development, did not include a separate concept of gender identity. We follow the suggestion of Tyson and Tyson (1990) in adopting distinctions among gender identity (understanding that you belong irrevocably to one gender), gender-role identity (tendency to behave in 'masculine' versus 'feminine' behaviours), and sexual partner orientation (heterosexual, homosexual, bisexual) to understand the feelings and behaviours associated with an individual's sense of self as a girl/woman or boy/man. Boys and girls face different tasks in the domain of gender development. For example, girls may be seen to have a relatively easier time achieving a core sense of gender identity. This is because to achieve their core feminine gender identity they must identify with their primary attachment figure, their mother. By contrast, for boys, in order to achieve a core masculine identity they must turn away from their primary love for the mother, and identify with the father. These tasks for girls and boys alike are complicated by the intense positive and negative emotions felt toward both parents, a situation well captured by Freud and his followers in their account of three-person oedipal dynamics.

For Freud, the crucial phase of psychosexual development was the oedipal phase. The dynamics of the oedipal phase have been charted by Edgecumbe and Burgner (1975) who sub-divided the oedipal phase (3–6 years) into the phallic–narcissistic phase (3-4 years) and the oedipal phase proper (5–6 years). In the phallic–narcissistic phase, pride in one's gender and exhibitionistic displays of the body are thought to be normal. Phallic–narcissism is an apt term for the consolidation of an understanding of the anatomical differences between the sexes which proceeds in line with the acquisition of early conservation skills described by Piaget (*see* Chapter 6) when children show that they realize their gender stays the same despite superficial changes (e.g. of dress, hairstyle etc.). In the preschool years, children often delight in their bodily prowess, readily displaying how well they can run, jump, ride or otherwise be competent in a physical manner. Girls may take a particular pleasure in displaying feminine qualities to their fathers, whereas boys may be prone to demonstrating their masculine strength to their mothers. At times this may become a desperate craving for closeness with the opposite sex parent (the positive oedipal complex). At other times proximity is desperately sought with the same sex parent (the negative oedipal complex). Whether the oedipal situation is positive or negative there is always fear of rejection from the desired parent, and retribution from the other parent. Appropriate emotional availability of parents is a crucial component to the successful resolution of these intense rapidly changing feelings in young children.

Most contemporary psychoanalytic approaches do not regard the oedipal-phase concept as an accurate description of children's sexual desires. Instead, the concept is utilized as a metaphor for the intense and often complicated thoughts, feelings and interactions that occur among three people (child, mother, father), each with profound emotional ties to the other. Nonetheless, the psychoanalytic approach regards it as important for children's gender development that their parents chart a middle-ground between under-gratifying and over-gratifying the sensual interests of their children. A benign positive presence by both the same-sex and opposite-sex parent will help protect children from undue burdens of guilt for their passionate positive feelings and/or jealousy-driven negative feelings, and grant them a deserved sense of pride in their gender-related feelings. This leads to an early consolidation of children's gender identification, encouraging boys and girls toward healthy transformed relations with their parents (and peers) at the end of the oedipal phase, the start of formal school learning.

The feelings of the early school-aged boy are normally governed by a wish *to be like* his father (no longer wanting to replace him) as shown in the preference of school-aged children for playing with same-sex peers. This is supported by positive encouragement from other boys who are adopting a masculine identity, and by non-parental male role models. Similar processes are involved for girls, who by the school-aged years show a clear preference for affiliating with other girls, and no longer battle quite so much with their mothers as they did in the immediately preceding years (or as they will in the adolescent years).

Psychoanalytic approaches differ from many mainstream psychological approaches to gender development issues in general, and the adolescent experience in particular. This can be seen in the closer attention paid by psychoanalysts to the intense emotional conflicts likely to be felt by children/teenagers, and the assumption that sexual identity, gender-role behaviour and partner-orientation are all core aspects of personality development and functioning with roots in early childhood experiences. Thus, from the psychoanalytic perspective, puberty presents the young person with enormous challenges. The radical changes in body size and functioning (menarche/spermarche) must be integrated with a renewed sense of gender identity, gender role behaviours, and sexual partner choice. Old (pre-oedipal) relationship issues (e.g. intense dependency needs) involving parents are reawakened and children must negotiate a new sense of autonomy from parents as they take their initial steps toward their choice of sexual partners.

The long-term influence of early family experiences upon personality development

The classic psychoanalytic view of emotional disturbance in adulthood was that individuals' problems invariably stemmed from difficulties in resolving the ambivalent feelings that characterize the oedipus complex. This oedipal-centred view of emotional development has shifted as more and more psychoanalytic authors proposed accounts of development that gave pride of place to the assumption that the infant's experiences with mother makes the fundamental and enduring contribution to social and emotional development. The plausibility of this revised psychoanalytic view stems from two sources. First, the mother who provides appropriate, sensitive and responsive care in the child's first year is highly likely to be the kind of woman who knows well how to modify her parenting behaviour to suit the changing needs of the child in subsequent developmental phases. Second, children's emotional and cognitive responses to their early interactions with their mothers are stored in mental representations that shape the development of a moral self, and guide the child's responses to new social experiences.

The understanding that development is based firmly on the *actual* quality of care children receive has been elaborated by many psychoanalysts (e.g. Emde, Erikson, Stern and Winnicott) but none have put it so plainly or with such fierce determination as Bowlby (1951, 1958, 1969, 1979, 1988). Drawing upon a set of diverse scientific theories concerning parent-child relations, Bowlby advanced a psychoanalytic model of self and moral development that has yielded a number of testable hypotheses, many of which have been robustly confirmed (*see* Bretherton, 1995; Sroufe, 1986; *also* Chapter 5). Bowlby's attachment theory has much in common with the first model of the mind advanced by Freud (*see* Sandler et al., 1972) which looked primarily at the environment in which the child lived for clues as to its inner world and moral sensibilities. And, while Bowlby incorporated aspects of Freud's later thinking, especially the suggestion that anxiety is best understood as longing for a lost person, or person whose loss is feared (*after* Freud, 1926), his attachment theory did not include Freud's ideas about instinctual drives of sexuality and aggression (*see* Steele and Steele, 1998).

Unlike Bowlby, his fellow British 'independent' psychoanalyst Donald Winnicott (e.g. 1965, 1967) did not seek a clean break from instinctual drive theory and was thus in a position to more strongly influence other psychoanalytic views of development. Winnicott used the unforgettable phrase that 'there is no such thing as a baby', urging his listeners to give full attention to the fact that development exists, proceeds, and depends, upon the context of the mother–child relationship. How mother looks at, and looks to, the baby was, for Winnicott (1967) the crucial formative influence upon self development. He believed that infants who are regarded with respect and genuinely loved will acquire an authentic sense of self, capable of experiencing a wide range of emotions and develop an integrated positive representation of self and others. In contrast, self-development may be set on a fundamentally insecure track by a mother whose own unmet relationship needs and psychological defenses interfere with her capacity to reflect accurately upon her infant's thinking. These children see too much of a mother's emotional conflicts, and not enough of her love and understanding. As a result, they have less capacity to understand and love the self or others. In response to repeated rejection and/or neglect, such children develop a false-self to protect the deeply hurt and fractured, yet true, inner self. The false-self is likely to be manipulative, seductive, untrusting of others and hostile – prone to launching pre-emptive attacks on others in the misguided hope of protecting the self.

Although it may sound like Winnicott was placing a huge burden upon mothers in terms of the need for them to fulfil their maternal roles 'perfectly', this was not the tone of his message. The type of mother Winnicott celebrated and encouraged was not the perfect mother, but the 'good-enough mother'. This was the mother who could cope well enough with her own mental conflicts and accept the inevitability of ambivalent feelings and conflicts in her children. The good-enough mother facilitates her children's capacity to resolve mental and social conflicts by knowing when to help her children but also, and equally important, knowing when to introduce frustration or challenge – knowing when and how to say 'no'. Curiously, as Winnicott was poetically etching his psychoanalytic account of good-enough parenting, in the world of psychology Baumrind (1967) was developing and testing her theory of parenting which bears a striking resemblance to Winnicott's ideas. In Baumrind's terms, the good-enough mother is the parent who is high on the dimensions of warmth and control – the authoritative parent; the not-good-enough mother is the parent low on warmth and either low or high on control – Baumrind's ineffectual or authoritarian types; whereas the too-good mother is the parent high on warmth but low on control – the permissive type (*see* Chapter 16). Notably, Bowlby (1973) himself recognized an affinity between Baumrind's research and his thinking about family experiences, secure attachment, the growth of self-reliance and a mature moral sensibility.

Dorothy Burlingham and Anna Freud (1944) pointed to these challenges of parenting, and the challenges of growing up when they noted how invariably and enthusiastically positive most parents are of very young children. They noted that to any objective observer the praise and adoration heaped upon infants is often out of all proportion to the acts performed or their characteristics. But this, they add, is how it should be when the child is very young because it will not be long until the parents nag and criticize their children for displaying some of the very same 'babyish' behaviours which were previously praised! Development demands that we give something up, just as we gain something else – the value of which is not always clear. Psychoanalytic views about development capture this inevitable paradoxical tension in psychological and social life, urging us to reach forward with trust, and to look inward with awareness at our characteristic emotional reactions to the world for these reflect our past understandings of self and others. The psychoanalytic literature on development, from Freud's day forward, underlines the persistent human wish to transfer into *present* social circumstances understandings and expectations acquired in the context of *past* relationships. This phenomenon, known as 'transference', is rather like Piaget's notion of assimilation, i.e. interpreting new experiences in light of past understandings. The psychoanalyst is a keen observer of the social and emotional manifestations of this tendency.

Ultimately, human development demands awareness of this powerful tendency to repeat the past, accommodation to the present, and the generation of new models to help permit the achievement of still more adaptive solutions in the future.

Although Freud's original thinking about development was based on reconstructions of childhood experiences from accounts provided by his adult patients, contemporary psychoanalytic views of development are based firmly on observations of children, many of whom are then studied in prospective longitudinal designs. Very different conclusions have arisen from the prospective investigations, as compared to the conclusions drawn from looking backward into the life experiences of disturbed adults. Early experiences appear to have a strong, almost inexorable, influence on later developmental outcomes *but only* when we are looking backward to the previous experiences of dysfunctional, emotionally disturbed individuals. Looking forward from infancy, early adverse social relations (even abuse) does not inevitably lead to continuing adversity and the repetition of it in the next generation (*see* Clarke and Clarke, 1999). There are multiple developmental pathways leading on to a more or less normal life course for those children who begin life in adverse circumstances. Each of these restorative pathways is, however, likely to require the establishment and maintenance of a long-term relationship with at least one caring and supportive other person. From this base adaptive developments involving satisfying work- and love-relations with others can and do proceed. An undeniable feature of contemporary psychoanalytic perspectives on development is the great care devoted to understanding the meaning children derive from, and the meaning children bring to, their real-life social experiences with others.

Chapter summary

This chapter has suggested that developmental theorizing may be enriched by taking into account a contemporary psychoanalytic perspective. The benefit may be found in the picture gained of the possible inner workings of the mind as they concern self and gender development, affect-regulation and the question of health versus psychopathology. Additionally, it should be clear that there is no single psychoanalytic perspective. The chapter provides an overview of the differences between Freudian dual-instinct theory and contemporary object-relations theories which have many points of convergence, but begin from distinct starting points in their conceptualization of what motivates development. From the classical Freudian perspective, it is self-interest as manifest in sexual and aggressive impulses; whereas from the contemporary object-relations perspective, it is an interest in social relations as manifest in the newborn's interpersonal orientation, and implicit understanding that inner security or safety stems from being cared for. Out of positive early experiences of being cared for well-enough, children manifest the capacity to care for others and healthy social and emotional development is likely to follow. Early experiences are often not good-enough and infant development thus begins from a less than beneficial starting point. We have considered some psychoanalytic observations on the consequences of this for the child's inner world, and the potential for returning to a path of normal development is highlighted. A central feature of all psychoanalytic perspectives on child development is the consideration given to each parent's responsibility and long-term influence.

Seminar questions

1. Discuss the characteristic features of psychoanalytic object-relations theories.
2. Compare and contrast Melanie Klein's with John Bowlby's view of early emotional development.
3. Provide a psychoanalytic account of life-span development.
4. Prepare an essay concerning some similarities and differences between psychoanalytic and psychological perspectives on development.

Further reading

Freud, A. 1965. *Normality in childhood*. Harmondsworth: Penguin Books. For a classic (yet still relevant) psychoanalytic account of the distinct, yet related, lines along which development unfolds, see the chapter on 'Developmental Lines'.

Steele, H., Steele, M. 1998. Psychoanalysis and attachment: time for a reunion. *Social Development* **7**, 92–119. For a comparison and contrast among the psychoanalytic theories of Melanie Klein, Anna Freud, Margaret Mahler and John Bowlby.

Bowlby, J. 1979. *The making and breaking of affectional bonds*. London: Tavistock Publications.

Bowlby, J. 1988. *A secure base. Clinical application of attachment theory*. London: Routledge. For accessible readings on attachment theory and research.

Sandler, J., Sandler, A.M. 1998. *Internal object revisited*. London: Karnac Books. For a complex integration of classical and contemporary psychoanalytic perspectives, which also conveys much fascinating detail about the history of psychoanalysis.

Erikson, E. 1950. *Childhood and society*. New York: Basic Books. The original account of the psychosexual stages elaborated in Box 13.3.

14 Emotional development

MARK MEERUM TERWOGT AND HEDY STEGGE

Editors' preface

The extremes of emotion can often be seen in childhood, either the desolation of inconsolable crying or joy shown by laughter and pleasure. From this perspective it would seem that adults have learnt to suppress and hold in check many emotions (see the previous chapter for a psychoanalytic view of these processes). In this chapter by Drs Mark Meerum Terwogt and Hedy Stegge we see how emotional development is linked to wider cognitive advances. The starting point is the observation that infants throughout the world show the same facial expressions which correspond to what is often called the primary emotions. It also seems to be the case that infants are able to discriminate between various emotional states. What is less certain is whether infant facial expressions are the result of related emotional feelings, whether infants have any understanding of the emotional states of others. These are all difficult questions as answers have to be based on observation and inference.

In the pre-school years children become much more aware of emotions. Here, we see links between the understanding of emotions and the understanding that others can have different beliefs to one's self. Both processes appear to involve the possession of a theory of mind (*see* Chapter 12), which involves at about four years of age an appreciation that the minds of others do not always correspond to one's own thought processes. However, it takes time before the full implications of this cognitive advance are incorporated into the behaviour and beliefs of children. For example, even at six years of age children do not seem to understand that emotional states are not merely the result of circumstances (e.g. people are happy on their birthday), and that people may react differently to the same event. Similarly, there are thought to be links between the development of emotions and moral reasoning (*see* Chapter 15).

In their chapter Mark Meerum Terwogt and Hedy Stegge show that the development of emotions is not a simple linear progression. Rather, there are a number of issues to be addressed during development and these are influenced by, and probably influence, cognitive processes. They also raise questions about whether differences in temperament influence emotional development and whether in extreme cases this can be considered as psychopathology.

Introduction

Emotions usually concern a wide variety of behaviours in combination with an equally wide variety of situations. The hypothetical construct that we put in between an eliciting emotional event and the emotional reaction is referred to as the **emotional state**.

Evolutionists assume that we start out with a limited set of discrete **emotional states**, which connect a set of prototypical situations to a prototypical reaction pattern. The (mainly subcortical) emotional state has to be distinguished from its cortical representation: the **emotional experience**. The emotional experience refers to the *cognitive interpretation* of the bodily signals accompanying the emotional state in terms of the actual situation and the felt action tendency (stomach contractions in confrontation with a large dog are interpreted as 'This animal frightens me; I want to get out of here', or something similar). From this perspective, the quality of the child's emotional experience can be considered an indication of emotional understanding. As a function of growing cognitive competence, children start to reflect more explicitly on their own emotional processes as well as the emotions of others. This will result in a more elaborate and more differentiated understanding of the emotion process. The present chapter will deal with these developments in more detail.

The chapter aims to clarify how children learn to understand their own emotional states and those of others, how new emotion patterns arise and how children learn to cope with their emotions. The chapter ends with a discussion of individual differences in emotionality and their role in psychopathology.

Expression and recognition of emotion in infancy

There is a restricted set of emotional states (happiness, sadness, anger, fear, surprise and disgust), which show up very early in life and are character-ized by a unique facial expression, that is identical all over the world (Ekman and Friesen, 1971). Darwin (1872), who first observed this phenomenon, therefore argued that there is an universal and innate basis to the expression of these **basic** or **primary emotions**. He furthermore believed that children are also equipped with an intuitive knowledge of the meaning of these expressions in others. In the next two sections we will examine the evidence for both claims.

FACIAL EXPRESSION OF EMOTIONS

Even in infancy, emotional expressions seem to have a discrete quality: babies look happy, sad or angry. It is not clear, however, whether the expressions are systematically produced in response to an appropriate stimulus situation (Wolff, 1987). In the literature, there is agreement about the occurrence of a positive emotion. Smiling, which is easy to detect, really seems to follow a happy event (Izard and Malatesta, 1987; Oster et al., 1992). There is less consensus, however, about distinctive quality of negative emotions. Whereas Izard and Malatesta (1987) claim that the expressions of fear, anger and sadness can be differentiated in early infancy, Oster et al. (1992) argue against this interpretation. Moreover, the connection with appropriate eliciting events is less clear than in the case of smiling, especially with expressions suggesting fear (Hiatt et al., 1979). For this reason, some authors argue that early emotional expressions should not be seen as signals of an underlying, discrete emotional state. Instead, they point to the important role of imitation. As it has been shown that babies can imitate facial expressions within a few days after birth (Field et al., 1982), it might be that they look angry or sad since they have seen others producing these emotional expressions. So, even if we accept that babies have an inborn ability to produce discrete emotional expressions, it is still debateable whether these expressions reflect the matching emotional states.

REACTIONS TO OTHER PEOPLE'S EMOTION SIGNALS

Empirical work has convincingly shown that infants are able to *discriminate* among various basic expressions in others (*see* Box 14.1). Children have proved to be fairly sensitive to different emotion signals from a very young age. The question is whether they also grasp the *meaning* of these signals. If they do, we would expect them to show appropriate reactions. A study by Haviland and Lelwicka (1987) has found that even ten-week-old babies tend to react with a happy expression on seeing a display of happiness. In contrast, they look angry or remain still when the mother displays anger. Clearly, these are adequate, or at least natural reactions in the prevailing situation, which might suggest that the children really have grasped something of the meaning of the mother's behaviour. A symmetrical reaction pattern, however, can also be explained by imitation and therefore does not necessarily imply real understanding. But even then, it is clearly no 'mindless' imitation: the infant does not imitate just any emotional expression at any point in time. When we observe mothers and their children as dyadic systems, the impression is strengthened that there really is something happening like a 'dialogic exchange' (Trevarthen, 1993): 'the analysis of the behaviours of partners in the "best" or most organized and co-ordinated engagements shows that infant and adult meet with the same standards of emotion that define "good" or "bad" expression and reply and that is why each is ready to gain immediate emotional support from appropriate responses of the other' (p. 68).

BOX 14.1 Discrimination of facial expressions

Studies that aim to demonstrate the infant's ability to discriminate among different emotional expressions all use the habituation paradigm. A well designed study of this type is the one by Caron et al. (1982), that focuses on the discrimination between happiness and surprise. Four- to seven-month-old babies were presented with pictures of several women expressing the same emotion (either happiness or surprise). Notwithstanding individual differences in appearance between the women in question, habituation on the general configuration of the emotional expression caused a decrease in inspection time with each following picture. However, even in four-month-old subjects, the introduction of a picture of one and the same women exhibiting another emotional expression immediately elicited an increase in inspection time, indicating that the infants could discriminate between the two emotional expressions.

A reaction pattern that clearly goes beyond imitation is **social referencing**: a process in which children spontaneously use (facial) information from the caregiver to direct their own actions. A one-year-old child will crawl over the 'drop' in a 'visual cliff' (a landscape that looks like a sharp drop, which is in fact covered with a flat glass surface), when there is a smiling mother at the other side. However, the same child refuses to cross when the mother looks fearful or angry (Sorce et al., 1985). Although the child's reaction can be interpreted in terms of a general effect of the mother's reaction on the child's exploratory behaviour (Bowlby, 1973), the social referencing hypothesis provides a more specific explanation, by assuming that the child has made a connection between the mother's emotional reaction and a particular object or event (e.g. the visual cliff). Playroom observations have supported an interpretation in terms of social referencing by showing that infants avoid a particular toy when the experimenter expresses anger at the moment they try to grab the toy, but nevertheless they go on exploring other toys (Bradshaw et al., 1986).

Another sign of early emotional understanding is provided by the emphatic reaction. Some authors (e.g. Hoffman, 1982; Trevarthen, 1993) are willing to accept the infant's contingent emotional response (for example, crying when another child cries) as the first manifestation of this fundamental quality. However, as has been argued before, the level of understanding implied by this symmetrical behaviour cannot easily be determined. Real **empathy**, that can be defined as 'the ability to put yourself into the feeling state of another person', is demonstrated by the appearance of asymmetrical reactions during the second year of life with the first clumsy attempts to comfort younger siblings in distress (Dunn, 1988), but also with examples of deliberate hurting and teasing. Both types of behaviour not only indicate the two-year-olds' capacity for perspective-taking, but also signals their appreciation of the way in which they themselves can influence the emotional reactions of others (Harris, 1989).

DISCUSSION POINT

Darwin claimed there is an innate ability to both produce and understand the facial expressions of basic emotions. Which of the two claims is the most hard to substantiate? Why is this?

Acquisition of emotional knowledge

In the course of the first two years, children may have discovered certain connections between emotional situations and emotional behaviours by means of their own information processing activity, but they still lack the interconnecting linguistic concepts for emotional states or emotional experiences that firmly link the two together. In the next few years they will gradually acquire a more mentalistic conception of emotion (Harris and Olthof, 1982). They learn to understand that people do not react on the situation *per se*, but on their subjective mental representation of that situation. Emotions become a part of the child's **'theory of mind'** (Wellman, 1990), which mandates that people's behaviour has to be understood in terms of their subjective beliefs and desires (Harris et al., 1989): you expect people to be happy when their *desires* become fulfilled, or when you know that they *believe* that their desires will be fulfilled.

In this section, it is described how early conversation helps children understand that emotion labels refer to inner processes and how they discover the link between these inner experiences, on the one hand and distinctive eliciting situations as well as distinctive behavioural expressions, on the other. Later on, we will see how a mentalistic conception of emotions (people perceive a situation in their own way and it is this subjective appraisal that determines the subsequent emotion!) stimulates children to question the assumption of one to one connections. They will learn that one and the same situation may elicit different emotions in different people, or even within one person ('mixed emotions') and also that an emotional expression may not fit the emotion as it is actually felt ('conflicting emotion cue's').

TALKING ABOUT EMOTIONS

Around the age of two children start to talk about emotions (Bretherton et al., 1986; Smiley and Huttenlocher, 1989). Such conversations result in a fast accumulation of emotional knowledge. Children do not have to figure out everything for themselves anymore. When your Mum tells you that she is angry because you took a cookie without asking first, while showing an explicitly 'angry' face, it is much easier to work out a causal relationship between the different elements. So, when children become part of the verbal community, they also become the 'passive' recipient of whole chunks of more or less structured knowledge (see Box 14.2).

BOX 14.2 Sources of knowledge

Harris and Olthof (1982) distinguish three different sources for the acquisition of emotional knowledge:

- The **solipsistic source**: monitoring one's own physiological phenomena and mental processes.
- The **behaviouristic source**: the observation of emotional behaviour and the situations in which these behaviours occur (in others as well as regarding one's own behaviour).
- The **socio-centric source**: the information that reaches the child by (verbal) communication with knowledgeable others.

Full insight, of course, requires combining the information of all three sources.

Children's questions are an important marker of their growing understanding of the central role of mental states. Questions about other people usually concern their actions, whereabouts, inner states (including emotions) or the application of rules. Dunn (1991) reports that, around the age of two, almost no questions belonging to the two latter categories are asked. By the age of three, on the contrary, a growing interest in mental processes and emotional states can be observed, as almost 30 per cent of the questions three-year-olds ask concern the identifications of other people's intentions and emotions. It is not until much later, however, that children think of internal states as an essential part of the concept of emotion (Harris et al., 1981). Even six-year-olds tend to define an emotion primarily in terms of the eliciting event (you are happy 'when it is your birthday') or the expressive component (you are happy 'when you cheer and laugh'). In the course of development children learn that these elements, although they are perfectly good descriptors, are not always decisive. Not all people are happy on their birthday. And laughing does not always imply real happiness. Ten-year-olds therefore tend to give priority to the emotional state: you are happy 'when you *feel* happy (inside)'.

KNOWLEDGE ABOUT THE SITUATIONS THAT PROVOKE EMOTIONS

Harris et al. (1987) asked 5–14-year-old children to describe a prototypical situation for a wide range of emotions. Even among the youngest children, a firm consensus was found of the kind of situations that provoke the emotions happiness, sadness, anger and fear. Note that these are emotions that belong to the category of basic emotions. It might be that the acquisition of conceptual knowledge about this set of emotions is facilitated by the fact that they can be identified on the basis of a unique facial expression (Meerum Terwogt and Olthof, 1989). However, given that the situational determinants of another basic emotion, disgust, are not clearly acknowledged before the age of seven, other variables seem to play a role as well. An interesting finding in this respect concerns young children's relatively advanced understanding of the concept of shyness – an emotion that is not characterized by an emotion specific expression. Like happiness, sadness, anger and fear, shyness is a frequent topic in the conversation between caregivers and young children. This suggests that early conceptual knowledge about emotion is facilitated by verbal explanation.

The situational determinants eliciting emotions such as gratitude, pity, pride, guilt and shame are usually not fully understood before the age of ten. These emotions do not simply depend on the attainment or loss of a desirable outcome but also on the way that outcome is reached. A certain amount of social knowledge (especially with respect to norms and values) is needed, as well as the ability to combine several perspectives on one and the same situation: the child's own interests, the goals of the interaction partner, or even the concerns of a whole group, which may range from the well defined goals of your own football team to the unwritten norms and standards of an anonymous society (*see* Box 14.3).

BOX 14.3 The understanding of complex emotions. A two-stage model

Graham and Weiner (1986) claim that the understanding of complex emotions such as gratitude or shame requires a two-stage processing strategy. First, we analyse the situation in terms of the *outcome* (favourable for ourselves or not?), and subsequently we examine the causal chain of events (how was the outcome brought about?). Even three-year-olds are able to make the first step: you are *happy* whenever you get something you like. But it usually takes some years before children realize that, for instance, *gratitude* is the appropriate emotion in cases where this outcome is reached by the help of others. Note, that a 'simple' emotion like happiness may result from an evaluation of the outcome, but also from a further analysis of the event ('I was just lucky to win the lottery'). Empirical evidence for this two-stage model was provided by Graham (1988). She presented children with two versions of a story about an accident. The difference between the two was that the protagonist could have easily prevented the accident in the first version, whereas in the second the accident could hardly be avoided. Six-year-old children proved to be able to identify the difference in responsibility correctly. None the less, they predicted that the protagonist would feel equally guilty after both accidents. So, although they can figure out whether someone is to blame or not, they completely focus on the outcome in their emotion predictions. Their concept of guilt is still incomplete.

ACKNOWLEDGEMENT OF MIXED FEELINGS

Although four-year-old children already acknowledge that one and the same situation may create different emotional reactions in different people (Harris et al., 1989), children find it hard to understand that certain situations may create emotional ambivalence within one and the same person. Harter (1983; Harter and Buddin, 1987) was the first to tackle the topic of **mixed feelings**. She asked children whether it would be possible to experience two feelings at the same time and to provide a typical example of this. Six-year-olds sometimes produced situations with a dual emotional impact, but in these cases one emotion usually *followed* the other. At the age of eight, children were able to come up with situations that provoke *simultaneous* emotions, but their examples were limited to events in which two emotions of the same *valence* were experienced (for example, sadness and anger). It was only at the age of ten that children proved to be able to integrate two opposite feelings (for example, happiness and sadness). Harter's results seem to indicate a fundamental problem with the acknowledgement of mixed feelings. But, as Harris (1989) pointed out, it might be that Harter's findings mainly reflect a production deficit: young children may know about mixed emotions but have difficulty in remembering or constructing illustrative situations.

This problem can be avoided by starting the other way around. Instead of asking the child to produce a situation with a dual emotional impact, we can ask them to evaluate the affective consequences of an ambiguous situation. This procedure was adopted by Meerum Terwogt et al. (1986) and by Olthof et al. (1987). The results of these studies fit Harter's findings surprisingly well. Before the age of seven most children focused on one emotional aspect only. After that, children first came to acknowledge the prevalence of successive emotions, whereas the possibility of simultaneous emotions was accepted only later on. Finally, in line with Harter's findings, the co-occurrence of emotions of the same valence was easier to accept than the co-occurrence of emotions of opposite valence.

Why does it take children such a long time to acknowledge the possibility of mixed feelings? One plausible explanation is put forward by Harris (1989), who suggests that the existence of mixed feelings does not fit within the child's early theory about emotion. Having noticed that situations typically elicit either positive or negative feelings, they have constructed a 'theory' that assumes a one to one correspondence between situation and emotion. For a long time, this general assumption prevents them from analysing the situation in greater detail. The first possible interpretation on the situation that comes to mind is adopted, consequently it is only in the course of development that 'Their phenomenal experience of shifting feelings gradually intrudes and breaks down their insistence that two types of feeling are quite separate' (Harris, 1989, p. 125).

CONFLICTING EMOTION CUES

Just as the detection of discrepancies between emotions 'as reported' and emotions 'as felt' results in an understanding of mixed emotions, the appreciation of other discrepancies may bring about further reconceptualizations. Children are often confronted with a conflict between situational cues and an emotional expression. For example, they may see someone smile who apparently just hurt his knee. Gnepp (1983) has shown that young children tend to rely on the emotional expression in these kinds of situations and do not seem to be aware of the conflict between the emotional expression and the situational determinants. A more thorough analysis of the prevailing situation may draw their attention to the inconsistencies and subsequently encourage them to question the one to one correspondence between emotional expression and emotional state. As they are surely aware of the link between pain and sadness, they may ask themselves why the protagonist's face does not show any signs of sadness. Meanwhile, social experience may have taught the child that the expression of emotion sometimes is prohibited ('Don't be a cry-baby!'). They then may put two and two together and conclude that the protagonist probably *masks* his true sadness.

ANTICIPATION OF THE BEHAVIOURAL EFFECTS OF EMOTIONS

Apart from the direct behavioural correlates, emotions tend to influence behaviour in a much wider sense. Some of these effects are acknowledged by children quite early. Six-year-olds, for instance, claim that a negative emotion will impair task motivation, whereas a positive emotion will improve performance. Furthermore, they appreciate that a negative emotion will bias their social judgements about others in a negative way, whereas a positive emotion will result in a more positive attitude (Harris et al., 1981; Stegge, 1995).

Knowing the consequences of an emotional state is important in that it may help us to take measures to eliminate the anticipated undesirable consequences of a prevailing emotion. Whenever we experience a certain emotion, the simple fact of knowing that we are emotional can then serve as a warning signal that action has to be taken. In older children, this mechanism seems to work quite well. After the induction of a negative mood state, ten-year-olds were able to keep their performance on a memory task at an optimal level, whereas the performance of five-year-olds clearly decreased. However, when this latter group was questioned about the possible effects of a negative emotion on performance just before the mood induction, the deteriorating effect disappeared (Meerum Terwogt, 1986). A simple priming of these young children's latent knowledge thus seems to be sufficient to elicit a compensating effort.

Even more important than knowing the indirect behavioural effects of emotions, is the realization that emotions automatically elicit direct action tendencies that may be functional from a personal point of view, but often far from advisable from a social perspective. Anger, for instance, elicits a primitive aggressive response. In an uncontrolled way, hitting and kicking may remove a perceived obstacle. But, as children will quickly notice, such actions are often disapproved of. In the next section we will see how children try to solve the dilemma between personal and social goals, when we discuss their understanding of different options to cope with negative emotions.

DISCUSSION POINT

Beliefs and desires are supposed to be the keystones of a theory of mind. How do emotions fit in?

Regulation of emotion

In the course of development children have to learn express their feelings in a way that not only serves their own interests but is also accepted by the social environment. When children get older, they are confronted with an increasing amount of social restrictions. Basically, there are two ways of dealing with environmental demands. One may try to change the emotional impact of the situation in such a way that the resulting feeling state can be expressed without endangering one's social interests. Alternatively, one may try to mask a socially less acceptable emotion. That is, one can limit control to the expressional component only. In this section, we will discuss the most important age changes with respect to each of these two regulation options.

COPING WITH NEGATIVE EMOTIONS

In the literature, several attempts have been made to classify the kinds of strategies people use in reaction to stressful situations. Lazarus and Folkman (1984) distinguish two types of coping behaviours: **problem-focused** and **emotion-focused** strategies. Problem-focused coping aims at removing or diminishing the actual problems presented by the situation, whereas emotion-focused strategies seek to improve the resulting emotional state. As the use of problem-focused coping changes the emotional state as well, albeit indirectly, both types of strategies can be seen as equally effective from an emotion perspective (*see* Box 14.4).

It has been suggested that initially peoples try to tackle the problem directly by changing the actual situation to their advantage. Alternative options will be considered only after these attempts seem to be blocked. Authors such as Rothbaum et al. (1982) therefore prefer to talk about effectively the same bipartition at the one made by Lazarus and Folkman

---

BOX 14.4 Guilt and shame

Emotions have to be socialized. However, the issue of socialization also has a counterpart: some emotions have a socializing effect. Well-known examples of emotions that can be considered the guardians of societal norms and values are guilt, shame and pride. These so-called social or reflexive emotions are elicited by a process in which the person compares their behaviour or accomplishments to normative standards of conduct. Shame signals a perceived failure to be what one would ideally like to be. Guilt, on the other hand, results from a discrepancy between one's behaviour and moral norms and values. Both shame and guilt serve important intra-personal and inter-personal functions, as they foster self-improvement and strengthen social relationships (Ferguson and Stegge, 1995, 1998). When the internalization of norms and values is completed in the course of development, the proximity of witnessing others is no longer critical (Harter et al., 1987). Children now have constructed a new audience; they no longer need others to tell them what's right or wrong, but have become their own guardians. This is nicely illustrated in a study by Harter and Whitesell (1989), in which children were asked about the affective states of guilt and shame. Young children primarily referred to the judgements of other people (My mum was ashamed of me when I . . .), whereas eight-year-olds talk of themselves as feeling guilt or ashamed (I felt ashamed when I . . .).

(1984), in terms of **primary** as opposed to **secondary** coping. Secondary (or emotion-focused) strategies are particularly useful in situations that are beyond a person's control. If we are, for instance, confronted with the death of a close friend, we can only learn to live with it; or, as Rothbaum et al. (1982) phrase it 'to maximize our goodness of fit with the conditions as they are'. Secondary control options are also effective in situations in which primary solutions are expected to have social repercussions. Although it may be unwise to leave a boring meeting, nothing prevents us from shortening the time by thinking of more interesting things.

Generally, it can be argued that most secondary or emotion-focused strategies appear later in life. Whereas six-year-old children are able to produce a wide variety of primary strategies, they rarely claim to use secondary strategies. Reactions like avoidance, direct behavioural intervention and asking the help of powerful others are considered earlier in life than mental distraction or a cognitive reappraisal of the situation (Band and Weisz, 1988). Although this developmental trend can be explained along social lines (young children may be confronted with social restrictions to a lesser extent, or not be as aware of the consequences of their primary attempts), we have to consider the impact of yet another factor: the growing understanding of emotion as a mental phenomenon.

Instead of using one's *aim* (improving the actual situation or improving the emotion) or using the *result* (a changed situation or an improved mood state within an unchanged situation) as the dividing criterium, one can classify a set of coping options according to the *means* that people use to reach their goals. Changing the actual situation for the better acquires some kind of **behavioural** action, whereas one can only diminish the emotional impact of actually unchanged situation by some kind of **mental** manipulation. For instance, if your little bother has broken one of your toys, you can always try (or ask your parents) to mend it. However, it may also help to remind yourself that 'it wasn't one of your favourite toys anyway'; a mental strategy normally known as 'cognitive reappraisal'. Your toy is still broken but your sadness will probably diminish now that there is no desire at stake anymore. Moreover, if you are also able to convince yourself that your little brother 'did not do it on purpose' the reason for anger vanishes too. It is mainly this mental aspect that explains why secondary strategies are not only secondary in the sense that they are considered only when primary options seem to fail but also secondary in the sense that they develop later in life (Meerum Terwogt and Stegge, 1995).

The bottom line is that children's understanding of mental strategies is directly related to their acknowledgement of the representational nature of mental phenomena; that is, to the development of a theory of mind (Harris et al., 1989; Meerum Terwogt and Stegge, 1995). Before children understand the possible usefulness of mental strategies, they have to understand that people do not react to the situation, but on their subjective representation of the situation. A slightly different appraisal of the same situational elements therefore can change the (emotional) impact of an actually unchanged event. Once children are aware of this phenomenon, they may start to look for an acceptable 'reappraisal' that enables them to resign themselves to the situation as it is.

MASKING EMOTIONS

Previously, we have argued that young children tend to assume a one-to-one relationship between the inner emotional state and outer emotional expression. Older children, in contrast, clearly appreciate the possibility of concealing or faking emotions. Since faked emotions can hardly be distinguished from genuine displays (DePaulo and Jordan, 1982), Harris (1989) argued that children's understanding of the potential privacy of their emotional experience is a cognitive discovery rather than a refinement of their observational skills.

The deliberate concealment of own's feelings, or the substitution of one emotion by another, starts in the early school years. At this time, children begin to learn that the expression of one's emotion, which may satisfy an immediate urge, has social consequences as well. You may not feel well, but if you complain about it, your mother most likely will forbid you to go outside. And if you show your fear at the high diving board, your friends will probably laugh at you. By the age of seven, children start to appreciate that to behave adaptively in social situations, one needs to take into account the consequences of a genuine display of emotion for both the self and others. In subsequent years, children's understanding in this respect improves in important ways (Saarni, 1979) *(see* Box 14.5).

BOX 14.5 Understanding of display rules

Cole (1986) carried out an experiment that suggests that even three-year-olds are able to conceal their emotions deliberately. She gave children (girls only) a very disappointing gift as a reward for their participation in an experiment. As long as the experimenter was present the children reacted with a 'half-hearted' smile, but in her absence their disappointment was clearly visible. Harris (1989) pointed out a simple explanation for this amazing accomplishment. He argued that these young children's reactions are the direct result of parental indoctrination. Children are told again and again to smile and say 'thank you', whenever they get something. Cole's three-year-olds are probably scarcely aware of the fact that they displayed an emotion that did not correspond to what they actually felt in the prevailing situation.

When children grow older, their knowledge of display rules makes it quite clear that they are well aware of this discrepancy. They anticipate the consequences of their expressive behaviours. Children aged 7–13 (Saarni, 1989) argued, for example, that it is allowed to show your emotions under conditions of limited control, even if negative interpersonal consequences are to be expected. Limited control may have to do with the nature of the eliciting situation, the age of the actor (young children are not expected to show the same amount of control), or the intensity of the emotion (intense feelings supposedly are hard to control). Furthermore, those children who argued that they would not show their real feelings to adults, justified their answers by referring to the possibility that powerful people might use such expressions of 'weakness' against them. Within the peer-group, the loss of status was considered to be especially dangerous. Finally, children were of the opinion that you should show your true feelings to close friends or parents rather than to acquaintances or strangers.

DISCUSSION POINT

What are the possible costs and the benefits of a mental as opposed to a behavioural way of coping with negative emotions?

Individual differences in emotionality

People differ greatly in the extent to which they are able to experience different emotions. Malatesta and Wilson (1988) discuss two types of deviancy that involve either the over-use or the under-use of particular emotions. A **surfeit bias** refers to a situation in which a certain emotion has come to dominate the affective life of the individual and is used indiscriminately. In the case of a **deficiency bias**, on the other hand, a particular emotion is absent in the person's affective experience, either because of the use of defence mechanisms, or because the person simply never developed the capacity to experience the emotion.

In the remainder of this section, we will first discuss possible sources of individual differences in emotionality. We then will discuss some examples of emotion traits well-known within the field of clinical child psychology.

SOURCES OF INDIVIDUAL DIFFERENCES

Some authors assume that there are biologically based individual differences in people's emotional reactions to certain events. In the literature, this patterning of emotion, which is assumed to have a relatively stable physiological basis, is referred to as **temperament** (Goldsmith, 1993). Empirical studies have investigated different temperamental qualities, such as irritability, smiling or sociability, the ease with which a baby can be soothed, or the extent to which children are inclined to react to novel stimuli with approach or avoidance. One well-known distinction in the temperament literature is based on the work of Kagan and his colleagues (Kagan, 1994; Kagan and Snidman, 1991), who described inhibited children as opposed to uninhibited children. Based on the reactions of a large group of children in different laboratory situations, these researchers concluded that one temperamental group (the uninhibited children) easily experiences positive emotions, like joy or happiness, whereas the reactions of the other temperamental group (the inhibited children) are relatively dominated by fear and anxiety. It has been shown that these temperamental qualities are modestly stable. Whether inhibited children retain their problematic temperamental style is largely dependent on environmental factors. Kagan (1994) argues that caretakers can play an important role in reducing anxious reactions by discouraging timidity and encouraging the child to approach unfamiliar situations.

Other research has examined how individual differences in emotionality are a function of differences in socialization experiences. According to Magai and McFadden (1995), parental attitudes towards emotional experiences play an important role in this respect. These authors stress the importance of a rewarding socialization of emotions, by which they mean that the parent should not teach the child to suppress negative affective experiences, but instead help them by empathizing with the negative experience and help the child cope. In this way, the parent may encourage the child to develop the full emotional repertoire. In a punitive environment, in contrast, the parent's rejecting attitude towards certain emotional experiences might cause serious problems for the child's emotional development. It has been suggested, for example, that the punitive socialization of shame (for example, by showing contempt) actually magnifies the experience of shame in the child (Ferguson and Stegge, 1995; Magai and McFadden, 1995).

The affect dynamics already described in this chapter may also play an important role in the acquisition of an emotion bias. According to Magai and McFadden, children's tendency to mimic another person's emotional experience/expression should be considered one such powerful social factor. The implications for the young child's emotional life can easily be seen. It has been shown, for example, that infants begin to show depressed-like affect after exposure to simulated maternal depression (Tronick and Giannino, 1987). Similarly, it has been shown that children who were exposed to angry conflicts between adults showed higher levels of anger themselves (Cummings et al., 1991).

EMOTION TRAITS AND PSYCHOPATHOLOGY

Within the normal range, there is some flexibility in the expression of emotional traits (Magai and McFadden, 1995). Individuals may be inclined to react with one or the other emotion, but they will not do so regardless of the situation. In the case of pathological functioning, flexibility is significantly reduced and a person gets trapped in a negative cycle, in which cognition, affect and behaviour sustain one another. Within the field of clinical psychology, the dysfunctional emotion traits of anger, sadness and fear have been long recognized and are assumed to play a dominant role in conduct disorders, depression and anxiety, respectively.

Anger

In the DSM-IV, the essential feature of a conduct disorder is a repetitive and persistent pattern of behaviour in which the basic rights of other people or societal norms or rules are violated. Important symptoms are: physical harm to other people or animals, property damage, deceitfulness or theft and serious violations of rules. In this description, deviant behaviours are emphasized, most notably aggression. In terms of the emotion model introduced by Magai and McFadden (1995), one might describe the problems of this clinical group in terms of a **disposition** for anger. In empirical research, evidence has been found for an emotion bias on the cognitive level, the level of affect and the behavioural level. Aggressive children were shown to report higher levels of anger to a broad range of situations, to ascribe more hostile attributions to others and more often interpret situations in terms of threat, to easily generate aggressive solutions to interpersonal problems and also to more often respond aggressively (Crick and Dodge, 1994).

Fear/anxiety

Analogous to the research conducted with aggressive children, anxiety-related disorders have recently been studied from a cognitive emotion perspective as well. It has been shown that, in line with the assumption of a dominant fear disposition, anxious children pay more attention to and are more easily distracted by threat-related information. They are also inclined to interpret ambiguous situations more often as dangerous and do so only on the basis of a superficial screening of the information available. Behaviourally, these children respond with avoidance and/or distraction and claim that fear reduction is an important goal (Daleiden and Vasey, 1997).

Sadness/depression

From a functionalist perspective, sadness is an appropriate reaction to loss. In the case of depression, however, the emotional reaction has lost its functional value due to its pervasiveness. Depressed children generally show high levels of persistent negative affect and low levels of positive affect (Clark and Watson, 1992). In addition, recent studies focusing on the role of shame and guilt in depression, suggest that depressed children show increased levels of these related negative emotion dispositions as well (Ferguson and Stegge, 1995, 1998). Evidence for cognitions and behaviours consistent with the depressed mood has also been found. Depressed children show feelings of low self-esteem (Hammen, 1990; Harter, 1987). Furthermore, they experience little control over the outcome of relevant events, an attribution tendency that has been labelled 'learned helplessness' (Seligman, 1975). On the behavioural level, depressed children's negative cognition results in a preference for avoidance rather than active problem solving (Garber et al., 1991).

To conclude, emotion traits seem to play an important role in the major disorders of childhood. It is of great importance that future research systematically examines individual differences in emotionality, so that we are able to specify normal variations in emotional development and determine the possible pathways to emotional psychopathology.

Summary

Newborns are equipped with a number of functional basic emotion patterns. Learning to understand the constituent elements of these patterns in oneself and others is an important developmental task. With age, children increasingly acknowledge the significance of the emotional state as a key element that connects a variety of emotional situations with a variety of emotional behaviours. In early theorizing about emotion, children assume a one-to-one relationship between the eliciting situation and the emotional state. Similarly, they expect a perfect correspondence between the inner emotional state and it's outer expression. It is only when this early conception of emotions is left that children come to acknowledge the occurrence of mixed feelings and the masking of emotion.

An increased acknowledgement of emotions as mental phenomena has important consequences within the domain of emotion regulation as well. As children come to realize that emotions are not elicited by 'the situation as it is', but by 'the situation as it is seen', this allows for the strategic use of cognitive strategies to change one's feeling state. One needs to realize, however, that the cognition–emotion relationship works two ways. Not only is emotion regulated by cognition, cognition is also influenced by emotion. Sad people tend to perceive their environment somewhat differently from, for instance, angry or anxious people. A person's tendency to react with a particular emotion may become consolidated in a more or less stable emotion disposition, in which case a rigid structure is formed where affect, cognition and behaviour influence each other in a recursive loop. Eventually, the loss of flexibility regarding one's emotional life may even result in psychopathology.

Seminar questions

1. Imagine a child who tries to understand his mother's angry reaction when he has taken a cookie out of the cookie jar. Discuss how each of the three sources of knowledge mentioned in Box 14.2 can help him to grasp the situation in an emotional sense. Do the same for a few other examples of your own invention. How is it that the combined influence of all three sources facilitates progress from a behavioural to a mental conception of emotion?
2. Knowledge of emotion is considered to be an important dynamic factor underlying the development of adequate emotional functioning. On the other hand, behaviour often precedes understanding: you have to be able to *do* something before you *know* that you can do it. Now why is it that emotional understanding can be important? In what ways can psychological understanding contribute to behavioural change?
3. The finishing section on individual differences focuses on the biasing influence of the emotion traits of anger, sadness and fear. What would be the effects of other emotion traits? How would shame as a trait, for example, bias one's cognitions and behaviours? Or happiness?

Further reading

Harris, P.L. 1989. *Children and emotion. The development of psychological understanding.* Oxford: Blackwell. Provides the most clear and concise argument on how children gain an insight into emotions.

Dunn, J. 1988. *The beginning of social understanding.* Oxford: Blackwell. A well written account of children's emotions in social interaction.

Garber, J. and Dodge, K.A. (eds) 1991. *The development of emotion regulation and dysregulation.* Cambridge: Cambridge University Press. A number of leading emotion specialists discuss the intra- and interpersonal origins of emotion regulation and dysregulation from every possible perspective.

Cole, P.M., Michel, M.K. and O'Donnell Teti, L. 1994. The development of emotional regulation and dysregulation: A clinical perspective. In Fox, N.A. (ed.) The development of emotion regulation. *Monographs of the Society of Research in Child Development* **59** (Serial No. 240), 73–103. A helpful taxonomy on emotion regulation in childhood disorders.

Magai, C. and McFadden, S.H. 1995. *The role of emotions in social and personality development.* New York: Plenum. An extensive work on individual differences in emotionality and their continuity through the life span.

15 Socio-moral development

LUTZ H ECKENSBERGER

Editors' preface

As we have seen in the first chapter of this section, psychoanalytic the-ories have provided a view of moral development where emphasis is given to the way a child 'identifies' with parents, and the way that the formation of a 'superego' restricts and rechannels primitive drives; from this perspective emphasis has been given to broad operations of the mind in the context of dealing with strong instinctual urges. A contrast to this approach comes from cognitive psychology which treats moral develop-ment as an aspect of children's and adults' reasoning. As a result, Piaget (*see* chapters 3 and 6) is often seen as providing a very different perspective to that provided by psychoanalysis. However, in this chapter, Professor Lutz Eckensburger argues that in Piaget's writings about moral develop-ment involves more than a consideration of cognitive processes, Piaget also was interested in the way feelings for others play a part in the development of moral judgements. Another significant 'cognitive view' about moral development has been provided by Kohlberg. Because of the importance of Kohlberg's ideas a major part of this chapter involves a consideration of his theory, as well as subsequent investigations which have evaluated his ideas. These more recent investigations provide evidence about the way that social and cultural processes can influence the way individuals make progress in their ability to reason about moral dilemmas.

Introduction

This chapter deals with 'normative standards for social actions', rather than with social actions themselves. **Morality** is one of these standards and with reference to psychological research it is probably the most central one. Beyond its societal relevance, this subject is dealt with in virtually all 'schools' (or paradigms) of psychology: in classical psychoanalysis, in learning theory, personality or character theories as well as in cognitive development approaches. However, these approaches not only focus upon different aspects of morality (emotions, cognition or behaviour) but also assume different mechanisms of development.

A full understanding of current research and discussions on moral development presupposes knowledge of at least some earlier research. Thus Piaget's work will be summarized first. Then we will focus on the work of Lawrence Kohlberg, who compiled a very influential theory on the development of 'moral judgements'. Finally, we turn to some post-Kohlbergian issues, such as roots of morality in early childhood, and to the distinction of additional types of normative frameworks in social actions like personal concerns or preferences and social conventions. We also refer to some cross-cultural data in order to discuss the generality of our knowledge.

DISCUSSION POINT

How do you think morality develops?

General conceptions of morality in psychology

In classical *psychoanalysis* (cf. Chapter 13), morality is understood as one result of the solution of the oedipal situation, in which the child (son) tries to solve the conflict between his desire for his mother and his anxiety and jealousy of his father by **identifying** with him (Freud, 1925/1959). By the very nature of this process the child also *internalizes* the values of his father's (culture), which then constitute the **conscience** (in psychoanalytic terms: the *superego*) of the child.

Emotions are indicators of morality (of a strong *superego*), or more precisely, negative emotions like *anxiety, guilt* and *shame*. In this view, morality counterbalances natural primitive desires in humans. This focus on the development of the son was the reason why Freud believed that women have a less developed superego than men (Freud, 1925/1959, p. 196), an assumption, which since then has come under heavy attack for various reasons.

Learning theories (*see* Introduction), by their very nature focus much more on behaviour, but some also refer to guilt responses. In these theories the family context and the behaviour of parents play a central role, because it is assumed that behaviour 'learned' in the family generalizes to other situations. And again morality is understood as a concept that counterbalances the natural (immoral or egoistic) tendencies in humans. Learning theories differ primarily in the assumed mechanisms about how morality develops. One early but influential approach, for instance, focused on learning *good habits* (Hartshorne and May, 1928–1930) on the basis of reinforcement schedules (punishment, positive and negative reinforcement), others assume modelling (*see* Introduction) as the prime factor. In some approaches (Eysenck, 1976) the conscience is understood as a conditioned anxiety response which varies according to hereditary differences in conditionability.

Kohlberg who in the early 1960s (e.g. 1963), carefully analysed the empirical literature on moral development, came to the conclusion that none of these approaches was a satisfactory explanation of moral development. Besides many methodical problems in measuring feelings of guilt, consistency in moral behaviours was low (someone who lies does not necessarily steal), which meant that the idea of a 'moral character' did not have a sound empirical foundation. In addition, childrearing antecedents derived from learning theory (punishment in the form of power assertion) or from psychoanalysis (love withdrawal) were not significantly related to morality (*see also* Hoffman, 1970).

Kohlberg himself argued that the development of morality is neither a matter of a superego/conscience nor a matter of learning/unlearning a particular behaviour, but that it is primarily based upon **cognitive (constructive) processes**. These are based upon experiences of the social environment 'which includes rules . . . which the child understands through conceptually organized role-taking' (Kohlberg, 1963, p. 313). All this is a **social cognitive process** that involves taking the perspective of another person. Broadly speaking, morality from this perspective was conceptualized as an *ego-function*.

So Kohlberg was one of the protagonists of the general 'cognitive turn' in developmental psychology. In a way this is astonishing because Kohlberg's own work relied very much on Piaget's ideas and research, but in Piaget's work on moral development – as we will see – the role that *emotions* play was much more pronounced than in the theory developed later by Kohlberg. And it is noteworthy that emotions are once again playing a much more important role in post-Kohlbergian research. But in these cases emotions are conceptualized differently than in psychoanalysis or learning theory: in Piaget's work as well as in present day research *positive emotions* (feelings of mutual respect and empathy) are underscored as a basis for moral development.

Some terminological clarifications

Before progressing further it is necessary to present some terminological clarifications. **Moral judgement** relates to two important terms: *ethics* and *morality*. The term **ethics** has its roots in the Greek term *ethos*, which basically had the same meaning. In philosophy an important distinction often is made between the two terms: The term morality or morals is derived from Latin and is usually reserved for customs and traditions that *in fact* exist in a particular social or cultural group, whereas the term ethics is used if *reasons* or *justifications* for customs or actions are given. *Ethics* in the narrow sense of the word therefore does not relate to how the world *is*, but how the world *should be*, not to how people act or *would* act in a particular situation, but how they *should* act. It is therefore an *ideal* which is not necessarily met in reality, yet it has a regulating function for customs as well as for social actions. As we will see, most research conducted on the development of 'moral judgements' in psychology should be called the development of 'ethical judgements' or 'ethical thinking', because it relates primarily to the development of ideas, reasons and justifications of how people *should* act. Developmental psychologists are interested in the complexity of these reasons, they therefore aim at an analysis of the *structure* underlying the judgements. Studies not only investigate whether lying, stealing, promise keeping etc. is good or bad, right or wrong, but primarily *why* this is so. Hence, in this research, the child or the adolescent is interpreted as 'a moral philosopher'.

It is also useful to define what it is that in the eyes of philosophers makes an opinion a moral or ethical judgement. According to Hare (1963) these are primarily two features: (a) it is **prescriptive**, that is it implies a *categorical obligation* to act; (b) it is **universalizable**, that is any (rational) human being could or should adopt such a point of view in a conflict situation.

Piaget's conceptions

Piaget's (1932) classical monograph on moral development is still a rich source of information. Comprehensive summaries and evaluations can be found in Lickona (1976), Modgil and Modgil (1976), Weinreich-Haste (1982) and Wright (1982). First we will discuss the most important theoretical perspectives in Piaget's work about moral development (for Piaget's general model, *see* Chapters 3 and 6). Then relevant empirical data will be summarized.

PIAGET'S GENERAL APPROACH TO MORAL DEVELOPMENT

Piaget's interest in moral development has to be understood in the context of his general **epistemological** interest in psychology (i.e. the study of the source, nature and limitations of knowledge). It is often overlooked that Piaget's interests in the psychological development of certain cognitive concepts like causality, space, number, time, logic etc., was basically a philosophical one: He was convinced that these *concepts* can only be understood properly, if one *understands their development*. His standpoint is therefore also called **genetic epistemology**, where 'genetic' is understood as developmental (Kesselring, 1981). This was also true for his interest in moral development. Consequently, he turned to the *historical development* of morality (and also of law) and he studied the *individual development* of moral judgements in order to understand its conceptual basis.

Second, Piaget's basic assumptions were based upon the *notion of biological systems which to a certain extent strive toward an* **equilibrium**. When

Piaget, was only 22 years old, he already conceptualized morality in terms of an *equilibrium* between society and individuals (and he looked upon the *individuals as parts* and the *society as the whole*). In addition, he distinguished between *real* and *ideal* aspects of this equilibrium. His idea was that morality is this *ideal equilibrium* to which society strives. So, although he used a different conceptual framework from philosophers, he, like them, understood morality as a *regulative idea.*

Two further issues are important in this context. Based upon the idea of a balance between the individual and society, Piaget did not think that the developmental trends he observed in Geneva would also necessarily be present in other cultures. On the contrary, he claimed that the essential issue was whether the cultural context would allow certain developments. It is noteworthy that this general orientation towards **contextualization** is again becoming more and more evident in current cross-cultural research. On the other hand, despite his systemic orientation, Piaget (1932) explicitly did *not* use the concept of **developmental stages** in the domain of moral development. Instead, he differentiated two *types* of moral orientation: **heteronomous** and **autonomous** moral judgements. The former being oriented towards *external rules* and obedience to authorities (which is based on *one-sided respect*), whereas the latter is oriented towards autonomous moral decisions (which are based upon *mutual respect, co-operation with and loyalty towards other persons*). As we will see, the first decreases and the second increases with age. Additionally, Piaget (1932) also tried to integrate sociology and psychology. Consequently, his basic intention was to solve the paradox, 'how the individual *autonomous* morality (can) develop out of the *imposed* morality of the "adult" world' (Weinreich-Haste, 1982, p. 182, *my italics*).

It is noteworthy that Piaget explicitly refused to explain the development of morality purely in terms of rational thinking. Particularly in his lectures at the Sorbonne University (1953–1954/1981) it is clear that he did *not* consider morality a form of cognition. Instead, he discussed the development of morality in the context of *affects* or *feelings.*

Finally, it is also important to note that from the very beginning Piaget (1932) understood the development of morality as taking place in *concrete action contexts*, that is he dealt with 'practical morality'. He assumed that morality at first involves implicit knowledge and is then reconstructed by the process of 'conscious realization' – an effort to understand rationally what one already has interpreted as being right or wrong.

METHODS AND FINDINGS

Piaget defined *morality as a system of rules and individual ethos as the respect for these rules.* So he first looked for a domain in children's activities that is governed by rules. This was the reason why he turned to children's *games*. He chose the game of marbles (for boys) and the game of hide-and-seek (for girls). Most of his data on games refer, however, to the game of marbles. He *observed* how children between two and 12 years of age played the game. He *offered to play himself* and *asked* children about the rules of the game – what precisely the rules were, where they came from and whether they could be changed. So he studied the 'practice' of rules as well as 'the understanding' or 'consciousness' of the rules. It is important to realize, however, that Piaget was quite aware of the fact that the rules of games were not really moral in nature but only formed an analogy to moral rules. Today one would interpret them as conventions.

Additionally, Piaget used more than 50 (!) small scenarios, short fictitious stories, which all represented a particular aspect of a moral problem or conflict. These scenarios were not really 'hypothetical' like the stories Kohlberg used (*see below*), but represented a morally relevant conflict for the child which was presented more clearly and simply than is usual in real-life.

These stories all dealt with facets of morality: they touch on the meanings of **responsibility** (when negative consequences occur by chance or because of negative intentions), of **lies** (what is meant by lies, what is bad about them, whether it is worse to lie to an adult than to a child etc.), of different aspects of **justice**, (a) **immanent justice** (whether negative events that follow an offence are unrelated to this act or are 'natural' consequences of the offence), (b) questions of **retributive justice** *(punishment)*, (c) questions of fairness and (d) of collective punishment.

Not all of these dimensions of morality have had the same influence on later research and the evidence about the process of their development is mixed. But many of the age *trends* (not necessarily the ages) Piaget described are supported by later research, including cross-cultural data (cf. Eckensberger and Zimba, 1997; Weinreich-Haste, 1982; Lickona, 1976 for detailed references).

One example of a story (which focuses on retributive/distributive justice) which illustrates Piaget's procedure is given in Box 15.1. As mentioned (*see* page 306), the developmental changes in the different aspects of morality were interpreted by Piaget as a developmental progression from *heteronomous morality* to *autonomous morality*. Since particular ages are not as important in Piaget's findings as the general age trend, ages will be omitted in the following descriptions. Generally in these studies the younger children were aged between five and eight years, the older children were between nine and twelve years of age.

Rules of games

The *use of rules* is first based upon imitation of others. Then co-operation, competition and mutual control result in rule variations, i.e. it is now possible to change rules, but only if there is agreement about the changes. Finally, rules are codified and controlled by the group. The rules can also be changed by agreement of the group.

The *awareness of rules* is first located in some authority. They are therefore even considered as 'sacred' and unchangeable. They are then derived from mutual respect and loyalty and also have to be followed because otherwise the 'spirit' of the game can not be realized.

BOX 15.1 A fictitious scenario Piaget (1932) used to investigate distributive justice as an aspect of moral development

There was a mummy, who went for a walk close to the river Rhone on a free afternoon. At four o'clock, she gave every child a roll. Each child started to eat, except the smallest one, whose roll fell into the water. What does/should the mummy do? Should she give him another roll? What do the older children say?

The children's answers were coded into three categories: (a) the child should not get another roll (i.e. it should be punished for losing it); (b) the target child should get another one, so that every child has the same amount to eat (that implies equal distribution, called *equality*); (c) the child should get another one, because it is the smallest child (this takes account of additional factors and is referred to as *equity*).

Age distribution of responses in percentages

Age (years)	Punishment	Equality	Equity
6–9	48	35	17
10–12	3	55	42
13–14	0	5	95

These developmental trends are generally supported by later research, but there are also some conflicting findings: (a) in a recent study in Germany, which used a game of playing cards, the rules did not emerge from an authority, instead children reported that they have to be followed, otherwise the game would not be fun and would not work; (b) there is evidence that at first young children do not distinguish between changing and breaking a rule, a distinction, which is, however, understood with increasing age (cf. Lickona, 1976); (c) a study by Havighurst and Neugarten (1955) found an interesting (reverse) age trend in some (American) Indian tribes. But this finding is compatible with Piaget's theory because he assumed that in 'traditional cultures' the rules have to be followed with *increasing* rigidity during development and they are also increasingly interpreted as being unchangeable. Piaget therefore predicted that in these cultures children would be the only ones relatively unconstrained by rules. Additionally, Havinghurst and Neugarten (1955) found that some rules had a *religious* meaning and could not be changed. This aspect gives a hint about the importance of distinguishing between different 'rule systems' such as moral and religious ones.

Responsibility

According to Piaget responsibility for an action is first interpreted as being 'objective' (the greater the damage of an act the worse it is), then it is 'subjective', i.e. *intentions* of the actor are taken into consideration in the evaluation of an act. Many existing studies support this trend, they again also include cross-cultural studies, mainly from Africa (*see* Eckensberger and Zimba, 1997).

Lies

Piaget suggested that at first lies are understood just as bad words, that the degree of punishment indicates the naughtiness of a lie and that it is considered worse to lie to an adult than to a friend. Older children take account of the intentions behind lying and that they destroy trust in others.

Immanent justice

The idea of *immanent justice* involves the belief that a bad act will be followed by some form of punishment (i.e. there is a causal relationship). This belief decreases with age and has been found in cross-cultural work. However, it is important that this idea is carefully separated from religious convictions (like the assumption that God is watching and punishes evil acts), failure to do this can obscure or even reverse developmental trends.

Retributive justice

The idea of *retributive justice (punishment)* is interesting because a similar trend can be observed in the historical development of law. Piaget claimed that at first, punishment is seen as being just (the harder the more just it is), then as *tit* for *tat*; later, circumstances are taken into consideration as well as compensation for the damage which the person to be punished caused.

Cheating and unfairness

The *meaning of cheating* also changes with development from an external interpretation (it is bad, because it is forbidden) to the notion that it is against the principle of equality.

Similarly, the idea of *unfairness* produces the feeling of injustice because of **inequality** in treatment.

PSYCHOLOGICAL PROCESSES

Piaget interpreted his data as indicating that autonomous morality does *not emerge* from a heteronomous orientation, but *from the experience of co-operation and mutuality among equals* (in interactions with other children etc.). Furthermore, he claimed that one-sided respect for another person such as an adult, *by its very nature* (or mechanism) *inhibits* the development of a feeling of equality (and mutuality). However, the experience of inequality (and also injustice) may still trigger feelings of justice and equality.

If one summarizes the psychological 'processes' or 'mechanisms' which Piaget mentioned rather unsystematically in his work, then one can state that he distinguishes external and internal conditions for development. The external ones refer to social experiences (first those involving asymmetrical power relations, such as adult–child relations, then interactions between equals such as those among children). The internal conditions for development involve cognitive and emotional transformations.

DISCUSSION POINT

What are the main features of Piaget's theory of moral development?

Kohlberg's concepts

Kohlberg's influence on the field can not be overestimated. His interest in morality was triggered by personal experiences[1] rather than by epistemological reflections. But later (since the late 1960s) he became very interested in the relationship between philosophy and psychology.

Kohlberg's theory (as well as his scoring procedure) also changed in many details over the years (Kohlberg, Levine and Hewer, 1983) and this complicates the evaluation of his work. When he first found inconsistencies in data he attributed this to the method of scoring not to weaknesses in his theory. So he continuously adapted his method to his theory. Hence, data collected at different times are difficult to compare. The present standard-scoring manual was basically finished in 1978, but it was only published in 1987 (Colby and Kohlberg, 1987a, b).

Although Kohlberg built on Piaget's work, his understanding of morality was slightly different. For him *respect* was not so much the core of morality, but **justice**, which he interpreted as the distribution of rights and duties, regulated by the concepts of *equity* and *reciprocity* (Kohlberg, 1976).

METHOD AND DEVELOPMENTAL TRENDS

Kohlberg's methods were much more restricted than those of Piaget. He only used **hypothetical dilemmas**, which basically represent a *typical*

---

1 In 1945 Kohlberg helped the Hagana to smuggle Jewish refugees from eastern Europe into the later Israel, and he was imprisoned in a detention camp in Cyprus by the British army for some time. In this 'enforced reflection phase' he dealt with the question of *justice* (of the parties involved, the Britons as well as the Hagana). Consequently, he started to study law for some time before he turned to psychology.

conflict between different claims and he developed a detailed manual to score the answers to the moral dilemmas. Because the famous Heinz-story is usually given as an example, we will consider another story to illustrate his method. It is taken from the manual (Colby and Kohlberg, 1987b) and is presented in Box 15.2.

BOX 15.2 The hypothetical dilemma 'Joe and his father' (Colby and Kohlberg, 1987, p. 3)

Joe is a 14-year-old boy who wanted to go to camp very much. His father promised him he could go if he saved up the money for it himself. So Joe worked hard at his paper route and saved up the $100 it cost to go to camp and a little more besides. But just before camp was going to start, his father changed his mind. Some of his friends decided to go on a special fishing trip and Joe's father was short of the money it would cost. So he told Joe to give him the money he had saved from the paper route. Joe didn't want to give up going to camp, so he thinks of refusing to give his father the money.

The first question which is asked is: Should Joe refuse to give the father the money? Why or why not?

Additionally some (standard) questions are given, such as:

- Does the father have the right to tell Joe to give him the money? (Why? Why not?) (No. 2)
- In general why should a promise be kept? (No. 6)
- In general, what should be the authority of a father over his son? (No. 9)
- What do you think is the most important thing a son should be concerned about in his relationship to his father? (No. 10)

According to Kohlberg the conflicting claims or values in this story involve a *'contract'* (between the father and his son) and an *'authority'* (of the father). Since philosophy is concerned with the *reasons* given for a moral decision and since Kohlberg was interested in lay persons' philosophy, he did not focus on the *decision* a person makes, but on the *reasons a person gives for the decision that is made*. One basic idea in Kohlberg's theory is that the decision in favour or against an action in a dilemma (giving the father the money or not) represents a **value judgement**, i.e. refers to the *content* of the dilemma, whereas the arguments, reasons or justifications given by a subject for their decision represent the **structure** of moral judgement. And it is this structure which varies systematically in complexity during development. Since morality is defined in terms of *prescriptivity* (*see* pages 304–5) these reasons should not refer to ideas of how fathers and sons deal with this conflict *in reality*, i.e. how Joe *would act* – but they should refer to convictions about how one thinks the son *should act*, what should be considered the *right action*.

These structures differ in quality and form a *developmental sequence*, since they form qualitative wholes, they are called *developmental stages*. In the example given, the stages differ according to the arguments in favour or against giving the father the money. Kohlberg used the 'socio-moral perspective' taken in these arguments (i.e. the kind and number of the arguments used) as a criterion to identify six stages of moral development, which he grouped in three levels (i.e. two stages in each level). Table 15.1 (*see* pages 314–15) presents a summary of them. The first column describes the levels and stages in broad terms, columns two and three contain examples of arguments given in the Joe-dilemma for five stages (stage six is not scored any longer).

Fig 15.1 illustrates the distribution of the stages over age groups. As expected in a developmental variable, the correlation of moral judgement stages and age was 0.78. Yet as fig 15.1 demonstrates, there is a tremendous variance of stages within age groups. Most of the ten-year-olds scored on stages one and two. In early adolescence (age 13–14 years) stage three increases in frequency. In late adolescence (16–18 years), stage three clearly dominates, but some people still score at stage two. From 20 to 36 years, stages three and four dominate. Stage five is rather infrequent even in adults (Colby and Kohlberg, 1983, p. 46f.).

KOHLBERG'S THEORY

Kohlberg's psychological theory was formulated using Piaget's ideas as a framework. Consequently, he used the ideas of accommodation, assimila-

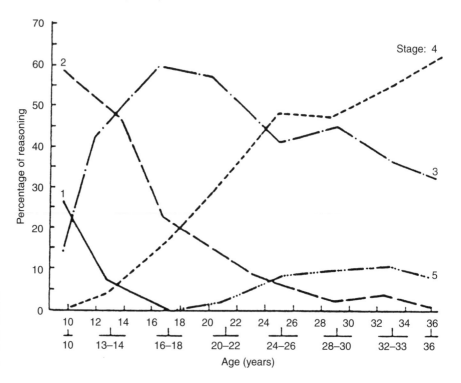

Figure 15.1 Mean percentage of moral reasoning at each stage for each age group (Colby et al., 1983).

tion and decentration (cf. chapters 3 and 6). However, with reference to stage assumptions Kohlberg was, in a way, more Piagetian than Piaget himself, because he transferred the *strong stage notions* Piaget had originally developed about logical structures to the domain of moral development. Kohlberg postulated (a) that later stages integrate (transform) the earlier ones, (b) that stages form 'holistic wholes', i.e. that a person at one stage would use structurally similar arguments irrespective of the topic being discussed, (c) that no stage can be skipped and most important, (d) that no stage regression exist, i.e. a person who argues on stage four at a particular age, will never argue on stage three again.

Later Kohlberg's ideas increasingly turned to the relationship between philosophy and psychology. This interest was grounded in theoretical issues as well as in practical problems. This rather complex discussion is summarized in Spielthenner (1996, pp 224–71). One of the reasons for Kohlberg's interest in philosophy was because of his involvement in educational processes about moral development. This is of course a tricky question for psychologists, because they usually do not make *ought statements* (how things *should be*). Rather as a descriptive science psychology deals primarily with *is-statements* (how things *are*). Ought statements are made in philosophy, hence it was quite natural to turn to the question how these two disciplines interrelate. The *empirical* finding that in the course of development the arguments of lay persons begin to resemble the *normative* positions (general ethical principles), taken in philosophy more and more closely, tempted Kohlberg first to argue that the philosophical and psychological perspectives are essentially *isomorphic* or *parallel* and second to propose that development itself (which ends up in these ethical positions) should be the *aim of education*.

DISCUSSION POINT

How does Kohlberg view the process of moral development?

TESTS OF PARTICULAR IMPLICATIONS OF THE THEORY

Empirical research was conducted by Kohlberg himself (primarily as a follow-up of the sample used for his dissertation, which was tested six times over a period of at least 25 years) but also by many others. Besides a huge amount of literature that deals with Kohlberg's theory in the USA and Europe (Modgil and Modgil, 1986), there are a tremendous number of cross-cultural studies from almost all parts of the world. What was the outcome of this research? We will discuss four major issues.

Table 15.1 Kohlberg's stages of development of moral judgment

Level and stage*	Example from 'Joe and his father'		What is right	General description	
	Joe should **not** give the father the money because**	Joe should **give** the father the money because		Reasons for doing right	Social perspective
LEVEL I PRE-CONVENTIONAL					
Stage 1 Heteronomous morality	. . . it is important to keep a promise, if you don't you'd be lying, it's a lie, it's bad	. . . you should do what your father or parents tell you to do	• Adherence to rules backed by punishment; obedience for its own sake	• Avoidance of punishment	• Egocentric point of view
Stage 2 Individualism, instrumental purpose, and exchange	. . . because it's Joe's money, he worked for it	. . . because his father will pay him back later	• Acting to meet one's own interests and needs and letting others do the same	• To serve one's own needs or interests	• Concrete individualistic perspective: right is relative, an equal exchange, a deal, an agreement
LEVEL II CONVENTIONAL					
Stage 3 Mutual interpersonal expectations, relationships, and interpersonal conformity	. . . because if Joe explains how hard he worked, his father will not ask for the money, (otherwise) it breaks the relationship	. . . because his father will be hurt or shamed by his friends if he cannot go	• Living up to what others expect	• The need to be a good person in one's own eyes and those of others	• Perspective of the individual sharing feelings, agreements, and expectations with others
Stage 4 Social system and conscience	. . . because the father is not asking for the money for the sake of the family welfare, he is misusing his authority	. . . because if there is to be family unity there must be an authority in the family	• Fulfilling the actual duties to which one has agreed • Upholding laws except in extreme cases when they conflict with other fixed social duties • Contributing to society, group, or institution	• To keep the institution going as a whole • What would happen 'if everyone did it?' • The imperative of conscience to meet one's defined obligations (easily confused with Stage 3 belief in rules and authority)	• Perspective of an individual in relation to the social group: takes the point of view of the system that defines roles and rules

LEVEL III
POST-CONVENTIONAL OR PRINCIPLED

Stage 5 A social-contract orientation, generally with legalistic and utilitarian overtones	. . because automony with respect to personal property is the right of every individual	. . if parental authority is legitimate and agreed to by both parties with informed consent***	• Being aware that people hold a variety of values and opinions, most of which are relative to the group that holds them • Upholding relative rules in the interest of impartiality and because they are a social contract • Non-relative values and rights, such as *life* and *liberty*, must be upheld in any society, regardless of majority opinion	• A sense of obligation to law because of one's social contract to make and abide by laws for the welfare of all and for the protection of all people's rights • A feeling of contractual commitment, freely entered upon, to family, friendship, trust and work obligations • Concern that laws and duties be based on rational calculation of overall utility, 'the greatest good for the greatest number	• Prior-to-society perspective: perspective of a rational individual aware of values and rights prior to social attachments and contracts • Integrates perspectives by formal mechanism of agreement, contract, objective impartiality, and due process • Considers moral and legal points of view; recognizes that they sometimes conflict and finds it difficult to integrate them
Stage 6 Universal ethical principles	not scored empirically	not scored empirically	• Following self-chosen ethical principles because they are universal principles of justice: the equality of human rights and respect for the dignity of human beings as individual person • Judging laws or social agreements by the extent to which they rest on such principles • When laws violate principles, acting in accordance with the principle	• A belief in the validity of universal moral principles • A sense of personal commitment to those principles	• Perspective of a moral point of view from which social arrangements derive: perspective is that of any rational individual recognizing the nature of morality or the fact that persons are ends in themselves and must be treated as such

* The description of the summary – tables of moral levels and stages changed from Kohlberg's dissertation (1958) to his latest publications (1986). These changes also indicate some changes in the theory. The most detailed analyses of these variations was presented by Bergling (1981).

** The examples are drawn from the Standard Issue Scoring Manual (Colby and Kohlberg (1987) pp. 187–94 (con), and pp. 235–43 (pro)).

*** Interestingly, no example is given in the manual for an argument in *favour* of giving the money to the father (as a first answer to the dilemma) at stage 5. The example given is taken from answers to an additional question (No. 10: What do you think is the most important thing a son should be concerned about in his relationship to his father?).

If stages are structured wholes, then there should be a high consistency in reasoning about different dilemmas

The data on this aspect are contradictory. Kohlberg and his colleagues found high consistencies in the longitudinal US-sample (Colby and Kohlberg, 1987b). The same is true for some Taiwanese data of Lei (1994). Others, particularly some German studies (Burgard, 1989; Eckensberger, 1989; Teo et al., 1995), however, found systematic inconsistencies. In some age groups (particularly adolescence) those dilemmas which contain interpersonal relations (father–son; sisters–mother) obtained lower stage scores than the other dilemmas. This is problematic for Kohlberg´s ideas.

The absence of stage skipping and regressions

Kohlberg claimed that there is no reason for regression to an earlier stage. Since this can only be tested by longitudinal data, there is limited data. Kohlberg and Kramer (1969) reported that 20 per cent of their 14 subjects in a longitudinal study showed regression from stages four and five to stage two between high school age and college. Similarly, Holstein (1976) in a study of 13-year-olds and their parents over a three year period found 25 per cent of 13-year-olds and parents regressed from a higher stage (four, five or six) to a lower stage (one, two or three). However, if one restricts discussion to the studies which were conducted using the latest manual, then regressions remain within an acceptable range (the reliability of scoring is high, the number of regressions do not exceed the unreliable cases and they only occur in adjacent stages). There has been no indication that stages are skipped.

Universality of the moral stages and conditions which assist or restrict moral development

Kohlberg claimed his stages were universal. On the grounds given above:

- Stages represent a progression in logical complexity.
- The dilemmas focus on unusual issues in social interaction, relating to life, property, authority and trust and can be modified to represent culturally relevant work.
- All groups share the problem of social control involving categories of right and wrong, obligation, responsibility, trust and blame.

Although he did not expect the same distribution and occurrence of the stages in all cultures, he expected the same developmental sequence. It is evident that this assumption is one which really runs counter to most ideas that norms and values differ among cultures (are culturally relativistic). Yet, generally, Kohlberg's claim has been validated in many studies. Although it should be admitted that stages one and five are rare and four is also only found under specific conditions.

There is some recent evidence that some differential variables like impulsiveness and shyness influence moral development. It is also evident that the social environment can assist moral development. Eckensberger (1998) summarizes the existing literature as follows.

There is some evidence of *global antecedent conditions* (Snarey, 1985; Eckensberger and Zimba, 1997): The theory is not as 'Western biased' as some critics claimed because the highest stages can also be found in India, Taiwan, Israel. It would seem that the 'complexity' (industrialization) of a culture and not 'Westernization' assists development to higher stages. Furthermore socio-economic status and religious fundamentalism correlate with moral development, the former positively, the latter negatively. Education and occupation, or generally speaking, *participation in social systems* seem to trigger the development of stage four. 'Face-to face-societies' (small tribal societies) on the other hand seem to remain at stage three.

The following *intra-familial and peer experiences* seem to influence moral development (Lempert, 1988):

- *Generally positive effects on moral development are*: role-taking opportunities, participation in co-operative decisions, the experience of taking responsibility and an open confrontation of social conflicts.
- *General negative effects are*: absence of positive experiences and instead a repression of contradictions in the social domain, power oriented 'mechanical' communication.
- Development *from pre-conventional to conventional level* seems to be influenced *positively* by: stable, emotional acceptance by parents, receiving social esteem from authorities and peers and emphasis on the consequences of actions for others by caretakers. This developmental transition is affected *negatively* by: inconsistent behaviour by authorities, unjust demands for obedience, instrumental misuse of power and withdrawal of love.
- The development from *the conventional to the post-conventional level* seems to be influenced *positively* by: confrontation with conflicting roles/ norms; experiences of responsibility in institutions and of autonomy. This transition seems to be affected *negatively* by: confrontation with diffuse social structures or completely incompatible social standards, absence of responsibility.

Moral judgement and behaviour

The relationship between moral judgement and behaviour is not central to Kohlberg´s theory (in fact, he spent much effort arguing that morality cannot be defined by behaviour). However, he turned to this issue in the 1980s, perhaps because it is still considered *the* test of a theory in psychology. The most comprehensive summary of relevant research was done by Blasi (1980). According to this review, many findings support the relationship between moral thinking and actions, although some data show inconsistencies. Generally, there was a high correlation between moral stages and honesty, altruistic (helping) behaviour and resisting conformity. Kohlberg and Candee (1984), after some re-analyses of their own data, propose the following 'model' to predict overt behaviour from moral judgements:

- In a first step the situation is analysed by the actor in the framework of his moral stage.
- A decision to act or not to act is made.
- A judgement of one´s own responsibility or duty to act is triggered. Beyond this, ego-functions like intelligence, attention etc. are important.

So, there is much empirical evidence supporting the theory. Nonetheless a couple of problems and open questions exist, to which we will now turn.

Open issues and present trends

THE MORALITY OF CARE AND RESPONSIBILITY

One of the most serious and salient critiques of Kohlberg's theory was formulated by Gilligan (1982). She criticized Kohlberg's justice-oriented theory and method for having a 'sex bias', favouring boys/men to girls/women. She introduced a **'morality of responsibility and care'**, which was assumed to be gender-related, representing 'a different voice' of women. Yet, a careful analysis of almost 200 studies (Walker, 1984; Walker and De Vries, 1985) did not reveal evidence of gender relatedness, although the two moral orientations (justice versus responsibility and care) seem to represent different aspects of morality. Nor did Snarey's (1985) review of cross-cultural studies support the assumption of a gender bias in Kohlberg's theory. Yet, on the whole this discussion (among other aspects) has lead to a rediscovery of the aspect of *benevolence* (care and responsibility) and its relationship to *justice* in moral development. Particularly in cross-cultural research the question arises whether in other cultures there exist other moral principles besides the justice principle, on which Kohlberg's theory is based.

IS THERE REALLY NO WESTERN BIAS IN THE THEORY?

Although the manual allows one to score individuals from different cultures, cross-cultural research also reveals problems as yet unsolved by the theory. Some stages (one and five) are really rare in some cultures, in addition questions exist practically at every stage: *Stage two* which is primarily based upon *instrumental* exchange, also seems to be based on *emotional expectations* (which usually are a major feature of stage three) (Keller et al., 1989). *Stage three* is quite frequent, it even seems to represent a 'culturally balanced' system in some traditional cultures. It therefore seems to be a stage which is much more mature than is suggested by Kohlberg´s descriptions of this stage (Setiono, 1994). *Stage four* seems to be too narrowly defined in terms of an institutionalized (written) law. The systems perspective, involved in this stage, also seems to be possible without this narrow criterion (Edwards, 1978). Beyond this, there is much evidence that the transition from stage three to stage four is very critical. This is one of the reasons why I (Eckensberger and Reinshagen, 1980) proposed to affiliate stages one, two and three into one (interpersonal) level that deals with conflict solutions among acting subjects, and stages four and five on a second (transpersonal) level that refers to relations between individuals and wider social systems (roles, societal positions).

The most challenging result is from cross-cultural research, however, that the most interesting material seems to be that which *cannot be scored* in terms of Kohlberg´s manual. This material points to some normative orientations (ethical principles within a culture) which differ from Kohlberg's justice orientated scheme (*see* Snarey, 1985; Eckensberger and Zimba, 1997). An outline of three of these ethical principles quoted in cross-cultural research illustrates distinctive normative orientations.

- In Hindu and Buddhist cultures, morality is embedded in **conceptions about the nature** of human existence itself. There, especially the law of **karma** (i.e. adding up of good (**dharma**) and bad (**adharma**) actions which may also have been committed in earlier lives) is regarded as crucial. It leads to types of moral reasoning which are totally different and not recognized in Kohlberg's stage theory and manual. It relates to the Indian **ethic of duty**, and it implies the principle of *respect for all life* which leads to the principle of **non-violence** (*ahimsa*) in Hinduism.
- The Javanese principles of **hormat** (respect for older people) and **rukun** (harmonious social relations), which also relates to the Taiwanese types of *'collective conflict-solving strategies'* is not mentioned by Kohlberg.
- The principles of *collective happiness* in the Kibbutz.

WHAT IS THE ROLE OF AFFECTS/FEELINGS IN MORAL JUDGEMENTS?

The analysis of the development of *altruism* (helping behaviour) by Eisenberg (1986) and others has resulted in a shift of focus to emotions, but this time to clearly *positive emotions*, to attachment, bonding and love, but particularly to sympathy and empathy. **Empathy** is an emotion that relates to another person's emotional state. It can, however, result in 'empathetic distress' or sympathy. **Sympathy** implies a feeling of concern for the other person's well-being. Because there is empirical evidence that these feelings are related to prosocial actions, they are highly relevant to moral development. Furthermore, these ideas contradict the basic idea that children are selfish unless they are socialized by parental discipline. Hoffman (1984) has discussed the way in which empathy is a major influence on morality. Although he assumes that the basis for this emotion is biological, he proposes 'stages' which represent (largely cognitive) transformations of empathy during development. These stages are largely based upon Piaget's theory of cognitive development. Although the empirical basis of these stages rests mainly on episodes and on the spot observations, these stages are consistent with other findings about cognitive development.

The *first stage* (first year) is characterized by *global stress* which implies a *confusion* of one's own feelings with those of others. At the *second stage* (second year) the child demonstrates *egocentric empathy*, which is based upon object permanence and upon the fact that others are experienced as different from the self (although the child does not fully distinguish his or her own feelings from those of others). There seem to be no feelings of guilt at this stage. It is only at the *third stage* (age 2–3 years) that the child has *empathy for another person's feeling*. Hence the child reacts to a variety of feelings of others. Feelings of shame and guilt occur, if the child harms another. At *stage four* (late childhood), when the child is able to think at the concrete operational stage and is able to 'conserve', children are able to see others as 'continuous' and 'unique' persons with a particular history. Therefore they can empathize with more *general life circumstances*. They also can feel guilt for omissions. When people reach the level of formal operations they can empathize with groups and general cases, which means they can feel solidarity. At this level existential guilt is also possible, a feeling of guilt which is not related to one's own actions but results from complex social comparison processes (like having survived in a concentration camp). It is particularly the close relation to cognitive development, which defines the transition of empathy which – exactly as Piaget elaborated in his Sorbonne lectures – demonstrates the synthesis of judgments and emotions. Hence, in a way, theory and research returns to a Piagetian perspective.

A SEQUENCE OF MORAL LEVELS VERSUS DOMAINS OF THOUGHT: VERTICAL OR HORIZONTAL DISTINCTIONS OF MORAL JUDGEMENTS?

Recently, a number of authors criticized Kohlberg's theory for being too global or undifferentiated as it confounds levels of development with dif-

---

BOX 15.3 Features of personal concerns and conventions

Personal concerns
Are considered to be private, one's own business, idiosyncratic and subjective. They change more or less according to the situations encountered during personal development, in western cultures, say, according to in vogue fashion styles or in changing predilections in the choice of friends.

Conventions
On the other hand, are obligations which are based on cultural consensus; they evolve in the course of history and serve to stabilize a group or society, to co-ordinate its social interactions. Conventions are tied to historical developments of a specific culture and, of course,

these histories differ. They are acquired by the individual subject in the course of ontogeny, specifically by imparted customs, e.g. table manners, how to address superiors, rules encountered in going to school and taking up a job.

ferent domains of thinking, which are distinguished very early in life (three to four years of age) namely pre-moral stages with *personal concerns* (Nucci, 1981) and *conventions* (Turiel, 1983), *see* Box 15.3.

These criticisms question the essence of the Kohlberg's theory regarding the validity of the developmental sequence. This is so because what is assumed to represent a 'vertical' sequence in Kohlberg's theory (first pre-conventional = personal and instrumental, then conventional and only then moral, cf. Table 15.1) seems rather to be a 'horizontal' (early and simultaneously existing) domain specificity of thinking.

Two cautions, however, have to be kept in mind in regard to this criticism. First, it is not possible to find *behaviour* which can exclusively be defined as personal concerns, conventions or morals. Rather, any assessment of behaviour according to these categories always rests on *personal interpretation*. For instance, in the US, premarital sex is most frequently considered a personal concern, whereas it is seen as a moral event in Zambia (Africa). Why? Because in Zambia a specific theory of illness exists assuming that sexually active (hot) individuals somehow make sexually inactive (cold) individuals (children, elderly) ill by practising premarital sex. So there is a *culture specific interpretation scheme* mediating and explaining this moral judgement. On the other hand, one can easily imagine that, even in Zambia, premarital sex would turn into a personal concern or a generally accepted convention if the theory of illness were replaced by a more 'modern' view. However, what is true at a cultural level is also true at an individual level: the same behaviour in a particular situation can be interpreted by one person as a personal concern, whereas another person may consider it a convention and still another one may feel moral dimensions are involved.

Second, we have to remember that Kohlberg's dilemmas purportedly all refer to problems, which are of *direct moral relevance* to everyone. The dilemmas refer to stealing, killing a person, keeping promises etc. and not to table manners (convention) nor haircuts (personal concern). Therefore, in principle, subjects are assumed to attribute Kohlberg's hypothetical dilemma situations to the moral domain.

In order to reject the criticism, one can therefore argue that children really give explanations about dilemmas by *referring to* the personal interests of the agents involved (Joe should not give the father the money because he worked for it), that most adolescents and many adults really explain moral standards by means of their *functionality in regulating personal relationships* (Joe should not give the father the money otherwise it breaks the relationship), or by referring to the organization of small groups and society as a whole (Joe should not give the father the money because the father is not asking for the money for the sake of the family welfare), but this does not make the moral judgements a personal concern or convention. Instead, children seemingly *individualize* morality and adolescents *conventionalize* morality. Therefore it would also be incorrect to say that in Kohlberg's theory morals ultimately *emerge* from conventions.

Yet, the distinction between morality and conventions has already had a very stimulating influence on the question of conditions which foster the development of social rule systems. To give just some examples: by the age of three children start to argue with their mothers on matters such as aggression, rights, needs and manners. What is interesting is that they react with anger and distress when they argue about their rights and needs. Mothers also seem to vary their practices and arguments depending on the kind of transgression involved. Mothers of toddlers refer to harm done to others, when moral questions were involved; they refer to social order if conventions were transgressed. They also combine power assertion and reasoning if stealing and lying was the problem, but they used reasoning when children did not show concern for others.

Chapter summary

This chapter deals with the development of normative standards for social actions. It focuses on moral development. After some terminological clarifications of the concept of morality, the two major theories and methods of Jean Piaget and Lawrence Kohlberg are explained in terms of their theoretical assumptions and developmental mechanisms. The main results, forming the basis of these theories, are summarized. Antecedents (the conditions that facilitate or impede development) are presented as well as the consequences for behaviour. The generality of our knowledge is checked by references to cross-cultural data. The chapter closes by discussing some current trends and open questions in the field. In this context the possible 'Western bias' of these theories is re-addressed. But additional theories are also touched upon like Gilligan's work on an ethic of responsibility and care, Hoffman's focus on positive emotions (sympathy) in moral development. Finally, the relationship between different domains of social cognitions (personal concerns, conventions and morality) and moral developmental stages are discussed.

Seminar questions

1. How is the relationship between cognition and behaviour interpreted by Piaget and Kohlberg?
2. What is meant by heteronomous and autonomous morality?
3. What are the stages of moral development in Kohlberg's theory?

Families and their role in children's lives and development

16

ANNE WOOLLETT

Editors' preface

Psychology is often defined as the scientific study of mental and behavioural processes related to individuals. This gives emphasis to the functioning of the isolated individual, and some theories of development, such as Piaget's (*see* chapters 3 and 6), have been criticized on precisely these grounds, that not enough account is taken of inter-personal and social processes. Even more general criticisms of developmental psychology have been made about the general failure to take account of the broader cultural processes (*see* chapters 12, 18 and 21). Thus, there is an appreciation that developmental psychology needs to investigate processes beyond the individual if a more complete picture of children is to be obtained.

As Professor Anne Woollett argues in this chapter, the nature of families and family life are generally accepted as being powerful influences on child development. However, as she indicates, developmental psychology is only recently beginning to investigate the complexity of family functioning. The chapter shows that many previous studies of families have involved examination of the mother's effect on children, and often the effect of other family members have not been given sufficient attention. This seems to be partly a result of limited conceptualization of family processes, and partly a result of the lack of resources to fully study the complexity of family functioning. Those studies which have taken a more complete view of family processes have built up a set of interesting findings and emphasize the need to go beyond investigations of simple processes of the effect of one family member on another. They also emphasize the need to see the family as an evolving structure both in the comparatively short time during which a single family develops, and over longer historical time periods where we see changing social structures.

Introduction

Families are considered to play a major role in children's lives and development. Whereas most families comprise mothers, fathers and their biological children ('nuclear families'), families are more diverse and change over time, increasingly as the result of family breakdown and remarriage. Families are positioned in the wider social context of schools, friendships and neighbourhoods. Family life is experienced directly but also as filtered through the presentation of families on television and in the mass media. Ideas about children and families vary, associated with social and economic factors and, reflecting the multi-cultural nature of modern societies, 'race' and ethnicity.

The main focus of psychological approaches to families are children and mothers. For this reason mothering and the role of mothers in children's lives and development has a prominent place in this chapter. However, reflecting current interest in other family influences, children's relations with fathers and siblings are also considered. The chapter starts by examining some ways in which families and their role in children's lives and development are theorized.

Approaches to families and their roles

In this section families and their roles are considered with particular reference to change and diversity as well as the influence of families, but the section starts by examining some ways in which families are conceptualized.

WAYS OF CONCEPTUALIZING FAMILIES

Psychological approaches to families concentrate largely on dyadic or one-to-one relations between mothers and children. However, relations with fathers and siblings (i.e. brothers and sisters) and other family members are increasingly being considered. The focus in these studies is often on 'difference': between mother–child and father–child and sibling relations and in the ways in which family members influence children's development (Burman, 1994; White and Woollett, 1992).

In contrast, systems theory and family therapy conceptualize families and family relations in more complex ways. They consider the ways in which relations between two family members are influenced by the relations each has with third, fourth and other family members, emphasizing indirect as well as direct influences of family members on one another (Minuchin, 1985; Sillars, 1995). So, for example, when relations between parents are good, mothers and fathers support one another and their parenting is sensitive and effective, but when parental relations are poor, parenting is more restrictive and coercive (Gable et al., 1992; Gano-Phillips and Fincham, 1995). Approaches such as these argue that parenting and parent–child relations are best understood within the context of other family relations (Dunn, 1993).

Systems theory also theorizes families as groups of people who interact together with a distinctive family 'culture'. In this way analysis is not limited to interactions and relations between individuals or groups *within* families, but considers each family as a unit with its own ways of functioning (as, for example, 'supportive', 'communicating about issues', 'isolated and with distinct boundaries') (Gable et al., 1992; Sillars, 1995). The family culture influences how family members relate to one another and make sense of family relationships and whether, for example, conflict between parents is considered as a 'normal' part of everyday life or as indicating a breakdown of parental relations (Dallos, 1995; Gano-Phillips and Fincham, 1995).

DISCUSSION POINT

Consider two families you know or families from soap operas. Think about how each family operates as a group and how you might characterize their family 'culture'.

CHANGE AND DIVERSITY IN FAMILIES

Families are usually considered to comprise mothers, fathers and their biological children. However families are more diverse. Although most families are created through the birth of children, others result from adoption or the use of the new reproductive technologies, or from remarriage. Families may also include grandparents or relatives (see Figure 16.1). Families change over time. The birth of a child creates new relationships but family relations also change as children grow up. In the early years, parents can control children's lives fairly easily. When children go to school they form relationships independently of parents and begin to reflect on their families and compare them with others (Moore et al., 1996; Newson and Newson, 1976). By adolescence the influence of friends, school and the media competes strongly with that of families (Allatt, 1996; Brannen et al., 1994). Families also change as a result of death, illness or handicap of family members and the separation or divorce of parents. Increasing rates of family breakdown mean that a substantial minority of children are brought up in families headed by one parent rather than two (usually but not always mothers). One parent families are often shortlived, with parents entering new relationships, thereby creating new families with new parents and sometimes step-siblings (Hetherington, 1989).

Psychological interest in family change has focused on family breakdown. Parental discord and conflict are identified as problematic because they are associated with a reduction in the quality of parenting, children's well-being, performance at school and relations with friends (Hetherington, 1989; Gano-Phillips and Fincham, 1995). This is the case especially when children become isolated from potential sources of support, including grandparents, siblings and friends. But there are also positive outcomes, particularly when family breakdown means an end to domestic violence and abusive family relations (Erel and Burman, 1995; Gable et al., 1992; Gano-Phillips and Fincham, 1995).

However, in spite of the diversity of family forms, psychological theorizing about 'normal' families and family life draws largely on research with nuclear families and assumes that they necessarily provide the best context for children and their development. Other family forms are either largely absent from research or are included only when the focus is 'problems' (antisocial behaviour, poor performance at school, or inadequate family functioning), thereby reinforcing views about the problematic nature of non-nuclear/'other' kinds of families (see Figure 16.2). As a result we know less about the resilience of children in single parent families and the problems experienced by children in two parent families. Approaches which exclude 'other' families marginalizes them and adds to the sense of stigma experienced by parents and children in families which do not conform to the nuclear family model (Garcia Coll et al., 1996; Phoenix and Woollett, 1991).

DISCUSSION POINT

Consider how relations in families change by comparing families with children under five years with those with children in their teens, or relations in families before and after breakdown of parental relations.

INFLUENCE IN FAMILIES

Psychologists conceptualize the influence of families in a variety of ways. Some focus on 'nature' and consider the genetic and biological basis of development and individuality (*see* Chapter 1). Others concentrate on 'nurture' and especially families, often arguing that because families are children's first/early environment they set the scene for later development. Mothers are considered the major influence on children, although fathers and siblings and other family members are seen to have a role. Influence is conceptualized in a number of ways (Dallos, 1995), see Box 16.1.

Mothers, fathers and siblings behave somewhat differently with children and these differences are used to argue for differences in influence.

Figure 16.1 A view about the 'immediate family'. Reprinted by permission of the Peters Fraser & Dunlop Group Ltd

Figure 16.2 A comment on the range of family structures in our society. Reprinted by permission of the Peters Fraser & Dunlop Group Ltd

---

BOX 16.1 Kinds of influence in families

Linear	Mother influences child Children change as a result of what mothers do
Reciprocal	Mother influences child and child influences mother Mothers and children both change because they influence one another
Circular	Mother influences child, child influences mother, mother influences child etc. Mothers and children are continuously changing in in response to one another

---

However, differences between mothers and fathers **within** a family are often small compared with differences **between** families: a Black mother may have more in common with her Black partner than she does with many white mothers (Wetherell, 1995). The influence of mothers and fathers is often examined separately, but it is important to recognise that parents influence one another (Gable et al., 1992). This can be seen in research on the impact of maternal employment which suggests that when mothers are employed outside the home, fathers tend to be more involved with child care than is the case when mothers are full-time carers (Bronfenbrenner, 1986). A number of factors operate in combination here: men with less traditional gender roles are more involved in child care and this help enables mothers to work outside the home. But women who are employed outside the home also make greater demands on men for assistance with child care and are more supportive of men's involvement (Parke, 1995).

It is also the case that maternal employment, divorce and single parenting often intersect with one another and with other factors and so do not influence children in single or direct ways. Divorce, for example, impacts on children's lives in large part because associated with it are a number of stressors such as reduction in family income, moving house and the loss of close relationships (Hetherington, 1989; Gable et al., 1992). Analysis of maternal employment, divorce and one parent families usually draws on stress models, emphasizing the risks and negative impact for children. Resilience models, however, provide a balance by emphasizing children's well-being, identifying factors associated with good adjustment and considering ways in which children who are experiencing family problems can be supported (Gano-Phillips and Fincham, 1995; Schaffer, 1996).

An additional and complicating factor is that different developmental routes can be detected in the ways in which boys and girls respond to divorce and remarriage. Girls cope better after divorce, often because they form close relations with mothers and are encouraged to take responsibility, whereas conflict between mothers and boys increases. By contrast boys cope better than girls with remarriage, often responding well to their step-fathers, whereas for girls remarriage is sometimes experienced as a loss of close relations with mothers (Hetherington, 1989).

Analysis which draws on both stress and resilience illustrates the variety of paths development may take and the different ways in which influence operates. However, research tends to examine group means (children in divorced/intact families, two/one parent families) and *overall* correlations and so diversity in children's coping strategies and patterns of development are not often explored. Parenting which enhances one skill may detract from the development of others. So for example, closed questions such as 'What's this called?' or 'What colour is this?' may encourage children to label objects but may discourage their use of more complex conversational skills.

CHILDREN: THEIR INFLUENCE AND PERSPECTIVE

Research about families considers a variety of child outcomes but the perspectives and accounts of children and young people themselves are less often examined. Children and young people are not just passive recipients of family relations and influence, but seek to understand and make sense of their families (Moore et al., 1996; Phoenix, 1997). In doing so they suggest some of the ways in which family relations operate and how family influence is mediated and why, for example, boys and girls experience divorce and remarriage somewhat differently (Dallos, 1995; Oppenheim et al., 1997). Their accounts also demonstrate that families are differently experienced by family members and that children's ideas and perspectives on family events are not necessarily the same as parents (Dunn, 1993, *see also* Chapter 1). Children influence families in a number of ways, for example, children who enjoy being cuddled or talking are more likely to elicit and encourage affection and conversation than are children who are construed as 'irritable' or 'difficult' (Das Gupta, 1995).

Consideration of the perspectives of children and other family members has implications for the ways in which families are researched (*see* Maccoby and Martin (1983)). Research which employs observation as a method provides information about what parents and children do and the ways in which they respond to one another in particular settings. But such research does not provide information about why family members behave as they do and how parents make sense of what children do and vice versa. To understand family relations and family influence we need to consider BOTH what people do AND their ideas and accounts (Dunn, 1988).

Parents: mothers and fathers

As has already been suggested, most research about families examines parents and particularly mothers. In most families (both one and two parent families) mothers have responsibility for child care and so are theorized as the major influence on children. Fathers who live with children vary considerably in their involvement, with fathers more involved with older than younger children and with boys more than girls (Parke, 1995). The increasing number of mother-headed families means that a substantial minority of fathers do not live with their biological children and are minimally involved in their lives (Burman, 1994; Wetherell, 1995).

Mothers and fathers parent in many similar ways: they control and monitor children's activities and often work together to create a family atmosphere which is, for example, child-centred or in which emotions can be safely expressed (Brannen et al., 1994; Sillars, 1995). But there are also some differences. Fathers are generally less involved with children and their involvement is largely through play and leisure activities (Russell and Russell, 1987). Fathers play in somewhat different ways than mothers, with more physical play and less verbal, educational and toy-mediated play, although fathers' play changes as children get older (Parke, 1995; Russell and Russell, 1987). Fathers' involvement in play makes them interesting and attractive to children and their influence is often considered to be mediated through play (White and Woollett, 1992). Fathering is often considered to be gendered, with fathers differentiating somewhat more than mothers in their relations with boys and girls and encouraging sex-typed behaviours more than mothers (Lytton and Romney, 1991). Fathers are therefore often considered to have a particular role to play in the development of children's gendered identities.

DISCUSSION POINT

Consider some reasons why mothers and fathers parent in similar and in different ways.

A number of aspects of parenting have been identified as having particular salience for children's development. These are considered here in terms of two themes: first, socialization of children to fit them to an adult world and second, fitting around and being sensitive to children.

SOCIALIZATION OF CHILDREN TO FIT THEM TO AN ADULT WORLD

In this section two aspects of parenting are considered: parental control and discipline and encouraging mature behaviour (*see* Das Gupta (1995) and Ribbens (1994)).

Control and discipline

Parents are expected to be responsible for the socialization of their children and to ensure that children behave in ways which are socially acceptable (Brannen, et al., 1994; Phoenix and Woollett, 1991). This is reflected in the accounts of mothers (as Newson and Newson (1968) and Ribbens (1994) discuss). In addition children and young people expect parents to exercise control and they often define 'good' parents as those who are 'understanding *and* strict' and 'keep . . . you on the right road' (Allatt, 1996; Goodnow and Burns, 1985). Psychological research points to the complexity of 'control', differentiating between how much control parents exert (how strict parents are or how much they monitor children's activities) and the strategies parents adopt.

Two parental strategies are often contrasted: power assertive techniques (such as physical punishment and smacking, shouting, forceful commands and threats) and psychological forms of control and discipline (such as threats to withdraw love, praising, exploiting the children's vulnerability, reasoning with and involving the child) (*see* Das Gupta, 1995; Grusec and Goodnow, 1994; Schaffer, 1996). Which of these strategies mothers employ depend on a range of factors. These include social class (middle class families employ psychological techniques more than working class families (Newson and Newson, 1976; Tizard and Hughes, 1984)), what mothers consider to be effective (some mothers consider that being restrictive is the most effective way of ensuring that children are well-behaved, whereas others argue that explanations are more effective) and factors to do with children (such as their age, gender and the reasons why mothers consider they have misbehaved (Dix, 1991)). Psychological techniques of control seem to be more effective because they provide children with information about how 'good' behaviour is defined in a particular family or setting and encourage children to internalise family rules and become 'self-controlled' rather than 'other-control' (Schaffer, 1996).

When considering issues of control and discipline it needs to be recognized that families vary in their ideas about what it means for a child to be 'well behaved' or 'competent'. Independence, assertiveness and the effective and confident expression of ideas are valued by many parents, although these ideas and values are also often linked to children's gender. Language skills are encouraged in girls more than boys and parents are more tolerant of boys' aggressive and disruptive behaviour (Lytton and Romney, 1991; Wetherell, 1995; Woollett and Phoenix, 1996). However, these values are not universal. In many families and especially working class families and minority families in USA, UK and Australia, independence and assertiveness are less highly valued than conformity, obedience and respect for parents (Das Gupta, 1995; Greenfield and Cocking, 1994; Newson and Newson, 1968).

DISCUSSION POINT

Consider why qualities such as independence and conformity are valued for children in some families but not others.

Modelling and encouraging 'mature' behaviour

Parents are often theorized as socializing children by providing models and 'teaching' children about their physical and social worlds (Das Gupta, 1995; Woollett and Phoenix, 1996). So, for example, parents engage with children's language development by presenting models of language which is well articulated, complies with grammatical rules and is appropriate to its context. This is linked to children's expression of ideas, their ability to construct sentences and to conduct conversations (Barton and Tomasello, 1994). Parents also influence children's development by encouraging them to behave and talk in ways which are considered appropriate for their age, gender and social situation and which take account of the perspective and knowledge of others (Kucynski and Kockanska, 1995). Comments from parents such as 'now do the next one' or 'What do you mean?' encourage children to be persistent and work at tasks and to convey information in ways which are meaningful to others. This demanding quality of parenting is acknowledged by children in comments such as 'They shouldn't do it all for you'. 'They (children) need to learn now or later on they won't even try' (Goodnow and Burns, 1985, p.32). Parental demands are often linked with children's academic achievement, their social competence, prosocial behaviour and concern for others (Maccoby and Martin, 1983).

FITTING AROUND AND BEING SENSITIVE TO CHILDREN

A second theme of parenting is that of parents fitting around children, being involved with them and sensitive to their feelings and competence. This theme incorporates two aspects of parenting: warmth and emotional involvement and sensitivity and child-centredness.

Warmth, emotional involvement and closeness of family relations

Ainsworth et al. (1974), drawing on the attachment theory of Bowlby (1969) (see Chapter 5), argued that warmth and affection were key aspects of parenting and (with sensitivity) were linked to the security of children's attachment and their later social and cognitive development. Children become attached to both mothers and fathers and close relations with one parent can buffer children against poor relations with the other parent (Schaffer, 1996). Mothers, fathers and children value the closeness and emotional intensity of family life, although young people report feeling closer to mothers than fathers (Brannen et al., 1994).

Families vary in their expression of emotional intensity and the extent to which they discuss emotions (Dunn et al., 1991; Oppenheim et al., 1997). From their study of mothers and four-year-old girls, Tizard and Hughes (1984) argue that in the emotional intensity of arguments with children, mothers give powerful expression to their feelings about what children are doing and in doing so provide children with clear demonstrations of the links between their actions and parents' feelings. Family relations also provide children with a context in which to learn about the emotions and feelings of others and manage conflict in ways which facilitate their social and cognitive development (Denham, 1993; Dunn, 1988).

SENSITIVITY AND CHILD-CENTREDNESS

Sensitivity, responsiveness or child-centredness are often seen as important aspects of parenting, in line with current ideas about the value of respecting children, their feelings and individuality (Woollett and Phoenix, 1996; Ribbens, 1994). Definitions vary but a common element is that children (rather than adults) are centrally positioned (hence the term 'child-centred'). In attachment studies 'sensitive' parents are those who respond warmly and quickly to children's distress and in studies of language and cognitive development as those who reply to children's questions in ways which reflect children's competence (Burman, 1994; Woollett and Phoenix, 1991). This aspect of parenting is valued by children and young people ('cook the things *you* like' and 'make you feel special') (Goodnow and Burns, 1985).

Parents vary in their degree of sensitivity: mothers are usually considered to be more sensitive than fathers, because they are more involved with children and know them better (Brannen et al., 1994). Being employed outside the home is not necessarily associated with a reduction in mothers' sensitivity (Greenberger et al., 1994). Parents (and especially fathers) are less sensitive when marital relations are poor and mothers are less sensitive after separation or divorce, initially at least (Gano-Phillips and Fincham, 1995; Hetherington, 1989).

Parental sensitivity is linked to the security of children's attachment, cognitive development and perspective taking and their prosocial behaviour and social relations. Sensitive parenting provides children with models which match their competence and interests and encourages them to use parents as a secure base from which to explore their worlds (Dunn, 1988; Schaffer, 1996). However, the development of perspective taking is linked to both sensitivity on the part of mothers AND insensitivity on the part of fathers (White and Woollett, 1992; Barton and Tomasello, 1994).

DISCUSSION POINT

What is it about mothers' sensitivity and fathers' insensitivity which relates to children's perspective taking?

PARENTING STYLES

The different aspects of parenting that have been discussed are linked to one another in ways which suggest patterns or styles of parenting (Maccoby and Martin, 1983). The most influential proponent of this approach is Baumrind (1973). From a mix of observations and interviews with US parents, she identified three main patterns of parenting: authoritarian, permissive and authoritative (a fourth, neglectful, is sometimes included), *see* Box 16.2.

One advantage of considering 'parenting styles' is to recognize patterns and consistencies in parenting and parents' ideas and values. How parents behave, their values and ideas and the ways in which they make sense of what children do are all important for understanding children's lives and

---

BOX 16.2 Baumrind's parenting styles

Diane Baumrind postulates three main parenting styles: authoritative, authoritarian and permissive.

AUTHORITATIVE PARENTS are those who encourage discussion and explain the reasoning behind their ideas. They demand mature behaviour and guide their children's activities, exerting control when their ideas clash with those of their children but they are not restrictive. Authoritative parents are prepared to confront children and expect them to respect their values. They are responsive in the sense of being loving, supportive and committed, they provide a stimulating and challenging environment and recognize their own and their children's individual interests. Children learn to use their initiative, deal with the consequences of their actions and recognize the perspectives of others and as a result, they perform well on measures of social and cognitive competence.

AUTHORITARIAN PARENTS score highly on measures of control, set high standards of behaviour and value respect for authority and obedience. They favour power assertive methods when children's actions or beliefs conflict with their own or their culture's standards. Authoritarian parents do not encourage discussion, believing instead that children should accept what parents say. Children of authoritarian parents tend to be lacking in independence, assertiveness, social and cognitive competence.

PERMISSIVE PARENTS are warm, avoid the exercise of control and grant children autonomy. They respond in non-punitive, accepting and affirmative ways to children. They present themselves as resources for children but not as shaping their children's behaviour. They allow children to regulate their own activities, make few maturity demands and do not insist that children obey externally defined standards. By failing to express their feelings and especially their anger, permissive parents protect children from the outcomes of their behaviour. Children of permissive parents are less achievement oriented and girls are less socially assertive.

DISCUSSION POINT

Take a particular issue, such as trying to stop children fighting, or ensuring that children have everything ready for school in the morning and consider how 'authoritarian', 'authoritative' or 'permissive' parents might deal with it.

development (Goodnow and Collins, 1990). Some ways in which parental practice and parents' ideas are related to one another are illustrated in Box 16.3.

BOX 16.3 Mothers' practices and ideas

By failing to respond to what their child is doing and saying, two mothers behave in similar ways.

The first mother describes her child as 'only playing' and she does not consider that play provides a context for learning. She does not believe that her engagement in her child's play has any developmental significance.

The second mother says she believes that her child learns best if she is sometimes able to have 'space' to do things for herself and to become self-reliant.

On the basis of their observed behaviour these mothers could both be rated as 'insensitive' or 'unresponsive'. However, although their behaviour is similar, the accounts of the two mothers suggest somewhat different views of children and their development and provides information about *why* the mothers behave as they do. Children are likely to take away somewhat different messages from what is seemingly similar behaviour.

At the same time, parenting is influenced by a range of often conflicting demands, so when, for example, mothers are in a hurry to get children to school or children are resisting their suggestions mothers may shift from their preference for explanation and use power assertive techniques (Das Gupta, 1995). Parents' accounts and understandings of what a child is doing (for example, whether they interpret something as 'standing up for themselves', 'trying to help' or 'deliberately disobedient') may be more important to parents than the child's behaviour.

Aspects of parenting examined in psychological research have been discussed. A central finding of this research is that children's social and cognitive development and their emotional security are related to parental demandingness AND parenting which is sensitive and child-centred. There is substantial variability in parenting and parental style associated with a range of social and economic factors such as maternal employment, the quality of parental relations and family breakdown. In addition the parenting of mothers is considered in general to be more sensitive and child-centred than that of fathers. Although there are associations between parenting and child outcomes, these are not always strong nor consistent and understanding influence in families requires analysis of both parenting and of parents' ideas.

The wider family

Examination of children in their families has suggested some ways in which wider family and contextual factors influence children. The influences to be discussed in this section include siblings and the social, economic and cultural contexts in which families live.

SIBLINGS

Fewer children are now born into families than was the case, but the majority of children are still brought up in families with one or more sibling and increasingly with step-siblings. As Dunn (1993) argues, the birth of a new baby brings about changes and creates new relationships for all family members, including older siblings and sibling relations have a major impact on children's experiences of family life. Psychodynamic approaches emphasize the negative aspects of sibling relations such as sibling rivalry and jealousy. However, siblings relations are also viewed more positively as encouraging and facilitating children's own development (Dunn and McGuire, 1992). Because siblings spend a great deal of time together they have much in common, they can provide sensitive support and companionship for one another and act as attachment figures especially in times of stress, such as family breakdown (Gano-Phillips and Fincham, 1995). Their close knowledge of one another enables children to see their sibling(s) as separate individuals with differing perspectives, in ways which impact on their perspective taking and cognitive development more generally (Dunn, 1988). There is considerable variability in sibling relations: whereas relations between some siblings are predominantly positive and supportive, others are more negative (Dunn, 1993).

Sibling relations change over time as children become more competent. In the early years there is an uneven balance of skills and knowledge: younger children are less competent and they watch and imitate older siblings. Older siblings talk more, are nurturant and bossy to their younger siblings. With increasing age, the balance changes: younger siblings talk more, they are more able to resist the bossiness of older siblings and play a more active role in sibling interactions (Dunn and McGuire, 1992).

Relations between siblings differ in a number of respects from children's relations with parents. Sibling relations are less sensitive and more competitive. Sibling relations are characterized by greater expression of emotions and especially of hostility and so provide children with the experience of

DISCUSSION POINT

Consider some ways in which the dynamics of sibling relations may change as children reach adolescence.

expressing and managing intense feelings and opportunities for developing skills of argument and negotiation (Barton and Tomasello, 1994). Children play more with siblings than with parents and the nature of their play differs: play with parents is more educational, but in play with siblings there is more expression of vulgarity and pretend and role play are more common. Play therefore is seen as a major route through which siblings engage with and influence one another. Sibling relations are more reciprocal than those with parents and provide them with experience of reciprocity as they share responsibility for maintaining interactions and conversations (Dunn and McGuire, 1992; White and Woollett, 1992).

Sibling relations influence and are influenced by other family relations. When there are two or more children in a family siblings have each other for company but they have fewer opportunities for one-to-one interactions with parents than do only children (Dunn, 1988). Although they have less opportunity for interactions with mothers, young children monitor relations between mothers and older children. By overhearing these conversations children are presented with models for complex language use which demonstrate ways of gaining the attention of people and sustaining conversations (Barton and Tomasello, 1994). Relations between mothers and children and the differential treatment of siblings by parents influence sibling relations. When mothers treat children very differently and make derogatory comparisons of children (for example about a child being spiteful, stupid or less loved than their sibling(s)) relations between children are more antagonistic (Dunn and McGuire, 1992; Gano-Phillips and Fincham, 1995).

DISCUSSION POINT

Consider some ways in which the differential treatment of children may influence how siblings feel about one another.

FAMILIES IN THE WIDER CONTEXT

Families do not operate in isolation but are positioned in their social, economic and cultural contexts. The economic context includes parental employment which influences family income and the amount of time parents have to spend with children and hence how feasible it is for parents to be involved and sensitive (Bronfenbrenner, 1986; Greenberger et al., 1994). Divorce usually means less contact with fathers, but the gap left by fathers is sometimes filled effectively by grandparents, neighbours and other relatives (Hetherington, 1989). Divorce is also associated with changes in a family's economic circumstances which sometimes requires that families move house, disrupting children's routines, friendships and schooling. A reduction in family income often means that mothers find employment outside the home. This is associated with changes in parenting: mothers become less sensitive, they demand more help around the house and expect children to take more responsibility for themselves. Although children often respond positively to these demands, they also resist them, increasing conflicts between mothers and children and especially boys (Erel and Burman, 1995; Hetherington, 1989).

DISCUSSION POINT

Consider some of the ways in which maternal employment may influence family members and relations within the family.

Parenting and family relations are shaped by the social and cultural context (Newson and Newson, 1968). Culture, 'race' and ethnicity often intersect with other factors: Black families in the UK, for example, are more likely to be working class, to earn less and to live in urban areas than white families, although this is by no means always the case (Modood et al., 1997; Garcia Coll et al., 1996). Social class, economic circumstances and culture are associated with some differences in parenting. Parenting changes over time, often reducing any differences between minority families and those of the dominant culture. However, this is not always the case: many minority parents and young people are rediscovering and reasserting their culture and religion (Modood et al., 1997).

Research on parenting in minority families questions the universality of associations between authoritative parenting and children's outcomes. Ideas about children vary considerably with some families valuing qualities such as independence and assertiveness while others value co-operation, respect for others and 'fitting in' (Greenfield and Cocking, 1994; Ribbens, 1994). Good achievement at school and prosocial behaviour (and not engaging in 'delinquent' behaviour) are mediated in somewhat different ways for different groups of children (and for boys rather than girls; Phoenix, 1997). For Afro–American and Asian–American families these outcomes are associated not so much with authoritative parenting but through the use of firm control, close monitoring of children and authoritarian parenting (Greenfield and Cocking, 1994; Lamborn et al., 1996). Firm/strict control may be associated with these positive outcomes because it enables young people to resist the influence of peers and supports their educational aspirations (Darling and Steinberg, 1993). In addition, parenting and parental control are interpreted in somewhat different ways. Many Afro–American and Asian–American children and young people interpret their parents' firm control and careful monitoring not so much as restrictive and interfering (as might children in more affluent and in authoritative families), but as indicating their concern and commitment (Lamborn et al., 1996; Mason et al., 1996). Careful monitoring helps to protect young people from involvement in deviant activities and means they are less likely to be noticed by the police and excluded from regular schooling (Lamborn et al., 1996).

Findings such as these point to the diversity of effective parenting and argues against generalizing about parenting and family influence across social and cultural groups. The findings indicate influences from outside as well as within families and the ways in which families and family relations are positioned within their wider social and economic context. The meanings of families for parents, children and young people and their appraisals of family relations suggest ways in which influence is mediated (Dallos, 1995; Gano-Phillips and Fincham, 1995).

Chapter summary

A variety of ways of considering parenting and its influence on children have been examined. Children's relations with mothers, fathers and siblings and their influence on children's lives and development have been considered. It has been argued that the significance of children's relations with parents and siblings needs to be considered not in isolation but in terms of the network of relations within families and more widely in terms of the social, economic and cultural contexts in which families operate. Influence operates in complex ways: some associations between parenting and children's development have been reported but the limitations of these associations have been discussed, raising issues about the ways in which influence is identified and mediated. Research drawing on a number of theoretical and methodological traditions has been examined to consider both family interactions and the ways in which different family members appraise and make sense of families and family relations.

Seminar questions

1. Consider some of the ways in which children living in the same family may experience their families differently. What factors may be associated with such differences?
2. Consider some ways in which children's individual characteristics (e.g. their gender, temperament, able-bodiedness, physical health) influence parents and how parents may interpret or 'read' children.
3. Give examples of linear, reciprocal and circular family influence and consider some ways in which they may be examined.
4. Role play an issue which generates considerable family debate (such as what time young people come home at night, an eight-year-old's fear of going to school, quarrels between siblings, how the family are going to spend a day out) with each person taking the part of one family

member. Think about the ways in which your position in the family influenced your choice of arguments and the extent to which you felt people were prepared to listen to/accept your arguments.

Further reading

White, D., Woollett, A. 1992. *Families: a context for development*. London: Falmer. The issues raised in this chapter are treated in greater detail in this book. It considers the perspective of parents, issues raised by the diversity of family forms, including families created by adoption and new reproductive technologies and children's health and illness.

Schaffer, H.R. 1996. *Social development*. Oxford: Blackwell. Children's development is positioned within the context of their social lives. It considers important issues for understanding children and their development, such as their sense of self and the shift from 'other-control to self-control'. It has an excellent last chapter on issues such as the reversibility of development and resilience.

Greenfield, P.M. and Cocking, R.R. 1994. *Cross-cultural roots of minority child development*. Hillsdale, NJ: Lawrence Erlbaum Associates. This is an edited collection of studies of children from a large number of ethnic communities in the USA. Their analysis emphasizes 'normality' and coping and hence provides a good counter-balance to approaches which emphasize problems and pathology. There is an excellent first chapter which sets the scene and raises the key issues, but unfortunately the book examines only US children and communities.

Brannen, J., O'Brien, M. 1996. *Children in families: research and policy*. London: Falmer Press. An interesting multi-disciplinary collection of chapters from UK and from Europe which look at children's and young people's experiences and ideas about families and the demographic and economic circumstances in which children grow up. There is a strong focus on social policy.

Dunn, J. 1993. *Young children's close relationships: beyond attachment*. London: Sage. This book examines children's relationships with parents, siblings and with peers. It includes two excellent chapters on connections between relationships within families and on the ways in which family relations impact on children's peer relations.

Bullying in school children

17

DIETER WOLKE AND KATHERINE STANFORD

Editors' preface

Violence is a powerful issue in relation to child development. The presentation of violence, especially on television, attracts debate and controversy (*see* Chapter 18). Similarly, in the last decade, bullying in schools has become an issue investigated by psychologists and a focus of attention in the media. Bullying has an immediate effect on those involved and is also likely to have longer term consequences.

Professor Dieter Wolke and Katherine Stanford review the findings from psychological research on bullying. They first consider definitions and prevalence, then discuss the origins and consequences of bullying and lastly they evaluate the effectiveness of programmes to prevent bullying. In addition, attention is paid to important methodological issues when collecting information on sensitive topics such as this and the way that different methods of data collection can result in different findings. This discussion of bullying connects with other chapters in showing the relations between aggressive behaviour and insecure attachments (*see* Chapter 5), between aggressive behaviour and parenting styles (Chapter 16) and between bullying and the ability to read others' minds (Chapter 12).

Definition of bullying and prevalence

Since the late 1960s, Dan Olweus has carried out pioneering quantitative assessment to investigate the nature, causes and consequences of bullying in Scandinavia. He has given this definition:

> A student is being bullied or victimised when he or she is exposed *repeatedly* and *over time* to *negative action* on the part of one or more other students (Olweus, 1991).

1. The behaviour must be *intentional*, to cause harm to the victim (Farrington, 1993; Smith and Thompson, 1991).
2. It can be physical (hitting, kicking, pinching, taking money or belongings etc.), verbal (name calling, cruel teasing, taunting, threatening etc.) or it can be psychological (social exclusion, isolation, malicious gossip etc.) (Bjorkqvist et al., 1992; Crick and Grotpeter, 1995).
3. Bullying must be a *repeated action* and *occur regularly over time*. Thus, occasional negative behaviours cannot be seen as victimization. Conflict between children is normal and natural behaviour, which can lead to learning experiences and the development of coping strategies.
4. Bullying must involve a real or perceived *imbalance in strength/power* (either physical or psychological). The victims feel helpless and unequipped to defend themselves.

DISCUSSION POINT

According to this definition, did you ever bully other children or were you a victim when you went to school?

PREVALENCE

Surveys carried out in different countries over the last decade suggest that bullying affects almost one in five school children. Table 17.1 details the prevalence of bullying in primary and middle schools in different countries and Table 17.2 the prevalence in secondary schools.

DIFFERENCES BETWEEN STUDIES

There is a lack of consistency between studies. For example, studies of 8–12-year-olds show large variation in children who bully (from 3 per cent to 23 per cent) and in those who are victimized (from 8 per cent to 46 per cent). This could partly be explained by the variations in instruments and methodologies (*see* Box 17.1).

Bullying is an emotive issue and sensitive instruments are necessary to gather accurate information. The most frequently used method of data collection for children aged over eight years is by anonymous questionnaire. For a national study in Norway, Olweus (1978, 1991) designed a questionnaire which subsequently has been used (or adaptations of it) to collect much of the data. These questionnaires are usually administered to whole classes (Smith, 1991). However, different adaptations of the questionnaire by different investigators may explain some of the inconsistencies across studies.

Table 17.1 Rates of bullying and victimization in primary and middle schools in different countries

Study	Age range (Years)	Country	Results			Frequency category
			Bully (%)	Victim (%)	Bully/victim	
Boulton and Underwood (1992)	8–12	UK	17	21		Sometimes or more often
Boulton and Smith (1994)	8–9	UK	13	17		(Not specified)
Garcia and Perez (1989)	8–12	Spain		17.2		Bullied often
Genta et al. (1996)	8–11	Italy: Florence/ Cosenza	23/20	46/38		Sometimes or more often
			9/7	20/14		Once a week or more often
Hirano (1992)	10–11	Japan	12	15		(Not specified)
Olweus (1984)	8–11	Norway	7	9		Now and then/or more
O'Moore and Hillery (1989)	7–13	Ireland	3	8		Once a week or more often
Perry et al. (1988)	7–13	USA		10		Extreme victims
Wolke and Schulz (1997)	7–8	Germany	17	21		At least four times in last six months
			5	8		At least once a week
Smith and Levan (1995)	6–7	UK	10	23		Bullied 'that week'/Bullied 'a little'
Whitney and Smith (1993)	8–11	UK	12	27		Sometimes or more often
			4	10		Once a week/or more often

A peer nomination technique has been used in other studies to identify children who are often victimized or who actively bully in a class. Schwartz *et al.* (1997) used this technique to identify victims. This involves children being asked to nominate peers who are involved in bully or victim

Table 17.2 Rates of bullying and victimization in secondary schools in different countries

Study	Age range (Years)	Country	Results Bully (%)	Victim (%)	Bully/victim	Frequency category
Ahmad and Smith (1989)	13–16	UK	11	18		Sometimes or more often
			4	8		Once a week or more
Genta et al. (1996)	11–14	Italy: Florence/ Cosenza	14/19	27/30		Sometimes or more often
			4/7	10		Once a week or more often
Hirano (1991)	12–14	Japan	14	10		(Not specified)
Olweus (1984)	13-16	Norway	7	4		Now and then/or more
Yates and Smith (1989)	11–16	UK	12	22		Now and then or more frequently
Mellor (1990)	11–16	Scotland	6	4		Sometimes or more often
Lagerspetz et al. (1982)	11–16	Finland	6	4		–
Whitney and Smith (1993)	11–16	UK	6	10		Sometimes or more often
			1	4		Once a week/or more often

behaviour. Once every child in the class has been interviewed it is possible to calculate a score for each child on each variable (i.e. bully and victim) by adding the nominations received (*see* Table 17.2).

Individual interviews have also been conducted and provide valuable insight into changes in forms of aggression during the primary school years. Self-report questionnaires are not suitable for children below eight years of age because of a lack of reading skills. Some individual interviews have been administered which are structured largely upon modified versions of the Olweus questionnaire, but which use simple questions and pictures to elicit information (Ahmad and Smith, 1990; Smith and Levan, 1995; Wolke and Schulz, 1997).

BOX 17.1 Methods of researching bullying in schools[1]

	Advantages	Disadvantages
Self-report questionnaire	• Whole-class administration (quick and economical) • Ideal for quantitative surveys • Anonymous (honest information) • Reliable	• Differences in measures lead to varying frequencies • Reliance on reading and comprehension skills (not suitable for young children) • Self-perception bias
One-to-one interview	• Can be used with young children • In-depth enquiry, e.g. reasons for bullying and attributions • Probing if inconsistent information is given	• More expensive • Time-consuming • Cannot be anonymous (older children may not own up to being bullies/victims)
Peer-nomination technique	• Whole class administered in older children (quick and economical) • Anonymous (honest information) • High re-test reliability • Whole class perception	• Time-consuming with young children (interview) • Liable to 'reputation effect' • Children talking about their nominations between each other
Observation technique	• Offers qualitative detail which survey studies may miss • Material for interviewing about bullying situations • Capturing bullying in social context	• Expensive • Time-consuming • Observer effect/bias • Not useful for prevalence investigations (e.g. hidden bullying)

[1]The convergence (agreement) in classification of bullies, victims and bully/victims, for example, between methods has been found to only be low to moderate

Natural observations have obvious practical limitations (costly, time-consuming, bullying occurring out of sight etc.). However, they are useful, for example, to understand: whether provocation has occurred; the role of bystanders; how conflicts are negotiated; and to learn about the social perception of bullies and victims (Pepler and Craig, 1995; Howe et al., 1998).

COMMON FINDINGS

Despite variations in prevalence estimates, certain common and cross-culturally consistent findings have emerged (Table 17.3). There is a steady and consistent decrease in being bullied between the ages of eight and 16 years (Manning et al., 1978; Olweus, 1991; Boulton and Underwood, 1992; Whitney and Smith, 1993). For example, although 13 per cent of girls and 18 per cent of boys report being bullied once a week or more when aged nine, only 8 per cent were found at age 14 (Hanewinkel and Knaack, 1997). Generally, bullying behaviour does not appear to vary so much with age, if anything there appears to be an slight increase as children get older (Olweus, 1991; Smith, 1991; Boulton and Underwood, 1992; Hanewinkel and Knaack, 1997).

Structural factors such as the size of the school or class or whether the school is in a rural or an urban location have not been found to be related to bullying behaviour (Stephenson and Smith, 1989; Olweus, 1991; Whitney and Smith, 1993; Wolke and Schulz, 1997) (Table 17.3). Gender differences in types of bullying behaviour have been established (Lagerspetz et al., 1988; Schäfer et al., submitted).

Dichotomy of bully versus victim

Traditionally children have predominantly been classified as bullies, victims or not involved in either bullying or victimization. The findings reviewed so far are based on this dichotomy which, however, appears to be an over-simplification. A sizeable group of children cannot be classified simply as bullies or as victims, but appear to both bully other children and

Table 17.3 Common findings across studies	**Common findings**	Age factors – victimization	Most prevalent in younger children
		Age factors – bullying	Does not vary significantly with age
		Gender distribution	Boys are more often perpetrators and victims of direct bullying, girls of relational/indirect bullying
		In groups or in isolation?	Much of bullying is carried out by groups of children
		Size of school	Little or no effect
		Size of class	Little or no effect
		Location of bullying	Bullying takes place in public places, i.e. the playground, the classroom or the corridor
		Location of school	Little or no effect

be victimized. These children (up to half of all victims) have been labelled 'bully/victims' (Stephenson and Smith, 1989; Boulton and Smith 1994; Bowers et al., 1994; Gasteiger-Klicpera and Klicpera 1997; Wolke and Schulz, 1997; Sutton and Smith, in press). In earlier research these children were assumed to be only a small group and have been described as provocative victims (Olweus, 1978, 1984, 1993; Pikas, 1989), aggressive victims (Schwartz et al., 1997) or most recently as reactive/proactive aggressors (Vitaro et al., 1998). Specific characteristics of bully/victims are discussed more fully below (Table 17.4).

Roles taken in bullying

Bullying can be regarded as a subcategory of aggressive behaviour but is also distinct from aggression in a number of ways. Aggressive behaviour often refers to a construct involving individual differences, that is one child is different from another in the tendency to react or show aggressive behaviour. Bullying, in contrast is social in nature and takes place in a relatively permanent social group (the class), in which the victim has little opportunity to avoid their tormentors and the bully often gets support from other group members, i.e. their role becomes defined (Lagerspetz et al., 1982; Bowers et al., 1994; Olweus, 1994; Salmivalli et al., 1996). Bullying is not simply aggression but a systematic abuse of power.

Salmivalli et al. (1996) distinguished six different roles children can take in bullying situations: the bully (leader), the reinforcer (encourages and provides the audience), the assistant (follower/helper, e.g. holds the child down), the defender, the outsider (staying away from bullying situations) and the victim. Sutton and Smith (in press) determined the participant roles in 7-10-year-old British children. They found that the three roles: bully, reinforcer and assistant are closely correlated with each other. That is bullies start the bullying and at other times reinforce or assist. Those who are primarily involved in the action of bullying (bully and assistant) rarely become victims, whereas reinforcers (those who yell and laugh) are more likely to also be victims at times. The bully and assistant appear to be what is called in other distinctions the 'Bully'. The reinforcer is likely to be a 'Bully/victim'. The defender and outsider rarely engage in any bullying and are neutral.

A second important finding is that self-reports of the pupils showed little correlation with peer nominations (pupils being asked about the roles of each child) (Schuster, 1997). Only 20 per cent of those nominated by peers as bullies reported themselves as being bullies. Sixty per cent of the peer-nominated bullies perceived themselves as defenders, helping others in trouble and fights (Sutton and Smith, in press). In fact, most children when asked to name their role saw themselves as defenders. Only the peer-nominated victims also perceived themselves as predominantly victims.

The classification of children's bullying in terms of roles can be potentially useful for intervention. Rather than focusing on the bullies and

Table 17.4 Concurrent characteristics of bullies, bully/victims and victims

	Bullies	Bully/victims	Victims
Individual differences	Little anxiety, good self-esteem, not easily angered and well regulated physically strong (boys)	Highly reactive and angry, irritable and hot-tempered, impulsive, hyperactive/short attention span	Withdrawn, anxious, insecure, low self-esteem, unassertive easily emotionally upset, often physically weak
Social cognition	Considers aggression a means to dominate others; 'cool cognition', good understanding of social situations (theory of mind), little empathy	Positive attitude to aggression, interpret others' ambiguous provocations as hostile, low to moderate understanding of social situations	Negative attitude to violence, poor social understanding (theory of mind), poor in finding conflict resolution alternatives
Sociometric status	High social impact, number of friends (followers), ring leader, both popular and rejected (controversial)	Moderate to high social impact, few friends, often reinforcer or assistant, highly rejected by peers	Low social impact, no friends or only single friend (lonely) rejected or neglected by peers
Family functioning	Harsh discipline style, but no violence against them, disengaged or distant family structure, negative relations between siblings (dominance struggles), father more likely to have been bully himself	Experience of violence against them or exposure to violence between adults, inconsistent discipline and parenting, poor monitoring of child, often marital conflict, most troubled or dysfunctional families, often father absent	Overly protective mothers, enmeshed/overly close family allowing little independence, close relationship to siblings; or fathers distant, negative, cold and not a role model

victims, strengthening the usually popular and influential defenders and outsiders may help reduce bullying incidences (Cowie and Sharp, 1996).

Physical versus relational bullying

Bullying typically occurs more often in boys than girls (Table 17.3). Most research has focused on physical bullying such as hitting, fighting or blackmail. It has been suggested that there is an under-reporting in girls' bullying, as it usually takes the form of more subtle behaviours such as name-calling, slandering, the spreading of rumours and manipulation of friendship relationships (Lowenstein, 1977; Bjorkvist et al., 1992; Boulton and Underwood, 1992). Crick and Grotpeter (1995) called this form of bullying 'relational aggression' and defined it as 'harming others through purposeful manipulation and damage of their peer relationships'. They found that relational and physical aggression are distinct constructs and that girls engage in relational aggression four to five times more frequently than boys. They suggested that both boys and girls are equally aggressive but that boys engage in overt and girls in predominantly relational aggression (*see also* Schäfer et al., submitted).

The 'bullying' behaviour of girls seems to have been under-estimated in previous research for the following reasons:

- Children may understand the word 'bully' to refer to the physical forms of bullying rather than non-physical forms (Boulton and Smith, 1994; Smith, 1991).
- Relational aggression is more complex and subtle in nature. Screening questionnaires may therefore miss this form of peer aggression. It is thus crucial that relational bullying is adequately investigated using instruments designed specifically for this purpose. First replications indicate that relational and physical bullying are indeed distinct constructs (Schäfer et al., submitted).

DISCUSSION POINT

- How upsetting did you find it when you were left out by other children or gossiped about when you were at school?

Concurrent characteristics

A number of characteristics have been identified as being related to bullying status. These have been primarily investigated in secondary school children. The major findings are summarized in Table 17.4 and Box 17.2 and are reviewed below.

INDIVIDUAL CHARACTERISTICS AND SOCIOMETRIC STATUS

The typical victim is described in Table 17.4. (e.g. Boulton and Underwood, 1992; Slee and Rigby, 1993; Olweus, 1994). There are inconsistent findings whether physical characteristics such as hair colour (e.g. red hair), colour of skin, physical growth or physical stigmata (ranging from wearing spectacles to neurological disabilities) are related to victimization. Olweus (1994) in Scandinavia and Wolke and Schulz (1997) in Germany found that physical or ethnic characteristics do not predispose children to become victims of bullying. In contrast, studies in the UK and USA suggest that physical characteristics, including clumsiness, obesity, below average attractiveness, speech problems and special educational needs, are related to victimization (Whitney et al., 1994; Mooney and Smith, 1995). Thus, cultural differences between America and the UK and other European countries are apparent. Dawkins (1996) showed that it may not be the visible disability that is associated with victimization – disabled children are more often males, have few friends and more often have learning problems, all factors that are also related to victimization in non-disabled children.

Bully/victims (provocative victims) are easily provoked, involved in angry outbursts in response to provocation (reactive aggressiveness) and they initiate aggression towards others on other occasions (proactive aggressiveness) (e.g. Olweus, 1978, 1994; Stephenson and Smith, 1989; Vitaro et al., 1998). They are usually well known by other pupils (high social impact) but are most strongly rejected by the majority (*see* Box 17.2).

Bullies have been described as being more aggressive not only towards peers but also adults. They have a more positive attitude towards violence. Male bullies are often physically stronger than their age-mates. They often have unusually little anxiety and insecurity and do not suffer from negative self-esteem (Pulkkinen and Tremblay, 1992; Olweus, 1994). Non-victimized bullies tend to display more organized and goal-directed aggressive behaviour to dominate others, but rarely engage in retaliatory behaviours or get angered. Bullies are more popular than victims and are usually surrounded by a small group of children who support them and thus are generally controversial in their peer status, i.e. liked by some (their followers) and rejected by others (Wolke and Schulz, 1997; Cairns et al., 1988). Bullies are ring leaders (Bowers et al., 1994).

SOCIAL COGNITION

Social cognition refers to the process of encoding, interpreting and acting appropriately on social cues in social situations (Crick and Dodge, 1994). Aggressive or conduct disordered children have been found to use fewer social cues of any type to interpret social situations and to be more likely to attribute hostile intent to peers. They often want to 'get even' or dominate others. They have little knowledge of how to influence others and thus repeatedly use aggression to reach their goals (social skills deficit) (Besag,

BOX 17.2 The Munich Bullying Study (MBS)

The MBS (Wolke and Schulz, 1997) conducted in Munich (Germany) and the surrounding rural area found in individual interviews with 1538 eight-year-old children the following prevalence: *boys*: 13.7 per cent victims, 18.4 per cent bully/victims (B/V) and 12.3 per cent bullies and in *girls*: 18.4 per cent victims, 7.5 per cent bully/victims and 5 per cent bullies. B/V reported most often (even more than only victims) that they have been beaten, threatened/blackmailed and shouted at. According to the peer nominations the different bully and victim groups fell into the following sociometric categories.

Status	Popular	Rejected (%)	Neglected (%)	Controversial (%)	Average (%)
Victim	22.5	24.2	20.5	12.0	20.8
Bully	11.9	24.9	8.8	34.9	19.5
Bully/Victim	7.4	31.8	14.6	28.3	17.9
Neutral	23.5	15.5	22.9	17.8	20.3

The B/V were the least popular and most rejected children. Bullies were the most controversial children, the least likely to be neglected and not very popular. Victims were the least controversial and similarly to the bullies, they are often rejected by some and popular with other children. Children were most frequently frightened of bullies (32 per cent) and B/V (27 per cent) and the least frightened of victims (19.3 per cent).

1989; Happé and Frith, 1996). Applied to bullies, this would mean that they are socially deficient or even socially blind (Randall, 1997).

New evidence indicates that equating social maladjustment (e.g. rejection in peer nomination) or aggressive behaviour with bullying (which is aggressive behaviour within a particular social context) may be *vastly misleading*. Rather (*see* Table 17.4), ring leader bullies (non-victimized) have been found to be superior to any of the other groups in their ability to read the mind of others (*see* Chapter 12) and to use this to manipulate and dominate others without empathy (Sutton et al., 1997; Sutton et al., in press). Victims showed the poorest performance in the social cognition tasks.

Theory of mind studies have also consistently found a sex difference in favour of girls (*see* Chapter 12) and there may be a genetic basis for it (Skuse et al., 1997). This may explain why girls use this superior ability in social understanding and intuition to relationally bully others more often than boys.

These recent findings have a number of implications:

- Ringleader bullies who are not victimized appear to be superior in their understanding of social relationships and use their ability to manipulate social situations without concern for the victims (cool cognition).

- Victims are particularly poor in their social understanding of groups.
- Bully/victims who are mostly followers seem to be torn in their roles as they show an understanding of social situations and also an understanding of feelings.

Thus bullying as a social construct has to be distinguished from aggression as an individual differences construct. The similarities between the development of aggression and bullying behaviour are not yet well understood.

FAMILY CHARACTERISTICS

There are conflicting findings regarding the perception of family characteristics of bullies and victims (Smith and Myron-Wilson, in press; Bowers et al., 1992, 1994; Schwartz et al., 1997). This is partly due to three factors:

- Findings from studies on aggressive children have been generalized to bullying behaviour.
- Some studies just discriminated bullies and victims but not the sizeable group of bully/victims.
- The pathways to the different roles in bullying appear to be different for boys and girls.

As summarised in Table 17.4, the families of *bully/victims* have been found to be most dysfunctional and troubled, followed by *bullies*, who often experience harsh discipline but rarely violence against themselves. Farrington (1992) found that the parents of bullies are much more likely to have been bullies themselves and thus, although not endorsing bullying are more likely to turn a blind eye to bullying. Bullies and bully/victims describe little positive affect (warmth) and positive communication in their families (Lowenstein, 1977; Batsche and Knoff, 1994). These families are more often lacking a father figure (Rigby, 1994; Bowers et al., 1994). The families of (*passive*) *victims* are not particularly conflictual or troubled, rather the mothers are often over-protective, in particular, towards children perceived as emotionally vulnerable (e.g. Bowers et al., 1992, 1994; Olweus, 1993; Rigby, 1994).

Paternal and maternal behaviour is related to victimization in different ways between the genders. Boys are more prone to become victims when the father is highly critical and distant in his attitude towards his son, the relationship is dysfunctional and the father is not providing a satisfactory role model (Olweus, 1993; Rigby, 1993). Victimization in boys is also associated with maternal over-protectiveness, in particular, when the boys felt afraid and compelled to submit to their mothers during conflicts (Finnegan et al., 1997). In contrast, victimization in girls is related to maternal hostility, especially for girls seen as lacking physical strength (Rigby, 1993). It is likely that a common pathway towards victimization occurs when maternal behaviour hinders boys' and girls' progress towards the relevant social and developmental goals. Smith and Myron-Wilson (in press) speculate that for girls, mothers' hostility may decrease their sense of connectedness in relationships (leading to anxiety) (Rigby, 1993), whereas for boys a mother's over-protectiveness may hinder their search for autonomy and independence.

Little is still known about the role of sibling relationships in the development of aggression or bullying. Sibling relationships with high levels of conflict and little warmth have been shown to be related to lower adjustment and more aggression towards peers (Stormshak et al., 1996). Play fighting with fathers who set clear roles when the play becomes too aggressive can be a good way of learning social understanding and modulating aggression (Boulton, 1993). Perlman and Ross (1997) reported that when parents choose to intervene in the most intense fights between their children, this led to the reduction of aggressive strategies and the use of more non-violent negotiations. Thus rehearsing using pretend play or play fighting and adequate parental control are important factors in learning conflict resolution strategies.

SOCIO-ECONOMIC CONDITIONS

There is disagreement regarding the role of socio-economic status of children involved in bullying and victimisation. British studies (Whitney and Smith, 1993; Stephenson and Smith, 1989) report that social disadvantage is a correlate of such difficulties and lower socio-economic status (SES) is correlated with more bullying. Studies in Ireland (O'Moore and Hillery, 1989), Germany (Wolke and Schulz, 1997) and Scandinavia (Olweus, 1980) find that socio-economic status is not related to the degree of bullying or victimization.

Limitations of correlational studies

Concurrent studies are important in understanding family dynamics and to plan interventions. However, concurrent associations do not explain why some children become victims or bullies – the differences in family dynamics may be a result rather than a cause of the bullying status of the child. For example, a difficult child challenges the parents' resources, putting stress on the parents and this leads to dysfunctional family relationships. Thus any concurrent association between difficult temperament and bullying does not give us any indication of causality. In fact, they may be misleading. For example, it has been observed that with the reduction of storks in Northern Europe the birth rate has fallen in these countries (Hofstaedter and Wendt, 1974). However, from our knowledge of reproduction, we know that these two facts may be statistically but not causally related.

To understand bullying status, it is necessary to study individual and family characteristics before children show bullying behaviour and follow them until the time bullying is detected (e.g. middle childhood or adolescence) using a prospective design. Prospective studies have the advantage of being able to describe the way different characteristics work together, i.e. lead to victimization. For example, being physically fragile may lead to altered care taking (e.g. over-protection) in early childhood. Over-protection may deprive the child from learning strategies for conflict resolution with peers. That is, the child may not become victimized because of a physical weakness which they may have outgrown but because they never learned strategies to deal with peers. These types of studies are very expensive as a large group of children needs to be followed.

To save time, money and the difficulties of doing a follow-up study, retrospective designs are often used; i.e. those who experienced bullying are asked how they grew up, what type of person they were before it happened etc. (KIDSCAPE, 1998). Retrospective studies are liable to biases. These are sample selection biases (i.e. only those who still feel strongly about bullying are included in the sample) and biases in remembering actual events and the quality and feelings during these events. Retrospective studies often find links between early factors and later behaviour which have not been replicated in prospective studies (e.g. Sameroff, 1975).

Precursors of bullying

Other than one recent study (Schwartz et al., 1997), there are *no* investigations into precursors of bullying behaviour. As bullies have aggressive reaction patterns, models for explaining their development have borrowed from the general research on aggression, delinquency and conduct disorder. This is not satisfactory but represents the current state of knowledge. We will first describe what is known about the development of aggressive behaviour patterns and conduct problems and then discuss how this evidence may be helpful in explaining the development of bullying behaviour.

The following major factors have been identified to facilitate the development of aggression, conduct problems or delinquency in boys (e.g. Olweus, 1980; Loeber and Stouthamer-Loeber, 1986; Loeber and Hay, 1994) (Box 17.3).

Prospective longitudinal studies (e.g. Loeber et al., 1993; Farrington, 1995; Moffitt et al., 1996; Newman et al., 1997) have found that neither individual child, family or neighbourhood characteristics on their own predict aggression and social maladjustment, rather the accumulation and interaction between these factors does.

It is not clear whether the findings explain why some children become bullies or bully/victims. Furthermore, they do not explain why some children are more likely to become victims and what are the precursors of the more subtle, relational bullying (Bjorkqvist et al., 1992). Schwartz et al. (1997) provide the first prospective study on the early socialization of aggressive victims (bully/victims), passive victims (victims) or non-victimized aggressors (bullies). They found that children classified as

> **BOX 17.3 Factors which facilitate aggression, conduct problems or delinquency in boys**

Child characteristics
Difficult temperament (i.e. early under-controlled behaviour as expressed by high reactivity to stress, excessive crying and irritability, poor consolability). In infancy and toddlerhood, difficult temperament has been found to be a significant precursor of aggressive behaviour and poor social functioning in middle childhood (e.g. Sanson et al., 1993; Eisenberg et al., 1997) and even into early adulthood (Moffitt et al., 1996; Newman et al., 1997). In middle childhood, *low intelligence and attainment* (Farrington, 1995) and *hyperactivity/attention problems* (e.g. Schachar, 1991; Hinshaw et al., 1997) have been found to predispose peer rejection, conduct problems and delinquency.

Attachment security
Early insecure attachment has been related to poorer peer relationships, lower social competence and more aggressive relationships in observed play situations (Bost et al., 1998; Fagot and Kavanagh, 1990). Lyons-Ruth (1996) found that disorganized attachment behaviours predict aggression in school-aged children (*see* Chapter 5).

Parenting Style
The following parenting styles have been found to lead to more aggressive behaviour in children (e.g. Farrington, 1995; Loeber and Hay, 1994; Olweus, 1994; McGuire et al., 1995) (*see* Chapter 16, *Families and their role in children's lives and development*):

- *Authoritarian parenting*, which is characterized by negative emotional attitude, lack of warmth and involvement (Hinshaw et al., 1997; Olweus, 1980).
- *Parenting is permissive and tolerant* without setting clear limits on aggressive behaviour towards siblings, peers and other adults (Olweus, 1994; Loeber and Hay, 1994).
- *Parents who have high levels of parental disagreement* regarding caretaking (e.g. Henry et al., 1993), use highly power-assertive methods such as *harsh physical punishment* and violent emotional outbursts (Cichetti and Bukowski, 1995) and generally provide an aggressive role model (Bandura, 1973).

Neighbourhood contexts
Socio-economic conditions such as poverty, single parent household, minority ethnic status and exposure to high stress levels (e.g. Farrington, 1995; Kupersmidt et al. 1995; Fergusson et al., 1990) have also been found to be related to aggressive behaviour. However, socio-economic conditions are most predictive in association with certain family and neighbourhood contexts (i.e. the opportunities to associate

> with other delinquent peers, Keenan et al., 1995). For example, moving out of a poor neighbourhood with a high prevalence of delinquent peers or living as a poor, single parent family in a predominantly middle class area have been found to be protective against aggressive behaviour and delinquency (Farrington, 1995; Kupersmidt et al., 1995).

aggressive victims at age 10 were significantly more likely than the other groups to have had experiences of harsh, disorganised and potentially abusive home environments five years earlier. Mother–child interactions at five years were characterized as hostile and restrictive or overly punishing. In contrast, the non-victimized aggressors had a history of greater exposure to adult aggression and conflict, but not victimization by adults. The passive victim group were little different than the normative sample.

Both the pattern of concurrent associations and the Schwartz et al. (1997) study on precursors suggests that those described as bully/victims grow up in dysfunctional families and resemble chronically aggressive children (Kupersmidt and Coie, 1990; Rigby, 1994). In contrast, the superior social cognitive skills found in non-victimized bullies suggest that these children use bullying for dominance. Apart from concurrent findings of more protective parenting (e.g. Bowers et al., 1992, 1994; Finnegan et al., 1997) and social withdrawal in peer situations, relatively little is known about the early development of (passive) victims.

DISCUSSION POINTS

- Do you remember any bullies at your school? Why do you think they became bullies?
- Do you remember any victims at your school? Why were they always picked on? What were they like?

Consequences of bullying and victimization

Media reports and retrospective research have emphasized the adverse effects of victimization, including the severe emotional consequences (low self-esteem, depression, suicide) and social adjustment difficulties (poor friendship patterns, limited success in relationships, poor educational achievement) lasting into adolescence and adult life (KIDSCAPE, 1998). Short term prospective studies (e.g. Rutter, 1987; Alsaker and Olweus, 1993; Slee and Rigby, 1993; Neary and Joseph, 1994; Callaghan and Joseph, 1995) have confirmed short term emotional consequences for victims, such as lowered self-esteem, higher levels of depression and negative self-appraisal of interpersonal competence and the increased risk of depression and social withdrawal in adulthood. However, Olweus (1993) also found that most children 'normalize' as they become older when they can choose whom to socialize with to a greater extent.

Bullies are more likely to engage in problem behaviours such as criminality, violence, alcohol abuse and dropping out of school in adolescence (Loeber and Dishion, 1983; Loeber and Strouthamer-Loeber, 1987; Magnusson, 1987; Parker and Asher, 1987; Farrington, 1993; Olweus, 1993). Tattum (1993) has proposed a 'Cycle of Violence Model' which involves the development from childhood bullying through to juvenile delinquency, adult criminality and later abusive behaviour in families. In a 22-year longitudinal study, Eron (1987) found that children who demonstrate bullying behaviour have a one in four chance of having a criminal record by the age of 30, compared to a one in 20 chance of children not involved in bullying. Olweus (1991) reported that approximately 60 per cent of boys identified as bullies in Grades 6–9 had at least one conviction at the age of 24 and 35 per cent to 40 per cent had three or more criminal convictions. Victims were less likely than control subjects or bullies to have a criminal record.

Social maladjustment is common in both bullies and victims. Gilmartin (1987) found that childhood victimization increased the risk of impaired adult relationships in young men. Eron (1987) found that bullies were much more likely to produce aggressive children and also to physically abuse their wives and children in adult life. Tattum (1993) and Farrington (1992) highlighted an increased risk in adult males who bullied at school to have offspring who themselves are bullying their peers.

Much less is known about the consequences of relational bullying. Crick (1996) indicated in a short-term follow-up study that relational bullying maybe an even stronger predictor of future social maladjustment than overt aggression. It has not yet been established whether relational forms of bullying have different effects to those of physical bullying, i.e. lead to more internalizing problems and failures in academic achievement. Williams et al. (1996) recently reported a three to four time increased risk for commonly reported health problems in primary school children who reported any bullying (e.g. headaches, tummy aches). A causal pathway cannot be presumed as it is not possible to conclude whether the victimization is a cause of the reported illness, or a consequence of being a 'sickly' child.

Intervention

In Bergen, Norway, Olweus (1991, 1992, 1993) first studied the effects of an intervention programme. The goals of the nationwide programme were to reduce bullying and to minimize the development of new problems.

Olweus' key concept is that the *whole school* (i.e. the entire population of the school – no particular identification or focus on bullies or victims) should be targeted. A set of rules, communication strategies, routines and action plans are developed which outline clear guidelines for dealing with current and future bullying. This is approached in various ways at the *school level* (better supervision, parent–staff meetings etc.), at the *class level* (class rules, role-playing, class discussion etc.) and then at the *individual level* (talks with victims and bullies, parental input, discussion groups for participants). A resource pack was given to every participating school to offer advice for parents and teachers and a video for children to assist with developing a whole school policy.

This intervention programme led to reported reductions of 50 per cent or more over a two-year period in both direct and indirect bullying in boys and girls of all ages (Olweus, 1991, 1992, 1993). It also led to a subsequent reduction in bullying problems and a general increase in reported levels of happiness at school. There did not appear to be any 'displacement' in terms of increases of other anti-social behaviour. In contrast, evaluation by Roland (1993) in Stavangor, Norway, three years into the programme, reported much less improvement, with some schools even showing more bullying.

Sharp and Smith (1991, 1995), and Smith and Sharp (1994) adopted the 'Whole School Policy' intervention programme for Great Britain. In addition, schools could also choose from extra optional techniques such as curriculum-based strategies and playground/environment interventions. This policy was assessed two years later and it was concluded that the programme had a positive effect in most schools (reductions in bullying, increases in helping behaviour, increased feeling of support from school), with most effects being seen in those who did most and in primary schools. However, the reduction in bullying behaviour in primary schools was only around 7 per cent and in victimization 17 per cent thus much less than in Olweus' original Norwegian programme. Although bullying behaviour changed much less than anticipated, most pupils and teachers perceived that the bullying situation had improved. Eslea and Smith (1998) were able to follow up in 1994 four of the 16 primary schools who started the intervention in 1990. The findings are generally disappointing. Two schools had a consistent decline in reported bullying (7–10 per cent), one experienced a consistent rise and the other an initial fall and subsequent rise. All four schools had reduced bullying among boys, but three experienced a rise in bullying among girls. No school had raised the proportion of victims who had told staff about being bullied. The authors concluded that special efforts are necessary to raise awareness and promote honesty among girls – too much has focused on the male stereotype of bullying.

Whole school intervention programmes have demonstrated that bullying problems can be tackled in the short term by schools, however, the effects are smaller and less enduring than initially thought. A whole-school approach may thus not be sufficient and may for some groups be even contra-effective, i.e. training bullies who have good social cognition in how to understand others' feelings may lead to even more effective bullying. Thus action pacts focusing on teachers, parents and role-playing have been developed (Elliott, 1991, Cowie and Sharp, 1994, 1996), but not widely evaluated yet. Furthermore, considering the family influence on the development of such behaviours, parents and families may need to be much more involved (Oliver et al., 1994). Knowledge of the roles taken in bullying may be utilized to reduce bullying. For example, the outsiders and defenders who have a high social standing in the class could be useful in preventing and helping others in bullying situations. Furthermore, preventative strategies focusing on pre-school children or children in the early primary school years could help reduce the number of children who enter school with a predisposition for aggressive behaviour or the vulnerability to be bullied.

Chapter summary

Persistent bullying has adverse consequences for both victims and bullies. Many victims, once free to choose their own peers, may recover from their early experiences of humiliation. Little is still known about the precursors of bullying, however, individual differences in temperament, social cognition, family relationships and school environment are all contributing to the development of bullying problems in children.

Children have a right to go to school without being subjected to bullying. By using the knowledge generated from research to design intervention programmes, schools are likely to become less threatening places for the most vulnerable and help to change the socially maladaptive career of some of those engaging in bullying.

Seminar questions

1. All children have conflicts. How is bullying different?
2. How do bullies differ from those children who both bully and get victimized (bully/victim)?
3. Why is bullying of concern to parents, children and teachers?
4. Adults have reported about their experiences of bullying in childhood (KIDSCAPE, 1998). Many feel that their life could have turned out differently but for these experiences. How much can we rely on these retrospective reports? How do we know that these individuals were not already different as children? How would this best be studied?
5. What could you do to prevent bullying or to intervene when someone is being bullied?

Further reading

Olweus, D. 1993. *Bullying at school: What we know and what we can do.* Oxford: Blackwell. Easy to read. A general overview of the Scandinavian experience.

Smith, P.K., Sharp, S. 1994. *School bullying: insights and perspectives*. London: Routledge. A general overview of the research in Europe and the main intervention approaches.

Newcomb, A.F., Bukowski, W.M., Pattee, L. 1993. Children's peer relations: a meta-analytic review of popular, rejected, neglected, controversial and average sociometric status. *Psychological Bulletin* **113**, 99–128. Describes the method for determining sociometric status, a key approach to peer research.

Moffitt, T.E., Caspi, A., Dickson, N., Silva, P., and Stanton, W. 1996. Child-onset versus adolescent-onset antisocial conduct problems in males: natural history from ages 3 to 18 years. *Development and Psychopathology* **8**, 399–424. A good paper distinguishing different pathways to conduct problems. Indicates the importance of early individual differences in temperament.

The uses and significance of electronic media during development

18

CHARLES K CROOK

Editors' preface

Ethical considerations often prevent experiments being conducted with children because one cannot randomly give some children an experience and deny the experience to others (*see* the *Introduction*). In addition, there are arguments that experimental research designed to evaluate the effect of one variable on another often can fail to do justice to the complexity of the phenomena. Such arguments link to wider concerns about the way we conceptualize science and the determinants of human behaviour (*see also* Chapter 21), as well as the way we conceptualize the operation of influences on humans (for example, the way we think about matters such as 'free will').

Dr Charles Crook provides a careful argument about why we should take these matters seriously when we consider child development and the electronic media. He criticizes experiments into the 'effects' of the media on children as only providing a limited understanding of the phenomena. Instead he suggests we need to re-conceptualize the processes that are occurring and the questions that we can ask. His solution is to use the perspective supplied by 'cultural psychology' to move away from a simple mechanistic view of the world. This involves locating events and experiences in the wider context of human culture (*see also* Chapter 21). As a result electronic media should not be seen as a cause of certain behaviours, but as a new tool which inevitably changes the organization, format and even the setting of children's behaviour. Furthermore, cultural psychology suggests that we should move away from attempts to understand causality by asking how the electronic media affect children. Instead we should see electronic media as the creation of our culture which is both a response to human needs and an influence on our behaviour. This provides a more difficult, but more sophisticated view of the processes involved in child development and has important implications for other areas of developmental research.

Introduction

It is frequently said that children grow up in a world dominated by technologies for communication. Indeed, the slang used to characterize children born in the last 50 years persistently refers to electronic media. So my own peer group has been variously identified as the 'TV', the 'plugged-in' and the 'wired' generation. How should the prominence of these technologies be incorporated into theories and studies of psychological development?

Developmental psychology has paid little serious attention to this question. In most text books of human development, media and technology are treated as marginal issues: they provoke little serious analysis. This neglect cannot be due to a simple scarcity of empirical research. There is a substantial volume of such research, albeit scattered across various disciplines. Perhaps it is this multi-disciplinarity that deters developmental psychologists from making a distinctive contribution. Certainly, there is a failure to use frameworks that would allow empirical studies of media and technology to be assimilated into the mainstream of developmental psychology. So, with an unfortunate circularity, empirical research is too rarely guided or inspired by serious developmental theorizing – and developmental theorizing is too rarely motivated by attention to media research studies.

Here, the focus is on electronic media (particularly television and computers). The motive is not to make inflated claims about how much these technologies matter in psychological development. As it happens, they are important, but readers will reach their own views about just how important. A more significant motive here is to use the case of electronic media as a vehicle: as an excuse for emphasizing a more general (a 'mediational') perspective on development. This is the approach of 'cultural psychology'. It is an approach that is greatly inspired by the re-discovered writing of the Soviet psychologist Vygotsky (1978). Thus, in what follows a traditional literature review is not attempted. Instead, the aim is to introduce a helpful theoretical framework: one that can guide an empirical approach to the issue of children and technology. Although what follows will not be a comprehensive review, plenty of research examples are mentioned and these may furnish a starting point for readers wishing to explore further.

Before introducing cultural psychology and before arguing for its value in addressing the topic of this chapter, we identify certain approaches that have *not* been so helpful. So, in the following section we caution against those analyses of electronic media that refer to 'effects' on children. The argument will help to clarify why a novel theoretical orientation is called for (i.e., a cultural psychological orientation). Accordingly, the second section sets out such an alternative. Then, in the remainder of the chapter, we mobilize this cultural perspective and illustrate the research questions it provokes.

MEDIA EFFECTS: A NARROW CONCEPTION

Popular concern and much academic research has been preoccupied with the 'effects' on children of exposure to certain literature, film or television.

BOX 18.1 A history of disquiet

Up until the early years of the twentieth century, print was the only medium whereby a large audience might easily be addressed. Postman (1982) argued that the printed word played a significant role in keeping separate the worlds of children and adults. On this view, print has been one mass media that has greatly influenced psychological development. It is argued that when public communication was governed by writing, so the experience of childhood was prolonged. The time it takes to become literate effectively insulates young people from the private and complex world of their elders – as it might be revealed in the written word. Of course, the expansion of electronic broadcasting during the twentieth century has ensured that growing up in the current era involves earlier contact with a much richer array of communication media. Such media are more accessible; but they are also more vivid and more explicit in their portrayal of the adult world. For commentators such as Postman (1982) and Meyrowitz (1985) these trends have dramatically influenced psychological development by eroding the separate world of childhood. Whether we are persuaded by this particular theorizing, it certainly exemplifies a very widespread class of beliefs: namely, that children's exposure to modern mass media has had powerful *effects* – and, for many commentators, not very wholesome effects.

Some of the earliest public disquiet over such matters was documented 100 years ago, when the negative influence of popular dime novels was vigorously debated (Barker, 1989). Spigel (1992) traces almost a century of growing public disappointment at how readily children's curiosity is seduced by media content of low quality – and how willingly media authors have pandered to the various lurid interests of young people. Understandably, social scientists were encouraged to comment on this situation. For example, the emergence of modern cinema precipitated the Payne Fund research studies: the first of a number of large-scale commissioned investigations into the role of mass media in children's lives. Later, the development of television released a further wave of public concern and, thus, another set of research reviews – notably, the US Surgeon General's Report (1972) on the impact of television.

Yet, research has never led to generalizations that were very confident or prescriptive. It proved hard to trace the causal links between exposure to media content and particular psychological characteristics of 'viewers'. Certainly, there emerged from this work co-relations that were worrying or provocative, but this was not enough to demonstrate the *causal* relations suspected by commentators. In the 1960s this uncertain state of affairs implied to some that what was needed was the application of experimental methods to the problem. This is a view that still enjoys good currency. One distinguished psychologist reflecting recently on the psychological impact of media violence remarks: 'The problem with most socially important questions is that they are virtually impossible to solve by good experiments' (Morgan, 1994, p. 9). Morgan encourages us to leave them alone until this is possible. Yet, experiments have certainly been conducted on this topic. Moreover, many of them seem to have been 'good' experiments. At least, their design has been rigorous and they have been executed with care and professionalism. But, of course, this is not all we demand of good empirical research. The problems with research have not been about the niceties of methodology, but the logic of extrapolation. The reactions of children viewing media within certain laboratory arrangements have been well enough explained. Yet generalizing beyond these narrow scenarios can be precarious.

The seminal work of Bandura and colleagues in this area deserves mention (e.g. Bandura et al., 1965). A central strategy of their research was to analyse the free play content of children who had just watched a sequence of television drama. Relations were sought between the form of the children's activity and the themes portrayed in the drama. Their widely known claim concerns an association between violent media themes and violence expressed in play. This work attracted much attention. In part because it deployed the experimental method to reveal strong causal relationships and in part because Bandura's theoretical focus on *imitation* challenged the associative theories of learning that were so influential at that time (imitation was hard to assimilate into a conceptual framework that prioritized reward and punishment). Finally, perhaps these claims simply resonated with everyday experiences and observations. We know powerful dramatic depictions can leave us in empathic psychological states. Furthermore, we may have seen our own children modelling action sequences they have witnessed as media representations.

Possibly for these reasons, the research procedure just described proved seductive to those interested in the psychological significance of mass media. Yet the methodology is problematic. A central difficulty is that an experiment is itself a distinctive situation: it is merely another way of organizing events in the world. It invites participants to construct idiosyncratic interpretations of what is happening to them. In short, an experiment does not necessarily 'sample' some core psychological process in a transparent way. For example, participants might understand an experimental script and its props to imply that the reproduction of witnessed media aggression is actually condoned or required by the experimenters. Such complications need not render experiments in this area useless, but they are a problem.

One way forward might be to observe young people's reactions to media content in situations where they are unaware that an experiment has been orchestrated around them. Studies that recruit such innocent participants have been summarized. Wood et al. (1991) catalogue findings that show how a period of viewing violent media programming can be followed by detectable changes in unconstrained (but discretely observed) behaviour. Alternatively, 'natural experiments' may be possible in which a telling but unplanned comparison is made possible. A good example is the case of adjacent communities, one of which has been deprived of television broadcasts (for geographical reasons). What happens when the deprived group has normal access? Research reveals distinct social consequences for children (Murray and Kippax, 1978; Williams and Handford, 1986). A striking finding is that those children spend less time in organized activities in the local (extra-familial) community. Thus, experimental paradigms may still have a part to play in a research strategy directed at media and development – but only if we are vigilant about how the scenarios researchers create are understood by the participants.

The apparently successful application of experimental method may have encouraged adoption of a more bullish discourse about 'media effects'. Arguably this confidence is misplaced. Many have cautioned against making hasty causal links between media content and social behaviour, or denied the possibility of doing so at all (e.g. Buckingham, 1994; Cumberbatch and Howitt, 1989). Even where experiments are well designed *and* unobtrusive, they may remain problematic. For one thing, the paradigm is over-concerned with operationalizing and quantifying. This means that complex psychological circumstances tend to be portrayed as circumscribed, visible events and only simple, recordable behaviours are considered. This may trivialize rich psychological phenomena. It may also distort research: encouraging an exclusive concern with topics capable of analysis in this reductionist manner. Thus, the effect of media on children's *aggression* has become a research preoccupation because both the media manifestation and the putative effects are readily operationalized as (countable) violent acts. Yet counting violent acts is hardly a sophisticated analysis of 'aggression' – its representations or its enactments. Moreover, a further consequence may be the neglect of other important psychological themes; for example, the educational significance of TV programming such as 'Play School', or the prosocial effects of TV programming such as 'The Waltons' (Baran et al., 1979).

The pressure on experimentalists to operationalise 'stimuli' and 'responses' creates a further problem: it frames engagement with media as a passive process. It may be harsh to claim that most researchers regard children as 'mere blank slates on which television scrawls its harmful and indelible messages' (Buckingham, 1994, p. 81). Yet it does seem fair to claim that the operationalizing approach tends to distract researchers from taking seriously the interpretative disposition of the viewer.

Finally, the most problematic consequence of reducing media to sets of 'variables' having discrete 'effects' is that it encourages us to think of the relationships documented as being neatly self-contained. Suppose that research does lead to a claim about developmental relevance for certain media content – how do we explain the initial potency or appeal to children of this particular content? Why is it broadcast? If we wish to appreciate the significance of some particular media representation, our progress will be very limited if we merely propose a mechanical impact on those exposed to it. Progress arises from recognizing that such encounters occupy space within a larger web of causality. What happens to be depicted in mass media is inspired by the full cultural context characterizing the way we live at the time. What then happens to children, as users of media, depends on all the various ways they interpret those depictions.

The risk of being so sceptical about method and theory is that we simply dismiss large bodies of research because we are disappointed in the standard interpretations. When scepticism becomes radical, we run a more serious risk: namely, supposing that media exposure is simply irrelevant to psychological development. At present, progress requires a more sophisticated theoretical framework. Such a framework should allow us to unpack tidy questions about 'effects'. Then it should inspire and direct the design of more versatile research strategies.

Arguably media researchers now have moved towards more fertile theoretical approaches. This is apparent in various recent positions that conceptualize media as a resource that is 'used'. An early expression of the contrast that this entails is Katz's (1959) invitation to transform the question 'What do the media do to people?' into the question 'What do people do with the media?'. In practice, the shift seems to have cultivated a more cognitive style of theorizing. The early effects literature was guided by behaviourist conceptions – imitation and reinforcement. More recently, theoriests have invoked intervening cognitive states. An emphasis on 'use' liberates the theorist to address individual differences that are brought to media encounters: variations in understanding that reflect different personal histories of interpreting the world. Thus the significance of media experiences may now be framed in terms of semantic networks (Berkowitz, 1984) or script theory (Huesmann, 1986). A good illustration of cognitive theorizing is the idea that media users evolve distinct cognitive dispositions such as the 'Mean World Syndrome' (Gerbner and Gross, 1976). So it is claimed that the particular experience of media violence leads to beliefs about the world being a 'mean' place: beliefs arising from distorting media representations that suggest the world is driven by violence and mayhem.

What is effected is cognitive, a belief. This may or may not be manifest in violent behaviour – depending on other aspects of the individual and their context.

Yet in these conceptual shifts there is still a lingering sense of 'effects': distinct psychological impacts rather tightly associated with media experiences. To be sure, these effects are understood as mediated by a richer set of (cognitive) concepts but the perspective still implies a rather mechanical causal pattern. It also provokes a narrow and familiar research strategy – in which measures of media contact are correlated with psychological measures of the 'viewer' at some later time. In my view, these theoretical developments represent a degree of progress. Thus, they do encourage thinking of media users as 'active' – each making their own *sense* of media experiences. On the other hand, the focus of theorizing is very much on *individuals* and their private cognitions. 'Media use' is thus a rather solitary affair. It may miss much that is psychologically interesting about the process of engaging with media. My reasons for now introducing a cultural perspective is that I believe it can take us beyond these limitations.

DISCUSSION POINT

List the problems of investigating the direct effects of media on children.

A MEDIATIONAL PERSPECTIVE: CULTURAL PSYCHOLOGY

On the current landscape of psychology there is a group of theoretical perspectives which, although not overlapping, enjoy a certain family resemblance. These are (with notable advocates identified in parenthesis) 'situated cognition' (Suchman, 1993), 'discursive psychology' (Edwards and Potter, 1992), 'socio-cultural psychology' (Wertsch, 1991) and 'cultural psychology' (Shweder and Sullivan, 1993). Put simply, these theoretical traditions share a concern with 'context'. They characterize human action in relation to the settings in which it is located. By contrast, they are suspicious of analyses that conjure up (de-contextualized) psychological processes which are then framed as properties of individuals, free of contextual embedding. So the cultural approach tends not to isolate psychological states or characteristics – the traditional dependent variables of laboratory-style research. It is argued that traditional analyses in psychology reduce human actions to a set of 'variables': a set from which researchers may systematically select, control and parametrically manipulate – in order to explore various 'effects'.

An important part of this alternative position is the concept of 'culture'. It is useful to recall the biological sense of this key concept. For biologists, a 'culture' is the medium in which some life or other is supported. Within biology it makes little sense to characterize an organism without reference to the culture which sustains it. Similarly, any statement about a (psychological) organism must refer to a supporting culture. Human individuals derive their nature from such embedding. In the psychological domain, a culture will embrace the various accumulated artefacts (e.g. weapons), technologies (e.g. printing), symbol systems (e.g. algebra), rituals (e.g. weddings) and designs-for-living (e.g. university campuses) that have evolved within the social group of an individual. The design of the spaces, tools and technologies around us embody a history of human activity: they invite us, now, to exploit their design for distinctive new forms of action. This roughly captures the agenda for cultural psychology – a modern movement that owes much to the influence of Vygotsky's writing on psychological development.

At this point, another important concept is needed: namely, that human actions are typically 'mediated'. Between us and the material or social world are various cultural resources. Everywhere, the intelligent activity of human beings is mediated – through various artefacts (such as electronic media), symbols systems (such as mathematics), rituals (such as story telling), spaces (such as theatres) and so forth. So any psychological analysis should frame the individual as 'a person acting with mediational means'. The challenge from cultural theorizing is to understand how the inclusion of some new such means (e.g. computers) into an activity system makes a difference: how it serves to re-mediate that system. In studying individual lifetimes, this amounts to a concern for the circumstances in which children are exposed to these resources and how they are thereby incorporated into a child's activities. Unsurprisingly, cultural psychologists are especially interested in development; and also in education – the deliberately managed use of a cultural's mediational resources. It is helpful to see electronic media as 'mediating' in the sense developed above.

We have sketched an approach to theorizing: one that is useful for thinking about children and media. We must now make a link between theory and actual research questions. A simple structuring device for the necessary discussion may help. Three principled concerns that recur within cultural psychology are suggested. In what follows, each will then serve as an anchor for noting possible research strategies – as well as for outlining some of the claims that have already been made from this research. Together, these concerns reveal the general strategy of putting cultural artefacts at the centre. However, once such a commitment is made, each of these three concerns illustrates a different research focus: individual actions, interpersonal exchanges and the ecological setting.

First: individual actions. Cultural psychology regards individual human competence as rooted in cultural artefacts. Whereas other animals act directly (immediately) on their world, our actions are invariably mediated. Our successes depend upon cultural tools (technologies and symbol systems) that lie between us and the material world. Becoming competent thereby translates into the appropriation and effective deployment of such resources. Where the actions and achievements of individuals are taken as research focus, then this insight about tools suggests we should consider how those actions are re-mediated by access to new cultural technologies. Electronic media are prime candidates in this process. Below are sketched examples from educational contexts in which our individual exploratory activities are potentially re-configured by new media.

Second: interpersonal experience. The cultural perspective highlights social interaction as central to human experience and development. This follows from the significance attached to language as the prime cultural tool for acting on the world. Personal meanings are negotiated, created and enriched within inter-personal exchanges. It follows that we should view new technologies as potentially prominent in this: potentially mediating new forms of social interaction and, thereby, new undestandings.

Third: the ecological setting. Individual and social action occurs within environments. Culture has evolved spaces that are specialized to suppport our various styles of living. In this sense there is an ecological dimension to human experience. Thus, we should ask how new technologies create new designs for living – new constraints and opportunities for acting on the world or co-ordinating with other people.

Related to the third theme, we might acknowledge that all of this is framed at an institutional or societal level. Living in a culture involves engaging with practices and rituals that have evolved to orchestrate social life. Most obviously, there are legal, commercial and educational structures that we experience as institutional forces influencing our experiences and our psychological development. This is an important further dimension to a proper cultural analysis of media in development – but not one that we have space to pursue here.

The three-part list defines recurring concerns of cultural psychology. The second of them (social interaction) is most widely associated with this theoretical approach – most notably through the influence of Vygotsky's conception of the zone of proximal development. However, while inter-change with others is a central aspect of our relation to culture, it clearly is not all there is to study. Thus, tools, spaces and rituals are also important and foregrounding their role in human development is as significant to a cultural analysis as any stress on interpersonal processes (Vygotsky, 1930/1994). It might also be noted that this approach refers to the external more than the internal (such as is implied by a more traditional cognitive analysis). Certainly, cultural psychology does dwell on how psychological functioning is distributed across artefacts, set within environments and governed by societal practices. Yet this is not 'externalizing' in the sense championed by behaviourism and illustrated by the early media effects lit-erature mentioned above. It is not a framework of reacting to stimuli, but one of understanding how human action is *co-ordinated* with a cultural environment. We now turn to illustrating how the three-way structure of this theoretical frame can guide questions and research about children using electronic media.

DISCUSSION POINT

How would you characterize the concerns of cultural psychology?

Cultural tools: re-mediating exploratory activity systems.

Let us begin with a simple (if macabre) example discussed by Cole and Griffen (1980). Suppose a traditional society has established tools and rituals for hunting. We may introduce them to the gun. Our new tool extends their capacity as hunters. More beasts are killed. Although we might want to say that their killing capacity is 'amplified', Cole and Griffen caution against any account that implies they are now 'generally' empowered – changed even when the tool is not 'to hand'. The point is that some new technology (a weapon) has re-mediated the practice of hunting. This will be witnessed in various details about, perhaps, stalking and capturing as well as details to do with the social organization of the hunt. In sum, we have an activity system (hunting) and various tools that exist within it – or that may be introduced to reconfigure it. The suggestion here is that the psychological relevance of electronic media to children may, in part, be approached as varieties of such re-mediation.

For children growing up, what are the activity systems parallel to hunting and what is the role of media? The most potent examples will arise from experience at school. For it is here that society formally organizes participation in activities that aim to introduce culturally valued skills. Thus it is important to notice the way in which electronic media (particularly computers and broadcasting) are functioning in these contexts. We comment on this in the context of two educational activity systems: private study and simulations (*see* Box 18.2).

BOX 18.2 Remediation for two kinds of learning

Private study

Private, reflective study may express society's canonical image of the learner: a young person engrossed by some text or engaged with some apparatus. How do technological artefacts re-configure such autonomous study? How is the *activity* of independent learning carried out in new ways? We should notice how this new technology affords quite novel forms of interaction – in comparison with books. So the '*electronic* book' demands that reading – as a learning activity – is conducted differently. This is partly determined by the screen-based nature of the delivery. As Gaver (1996) has illustrated, screens and printed pages afford very different approaches to the searching, annotation and archiving of recorded information. Such new demand on 'readers' also arises from innovation in methods for organizing the *structure* of stored information on computers: specifically, as hypertext or hypermedia. Plowman (1996) reviews how new learning media undermine the traditional sequential narrative organization of texts. Through classroom field studies, she illustrates how the less linear structure of study materials demands novel forms of study practice from pupils. Taylor and Laurillard (1995) provide a complementary perspective: they stress more how electronic media extend the learning resource base itself. Networked hypermedia in particular dramatically extends the pupil's 'library' of source material. Children growing up in classrooms with these rich opportunities must adopt a circumspect and reflective approach to discovery learning.

Regrettably, we know little about the influence of these technological innovations. We know little of how computer-based private study gets managed by pupils or of how teachers (and parents) co-ordinate and support such study. Early research in this area conforms to the traditional psychological model of evaluation: manipulating access to learning resources and, then, assessing pupil outcomes in formal academic tests. So, for example, Large et al. (1994) exploit the fact that some encyclopaedias are available both in traditional book form and as CD-ROMs. When groups of children study these different resources, the researchers find no dramatic influence of presentational medium on test results. This is useful (sobering perhaps) but the design of such studies does side-step questions of how such electronic media are used: how is the activity of pupil research, synthesis, investigation re-mediated. Partly this will demand looking more at the learning as it happens – with the media to hand. Partly it will demand recognizing that these experiences are not de-coupled from the larger classroom agenda: teachers will more or less effectively weave them into other tutorial conversations in the learning environment. Perhaps it is this contextualizing work that determines much of a new media's cognitive impact.

Simulations

As well as involving texts, private study may also be more participatory: it may involve experiment with materials or models. In the early period of computer-based learning it was anticipated that technology would transform classrooms into more exploratory and discovery-oriented places. The computer was promoted by many as a machine-to-think-with; a device that might itself become a 'pupil' (rather than a tutor), as children used classroom knowledge to 'teach' it to do things (Papert, 1980). Now there is some consensus that this vision has not been realized; that the cognitive impact of manipulating so-called computer simulations or 'microworlds' is limited (Pea and Kurland, 1987). Although the 'exploratory tool' remains an intriguing role for technology in children's learning, the notion is problematic in other ways. This relates to the whole principle of *simulation* as a resource for learning. Computers offer very seductive opportunities in this respect.

Designers can create working models of systems that children need to understand. Pupils then can notice what happens as they manipulate the parameters of these models – thereby using the principled bodies of knowledge we urge them to acquire. The advantages of such experiences have been well rehearsed for undergraduates learning with computers (e.g. Turkle, 1994). Yet, in practice, the strategy is controversial: the teachers of such students worry that simulations cultivate understandings of systems that are dangerously divorced from reality (Turkle, 1996): understanding gets rigidly linked to simplistic assumptions derived from the software authors' creation of the system. This may be particularly unfortunate when the systems explored are social (economies or businesses say). Simulation may encourage too mechanical and rigid a model of how such systems function. We know little of the distorting or empowering effect for younger children of allowing computers to re-mediate activity systems of private exploration and experiment.

The culture of social interaction: using media to create intersubjectivities

The issue to be considered here is how electronic media co-ordinate or resource social communication in ways that are developmentally interesting. Although children may create meanings through their solitary but mediated explorations with devices such as computers (as illustrated in the previous section), much of their meaning-making originates in social discourse. So, under the present heading we may consider situations where technology takes the role of a conversant and situations in which it serves to transform existing patterns of person-to-person communication. In either case we are investigating intersubjectivies: states of mutual awareness upon which the enterprise of building understanding can proceed. First, can this be achieved in communication with machines (*see* Box 18.3)? And, second, in traditional interaction with real people, can machines mediate our efforts?

BOX 18.3 Can teaching technology communicate?

Education again provides a good reference point for communication with machines. A basic format for educational practice is exposition: people telling you things. Electronic media might take over this expository role for pupils: but through what sort of activity system and with what impact? The most significant technologies for exposition are educational film, video and broadcasting. Of course these are the very media which, outside of school, generate so much anxiety over influence – but influence that is more harmful than instructional. This makes their fate within educational practice all the more interesting. In effect, what we discover is a mismatch between popular theories of educational television and popular theories of entertainment television. Teachers are not so committed to the positive effects of the former as parents and others are concerned for the negative effects of the latter. If teachers *were* so persuaded, then broadcast media would surely play a more central part in classroom life than is actually the case. Yet such media do play *some* part in modern classroom life. In short, the status of educational TV, video and film is precarious. They have not evolved to be a powerful force for learning, but they remain a persistent ingredient of modern curricula.

In the debates that surround educational technology there is often invoked a certain metaphor. These educational resources, it is claimed, are not 'magic bullets'. They can not behave as certain medicines do: ingeniously seeking out and acting upon under-nourished tissue. Perhaps irrationally, commentators are more comfortable with this caution for educational programming than for recreational programming. It is not expected that exposing a child to hours of, say, 'Sesame Street' sketches on words and letters is going to accelerate dramatically that child's reading. If it does seem to make a difference we start to notice all the ways in which that influence may be very indirect. Thus, such programming can be argued to make a difference through recurrently reinforcing positive images of schooling – thereby effecting a stronger engagement with reading instruction *in class*. Or it may make a difference because of the ways in which the images portrayed are drawn by teachers into some broader discourse of classroom instruction – used as reference points in teaching talk going on at times *after* the TV has been seen (and shared).

In the case of learning from educational broadcasting, it may be of only limited value to study just the moment of viewing – as if this were all the activity system entailed. To be sure, there will be aspects of this that are psychologically interesting (the taking of notes, strategic patterns of attending and so forth). However, suppose the media experience is promptly followed by a directed class discussion? A researcher should surely include such elaborations in any effort to characterize how the media is entering into a pupil's learning. Unfortunately, the elaborating discourse may occur much later on and, thereby, be more difficult for the researcher to track when describing a process of influence. This example reminds us that teachers are always and everywhere drawing earlier fragments of learning experience into their current discussion. Edwards and Mercer (1987) document a persistent effort at constructing and agreeing such 'common knowledge' within a classroom of learners. Such elaboration will be very relevant to understanding the 'effects' of experiences that arise from electronic media.

The discussion in Box 18.3 concerns the limits in how far technology will play a social role in being a communicative *partner*. Yet there is a second, more familiar, interpersonal theme to which technology relates. This concerns the role of electronic media in catalyzing or mediating more traditional communication – conversation among people. We should ask how media is mobilized as a point of joint reference within the broader flow of social exchange among young people.

We surely recognize that children may recruit media characters and media narratives into their *solitary* play (hence the successful marketing of Disney or Star Wars paraphernalia). Indeed, it has been argued that incorporations of these toy tie-in characters into playful pretence is unwelcome: they serve only to constrain the creative element of socio-dramatic play (Kline, 1993). Although, children's explorations of media themes may often be private in this sense, it may also take place with friends or siblings (Singer and Singer, 1981; Davie et al., 1984). It is the occasions with a social dimension that we are more concerned with here, the collaborative interpretation of the world with peers and others. This is termed 'intersubjective' work in order to link with contemporary interest in the human ability to project psychological states into other people. Doing so enables us to co-ordinate our own mental state with that of others – to achieve a degree of intersubjectivity (*see* chapters 4 and 12). Social life acquires coherence from this ability but this ability is grounded on opportunities to reference common experiences. Thus events and objects that have been shared by people become anchors for efforts to establish and elaborate intersubjectivity among this group of people (e.g. as in discussing a sporting event).

Perhaps media events play a significant role as 'anchors' of this kind. Common sense suggests that we do indeed make frequent reference to such events in our everyday social talk. However, there is rather little research on such habits as developmental phenomena. To what extent and in what manner do media portrayals and activities enter into children's discursive elaborations of their experience? Buckingham (1993) has carried out interviews with young people in which they are invited to talk freely about their media interests. The records of these encounters indicate, unsurprisingly, an emphasis on television. They demonstrate how media programming gives reference points for the exploration of a number of personal identity issues. They also show how shared media experience is used to provide a context for positionings and counter-positionings on issues of class, gender and race.

These reflections by young people do support the general idea that media experiences make a difference through their role in stimulating intersubjective work in conversation. On the other hand, the primary data are 'reflections'. Theoretical conclusions from them involve inferences about what will be going on at times when these young people are not being interviewed – when they are actually doing the intersubjective work. What would be useful is ethnographic records of this process. There is some research in this tradition. For example, Walkerdine (1993) documents how characterizations from a video drama serve as a resource for members of one stressed family: allowing them to make a sense of their own predicaments.

The example records and illustrates the use of shared media experience as a framework for everyday sense-making. Moreover, it identifies children in this family as actively participating in this enterprise.

The culture of spaces: media and designs for living

Here, we consider how engagement with technology (say televisions or computers) has implications for how we spend time and how we use space. The issues certainly concern recreational and home life but, as above, we lead with a consideration of schooling. So: what does it mean to claim that a technology re-configures the designs within which we live (and learn)?

In the context of school, there has been a persistent fear that encouraging pupils to learn with computers would create a-social classrooms: dislocated children absorbed in solitary activity. Populating classrooms ('*learning* spaces') in that sort of way would be one controversial form of re-configuration arising from media use. However, what has actually happened does not match this prediction. A significant fact about the introduction of computers into schools is that the ratio of machines to pupils is not very favourable – although the political pressure to get children using this technology has been great. The solution discovered entailed organizing children to work *together* at this resource and, serendipitously perhaps, teachers noticed a potential in computers for mediating collaborative learning (Crook, 1994).

However, joint work can be realized in ways other than through the intimate, small group with its focus on a single problem. Again, electronic media may be implicated in designing learning spaces that afford alternative versions of collaborating. I have in mind those informal or unplanned exchanges that arise from learners being engaged in close but merely parallel activities. Such casual collaborative opportunities are well documented in workplaces (particularly open-plan arrangements) – and computer-based work has been identified as an environmental design feature that facilitates such patterns of work (Bannon, 1986). The creation of networked computer spaces in schools can be expected to have similar impacts. Early observation of such innovation suggests that this configuration for working does vitalize a interesting form of pupil exchange (Kafai and Harel, 1991).

DISCUSSION POINT

Do you think schools and classrooms will become less necessary as information technology advances?

Enthusiasm for connecting pupils to wide area computer networking may prove a yet more dramatic example of how media is shaping new experiences of learning (e.g. by using the World Wide Web). In this case, it is too early to anticipate particular outcomes. However, on certain visions of this future, schooling could become a very different class of experience: perhaps the change will be towards learning that is less orchestrated by adults and teaching that is less didactic. On the other hand, such media-induced de-schooling (Illich 1973) could undermine something precious, such as the community feeling from participation in learning that is typical of the traditional classroom (Crook, 1999). The point here is more to recognize the sense in which how we use media re-designs the environments we learn and work in – and how such media intrusions have developmental significance. This dynamic should be an important focus for psychological research.

Such influences have a domestic version: where they may be more quickly recognized. The leisure uses of electronic media impact on both the temporal and the spatial dimensions of children's experience. Activities associated with new media re-distribute the use of time and re-define the use of space. This, in turn, has created changes in children's social interactions, particularly in relation to family members. Television, in particular, has evolved into what some have analysed as 'a thief of time' (Condry, 1993) – estimated for US children as the third most common activity (after sleeping and school). From those rare studies of communities where television has arrived late, we learn that one of TV's highly significant impacts is to displace participation in other community activities – particularly sport (Williams and Handford, 1986).

DISCUSSION POINT

List the ways that television viewing can distinctively shape the pattern of family interaction.

Of course this shift towards 'staying indoors' should not simply be seen as undermining social life: it merely creates a new version of it. Spigel (1992) has traced the history of television's impact on family interactions suggesting that in the early years it was seen as a resource for cementing family bonds. Indeed, 15 years ago, television was the most commonly shared feature of family life (Timme et al., 1985). The video recorder and the cheap television set are new forms of technology that make this observation less likely to be true today. Children may have sets in their bedrooms: family members may manage their viewing so as not to create simultaneous demands. These are good illustrations of how media use re-designs contexts for social life in the sense considered here. To reinforce further the psychological theme of this section, we invoke some concrete examples: they serve to illustrate how media use configures distinct patterns of social interaction.

First, we can consider how media use bears on the absolute amount of social interaction in children's lives. The bedroom television is a configuration of resources that invites gravitation towards private space. The currently popular hand-held video games have similar significance (Provenzo,

1991). Although these games can support multi-user play, typically they are a solitary pursuit. Their 'stay indoors' quality is more isolating than television. It is risky to propose the psychological significance of any one game format when the underlying technology changes so rapidly. What little evidence there is suggests that young users of video games are not prone to difficulties in social interaction or social understanding (Sakamoto, 1994). However, this generalization may not hold up if the present pattern of electronic game use is sustained or extended. On the other hand, the present pattern may shift towards more multi-user, interactive games such as could accompany widespread Internet access. In which case the impact on children's social development of interacting in virtual environments could be still more dramatic (Turkle, 1996).

In addition to influencing the amount of social interaction, patterns of using electronic media are also relevant to the quality of such interactions. Here, just two examples will serve to illustrate the possibilities. First, from Buckingham's (1993) interviews with school children, it is clear that television can be a significant focus for family tension and disputes – particularly in relation to the policing by parents of viewing policy, but also the arguments between siblings over what should be watched. Given claims about the psychological significance of sibling dynamics (Dunn, 1988), media may be one important focal point within which tensions are expressed and negotiations are pursued. A second example relating media to the quality of interactions is the case of 'co-viewing'. The developmental significance of adults and young children reading books together is well documented (e.g. Ninio and Bruner 1978). Although most children's television viewing is not accompanied by adults (St. Peters et al., 1991), researchers have demonstrated how rich co-viewing of adults and children *can* be in terms of conversational possibilities (Lemish and Rice, 1986).

Chapter summary

We have reinforced a caution that runs through the psychological literature on media and development. That caution concerns how we implicate media experiences in accounts of children's behaviour or explanations of their developmental trajectories. It is argued that we should be wary of invoking 'effects' of media on children: wary of claiming a cause for this or that behaviour (usually problematic behaviour). These are important cautions. However, the resistance to talk of 'media effects' might lead to a misconception that children's media exposure was of *no* significance: that it was simply not relevant to their development. This, in turn, might lead researchers to neglect the field of inquiry. Electronic media must be a central interest for students of psychological development: the fact that it is not reminds us of the need to establish strong theoretical frameworks in which a suitable research agenda can evolve. We have proposed cultural psychology as one such framework. The cultural psychology of development orients towards artefacts as central to understanding our relationships with the world. This *cultural* context of development embraces tools, symbol systems, technologies, institutional spaces and various genres of communication. Psychological development entails appropriating these resources and adapting to these settings as we encounter them through socialization. In this way each of us becomes equipped with mediational means and with scripted knowledge for acting creatively on the material and social world.

A culturally influenced analysis need not be in tension with other theoretical frameworks addressing these problems. Thus, our tendency to learn by imitation is well enough accepted in a cultural analysis (e.g. Tomasello et al., 1993) – it is simply regarded as a low level form of learning that is of limited significance outside of its elaborations within richer social contexts. Similarly, cultural psychology acknowledges that meanings can be constructed within private reflections – some of which may be resourced by media encounters. Thus, Cole is able to embrace the rather cognitive notion of 'script' into a cultural agenda (1996). So the themes stressed in the present chapter are not exhaustive perhaps. But they are significant. Moreover, we must look to this new framework given the modest progress made by the previously dominant theoretical approaches to media and development – approaches promoting either imitation/reinforcement or purely cognitive intermediaries.

Possibly the best hope for summarizing some of the themes raised above is to resort to a hypothetical example: one that might rehearse at least some of the significant claims. We conclude in this spirit.

A six-year-old child known to me keenly watches the television series 'Power Rangers'. His politically proper thinking parents are aware of the need to be cautious about invoking 'media effects'. So they tolerate the child's enthusiasm but choose not to share it. Yet it is painful for them to sustain a liberal attitude towards this programming and its psychological significance. Immediately after each viewing, the child will be found vigorously shouting and kicking in the style of the Power Ranger characters. Confronted with such vivid spectacles it is hard to suppress an appeal to the 'effects' of this programme. Moreover, the child is anxious to own the toy tie-ins and will recruit friends into elaborate games based upon them. Everywhere adults must be witnesses to such correlations of viewing and acting and, so, it is unsurprising that the psychological impact of media remains a matter of public interest.

Psychologists, however, have been unimaginative in their empirical approaches to these matters. They have been preoccupied with the watch–act correlation (as in 'watch Power Rangers' > 'kick/shout/etc.'). The reductionist/analytic orientation of mainstream psychology has encouraged studies of such short term behavioural expressions of media programming. Otherwise, much research has simply articulated these correlations over longer intervals – using survey and observational methods rather than laboratory simulations. Yet the case sketched above surely does invite a wider range of research approaches.

For example, the very existence and appeal of a programme like Power

Rangers has to be analysed – before we hold it comprehensively responsible for certain observed behavioural correlates. This requires noticing the wider cultural context in which, for instance, Cyborgs have emerged as a phenomenon that resonates for us. The particular television programme is tapping into something more extensive in the prevailing culture. Thus it is unwise to isolate that programme in our determination to find root causes for certain species of unimaginative or unwholesome child behaviour.

We should also consider the social context of this viewing: the participation (or de-coupling) of parents and others potentially involved in sharing or interpreting the programme. This involves asking how the event is used as an organising element within family life: how its influence is thereby filtered or modified by such a status. The social context is also relevant *beyond* the occasion of viewing. Here we would dwell upon the way in which the props and narratives of the programme are used by the child to resource play with peers at other times. Furthermore, how does that format of play serve to locate and distinguish a group of children in relation to their peer group? How does it reinforce a teacher's categorizing of pupils? It is clear that even whole genres of media programming demand consideration in just such a full cultural context. Rather than attempting to isolate them as unqualified sources of anti-social or prosocial development, we must locate them in a broader web of causality. This demands more sophisticated research designs and less easy generalisations about developmental influences. This is harder work for us but at least the work becomes more intellectually honest and, probably, more rewarding.

Seminar questions

1. Might a child equipped with a multimedia PC and a modem dispense with the need for going to school? What research would help us understand such possibilities?
2. Should media education be a National Curriculum subject in schools?
3. Characterize the possible significance of the telephone in cultural psychological terms.
4. Take a home (or classroom) to which you have access and make some field notes about how electronic media are used there. How does media shape the format of daily events? Interpret your observations in psychological terms.

Further reading

For further reading I have selected four books each of which provides a distinctive form of background for thinking about this difficult topic. Only the first approximates a more detailed review of the research literature.

Meyrowitz, J. 1985. *No sense of place*. New York: Oxford University Press.

This is a big book but it is agreeably controversial and written with style and pace. Moreover, the substantial research literature (at least up until the mid-1980s) is well reviewed in the course of developing a distinctive and intriguing thesis about the psychological importance of media.

Spigel, L. 1992. *Make room for TV. Television and the family ideal in postwar America*. Chicago: Chicago University Press.

The story of television and its significance for American family life told in a most engaging way. This leaves the reader with a rich example of the socially remediating effect of modern electronic technologies.

Cole, M. 1996. *Cultural psychology*. Cambridge, MA: Harvard University Press.

This book gives a rich and scholarly treatment to the theoretical tradition that I have used in the present chapter – although it says little about electronic media as a particular case for research.

Winston, B. 1986. *Misunderstanding media*. London: Routledge and Kegan Paul.

An historical perspective is very valuable in this arena. Winston traces the history of most modern communications technology across the last 100 years. The book is not explicitly psychological – it is more about the *societal* appropriation of technology. However, recognizing recurring patterns in technological change provides a sobering orientation to the more psychological questions addressed here.

Part  5

TOWARDS ADULTHOOD

Adolescence in Europe – an important life phase?

19

LEO B HENDRY AND MARION KLOEP

Editors' preface

Adolescence is usually taken as the period between childhood and adulthood. It is relatively easy to define in broad terms like the ones we have just used, but as we will discover in this chapter there are problems in formulating a more precise definition.

In the past, adolescence has been claimed to be a period of 'storm and stress' and this has been related to the marked biological changes associated with puberty which could cause such disruption. A different perspective about storm and stress has been provided by psychoanalysis and those interested in social processes which suggest that issues about identity formation are a key feature of adolescence (*see* chapters 13 and 21). Undoubtedly, adolescence is a period of change and challenge. There are many new tasks to be negotiated: sexual relationships, independence from family, careers, and many, many more.

As you will see in this chapter, Professor Leo B. Hendry and Dr Marion Kloep, do not subscribe to the 'storm and stress' view of adolescence. They think it is more useful to move to an agenda which considers the tasks that young people face, as well as the resources available to help them cope with these tasks. The authors argue that there are a number of 'normative' shifts which occur in adolescence, and these are experienced by most individuals in Western societies. The authors also argue that many adolescents possess a set of skills and resources which enable them to successfully cope with these normative shifts (*see also* Chapter 21). This discussion sets the stage for the next chapter (which is by the same authors), here there is a discussion of the reasons why some adolescents have problems in successfully overcoming tasks that face them.

Introduction

This chapter sets out to describe 'normal' adolescent development. In it, we address the question of how adolescence could be defined and why this period of the life span is – or is regarded as – specially important.

The first problem we meet in describing 'normal' adolescent development is the variety of circumstances within which young people grow up. Culture, gender and the historical time period all have powerful influences on adolescent development (*see* Box 19.1).

BOX 19.1   Adolescents in different cultures

There is a 16-year-old girl in Northern Sweden. She has just started secondary school and moved into her own flat in the city. She is not going to marry before her late twenties, when she has established a career. She is not at risk from a premature pregnancy, because the State provides her with free contraceptives . . .

There is another girl of the same age in Manchester, England, who often thinks about leaving her parents' home even though she doesn't know where to go. She can't stand the verbal abuse of her unemployed father. She is on the dole herself . . .

Yet another girl has found a job in one of the big factories in the Ruhr-area of Germany. Her wage is too small to allow her to move away from her family. She has no boyfriend yet, but dreams about the man who will come and marry her, so that she can stop working and become a housewife and mother . . .

This dream has already come true for another girl in the rural area of Turkey. She is pregnant with her first child. She lives with the husband her parents have chosen for her and her parents-in-law in the village where she was born and will never leave . . .

In southern Italy a girl concentrates on piano-lessons in her parents' luxury villa. She is looking forward to finishing secondary school in two years time. She hopes that becoming a student at the University of Rome will help her to escape from her brothers' and father's surveillance . . .

These are all fairly typical young women in mid-adolescence, yet they lead different lives in different cultural and social contexts. This is equally true for young men:

There is a Scottish boy, who – though occasionally wearing the kilt to support the national rugby team at Murrayfield stadium – wants nothing more than to leave his boring highland village and move to the big city; an Albanian teenager who fires his self-repeating rifle into the air to defend his country against he-knows-not-what; or the Amsterdam yuppie who has already begun his economic career through Internet dealings . . .

How can we talk about 'normal' development in adolescence if all that different European adolescents have in common is age? Or can we discover other characteristics that they all possess?

WHAT *IS* ADOLESCENCE?

We do not have a clear definition of 'adolescence'. For some, adolescence may begin at 13, the first 'teen' year, while for others it may be the start of secondary school (in Britain around 11 years, in Germany nine years and in Sweden 16 years of age). For those who prefer a physical marker, the commencement of puberty is the obvious start, yet puberty itself is a very complex phenomenon, with different elements – the growth spurt, menarche and so on – occurring at different times. For some girls, puberty starts as early as nine or ten years, for others it is delayed until they are 15 years old.

As difficult as defining the beginning of adolescence, is determining when it ends. Some sociologists use status transitions as a marker: adulthood is reached when young people have left their parents' home, found a job and started a family of their own (Zinnecker, 1991). Yet, today there are large intercultural and psycho-social differences in these status transitions.

Looking at the transition from adolescence to adulthood from a legal standpoint does not clarify the picture. Although some young people are allowed to die for their country as early as 16 years, they may not be entitled to vote before 18 years, to purchase alcoholic beverages before 20 years (Sweden), or to receive housing benefits until they are 26 years old (Great Britain).

The picture is further complicated by the increasing flexibility of the life course in industrialized countries: instead of marrying one partner, young adults tend to have a number of serious relationships and marry 'late' (i.e. around 30 years) or not at all. Instead of choosing one job for life, they may be made redundant or return to further education and then seek re-employment in a new career. Even leaving the parental home need not be an early or irrevocable decision.

So, like childhood, adolescence is a socially constructed phenomenon which is redefined by each succeeding generation (France, 1995) and defined differently for different groups (Griffin, 1993). Additionally, adulthood becomes an equally problematic concept in an uncertain, complex changing society. Koops (1996) argues that the boundaries between adolescence and adulthood have become blurred to a degree that 'adolescence will lose its most characteristic meaning, namely being the bridge between childhood and adulthood' (p. 10).

PERSPECTIVES ON ADOLESCENCE

Earlier 'classical' theories of adolescence established certain trends, emphases and biases which seem still to be reflected in modern views. Lloyd (1985) outlined a number of key historical theories which have helped to create public 'images' of adolescence. Amongst earlier theories, Hall's view of adolescence as being a time of 'storm and stress' still maintains currency in the public's mind.

Across the years, different branches of developmental psychology have tried to demonstrate that children and youths think in qualitatively different ways from adults (Inhelder and Piaget, 1955; *see* Chapter 6), that they have different moral values (Kohlberg, 1969; *see* Chapter 14), that they are egocentric (Elkind, 1967) and most of all, that as a normal feature of development, they are subject to psycho-social stresses (Erikson, 1968, Kohnstamm, 1996; *see* Chapter 21). They are seen to have problems in school, with their self-identity and sexuality and particularly with becoming socialized into society – as if they were not yet a part of that society (Qvortrup, 1994)! This view of adolescents as immature trouble-makers has been used to justify treating them as an underprivileged group in society without any influence in the decision making processes of the adult world (Jones and Wallace, 1992).

More recently, youth researchers have applied findings from an array of studies to change this view of adolescence as a time of 'storm and stress'. For instance, Coleman and Hendry (1990) wrote:

> . . . there is no evidence to suggest that during adolescent years there is a higher level of psychopathology than at other times . . . the great majority of teenagers seem to cope well and to show no undue signs of turmoil or stress. (p. 201)

Other youth researchers have come to similar conclusions, opening up the possibility of concentrating research on young peoples' potential for development instead of on their claimed problems and shortcomings. In other words: treating them as 'human beings' instead of 'human becomings' (Qvortrup, 1994).

Discussion point

Can you recall any incidents of an 'identity crisis' or particular 'storm and stress' from your own adolescence?

APPROACHES TO UNDERSTANDING 'MAINSTREAM' ADOLESCENT TRADITIONS

Among present-day theories, there are three broad approaches that appear to have a major influence within developmental psychology. These are psychoanalytical approaches, social learning theories and ecological perspectives.

Psychoanalytical approaches

The psychoanalytical approaches are mainly elaborations of Erikson's (1976) theory of identity formation (e.g. Blos, 1967; Marcia, 1980). Development occurs around the basic personal and social tasks that need to be resolved at each stage of development. Usually, eight stages of development are postulated, which have to be passed in order to reach 'genuine' maturity (Erikson, 1968). At each stage, there is a characteristic crisis and the way in which the individual meets and solves the problem at each stage determines the kind of person they will become. Conflict is important for optimal ego development, so the individual has to pass through a series of identity-crises during his or her life-span. Adolescence, for example, is a normative crisis focused on self-identity. However, the assumption of an adolescent crisis has been criticized for lacking empirical support:

> ... some of the dominant psychological theories, Erik Erikson's identity crises for example, may be partly responsible for the widespread acceptance of adolescence as a deviant category ... Certainly, none of our sample nor for that matter any of the three authors, had experienced a life crisis in adolescence; nor did any of us know of anyone who had such an emotional disturbance in their late teens or was likely to. (Coffield et al., 1986 p. 211)

Social learning theory

Social learning theory is mainly associated with the work of Skinner (1953) and Bandura (1989). Development is seen as a continuous reciprocal interaction between the individual's behaviour and the environment. Changes occur gradually through a lifetime of learning, and even development that seems to occur in stages need not be caused by biological maturation: age-related changes in the environment can produce age-related changes in behaviour (Bijou and Baer, 1965). Consequently, there is no 'normal' course of development, so instead of trying to describe THE period of adolescence within this theoretical framework, one should concentrate on the mechanisms through which behaviour can change over time. This means applying basic learning principles (for example shaping processes, or, as Bandura (1989) described them, imitation and modelling) to understand how specific individuals change in response to changes in their environment and how they change the environment as a consequence of their actions. In practice this means finding out which skills young people need to cope with the special tasks they encounter in the process of growing up and how these skills can best be taught (e.g. Fürntratt and Möller, 1982).

Ecological perspectives

Like social learning theory, an ecological approach, represented for example by Bronfenbrenner (1986), Lerner (1985) and Coleman and Hendry (1990), stresses the dynamic interactions between the individual and the environment and draws attention to the adolescent as a self-agent in three modes: as stimulus (eliciting different reactions from the social environment); as processor (in making sense of the behaviour of others); and as agent, shaper and selector (by doing things, making choices and influencing events) (Lerner, 1985). In Bronfenbrenner's terms, development is seen as an interactional process between the individual and various environmental systems, such as the microsystems (the actual settings in which the child lives, e.g. family or peer group), the mesosystem (the inter-relations among contexts of the microsystems, e.g. the parents' relationships with the child's peers), the exosystem (settings that influence a child's development but in which the child does not play a direct role, e.g. the parents' work place) and the macrosystem (the cultural and ideological patterns surrounding the child, e.g. religion or form of government). In addition, the ecology of development is never static, but encompasses the interactions of the changing individual with a changing matrix of systems.

Coleman and Hendry (1990) suggested that at different periods across adolescence particular sorts of relationship patterns come into focus. The fact that most adolescents do not usually have to cope with such crises at the same time, but can meet them sequentially using and developing their psychosocial skills, means that the majority of young people make the transition to adulthood in a relatively unproblematic way.

A changing research focus

Though some of the approaches described above explicitly stress the importance of cultural and other differences, many theories are still biased in particular ways towards white, middle-class, urban males in Western industrialized societies. Young women, ethnic groups, adolescents living in rural areas or in other than highly industrialized countries receive little research attention, yet are implicitly subsumed into the existing theories.

For instance, as Marcia (1996) pointed out, striving for autonomy, which plays a central role in identity theory, might neither be existent nor needed in societies that do not emphasize personal autonomy. How stage theories reflect an ethnocentric Western point of view can be juxtaposed to the fact that the majority of the world's population does not live long enough to experience all the eight stages postulated by Erikson!

However, the focus of youth research is changing: McRobbie and McCabe (1981), Phoenix (1992), Griffin (1993), among others, have introduced a strong gender perspective into developmental psychology, whereas Zinnecker (1991), Chisholm et al. (1995) and others have begun to look cross-culturally at youth development, including rural youth (Hendry et al., forthcoming).

Though originating from different theoretical traditions, all these more recent approaches have important aspects in common: they all emphasize that adolescents are confronted with a number of challenges (or 'tasks' according to Havighurst, 1972) which they have to meet and the way they cope with them will influence their subsequent development. In order to solve these tasks, adolescents need certain skills and in the process of resolving 'tasks', they will acquire new skills or refine and extend existing abilities. These skills can be effective (i.e. solving the issue in an optimal way), or they can be less than effective (not solving the problem, or solving it but creating new problems in the process) or even producing harmful effects in the long term. Another aspect on which there seems to be full agreement is that such developments are part of a life-long learning. In this way, childhood and adolescence are no longer viewed as simply formative periods that directly dictate later stages of development.

IMPORTANCE OF STUDYING ADOLESCENCE

The transitional processes of growing up mean having to cope with the sociocultural effects of fairly dramatic bodily changes. But these occur also later in life – detecting one's first grey hairs might be even more dramatic than discovering one's first pubic hairs! Adolescence brings with it a great number of 'first experiences' such as the first date, first experiences with sex, first time living away from home. But so do other age stages: first step, first word, first day in school, first adultery, first promotion, first time real-izing that one can't run up the stairs anymore . . . and everybody feels uncomfortable and can experience low self-esteem in new situations until the necessary coping-skills are learned. We would agree with Marcia (1996) that even the search for identity 'remains an issue throughout the life-span'.

What makes adolescence special is that it is a period early in one's life and thus can be decisive for the way the remaining years may be managed. The way a problem is tackled the very first time it occurs influences further problem-solving. Coping-skills once learned can be repeated in similar sit-uations and failed attempts to solve problems create a potential for subse-quent failure. As a teenager, one has greater possibilities to experiment and fail occasionally and 'childish' attempts to tackle a problem are tolerated to some extent. These chances for training and the 'freedom' for trying out skills diminish over the years, as does the broader array of resources avail-able to young people. Once adult, society expects its members to tackle their problems in a fairly independent, competent fashion. Thus adoles-cence is a period which provides the opportunity to learn (and be helped to learn) essential life-skills in a relatively supportive environment (though *see* Box 19.2). Furthermore, modern society demands that young people begin to develop such competencies as early as possible. As Clausen (1991) puts it:

> '. . . possessing a reasonably clear idea of who and what one is and wants to be, now gives not only a head start but an acceleration that makes it difficult for late bloomers without special talents to catch up.' (p. 807)

BOX 19.2 What is distinctive about adolescence?

Hendry (1983) has suggested that what is truly distinctive about ado-lescence is the importance placed by various European societies on the child/adult distinction. In this context adolescence may be seen as an attempt by every society to prolong childhood, and the reaction of adolescents to this is a striving towards adult status.

Reasons for the ascribing of roles which accentuate the child/adult distinction are complex. First, this may result from a 'deficiency' view of childhood – the view that children are incompetent interpreters of the social world. This may lead to an attitude which is possessive or protective. It implies that adults 'define the situation' and denies the validity of childhood perceptions or culture. A second, contradictory view would be to 'let them stand on their own two feet' and may be seen as premature ascription of adult status. Third, straightforward commercial gain provides a vested interest in creating an adolescent consumer group. Finally, there is a perhaps more sinister rationale in terms of power or domination by institutions. Apple (1979) wrote that the (adult) social purpose was to:

> . . . help create people (with the appropriate meanings and values) who see no other serious possibility to the economic and cultural assemblage now extant.

These facts make it necessary to more closely look at what 'tasks' young people need to face up to during their adolescent years – and what psychosocial skills they need to cope successfully within society.

New situations demand new skills?

'NORMATIVE' SHIFTS

There are a variety of tasks to be achieved in adolescence – personal development, social relationships, leaving school, seeking qualifications and employment (or coping with unemployment), leisure pursuits, creating a particular life-style, becoming independent, amongst others (Havighurst, 1972).

Some of these tasks will be common for most adolescents. These stem from biological, age-related, 'normative' events that occur in everybody's life, such as the onset of menarche for girls or 'breaking of the voice' for boys. Other events are common for adolescents living in similar societal settings, the 'normative' events programmed by these societies such as schooling or the legal status of youth. Finally, there are a range of 'non-normative shifts' that can present some young people with extraordinary tasks. Here, we will consider mainly the tasks and challenges most young people meet in the normal course of development, namely '**normative shifts**': body changes, the development of gender identity, changing relationships with parents and peers, leisure, demands made by school and employment and their self-agency in society. (In the following chapter we will discuss issues associated with '**non-normative shifts**' – concerns that do not normally arise for most adolescents, but can occur for some.)

'MAINSTREAM' ADOLESCENT DEVELOPMENT

Puberty and its sociocultural meaning

The impact of physical changes at puberty not only have a profound impact in themselves but are closely linked to other forms of adjustment and change (Coleman and Hendry, 1990). Changes in body shape, size, different rates of growth in primary and secondary sexual characteristics and hormonal changes may all lead to some physical awkwardness. The timing of such changes may also provoke social unease. How the body is perceived, interpreted and presented to the self and others will be influenced by a range of factors which include individual, cultural and social dimensions (Goffman, 1971).

The transformation of a girl's body into a young woman's demands a range of new behaviours from the teenage female: while some societies encourage her to reveal her new womanhood and to enhance it by the use of make-up, bras and high-heeled shoes, other societies 'force' her to cover her body or even her face to conceal her emerging femininity. In all societies though, she has to understand and cope with social – and particularly male – reactions to her changing body. In addition to other adolescent 'tasks', she has to learn that a female body can become target of male aggression (Martin, 1996). This, with the onset of menstruation – which is perceived by some young women to be a taboo topic socially – makes puberty for many girls a less than positive experience, as Martin (1996) describes in a series of illuminating interviews with teenagers.

Restricted by fewer societal norms, body changes in males lead to fewer complications, though concerns – both voiced and kept secret – about body build and penis size occupy many men's minds far beyond puberty. Adolescent males may be faced with problems and feelings of guilt about their emerging sexuality, particularly in agrarian societies where masturbation and an early interest in females meet with social disapproval. Overall, however, adolescent males are more likely to regard the transition to manhood as a positive experience (Martin, 1996).

Gender identity

The beginnings of sexual activity mean that masculinity and femininity have to be renegotiated in adolescent terms (Bancroft, 1990). Sexual identity is intimately connected to how gender identity is perceived within the culture (*see* Chapter 21). It is therefore not surprising that young people may try a number of different sexual roles, the nature of which will be closely connected to their attempts to develop a separate identity in the context of and sometimes in opposition to, their families. Particularly with girls, some 'male' behaviours might have been tolerated during childhood, but when growing into a young woman, the 'tomboy' is expected to readjust according to the gender-stereotypes prevailing in that society.

Experimentations with new roles often include, at least in fantasy, experimenting with sex roles. From a developmental point of view, sexual variations, including homosexuality or 'crushes' on admired adults may best be considered in terms of the young person exploring which 'elements' of sexual behaviour are to become their own in the process of growing up.

Adapting a female gender role seems to be more difficult and problematic than accepting a male role in most societies: asked to write an essay about how they would react if one morning they wakened up to find they had transformed into a member of the opposite sex, the majority of male adolescents described feelings of panic and suicidal thoughts, whereas most of the girls were willing to accept their new role (Gunnarsson, 1994).

DISCUSSION POINT

How is your relationship to your parents today? How has it changed since you were an adolescent?

Family relationships

Repeated studies from different countries have found that despite common-sense assumptions to the contrary, young people get along well with their parents (Hendry et al., 1993; Kloep and Tarifa, 1993), adopt their views and values and perceive their family members as most important 'significant others' in their lives (McGlone et al., 1996). Furthermore, Stattin and Klackenberg (1992) showed that the majority of adolescents who have conflicts with their parents already had a poor relationship with them earlier during childhood.

Disagreements between young people and their parents are similar everywhere in Europe. Whether in Greece (Besevegis and Giannitas, 1996), Italy (Jackson et al., 1996), Scotland (Hendry et al., 1993), Germany (Fischer et al., 1985), Albania or Sweden (Kloep and Tarifa, 1993), young people have day-to-day quarrels with their parents about how long and how often they may stay out, how much they should help at home, the tidiness of their bedrooms, the volume of their music and about their achievement at school.

Jackson et al. (1996) outlined these conflicts as follows:

- Disagreements which arise because parents expect more independence of action from the adolescent.
- Disagreements which occur because parents don't want to grant as much autonomy as the adolescent demands. Even in the most gender-emancipated countries in Europe, young women have more conflicts with their parents than young men about independence.
- Disagreements which arise because of differences in personal tastes and preferences.

The 'task' to accomplish regarding family life is for adolescents to learn new roles in relation to parents (which is as difficult for parents as it is for adolescents). When children are younger, parents usually solve controversies by explaining their decisions and/or by using their authority. Adolescents learn to argue back and authoritarian threats are no longer accepted (Jackson et al., 1996). Both parties have to acquire new ways of negotiating and until these skills are developed, some disagreements occur.

School and post-school trajectories

As Jeffs (1994) has pointed out, most schools are 'depressing places' for those sympathetic to young people's rights. Moreover, it is claimed that failure to treat young people as emerging adults leads to increasing numbers of truancies, expulsions and suspensions as well as to the breakdown of discipline. Truancy in schools, according to Demarco (1978), occurs because pupils are simply 'voting with their feet' about schools and what passes for education.

Nevertheless Claxton (1984) comments that for many pupils school does work – 'it meets their needs, feeds their interests, creates opportunities. For others school holds out rewards that they know they will not get and do not even want.' Not surprisingly, many pupils are dissatisfied with the content and quality of lessons and with the influence they have in various aspects of school life (Jeffs, 1994; Barnombudsmannen, 1995).

Their reasons for dissatisfaction are threefold:

1. Lack of influence: if we wish to change 'school climate' and provide self and social management skills for young people we need to take real account of the ways they think about school and to enable them to exercise a more positive influence over their own destiny.
2. Traditional teaching methods: whole class teaching with 'fact-giving' may not correspond to the needs of modern society. Pupils require information-seeking and 'learning-to-learn'-skills to cope with an ever changing world:

   > School must . . . start very early in training the students to take their own responsibility for their learning. Teachers should not teach; students should learn (Andersson, 1995, p. 111).

3. Involuntary prolongation of schooling due to the labour market situation: the trend through the 1980s and 1990s has been towards more young people 'staying on' at school and going on to further and higher education while youth schemes have replaced *real* jobs in many countries. However, 'more' education does not necessarily mean 'better', in particular when pupils' motivation is zero and career trajectories problematic (Roberts and Parsell, 1990).

Given the conditions of today's schools, the tasks for adolescents are mainly to access as much knowledge and qualifications as possible and to acquire many learning skills, not only *because* of the range of lessons they are forced to attend, but also *in spite* of them! Given their subordinate and dependent positions, they should learn a range of diplomatic negotiating skills as well as academic skills and a range of coping skills for future life events.

By contrast to earlier generations, young people leaving school are confronted with a wider range of 'tasks'. Not only do they have to learn new forms of discipline, team work and specific skills associated with working life but also initiative and creativity if they want to find a job at all. Furthermore, leisure skills grow in importance as a positive source of development for young people when most other aspects of society change rapidly beyond the individual's control.

DISCUSSION POINT

In what ways does teaching and learning at university differ from your school experiences? Which context is better? Why?

Peers

As a consequence of different socialization patterns, peer relationships have a different meaning for young men and women. Golombok and Fivush (1994) described boys' and girls' development of peer relations as follows: during the first years of primary school boys and girls play separately. Girls have a best friend with whom they talk a lot and share small secrets. They also play, but games are not of great importance to them. If a conflict arises they end the game in order to regain harmony in the relationship.

Boys, on the other hand, play in groups and do not have a single best friend. They play competitive games with clear rules. If conflicts arise, they are resolved in order to continue the game. Boys do not have long conversations with their peers, if they talk they talk about the game and its rules.

Thus, boys learn to negotiate, to co-operate with a group and to compete. By comparison, girls learn to communicate, to listen and to keep a relationship going. These different gender relationships can be observed for the rest of their lives. Girls have deeper, more emotional and personal relationships, whereas boys have more instrumental, action-centred relationships (Griffin, 1993; Shucksmith and Hendry, 1998). If boys or men are interested in deeper conversations – they seek a woman to talk to!

Perhaps at this stage it is important to distinguish between friendship groups (established around mutual interests) and peer groups which set 'norms', provide comparisons and pressures to conform to 'expected' behaviours. Friendship groups (embedded within the wider network of peer groups) re-affirm self-images and enable the young person to experience new forms of intimacy (Coleman and Hendry, 1990), learn social skills such as initiating contact, discussing and solving conflicts, helping, sharing, asserting oneself. Such groups can offer the opportunity to expand knowledge, to develop a new identity and to experiment away from the watchful eyes of adults and family. But the groups are also contexts for lying, showing off, dominating and 'scapegoating'. In such a setting young people can construct their own styles and perspectives within a relatively 'safe' context. Adolescent groups often act as a site for trying out particular social strategies. In this way (sub-cultural) groups may establish a collective identity distinctive from other groups.

One of the key 'tasks' of adolescence is the development of romantic and sexual relationships. In more patriarchally oriented areas of Europe, such as the Balkans, meeting male friends without parental supervision is a privilege for young men, whereas meeting members of the opposite sex in informal settings is an impossibility for both genders. Kloep (1994) found that premarital sexual experiences were extremely rare for Albanian women and Ford and Bowie (1989) stated that a smaller percentage of youngsters in rural areas were sexually experienced compared to urban adolescents.

For both genders, the acquisition of romantic strategies and sexual techniques is problematic. Unlike other aspects of social learning, little help and support is offered to young people by family, schools or even peers. Sex education, if given at all, is often restricted to issues like contraception and sexually transmitted diseases and often inappropriately taught from the adolescents' perspective (Shucksmith and Hendry, 1998). Questions like what is required to be a good lover, how to make a socially competent (sexual) approach or how to end a relationship are only covered inappropriately in the pornographic material young men may access. Perhaps young women are better served in this regard by the available array of women's magazines. The point we wish to make here is that adolescents are usually left to find out such information for themselves.

Leisure

Nowadays, as Ingham (1987) has suggested, leisure may be more significant in creating opportunities for identity development, competence and intrinsic satisfaction. Adolescents should learn planning and organizational skills in the social and leisure domains as well as in cognitive and work-related spheres in order to develop a clear-cut personal and social identity.

Leisure activities may be chosen for their personal meaning and for social expression. These choices are, in turn, coloured by influences such as the family, peers, the educational system, the media, leisure promotion industries and changes in wider society such as employment opportunities. A crucial point to stress in all this is the way the interplay of factors determining choices varies as the focus of social interests changes across the adolescent years. Changes and continuities in adolescents' leisure preferences can be noted (*see* fig 19.1).

From a certain age, adolescents want to meet without adult surveillance to experiment with developing new social roles. In warmer countries, such

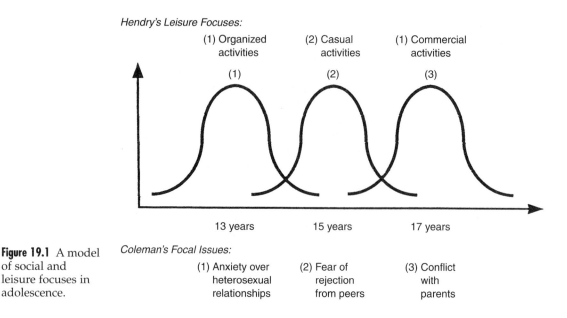

Hendry's Leisure Focuses:

| (1) Organized | (2) Casual | (1) Commercial |
| activities | activities | activities |

Figure 19.1 A model of social and leisure focuses in adolescence.

Coleman's Focal Issues:

| (1) Anxiety over heterosexual relationships | (2) Fear of rejection from peers | (3) Conflict with parents |

as Italy, these casual leisure meetings happen in the street. Seventy-eight per cent of Italian 16-year-olds claimed to meet their preferred peers in the street, whereas that of Austrian 16-year-olds was only 50 per cent (Kirchler et al., 1991, 1992). In cold countries such as Sweden, young people desperately need a place to meet. They are 'confined' to organized activities, though sports and youth clubs have become 'too tame' and adult-dominated for them. Yet legal and economic obstacles prevent them from meeting in more commercial surroundings such as night-clubs, pubs and bars (Hendry et al., 1993). In rural areas, transport provides an additional problem. Consequently, young people there spend less time with friends than in other areas, until they are old enough to drive legally. Such factors clearly influence the transitional patterns of the model in fig 19.1.

Young people's rights and self agency

The issue of children's rights highlights the paradox of views held about children and young people within contemporary European society. The UN Convention of the Rights of the Child, adopted in 1989, underlines the rights of young people 'up to the age of 18'. Has this emphasis extended young people's autonomy or has it simply reinforced notions of powerlessness and the need to protect them from both their own-risk taking propensities and from the 'uncivil' society (Wyness, 1994)? It may seem peculiar that youths are explicitly excluded from participating in democratic procedures by not having the right to vote.

They may exert freedom of speech; but their access to all types of written and spoken expression is limited, since censorship is practised towards them in a number of cases. Children's freedom to organise is nowhere prohibited, but it is limited in the sense that they cannot as minors provide the necessary signatures. (Qvortrup and Christof-fersen, 1991, p. 44).

So young people, as they grow up, find themselves in the trap of having to respond more and more to society's demands in a 'responsible' adult way while being treated as immature and not capable of holding sound opinions on a wide range of social matters.

> We must, of course, acknowledge the protectionist background for the exclusion of children from a number of rights. Yet it is not always clear whether it is children or adult society which are the primary object of protection. (Qvortrup and Christoffersen, 1991, p. 44)

Coping with this societal double standard is not easy for young people. They have to learn to submit to authority or to find forms of protest which are acceptable to adults. Otherwise they are vulnerable to being harshly judged, with their future put at risk. At the same time, young people are expected to develop as democratic citizens and to participate actively in the political life of their society, as soon as they are legally entitled to do so. More often than not, young people have lost an interest in politics and their trust in politicians by the time they reach voting age (e.g. Zinnecker, 1992 in Germany; Roe et al., 1994 in Sweden; Furnham and Gunter, 1988 in Britain).

Successful coping

Now that we are more aware of the tasks and challenges adolescents face in growing up, it is of interest to see what enables young people to deal with such issues. The following list of elements describes the decisive mediators for the successful coping of 'normative' shifts:

- *'Steeling experiences'* (Rutter, 1996a): resilience does not reside in the avoidance of a risk experience, but in successfully coping with it. Rutter compared exposure to psychosocial adversities with the controlled exposure to pathogens in medical immunization: if exposed to poten-tially harmful stimuli in low doses and under favourable conditions, the individual learns to cope with this situation and later the experience can generalise to more difficult contexts. This makes the individual feel more in control and provides a 'steeling' experience towards future events.
- *Spacing out of issues*: 'focal theory' (Coleman and Hendry, 1990) offers an explanation as to why the majority of young people cope successfully with the substantial social and psychological adjustments demanded of them: they cope by dealing with one issue at a time. Adaptation covers a number of years, with the adolescent attempting to solve one issue, then the next. Any stresses resulting from the need to adapt to new models of behaviour are rarely concentrated at one time. Those who, for whatever reason, do have more than one issue to cope with at one time

are most likely to have problems of adjustment. Thus, if normative transitions coincide with non-normative shifts the situation is even more problematic.

- *Social network resources*: it has often been shown that young people who are able to form strong relationships have demonstrated a facility for moving out of adverse social circumstances (e.g. Rutter, 1996; Philip and Hendry, 1996). Individuals within relationships can function as sources of emotional support, of advice and instrumental help, as mediators and mentors and as role models for learning social skills, so crucial in problem-solving. Werner and Smith (1981) for instance showed that resilient youths generally had a 'higher degree of social maturity' than their age-mates.
- *'Self-esteem'*: self-esteem or the belief of being able to solve one's own problems stems from successful task accomplishment. Succeeding in one set of tasks creates the confidence necessary to face other tasks. Successful experiences in school (not necessarily academic ones) increase the probability that children can tackle other kinds of problems as well (Rutter, 1996).
- *Problem-solving skills*: Quinton and Rutter (1988) demonstrated that the existence of 'planning-skills' in some young people makes a difference to their future lives, even if their earlier experiences were disadvantageous. Similarly, Clausen (1991) found through an analysis of longitudinal data that competent adolescents with planning skills had fewer disruptions in their marriages and careers in middle age than less skilful individuals.

Chapter summary

In this chapter we have argued that throughout Europe (and in other Western societies) adolescence is a significant life stage. Yet, in adolescence young people share many experiences in common with other life periods. Most theories propose that the most important factor of adolescence is concerned with the resolution of various psychosocial 'tasks'. The most obvious challenge adolescents have to meet is the body changes caused by puberty and the social implications this has for being regarded as an adult woman or man. These include different social relations with parents, peers and the opposite gender, which all have to be learned and negotiated. In connection with this, new types of leisure skills are acquired. Furthermore, becoming an adult means having to meet demands and responsibilities in the transition from school to university and to employment or unemployment, at a time when the adult world is not totally ready to accept the adolescent as a full member of society. This can lead to conflicts and/or negotiations about self-agency and democratic rights.

Being confronted with these various challenges and successfully solving them, are important steps in the individual's development. Towards the end of the chapter we outlined some factors which appear to be decisive in preparing young people to meet different developmental issues: namely steeling experiences, timing and spacing of issues, social support, self-esteem and problem solving skills.

To some degree, adult society is prepared to help and guide young people through adolescence, giving them time and space, support and tuition in trying to solve their developmental tasks. However, apart from the foreseeable normative shifts, which we have discussed in this chapter, there can be additional problems, for which young people are less well prepared. It is to these 'non-normative shifts' and ways of dealing with them we turn in the next chapter.

Seminar questions

1. Is it only the *kind* of 'tasks' that makes adolescence different from both adulthood and childhood? What other factors make adolescence distinctive?
2. Can you think of other 'tasks' which young people meet and which have not been mentioned in this chapter? Why would you include these if you were the authors?
3. Can parents/teachers/youth workers do anything to prepare pre-adolescents for the developmental tasks ahead? What would you suggest that parents and professionals do to facilitate 'successful' adolescent transitions?

Further reading

Chisholm, L., Büchner, P., Krüger, H.-H., du Bois-Reymond, M. (eds) 1995. *Growing up in Europe*. Walter de Gruyter: Berlin. This book gives an introduction to how adolescent transitions can be different across European countries.

Griffin, C. 1993. *Representations of youth*. Polity Press: London. An effective feminist critique of youth research and of youth in society.

Morrow, V. and Richards, M. (1996) *Transitions to adulthood*. Joseph Rowntree: York. This reviews recent research on key transitions to adulthood and the role of family support in making these transitions.

20 Challenges, risks and coping in adolescence

MARION KLOEP AND LEO B HENDRY

Editors' preface

The previous chapter discussed various tasks faced by individuals in the adolescent years involving 'normative' shifts such as coming to terms with biological changes and the impact of new family relationships. In this chapter there is a focus on non-normative shifts which occur when an individual is faced with an unpredictable task or life event. In this chapter, Dr Marion Kloep and Professor Leo B. Hendry conceptualize the tasks facing adolescents as involving both challenges and risks. They do not make a rigid distinction between these two processes, but they suggest that challenges are often those tasks which an individual can successfully accomplish because of their existing psychosocial skills, whereas a risk is less likely to result in such success. However, they also draw attention to the way that challenges and risks can have different meanings depending on the perspective that is adopted. From the outside, some individuals appear to successfully deal with challenges and risks, others find it difficult to achieve the same success with the same task; furthermore, what is considered as a challenge or risk may change from individual to individual and from whether the view is from the individual's perspective or from the outside. A further complication is that sometimes even where a task is a difficult one this can result in gain and personal growth (*see also* Chapter 21). The authors conclude with proposals about the need in education and in society for a new set of 3Rs, involving responsibility, reflection and relations, to help young people deal with the many challenges and risks that face them.

Introduction

At the beginning of this chapter, we will discuss concerns that are created for young people such as matching up to cultural images of attractiveness, family relations, school and romantic love, then proceed to look at problems young people might create for themselves – risk-taking behaviours such as alcohol use or delinquent activities. Finally, we will outline a theoretical model of how the development of meta-awareness skills may be a powerful coping device, while admitting that research has not yet fully uncovered the processes and mechanisms involved. Thus, this chapter does not present a detailed review of research on adolescence. Rather, taken together the ideas in both this and the previous chapter can create a reasonable framework for integrating information and findings about adolescent development and so enhance our understanding of this transitional period of the lifespan.

Normative events and non-normative shifts

In the previous chapter, we examined the variety of 'tasks' adolescents have to deal with. Apart from 'normative' events that most adolescents encounter, some also experience 'non-normative shifts' which are problems that arise from the social environment, from unsuccessful coping (Rutter, 1996a) or from special life events such as a death in the family. Although all adolescents have to cope with the psychosocial challenges associated with their maturing body, new relationships with parents and peers, with school and the transitions towards employment, a growing number encounter additional problems like family disruption, economic deprivation or social or cultural changes (*see* Box 20.1). Sometimes, a normative shift can turn into a non-normative one, if it is dealt with unsuccessfully, or if there are other circumstances that cause a normal developmental 'task' to become more difficult. If the onset of puberty, for example, occurs too early or too late (compared to age-norms), or if conflicts with parents cannot be resolved, these basic 'normative shifts' can turn into 'non-normative' ones for particular adolescents.

DISCUSSION POINT

Identify some normative changes that occur in adolescence and think about the way these can become non-normative shifts for some individuals.

BOX 20.1 Normative and non-normative shifts during adolescence

- *Normative, maturational shifts*: growth spurt, menarche, first nocturnal emissions, voice breaking, changes in sexual organs, beginnings of sexual arousal, changed romantic relationships, gender role identity, changed relationship with adults, increasing autonomy, independence and responsibility (e.g. for own risk-taking behaviours) etc.

- *Normative, society-dependent shifts*: changing from primary to secondary school, leaving school, getting started in an occupation, acquisition of legal rights for voting, purchasing alcohol, sexual relationships, driving licence, military service, co-habitation, etc.
- *Non-normative shifts*: divorce of parents, death of close relative, illness, poverty, natural disasters, war, changes in society, incest, emigration, disruption of peer network, risk-taking behaviours, 'disadvantage' because of gender, class, regional or ethnic discrimination, physical and/or mental handicaps, maturation 'out of phase' etc.

RISKS OR CHALLENGES?

Normative and non-normative shifts that young people are likely to encounter can turn out to be either challenges or risks, depending on their psychosocial properties. In order to find out what makes specific events or circumstances into a challenge or a risk we need to differentiate between risk indicators and risk mechanisms (Rutter, 1996a). Rather than simplistically assigning certain events like family break-up as a risk, we should try to understand what mechanisms are involved which turn these events into problematic contexts for some, whereas the same events leave other adolescents unharmed or may even lead to personal growth.

Having briefly described the different functions of developmental challenge and risk, we want to illustrate this with a few examples in relation to psychosocial functions in young people's lives.

SOME EXAMPLES OF RISK AND CHALLENGE

Aspects from the social environment

Cultural body images

Amongst others, Davies and Furnham (1986) have shown that the average adolescent is not only sensitive to, but also critical of their changing physical self. Because of gender and sexual development young people are inevitably confronted, perhaps for the first time, with cultural standards of beauty in evaluating their own 'body image'. Direct influences may come, for instance, via media images or by the reactions of others, as we can illustrate with some quotes from a qualitative study by Shucksmith and Hendry (1998):

> 'You look in these magazines and you see all these super models. You don't see any that are 22 stone! They're all about seven stone.' (Girl, age 15)

> 'O God, where did all this fat come from. It never used to be there or I never noticed it. I used to be able to eat lots of sweets and the only thing that grew were my feet.' (Girl, age 15)

That this may lead to a non-normative shift is seen by the fact that concerns about weight and body shape are frequently associated with dieting practices and sometimes by serious eating disorder. In the Mayfly study (Balding, 1986), over half of the girls and 20 per cent of the boys had tried to exert control over their weight, whereas Coleman and Hendry (1990) described how young people may be especially vulnerable to teasing and exclusion if they are perceived by peers as either over- or underweight. Fear of such teasing can itself lead to feelings of self loathing and isolation (Shucksmith and Hendry, 1998) and thus implies a clear risk for further development.

Realizing that you lack the physical attractiveness to make friends *just* by being good-looking can become a challenge leading to the development of alternative skills to gain peer acceptance. Being helpful, having listening skills, having a sense of humour or possessing 'entertainment' skills like playing an instrument, or being good at highly regarded sports, are all accomplishments that can outweigh physical attractiveness (Hendry et al., 1993).

Family life and traditional values

Turning to family life, we have seen that adolescence is a time for renegotiating roles. If done skilfully on both sides, this will lead to heightened autonomy and the development of many necessary life-skills like managing one's own economy, personal hygiene, short- and long-term planning and a continuing warm relationship with parents. Done in an unskilled way, this can result in less effective solutions and may lead to further problems – running away, marrying or becoming pregnant early, joining a religious cult, drug abuse or self-harm and suicide attempts.

Another factor that can disturb parent–adolescent relationships is the 'non-normative shifts' that affect family-life. Examples of this are economic hardship, which can weaken the marital bond and, as a consequence, distort parental styles (Silbereisen et al., 1990), or sudden value changes in society after political unrest (e.g. Kloep and Hendry, 1997), or in some traditional south-European countries, media-influence (Georgas, 1991; Deliyannis-Kouimtzi and Ziogou, 1995). Young people, in particular girls, who readily adapt to new Western ways, find themselves in conflict with their parents and the older generation over traditional values (Pais, 1995). In families with a supportive climate, parent–adolescent discussions can be an opportunity for the development of social and intellectual skills, whereas in families where conflicts are numerous, an additional issue can be disastrous.

Similarly, a non-normative shift like parental divorce can have positive or negative implications for a young person, depending how the separation is conducted. Research has shown that children of a 'happy' divorce are better adjusted than children of unhappy marriages (Hetherington, 1989). If there is conflict between the parents and particularly if adolescents are involved in the conflicts, they are likely to suffer (Kloep et al., 1995). Further, the young person's coping style seems to make a difference: avoidance of dealing with their parent's divorce either cognitively or behaviourally or even blaming themselves for the incident seems to be related with poorer functioning (Emery and Forehand, 1996). Box 20.2 summarizes protective factors identified from research about child resilience in divorce.

BOX 20.2 Protective factors identified in child resilience research

Individual factors	Family factors	Extrafamiliar support systems
Temperament (e.g. active, cuddly, good-natured)	Warm supportive parents	Supportive networks (e.g. grandparent, peers)
Gender (being female prior to adolescence and male during adolescence)	Good parent–child relations	Successful school experiences
Age (being younger)	Parental harmony	
IQ		
Self-efficacy		
Social skills		
Interpersonal awareness		
Feelings of empathy		
Internal locus of control		
Humour		
Attractiveness to others		

Adapted from Emery and Forehand (1996)

On the other hand, divorce can give youths the opportunity to assume a responsible role in the family, helping them to 'grow up faster'. Hetherington (1989) concluded:

> 'Depending on the characteristics of the child, available resources, subsequent life experiences and especially interpersonal relationships, children in the long run may be survivors, losers, or winners of their parents' divorce or remarriage.'

When young people leave their parents' home, many of them continue to live locally, often deriving help from an extended kin network (Harris, 1993). It is those who do not enjoy this family support who are at risk, for example, of becoming homeless. The pervasive influence of unemployment has created a shifting population of homeless people who inhabit the 'cardboard cities' of many European towns. Voluntary organizations estimate that 200,000 young people experience homelessness each year in Great Britain alone (Killeen, 1992). This last example shows how a 'non-normative shift' like the liberalisation of 'market forces' has an enormous impact on the life of young people – though varied for different adolescents (*see* Box 20.3).

BOX 20.3 Factors influencing the experience of unemployment

Risks			*Challenges*
Unsuccessful coping			**Successful coping**
Low, guilt, self-blame	←	SELF-IMAGE →	Defensively high
Devalued, low	←	ASPIRATIONS →	High
Isolation		SOCIALIZATION	Contact
	←	WITH PEERS →	with peers
No freedom, low structure	←	TIME USE →	Structure, purpose, self-responsibility
Pressure, stress	←	FAMILY →	Support, sympathy
Not 'adult', frustrating	←	LEISURE →	'Appropriate', acceptable
Not useful	←	EDUCATION →	Helpful, useful
Rejected, hostility		TRAINING	Involvement
	←	SCHEMES →	
			adapted from Hendry (1987)

The omnipresence of multinational companies, consumerism and the ascent of service industries enable individuals to access the global market-place to create and sustain a variety of lifestyles – if they have available financial resources. As Büchner et al. (1995, p. 57) concluded:

'. . . apart from those 'winners' of modernisation who are able to integrate modern life style features into their everyday lives, there are also quite a number of children who must be regarded as 'losers' of modernisation. Such children do not have the necessary material or personal resources at their disposal nor do they have adequate support networks to live modern individualised lives. Rather they are at risk, both socio-economically (for example, new poverty) and personally (for example, deviant, psychosomatic syndrome)'.

Not only large sections of working class youth in affluent nations, but also the majority of young people in former socialist countries find themselves so trapped: Cashmore (1984) called this the 'luxury gap'.

This situation constitutes a risk rather than a challenge for most young people. There are only a limited number of strategies at their disposal which may be approved of by adult society. So, a small number make their way by succeeding in a sports- or arts-career, by obtaining outstanding academic qualifications or, as in the case of many poorer countries, by emigrating. Others are left to adopt potentially damaging strategies: turning to delinquency, rioting, drugs or becoming totally apathetic.

Romance and sexuality

Young people's awakening sexuality creates possibilities of both challenge and risk. If first sexual experiences are positive ones, this can provide a basis for learning the new skills of intimate relationship (such as respect, intuition, negotiation and 'give and take', conflict prevention and

resolution, developing a positive relationship to one's own body and specific sexual skills). These can provide a firm foundation for future interpersonal understanding. Even the pain of ending a love-relationship can be
an important learning experience for coping with loss or for helping to
make a future better choice. Yet, having sex with the 'wrong' partner
and/or under the wrong circumstances can be such a traumatic experience
that it may lead to difficulties in establishing and maintaining future
romantic, or even friendly, relationships (Martin, 1996). Such an experience
was summed up by a 15-year-old young woman who said:

> 'Then I went on holiday and I had sex with this guy and it was a total
> mistake and then I came back and I wished I hadn't done it. There's
> nothing special to it. There's nothing to look forward to ...'
> (Shucksmith and Hendry, 1998)

Hendry et al. (1991) have shown that power and intimacy are two dimensions around which young people need guidance and help to understand
the ways in which romantic and sexual relationships are negotiated. In particular, the dangers of learning a masculine role which separates sexual
practices from emotional feelings cannot be overstated. For young men, the
threat of loss of a precarious masculine identity makes them reluctant to
engage emotionally with sexual partners or to acknowledge their needs.
The importance of assertiveness in young women's refusal of unwanted
sexual advances has to be pointed out because rational models of decision-
making can be affected by a number of interpersonal and social factors.
Hendry et al. (1991) found that amongst their sample of young women,
being seen to carry condoms, to be assertive about their own sexual needs
or to be defined as sexually active would be interpreted as a loss of reputation as being 'respectable' and make them vulnerable in other areas of their
lives. The creating and sustaining of an acceptable sexual reputation is clearly
highly gendered. Moreover, this reputation will have a significant impact
on attitudes and beliefs in other social contexts and activities (Wight, 1992).

All the foregoing relates to heterosexual activity. Kent-Baguley (1990)
noted that not surprisingly the majority of young lesbians and gays feel
marginalized, isolated and unhappy at school and are often feeling obliged
to pretend to participate in 'queer bashing' talk to avoid self-revelation:
gender orientation carries with it particular risks and challenges.

In this section, we have looked at normative and non-normative shifts in
adolescence and given some examples of influences from interpersonal
relations, from primary groups like the family and from wider society
which turn transitional 'tasks' into challenges or risks – or normative shifts
into non-normative ones.

Behavioural aspects

Such examples from the social environment lead us to problems adolescents might build up for themselves by engaging in behaviours that might
be a risk for their health or their psychosocial development.

DEFINING RISK-TAKING

At this stage, it is important to stress the distinction between problems from the social environment and actions taken by the adolescent (i.e. behavioural aspects). With regard to behavioural aspects we mean activities which are normally referred to in the literature as adolescent risk-taking. The concept of risk-taking is ill defined. Is it part of the psychological make up of youth – a thrill seeking stage in the developmental transition – or a necessary step to the acquisition of adult skills and self-esteem? Or is it a consequence of a societal or cultural urge by adults to marginalize youth because in their transitions from controllable child to controlled adult they are seen as troublesome and a threat to the stability of the community?

Before we even try to answer such questions, we need a clearer definition of what is meant by risk-taking. Hendry and Kloep (1996) offered the following three categories of risk-taking behaviour:

First, there are *thrill-seeking behaviours*. These are exciting or sensation-seeking behaviours which arouse and test the limits of one's capacities. Such behaviours can be observed in children as well as in adolescents and adults. Children, though, lack resources such as money or non-supervised time to engage in these behaviours. Most adults, on the other hand, know their limits reasonably well after years of experimentation and do not need to engage in so much risk-taking behaviour, beyond meeting new challenges. What distinguishes adolescent thrill-seeking behaviour is a combination of:

- *Frequency* – they engage in these activities more often than adults to test themselves and learn.
- *Resources* – they have more access than children to money and time.
- As a result of limited experience, they *lack judgement* of their own capacities and the extent of risk they are undertaking.

Next, there are *audience-controlled risk-taking behaviours*. In order to be accepted, to find place in a peer group and to establish a social position, people have to demonstrate certain qualities and abilities. Thus, it is obvious that most risky behaviours need an audience. This may be the reason why adults do not engage so often in demonstrative risk-taking: they have symbolic means of displaying their status in titles, expensive clothes or sports cars.

There is a special sub-category of audience-controlled risk-taking behaviour that young people engage in with the intention of impressing or provoking other people. These 'other people' can be peers, parents or adult authority figures. Adults restrict many adolescent behaviours and activities and defying norms is for many adolescents a step in the development of independence. Eager to break adults' dominance by refusing to obey their commands and prohibitions, adolescents may not always be able to discriminate which rules were made to suppress them and which were in their best interests. This can lead to risk-taking (i.e. *norm-breaking*) behaviours, reinforced by adults' negative reactions.

Third, there are risk-taking behaviours which are *irresponsible behaviours.* These are not performed because of the risk they imply, but in spite of it, in order to achieve other desired goals. Such irresponsible behaviours demonstrate the inability of individuals to see long-term consequences, or, if these are apparent, to be unwilling to abstain from them because of perceived short-term advantages. Examples of such behaviours are smoking and drinking, abstaining from exercise, or engaging in unprotected sex. It is obvious that behaviours such as getting drunk or failing to use condoms are not attractive because of the risks they imply, but are pursued for other reasons that are temporarily more important than these consequences (*see* Box 20.4). As Arnett (1998) has suggested, cultures must accept a trade-off in socialization between promoting individualism and self-expression on the one hand and in promoting social order on the other. Societies such as ours pay the price for promoting individualism and achievement by having higher rates of adolescent risk-taking in response to adult culture.

BOX 20.4 Types of risk-taking behaviours

THRILL-SEEKING:

Examples:	most alcohol and drug use, risky sports, some delinquent acts
Adolescence-specific:	partly
Prevention:	opportunities for less harmful 'thrilling' behaviour

AUDIENCE-CONTROLLED:

Examples:	vandalism, provocation, dangerous driving
Adolescence-specific:	predominantly
Prevention:	self-esteem enhancing measures, social skills

IRRESPONSIBLE:

Examples:	unprotected sex, drunk-driving, sunbathing
Adolescence-specific:	not at all
Prevention:	information, self-management training

Alcohol and other drugs

Hendry et al. (1993) showed that five per cent of 13–14-year-old Scots and nearly 50 per cent of 17–18-year-olds were frequent drinkers (once a week or more often), and Kloep (1998) found similar figures in Swedish rural youth (nine per cent of 13–14-year-olds and 45 per cent of 17–18-year-olds had been drunk at least once during the last four weeks). Looking at drug use: 15 per cent of young people in Stockholm (Barnombudsmannen, 1995), 18.5 per cent of English youth (Coleman, 1997), and 4 per cent of Swedish rural youth (Kloep, 1998) admit that they have tried Marihuana at least once. As Hurrelman and Losel (1990) have suggested, personal behaviours in adolescence can contribute to morbidity and mortality: smoking, drinking, using illegal drugs, precocious and unprotected sexual activity, little involvement in sports and exercise, delinquent activities 'indicate that the image of healthy adolescence is inaccurate'. Gofton (1990) examined the practices of young drinkers in the North of England, and found that their aim with drinking was principally 'to get out of it' at the weekend and to lose control. Courtship, or the search for 'talent' and sex were important possible outcomes for both young men and women, and discourses of spontaneity and 'getting carried away' were drawn on to excuse risky behaviours. The search for a 'high' and for 'magical' transformations from the reality of the ordinary work-a-day world was highly prized.

Assessing patterns of illicit drug use among youth is notoriously difficult, due to illegality and the low numbers seeking treatment from drug agencies. Traditional assumptions derive from beliefs that young people are manipulated by a range of factors – peer pressure, insecurity, the desire to be different, and so on. More recently, researchers have suggested that this perspective is overly simplistic and unhelpful in teasing out the dimensions of drug misuse (Coggans et al., 1993). Often this has been matched with explanations given by young drug users who do not see themselves as weak or manipulated but rather actively involved and purposeful in their assessment of the risks, costs and benefits of particular substances. For some young people the desire for 'flow', for a transformation of reality, for going beyond the day-to-day grind, or for belonging to a leisure subculture may be important and may be compared to some adults' rationalisations for use of alcohol. As in many contexts, the risks created by society for young drug users by criminalising them may be far beyond the risks of drug usage itself (e.g. Christie and Bruun, 1985).

The degree to which the adolescent's contact with alcohol and other drugs is a risk or challenge depends on which functions they fulfil for the individual, to what degree the young person is able to derive similar experiences by less harmful means, and by the young person's variety of skills around which they can make reasoned choices in leading a 'balanced' life. Where alternative behaviours are not possible and drugs are perceived as the only means of reaching desired gratification, they will be a serious risk factor, especially when the adolescent lacks self-control skills.

Given the necessary self-control and a wide range of behavioural alternatives (to create excitement in one's life and to gain the respect of one's friends), the possibilities of over-indulgence may be lessened. Then an occasional bottle of beer or wine, for example, is just another step in learning 'sensible' drinking and adding some pleasure to one's life. Yet:

> Among the young people we met, the non-drinker is the deviant and talk about sensible drinking is openly ridiculed. . . . (Young people)

tend to dismiss any possible health risks because they 'bounce back' so quickly and without any apparent ill-effects.

(Coffield, 1992: 2)

As Berndt (1998) has suggested, adolescents are influenced by their friends' attitudes and behaviours, but adolescents can also influence their friends: over time this mutual influence increases similarities.

What is being suggested in this section is that both legal and illegal drugs are used by young people (and adults) as transformation. Additionally, for adolescents, they can be symbolic (e.g. looking 'cool' or 'grown up'). As with other behaviours, the circumstances of learning to drink present young people with a risk or challenge within cultures where adult drinking is approved.

Delinquent behaviour

Delinquent behaviour is regarded by many as the most prominent form of adolescent risk-taking (Farrington, 1995). The majority of those convicted for car-theft, vandalism, shoplifting, theft and burglary are young men between 14 and 17 years. Yet, the media picture of the dangerous, criminal teenager is exaggerated and may be a sign of perceived hostility by adults towards adolescents (Davis, 1990). Together with the fact that it is not *many* young men who commit *some* crimes, but relatively *few* young men who commit *many* crimes (e.g. Farrington and West, 1993), this begins to suggest that juvenile delinquency may be less of a problem than is perceived by most adults.

To these views should be added a perspective that crime and delinquency in our society are in some measure the cost of certain kinds of social development. It has been argued that the predominant ethic of our society is acquisitiveness and desire for success. The values underlying juvenile delinquency may be far less deviant than commonly assumed. A number of theorists have emphasized the role of identity processes in determining delinquent behaviour (e.g. Emler and Reicher, 1995). The desire to identify with a peer group requires adherence to particular types of behaviour even when anti-social actions may result. Thus, delinquency can have different functions for different adolescents: for some, it may be socially controlled in helping them to attain status in the peer-group or to enable them to challenge adult society, for others it may be the thrill of sensation-seeking or a means of survival in a society stressing individual achievement and gain.

Sports

One activity which *is* socially approved and can provide self control, sensation-seeking and peer approval, yet is seldom regarded as true risk-taking behaviour, is sports participation. Yet it is a useful example of how almost any activity can be viewed as a challenge or a risk, depending on the psychosocial circumstances. If sport is experienced as the only way of gaining peer acceptance and/or adult approval, the adolescent may invest too much time and effort, to the neglect of other achievements like scholastic endeavour, or 'success' may be enhanced by cheating and illegal means, creating a 'hidden curriculum' in sports (e.g. Hendry, 1992). If sport is the *only* way of experiencing 'thrill', the young person may take higher risks, influenced by the 'negative' elements inherent in many sport activities: high skill demands, parental pressure, 'insensitive' coaches or physical education teachers focusing only on talented athletes (Hendry, 1992).

As Hendry et al. (1993) have noted, organized sports and physical activities are not particularly attractive to certain adolescent groups (e.g. young women) nor at certain times during adolescence (e.g. leaving school). Yet casual fun-oriented sports can be popular, especially with young women, when there is more focus on sociability, enjoyment and competence rather than on competition. Longer term goals related to cardiovascular health do not seem to be a potent impetus to participation. 'Competing' leisure and social interests and the influence of mass media in projecting 'desirable' adult role models may direct young people away from sports despite their initial positive attitudes.

Risk-taking behaviours in adolescence serve a variety of developmental functions which seem to be related to seeking 'escape', identification or 'fitting in' with peers and with seeking adult status. Within this we have outlined that different functions of risk-taking can be thrill-seeking, audience-controlled or irresponsible behaviours (*see* Box 20.4). Outwardly similar behaviours can be totally different functionally, while seemingly different behaviours can serve the same psychological purpose.

DISCUSSION POINT

Given the classification of risk-taking behaviours in Box 20.4: have you ever engaged in risk-taking as an adolescent? What kinds of risk-taking behaviours were these? Are you involved in similar risk-taking now? What do you consider to be the differences between adolescent and adult risk-taking?

Developing meta-skills

Throughout this chapter we have argued that one of the most important factors that turns risks into challenges and vice versa, is the competency level of young persons themselves. If they have a variety of skills with which to tackle psychosocial tasks, the danger of engaging in certain potentially risky behaviours such as unprotective sex, joy riding, excessive dieting diminishes. If the young person has self-management and self-control skills, they can cope with occasional 'irresponsible' acts and if the young person has experiences in successful problem-solving, new tasks will more likely be seen as a challenge rather than a risk. Thus, one thing adults could do to help young people's transitions to adulthood, would be to encourage and enable them to develop an appropriate repertoire of psychosocial life skills. This repertoire might encompass *basic living skills* for societies such as ours, like computing, reading, writing, personal economy, understanding directions and time-tables, domestic capacities and *interpersonal social skills*. Adolescents should also acquire a wide range of skills to ensure a satisfying *leisure-time and occupational life*. Fürntratt and Möller (1982) proposed the main goal of education as the creation of 'homo excercens': the acting person, rather than 'homo sapiens', the (passively) knowing person.

Clausen (1991) emphasized that a 'socialization for competence' should enhance knowledge, abilities and controls: knowing something about one's own intellectual abilities, social skills, about available options and how to maximize or expand them, with the ability to make accurate assessments of the actions and reactions of others. Most importantly, one should be able to apply these 'competences' to everyday living. What skills should these be? Some clues might be given by our earlier discussions of normative changes: assertiveness, negotiating, giving and taking feedback, listening, discussing, legitimate protesting, coping with injustice, hobby skills, educational skills, sexual skills and so on.

Yet, the key question in all this is: how can we empower youth to prepare for 'non-normative shifts', for all the unpredictable problems they may meet throughout life? As with learning strategies in schools (Nisbet and Shucksmith, 1984) we cannot teach every life skill. So we propose that we teach 'learning to learn' strategies, meta-skills which enable young people to learn whatever they need by organizing their learning themselves (e.g. Hendry, 1993; Kloep, 1984).

THE NEW 3 R'S?

If we can support and encourage learning processes and experiences which enhance self-esteem and self-efficacy, we may avoid the complex, fragmented transitions from youth to adulthood which are heavily influenced by systematic social inequalities. Hendry (1993), for instance, proposed a new emphasis in education – a new 3R's for pupils to learn: Responsibility, Reflection and Relationships. Here we elaborate on this model (*see* fig 20.1).

Responsibility essentially means an enhancement of the young person's self-agency. As shown in fig 20.1, these qualities demand the employment of 'meta-awareness': the ability to see a contingency between self-initiated behaviour and the consequences it produces. This ability is mainly acquired by successful experiences, by actually seeing that one's actions lead to the desired outcome. But it can also be trained by mental trial-and-error exercises.

Reflection implies the cognitive skills that allow the transfer of knowledge or behaviours from the context in which they were first learned to new or problematic situations. This involves the abilities of discrimination (i.e. seeing the differences between two contexts) and generalization (i.e. seeing the

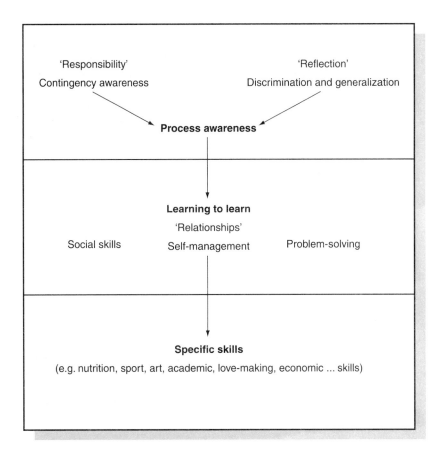

Figure 20.1 Meta-skills as the basis of development, the 'three R's'.

similarities between two contexts), notions that are related to the Piagetian concepts of accommodation and assimilation. Usually, pupils are not taught to take responsibility for monitoring the way or the contexts in which skills can be used. Thus adolescents have trouble applying them again in new situations on their own initiative. Nisbet and Shucksmith (1984) suggested a hierarchical (classroom) learning model which distinguishes task-oriented, *highly specific skills* from *learning strategies*. Strategies represent super-ordinate skills, generalized procedures or sequences of activities such as self-monitoring, reviewing and self-evaluating. Many of these strategies are meta-cognitive in character, that is they involve individuals in being aware of their own preferred learning and thinking styles, orientations to learning contexts and awareness of alternative strategies, thus placing them in a position of choice within a framework of 'learning to learn'. In our model, 'Responsibility' and 'Reflection' can thus be regarded as 'process-awareness' skills, or, as Fürntratt and Möller (1982) described them, as skills 'that support task-solution'.

'*Relationships*' in the original 3 R's- model (Hendry, 1993) referred to the competent youngster having an understanding of, and skills needed for, successful social relationships: thus it is the *application* of meta-skills to the broad social context of inter-personal encounters that is important in learning with, from and about others. We agree with Gardner's (1984) broad definition of intelligence as a set of 'appropriate skills' related to exploring and solving problem, not only in the cognitive domain, but also in psychomotor, artistic, musical, leisure and social spheres and in other aspects of life. Therefore, as fig 20.1 shows, we should add to social skills other 'learning to learn' strategies, like self-management (skills such as planning, time-management, setting objectives, self-reinforcement) and the skills of general problem-solving (e.g. operationalization of goals, information-seeking, decision-making).

Then, these meta-skills, with a high degree of process-awareness, should enhance the acquisition of more *specific skills* (*see* fig 20.1) needed for every-day life, in leisure and working-life, and provide young people with an arsenal of tools to meet whatever challenges and risks they are likely to find on their way to becoming an adult – and beyond.

DISCUSSION POINT

Which of the skills learned during your present studies are 'learning strategies'? To which contexts could they be transferred? (See the 'reflection' section)?What learning strategies do you consider to be important for adolescents?

Chapter summary

Within these two chapters, we have proposed that adolescents' psychosocial 'tasks' can be categorized at three levels: 'maturational shifts', 'normative shifts' and 'non-normative shifts', and that these 'tasks' present adolescents with both challenges and concomitant risks.

To some extent we can enable young people to acquire appropriate skills to successfully work through 'tasks' at the first two levels, since the onset of these is fairly predictable and sequential. However, 'non-normative shifts' are more problematic especially with rapidly changing 'globalized', technologically oriented societies which influence and are influenced by individuals within them.

We have argued that meta-skills can best enable adolescents to 'fit in' to the culture in which they are growing up. This also requires the use of meta-awareness (*see* fig 20.1) in understanding the social parameters of a particular culture, so that the individual adolescent knows when they 'drift' across value-boundaries into alternative – and perhaps illegal – ways of life. Additionally, they can empower adolescents to become more proactive in their own development and be potential 'societal agents for change'.

Opportunities need to be found for the development of an *individual* identity, the creation of *personal* social meanings and the acquisition of *self* – competency. These permit the flexibility and resilience necessary to cope with the more unpredictable 'non-normative shifts', cultural changes or social 'dislocations' in life.

Although we cannot predict future 'paradigm shifts' with any certainty, the development of meta-skills puts the individual in a stronger position to face challenges by having a range of choices from which to select a range of generalizable competences.

It has to be said that at present developmental psychologists have not begun to consider in any detail what these meta-skills, mechanisms and processes are which enhance (or hinder) young peoples' ability to meet challenges and risks. It is this area to which researchers should now turn their attention (*see also* Rutter, 1996b).

Thus adolescence differs from earlier years both in the nature of challenges (and risks) encountered and in the capacity of the young person to respond effectively to these. Adolescence is a particular phase of life stimulating and requiring adult-like patterns of coping behaviours in relation to various tasks, in creating opportunities to 'try out' strategies and to experiment in relatively supported contexts and hopefully in giving young persons the skills with which they can confidently start their journey through adult life.

Seminar questions

The chapter gives only a few examples of 'non-normative shifts' that might occur during the adolescent period. Try to find additional examples, taking account of ethnic, cultural and gender differences.

1. How can you determine if a risk-taking behaviour (e.g. speeding) for a certain individual is thrill-seeking, audience-controlled or irresponsible behaviour? Once you have determined this: what are the ways psychologists and youth professionals could provide preventions/treatments for adolescents?

2. In what ways do schools/universities need to change in order to teach and enable young people to build up meta-skills that are appropriate for their particular life-course development?

Further reading

Coleman, J. 1997. *Key data on adolescence*. London: Routledge. A rich array of facts and figures about various aspects of the life of British teenagers.

Haggerty, R.J., Sherrod, L.R., Garmezy, N., Rutter, M. (eds) 1996. *Stress, risk and resilience in children and adolescents*. Cambridge: Cambridge University Press. (This book deals with the complexity of the processes that impact on coping and resilience. It covers physical and mental disorders, protective factors, divorce, minority adolescence and explores the potentials for intervention.

Verhofstadt-Denève, L., Kienhorst, I., Braet, C. (eds) 1996. *Conflict and development in adolescence*. DSWO Press: Leiden. A recent and useful collection of European research on different aspects of adolescent development.

Personal growth and racialized identities

THE INEXTRICABLE LINKING OF THE PERSONAL AND THE SOCIAL IN EVERYDAY PRACTICES

ANN PHOENIX

Editors' preface

As we have already seen throughout this book, an understanding of the process of development involves drawing on many different perspectives. In this chapter Dr Ann Phoenix discusses the idea of personal growth (*see also* Chapter 13) and the way that it can be applied to the development of self-esteem and identity in the adolescent years (and beyond). This provides a platform for arguments about the process of personal growth in relation to the tensions present within multi-cultural societies which contain racisms. Running through this discussion is an emphasis on the way that personal growth is a constructive process which does not always involve consistent or static identities. In addition, emphasis is given to the argument that personal identity and the growth of this identity develop in a variety of ways and levels. These views are important in helping us to understand dynamic and non-deterministic ideas about development, as well as the way that the wider context of social experiences can influence ideas about our self and others (*see also* Chapter 18). The chapter also is important in illustrating the methodological difficulty of gaining information about other people's ideas of their self; the discussion makes it apparent that interviews and conversations can provide valuable insights and information about these processes.

Introduction

This chapter discusses the ways in which the racialized identities of children and young people have an impact on their 'personal growth'. Personal growth has frequently been treated as if it is an individualistic process. However, the chapter argues that it is necessarily a social process.

The late twentieth century may be said to be characterized by a concern with personal growth and identity. Numerous self-help manuals provide advice on how to improve relationships, understand oneself and others better and to achieve a variety of life goals through self-directed personal growth. Although much self-help material is aimed at adults, the concept of 'personal growth' and identity are, arguably, equally relevant to young people going through the period referred to as 'adolescence'. This is because many people consider that identity achievement is a central task of adolescence and that, at the heart of personal growth, lies identity and, hence, the associated notions of:

- Self-awareness
- Self-concept
- Self-esteem.

In addition, some theorists suggest that one of the central tasks of adolescence is to make choices which can have far-reaching consequences (e.g. about education, employment, accommodation and sexual partners). Indeed, the establishment and maintenance of relationships are central to young people's lives (Brown, 1998; Brown and Gilligan, 1992; Salmon, 1998) as well as to the notion of personal growth (Stevens, 1996). The necessity of making commitments to particular identities is argued to generate 'crises' for young people (Erikson, 1968). However, since certain kinds of crisis can stimulate personal growth (Gilligan, 1982; Skoe, 1998), young people may be well placed to make advances in personal growth.

This chapter argues that a consideration of young people's personal growth must include a consideration of the wider social context in which they live. The first part of the chapter discusses the concept of personal growth. It then considers the ways in which identities, self-concept and self-esteem (as the underpinnings of personal growth) have been theorized. The final part of the chapter uses the example of the *racialization* of adolescence (an area little studied in developmental psychology) to demonstrate the centrality of macrosocial issues to personal growth. It argues that personal growth in development can only be understood in the context of the complex, and multiple, ways in which people are positioned.

What is personal growth?

Personal growth is an important concept within the area known as humanistic psychology. In the 1940s, even before the term 'humanistic psychology' was coined, the psychotherapist Carl Rogers (1942, 1951, 1961) developed 'client-centred', ' person-centred' or 'self-actualization' theory and therapy. Rogers was dissatisfied with a focus on pathology in studies of personality and wanted psychology to be concerned with developing human potential. Rogers called this approach a 'third force' in psychology (to counterbalance the two major forces of the time – behaviourism and psychoanalysis). Maslow's (1968) concept of 'self-actualization' and his 'hierarchy of needs' which suggested that when material needs were met, humans had higher level needs for 'self-fulfilment' also made important contributions to this perspective.

Rogers believed that the ways in which our self-perceptions are structured are crucial to personal growth (*see* Box 21.1). His (1951, 1961) approach is humanistic in that it emphasizes an understanding of how people experience themselves and the world around them (i.e. it is phenomenological). It opposes what humanists see as the bleak pessimism of psychoanalysis or the social determinism and lack of self-will of behaviourism. It is an optimistic philosophy as it concerns and takes for granted, people's potential for growth.

BOX 21.1 Rogers' (1942, 1951, 1961) client-centred/person-centred theory

Rogers' theory was based on five basic tenets:

1. People want agreement between their experiences and their self-concept. Therefore, they behave in ways designed to maintain and confirm their perceptions of themselves.
2. Individuals deny and distort their experiences if events do not fit with their view of themselves. Rogers believed that psychological defences are not just the result of 'bad' experiences, but also are the results of a lack of fit between a *self-concept* and experiences. This leads to defensive behaviour which can be psychopathological. Such defensive behaviours include: *rationalization* (which, for example, allows a person to attribute their mistakes to something or someone else); *fantasizing* that the self and circumstances are more satisfactory than they are; and *projection* of, for example, frightening, evil, hateful thoughts onto someone else. Rationalization, fantasizing and projection facilitate *denial* (another defence).
3. Rogers considered that the fit (discrepancy or agreement) between *actual* and *ideal selves* was a measure of psychological adjustment.
4. People have a need for 'unconditional positive regard' in order to grow and be *'self-actualizing'*. So, if children misbehave, parents should make it clear that they disapprove of the behaviour, not the child and make their children feel that they will always be loved and approved of, no matter what they do – i.e. they do not have to earn their parents' love. However, Rogers argued that the process

> of development teaches us that love and acceptance by others is usually conditional.
> 5. Each individual has a basic striving towards self-actualization, growth and congruence between their self-concept and their experiences. Rogerian inspired psychotherapy aims to build on this striving.

Humanist psychology, inspired by Rogers' ideas, popularized notions that people's lives are not determined by their circumstances or upbringing. Instead, everybody is potentially capable of taking responsibility for enhancing their own lives (and their relationships) through emotional development. It is possible for everybody to exercise autonomy and choice in their lives and relationships by a commitment to openness, authenticity and growth. Rogers' ideas about personal growth have sometimes been linked with other theories of interpersonal relationships such as those of the psychologist Eric Berne (1968) and the psychoanalyst Erich Fromm (1968).

PROBLEMS AND POSSIBILITIES IN THEORIES OF 'PERSONAL GROWTH'

The above discussion may suggest that the concept of 'personal growth' is straightforward. However, it is far from precise since 'personal growth' can be said to encompass the whole of psychological development. The ways in which the concept is applied raise a number of problems:

1. The very term 'personal growth' suggests an individual process and, while the management of relationships is central to the notion of personal growth, these are often treated as if they are purely personal matters. Yet, personal growth can only occur within social contexts. Thus, the possibilities for personal growth differ, for example, in relation to 'race', ethnicity, gender, social class and physical capacities as well as the choices made by each person. Personal growth is, therefore, always circumscribed by social positioning. Notions of personal growth can lead to 'victim-blaming' if it is assumed that everybody has the same opportunities and hence responsibilities, for self-development (Allwood, 1996; Heenan, 1996).
2. Many formulations (even Rogers') imply that personal growth involves a search for the 'true' or 'real' self. However, recent theories suggest that, even though people generally feel themselves to be consistent, there is no unitary, 'real' self but, rather, multiple selves (see the discussion below).
3. The term 'personal growth' suggests that, as with physical growth, there is an accepted, unidirectional trajectory of development. This implies that all personal growth can, unequivocally, be considered good. Yet, there are no agreed standards and different people may have different (and contradictory) visions of what constitutes personal growth. This

imprecision is increased by dependence on other theoretical constructs which are themselves complex (e.g. self-concept; self-esteem and identities). Similar criticisms have been made of the notion of 'development' (e.g. Burman, 1994; Morss, 1996).

4. Humanism (the philosophy from which ideas about personal growth developed) has frequently been criticized for constructing an idealistic 'universal subject' which serves to maintain the political status quo in liberal democratic societies by, for example, addressing the interests and needs of those already powerful within society (often white, middle class men in northern societies) while claiming universal applicability (*see*, e.g., Henriques et al., 1984).

Such critiques have made some people consider that humanism and concepts such as 'personal growth' are outmoded (e.g. St Pierre, 1997). However, notions of personal growth can also fit with more recent, social understandings of development in the following ways:

1. The emphasis on relationships makes it possible to consider a range of social relationships (including 'race' and gender) and the ways in which they intersect with personal growth.
2. Since emphasis is put on changing how people understand themselves, the notion of personal growth fits with ideas that the self is *socially constructed*, rather than naturally occurring.
3. Although the use of the term 'growth' is problematic, it does allow human life to be viewed as a process, rather than as static.
4. The emphasis on personal growth as possible for everybody, regardless of the circumstances of their birth and origins is (as Rogers intended) optimistic in being non-determinist.

DISCUSSION POINT

Try to think of some concrete examples of what you would term 'personal growth'. How useful do you think the concept is in practice?

The building blocks of personal growth: self-concept, self-esteem and identities

Since personal growth requires conscious choice in order that emotional development can be enhanced, it necessarily demands a degree of self-awareness. Consequently, for personal growth to occur, people must have a concept of themselves (the *self-concept* or *self-image*). The development of the self-concept is a continuous process which developmental psychologists suggest has begun by the end of the first year, but which becomes pronounced during adolescence. Once children are able to think about themselves (i.e. they have a self-concept), theories of the self suggest that everyone evaluates themselves either positively or negatively (i.e. they develop *self-esteem*). It can be said that self-esteem provides the impetus for personal growth in that the need to think of themselves positively is likely to make people want to enhance their emotional development and relationships. The ways in which people reflect on their selves is central to the notion of *identities* (which is sometimes divided into 'social' and 'personal'). Thus, self-concept, self-esteem and identity are hierarchically organized, with identities incorporating self-esteem which, in turn, incorporates the self-concept. All three can be considered as the 'building blocks' of personal growth.

However, one of the difficulties in understanding personal growth is that the conditions thought essential to it can also be viewed as its products. Thus, for example, self-concept (and the self-awareness it requires), self-esteem and identity have to be in existence to facilitate personal growth. At the same time, shifts in the self-concept; self-esteem and identities are generally considered an important outcome of personal growth.

THE SOCIAL ROOTS OF SELF-AWARENESS AND THE SELF-CONCEPT

Self-awareness (sometimes referred to as reflexivity or subjectivity – i.e. the ability to think about ourselves as we think about other objects in the world) is a social process. This may seem strange because people often believe themselves to be private individuals who think independently and sometimes secretly, of themselves. However, even when we engage in private self-reflection, we are using standards and criteria that other people have used to evaluate us or that we know they use to evaluate other people. Regardless, therefore, of whether we accept or reject the judgements made by other people, self-awareness is a product of social interaction.

Box 21.2 uses two pieces of autobiographical writing to demonstrate the dramatic ways in which self-awareness and reflexivity can develop in adolescence and how it develops socially.

BOX 21.2 Autobiographical reflections on the development of self-awareness

Children ten years old wake up and find themselves here, discover themselves to have been here all along; is this sad? They wake like sleepwalkers, in full stride; they wake like people brought back from cardiac arrest or from drowning; *in medias res*, surrounded by familiar people and objects, equipped with a hundred skills . . .

I woke in bits, like all children, piecemeal over the years. I discovered myself and the world and forgot them and discovered them again / . . . /

> . . . I myself was both observer and observable and so a possible object of my own humming awareness.
>
> Dillard (1987, pp. 11–12)
>
> When I was 11 there were no bad films, just films that I didn't want to see, there was no bad food, just Brussels sprouts and cabbage and there were no bad books – everything I read was great. Then suddenly, I woke up in the morning and all that had changed. How could my sister not hear that David Cassidy was not in the same **class** as Black Sabbath? Why on **earth** would my English teacher think that *The History of Mr Polly* was better than *Ten Little Indians* by Agatha Christie?
>
> Hornby (1992, p. 29)

George Herbert Mead (1934) was one of the earliest thinkers who recognized that reality and the self are created in everyday symbolic activity (such as language). He argued that the individual is formed in society and that consciousness arises from social behaviour as well as being a function of evolutionary adaptation. According to Mead, the better we understand other people's attitudes, the better we can predict what they are likely to do. This, in turn, helps the development of self-awareness and, hence the concept of the self. This did not mean that self-awareness was determined by social interactions. Mead argued that, although people are affected by their circumstances, they can change and recreate their own environments.

These ideas connect with current research in developmental psychology. It has increasingly come to be accepted that success in dealings with other people requires empathy, anticipation and understanding of others, as well as the ability to see things from other people's points of view (i.e. *perspective-taking)*. The substantial body of work on children's theory of mind (the ability to attribute independent thought to oneself and others) and social cognition indicates the importance of such social understandings to self understandings and social relationships (*see* Chapter 12). Perspective-taking is thus a skill which, because it is central to the development of self-awareness and the self-concept, facilitates, and is facilitated by, personal growth. Both perspective-taking and symbolic understandings are relevant to self-awareness, in that people do not literally see themselves from other people's points of view. Instead, they actively (rather than passively) *infer* other people's views in terms of abstract qualities like sincerity, truthfulness etc. Once people are able to reflect on their selves, they develop a concept of the self.

Although 'the self' is often discussed in the singular, recent conceptualizations of selves (and of identities) consider selves to be relational and plural as well as socially constituted (e.g. Mama, 1995; Wetherell, 1996; Rattansi and Phoenix, 1998). Box 21.3 below discusses different psychological theories of identities.

BOX 21.3 Theories of identities

Psychological work has been very influential in producing theories of identity. There has, however, been a tendency to focus on 'personal identity'. 'Social identities' (e.g. gender, 'race' and social class) have received less attention. The individualizing of identity and the treatment of it as singular, partly results from the influence of Erik Erikson's (1968) ego identity approach, which built on the work of James (1890) and of Mead (1934). Erikson theorized identity as the main task of adolescence and as having the integrity and continuity necessary to keeping the internal and external worlds in line with each other. Following Erikson, many psychologists construct identity as an inner core (the self) which requires continuity if it is not to experience threat (Breakwell, 1986). There is a preoccupation, particularly in the USA, with identity as a marker of healthy psychological adjustment related to *self-esteem*. James Marcia (1980, 1994, 1998) built on Eriksonian theory to identify a process of identity development in which the highest level is individual *identity achievement*.

The notion of coherent, stable identities is, however, increasingly being challenged (e.g. Wetherell, 1996), even by those who are proponents of Erikson's approach, on the grounds that each person has *plural identities* (e.g. of gender, ethnicity, sexuality and adoption). *Social identity theory* initiated by Tajfel (1978) aimed to produce a genuinely social theory of identity (*see* Hogg and Abrams, 1988). Unfortunately, the continued emphasis on laboratory experiments as the major means of testing and contributing to social identity theory reduces its relevance to understandings of social relations and inequities in power relations outside the laboratory (but *see* Reicher (1987) and Kelly and Breinlinger (1996) for exceptions). Social identity theory has had little to say about the identities of young people.

Despite more complex theorizing of social identities, the notion of unitary, stable identities is one which is taken-for-granted in much psychological work on *'ethnic identity'*. Ethnic and *'racial' identity* are generally treated as if they possess clearly identifiable, static qualities, without which members of minority ethnic groups are likely to suffer damage. For members of minority ethnic groups (but not for the majority ethnic group) ethnic identity (measured on standardized tests) is assumed to be highly placed in a hierarchy of identities which must, essentially, be positive (Phinney and Rosenthal, 1992). Yet, ethnic identities are plural, so that there are a variety of ways in which they may be experienced and may intersect with other identities. They are also important to white, majority ethnic groups (*see*, for example, Cohen, 1988; Frankenberg, 1993).

If, as many theories suggest, identities are important to healthy psychological functioning in the social world, it is not surprising that the concept is considered crucial to personal growth.

The process of becoming self-aware, developing a concept of ourselves and 'achieving' identities, also entails the evaluation of our selves and our identities. Box 21.4 discusses self-esteem, which can be seen as the evaluative aspect of the self-concept and which, in relation to social identities of 'race' and gender, is more complicated than is frequently thought.

BOX 21.4 Self esteem: the impetus for personal growth?

William James (1890) suggested that self-esteem is the positive or negative regard in which people hold their various identities. One could be proud of one identity (e.g. as an employee), but not another (e.g. as a parent). The notion that we evaluate our identities positively or negatively has permeated the huge body of work on self-esteem. There is general agreement that self-esteem requires comparison of aspects of the self, either with other individuals, or with groups. For example, social identity theory (e.g. Tajfel, 1981) proposes a fundamental individual motivation for self-esteem. This leads individuals to attempt to maximize the differences between their own group (the in-group) and others (out-groups) on those dimensions that favour the in-group. The individual works to maintain a positive social identity in comparison with members of other groups. Such theories would suggest that the striving to maintain self esteem provides the impetus for personal growth.

The racialization of adolescence: personal growth and social positioning

Psychological considerations of personal growth often focus on a limited view of social experiences (in the form of interpersonal relationships). However, more complex theories of identities conceptualize multiple, social selves as normal. This section explores differences in young people's personal growth which relate to the intersection of racialization and their individual biographies. It, therefore, addresses some of the ways in which development is necessarily social. Although it focuses particularly on 'race', other social positionings (i.e. of social class and gender) are equally important and are partly discussed below.

Since the terminology of 'race' is often complex, Box 21.5 addresses the ways in which they are used here.

BOX 21.5: Some definitions of racialized terminology

Ethnicity refers to a collectivity or community which shares common attributes to do with cultural practices and shared history. *Ethnic group* is sometimes used as if it refers to people who are in less powerful positions within society and who are often subjected to racism. However, *ethnicity* applies to everybody.

Race is often used to mean no more than 'black' and 'white', which are treated as opposites. People designated as belonging to the same 'race' are constructed as belonging to the same human stock. 'Race' is seen as inherited and evident in biological or physical differences or in culture. Skin colour, physiognomy, culture or territory have all been used as markers of the boundaries between 'races' (Anthias, 1996). Hence, 'race' overlaps with ethnicity. The way in which 'race' (and ethnicity) is designated shifts over time. Many people put the term 'race' into quotation marks to signify that it is socially constructed, rather than about 'natural', biological or cultural difference. Others have argued that for these reasons, the term should not be used (e.g. Banton, 1977). Although 'race' is a social construct, the fact that it continues to be treated as socially significant means that it has real effects through racism. It should not, therefore, be dismissed (Donald and Rattansi, 1992). The term *racialization* (Omi and Winant, 1986) includes the idea that 'racial' meanings are not static but are social processes.

Essentialism involves treating an ethnic group or 'race' as if it has unchanging characteristics which will forever differentiate it from other groups (i.e. an essence). This exaggerates differences and understates similarities between groups.

Racisms take many different forms and can range from the grossest practices of genocide and slavery, through harassment and denial of social rights, to name calling. They involve exclusion and, frequently, inferiorization and so are intimately connected with power relations since one group has to have the power to exclude another from power and resources. They thus involve a range of economic and political practices. It is now generally accepted that racisms have to be conceptualized in the plural since there are different forms of racism (Brah, 1996). Similarly, experiences of racism are differentiated by social class, gender, sexuality and able-bodiedness.

DISCUSSION POINT

When do you think that children first become aware of 'race'? Try to think of examples, from your own or other people's experiences, of when the process of racialization begins.

THE RACIALIZATION OF YOUNG PEOPLE'S LIVES

It is not uncommon for those who work with young children to suggest that they are too innocent to notice colour differences and so are 'colour blind'. However, research in Britain, the USA and Canada generally finds that 'race' and ethnicity are often salient from two or three years of age. The trajectory mapped by such research is one in which consciousness of colour and ethnicity is evident in the early school years, increases through the middle school years (Milner, 1983; Boulton and Smith, 1992, 1996; Troyna and Hatcher, 1992) and continues in secondary school (Griffin, 1985; Mac an Ghaill, 1988; Macdonald et al., 1989; Tizard and Phoenix, 1993). Since children from white majority ethnic groups are not generally subjected to racisms, it is sometimes not recognized that they too are racialized. Yet, from the earliest studies of 'race' in childhood, it has been clear that white, majority children are, to some extent, aware of the power relations associated with 'race' and ethnicity in northern societies and of their place in a racialized hierarchy (Clark and Clark, 1939; 1947; Carrington and Short, 1989; Holmes, 1995; Phoenix, 1997). Given that processes of racialization involve people of all 'races' and ethnicities, it would be surprising if this were not the case and if white children's personal growth was not also affected by racialization.

Although research is available which demonstrates that preschool children are not 'colour blind', it tends to be limited to studies of children's racialized awareness, cognition or preferences established either experimentally or through ethnographic observation (e.g. Aboud, 1988; Holmes, 1995, Hirschfeld, 1997). However, in the 1997 Reith lectures, Patricia Williams, a black professor of law in the USA used an example which demonstrates not only the existence of racialized differences between children, but also how well-intentioned attempts to deny that such differences have meaning can isolate and pathologize those who experience racism. It indicates the different possibilities for personal growth that racialization entails for children and young people of different colours and ethnicities (*see* Box 21.6).

BOX 21.6 The racialization of early childhood

My son attends a small nursery school. Over the past year, three different teachers in his school assured me that he was colour blind. Resigned to this diagnosis, I took my son to an ophthalmologist who tested him and pronounced his vision perfect. I could not figure out what was going on until I began to listen carefully to what he was saying about colour.

As it turned out, my son did not misidentify colour. He resisted identifying colour at all. 'I don't know,' he would say when asked what colour the grass was; or, most peculiarly, 'It makes no difference.' This latter, this assertion of the greenness of grass making no difference, was such a precociously cynical retort, that I began to suspect some social complication in which he somehow was invested.

The long and the short of it was that the well-meaning teachers at his predominantly white school had valiantly and repeatedly assured their charges that 'colour makes no difference. It doesn't matter,' they told the children, 'whether you're black or white or red or green or blue.' Yet upon further investigation, the very reason that the teachers had felt it necessary to impart this lesson in the first place was that it *did* matter and in predictably cruel ways: some of the children had been fighting about whether black people could play 'good guys'.

My son's anxious response was redefined by his teachers as physical deficiency. This anxiety redefined as deficiency suggests to me that it may be illustrative of the way in which the liberal idea of colour-blindness is too often confounded. That is to say, the very notion of blindness about colour constitutes an ideological confusion at best and denial at its very worst. I recognize, certainly, that the teachers were inspired by a desire to make whole a division in the ranks. But there is much overlooked in the move to undo that which clearly and unfortunately matters just by labelling it that which 'makes no difference'. The dismissiveness, however unintentional, leaves those in this my son's position pulled between the clarity of their own experience and the often alienating terms in which they must seek social acceptance.

(Patricia J. Williams (1997:1) 'The Emperor's New Clothes.' Lecture 1 in the 1997 Reith Lectures **The Genealogy of Race: Towards a Theory of Grace**. BBC Radio 4.)

For all the children involved, this episode is likely to have produced a fragmentation of racialized identities. For some of the white children 'race' will probably not have become an issue of conscious note. If so, that lack of consciousness may well be akin to the way in which the white US women reported in Frankenberg's (1993) study asserted that they had never known any black people in their childhoods and were shocked to remember that, as children, they had nannies or household servants who were black. Even if that is the case, this incident may have had an impact on the white children's racialized identities. For, at the very least, they will have learned to take their whiteness for granted and to naturalize the power relations such a taking-for-granted entails. In that case, whiteness, while silent, would have allowed a confidence in racialized social positioning. On the other hand, for a few white children, the whole episode may have signalled a shift to egalitarian, if not anti-racist, positions. In both cases, the incident is likely to have contributed elements necessary to personal growth – quiet confidence in positioning or self-conscious positioning as egalitarian.

For the black boy involved (and perhaps for others if any other black children were present), the questioning of whether black boys and men are allowed to be superheroes, with the denial that this is important made black racialized identity a source of anxiety. It is likely to have invested 'race' with significance and marked blackness out as a marginal identity position. Both 'race' (overtly) and gender (implicitly) are important in this example – black girls are probably less likely to be interested in being 'good guys'. This incident may, thus, have produced contradictory identities and encouraged a greater awareness of the self as racialized. Thus, despite the pain undoubtedly caused to him because he is black, this episode may have facilitated personal growth, through crisis and through allowing enhanced emotional security to the white children involved. That very young children face such complex issues indicates how much racialization is engaged with during the whole process of development. Research done by Troyna and Hatcher on mainly white British primary schools provides a further example of this.

Troyna and Hatcher (1992) conducted an interview study (referred to by the authors as ethnographic) of three mainly white primary schools. The study considered how racism features in children's lives and the ways in which 'race' enters their social relationships. It is innovative in arguing that racist practices among children have to be understood within the context of children's cultures and that young children's lives are racialized in a rather different way from those of adults. Troyna and Hatcher focus on racialized name-calling as the major way in which racism manifests itself in mainly white British schools. Drawing on the work of Michael Billig, they argue that racist name calling among children is complex, that its meaning varies according to the circumstances and intentions of the children involved and that children draw on different themes to adults with regard to racism. In doing so, the study uses qualitative methods to go beyond simple identification of the fact that black and other minority children are often called racist names (e.g. Kelly and Cohn, 1988).

The idea of 'language as action' assumes that utterances are not a transparent (or opaque) reflection of reality but contain contradictory interpretive repertoires (Potter and Wetherell, 1987; Wetherell and Potter, 1992). For example, it is common for adults to take pains to avoid charges of racism and hence often to use the disclaiming double-hander, 'I'm not racist, but . . .'. This demonstrates either a conflict between the speaker's deeply held 'real' cognitive beliefs and their 'impression management' (van Dijk, 1987; 1993) or the competing ideological themes which people routinely express (Billig et al., 1988; Billig, 1991).

Although the adults described by Billig and by van Dijk are keen to empty racist content from their utterances, according to Troyna and Hatcher (1992), children sometimes include racist material in their talk with the interactional goal of deliberately hurting and hence scoring a point. This 'hot' name-calling occurs regardless of whether children hold racist or actively anti-racist thematic ideologies. Thus there are a number of possible interactions for children; racism can be held as a belief, but never acted on; anti-racism can be held as a belief while racist name-calling is sometimes employed or children can use interactional strategies which are consistent with their thematic ideologies (of racism or anti-racism).

Troyna and Hatcher's (1992) analysis raises fundamental epistemological questions. It implies that the reality of racism or anti-racism can be inferred from interviews. This both represents a *realist epistemology* (that it is always possible to find truth and reality if one digs deep enough) and a fixed notion of racialized identity (as racist or anti-racist). By way of contrast, discourse analysts and many identity theorists argue for constructivist epistemologies; a treatment of subjectivities as changing over time and from situation to situation and a construction of individual actions and discourses, rather than individuals, as racist or not (Potter and Wetherell, 1992; Essed, 1988; Hall, 1992, 1996; Burman and Parker, 1993).

The question of whether and how discourses about 'race' or the attitudes inferred by researchers have an effect on what young people actually do is far from simple. Billig et al. (1988) demonstrate some of the complexity of this issue in the following extract about a secondary school student:

> Immediately after the interview, conducted at school, this young supporter of a racist party, and of compelling all of 'them' to leave 'our country', was to be seen walking arm in arm with a young Asian girl, chatting and laughing in easy friendship (Billig et al., 1988, p. 106).

WHAT CONSTITUTES PERSONAL GROWTH?

Viewing identities as multiple and people as multiply positioned suggests that young people's racialized (and gendered) identities consist of creative borrowing and mixing of elements from a range of ethnic and gender positions (syncretism). Hewitt (1986), Jones (1988) and Back (1996) have all shown how some young white people (particularly young men) are involved in black musical cultures and linguistic forms – even if, for most, this constitutes a temporary period in their lives. At the same time, Weekes (1997) and Sewell (1997) have demonstrated how young black women and men can be resentful of this borrowing on the part of young white people and want to maintain distinctively black cultures – just as some of the young white people studied by Hewitt (1986; 1996) wanted to be as separate as possible from black people. Syncretism and racism can thus co-exist, not only between young people, but sometimes as contradictions within young people. This contributes to the complexity and contradictions of racialized and ethnicized identities. These complexities are evident in work which demonstrates the range of 'Asian women's' identities (Brah, 1996) and young black men's identities (Alexander, 1996). A related finding is that second generation Irish young people have differing orientations to Irishness which relate to whether or not they consider themselves to be Irish (Ullah, 1985; 1990). Similarly, studies of Asian young people (Hutnik, 1991), of 'second-generation Bangladeshi' young people (Ahmed, 1997) and of black, white and mixed-parentage young people (Tizard and Phoenix, 1993) find different identities in young people who are from the same ethnic groups.

Difference and diversity raise issues about what constitutes personal growth for young people and this in turn involves problems inherent in notions of personal growth which were discussed earlier. For if young people differ in terms of 'race' (as well as gender, social class etc.) and those within racialized groupings have a range of different identities, there can be no single way in which personal growth would make sense for all. An example of research by Hewitt (1996) serves to make these dilemmas more concrete.

Hewitt studied young, working class, white Londoners living on a disadvantaged housing estate renowned for its reproduction of racist discourses and racist attacks. The young white people he talked to asserted their disadvantage in ways which made clear the inextricable linking of 'race' and class position in the construction of their identities. They justified their anti-black discourses by blaming black people for white people's poverty as in the following account from a 15-year-old young woman:

> 'I don't like blacks full stop, right. We brought 'em over 'ere for slaves but now they're getting all the money and taking it all off out, our money and then we can't pay for our water, tax or anyfing, [sic] so I think they should go back to their own country.' (Hewitt, 1996, p. 16)

Given current 'norms against prejudice' (Billig, 1991), few, if any psychologists, would consider such sentiments indicative of personal growth. Nonetheless, discourses such as this require serious attention if we are to understand what constitutes personal growth for young white people racialized in Britain. The contexts in which such discourses flourish are ones in which white working class young people find themselves disadvantaged educationally and with regard to employment, housing and other socioeconomic resources. In these situations, it has commonly been found that working class, white young people express resentment of black and Asian people. Thus, the report of the inquiry into the murder of an Asian boy by a white boy in a Manchester school argued that a major problem within the school was that the white, working class boys felt that they had no ethnic identity while Asian young people had theirs buttressed through multicultural education. The tensions that resulted were both unpleasant and dangerous (Macdonald et al., 1989). In a similar way, Cohen (1997) argues that the young white working class people he studied associated the deterioration of their circumstances and neighbourhoods with the black people who had increasingly come to live in the same neighbourhoods.

If we look closely at what the young woman quoted above actually says, it is possible to speculate about the ways in which racialized identities constitute resources which allow personal growth for her. She says, *'I don't like blacks full stop, right'*, thereby establishing herself as someone who is discerning and who has no need to like everybody. Her next phrase then positions her not as a lone individual, but as a member of a community which is superior to black people – *'We brought 'em over 'ere for slaves'* – before arguing that black people are exploitive of white people, *'but now they're getting all the money and taking it all off out, our money'*. This projects onto black people direct responsibility for the impoverished situation 'we' are experiencing – *'and then we can't pay for our water, tax or anyfing,* [sic]'. This then rationalizes and justifies her already avowed dislike of black people and makes reasonable her proposed solution, *'so I think they should go back to their own country.'*

Although this young woman's argument may appear simplistic and easily able to be deconstructed by reference to 'facts' and illogicalities, this short statement does a great deal of work in relation to the young woman's personal growth:

1. It enables her to maintain her self-respect as better than black people and as not responsible for the difficult circumstances in which she lives.
2. At the same time, it both constructs an enemy (black people) and a solution to the problems she identifies *'they should go back to their own country.'* This, arguably, allows her one way of dealing emotionally with her situation and of understanding, and valuing, her (racialized) place in the world (historically and currently).
3. Although her construction of the problem and its solution in racialized terms is unlikely to provide practicable long-term solutions, it does provide one way of contending with her situation and feeling that she has some control over it.
4. Since it supposedly proscribes friendships with black people, it also provides her with some guidelines for the initiation and conduct of relationships.

It may be, therefore, that racisms, as part of some white, working class young people's racialized identities allows possibilities for personal growth. As Hewitt (1996) argues, it is counterproductive to assume that rational argument can counter racist ideas. Instead, it is important to take seriously such discourses in order to understand the psychological work they are doing. The espousing of racist ideas may well allow white, working class young people one way out of the dilemma of how to achieve congruence between their positive views of themselves (self-esteem) and the negative socio-economic circumstances in which they live. Her 'doing "race"' is thus crucial to her 'identity projects'. Thus, while the above example may seem counterintuitive in relation to personal growth, it demonstrates an important feature of living in racialized societies for young people: learning to live with contradiction and complexity.

DISCUSSION POINT

Try to think of an example of a time when you became conscious of racialization. What possibilities for personal growth do you think were presented?

LEARNING TO DEAL WITH COMPLEXITIES: RACIALIZATION AS PERSONAL GROWTH IN PROCESS

Although many studies have searched for problems in the self-esteem and social identities of Black children as a result of racism, few find real differences between the self-esteem of black and of white young people (Phinney and Rosenthal, 1992; Tizard and Phoenix, 1993). Instead, studies repeatedly find that black and Asian young people manage the complexities of racialization and racisms – demonstrating the personal growth they have achieved – despite racisms. Hutnik (1991), for example, illustrates the ways in which minority ethnic identities are in reality flexible and diverse. She found that some young people of South Asian origin living in Great Britain simultaneously considered themselves to be both Indian and British, whereas others thought of themselves as Indian and yet others as British. Such self-categorizations did not fix young people in specific cultural practices. Thus, for example, young people who rejected the British label in favour of being only Indian, sometimes engaged in exactly the same cultural practices as those who rejected the label 'Indian' and thought of themselves as only British. The fact that there is no essential 'race'/ethnic identity means that knowing how young people label themselves does not indicate how they live their lives or what are their cultural practices. This was also demonstrated in a study of black, white and mixed-parentage young Londoners (Tizard and Phoenix, 1993).

Hutnik's (1991) findings are echoed by those of Modood et al. (1994) who found that young British people of Caribbean and Asian origin retained aspects of cultural practices which allowed them to feel Caribbean or Asian while expressing those practices as British Caribbeans or Asians. The study of Modood et al. (1994) demonstrated the situational specificity and active agency of the performance of identities, in that participants in the study said that they would acknowledge some identifications in some contexts, but not others. The study found evidence for the dynamic nature of racialized identities in that it found that 'hybrid' identities were emerging. Modood et al. (1994) concluded that the complexity of racialized identities amongst Britain's ethnic minorities did not fit with notions of 'culture-clash' which have commonly been applied to young black and Asian youth.

Alexander's (1996) study also demonstrates this diversity in an ethnographic account of the construction and negotiation of identities of 'race', class and gender. As an Asian woman, Alexander, 'hung out' with 'Black youth' aged 18–24, who were predominantly young men. Her account describes the ways in which young black men and women developed a variety of ways of life despite the prevalence of racism – a finding echoed in Sewell's (1997) ethnographic study of 'black masculinities' in London schools. Like Sewell, Back (1996) found that young people occupied different subject positions in different contexts. Racialization therefore, varied between settings and was different for different groups. Syncretism and racism both operated on the same site in unpredictable ways which contributed to the kaleidoscopic nature of racialized identities.

The conclusion to be drawn from these studies is that mostly, young black and Asian people are not crushed by racisms and processes of racialization, but actively steer different and complex paths through identities, self-awareness and relationships. Racialization may well force them into understanding and anticipating the actions of others and reflecting on themselves as different in different situations (*see*, for example, Westwood, 1990). Racisms generally restrict, rather than allow, autonomy and choice in relationships. However, many young people from minority ethnic groups enhance the choices they can make by working out the identity positions that best suit them and by constantly developing both self-awareness and awareness of others. Their negotiation of racisms and racialized identities may both provide the building blocks for personal growth and result from the personal growth impelled by racialization. White young people can also achieve personal growth through racialization – either through racist discourses (as discussed in the previous section) or through the development of anti-racist understandings (Phoenix, 1998). For both white and black young people, then, engagement with racialization may serve to enhance self-esteem.

Chapter summary

Personal growth is a psychological concept which has become increasingly popular since the development of Rogerian client-centred therapy in the 1940s. For personal growth to occur, the self-concept, self-esteem and identities must already be established but, in turn, personal growth alters people's conceptions of their own selves.

A major problem with the application of the concept of personal growth is often that it tends to limit social processes to the interpersonal. However, recent theories make clear that social positioning is central to understandings of identities and, hence, to personal growth. This chapter has used the example of the racialization of childhood and adolescence to argue that macrosocial issues (in this case racialization) are closely linked to social identities and are, therefore, central to considerations of personal growth. The chapter argues that, although it may seem counterintuitive, racisms and racialization allow possibilities for personal growth to children and young people from both minority and majority ethnic groups.

One way in which many young people from minority ethnic groups achieve personal growth is through having to engage with the pains and difficulties produced by racisms. Far from lacking self-esteem as a result (as often expected in psychological work on 'ethnic identities'), they learn to deal with complex social relationships and racialized identities. White young people can also achieve personal growth through processes of racialization. In some cases, this involves using racist discourses to bolster self-esteem while in others, anti-racist discourses serve the same function. In all cases, however, racialization provides young people with social resources to be drawn on in everyday practices (which necessarily involve racialization, regardless of whether or not this is conscious). As a result, racialization can, sometimes in surprising ways, produce personal growth. That this is possible highlights the importance, for developmental psychology, of analyses of 'race', gender, social class etc. and their intersections with processes, such as personal growth, which are often treated as individual or interpersonal. Theories which treat identities as multiple, complex, dynamic and contradictory are potentially useful in such analyses.

Personal growth has frequently been treated as if it is an individualistic process which is dependent on the development of individualistic 'personal identities'. However, racialized identities and racisms have an impact on 'personal growth' and, hence, allow different possibilities for children and young people who are racialized in different ways.

Seminar questions

1. Consider the concept of 'personal growth'. Discuss the difference between its conceptualization as a property of individuals who are personally responsible for their personal growth, compared with thinking of it as resulting from complex social processes.
2. The fact that personal growth can result from the reproduction of racist discourses raises potentially thorny ethical questions. Do you think that it matters how people achieve personal growth or is all personal growth to be encouraged? Why?/Why not?
3. Discuss the ways in which social processes of racialization produce different possibilities for personal growth depending on, for example, whether children are black or white, girls or boys.

Further reading

Essed, P. 1991. *Understanding everyday racism*. London: Sage.
Philomena Essed analyses the ways in which racism is produced and reproduced through the minutiae of everyday interactions. It is unusual in focusing on the everyday experiences of black women and the diverse ways in which different black women interpret experiences, depending on their theoretical knowledge, past experiences and geographical situation.
Stevens, R. (Ed.) 1996. *Understanding the self*. London: Sage.
This accessible text provides five different theoretical perspectives on how to understand the psychological concept of 'the self'. These are: biological; cognitive experimental; experiential; social constructionist and psychodynamic.
Wetherell, M. (Ed.) 1996. *Identities, groups and social issues*. London: Sage.
This Open University edited collection presents overviews of social psychological research on groups; the development of social identity; intergroup relations and making sense of social life.

References

Abbeduto, L., Rosenberg, S. 1980. The communicative competence of mentally retarded adults. *Applied Psycholinguistics* **1**, 405–26.

Abbeduto, L., Rosenberg, S. 1992. The development of linguistic communication in persons with mental retardation. In Warren, S., Reichle, J. (eds) *Perspectives on communication and intervention.* Baltimore, MD: Brookes, pp. 331–59.

Aboud, F. 1988. *Children and prejudice.* Oxford: Blackwell.

Acredolo, L.P. 1978. Development of spatial orientation in infancy. *Developmental Psychology* **14**, 224–34.

Adams, M.J. 1990. *Beginning to read: thinking and learning about print.* Cambridge, MA: MIT Press.

Ahmad, Y., Smith, P.K. 1989. Bully/victim problems among schoolchildren. Poster presented at the Conference of the Developmental section of the BPS, Guildford, September.

Ahmad, Y., Smith, P.K. 1990. Behavioural measures: bullying in schools. *Newsletter of the Association for Child Psychology and Psychiatry* **12**, 26–7.

Ahmed, B. 1997. *The identity of second generation Bangladeshis.* Unpublished Ph.D thesis: Department of Psychology, Sheffield University.

Ainsworth, M.D.S. 1967. *Infancy in Uganda: infant care and the growth of love.* Baltimore, MD: John Hopkins University Press.

Ainsworth, M.D.S. 1973. Development of infant-mother attachment. In Caldwell, B., Ricciuti, H. (eds) *Review of child development research.* Chicago, IL: University of Chicago Press.

Ainsworth, M.D.S., Bell, S.M. 1977. Infant crying and maternal responsiveness: a rejoinder to Gewirtz and Boyd. *Child Development* **48**, 1208–16.

Ainsworth, M.D.S., Bell, S.M., Stayton, D.J. 1974. Infant–mother attachment and social development: 'socialisation' as a product of reciprocal responsiveness to signals. In Richards, M.P.M. (ed.) *The integration of the child into a social world.* Cambridge: Cambridge University Press, 99–135.

Ainsworth, M.D.S., Blehar, M.C., Waters, E., Wall, S. 1978. *Patterns of attachment.* Hillsdale, NJ: Lawrence Erlbaum.

Ainsworth, M.D.S., Wittig, B.A. 1969. Attachment and exploratory behaviour of one year olds in a strange situation. In Foss, B.M. (ed.) *Determinants of infant behaviour.* London: Methuen, 113–36.

Alexander, C. 1996. *The art of being Black.* Oxford: Oxford University Press.

Allatt, P. 1996. Conceptualising parenting from the standpoint of children: relationship and transition in the life course. In Brannen, J. and O'Brien,

M. (eds) *Children in families: research and policy*. London. Falmer Press, pp 130–44.

Allwood, R. 1996. 'I have depression, don't I?': Discourses of help and self-help books. In Burman, E., Aitken, G., Alldred, P., Allwood, R., Billington, T., Goldberg, B., Gordo Lopez, A.J., Heenan, C., Marks, D., Warner, S. *Psychology Discourse Practice: From regulation to resistance*. London: Taylor and Francis, pp. 17–36.

Alsaker, F.D., Olweus, D. 1993. Global self-evaluations and perceived instability of self in early adolescence: a cohort longitudinal study. *Scandinavian Journal of Psychology* **34**, 47–63.

American Psychiatric Association 1994. *Diagnostic and statistical manual of mental disorders* (fourth edition) (DSM-IV). Washington, DC: American Psychiatric Association.

American Psychiatric Association. 1980. *Diagnostic and Statistical Manual of Mental Disorders* (third edition): DSM III. Washington, DC: American Psychiatric Association.

Andersen, E., Dunlea, A., and Kekelis, L. 1993. The impact of input: language acquisition in the visually impaired. *First Language* **13**, 23–49.

Anderson, J.R. 1983. *The architecture of cognition*. Cambridge, MA: Harvard University Press.

Anderson, J.W. 1972. Attachment behaviour out of doors. In Blurton-Jones, N. (ed.) *Ethological studies of child behaviour*. Cambridge: Cambridge University Press, 199–215.

Anderson, M. 1992. *Intelligence and development: a cognitive theory*. Oxford.

Anderson, M. 1998. Individual differences in intelligence. In Kirsner, K. Maybury, M. Speelman, C. O'Brien-Malone, A. MacLeod, C. Anderson, M. (eds) *Implicit and explicit mental processes*. Hillsdale, NJ: Lawrence Erlbaum.

Anderson, M., Miller, K.L. 1998. Modularity, mental retardation, and speed of processing. *Developmental Science* **1**, 239–45.

Anderson, M., O'Connor, N., and Hermelin, B. In press. A specific calculating ability. *Intelligence*.

Andersson, B.-E. 1995. Does school stimulate young people's development? In Jonsson, B. (ed.) *Studies on youth and schooling in Sweden*. Stockholm: Stockholm Institute of Education Press, 91–113.

Anisfeld, E., Casper, V., Nozyce, M., Cunningham, N. 1990. Does infant carrying promote attachment? An experimental study of the effects of increased physical contact on the development of attachment. *Child Development* **61**, 1617–27.

Anthias, F. 1996. Rethinking social divisions: or what's so important about gender, ethnicity, 'race' and social class? Inaugural lecture. 15 February, Greenwich: University of Greenwich.

Apple, M. 1979. *Ideology and curriculum*. London: Routledge & Kegan Paul.

Arnett, J. 1998. The young and the reckless. In Messer, D., Dockrell, J. (eds) *Developmental psychology: a reader*. London: Arnold,

Arnheim, R. 1974. *Art and visual perception: a psychology of the creative eye. The new version*. Berkeley and Los Angeles: University of California Press.

Arnold, R., Yule, W., Martin, N. 1985. The psychological characteristics of infantile hypercalcaemia: a preliminary investigation. *Developmental Medicine and Child Neurology* **27**, 49–59.

Arts, W.; Hermkens, P., VanWijck, P. 1995. Anomie, distributive injustice and dissatisfaction with material well-being in Eastern Europe. *International Journal of Comparative Sociology*, 36: 1–16.

Asperger, H. 1944 'Die autistischen Psychopathen im Kindesalter', *Archiv fur Psychiatrie und Nervenkrankheiten* 117, 76–136. Translated by U. Frith in U. Frith (Ed). 1991 *Autism and Asperger syndrome*. Cambridge: Cambridge University Press, 37–92.

Atkinson, D., Ward, L. 1987. Friends and neighbours: relationships and opportunities in the community for people with a mental handicap. In Malin, N. (Ed.) *Reassessing community care*. London: Croom Helm.

Azmi, S., Hatton, C., Emerson, E., Caine, A. 1997. Listening to adolescents and adults with intellectual disabilities from South Asian communities. *Journal of Applied Research in Intellectual Disabilities* **10**, 250–63.

Back, L. 1996. *New ethnicities and urban culture: racisms and multiculture in young lives*. London: UCL Press.

Bailey, A., Le Couteur, A., Gottesman, I.I., Bolton, P., Simonoff, E., Yuzda, E., et al. 1995. Autism as a strongly genetic disorder: evidence from a British twin study. *Psychological Medicine* **25**, 63–77.

Bailey, A., LeCouteur, A., Gottesman, L., Bolton, P., Simonoff, E., Yuzda, E., Rutter, M. 1995. Autism as a strongly genetic disorder: evidence from a British twin study. *Psychological Medicine* **25**, 63–77.

Baillargeon, R. 1986. Representing the existence and the location of hidden objects: object permanence in 6- and 8-month-old infants. *Cognition* **23**, 21–41.

Baillargeon, R. 1987a. Object permanence in 3.5- and 4.5-month-old infants. *Developmental Psychology* **23**, 655–64.

Baillargeon, R. 1987b. Young infants' reasoning about the physical and spatial properties of a hidden object. *Cognitive Development* **2**, 179–200.

Baillargeon, R., DeVos, J. 1991. Object permanence in young infants: further evidence. *Child Development* **62**, 1227–46.

Baillargeon, R., Needham, A., DeVos, J. 1992. The development of young infants' intuitions about support. *Early Development and Parenting* **1**, 69-78

Baillargeon, R., Spelke, E.S., Wasserman, S. 1985. Object permanence in five-month-old infants. *Cognition* **20**, 191–208.

Baird, S.M., Mayfield, P., Baker, P. 1997. Mothers' interpretations of the behaviour of their infants with visual and other impairments during interactions. *Journal of Visual Impairment and Blindness* **91**, 467–83.

Balough, R.D., Porter, R.H. 1986. Olfactory preferences resulting from mere exposure in human neonates. *Infant Behaviour and Development* **9**, 395–401.

Balding, J. 1986. The Mayfly study. (HEA) University of Exeter. School of Education.

Baltes, P.B., Staudinger, U.M., Lindenberger, U. 1999. Lifespan psychology: theory and application to intellectual functioning. *Annual Review of Psychology* **50**, 471–507.

Bancroft, J. 1990. The impact of socio-cultural influences on adolescent sexual development. In Bancroft, J., Reinisch, J.M. (eds) *Adolescence and puberty*. Oxford: Oxford University Press.

Band, E.B., and Weisz, J.R. 1988. How to feel better when it feels bad: children's perspectives on coping with everyday stress. *Developmental Psychology* **24**, 247–53.

Bandura, A. 1973. *Aggression: a social learning analysis*. Englewood Cliffs, NJ: Prentice-Hall.

Bandura, A. 1989. Social cognitive theory. In Vasta, R. (ed.) *Six theories of child development*. Greenwich: JAI Press.

Bandura, Ross, Ross 1965. Imitation of film-mediated aggressive models. *Journal of abnormal and social psychology* **66**, 3–11.

Bannon, L.J. 1986. Helping users help each other. In Norman, D.A., Draper, S. (eds) *User centred system design*. Hillsdale, NJ: Lawrence Earlbaum Associates.

Banton, M. 1977. *The idea of race*. London: Tavistock.

Baran, S.J., Chase, L.J., Courtright, J.A. 1979. Television drama as a facilitator of prosocial behavior: 'The Waltons'. *Journal of Broadcasting* **23**, 277–84.

Barker, M. 1989. *Comics: ideology, power and the critics*. Manchester: Manchester University Press.

Barnes, S., Gutfreund, M., Satterly, D., Wells, D. 1983. Characteristics of adult speech which predict children's language development. *Journal of Child Language* **10**, 65–84.

Barnombudsmannen 1995. *Upp till . . . 18*. Halmstad: Statistiska Centralbyrån.

Baron-Cohen, S. 1995. *Mindblindness: an essay on autism and theory of mind*. Cambridge, MA: MIT Press.

Baron-Cohen, S. Leslie, A.M., Frith, U. 1985. Does the autistic child have a 'theory of mind'? *Cognition* **21**, 37–46.

Baron-Cohen, S., 1995. *Mindblindness: an essay on autism and theory of mind*. Cambridge, MA: MIT Press.

Baron-Cohen, S., Cox, A., Baird, G., Swettenham, J., Nightingale, N., Morgan, K., Drew, A., Charman, T. 1996. Psychological markers in the detection of autism in a large population. *British Journal of Psychiatry* **168**, 158–63.

Barraga, N. 1976. *Visual handicaps and learning: a developmental approach*. Belmont, CA: Wadsworth.

Barrett, M. 1995. Early lexical development. In Fletcher, P., MacWhinney, B. (eds) *Handbook of child language*. Oxford: Blackwell, 362–92.

Bartley, A.J., Jones, D.W., Weinberger, D.R. 1997. Genetic variability of human brain size and cortical gyral patterns. *Brain* **120**, 257–69.

Barton, M.E., Tomasello, M. 1994. The rest of the family: The role of fathers and siblings in early language development. In Gallaway, C., Richards, B.J. (eds) *Input and interaction in language acquisition*. Cambridge: Cambridge University Press, pp 109–34.

Bates, E., Bretherton I., Snyder, L. 1988. *From First Words to Grammar:*

individual differences and dissociable mechanisms. Cambridge: Cambridge University Press.

Bates, E., Marchman, V., Thal, D., Fenson, L., Dale, P., Reznick J.S., Reilly, J., Hartung, J. 1994. Developmental and stylistic variation in the composition of early vocabulary. *Journal of Child Language* **21**, 85–124.

Bates, E., O'Connell, B., Shore, C. 1987. Language and communication in infancy. In Osofsky, J. (Ed.) *Handbook of infant development* (second edition) New York: Wiley, 126–45.

Batsche, G.M., Knoff, H.M. 1994. Bullies and their victims: understanding a pervasive problem in the schools. *School Psychology Review*, **23**, 165–74.

Baumrind, D. 1967. Child care practices anteceding three patterns of preschool behaviour. *Genetic Psychology Monographs* **75**, 43–88.

Baumrind, D. 1973. The development of instrumental competence through socialization. In Pick, A.E. (ed.) *Minnesota symposium on child psychology*. Minneapolis: University of Minnesota Press, pp 3–46.

Bayliss, P. 1992. Language and integration: an investigation of students with severe learning difficulties in integrated and segregated settings. Unpublished PhD thesis, University of Bristol.

Beck, I.L., Perfetti, C.A., McKeown, M.G. 1982. Effects of long term vocabulary instruction on lexical access and reading comprehension. *Journal of Educational Psychology* **74,** 506–21.

Becker-Stoll, F., Fremmer-Bombik, E., Wartner, U., Grossmann, K.E. 1996. Attachment at age one, six and sixteen: A longitudinal study. Poster presented at the fourteenth Biennial ISSBD conference, Quebec City, Canada, August.

Behrend, D.A. 1990. Constraints and development: a reply to Nelson (1988). *Cognitive Development* **5**, 313–30.

Bell, M.A., Fox, N.A. 1992. The relations between frontal brain electrical activity and cognitive development during infancy. *Child Development* **63**, 1142–63.

Bell, R.Q. 1968. A reinterpretation of the direction of effects in socialization. *Psychological Review* **75**, 81–95.

Bell, S.M. 1970. The development of the concept of objects as related to infant–mother attachment. *Child Development* **41**, 291–311.

Bellugi, U., Bihrle, A., Jernigan, T., Trauner, D., Doherty, S. 1990. Neuropsychological, neurological and neuroanatomical profile of Williams' syndrome. *American Journal of Medical Genetics Supplement* **6**, 115–25.

Bellugi, U. Bihrle, A., Neville, H., Jernigan, T.L., Doherty, S. 1992. Language cognition and brain organization in a neurodevelopmental disorder. In Gunnar, M., Nelson, C. (eds) *Developmental behavioural neuroscience*. Hillsdale, NJ: Erlbaum.

Bellugi, U., Marks, S., Bihrle, A., Sabo, H. 1993. Dissociation between language and cognitive functions in Williams syndrome. In Bishop, D., Mogford, K. (eds) *Language development in exceptional circumstances*. Hove: Lawrence Erlbaum Associates, 132–49.

Bellugi, U., Wang, P., Jerrigan, T. 1994. Williams' syndrome: an unusual neuropsychological profile. In Broman, S.H., Grafman, J. (eds) *Atypical cognitive deficits in developmental disorders*. Hillsdale, NJ: Erlbaum.

Belsky, J., Rovine, M. 1987. Temperament and attachment security in the strange situation: an empirical rapprochement. *Child Development* **58**, 787–95.

Bench, R.J. 1992. *Communication skills in hearing impaired children*. London: Whurr.

Benjamin, J., Li, L., Patterson, C., Greenberg, B.D., Murphy, D.L., Hamer, D.H. 1996. Population and familial association between the D4 dopamine receptor gene and measures of novelty seeking. *Nature Genetics* **12**, 81–4.

Bennett, S.N. 1991. Cooperative learning in classrooms: Processes and outcomes. *Journal of Child Psychology and Psychiatry* **32**, 581–94.

Bergling, K. 1981. *Moral development. The validity of Kohlberg's theory*. Stockholm: Almquist & Wiksell International.

Berko, J. 1958. The child's learning of English morphology. *Word* **14**, 150–77.

Berkowitz, L. 1984. Some effects of thoughts on anti- and prosocial influences of media events: a cognitive-neoassociation analysis. *Psychological Bulletin* **95**, 410–27.

Berndt, T. J. (1998) Friendship and friends' influence in adolescence. In Messer, D., Dockrell, J. (eds.) *Developmental psychology: A reader*. Arnold: London.

Berne, E. 1968. *Games people play*. Harmondsworth: Penguin.

Bertenthal, B.I., Proffitt, D.R., Kramer, S.J., Spetner, N.B. 1987. Infants' encoding of kinetic displays varying in relative coherence. *Developmental Psychology* **23**, 171–78.

Bertrand, J., Mervis, C.B. 1997. Drawing by children with Williams' syndrome: a developmental perspective. *Developmental Neuropsychology* **13**, 41–67.

Besag, 1989. *Bullies and victims at school*. Milton Keynes: Open University Press.

Besevegis, E., Giannitsas, N. 1996. Parent–adolescent relations and conflicts as perceived by adolescents. In Verhofstadt-Denève, L., Kienhorst, I., Braet, C. (eds) *Conflict and development in adolescence*. Leiden: DSWO Press:, 93–116.

Besner, D., Twilley, L., McCann, R.S., Seergobin, K. 1990. On the connection between connectionism and data: are a few words necessary? *Psychological Review* **97**, 432–46.

Beveridge, M., Hurrell, P. 1980. Teachers' responses to severely mentally handicapped children's initiations in the classroom. *Journal of Child Psychiatry* **21**, 175–81.

Bigelow, A. 1987. Early words of blind children. *Journal of Child Language* **14**, 47–56.

Bigelow, A.E. 1996. Blind and sighted children's spatial knowledge of their home environments. *International Journal of Behavioural Development* **19**, 797–816.

Bijou, S.W., Baer, D.M. 1965. *Child development*. New York: Appleton––Century–Crofts.

Billig, M. 1991. *Ideology and opinions.* London: Sage.

Billig, M., Condor, S., Edwards, S., Gane, M., Middleton, D., Radley, A. 1988. *Ideological dilemmas: a social psychology of everyday thinking.* London: Sage.

Bishop D., Edmundsmon, A. 1986. Is otitis media a major cause of specific developmental language disorders? *British Journal of Disorders of Communication* **21**, 321–8.

Bishop, D. 1983. Comprehension of English syntax by profoundly deaf children. *Journal of Child Psychology and Psychiatry* **24**, 415–34.

Bishop, D. 1997. *Uncommon understandings.* Hove: Psychology Press.

Bishop, D.V.M. 1993. Annotation: autism, executive functions and theory of mind: a neuropsychological perspective. *Journal of Child Psychology and Psychiatry* **34**, 279–93.

Bjork, E.L., Cummings, E.M. 1984. Infant search error: stage of concept development or stage of memory development. *Memory and Cognition* **12**, 1–19.

Bjorklund, D.F., Harnishfeger, K.K. 1990. The resources construct in cognitive development: diverse souces of evidence and a theory of inefficient inhibition. *Developmental Review* **10**, 48–71.

Bjorkqvist, K., Lagerspetz, K.M., Kaukiainen, A. 1992. Do girls manipulate and boys fight? Developmental trends in regard to direct and indirect aggression. *Aggressive Behaviour* **18**, 117–27.

Blasi, A. 1980. Bridging moral cognition and moral action: a critical review of the literature. *Psychological Bulletin* **88**, 1–45.

Blos, P. 1967. The second individuation process of adolescence. *Psychoanalytic Study of the Child* **12**, 162–86.

Bohannon, J.N., MacWhinney, B., Snow, C. 1990. No negative evidence revisited: beyond learnability or who has to prove what to whom. *Developmental Psychology* **26**, 221–6.

Bohannon, J.N., Stanowicz, L. 1988. The issue of negative evidence: adult responses to children's language errors. *Developmental Psychology* **24**, 684–9.

Bolhuis, J.J. 1991. Mechanisms of avian imprinting: a review. *Biological Reviews* **66**, 303–45.

Bonvillian, J.D. 1999. In Barrett, M. (ed.) Sign language development. *The Development of Language.* Hove: Psychology Press.

Bornstein, M.H., Sigman, M.D. 1986. Continuity in mental development. *Child Development* **57**, 251–74.

Bost, K.K., Vaughn, B.E., Newell Washington, W., Cielinski, K.L., Bradbard, M.R., 1998. Social competence, social support and attachment: demarcation of construct domains, measurement and paths of influence for preschool children attending head start. *Child Development*, **69**, 192–218.

Bouchard, T.J., Jr., McGue, M. 1981. Familial studies of intelligence: a review. *Science* **212**, 1055–9.

Bouchard, T.J., Lykken, D.T., McGue, M., Segal, N.L., Tellegen, A. 1990. Sources of human psychological differences: the Minnesota study of twins reared apart. *Science* **250**, 223–50.

Boulton, J.B., Underwood, K. 1992. Bully/victim problems among middle school children. *British Journal of Educational Psychology* **62**, 73–87.

Boulton, M., Smith, P. 1996. Liking and peer perceptions among Asian and white British children. *Journal of Social and Personal Relationships* **13**, 163–77.

Boulton, M., Smith, P. 1992. Ethnic preferences and perceptions among Asian and white British school children. *Social Development* **1**, 55–66.

Boulton, M.J., Smith, P.K. 1994. Bully/victim problems in middle-school children: stability, self-perceived competence, peer perceptions and peer acceptance. *British Journal of Developmental Psychology* **12**, 315–29.

Boulton, M.J. 1993. Children's abilities to distinguish between playful and aggressive fighting: a developmental perspective. *British Journal of Developmental Psychology* **11**, 249–63.

Bower, T.G.R. 1982. *Development in Infancy* (2nd edition). San Francisco: Freeman.

Bower, T.G.R., Wishart, J.G. 1972. The effects of motor skill on object permanence. *Cognition* **1**, 165–72.

Bowers, L., Smith, P.K., Binney, V. 1994. Perceived family relationships of bullies, victims and bully/victims in middle childhood. *Journal of Social and Personal Relationships* **11**, 215–32.

Bowers, L., Smith, P.K., Binney, V. A. 1992. Cohesion and power in the families of children involved in bully/victim problems at school. *Journal of Family Therapy* **14**, 371–87.

Bowlby, J. 1951. *Maternal care and mental health*. Geneva: World Health Organization.

Bowlby, J. 1958. The nature of the child's tie to his mother. *International Journal of Psycho-analysis* **39**, 350–73.

Bowlby, J. 1969. *Attachment and loss: Vol. 1. Attachment*. London. Hogarth Press.

Bowlby, J. 1973. *Attachment and loss: Vol. 2. Separation: anxiety and anger*. London: Penguin.

Bowlby, J. 1979. *The making and breaking of affectional bonds*. London: Tavistock Publications.

Bowlby, J. 1984. *Attachment and loss: Vol. 1. Attachment* (second edition). London: Penguin.

Bowlby, J. 1985. *Attachment and loss: Vol. 3. Loss: sadness and depression*. London: Penguin.

Bowlby, J. 1988. *A secure base. Clinical application of attachment theory*. London: Routledge.

Bradley, L., Bryant, P.E. 1983. Categorising sounds and learning to read: a causal connection. *Nature* **301**, 419–21.

Bradshaw, D.L, Campos, J.J., Klinnert, M.D. 1986. Emotional expressions as determinants of infants' immediate and delayed response to prohibitions. Paper presented at the Fifth International Conference of Infant Studies, Los Angeles.

Brah, Avtar 1996. *Cartographies of diaspora: contesting identities*. London: Routledge.

Brannen, J., Dodd, K., Oakley, A., Storey, P. 1994. *Young people, health and family life*. Buckingham: Open University Press.

Breakwell, G. 1986. *Coping with threatened identities*. London: Methuen.

Bregman, J.D., Hodapp, R.M. 1991. Current developments in the understanding of mental retardation. Part 1 Biological and phenomenological perspectives. *Journal of the American Academy of Child and Adolescent Psychiatry* **30**, 707–19.

Bremner, J.G, Bryant, P.E. 1977. Place versus response as the basis of spatial errors made by young infants. *Journal of Experimental Child Psychology* **23**, 162–171.

Bremner, J.G. 1978a. Spatial errors made by infants: inadequate spatial cues or evidence for egocentrism? *British Journal of Psychology* **69**, 77–84.

Bremner, J.G. 1978b. Egocentric versus allocentric coding in nine-month-old infants: factors influencing the choice of code. *Developmental Psychology* **14**, 346–55.

Bremner, J.G. 1985. Object tracking and search in infancy: a review of data and a theoretical evaluation. *Developmental Review* **5**, 371–96.

Bremner, J.G. 1997. From perception to cognition. In Bremner, G., Slater A., and Butterworth G. (eds) *Infant Development: recent advances*. Hove: Psychology Press,

Bremner, J.G., Knowles, L.S. 1984. Piagetian stage IV errors with an object that is directly accessible both visually and manually. *Perception* **13**, 307–314.

Bremner, J.G., Moore, S. 1984. Prior visual inspection and object naming: two factors that enhance hidden feature inclusion in young children's drawings. *British Journal of Developmental Psychology* **2**, 371–76.

Bretherton, I. 1995. The origins of attachment theory: John Bowlby and Mary Ainsworth. In Goldberg, S., Muir, R., Kerr, J. (eds) *Attachment theory: social, developmental and clinical perspectives*. New York: Analytic Press, 45–84.

Bretherton, I., Fritz, J., Zahn-Waxler, C., Ridgeway, D. 1986. Learning to talk about emotions: a functional perspective. *Child Development* **57**, 529–48.

Bridges, A., Smith, J. 1984. Syntactic comprehension in Down's syndrome children. *British Journal of Psychology* **75**, 187–96.

Brittain, W.I., Chein, Y-C. 1983. Relationship between preschool children's ability to name body parts and their ability to construct a man. *Perceptual and Motor Skills* **57**, 19–24.

Brodmann, K. 1912. Neue Ergebnisse über die vergleichende histologische Lokalisation der Grosshirnrinde mit besonderer Berücksichtigung des Stirnhirns. *Anatomischer Anzeiger [Suppl.]* **41**, 157–216.

Broen, P.A. 1972. The verbal environment of the language learning child. *Monographs of the American Speech and Hearing Association*, No. 17.

Broman, Grafman, J. (eds) 1994. *Atypical cognitive deficits in developmental disorders*. Hillsdale, NJ: Erlbaum.

Bronfenbrenner, U. 1986. Ecology of the family as a context for human development. *Developmental Psychology* **22**, 723–42.

Brown, L. M. 1998. Voice and ventriloquation in girls' development. In. Henwood, K, Griffin, C., Phoenix, A. (eds) *Standpoints and differences: essays in the practice of feminist psychology*. London: Sage, pp. 91–114.

Brown, L. M., Gilligan, C. 1992. *Meeting at the crossroads: women's psychology and girls' development*. Cambridge, MA: Harvard University Press.

Brown, R. 1973. *A first language, the early stages*. Cambridge, MA: Harvard University Press.

Brown, R., Hobson, R., Lee, A., Stevenson, J. 1998. Are there 'autistic-like' features in congenitally blind children? *Journal of Child Psychology & Psychiatry* **38**, 693–703.

Brown, R., Hanlon, C. 1970. Derivational complexity and the order of acquisition in child speech. In Hayes, J.R. (ed.) *Cognition and the Development of Language*. New York: Wiley.

Bryson, S.E. 1996. Brief report: epidemiology of autism. *Journal of Autism and Developmental Disorders* **26**, 165–7.

Büchner, P., du Bois-Reymond, M., Krüger, H.-H. 1995. Growing up in three European regions. In Chisholm, L., Büchner, P., Krüger, H.-H., du Bois-Reymond, M. (eds) *Growing up in Europe*. Berlin: Walter de Gruyter.

Buckingham, D. 1993. *Children talking television. The making of television literacy*. London: Falmer.

Buckingham, D. 1994. Television and the definition of childhood. In Mayall, B. (Ed.) *Children's childhoods: observed and experienced*. London: The Falmer Press.

Buckley, S. 1985. Attaining basic educational skills: reading, writing and numbers. In Lane, D., Stratford, B. (eds) *Current approaches to Down's syndrome*. London: Holt Rinehart and Winston.

Buckley, S., Bird, G. 1993. Teaching children with Down's syndrome to read. *Down's syndrome: research and practice* **1**, 34–9.

Buckley, S., Sacks, B. 1987. *The adolescent with Down's syndrome – life for the teenager and for the family*. Portsmouth: Portsmouth Down's Syndrome Trust.

Burack, J.A. 1997. In Luthar, S. Burack, J. Ciccheti, D. et al. (eds) *Developmental psychopathology: perspectives on adjustment, risk, and disorder*. Cambridge: Cambridge University Press, 139–65.

Burack, J.A., Hodapp, R.M., Zigler, E. 1988. Issues in the classification of mental retardation: differentiation among organic etiologies. *Journal of Child Psychology and Psychiatry* **29**, 765–79.

Burgard, P. 1989. Consistencies in inconsistencies in moral judgments: microanalysis of stage variations within moral dilemmas. Poster presented at the poster session 'Moral Development' at the tenth biennial meeting of the ISSBD. Jyväskylä, Finland.

Burlingham, D., Freud, A. 1944. *Infants without families*. New York: International Universities Press, 1973.

Burman, E. 1994. *Deconstructing developmental psychology*. London: Routledge.

Burman, E., Parker, I. (eds) 1993. *Discourse analytic practice*. London: Routledge.

Bushnell, I.W.R., Sai, F., Mullin, J.T. 1989. Neonatal recognition of the mother's face. *British Journal Developmental Psychology* **7**, 3–15.

Butterworth, G. 1974. The development of the object concept in human infants. Unpublished DPhil thesis, University of Oxford.

Butterworth, G. 1975. Object identity in infancy: the interaction of spatial location codes in determining search errors. *Child Development* **46**, 866–870.

Butterworth, G. 1977. Object disappearance and error in Piaget's stage IV task. *Journal of Experimental Child Psychology* **23**, 391–401.

Butterworth, G., Jarrett, N., Hicks, L. 1982. Spatio-temporal identity in infancy: perceptual competence or conceptual deficit. *Developmental Psychology* **18**, 435–449.

Butterworth, G.E., Jarrett, N. 1991. What minds have in common is space: spatial mechanisms serving joint attention in infancy. *British Journal of Developmental Psychology* **9**, 55–72.

Cairns, R.B., Cairns, B.D., Neckerman, H.J., Gest, S.D., Gariepy, J.L. 1988. Social networks and aggressive behavior: peer support or peer rejection? *Developmental Psychology* **24**, 815–23.

Callaghan, S., Joseph, S. 1995. Self-concept and peer victimisation among school children. *Personality and Individual Differences* **18**, 161–63.

Campos, J.J., Bertenthal, B.I. 1988. Locomotion and psychological development. In Morrison, F., Lord K., and Keating D. (eds) *Applied Developmental Psychology*. New York: Academic Press, 176–98.

Carlson, E.A. 1998. A prospective longitudinal study of disorganized/disoriented attachment. *Child Development* **69**, 1107–28.

Caron, R.F., Caron, A.J., Myers, R.S. 1982. Abstraction of invariant face expressions in infancy. *Child Development* **53**, 1008–15.

Carrington, B., Short, G. 1989. *'Race' and the primary school*. London: NFER-Nelson.

Carroll, J.B. 1993. *Human cognitive abilities: a survey of factor analytic studies*. New York: Cambridge University Press.

Case, R. 1985. *Intellectual development: a systematic representation*. New York: Academic Press.

Case, R. 1985. *Intellectual development: birth to adulthood*. London: Academic Press.

Cashmore, E.E. 1984. *No future*. London: Heinemann.

Cazden, C. 1968. The acquisition of noun and verb inflections. *Child Development* **39**, 433–8.

Ceci, S.J. 1990. *On intelligence . . . more or less. A bioecological treatise on intellectual development*. Englewood Cliffs, NJ: Prentice Hall.

Chall, J.S. 1967. *Learning to read: the Great Debate*. New York: McGraw-Hill.

Champion, P., Lawson, R. 1996. Developmental competence in children with Down syndrome: a two part study. *The British Journal of Developmental Disabilities* **XL11**, 112–24.

Changeux, J.P., Dehaene, S. 1989. Neuronal models of cognitive functions. *Cognition* **33**, 63–109.

Chapman, R. 1995. Language development in children and adolescents with Down syndrome. In Fletcher, P., MacWhinney, B. (eds) *The handbook of child language*. Oxford: Blackwell, 641–63.

Chapman, R., Schwartz, S., Bird, E., Kay-Raining Bird. 1991. Language skills in children and adolescents with Down's syndrome; 1. Comprehension. *Journal of Speech and Hearing Research* **34**, 1106–20.

Charman, T., Baron-Cohen, S. 1993. Drawing development in autism: the intellectual to visual realism shift. *British Journal of Developmental Psychology* **11**, 171–85.

Chi, M.T.H. 1978. Knowledge structures and memory development. In Siegler, R.S. (ed.) *Children's thinking: what develops?* Hillsdale, NJ: Erlbaum, 73–96.

Chipuer, H.M., Rovine, M.J., Plomin, R. 1990. LISREL modeling: genetic and environmental influences on IQ revisited. *Intelligence* **14**, 11–29.

Chisholm, L., Büchner, P., Krüger, H.-H., du Bois-Reymond, M. (eds) 1995. *Growing up in Europe*. Berlin: Walter de Gruyter.

Chorney, M.J., Chorney, K., Seese, N., Owen, M.J., McGuffin, P., Daniels, J., et al. 1998. A quantitative trait locus (QT.) associated with cognitive ability in children. *Psychological Science* **9**, 159–660.

Chomsky, N. 1965. *Aspects of the theory of syntax*. Cambridge, MA: MIT Press.

Chomsky, N. 1968. *Language and mind*. New York: Harcourt, Brace & World.

Chomsky, N. 1981. *Lectures on government and binding*. Dordrecht: Foris.

Chomsky, N. 1988. *Language and problems of knowledge*. Cambridge, MA: MIT Press.

Christie, N. and Bruun, K. 1985. *Den gode fienden*. Stockholm: Rabén and Sjögren.

Chugani, H.T., Phelps, M.E., Mazziotta, J.C. 1987. Positron emission tomography study of human brain functional development. *Annals of Neurology* **22**, 487–97.

Cicchetti, D., and Bukowski, W. M. 1995. Developmental processes in peer relations and psychpathology. *Development and Psychopathology* **7**, 587–89.

Clahsen, H. 1992. Learnability theory and the problem of development in language acquisition. In Weissenborn, J. Goodluck, H., Roeper, T. (eds) *Theoretical issues in language acquisition*. Hillsdale, NJ: Erlbaum, 53–76.

Clark, A., Karmiloff-Smith, A. 1993. The cognizer's innards: a psychological and philosophical perspective on the development of thought. *Mind and Language* **8**, 487–519.

Clark, E.V. 1991. Acquisition principles in language development. In Gelman, S.A., Byrnes, J.A. (eds) *Perspectives on language and thought*. Cambridge: Cambridge University Press, 31–71.

Clark, H.H., Haviland, S.E. 1977. Comprehension and the given-new contract. In Freedle, R.O. (ed.) *Discourse production and comprehension*. Norwood, NJ: Ablex, 1–40.

Clark, K., Clark, M. 1939. The development of consciousness of self and the emergence of racial identity in Negro preschool children. *Journal of Social Psychology* **10**, 591–9.

Clark, K., Clark, M. 1947. Racial identification and prejudice in Negro children. In Newcomb, T.M., Hartley, E.L. (eds) *Readings in Social Psychology*. New York: Henry Holt, pp. 169–78.

Clark, L.A., and Watson, D. 1992. Tripartite model of anxiety and depression: psychometric evidence and taxonomic implications. *Journal of Abnormal Psychology* **100**, 316–36.

Clarke, A., Clarke, A. 1999. The prediction of individual development. In Messer, D., Jones, F. (eds) *Psychology for social carers*. London: Jessica Kingsley.

Clausen, J.S. 1991. Adolescent competence and the shaping of the life course. *American Journal of Sociology* **96**, 805–42.

Claxton, G. 1984. *Live and learn*. London: Harper and Row.

Coffield, F. 1992. Young people and illicit drugs. Northern Regional Health Authority and Durham University.

Coffield, F., Borrill, C., Marshall, S. 1986. *Growing up at the margins*. Milton Keynes: Open University Press.

Coggans, N., Shewan, D., Henderson, M., Davies, J. D., O'Hagan, F. J. 1993 National evaluation of drug education in Scotland. (SOED) Edinburgh.

Cohen, P. 1988. Perversions of Inheritance: Studies in the making of multi-racist Britain. In Cohen, P., Bains, H. (eds) *Multi-racist Britain*, London: Macmillan, pp. 9–118.

Cohen, P. 1997. *Rethinking the youth question: education, labour and cultural studies*. London: Macmillan.

Colby, A., Kohlberg, L. 1987a. *The measurement of moral judgment. Vol I. Theoretical foundations and research validation*. Cambridge, MA: Cambridge University Press.

Colby, A., Kohlberg, L. 1987b. *The measurement of moral judgment. Vol II. Standard issue scoring manual*. Cambridge, MA: Cambridge University Press.

Colby, A., Kohlberg, L., Gibbs, J., Lieberman, M. 1983. A longitudinal study of moral judgment. *Monographs of the Society for Research in Child Development* **48**, (1–2, serial no. 200).

Cole, M., Griffen, P. 1980. Cultural amplifiers reconsidered. In Olson, D.R. (ed.) *The social foundations of language and thought*. New York: Norton.

Cole, P.M. 1986. Children's spontaneous control of facial expression. *Child Development* **57**, 1309–21.

Coleman, J. 1997. *Key data on adolescence*. Routledge: London.

Coleman, J.C. 1979. *The school years*. London: Methuen.

Coleman, J.C., Hendry, L.B. 1990. *The nature of adolescence*. (second edition). London: Routledge.

Colombo, J. 1993. *Infant cognition: predicting childhood intelligence*. Newbury Park, CA: Sage.

Coltheart, M., Curtis, B., Atkins, P. , Haller, M. 1993. Models of reading aloud: dual route and parallel-distributed-processing accounts. *Psychological Review* **100**, 589–608.

Coltheart, M., Davelaar, E., Jonasson, J.T, Besner, D. 1977. Access to the internal lexicon. *Attention and Performance*. London: Academic Press, 535–55.

Comblain, A. 1994. Working memory in Down syndrome: training rehearsal strategies. *Down's Syndrome* **2**, 123–6.

Condry, J. 1993. Thief of time, unfaithful servant: television and the American child. *Daedalus* **122**, 259–78.

Conel, J.L. 1939–1967. *The postnatal development of the human cerebral cortex.* Cambridge, MA.: Harvard University Press.

Cooper, R.P., Aslin, R.N. 1990. Preference for infant directed speech in the first month after birth. *Child Development* **61**, 1584–95.

Corley, G., Pring, L. 1996. The inner life of visually impaired children. In Varma, V. (ed.) *The inner life of children with special needs*. London: Whurr, 1–14.

Couch, C.G. 1985. A test of Kohlberg's theory: the development of moral reasoning in deaf and hearing individuals. Unpublished doctoral dissertation, University of North Carolina at Greensboro.

Coulter, W.A., Morrow, H.W. (eds) 1978. *Adaptive behaviour: concepts and measurement.* New York: Grune & Stratton.

Cowie, H., Sharp, S. 1994. *Tackling bullying in your school*. London: Routledge.

Cowie, H., Sharp, S. 1996. *Peer counselling in school: a time to listen*. London: David Fulton.

Cox, M. 1992. *Children's Drawings*. London: Penguin.

Cox, M. 1993. *Children's Drawings of the Human Figure*. Hove: Lawrence Erlbaum Associates.

Cox, M., Parkin, C. 1986. Young children's human figure drawing: cross-sectional and longitudinal studies. *Educational Psychology* **6**. 353–68.

Cox, M.V. 1985. One object behind another: young children's use of array-specific or view-specific representations. In Freeman, N., Cox, M. (eds) *Visual order: the nature and development of pictorial representation*. Cambridge: Cambridge University Press, 188–200.

Craft, A. 1987. *Mental handicap and sexuality: issues for individuals with a mental handicap, their parents and professionals*. Tunbridge Wells: Costello.

Crick, N.R. 1996. The role of overt aggression, relational aggression and prosocial behaviour in the prediction of children's future social adjustment. *Child Development* **67**, 2317–27.

Crick, N.R., Dodge, K.A. 1994. A review and reformulation of social information-processing mechanisms in children's social adjustment. *Psychological Bulletin* **115**, 74–101.

Crick, N.R., Grotpeter, J.K. 1995. Relational aggression, gender and social–psychological adjustment. *Child Development* **66**, 710–22.

Crook, C.K. In press. Computers in the community of classrooms. In Littleton, K., Light, P. (eds) *Learning with computers: analysing productive interaction*. London: Routledge.

Crook, C.K. 1987. A social context for classroom computers. In Rutkowska, J., Crook, C. (ed.), *Computers cognition and development*. Chichester: Wiley.

Crook, C.K. 1992. Cultural artefacts in social development: The case of computers. In McGurk, H. (ed.), *Childhood social development: Contemporary perspectives*. Hove: Lawrence Earlbaum Associates.

Crook, C.K. 1994. *Computers and the collaborative experience of learning*. London: Routledge.

Crook, C.K. 1995. On resourcing concern for collaboration within peer interactions. *Cognition and Instruction*, 13, 541–547.

Crook, C.K. 1996. Schools of the future. In T. Gill (ed.) *Electronic children*. London: National Children's Bureau.

Csikszentmihalyi, M., Larson, R. 1984. *Being adolescent*. New York: Basic Books.

Cuban, L. 1986. *Teachers and machines*. New York: Teachers College.

Cullingford, C. 1991. *The inner world of the school: children's ideas about schools*. London: Cassell.

Cumberbatch, G., Howitt, D. 1989. *A measure of uncertainty: the effects of the mass media*. London: Libbey.

Cummings, E.M., Ballard, M., El-Sheik, M., Lake, M. 1991. Resolution in children's responses to interadult anger. *Developmental Psychology* 27, 462–70.

DHSS (Department of Health and Social Security). 1988. Causes of blindness and partial sight among children aged under 16, newly registered as blind and partially sighted between 1985 and 1987. *Statistical Bulletin No. 3/9/98*. London: HMSO.

Daleiden E.L., Vasey M.W. 1997. An information-processing perspective on childhood anxiety. *Clinical Psychology Review* 17, 407–29.

Dallos, R. 1995. Constructing family life: Family belief systems. In Muncie, J., Wetherell, M., Dallos, R., Cochrane, A. (eds) *Understanding the family*. London: Sage/Open University Press, pp 173–212.

Darling, N., Steinberg, L. 1993. Parenting style as context: An integrative model. *Psychological Bulletin* **113**, 487–96.

Darwin, C. 1872. *The expression of emotion in man and animals*. Chicago: University of Chicago Press.

Das Gupta, P. 1995. Growing up in families. In Barnes, P. (ed) *Personal, social and emotional development in children*. Buckingham: Open University Press, pp 83–129.

Das, J.P., Ojile, E. 1995. Cognitive processing of children with and without hearing loss. *Journal of Special Education* 29, 323–36.

Davie, C.E., Hutt, S.J., Vincent, E., Mason, M. 1984. *The young child at home*. Windsor: NFER.

Davies, D., Sperber, R., McCauley, C. 1981. Intelligence-related differences in semantic processing speed. *Journal of Experimental Psycholgy* **31**, 387–402.

Davies, E., Furnham, A. 1986. Body satisfaction in adolescent girls. *British Journal of Medical Psychology* **59**, 279–88.

Davis, A.M. 1985. The canonical bias: young children's drawings of familiar objects. In Freeman, N., Cox, M. *Visual order: the nature and development of pictorial representation*. Cambridge: Cambridge University Press, 202–13.

Davis, H. 1978. A description of aspects of mother–infant vocal interaction. *Journal of Child Psychology and Psychiatry* **19**, 379–86.

Davis, H., Anderson, M. 1999. Intelligence and development: one dimension or two? In Anderson, M. (ed.) *The development of intelligence*. Hove: Psychology Press.

Davis, J. 1990. Youth and the condition of Britain. London: The Athlone Press.

Davis, J.M., Elfbein, J., Schum, R., Bentler, R. 1986. Effects of mild and moderate hearing impairments on language, educational and psychosocial behaviour in children. *Journal of Speech and Hearing Disorders* **51**, 53–62.

Dawkins, J.L., 1996. Bullying, physical disability and the paediatric patient. *Developmental Medicine and Child Neurology* **38**, 603–12.

Dawson, G., McKissick, F.C. 1984. Self-recognition in autistic children. *Journal of Autism and Developmental Disorders* **14**, 383–94.

De Schonen, S., Mathivet, H. 1989. First come, first served: a scenario about the development of hemispheric specialization in face recognition during infancy. *European Bulletin of Cognitive Psychology* **9**, 3–44.

De Wolff, M.S., van IJzendoorn, M.H. 1997. Sensitivity and attachment: a meta analysis on parental antecedents of infant attachment. *Child Development* **68**, 571–91.

DeCasper, A.J., Fifer, W.P. 1980. Of human bonding: newborns prefer their mothers' voices. *Science* **208**, 1174–76.

DeFries, J.C., Plomin, R., Fulker, D.W. 1994. *Nature and Nurture During Middle Childhood*. Cambridge, MA: Blackwell.

DeMyer, M.K. 1975. Research in infantile autism: a strategy and its results. *Biological Psychiatry* **10**, 433–52.

DeMyer, M.K. 1979. *Parents and children with autism*. Washington, DC: Winston.

DePaulo, B.M., Jordan, A. 1982. Age changes in deceiving and detecting deceit. In Feldman, R.S. (ed.) *Development of nonverbal behaviour in children*. New York: Springer-Verlag.

Deary, I., Caryl, P. 1997. Neuroscience and human intelligence differences. *Trends in Neurosciences* **20**, 365–71.

Deary, I., Stough, C. 1996. Intelligence and inspection time. *American Psychologist* **51**, 599–608.

Dehay, C., Bullier, J., Kennedy, H. 1984. Transient projections from the frontoparietal and temporal cortex to areas 17, 18 and 19 in the kitten. *Experimental Brain Research* **57**, 208–12.

Dehay, C., Kennedy, H., Bullier, J., Berland, M. 1988. Absence of interhemispheric connectins of area 17 during development in the monkey. *Nature* **331**, 348–50.

Deliyannis-Kouimtzi, K., Ziogou, R. 1995. Gendered youth transitions in Northern Greece. In Chisholm, L., Büchner, P., Krüger, H.-H., du Bois-Reymond, M. (eds) *Growing up in Europe*. Berlin: Walter de Gruyter, 209–19.

DellaCorte, M., Benedict, H., Klein, D. 1983. The relationship of pragmatic dimensions of mothers' speech to the referential expressive distinction. *Journal of Child Language* **10**, 35–44.

Demarco, L. 1978. Obedience to authority. In Aikenhead, L. (ed.) *Children's rights*. Glasgow: SCCL.

Demetras, M.J., Post, K.N., Snow, C.E. 1986. Feedback to first language learners: the role of repetitions and clarification questions. *Journal of Child Language* **13**, 275–92.

Dempster, F.N. 1991. Inhibitory processes: a neglected dimension of intelligence. *Intelligence* **15**, 157–73.

Denham, S.A. 1993. Maternal emotional responsiveness and toddlers' social-emotional competence. *Journal of Child Psychology and Psychiatry* **34**, 715–28.

Denmark, J. 1994. *Deafness and mental health*. London: Jessica Kingsley.

Detterman, D.K., Daniel, M.H. 1989. Correlations of mental tests with each other and with cognitive variables are highest for low IQ groups. *Intelligence* **13**, 349–59.

Dholakia, R.R., Mundorf, N., Dholakia, N. 1996. New infotainment technologies in the home. New Jersey: LEA.

DiLalla, L.F., Gottesman, I.I. 1989. Heterogeneity of causes for delinquency and criminality: lifespan perspectives. *Development and Psychopathology* **1**, 339–49.

Diamond, A. 1985. The development of the ability to use recall to guide action, as indicated by infants' performance on AB. *Child Development* **56**, 868–83.

Diamond, A. 1988. Abilities and neural mechanisms underlying AB performance. *Child Development* **59**, 523–7.

Diamond, A. 1990. The development and neural bases of memory functions as indexed by the AB and delayed response tasks in human infants and infant monkeys. In Diamond, A. (ed.) *The Development and neural bases of higher cognitive functions*. New York: New York Academy of Sciences Press, 267–317.

Diamond, A. 1991. Neuropsychological insights into the meaning of object concept development. In Carey, S., Gelman, R. (eds), *The epigenesis of mind: essays on biology and cognition*. Hillsdale, NJ: Lawrence Erlbaum Associates, 67–110.

Dillard, A. 1987. *An American childhood*. New York: Harper and Row.

Dix, T. 1991. The affective organization of parenting: adaptive and maladaptative processes. *Psychological Bulletin*, **110**, 3–25.

Donald, J., Rattansi, A. 1992. Introduction. In Donald, J., Rattansi, A. (eds) *'Race', culture and difference*. London: Sage, pp. 1–8.

Donaldson, M. 1978. *Children's minds*. London: Fontana.

Dore, J. 1978. Conditions for the acquisition of speech acts. In Markova, I. (ed.) *The Social Context of Language*. New York: Wiley.

Downs, C., Craft, A. 1998. *Sex in context: a personal and social development programme for children and adults with profound and multiple handicaps*. Brighton: Pavilion & The Joseph Rowntree Foundation.

Dozier, M., Kobak, R.R. 1992. Psychophysiology in attachment interviews: converging evidence for deactivating strategies. *Child Development* **63**, 1473–80.

du Gay, P. 1996. *Consumption and identity at work*. London: Sage.

Dunlea, A. 1989. *Vision and the emergence of meaning: blind and sighted children*. Cambridge: Cambridge University Press.

Dunn, J. 1988. *The beginning of social understanding*. Oxford: Blackwell.

Dunn, J. 1991. Young children's understanding of other people: evidence from observation within the family. In Frye, D., Moore C. (eds) *Children's theories of mind*. Hillsdale NJ: Lawrence Erlbaum, 97–114.

Dunn, J. 1993. *Young children's close relationships: beyond attachment*. London: Sage.

Dunn, J., Brown, J., Beardsall, L. 1991. Family talk about feeling states and children's later understanding of others' emotions. *Developmental Psychology* **27**, 448–55.

Dunn, J., McGuire, S. 1992, Sibling and peer relationships in childhood. *Journal of Child Psychology and Psychiatry* **33**, 67–105.

Dunn, J., Plomin, R. 1990. *Separate lives: why siblings are so different*. New York: Basic Books.

Dunn, J., Stocker, C., Plomin, R. 1990. Non-shared experiences within the family: correlates of behavioral problems in middle childhood. *Development and Psychopathology* **2**, 113–26.

Dunst, C.J., Brooks, P.H., Doxsey, P.A. 1982. Characteristics of hiding places and the transition to stage IV performance in object permanence tasks. *Developmental Psychology* **18**, 671–681.

Dyck, D. van, McBrien, D., Mattheis, P. 1996. Psychosexual behaviour, sexuality and management issues in individuals with Down's syndrome. In Rondal, J., Perera, J., Nadel, L., Comblan, A. (eds) *Down's syndrome: psychological, psychobiological and socio-educational perspectives*. London: Whurr, 191–206.

Dykens, E.M. 1995. Measuring behavioural phenotypes: provocations from the 'new genetics'. *American Journal on Mental Retardation* **99**, 522–32.

Dykens, E.M., Hodapp, R.M., Leckmann, J.F. 1989. Adaptive and maladaptive functioning of institutionalized and noninstitutionalized fragile X males. *Journal of the American Academy of Child and Adolescent Psychiatry* **28**, 422–6.

Dykens, E.M., Hodapp, R.M., Leckmann, J.F. 1994. *Behaviour and development in fragile X syndrome*. Newbury Park, CA: Sage.

Eaves, L.J., Silberg, J.L., Meyer, J.M., Maes, H.H., Simonoff, E., Pickles, A. et al. 1996. Genetics and developmental psychopathology: 2. The main effects of genes and environment on behavioural problems in the Virginia Twin Study of Adolescent Behavioural Development. Journal of Child Psychology and Psychiatry **38**, 965–80.

Ebstein, R.P., Belmaker, R.H. 1997. Saga of an adventure gene: novelty seeking, substance abuse and dopamine D4 receptor (D4DR) exon III repeat polymorphism. *Molecular Psychiatry* **2**, 381–4.

Ebstein, R.P., Novick, O., Umansky, R., Priel, B., Osher, Y., Blaine, D. et al. 1995. Dopamine D4 receptor (D4DR) exon III polymorphism associated with the human personality trait of novelty seeking. *Nature Genetics* **12**, 78–80.

Eckensberger, L.H. 1989. Consistencies in inconsistencies in moral judgements: stage variations between dilemmas. Poster presented at the poster session 'Moral Development' at the tenth biennial meeting of the ISSBD, Jyväskylä, Finland.

Eckensberger, L.H. 1998. Die Entwicklung des moralischen Urteils. In Keller, H. (ed.) *Lehrbuch Entwicklungspsychologie*. Bern: Verlag Hans Huber, 475–516.

Eckensberger, L.H., Reinshagen, H. 1980. Eine alternative Interpretation von Kohlbergs Stufentheorie der Entwicklung des Moralischen Urteils. Ein Versuch ihrer Reinterpretation im Bezugsrahmen handlungstheoretischer Konzepte. In Eckensberger, L.H., Silbereisen, R.K. (Hg.) *Entwicklung sozialer Kognitionen. Modelle, Theorien, Methoden, Anwendung.* Stuttgart: Klett-Cotta, 65–131.

Eckensberger, L.H., Zimba, R. 1997. The development of moral judgement. In Berry, J.W., Dasen, P.R., Saraswathi, T.S. (eds) *Handbook of cross-cultural psychology. Vol. 2: Basic processes and human development.* Boston: Allyn and Bacon, 299–338.

Edgcumbe, R.M., Burgner, M. 1975. The phallic narcissistic phase: a differentiation between preoedipal and oedipal aspects of phallic development. *Psychoanalytic Study of the Child* **30**, 161–80.

Edwards, C.P. 1978. Social experience and moral judgement in Kenyan young adults. *Journal of Genetic Psychology* **133**, 19–29.

Edwards, D., Mercer, N. 1987. *Common knowledge.* London: Methuen.

Edwards, D., Potter, J. 1992. *Discursive psychology.* London: Sage.

Eisenberg, J.N. 1986. *Altruistic emotion, cognition and behavior.* Hillsdale, NJ: Erlbaum.

Eisenberg, N., Fabes, R.A., Shepard, S.A., Murphy, B.C., Guthrie, I.K., Jones, S., Friedman, J., Poulin, R., and Maszk, P. 1997. Contemporaneous and longitudinal prediction of children's social functioning from regulation and emotionality. *Child Development* **68**, 642–64.

Ekman, P., Friesen, W.V. 1971. Constants across culture in face and emotion. *Journal of Personality and Social Psychology* **17**, 124–9.

Elkind, D. 1967. Egocentrism in adolescence. *Child development* **38**, 1025–34.

Elliott, C. 1978. Factors influencing the response latencies of subnormal children in naming pictures. *British Journal of Psychology* **69**, 295–303.

Elliott, M. (ed.) 1991, *Bullying: a practical guide to coping for schools.* Harlow: Longman.

Ellis, A.W., Young, A.W. 1988. *Human cognitive neuropsychology.* Hove: Psychology Press.

Ellis, N.R. 1963. The stimulus trace and behavioral inadequacy. In Ellis, N.R. (ed.) *Handbook of mental deficiency.* New York: McGraw-Hill.

Elman, J., Bates, E., Johnson, M.H., Karmiloff-Smith, A., Parisi, D., Plunkett, K. 1996. *Rethinking innateness: a connectionist perspective on development.* Cambridge, MA: MIT Press.

Emde, R. 1981. Changing models of infancy and the nature of early development: remodeling the foundations. *Journal of the American Psychoanalytic Association* **29**, 179–219.

Emde, R. 1988. Development terminable and interminable: Part I, Innate and motivational factors from infancy. *International Journal of Psycho-analysis* **69**, 23–42.

Emerson, E., Bromley, J. 1995. The form and function of challenging behaviours. *Journal of Intellectual Disability Research* **8**, 272–95.

Emery, R.E., Forehand, R. 1996. Parental divorce and children's well-being. In: Haggerty, R.J., Sherrod, L.R., Garmezy, N., Rutter, M. (eds) *Stress, risk and resilience in children and adolescents.* Cambridge: Cambridge University Press, 64–99.

Emler, N., Reicher, S. 1995. *Adolescence and delinquency.* London: Blackwell.

Erel, O., Burman, B. 1995. Interrelatedness of marital relations and parent–child relations: a meta-analytic review. *Psychological Bulletin* **118**, 108–32.

Erikson, E. 1950. *Childhood and society.* New York: Basic Books.

Erikson, E. 1968. *Identity, youth and crisis.* New York: W.W. Norton and Co.

Erikson, E. 1976. *Identity and the life cycle.* New York: International University Press.

Eron, L.D. 1987. The development of aggressive behavior from the perspective of a developing behaviorism. *American Psychologist* **42**, 435–47.

Eslea, M., Smith, P.K. 1998. The long-term effectiveness of anti-bullying work in primary schools. *Educational Research* **40**, 1–16.

Essed, P. 1988. *Understanding everyday racism.* London: Sage.

Evans, W.F. 1973. The stage IV error in Piaget's theory of object concept development. Unpublished dissertation, University of Houston.

Eysenck, H.J. 1976. The biology of morality. In Lickona, T. (ed.) *Moral development and behavior. Theory, research and social issues.* New York: Holt, Rinehart and Winston,108–23.

Eysenck, H.J. 1988. The concept of 'intelligence': useful or useless? *Intelligence* **12**, 1–16.

Fagan, J.F. (1984) The intelligent infant: Theoretical implications. *Intelligence,* **8**, 1–9.

Fagan, J.F., McGrath, S.K. 1981. Infant recognition memory and later intelligence. *Intelligence* **5**, 121–30.

Fagot, B.I., Kavanagh, K. 1990. The prediction of antisocial behavior from avoidant attachment classifications. *Child Development* **61**, 864–73.

Farrar, M.J. 1992. Negative evidence and grammatical morpheme acquisition. *Developmental Psychology* **28**, 90–8.

Farrington, D.P. 1992. Understanding and preventing bullying. In Tonry, M., Morris, N. (eds) *Crime and justice: an annual review of research. Vol 17.* University of Chicago Press, 381–458.

Farrington, D.P. 1993. Motivations for conduct disorder and delinquency. *Development and Psychopathology* **5**, 435–47.

Farrington, D.P. 1995. The Twelfth Jack Tizard Memorial Lecture: The development of offending and antisocial behaviour from childhood: Key findings from the Cambridge Study in delinquent development. *Journal of Child Psychology and Psychiatry* **36**, 929–64.

Farrington, D.P. 1995. The challenge of teenage antisocial behaviour. In: Rutter, M. (ed.) *Psychosocial disturbances in young people.* Cambridge: Cambridge University Press.

Farrington, D.P., West, D.J. 1993. Criminal, penal and life histories of chronic offenders. *Criminal Behaviour and Mental Health* **3**, 492–523.

Fawcett, A.J., Nicolson, R.I. 1991. Vocabulary training for dyslexic children. *Journal of Learning Disabilities* **24**, 379–83.

Fawcett, A.J., Nicolson, R.I. 1996. *The dyslexia screening test: nonsense passage reading.* London: The Psychological Corporation.

Fawcett, A.J., Nicolson, R.I. Dean, P. 1996. Impaired performance of children with dyslexia on a range of cerebellar tasks. *Annals of Dyslexia* **46**, 259–83.

Felix, S. 1992. Language acquisition as a maturational process. In Weissenborn, J. Goodluck, H., Roeper, R. (eds), *Theoretical issues in language Acquisition.* Hillsdale, NJ: Erlbaum, 25–52.

Fenson, G.L., Dale, P.S., Reznick, J.S., Thal, D., Bates, E., Hatung, J., Pethick, S., Reilly, J. 1993. *The MacArthur Communicative Development Inventories; user's guide and technical manual.* San Diego: Singular Publishing Group.

Ferguson, C.A. 1964. Baby talk in six languages. *American Anthropologist* **66**, 103–13.

Ferguson, T.J., Stegge, H. 1995. Emotional states and traits in children: the case of guilt and shame. In Tangney, J.P., Fischer, K.W. (eds) *Self-conscious emotions.* New York: Guilford Press, 174–97.

Ferguson, T.J., Stegge, H. 1998. Assessing guilt in children: a rose by any other name still has thorns. In Bybee, J.A., (ed.) *Guilt and children.* New York: Academic Press, 19–74.

Fergusson, D.M., Horwood, L.J., Lawton, J.M. 1990. Vulnerability to childhood problems and family social background. *Journal of Child Psychology and Psychiatry* **31**, 1145–60.

Fernald, A. 1991. Prosody in speech to children: prelinguistic and linguistic functions. *Annals of Child Development* **8**, 43–80.

Fernald, A., Mazzie, C. 1991. Prosody and focus in speech to infants and adults. *Developmental Psychology* **27**, 209–21.

Field, T., Woodson, R., Greenberg, R., Cohen, D. 1982. Discrimination and imitation of facial expressions by neonates. *Science* **218**, 179–81.

Finnegan, R.A., Hodges, E.V.E., Perry, D.G. 1997. Victimisation in the peer group: Associations with children's perceptions of mother–child interaction. Paper presented at the SRCD Conference, Washington DC, April.

Fischer, A., Fuchs, W., Zinnecker, J. 1985. Jugendliche und Erwachsene '85. In Jugendwerk der Deutschen Shell (ed.) *Arbeitsbericht und Dokumentation.* Vol. 5. Leverkusen: Leske und Budrich.

Fitts, P.M., Posner, M.I. 1967. *Human performance.* Belmont, CA: Brooks-Cole.

Flavell, J.H. 1963. *The developmental psychology of Jean Piaget.* Princeton NJ: Van Nostrand.

Fletcher, J.M., Thompson, M., Brookshire, B.L., Bohan, T.P., Landry, S.H., Davidson, K.C., Miner, M.E. 1992. Verbal and nonverbal skill discrepancies in hydrocephalic children. *Journal of Clinical and Experimental Neuropsychology* **14**, 593–609.

Fodor, J.A. 1983. *The modularity of mind.* Cambridge, MA: MIT/Bradford Books.

Fogel, A. 1997. Seeing and being seen. In Lewis, V., Collis, G.M. (eds) *Blindness and psychological development in young children.* Leicester: British Psychological Society,

Fogel, A., Toda, S., Kawai, M. 1988. Mother–infant face-to-face interaction in Japan and the United States: a laboratory comparison using 3-month-old infants. *Developmental Psychology* **24**, 398–406.

Folstein, S., Rutter, M. 1977. Genetic influences and infantile autism. *Nature* **265**, 726–8.

Fombonne, E. 1996. Is the prevalence of autism increasing? *Journal of Autism and Developmental Disorders* **26**, 673–6.

Fonagy, P., Steele, H., Steele, M. 1991. Maternal representations of attachment during pregnancy predict the organization of infant–mother attachment at one year of age. *Child Development* **62**, 891–905.

Ford, N., Bowie, C. 1989. Urban-rural variations in the level of heterosexual activity of young people. *Area* **21**, 237–48.

Fortescue, M. 1984/5. Learning to speak Greenlandic: a case study of a two-year old's morphology in a polysynthetic language. *First Language* **5**, 101–13.

Foss, D.J., Hakes, D.T. 1978. *Psycholinguistics.* Englewood Cliffs, NJ: Prentice Hall.

Fox, N.A., Kimmerly, N.L., Schafer, W.D. 1991. Attachment to mother/ attachment to father: A meta-analysis. *Child Development* **62**, 210–25.

Fraiberg, S. 1977. *Insights from the blind.* New York: Basic Books.

Fraiberg, S., Adelson, E., Shapiro, V. 1975. Ghosts in the nursery: a psychoanalytic approach to the problems of impaired infant–mother relationships. *Journal of the American Academy of Child Psychiatry* **14**, 387–421.

France, A. 1995. Youth and citizenship in the 1990s. Paper presented at the Youth 2000 conference. Middlesborough.

Frankenberg, R. 1993. *White women, race matters.* London: Routledge.

Franklin, S., van Sommers, P, Howard, D. 1992. Drawing without meaning? Dissociations in the graphic performance of an agnosic artist. In Campbell, R. (ed.) *Mental lives: case studies in cognition.* Oxford: Blackwell, 178–98.

Freeman, N. 1980. *Strategies of representation in young children: analysis of spatial skills and drawing processes.* London: Academic Press.

Freeman, N., Cox, M. (eds) 1985. *Visual order: the nature and development of pictorial representation.* Cambridge: Cambridge University Press.

Freeman, R., Goetz, E., Richards, D., Groenveld, M., Blockberger, S., Jan, J., Sykanda, A. 1989. Blind children's early emotional development: do we know enough to help? *Child: Care, Health & Development* **15**, 3–28.

Freeman, R., Goetz, E., Richards, D., and Groenveld, M. 1991. Defiers of negative prediction: a 14-year follow-up study of legally blind children. *Journal of Visual Impairment and Blindness* **85**, 365–70.

Freud, A. 1936. *The ego and the mechanisms of defense.* New York: International Universities Press, 1946.

Freud, A. 1965. *Normality and pathology in childhood*. Harmondsworth: Penguin Books.

Freud, A., Burlingham, D. 1974. *Infants without families and reports on the Hampstead nurseries 1939–1945*. London: Hogarth.

Freud, S. 1905. Three essays on sexuality. In Strachey, J. (ed.) *Standard edition of the complete psychological works of Sigmund Freud*, vol. 7. London: Hogarth Press, 125–245.

Freud, S. 1907. Obsessive actions and religious practices. In Strachey, J. (ed.) *Standard edition of the complete psychological works of Sigmund Freud*, vol. 9. London: Hogarth Press, 115–27.

Freud, S. 1912. The dynamics of transference. In Strachey, J. (ed.) *Standard edition of the complete psychological works of Sigmund Freud*, vol. 12. London: Hogarth Press, 99–108.

Freud, S. 1914. On narcissism: an introduction. In Strachey, J. (ed.) *Standard edition of the complete psychological works of Sigmund Freud, vol 14*. London: Hogarth Press, 67–104.

Freud, S. 1917. Mourning and melancholia. In Strachey, J. (ed.) *Standard Edition of the Complete Psychological Works of Sigmund Freud Vol. 14* (pp. 237-259). London: Hogarth Press.

Freud, S. 1920. Beyond the pleasure principle. In Strachey, J. (ed.) *Standard edition of the complete psychological works of Sigmund Freud, vol. 18*. London: Hogarth Press, 7–64.

Freud, S. 1923. The ego and the id. In Strachey, J. (ed.) *Standard edition of the complete psychological works of Sigmund Freud*, vol. 19. London: Hogarth Press, 3–66.

Freud, S. 1926. Inhibitions, symptoms and anxiety. In Strachey, J. (ed.) *Standard edition of the complete psychological works of Sigmund Freud, vol. 20*. London: Hogarth Press, 77–172.

Freud, S. 1940. An outline of psychoanalysis. In Strachey, J. (ed.) *Standard edition of the complete psychological works of Sigmund Freud*, vol. 23. London: Hogarth Press, 141–207.

Freud, S. 1959. Some psychological consequences of the anatomical distinction between the sexes. In Freud, S. (ed.) *Collected papers*. New York: Basic Books, 186–97.

Friel-Patti, S. 1990. Otitis media with effusion and the development of language: a review of the evidence. *Topics in language disorders* **11**, 11–22.

Friel-Patti, S. 1992. Research in child language disorders: what do we know and where are we going. *Folia Phoniatrica* **44**, 126–42.

Friel-Patti, S., Finitzo, T. 1990. Language learning in a prospective study of otitis media with effusion in the first two years of life. *Journal of Speech and Hearing Research* **33**, 188–94.

Friel-Patti, S., Finitzo-Hieber, T., Conti, G., Brown, K. 1982. Language delay in infants associated with middle ear disease and mild fluctuating hearing impairment. *Pediatric Infections Disease*, **1**, 104–9.

Frijda, N.H 1986. *The emotions*. Cambridge: Cambridge University Press.

Frith U. 1989. *Autism: explaining the enigma*. Oxford: Blackwell.

Frith, U, Happé, F.G.E. 1994. Autism: beyond 'Theory of Mind'. *Cognition* **50**, 115–32.

Frith, U. (ed.) 1991. *Autism and Asperger syndrome*. Cambridge: Cambridge University Press.

Frith, U. 1985. Beneath the surface of developmental dyslexia. In Patterson, K.E., Marshall, J.C., Coltheart, M. (eds) *Surface dyslexia*. London: Lawrence Erlbaum.

Frith, U. 1989. *Autism: explaining the enigma*. Oxford. Blackwell.

Frith, U., Snowling, M. 1983. Reading for meaning and reading for sound in autistic and dsylexic children. *Journal of Developmental Psychology* **1**, 329–42.

Fromm, E. 1968. *The art of loving*. London: Unwin.

Fuchs, D., Fuchs, L., Benewitz, S.Y., Barringer, K. 1987. Norm-referenced tests: are they valid for use with handicapped students? *Exceptional Children* **54**, 263–71.

Furnham, A., Gunter, B. 1988. *The anatomy of adolescence*. London: Routledge.

Furrow, D., Nelson, K. 1986. A further look at the motherese hypothesis: a reply to Gleitman, Newport and Gleitman. *Journal of Child Language* **13**, 163–76.

Fürntratt, E., Möller, C. 1982. *Lernprinzip Erfolg*. Frankfurt: Peter Lang.

Gable, S., Belsky, J., Crnic, K. 1992. Marriage, parenting and child development. *Journal of Family Psychology* **5**, 276–94.

Galton, M. 1990. Grouping and group work. In C. Rogers and P. Kutnick (ed.), *The social psychology of the primary school*. London: Routledge.

Gano-Phillips, S., Fincham, F. 1995. Family conflict, divorce and children's adjustment. In Fitzpatrick, M.A., Vangelisti, A.L. (eds) *Explaining family interactions*. London: Sage, pp 206–31.

Garber, J., Braafladt, N., Zeman, J. 1991. The regulation of sad affect: an information processing perspective. In Garber, J., Dodge, K.A. (eds) *The development of emotion regulation and dysregulation*. Cambridge: Cambridge University Press, 208–40.

Garcia Coll, C., Lamberty, G., Jenkins, R., McAdoo, H.P., Crnic, K., Wasik, B.H, et al., 1996. An integrative model for the study of developmental competencies in minority children. *Child Development* **67**, 1891–914.

Garcia, I.F., Perez, G.Q. 1989. Violence, bullying and counselling in the Iberian Peninsula. In Roland, E., Munthe, E. (eds) *Bullying: an international perspective*. London: David Fulton, 41–52.

Gardner, H. 1983. *Frames of mind: the theory of multiple intelligences*. London: Heinemann.

Gasteiger-Klicpera, B., Klicpera, C. 1997. Aggressivität und soziale Stellung in der Klassengemeinschaft. *Zeitschrift für Kinder und Jugendpsychiatrie* **25**, 139–50.

Gathercole, V.C. 1987. The contrastive hypothesis for the acquisition of word meaning: a reconsideration of the theory. *Journal of Child Language* **14**, 493–531.

Gaver, W. 1996. Situating action II: affordances for interaction: the social is material for design. *Ecological Psychology* **8**, 111–30.

Gelman, S.A., Byrnes, J.A. (eds) 1991. *Perspectives on language and thought.* Cambridge: Cambridge University Press.

Genta, M.L., Menesini, E., Fonzi, A. 1996. Bullies and victims in Central and Southern Italy. *European Journal of Psychology and Education* **11**, 97–110.

Georgas, J. 1991. Intrafamily acculturation of values in Greece. *Journal of Cross-Cultural Psychology* **22**, 445–457.

George, C., Kaplan, N., Main, M. 1985. Adult Attachment Interview. Unpublished manuscript, University of California at Berkeley.

Gerbner, G., Gross, L. 1976. Living with television: the violence profile. *Journal of Communication* **26**, 173–99.

Giacquinta, J.B., Bauer, J.A., Levin, J.E 1993. *Beyond technology's promise.* Cambridge: Cambridge University Press.

Gibson, J.J. 1979. *The ecological approach to visual perception.* Boston, MA: Houghton Mifflin.

Gilbertson, M., and Kahmi, A.G. 1995. Novel word learning in children with hearing impairments. *Journal of Speech and Hearing Research,* **38**, 630–42.

Gilligan, C. 1982. *In a different voice: psychological theory and women's development.* Cambridge, MA: Harvard University Press.

Gillis, J.J., Gilger, J.W., Pennington, B.F., DeFries, J.C. 1992. Attention deficit disorder in reading-disabled twins: evidence for a genetic aetiology. *Journal of Abnormal Child Psychology* **20**, 303–15.

Gilmartin, B.G. 1987. Peer group antecedents of severe love-shyness in males. *Journal of Personality* **55**, 467–89.

Gnepp, J. 1983. Children's social sensitivity: inferring emotions from conflicting cues. *Developmental Psychology* **19**, 805–14.

Gnepp, J. 1989. Children's use of personal information to understand other people's feelings. In Saarni, C., Harris, P.L. (eds). *The child's understanding of emotion.* (pp 151-177). New York, Cambridge Univ. Press.

Goffman, E. 1971. *The presentation of self in everyday life.* Harmondsworth: Pelican.

Gofton, L. 1990. On the town: drink and the 'new lawlessness'. *Youth and Policy,* 29, 33–9.

Goldfield, B.A. 1985. Referential and expressive language: a study of two mother–child dyads. *First Language* **6**, 119–31.

Goldfield, B.A., Reznick, J.S. 1990. Early lexical acquisition: rate, content and vocabulary spurt. *Journal of Child Language* **17**, 171–83.

Goldiamond, I.E. 1974. Toward a constructional approach to social problems. *Behaviourism* **2**, 1–84.

Goldsmith, H.H. 1993. Temperament: variability in developing emotion systems. In Lewis, M., Haviland, J.M. (eds) *Handbook of emotions.* New York: Guilford, 353–64.

Golomb, C. 1995. Eitan: the artistic development of a child prodigy. In Golomb, C. (ed.) *The development of artistically gifted children: selected case studies.* Hillsdale, N.J.: Lawrence Erlbaum Associates, 171–96.

Golombok, S., Fivush, R. 1994. *Gender development.* New York: Cambridge University Press.

Gompertz, J. 1997. Developing communication: early intervention and augmentative signing from birth to five years. In Fawcus, M. (ed.) *Children with learning difficulties: a collaborative approach to their education and management*. London: Whurr, 97–129.

Goodman, R., Stevenson, J. 1989. A twin study of hyperactivity. II. The aetiological role of genes, family relationships, and perinatal adversity. *Journal of Child Psychology and Psychiatry* **30**, 691–709.

Goodnow, J.J., Burns, A. 1985. *Home and school: a child's eye view*. London: Allen & Unwin.

Goodnow, J.J., Collins, W.A. 1990. *Development according to parents: the nature, sources and consequences of parents' ideas*. Hillsdale, NJ: Lawrence Erlbaum Associates.

Goren, C.C., Sarty, M., Wu, P.Y.K. 1975. Visual following and pattern discrimination of face-like stimuli by newborn infants. *Pediatrics* **56**, 544–49.

Goswami, U. 1993. Toward an interactive analogy model of reading development – decoding vowel graphemes in beginning reading. *Journal of Experimental Child Psychology* **56**, 443–75.

Goswami, U.C., Bryant, P.E. 1990. *Phonological skills and learning to read*. Hove: Erlbaum.

Gould, S.J. 1996. *The mismeasure of man* (second edition). Harmondsworth: Pelican.

Graham, S. 1988. Children's developing understanding of the motivational role of affect: an attributional analysis. *Cognitive Development* **55**, 561–65.

Graham, S., Weiner, B. 1986. From an attributional theory of emotion to developmental psychology: a round-trip ticket? *Social Cognition* **4**, 152–79.

Gratch, G., Appel, K.J., Evans, W.F., LeCompte, G.K., Wright, N.A. 1974. Piaget's stage IV object concept error: evidence of forgetting or object conception. *Child Development* **45**, 71–77.

Green, C., Reid, D. 1996. Defining, validating and increasing indices of happiness among people with profound multiple disabilities. *Journal of Applied Behavior Analysis* **29**, 67–78.

Greenberg, J., Mitchell, S.A. 1983. *Object relations in psychoanalytic theory*. Cambridge, MA: Harvard University Press.

Greenberg, M.T., Kusché, C.A. 1997. Promoting social and emotional development in deaf children: the PATHS project. *Journal of Pediatric Psychology* **22**, 136–7.

Greenberger, E., O'Neil, R., Nagel, S.K. 1994. Linking workplace and homeplace: relations between the nature of adults' work and their parenting behaviors. *Developmental Psychology* **30**, 990–1002.

Greenfield, P.M., Cocking, R.R. 1994. (eds) *Cross-cultural roots of minority child development*. Hillsdale, NJ: Lawrence Erlbaum Associates.

Greer, M.K., Brown. F.R. 3rd, Pai, G.S., Choudry, S.H., Klein, A.J. 1997. Cognitive, adaptive, and behavioral characteristics of Williams' syndrome. *American Journal of Medical Genetics* **7**, 521–5.

Gregory, S. 1995. *Deaf children and their families* (second edition). Cambridge: Cambridge University Press.

Gregory, S. 1997. Deaf children's writing: the influence of British Sign

Language on written English. Paper presented to the International Symposium on Bilingualism, University of Newcastle on Tyne, April.

Gregory, S., Bishop, J., Sheldon, L. 1995. *Deaf young people and their families: developing understanding*. Cambridge: Cambridge University Press.

Gregory, S., Mogford, K. 1981. Early language development in deaf children. In Woll, B., Kyle, J.G., Deuchar, M. (eds) *Perspectives on BSL and deafness*. London: Croom Helm.

Gregory, S., Hindley, P. 1996. Communication strategies for deaf children. *Journal of Child Psychology and Psychiatry* **37**, 895–906.

Griffin, C. 1985. *Typical girls?* London: Routledge and Kegan Paul.

Griffin, C. 1993. *Representations of youth*. London: Polity Press.

Griffiths, M. 1994. *Transition to adulthood*. London: David Fulton.

Grosskurth, P. 1985. *Melanie Klein: her world and her work*. London: Basic Books.

Grossman, H. (ed.) 1983. *Classification in mental retardation* (third edition). Washington DC: American Association of Mental Retardation.

Grove, N., Porter, J., Bunning, K., Olsson, C. (Submitted for publication.) Interpreting the meaning of communication by people with severe and profound intellectual disabilities: theoretical and methodological issues.

Grove, N., Walker, M. 1990. The Makaton vocabulary: using manual signs and graphic symbols to develop interpersonal communication. *Augmentative and Alternative Communication* **6**, 15–28.

Grusec, J.E., Goodnow, J.J. 1994. Impact of parental discipline methods on the child's internalization of values: a reconceptualization of current points of view. *Developmental Psychology* **30**, 4–19.

Gunnarsson, Y. 1994. Livet på landet. In Fornäs, J., Boëthius, U., Forsman, M., Ganetz, H.. Reimer, B. (eds) *Ungdomskultur i Sverige*. Stockholm: Brutus Östlings Bokförlag, 103–24.

Gustafson, J.E. 1984. A unifying model for the structure of mental abilities.

Hagerman, R.J. 1991. Physical and behavioural phenotype. In Hagerman, R.J., Silverman, A.C. (eds) *The Fragile X syndrome: diagnosis, treatment and research*. Baltimore: Johns Hopkins University Press.

Hagerman, R.J. 1996. Biomedical advances in developmental psychology: the case of Fragile X syndrome. *Developmental Psychology* **32**, 416–24.

Hale, S. 1990. A global developmental trend in cognitive processing speed in children. *Child Development* **61**, 653–63.

Halford, G.S. 1982. *The development of thought*. Hillsdale, NJ: Lawrence Erlbaum.

Halford, G.S. 1993. *Children's understanding: the development of mental models*. Hillsdale, NJ: Erlbaum.

Halford, G.S., Maybery, M.T., Bain, J.D. 1986. Capacity limitations in children's reasoning: a dual-task approach. *Child Development* **57**, 616–27.

Hall, D. 1996. *Health for all children* (third edition). Oxford: Oxford University Press.

Hall, S. 1992. The questions of cultural identity. In Hall, S., Held, D., McGrew, T. (eds) *Modernity and its futures*. Cambridge: Polity, pp. 274–316.

Hall, S. 1996. Introduction: who needs 'identity'? In Hall, S., du Gay, P. (eds) *Questions of cultural identity*. London: Sage, pp. 1–17.

Hamer, D., Copeland, P. 1998. *Living with our genes*. New York: Doubleday.

Hamilton, C.E. 1994. Continuity and discontinuity of attachment from infancy trough adolescence. Unpublished manuscript, University of California at Berkeley.

Hammen, C. 1990. Cognitive approaches to depression. In Lahey, B.B., Kazdin, A.E. (eds) *Advances in clinical child psychology, vol. 13*. New York: Plenum, 139–73.

Hanewinkel, R., Knaack, R. 1997. Mobbing: eine Fragebogenstudie zum Ausmass von Aggression und Gewalt an Schulen. *Empirische Paedagogik* **11**, 403–22.

Hannon, P. 1995. *Literacy, home and school*. London: Falmer Press.

Hanson, V.L., Shankweiler, D., Fischer, F.W. 1983. Determinants of spelling ability in deaf and hearing adults: access to linguistic structure. *Cognition* **14**, 323–44.

Hanzlik, J.R., Stevenson, M.B. 1986. Interaction of mothers with their infants who are mentally retarded, retarded with cerebral palsy, or non-retarded. *American Journal of Mental Deficiency* **90**, 513–20.

Happé, F. 1994. *Autism: an introduction to psychology theory*. London: UCL Press Limited.

Happé, F., Frith, U. 1996. Theory of mind and social impairment in children with conduct disorder. *British Journal of Developmental Psychology* **14**, 385–98.

Hare, R.M. 1963. *Freedom and reason*. New York: Oxford University Press.

Harlow, H. 1958. The nature of love. *American Psychologist* **13**, 673–85.

Harris, C. 1993. *The family and the industrial society*. London: Allen & Unwin.

Harris, M. 1992. *Language experience and early development*. Hillsdale, NJ: Erlbaum.

Harris, M., Beech, J. 1992. Reading development in pre-lingually deaf children. In Nelson, K., Reger, Z. (eds) *Children's language, vol. 8*. Hillsdale, NJ: Lawrence Erlbaum.

Harris, M., Clibbens, J., Chasin, J., Tibbitts, R. 1989. The social context of early sign language development. *First Language* **9**, 81–97.

Harris, P.L. 1973. Perseverative errors in search by young infants. *Child Development* **44**, 28–33.

Harris, P.L. 1974. Perseverative search at a visibly empty place by young infants. *Journal of Experimental Child Psychology* **18**, 535–542.

Harris, P.L. 1989. *Children and emotion. The development of psychological understanding*. Oxford: Blackwell.

Harris, P.L., Johnson, C.N., Hutton, D., Andrews, G., Cook, T. 1989. Young children's theory of mind and emotion. *Cognition and Emotion* **3**, 379–400.

Harris, P.L., Olthof, T., Meerum Terwogt, M., Hardman, C.E. 1987. Children's knowledge of situations that provoke emotion. *International Journal of Behavioral Development* **10**, 319–43.

Harris, P.L., Olthof, T., Meerum Terwogt, M. 1981. Children's knowledge of emotion. *Journal of Child Psychology and Psychiatry* **22**, 247–61.

Harris, P.L., Olthof, T. 1982. The child's concept of emotion. In Butterworth, G., Light, P. (eds) *Social cognition; studies of the development of understanding* Brighton: Harvester Press, 188–209.

Harter, S. 1983. Children's understanding of multiple emotions: a cognitive–developmental approach. In Overton, W.F. (ed.) *The relationship between social and cognitive development.* Hillsdale, NJ: Erlbaum, 147–94.

Harter, S. 1987. The determinants and mediational role of global self-worth in children. In Eisenberg, N. (ed.) *Contemporary topics in developmental psychology.* New York: Wiley, 242–91.

Harter, S., Buddin, B. 1987. Children's understanding of the simultaneity of two emotions: a five-stage acquisition sequence. *Developmental Psychology* **23**, 388–99.

Harter, S., Whitesell, N. 1989. Developmental changes in children's emotion concepts. In Saarni, C., Harris, P.L. (eds) *The child's understanding of emotion.* New York, Cambridge University Press, 81–116.

Harter, S., Wright, K., Bresnick, S. 1987. A developmental sequence of the understanding of pride and shame. Paper presented at the Society for Research in Child Development Biennial Meeting, Baltimore.

Hartshorne, H., May, M.A. 1928–1930. *Studies in the nature of character. Vol. 1: Studies in deceit; Vol. 2: Studies in service and self-control: Vol. 3: Studies in organization of character.* New York: Macmillan.

Hartup, W.W. 1983. Peer relations. In Hetherington, E.M. (ed.), *Handbook of child psychology*, Vol. 4. New York: Wiley, 103–96.

Hasan, P., Messer D. 1997. Stability and instability in early cognitive abilities in children with Down's syndrome. *British Journal of Developmental Disabilities* **43**, 93–107.

Hastings, R. 1995. Understanding factors that influence staff responses to challenging behaviours: and exploratory interview study. *Mental Handicap Research* **8**, 296–320.

Havighurst, R.J. 1972. *Developmental tasks and education.* New York: McKay.

Havighurst, R.J., Neugarten, B.L. 1955. *American Indian and white children: a sociological investigation.* Chicago, IL: University Press.

Haviland, J., Lelwicka, M. 1987. The induced affect response: 10-week old infants' responses to three emotional expressions. *Developmental Psychology* **23**, 97–104.

Heenan, C. 1996. Feminist therapy and its discontents. In Burman, E., Aitken, G., Alldred, P., Allwood, R., Billington, T., Goldberg, B. et al. *Psychology discourse practice: from regulation to resistance.* London: Taylor & Francis, pp. 55–71.

Hemphill, L., Picardi, N., Tager-Flusberg, H. 1991. Narrative as an index of communicative competence in mildly mentally retarded children. *Applied Psycholinguistics* **12**, 263–79.

Hendry, L.B. 1983. *Growing up and going out.* Aberdeen University Press.

Hendry, L.B. 1987. Young people. In Fineman, S. (ed.) *Unemployment.* London: Tavistock, 195–218.

Hendry, L.B. 1992. Sports and leisure. In Coleman J.C., Warren-Adamson, C. (eds) *Youth policy in the 1990's.* London: Routledge, 62–87.

Hendry, L.B. 1993. Learning the new three Rs? *Aberdeen University Review* **189**, 33–51.

Hendry, L.B., Espnes, G.A., Glendinning, A., Ingebrigtsen, J.E., Kloep, M. Forthcoming. *Living at the edge?*

Hendry, L.B., Kloep, M. 1996. Adolescent risk-taking. Paper presented at the EARA Conference, Liège.

Hendry, L.B., Shucksmith, J., Love, J.G., Glendinning, A. 1993. *Young people's leisure and lifestyles.* London: Routledge.

Hendry L.B., Shucksmith, J., Philip, K., Jones, l. 1991. *Working with young people on drugs and HIV in Grampian region.* Grampian Health Board and Aberdeen University.

Henriques, J., Hollway, W., Urwin, C., Venn, C., Walkerdine, V. 1984/1998. *Changing the subject: psychology, regulation and subjectivity.* London: Methuen.

Henry, B., Moffitt, T., Robins, L., Earls, F., and Silva, P. 1993. Early family predictors of child and adolescent antisocial behaviour: who are the mothers of delinquents? *Criminal Behaviour and Mental Health* **3**, 97–118.

Hermelin, B., O'Connor, N. 1967. Remembering of words by psychotic and subnormal children. *British Journal of Psychology* **58**, 213–8.

Hermelin, B., O'Connor, N. 1986. Idiot savant calendrical calculators: rules and regularities. *Psychological Medicine* **16**, 885–93.

Hermelin, B., O'Connor N. 1990. Factors and primes: a specific numerical ability. *Psychological Medicine* **20**, 163–9.

Hermelin, B., O'Connor, N., Lee, S., Treffert, D. 1989. Intelligence and musical improvisation. *Psychological Medicine* **19**, 447–57.

Hesse, E. 1999. The Adult Attachment Interview: historical and current perspective. In Cassidy, J. Shaver, P. (eds) *Handbook on attachment theory and research.* New York: Guildford, 395–433.

Hetherington, E.M. 1989. Coping with family transitions: winners, losers and survivors. *Child Development* **60**, 1–14.

Hewitt, R. 1986. *White talk, Black talk.* Cambridge: Cambridge University Press.

Hewitt, R. 1996. *Routes of racism.* London: Centre for Multicultural Education, Institute of Education.

Hiatt, S., Campos, J.J., Emde, R.N. 1979. Facial patterning an infant facial expression: Happiness, surprise and fear. *Child Development* **50**, 1020–35.

Hill, A.L. 1978. Savants: mentally retarded individuals with special skills. In Ellis, N.R. (ed.) *International Review of Research in Mental Retardation,* Vol. 9. New York: Academic Press.

Hinde, R.A. 1982. Attachment: some conceptual and biological issues. In Parkes, C.M., Stevenson-Hinde, J. (eds) *The place of attachment in human behavior.* New York: Basic Books.

Hindley, P. 1997. Psychiatric aspects of hearing impairments. *Journal of Child Psychology & Psychiatry* **38**, 101–17.

Hinshaw, S.P., Zupan, B.A., Simmel, C., Nigg, J.T., Melnick, S. 1997. Peer status in boys with and without attention-deficit hyperactivity disorder: predictions from overt and covert antisocial behavior, social isolation and authoritative parenting beliefs. *Child Development* **68**, 880–96.

Hirano, K. 1992. Bullying and victimisation in Japanese classrooms. Paper presented at European Conference on Developmental Psychology, Spain.

Hirsch-Pasek, K., Treiman, R., Schneiderman. M. 1984. Brown and Hanlon revisited: mothers' sensivity to ungrammatical forms. *Journal of Child Language* **11**, 81–8.

Hirsch-Pasek, K. 1987. The metalinguistics of fingerspelling: an alternative way to increase reading vocabulary in congenitally deaf readers. *Reading Research Quarterly* **22**, 455–74.

Hirschfeld, L. 1997. *Race in the making: cognition, culture and the child's construction of human kinds.* Massachusetts: Massachusetts Institute of Technology Press.

Hobson, R.P. 1986. The autistic child's appraisal of expresssions of emotion. *Journal of Psychology and Psychiatry,* **27**, 321–42.

Hobson, R.P. 1993. *Autism and the development of mind.* Hove: Lawrence Erlbaum Associates.

Hobson, R.P., Brown, R., Minter, M., Lee, A. 1997. 'Autism' revisted: the case of congenital blindness. In Lewis V., Collis, G. (eds) *Blindness and psychological development in young children.* Leicester: BPS Books, 99–115.

Hodapp, R., Leckman, J., Dykens, E., Sparrow, S., Zelinsky, D., Ort, S. 1992. K-ABC profiles in children with Fragile X, Down's syndrome and non-specific mental retardation. *American Journal on Mental Retardation* **97**, 39–46.

Hoffman, L.W. 1991. The influence of the family environment on personality: Accounting for sibling differences. *Psychological Bulletin* **110**, 187–203.

Hoffman, M.L. 1970. Moral development. In Mussen, P.H. (ed.) *Carmichael's manual of child psychology (third edition).* New York, London, Sydney, Toronto: John Wiley and Sons, 261–359.

Hoffman, M.L. 1982. The measurement of empathy. In Izard, C.E. (ed.) *Measuring emotions in infants and children.* Cambridge: Cambridge University Press, 279–96.

Hoffman, M.L. 1984. Empathy, its limitations and its role in comprehensive moral theory. In Kurtines, W.M., Gewirtz, J.L. (eds) *Morality, moral behaviour and moral development: basic issues in theory and research.* New York: Wiley, 283–302.

Hofstaedter, P.R., Wendt, D. 1974. *Quantitative methoden der psychologie: deskriptive inferenz und korelationsstatistik (Vol. BD. 1,).* Frankfurt am Main: Johann Ambrosius Barth.

Hogg, M., Abrams, D. 1988. *Social identifications: a social psychology of intergroup relations and group processes.* London: Routledge.

Holmes, R. 1995. *How young children perceive race.* London: Sage.

Holstein, C.B. 1976. Irreversible, stepwise sequence in the development of moral judgment: a longitudinal study of males and females. *Child Development* **47**, 51–61.

Holt, J. 1984. *How children fail* (revised edition). Harmondsworth, England: Penguin Books.

Hood, B., Willatts, P. 1986. Reaching in the dark to an object's remembered position: evidence for object permanence in five-month-old infants. *British Journal of Developmental Psychology* **4**, 57–65.

Horn, G. 1985. *Memory, Imprinting and The Brain: an inquiry into mechanisms.* Oxford: Clarendon Press.

Hornby, N. 1992. *Fever pitch.* London: Victor Gollancz.

Horowitz, W.A., Kestenbaum, C., Person, E., Jarvik, L. 1965. Identical twin – 'idiots savants' – calendar calculators. *American Journal of Psychiatry* **121**, 1075–9.

Howe, M.J.A. 1990. *The origins of exceptional abilities.* Oxford: Blackwell.

Howe, M.J.A., Smith, J. 1988. Calendrical calculating in 'idiots savants': how do they do it? *British Journal of Psychology* **79**, 371–86.

Howe, N., Petrakos, H., Rinaldi, C.M. 1998. 'All the sheeps are dead. He murdered them': sibling pretence, negotiation, internal state language and relationship quality. *Child Development* **69**, 182–91.

Huesmann, L.R. 1986. Psychological processes promoting the relation between exposure to media violence and aggressive behavior by the viewer. *Journal of Social Issues* **42**, 125–39.

Humphrey, N. 1984. Consciousness Regained. Oxford: Oxford University Press.

Hunt, E. 1986. The heffalump of intelligence. In Sternberg, R.J., Detterman, D.K. (eds) *What is intelligence.* Norwood, NJ. Ablex, 101–7.

Hurrelmann, K., Losel, F. 1990. *Health hazards in adolescence.* DeGruyter: Berlin.

Hutnik, N. 1991. *Ethnic minority identity: a social psychological perspective.* Oxford: Oxford Science.

Huttenlocher, P.R. 1990. Morphometric study of human cerebral cortex development. *Neuropsychologia* **28**, 517–27.

Hyams, N. 1986. *Language acquisition and the theory of parameters.* Dordrecht: Reidel.

Hyams, N. 1992. A reanalysis of null subjects in child language. In Weissenborn, J., Goodluck, H., Roeper, T. (eds) *Theoretical issues in language acquistion.* Hillsdale, NJ: Erlbaum, 249–67.

Illich, I. 1973. *Deschooling society.* Harmondsworth: Penguin Books.

Ingham, R. 1987. Psychological contributions to the study of leisure. *Leisure Studies* **6**, 1–14.

Inhelder, B. 1943/1964. *The diagnosis of reasoning in the mentally retarded.* New York: John Day Company.

Inhelder, B., Piaget, J. 1958. *The growth of logical thinking.* London: Routledge and Kegan Paul.

Izard, C.E., Malatesta, C.Z. 1987, Perspectives on emotional development I: Differential emotions theory of early emotional development. In Osofsky, C.E. (ed.) *Handbook of infant development.* New York: Wiley, 494–554.

Jackson, S., Cicogani, E., Charman, L. 1996. The measurement of conflict in parent–adolescent relationships. In Verhofstadt-Denève, L., Kienhorst, I.,

Braet, C. (eds) *Conflict and development in adolescence*. Leiden: DSWO Press, 75–92.

James, W. 1890. *Principles of psychology*. New York: Holt.

Jarrold, C., Baddeley, A.D., Hewes, A.K. 1998. Verbal and nonverbal abilities in the Williams' syndrome phenotype: evidence for diverging developmental trajectories. *Journal of Child Psychology and Psychiatry* **39**, 511–24.

Jarrold, C., Russell, J. 1997. Counting abilities in autism: possible implications for central coherence theory. *Journal of Autism and Developmental Disorders* **27**, 25–38.

Jeffs, T. 1994. Children's educational rights in a new era? In Franklin, B. (ed.) *The handbook of children's rights: comparative policy and practice*. London: Routledge.

Jensen, A.R. 1982. Reaction time and psychometric *g*. In Eysenck, H.J. (ed.) *A model for intelligence*. Berlin: Springer-Verlag, 93–132.

Jensen, A.R., Schafer, E.W.P. Crinella, F.M. 1981. Reaction time, evoked potentials and psychometric *g* in the severely retarded. *Intelligence* **5**, 179–97.

Johnson, M.H. 1997. *Developmental cognitive neuroscience: An Introduction*. Oxford: Blackwell.

Johnson, M.H., Bolhuis, J.J., Horn, G. 1985. Interaction between acquired preferences and developing predispositions during imprinting. *Animal Behaviour* **33**, 1000–6.

Johnson, M.H., Dziurawiec, S., Ellis, H.D., Morton, J. 1991. Newborns' preferential tracking of face-like stimuli and its subsequent decline. *Cognition* **40**, 1–19.

Johnson, M.H., Vecera, S.P. 1995. Cortical differentiation and neurocognitive development: the parcellation conjecture. *Behavioural Processes* **36**, 195–212.

Johnson, M.H., Morton, J. 1991. *Biology and cognitive development: the case of face recognition*. Oxford: Blackwell.

Jones, G., Wallace, C. 1992. *Youth, family and citizenship*. Milton Keynes: Open University Press.

Jones, O. 1977. Mother–child communication with prelinguistic Down's syndrome and normal infants. In Schaffer, H. (ed.) *Studies in mother–infant interaction*. New York: Academic Press, 126–49.

Jones, S. 1988. *Black culture, white youth*. London: Macmillan.

Jordan, R.R., Powell, S.D. 1995. *Understanding and teaching children with autism*. Chichester: Wiley.

Kafai, Y, Harel, I. 1991. Learning through design and teaching: Exploring social and collaborative aspects of constructionism. In Harel, I., Papert, S. (eds) *Constructionism*. Norwood, NJ: Ablex.

Kagan, J. 1984. *The nature of the child*. New York: Basic Books.

Kagan, J. 1994. On the nature of emotion. In Fox, N. (ed.) The development of emotion regulation. *Monographs of the Society for Research in Child Development* **59** (Serial No 240), 7–24.

Kagan, J., Snidman, N. 1991. Infant predictors of inhibited and uninhibited profiles. *Psychological Science* **2**, 40–4.

Kail, R. 1988. Developmental functions for speeds of cognitive processes. *Journal of Experimental Child Psychology* **45**, 339–64.

Kail, R. 1992. Evidence for global developmental change is intact. *Journal of Experimental Child Psychology* **54**, 308–14.

Kanner, L. 1943. Autistic disturbances of affective contact. *Nervous Child* **2**, 217–50.

Karmiloff-Smith, A. 1988. The child is a theoretician, not an inductivist. *Mind and Language* **3**, 183–95.

Karmiloff-Smith, A. 1990. Constraints on representational change: evidence from children's drawings. *Cognition* **34**, 57–83.

Karmiloff-Smith, A. 1992. *Beyond Modularity: a developmental perspective on cognitive science*. Cambridge, MA: MIT Press.

Karmiloff-Smith, A. 1997. *Journal of Child Language.*

Katz, E. 1959. Mass communications research and the study of popular culture. *Studies in Public Communication* **2**, 1–6.

Katz, L.C., Shatz, C.J. 1996. Synaptic activity and the construction of cortical circuits. *Science* **274**, 1133–8.

Kay, J., Marcel, A.J. 1981. One process, not two in reading aloud: lexical analogies do the work of nonlexical rules. *Quarterly Journal of Experimental Psychology* **33A**, 397–414.

Kaye, K. 1982. *The mental and social life of babies*. Chicago, IL: University of Chicago Press.

Keenan, K., Loeber, R., Zhang, Q., Stouthammer-Loeber, M., Van Kamen, W.B. 1995. The influence of deviant peers on the development of boys' disruptive and delinquent behavior: a temporal analysis. *Development and Psychopathology* **7**, 715–26.

Keeney, T.J., Cannizzo, S.R., Flavell, J.H. 1967. Spontaneous and induced verbal rehearsal in a recall task. *Child Development* **38**, 953–66.

Kekelis, L., Sacks, S. 1992. The effects of visual impairment on children's social interactions in regular education programs. In Sacks, S. Kekelis, L., Gaylord-Ross R. (eds) *The development of social skills by blind and visually impaired students*. New York: American Federation for the Blind,

Kekelis, L.S., Prinz, D.M. 1996. Blind and sighted children with their mothers: the development of discourse skills. *Journal of Visual Impairment and Blindness* **90**, 423–36.

Keller, M., Eckensberger, L.H., von Rosen, K. 1989. Action theory and the structure of moral stages: the case of stage 2. *Journal of Behavioral Development* **12**, 57–69.

Kellogg, R. 1970. *Analyzing children's art*. Palo Alto, CA: Mayfield.

Kellogg, R. 1979. *Children's drawings, children's minds*. New York: Avon Books.

Kelly, C., Breinlinger, S. 1996. *The social psychology of collective action*. London: Falmer.

Kelly, E., Cohn, T. 1988. *Racism in schools: new research evidence*. Stoke-on-Trent: Trentham.

Kennedy, J.M. 1993. *Drawing and the blind: pictures to touch*. New Haven: Yale University Press.

Kent-Baguley, P. 1990. Sexuality and youth work practice. In: Jeffs, T., Smith, M. (eds) *Young people, inequality and youth work*. London: Macmillan.

Kernan, K., Sabsay, S. 1987. Referential first mention in narratives by mildly mentally retarded adults. *Research in Developmental Disabilities* **8**, 361–9.

Kernan, K., Sabsay, S. 1996. Linguistic and cognitive ability of adults with Down syndrome and mental retardation of unknown etiology. *Journal of Communication Disorders* **29**, 401–22.

Kesselring, T. (1981). *Entwicklung und Widerspruch. Ein Vergleich zwischen Piagets genetischer Erkenntnistheorie und Hegels Dialektik*. Frankfurt am Main: Suhrkamp.

Kestenbaum, R., Termine, N., Spelke, E.S. 1987. Perception of objects and object boundaries by three-month-old infants. *British Journal of Developmental Psychology* **5**, 367–83.

Kidscape Press Release 1998. World first study into long term effects of bullying. Presented at Kidscape Conference, 'Bullying: successful ways to stop it.' London, 21 April.

Kiernan, C., Reid, B., Jones, L. 1982. *Signs and symbols: a review of the literature and survey of the use of non-vocal communication systems*. London: Heinemann.

Kiernan, C.C., Qureshi, H. 1993. Challenging behaviour. In Kiernan, C.C. (ed.) *Research to practice? Implications of research on the challenging behaviour of people with learning disabilities*. Kidderminster: British Institute of Learning Disabilities, 53–87.

Killeen, L. 1992. Leaving home, housing and income. In Coleman, J.C., Warren-Adamson, C. (eds) *Young people in the 1990s*. London: Routledge, 189–202.

Kirchler, E., Palmonari, A., Pombeni, M.L. 1992. Auf der Suche nach einem Weg ins Erwachsenenalter. *Psychologie in Erziehung und Unterricht* **39**, 277–95.

Kirchler, E., Pombeni, M.L., Palmonari, A. 1991. Sweet sixteen . . . *European Journal of Psychology of Education* **6**, 393–410.

Klahr, D., Siegler, R.S. 1978. The representation of children's knowledge. In Reese, H. Lipsett, L.P. (eds) *Advances in child development*, Vol. 12. New York: Academic Press, 61–116.

Klein, M. 1946. Notes on some schizoid mechanisms. In *The writings of Melanie Klein*. London: Hogarth, 1975, 1–24.

Klein, R., Mannuzza, S. 1991. Long-term outcome of hyperactive children: a review. *Journal of the American Academy of Child and Adolescent Psychiatry* **30**, 383–7.

Kleiner, K.A. 1987. Amplitude and phase spectra as indices of infants' pattern preferences. *Infant Behaviour and Development* **10**, 49–59.

Kline, S. 1993. *Out of the garden. Toys and children's culture in the age of TV marketing*. London: Verso.

Kloep, M. 1984. Bildung als Lebensbefähigung. *Die Deutsche Schule* **6**, 487–93.

Kloep, M. 1994. Changing values in a patriarchal society. Paper presented at the International Conference on Family and Community Care, Hong Kong.

Kloep, M. 1998. *Att vara ung i Jämtland.* Österåsen: Uddeholt.

Kloep, M., Hendry, L.B. 1997. 'In three years we'll be just like Sweden!' *Young* **5**, 2–19.

Kloep, M., Olsson, S., Olofsson, A. 1995. 'Your mother doesn't love me anymore . . .' Paper presented at International Conference on Conflict and Development in Adolescence, Gent.

Kloep, M., Tarifa, F. 1993. Albanian children in the wind of change. In Wolvén, L.E. (ed.) *Human resource development.* Högskolan i Östersund, 85–116.

Knight, P. 1997. Bilingual nursery provision – a challenging start. *Deafness and Education,* **21**, 20–30.

Kobak, R.R., Sceery, A. 1988. Attachment in late adolescence: working models, affect regulation and representations of self and others. *Child Development* **59**, 135–46.

Koffka, K. 1935. *Principles of Gestalt psychology.* New York: Harcourt Brace.

Kohlberg, L. 1958. The development of modes of moral thinking and choice in the years ten to sixteen. Unpublished doctoral dissertation, University of Chicago.

Kohlberg, L. 1963. Moral development and identification. In Stevenson, H.W. (ed.) *Child psychology 62nd Yearbook of the National Society for the Study of Education.* Chicago: University of Chicago Press, 277–332.

Kohlberg, L. 1969. *Stages in the development of moral thought and action.* New York: Holt Rinehart and Winston.

Kohlberg, L. 1976. Moral stages and moralisation: the cognitive–developmental approach. In Lickona, T. (ed.) *Moral development and behavior. Theory, research and social issues.* New York: Holt, Rinehart and Winston, 31–53.

Kohlberg, L. 1986. A current statement on some theoretical issues. In Modgil, S., Modgil, C. (eds) *Lawrence Kohlberg: consensus and controversy.* London, Philadelphia: Falmer Press, 485–546.

Kohlberg, L., Levine, C., Hewer, A. (1983). *Moral stages: A current formulation and a response to critics.* Basel: Karger.

Kohlberg, L., Candee, D (1984). The relationship of moral judgment to moral action.. In W.M. Kurtines and J.L. Gewirtz (eds), *Morality, moral behavior and moral development,* 52, 73. New York: Wiley.

Kohlberg, L., Kramer, R.B. 1969. Continuities and discontinuities in childhood and adult moral development. *Human Development* **12**, 93–120.

Kohnstamm, D. 1996. A debate on the state of Dutch youth and on appropriate action to be taken in response to reported unhappiness. In Verhofstadt-Denève, L., Kienhorst, I., Braet, C. (eds) *Conflict and development in adolescence.* Leiden: DSWO Press, 183–7.

Koops, W. 1996. Historical developmental psychology of adolescence. In Verhofstadt-Denève, L., Kienhorst, I., Braet, C. (eds) *Conflict and development in adolescence.* Leiden: DSWO Press, 1–12.

Kranzler, J.H., Jensen, A.R. 1989. Inspection time and intelligence: a meta-analysis. *Intelligence* 13, 329–48.

Kucynski, L., Kockanska, G. 1995. Function and content of maternal demands: developmental significance of early demands for competent action. *Child Development* **66**, 616–28.

Kupersmidt, J.B., Griesler, P.C., De Rosier, M.E., Patterson, C.J., Davis, P.W. 1995. Childhood aggression and peer relations in the context of family and neighborhood factors. *Child Development* **66**, 360–75.

Kupersmidt, J.B., Coie, J.D. 1990. Preadolescent peer status, aggression and school adjustment as predictors of externalizing problems in adolescence. *Child Development* **61**, 1350–62.

Kusché, C.A., Greenberg, M.T. 1983. Evaluative understanding and role taking ability: a comparison of deaf and hearing children. *Child Development* **54**, 141–7.

Kyle, J., Woll, B. 1985. *Sign language: the study of deaf people and their language.* Cambridge: Cambridge University Press.

LaHoste, G.J., Swanson, J.M., Wigal, S.S., Glabe, C., Wigal, T., King, N. et al. 1996. Dopamine D4 receptor gene polymorphism is associated with attention deficit hyperactivity disorder. *Molecular Psychiatry* **1**, 128–31.

Lagerspetz, K.M., Björkqvist, K., Berts, M., King, E. 1982. Group aggression among school children in three schools. *Scandinavian Journal of Psychology* **23**, 45–52.

Lagerspetz, K.M.J., Björkqvist, K., Peltonen, T. 1988. Is indirect aggression more typical of females? Gender differences in aggressiveness in 11- to 12-year-old children. *Aggressive Behavior* **14**, 403–14.

Lamb, M.E., Thompson, R.A., Gardner, W., Charnov, E.L., Connell, J.P. 1985. *Infant-mother attachment: the origins and developmental significance of individual differences in strange situation behavior.* Hillsdale, NJ: Lawrence Erlbaum.

Lamborn, S.D., Dornbusch, S.M., Steinberg, L. 1996. Ethnicity and community context as moderators of the relations between family decision making and adolescent adjustment. *Child Development* **67**, 283–301.

Lancioni, G., Reilly, M., Emerson, E. 1996. A review of choice research with people with severe and profound developmental disabilities. *Research in Developmental Disabilities* **17**, 391–411.

Land, S.L., Vineberg, S.E. 1965. Locus of control in blind children. *Exceptional Children*, **31**, 257–60.

Landa, R., Folstein, S.E., Isaacs, C. 1991. Spontaneous narrative-discourse performance of parents of autistic individuals. *Journal of Speech and Hearing Research* **34**, 1339–45.

Landau, B. 1983. Blind children's language is not 'meaningless'. In Mills, A. (ed.) *Language acquisition in the blind child.* London: Croom Helm, 62–76.

Landau, B. 1997. Language and experience in blind children. In Lewis, V., Collis, G.M. (eds) *Blindness and psychological development in young children.* Leicester: British Psychological Society.

Landau, B., Gleitman, L.R. 1985. *Language and experience: evidence from the blind child.* Cambridge MA: Harvard University Press.

Lander, E.S, Shork, N.J. 1994. Genetic dissection of complex traits. *Science* **265**, 2037–48.

Landers, W.F. 1971. The effect of differential experience on infants' performance in a Piagetian stage IV object concept task. *Developmental Psychology* **5**, 48–54.

Large, A., Beheshti, J., Breuleux, A., Renaud, A. 1994. Multimedia and comprehension – a cognitive study. *Journal of the American Society for Information Science*, 45, 515–28.

Lazarus, R.S., Folkman, S. 1984. *Stress, appraisal and coping.* New York: Springer.

Le Prevost, P. 1983. Using the Makaton vocabulary in early language training with a Down's baby: a single-case study. *Mental Handicap* **11** (March), 28–9.

Lederberg, A. 1993. The impact of deafness on mother–child and peer relationships. In Marschark, M., Clark, M.D. (eds) *Psychological perspectives on deafness.* Hillsdale, NJ: Lawrence Erlbaum Associates, 93–122.

Lederberg, A.R., Rosenblatt, V.R., Vandell, D.R. 1987. Temporary and long-term friendships in hearing and deaf preschoolers. *Merrill-Palmer Quarterly*, **33**, 513–33.

Lei, T. 1994. Being or becoming moral in a Chinese culture: unique or universal? *Cross-Cultural Research* **28**, 58–91.

Lemish, D., Rice, M.L. 1986. Television as a talking picture book: a prop for language acquisition. *Journal of Child Language* 13, 251–74.

Lempert, W. 1988. Soziobiographische Bedingungen der Entwicklung moralischer Urteilsfähigkeit. *Kölner Zeitschrift für Soziologie und Sozialforschung* 40, 62–92.

Lepper, M.R., Cordova, D.I. 1992. A desire to be taught – instructional consequences of intrinsic motivation. *Motivation and Emotion* **16**, 187–208.

Lerner, R.M. 1985. Adolescent maturational changes and psychosocial development. *Journal of Youth and Adolescence* **14**, 355–72.

Leslie, A. 1994. ToMM, ToBy and agency: core architecture and domain specificity. In Hirschfeld, L., Gelman, S. (eds) *Mapping the mind: domain specificity in cognition and culture.* Cambridge: Cambridge University Press, 119–48.

Leslie, A.M. 1987. Pretense and representation: the origins of 'Theory of Mind'. *Psychological Review* **94**, 412–26.

Leudar, I. 1987. Communicative environments for mentally handicapped people. In Beveridge, M., Conti-Ramsden, G., Leudar, I. (eds) *Language and communication in mentally handicapped people.* London: Chapman and Hall.

Levitt, H., McGarr, N., Geffner, D. 1988. Development of language and communication skills in hearing impaired children. *ASHA Monographs* (No 26).

Levitt, M.J., Antonucci, T.C., Clark, M.C. 1984. Object-person permanence and attachment: another look. *Merrill-Palmer Quarterly* **30**, 1–10.

Lewis, H.B. 1973. *Shame and guilt in neurosis.* New York: International Universities Press.

Lewis, M., Feiring, C., Rosenthal, S. 1997. Attachment over time. Unpublished manuscript, Robert Wood Johnson Medical School.

Lewis, V., Collis, G.M. 1997. *Blindness and psychological development*. Leicester: BPS Books.

Lickona, T. 1976. Research on Piaget's theory of moral development. In Lickona, T. (ed.) *Moral development and behavior. Theory, research and social issues*. New York: Holt, Rinehart and Winston, 219–40.

Lieberman, A.F., Weston, D.R., Pawl, J.H. 1991. Preventive intervention and outcome with anxiously attached dyads. *Child Development, 62*, 199–209.

Light, P.H. 1985. The development of view-specific representation considered from a socio-cognitive standpoint. In Freeman, N., Cox, M. (eds) *Visual order: the nature and development of pictorial representation*. Cambridge: Cambridge University Press, 214–29.

Light, P.H., Humphreys, J. 1981. Internal relationships in young children's drawings. *Journal of Experimental Child Psychology* **31**, 521–30.

Light, P.H. 1997. Computers for learning: psychological perspectives. *Journal of Child Psychology and Psychiatry* **38**, 497–504.

Lipovechaja, N.G., Kantonistowa, N.S., Chamaganova, T.G. 1978. The role of heredity and environment in the determination of intellectual function. *Medicinskie, Probleing Formirovaniga Livenosti* **1**, 48–59.

Lloyd, M.A. 1985. *Adolescence*. London: Harper and Row.

Loeber, R., Wung, P., Keenan, K., Giroux, B., Stouthammer-Loeber, M., Van Kammen, W.B., et al. 1993. Development pathways in disruptive child behavior. *Developmental and Psychopathology* **5**, 103–33.

Loeber, R., Dishion, T.J. 1983. Early predictors of male delinquency: a review. *Psychological Bulletin* **94**, 69–99.

Loeber, R., Hay, D.F. 1994. Developmental approaches to aggression and conduct problems. In Rutter, M., Hay, D.F. (eds) *Development through life: a handbook for clinicians* Oxford: Blackwell Scientific Publications, 488–516.

Loeber, R., Stouthammer-Loeber, M. 1986. Family factors as correlates and predictors of juvenile conduct problems and delinquency. In Tonry, M., Morris, N. (eds) Crime and justice. Chicago: University of Chicago Press, 29–149.

Loeber, R., Strouthamer-Loeber, M. 1987. Prediction. In Quay, H.C. (ed.), *Handbook of juvenile delinquency*. New York: Wiley, 325–82.

Loehlin, J.C., Horn, J.M., Willerman, L. 1989. Modeling IQ change: evidence from the Texas Adoption Project. *Child Development* **60**, 993–1004.

Longstreth, L.E. 1984. Jensen's reaction time investigations of intelligence: a critique. *Intelligence 8*, 139–60.

Longstreth, L.E., Walsh, D.A., Alcorn, M.B., Szeszulski, P.A. Manis, F.R. 1986. Backward masking, IQ, SAT and reaction time: interrelationships and theory. *Personality and Individual Differences* **7**, 643–51.

Lowenstein, L.F. 1977. Who is the bully. *Home and School* **11**, 3–4.

Luquet, G.H. 1927. *Le dessin enfantin*. (Children's drawing). Paris: Alcan.

Lyle, R. 1959. The effects of an institutionalized environment on the verbal development of institutionalized children. *Journal of Mental Deficiency Research* **3**, 122–8.

Lynn, R., Hattori, K. 1990. The heritability of intelligence in Japan. *Behaviour Genetics* **20**, 545–6.

Lyons-Ruth, K. 1991. Rapprochement or approchement: Mahler's theory reconsidered from the vantage–point of recent research on early attachment relationships. *Psychoanalytic Psychology* **8**, 1–23.

Lyons-Ruth, K. 1996. Attachment relationships among children with aggressive behavior problems: the role of disorganized early attachment patterns. *Journal of Consulting and Clinical Psychology* **64**, 64–73.

Lytton, H., Romney, D.M. 1991. Parents' differential socialization of boys and girls: a meta-analysis. *Psychological Bulletin* **109**, 267–96.

Mac an Ghaill, M. 1988. *Young, gifted and Black: student teacher relations in the schooling of black youth.* Milton Keynes: Open University Press.

Maccoby, E.E., Martin, J.A. 1983. Socialization in the context of the family. In Hetherington, E.M. (ed.) *Handbook of child psychology: volume 4: personality and social development.* (fourth edition). New York. Wiley, pp 1–101.

Macdonald, I., Bhavnani, R., Khan, L., John, G. 1989. *Murder in the playground.* London: Longsight Press.

Magai, C., McFadden, S.H. 1995. *The role of emotions in social and personality development.* New York: Plenum.

Magnusson, D. 1987. Adult delinquency in the light of conduct and physiology at an early age: a longitudinal study. In Magnusson, D. Oehman, A. et al. (eds) *Psychopathology: an interactional perspective. Personality, psychopathology and psychotherapy.* Academic Press, 221–34.

Mahler, M.S., Pine, F., Bergman, A. 1975. *The psychological birth of the human infant: symbiosis and individuation.* New York: Basic Books.

Main, M. 1990. Cross-cultural studies of attachment organization: recent studies, changing methodologies and the concept of conditional strategies. *Human Development* **33**, 48–61.

Main, M., Goldwyn, R. In press. Adult attachment scoring and classification systems. In Main, M. (ed.) *Assessing attachment through discourse, drawings and reunion situations (working title).* New York: Cambridge University Press.

Main, M., Kaplan, N., Cassidy, J. 1985. Security in infancy, childhood, and adulthood: a move to the level of representation. In Bretherton, I., Waters, E. (eds) *Growing points of attachment theory and research.* Society for Research in Child Development, 66–104.

Main, M., Solomon, J. 1986. Discovery of an insecure–disorganized/disoriented attachment pattern. In Brazelton, T.B., Yogman, M.W. (eds) *Affective development in infancy.* Norwood, NJ: Ablex, 95–124.

Malatesta, C.Z., Wilson, A. 1988. Emotion–cognition interaction in personality development: a discrete emotions, functionalist analysis. *British Journal of Social Psychology* **27**, 91–112.

Mama, A. 1995. *Beyond the masks: race, gender and subjectivity.* London: Routledge.

Manke, B., Pike, A. 1997. The search for new domains of non-shared environmental experience: looking outside the family. Paper presented at the biennial meeting of the Society for Research in Child Development, Washington, D.C, April.

Manning, M., Heron, J., Marshall, T. 1978. Styles of hostility and social interactions at nursery, at school and at home: an extended study of children. In Hersov, L.A. Berger, M., Shaffer, D. (eds) *Aggression and anti-social behaviour in childhood and adolescence*. Oxford: Pergamon Press, 29–58.

Marchman, V., Bates, E. 1994. Continuity in lexical and morphological development: a test of the critical mass hypothesis. *Journal of Child Language*, **21**, 339–66.

Marcia, J. 1980. Identity in adolescence. In Adelson, J. (ed.) *Handbook of adolescent psychology*. New York: John Wiley, pp. 159–87.

Marcia, J. 1994. The empirical study of ego identity. In Bosma, H., Graafsma, T., Grotevant, H., de Levita, D. (eds) *Identity and development: an interdisciplinary approach*. London: Sage, pp. 67–80.

Marcia, J. 1998. Peer Gynt's life cycle. In Skoe, E., von der Lippe, A. (eds) *Personality development in adolescence: a cross national and life span perspective*. London: Routledge, pp. 193–209.

Marcia, J.E. 1996. The importance of conflict for adolescent and lifespan development. In Verhofstadt-Denève, L., Kienhorst, I., Braet, C. (eds) *Conflict and development in adolescence*. Leiden: DSWO Press, 13–19.

Margalit, M. 1991. Understanding loneliness among students with learning disabilities. *Behaviour Change* **8**, 67–173.

Marr, D. 1982. *Vision: a computational investigation into the human representation and processing of visual information*. San Francisco: W.H. Freeman.

Marschark, M. 1993. *Psychological development of deaf children*. Oxford: Oxford University Press.

Marschark, M. 1997. *Raising and educating a deaf child*. New York: OUP.

Marschark, M., Harris, M. 1996. Success and failure in learning to read: the special (?) Case of deaf children. In Cornoldi, C. and Oakhill, J. (eds) *Reading comprehension difficulties : Processes and intervention*. Hillsdale NJ; Lawrence Erlbaum Associates.

Martin, K.A. 1996. *Puberty, sexuality and the self*. London: Routledge.

Marvin, R.S., VanDevender, T.L., Iwanaga, M.I., LeVine, S., LeVine, R.A. 1977. Infant–caregiver attachment among the Hausa of Nigeria. In McGurk, H. (ed.) *Ecological factors in human development*. Amsterdam: North Holland, 247–59.

Maslow, A. 1968. *Towards a psychology of being*. (second edition). Princeton: Van Nostrand.

Mason, C.A., Cauce, A.M., Gonzales, N., Hiraga, Y. 1996. Neither too sweet nor too sour: problem peers, maternal control and problem behavior in African American adolescents. *Child Development* **67**, 2115–30.

Matthews, J. 1984. Children drawing: are young children really scribbling? *Early Child Development and Care* **18**, 1–39.

Maurer, D. 1985. Infants' perception of facedness. In Field, T.N., Fox, N. (eds), *Social perception in infants*, NJ: Ablex, 73–100.

Maurer, D. 1993. Neonatal synesthesia: implications for the processing of speech and faces. In B. de Boysson-Bardies B., de Schonen, S., Jusczyk, P., McNeilage, P., Morton, J., (eds), *Developmental neurocognition: speech and face processing in the first year of life*. Dordrecht, The Netherlands: Kluwer, 109–24.

Maurer, H., Sherrod, K. 1987. Context of directives given to young children with Down's syndrome and non-retarded children: development over two years. *American Journal of Mental Deficiency* **91** , 579–90.

Maxwell, M. 1990. Visual-centered narratives of the deaf. *Linguistics and Education* **2**, 213–29.

Mayberry, R.I., Eichen, E.B. 1991. The long-lasting advantage of learning sign language in childhood. Another look at the critical period for language acquisition. *Journal of Memory and Language* **30**, 486–512.

McCall, R.B. 1994. What process mediates prediction of childhood IQ from infant habituation and recognition memory? Speculations on the roles of inhibition and rate of information processing. *Intelligence* **18**, 107–24.

McCartney, K., Harris, M.J., Bernieri, F. 1990. Growing up and growing apart: a developmental meta-analysis of twin studies. *Psychological Bulletin* **107**, 226–37.

McClearn, G.E., Johansson, B., Berg, S., Pederson, N.L., Ahern, F., Petrill, S.A. et al. 1997. Substantial genetic influence on cognitive abilities in twins 80 or more years old. *Science* **276**, 1560–3.

McConachie, H., Moore, V. 1994. Early expressive language and severely visually impaired children. *Developmental Medicine and Child Neurology* **36**, 230–40.

McGlone, F., Park, A., Roberts, C. 1996. *Relative values*. Family Policy Studies Centre: BSA.

McGue, M., Bouchard, T.J., Iacono, W.G., Lykken, D.T. 1993. Behavioral genetics of cognitive ability: a life-span perspective. In Plomin, R., McClearn, G.E. (eds) *Nature, nurture and psychology*. Washington, DC: American Psychological Association, 39–76.

McGuffin, P., Gottesman, I.I. 1985. Genetic influences on normal and abnormal development. In Rutter, M. Hersov, L. (eds), *Child and adolescent psychiatry: modern approaches* (2nd ed.). Oxford: Blackwell Scientific, 17–33.

McGuire, S., Dunn, J., Plomin, R. 1995. Maternal differential treatment of siblings and children's behavioral problems: A longitudinal study. *Development and Psychopathology* **7**, 515–28.

McNeil, J.D. 1966. *The ABC learning activity: language of instruction*. New York: American Book.

McRobbie, A., McCabe, T. 1981. *Feminism for girls*. London: Routledge & Kegan Paul.

McShane, J. 1980. *Learning to talk*. Cambridge: Cambridge University Press.

McShane, J. 1991. *Cognitive development: an information processing approach*. Oxford: Blackwell.

Mead, G.H. 1934/1962. *Mind, self and society*. Chicago, IL: University of Chicago Press.

Meadow-Orleans, K.P. 1987. An analysis of the effectiveness of early intervention programs for hearing-impaired children. In Guralnick, M.J., Bennett, F.C. (eds) *The effectiveness of early intervention for at-risk and handicapped children*. New York: Academic Press, 325–57.

Meerum Terwogt, M. 1986. Affective states and task performance in naive and prompted children. *European Journal of Psychology of Education* **1**, 31–40.

Meerum Terwogt, M., Koops, W., Oosterhoff, T., Olthof, T. 1986. Development in processing of multiple emotional situations. *Journal of General Psychology* **113**, 109–19.

Meerum Terwogt, M., Olthof, T. 1989. Awareness and self-regulation of emotion in young children. In Saarni, C., Harris, P.L. (eds) *The child's understanding of emotion*. New York, Cambridge University Press, 209–37.

Meerum Terwogt, M., Stegge, H. 1995. Children's understanding of the strategic control of negative emotions. In Russell, J.A. Fernández-Dols, J. Manstead, A.S.R., Wellenkamp, J.C. (eds) *Everyday concepts of emotion: an introduction to the psychology, anthropology and linguistics of emotion. NATO ASI Series, Vol. 81*. Dordrecht: Kluwer Academic Publishers, 373–90.

Meier, R., Newport, E. 1990. 'Out of the hands of babes': on a possible sign advantage in language acquisition. *Language* **66**, 1–23.

Mein, R., O'Connor, N. 1960. A study of the oral vocabularies of severely subnormal patients. *Journal of Mental Defiency Research* **4**, 130–43.

Meisel, J. 1995. Parameters in acquisition. In Fletcher, P., MacWhinney, B. (eds) *Handbook of child language*. Oxford: Blackwell, 10–35.

Meldrum, W. 1990. Autism and adulthood, In Ellis, K. (ed.) *Autism: professional perspectives and practice*. London: Chapman & Hall, 123–52.

Mellor, A. 1990. Bullying in Scottish secondary schools. *Spotlights* **23**, Edinburgh: SCRE.

Meltzoff, A., Gopnik, A. 1993. The role of imitation in understanding persons and developing a theory of mind. In Baron-Cohen, S. Tager-Flushberg, H. and Cohen, D. (eds) *Understanding other minds – perspective from autism*. Oxford: Oxford University Press,

Meltzoff, A.N., Moore, K.M. 1977. Imitation of facial and manual gestures by human neonates. *Science* **19**, 75–8.

Meltzoff, A.N., Moore, M.K. 1992. Early imitation within a functional framework: the importance of person identity, movement and development. *Infant Behavior and Development* **15**, 479–505.

Meltzoff, A.N., 1988. Infant imitation after a 1-week delay: long-term memory for novel acts and multiple stimuli. *Developmental Psycholgy* 24, 470–6.

Meltzoff, A.N., Borton, W. 1979. Intermodal matching by human neonates. *Nature* **282**, 403–4.

Meltzoff, A.N., Moore, M.K. 1977. Imitation of facial and manual gestures by human neonates. *Science* **198**, 75–8.

Meltzoff, A.N., Gopnik, A. 1989. On linking nonverbal imitation, representation and language learning in the first two years of life. In Speidel, G.E., Nelson K.E. (eds) *The many faces of imitation in language learning*. New York: Spring-Verlag, 23–5.

Messer, D.J. 1981. The identification of names in maternal speech to infants. *Journal of Psycholinguistic Research* **10**, 69–77.

Messer, D.J. 1994. *The development of communication: from social interaction to language.* Chichester/New York: Wiley.

Messer, D.J., Vietze, P.M. 1988. Does mutual influence occur during mother–infant social gaze? *Infant Behaviour and Development* **11**, 97–110.

Meyrowitz, J. 1985. *No sense of place.* New York: Oxford University Press.

Millar, S. 1994. *Understanding and representing space: theory and evidence from studies with blind and sighted children.* Oxford: Clarendon Press.

Mills, A. 1988. Visual handicap. In Bishop, D., Mogford, K. (eds) *Language development in exceptional circumstances.* Edinburgh: Churchill Livingstone.

Milner, D. 1983. *Children and race ten years on.* London: Ward Lock Educational.

Minuchin, P. 1985. Families and individual development: provocations from the field of family therapy. *Child Development* **56**, 289–302.

Modgil, S. and Modgil, C. (eds), (1986). *Lawrence Kohlberg. Consensus and Controversy.* Philadelphia and London: Falmer Press.

Modgil, S., Modgil, C. (eds) 1976. *Piagetian research, Vol. 6.* Windsor: NFER.

Modood, T., Beishon, S., Virdee, S. 1994. *Changing ethnic identities.* London: Policy Studies Institute

Modood, T., Berthoud, R., Lakey, J., Nazroo et al. 1997. *Ethnic minorities in Britain: diversity and disadvantage.* London: Policy Studies Institute.

Moffitt, T.E., Caspi, A., Dickson, N., Silva, P., Stanton, W. 1996. Childhood-onset versus adolescent-onset antisocial conduct problems in males: natural history from age 3 to 18 years. *Development and Psychopathology* **8**, 399–424.

Mogford, K. 1988. Oral language development in prelinguistically deaf children. In Bishop, D., Mogford, K. (eds) *Language development in exceptional circumstances.* Edinburgh: Churchill Linvingstone,

Montanini-Manfredi, M., Fruggeri, L. 1978. Family behavioral patterns and the development of the deaf child in a strictly oral programme: some case studies. *Italian Journal of Psychology* **1**, 27–50.

Montanini-Manfredi, M.M. 1993. The emotional development of deaf children. In Marschark, M., Clark M.D. (eds) *Psychological perspectives on deafness.* Hillsdale, NJ: Lawrence Erlbaum Associates, 49–64.

Mooney, S., Smith, P.K. 1995. Bullying and the child who stammers. *British Journal of Special Education* **22**, 24–7.

Moore, V. 1985. The use of a colouring task to elucidate children's drawings of a solid cube. *British Journal of Developmental Psychology* **4**, 335–40.

Moore, D.G., Hobson, P., Anderson, M. 1995. Person perception: Does it involve IQ-independent perceptual processing? *Intelligence* **20**, 65–86.

Moore, M., Sixsmith, J., Knowles, K. 1996. *Children's reflections on family life.* London: Falmer.

Moore, V., McConachie, H. 1994. Communication between blind and severly visually impaired children and their parents. *British Journal of Developmental Psychology* **12**, 491–502.

Morgan, J.L., Travis, L.L. 1989. Limits on negative information in language input. *Journal of Child Language* **16**, 531–52.

Morgan, M.J. 1994. Sexpert Schmexpert. *The Guardian OnLine*, June 30th, p. 9.

Morss, J. 1996. *Growing critical: alternatives to developmental psychology.* London: Routledge.

Morton, J., Johnson, M.H. 1991. CONSPEC and CONLERN: a two-process theory of infant face recognition. *Psychological Review* **98**, 164–81.

Mottron, J., Belleville, S. 1993. A study of perceptual analysis in a high-level autistic subject with exceptional graphic abilities. *Brain and Cognition* **23**, 279–309.

Munakata, Y. 1997. Perseverative reaching in infancy: the roles of hidden toys and motor history in the AB task. *Infant Behavior and Development* **20**, 405–16.

Munakata, Y. 1998. Infant perseveration and implications for object permanence theories: a PDP Model of the AB task. *Developmental Science* 1, 161–84.

Munakata, Y., McClelland, J.L., Johnson, M.H., Siegler, R.S. 1997. Rethinking infant knowledge: toward an adaptive process account of successes and failures in object permanence tasks. *Psychological Review* 104, 686–713.

Mundy, P., Kasari, C. Sigman, M., Ruskin, E. 1995. Nonverbal communication and early language acquisition in children with Down syndrome and in normally developing children. *Journal of Speech and Hearing Research* **38**, 157–67.

Mundy, P., Sigman, M., Kasari, C., Yirmiya, N. 1988. Nonverbal communication skills in Down syndrome children. *Child Development* **59**, 235–49.

Murphy, C.M., Messer, D.J. 1977. Mothers, infants and pointing: a study of a gesture. In Schaffer, H.R. (ed.) *Studies in mother–infant interaction.* London: Academic Press, 325–54.

Murphy, G.L., Medin D.L. 1985. The role of theories in conceptual coherence. *Psychological Review* **92**, 289–316.

Murray, A.D., Johnson, J., Peters, J. 1990. Fine-tuning of utterance length to preverbal infants: effects on later language development. *Journal of Child Language* 17, 511–25.

Murray, J.P., Kippax, S. 1978. Children's social behavior in three towns with differing television experience. *Journal of Communication* **28**, 19–29.

Naigles, L., Fowler, A., Helm, A. 1991. The endpoint of syntactic bootstrapping? The comprehension of ungrammatical sentences by normal-IQ and Down's syndrome schoolchildren. In *Biennial Meeting of the Society for Research in Child Development.* Seattle.

Nathwat, S.S., Puri, P. 1995. A comparative study of MZ and DZ twins on Level I and Level II mental abilities and personality. *Journal of the Indian Academy of Applied Psychology* 21, 87–92.

Neary, A., Joseph, S. 1994. Peer victimisation and its relationship to self-concept and depression among schoolgirls. *Personality and Individual Differences* **16**, 183–6.

Needham, A., Baillargeon, R. 1993. Intuitions about support in 4.5-month-old infants. *Cognition* 47, 121–48.

Needham, A., Baillargeon, R. 1997. Object segregation in 8-month-old infants. *Cognition* **62**, 121–49.

Neilson, I. 1977. A reinterpretation of the development of the object concept in infancy. Unpublished PhD thesis, University of Edinburgh.

Nelson, C.A., Ludemann, P.M. 1989. Past, current and future trends in infant face perception research. *Canadian Journal of Psychology* **43**, 183–98.

Nelson, K. 1973. Structure and strategy in learning to talk. *Monographs of the Society for Research in Child Development* **38**.

Nelson, K. 1988. Constraints on word learning? *Cognitive Development* **3**, 221–46.

Nettelbeck, T. 1987. Inspection time and intelligence. In Vernon, P.A. (ed.) *Speed of information processing and intelligence*. New York: Ablex, 295–346.

Nettelbeck, T. 1999. Savant syndrome: rhyme without reason. In Anderson, M. (ed.) *The development of intelligence*. Hove: Psychology Press.

Nettelbeck, T., Brewer, N. 1981. Studies of intellectual disabilities and timed performance. In Ellis, N.R. (ed.) *International review of research in intellectual disabilities*. New York: Academic Press, 61–106.

Nettelbeck, T., Young, R. 1996. Intelligence and savant syndrome: is the whole greater than the sum of the fragments? *Intelligence* **22**, 49–67.

Nettelbeck, T., Young, R. In press. Savant syndrome. In Glidden, L. (ed.) *International Review of Research in Mental Retardation. Vol. 22*. London: Academic Press.

Neville, H.J. 1991. Neurobiology of cognitive and language processing: effects of early experience. In Gibson K.R. Petersen A.C. (eds), *Brain maturation and cognitive development: comparative and cross-cultural perspectives*. Hawthorne, NY: Adaline de Gruyter Press, 355–80.

Newell, A., Simon, H.A. 1972. *Human problem solving*. Englewood Cliffs, NJ:

Newman, D.L., Caspi, A., Moffitt, T.E., Silva, P.A. 1997. Antecedents of adult interpersonal functioning: effects of individual differences in age 3 temperament. *Developmental Psychology* **33**, 206–17.

Newson, E. 1984. The able autistic child: persisting barriers. *Communication* **18**, 30–8.

Newson, J., Newson, E. 1968. *Four years old in an urban community*. Harmondsworth: Penguin.

Newson J., Newson, E. 1976. *Seven years old in the home environment*. Harmondsworth: Penguin.

Nicolson, R.I. 1998. Learning and skill. In Scott, P.J., Spencer, C.P. (eds) *Psychology: a contemporay introduction*. Oxford: Blackwell, 294–343.

Nicolson, R.I., Fawcett, A.J. 1990. Automaticity: a new framework for dyslexia research? *Cognition* **35**, 159–82.

Nicolson, R.I., Fawcett, A.J. 1996. *The dyslexia early screening test*. London: The Psychological Corporation.

Ninio, A., Bruner, J.S. 1978. The achievement and antecedents of labelling. *Journal of Child Language* **5**, 1–16.

Nisbet, J., Shucksmith, J. 1984. *Learning strategies*. London: Routledge & Kegan Paul.

Norgate, S. 1998. Research methods for studying the language of blind children. In Hornberger, N.H. and Corson, D. (ed.) *Vol 8 Research Methods in Language and Education.* Kluwer Academic Publishers, The Netherlands.

Norgate, S., Collis, G.M., Lewis, V. 1998. The developmental role of rhymes and routines for congenitally blind children. *Cahiers de Psychologie Cognitive/Current Psychology of Cognition,* **17** (2), 451–77.

Norman, D.A. 1982. *Learning and memory.* San Francisco: Freeman.

Norris, D. 1990. How to build a connectionist idiot (savant). *Cognition* **35**, 277–91.

Nucci, L.P. 1981. Conceptions of personal issues: a domain distinct from moral or societal concepts. *Child Development* **52**, 114–21.

Nunes, T., Moreno, C. 1998. Is hearing impairment a cause of difficulties in mathematics? In Donlanc, C. (ed.) *The development of mathematical skills.* Hove: Psychology Press.

O'Connor, N., Hermelin, B. 1984. Idiot savant calendrical calculators: math or memory? *Psychological Medicine* **14**, 801–6.

O'Connor, N., Hermelin, B. 1990. The recognition failure and graphic success of idiot savant artists. *Journal of Child Psychology and Psychiatry* **31**, 203–15.

O'Connor, N., Hermelin, B. 1991. A specific linguistic ability. *American Journal on Intellectual Disabilities* **95**, 673–80.

O'Connor, N., Hermelin, B. 1992. Do young calendrical calculators improve with age? *Journal of Child Psychology and Psychiatry,* 5, 907–12.

O'Leary, D.D.M. 1989. Do cortical areas emerge from a protocortex? *Trends in Neuroscience* **12**, 400–6.

O'Moore, A.M., Hillery, B. 1989. Bullying in Dublin schools. *Irish Journal of Psychology* **10**, 426–41.

Ochs, E., Schieffelin, B.B. 1984. Language acquisition and socialization. In Shweder, R.A., Levine, R.A. (eds) *Culture theory.* Cambridge: Cambridge University Press,

Odom, P.B., Blanton, R.I., Laukhuf, C. 1973. Facial expressions and interpretation of emotion-arousing situations in deaf and hearing children. *Journal of Abnormal Child Psychology* **1**, 139–51.

Oliver, R., Oaks, I.N., Hoover, J.H. 1994. Family issues and interventions in bully and victim relationships. *The School Counselor* **41**, 199–202.

Olthof, T., Meerum Terwogt, M., Van Eck, O., Koops, W. 1987. Children's knowledge of the integration of successive emotions. *Perceptual and Motor Skills* **65**, 407–14.

Olweus, D. 1978. *Aggression in schools: bullies and whipping boys.* Washington, DC: Hemisphere.

Olweus, D. 1980. Familial and temperamental determinants of aggressive behaviour in adolescent boys: a causal analysis. *Developmental Psychology* **16**, 644–60.

Olweus, D. 1984. Aggressors and their victims: bullying at school. In Frude, N., Gault, H. (eds) *Disruptive behaviour in schools.* New York: John Wiley, 57–76.

Olweus, D. 1991. Bully/victim problems among schoolchildren: basic facts and effects of a school based intervention program. In Pepler, D., Rubin, K. (eds) *The development and treatment of childhood aggression*. Hillsdale, NJ: Erlbaum, 441–48.

Olweus, D. 1992. Victimization among schoolchildren: intervention and prevention. In Albee, G.W. Bond, L.A., Cook Monsey, T.V. (eds) *Improving children's lives: global perspectives on prevention*. Newsbury Park: Sage Publications, 279–295.

Olweus, D. 1993. *Bullying at school: what we know and what we can do*. Oxford: Blackwell.

Olweus, D. 1994. Annotation: bullying at school: basic facts and effects of a school based intervention program. *Journal of Child Psychology and Psychiatry* **35**, 1171–90.

Omi, M., Winant, H. 1986. *Racial formation in the United States: from the 1960s to the 1980s*. New York: Routledge and Kegan Paul.

Oppenheim, D., Emde, R.N., Warren, S. 1997. Children's narrative representations of mothers: their development and associations with child and mother adaptation. *Child Development* **68**, 127–38.

Oster, A-M. 1995. Principles for a complete description of the phonological system of deaf children as a basis for speech training. In Plant, G., Spens, K.-E. (eds) *Profound deafness and speech communication*. London: Whurr, 441–60.

Oster, H., Hegley, D., Nagel, L. 1992. Adult judgements and fine-grained analysis of infants facial expressions: testing the validity of a priori coding formulas. *Developmental Psychology* **28**, 1115–31.

Owens, R., Macdonald, J. 1982. Communicative uses of the early speech of non-delayed and Down syndrome children. *American Journal of Mental Deficiency* **86**, 503–10.

Ozonoff, S., Pennington, B.F. Rogers, S.J. 1991. Executive function deficits in high-functioning autistic individuals: relationship to theory of mind. *Journal of Child Psychology and Psychiatry* **32**, 1081–105.

Pais, J.M. 1995. Growing up on the EU periphery: Portugal. In: Chisholm, L., Büchner, P., Krüger, H.-H., du Bois-Reymond, M. (eds) *Growing up in Europe*. Berlin: Walter de Gruyter, 195–208.

Pal, S., Shyam, R., Singh, R. 1997. Genetic analysis of general intelligence 'g': a twin study. *Personality and Individual Differences* **22**, 779–80.

Papert, S. 1980. *Mindstorms*. Brighton: Harvester Press.

Pappas-Jones, C., Adamson, L.B. 1987. Language use in mother–child and mother–child–sibling interactions. *Child Development* **58**, 356–66.

Park, K. 1997. How do objects become objects of reference? A review of the literature on objects of reference and a proposed model for the use of objects in communication. *British Journal of Special Education* **24**, 108–14.

Parke, R.D. 1995. Fathers and families. In Bornstein, M.H. (ed.) *Handbook of parenting. Volume 3: Status and social conditions of parenting*. Hillsdale, NJ: Lawrence Erlbaum Associates.

Parker, A., Rose, H. 1990. Deaf children's phonological development. In Grunwell, P. (ed.) *Developmental speech disorders*. London: Whurr, 83–108.

Parker, J.G., Asher, S.R. 1987. Peer relations and later personal adjustment: are low-accepted children at risk? *Psychological Bulletin* **102**, 357–89.

Pascual-Leone, J. 1970. A mathematical model for the transition rule in Piaget's developmental stages. *Acta Psychologia* **32**, 301–45.

Pea, R.D., Kurland, D. 1987. On the cognitive effects of learning computer programming. In Pea, R., Sheingold, K. (eds), *Mirrors of the mind: patterns of experience in educational computing*. Norwood NJ: Ablex.

Peeters, T. 1997. *Autism: from theoretical understanding to educational intervention*. London: Whurr.

Penman, R., Cross, T., Milgrom-Friedman, J., Meares, R. 1983. Mothers' speech to prelingual infants: a pragmatic analysis. *Journal of Child Language* **10**, 17–34.

Penner, S.G. 1987. Parental responses to grammatical and ungrammatical child utterances. *Child Development* **58**, 376–84.

Pepler, D.J., Craig, W.M. 1995. A peek behind the fence: naturalistic observations of aggressive children with remote audiovisual recording. *Developmental Psychology* **31**, 548.

Perez-Pereira, M. 1994. Imitations, repetitions, routines and the child's analysis of language-insights from the blind. *Journal of Child Language* **21**, 317–37.

Perez-Pereira, M., Castro, J. 1992. Pragmatic functions of blind and sighted children's language: a twin case study. *First Language* **12**, 17–37.

Perlman, M., and Ross, H.S. 1997. The benefits of parent intervention in children's disputes: an examination of concurrent changes in children's fighting styles. *Child Development* **68**, 690–700.

Perry, B. 1997. Incubated in terror: neurodevelopmental factors in the 'cycle of violence'. In Osofsky, J. (ed.) *Children in a violent society*. New York/London: Guildford Press, 124–49.

Perry, D.G., Kusel, S.J., Perry, L.C. 1988. Victims of peer aggression. *Developmental Psychology* **24**, 807–814.

Peterson, S., Fox, P., Posner, M.I., Mintun, M., Raichle, M. 1988. Positron emission tomographic studies of the corical anatomy of single-word processing. *Nature* **331**, 585–9.

Pettito, L.A., Marentette, P.F. 1991. Babbling in the manual mode: Evidence for the ontogeny of language. *Science* **251**, 1493–6.

Philip, K., Hendry, L.B. 1996. Young people and mentoring. *Journal of Adolescence* **19**, 189–201.

Phillips,W.A., Inall, M., Lauder, E. 1985. On the discovery, storage and use of graphic descriptions. In Freeman, N., Cox, M. (eds) *Visual order: the nature and development of pictorial representation*. Cambridge: Cambridge University Press, 122–34.

Phinney, J., Rosenthal, D. 1992. Ethnic identity in adolescence: process, context and outcome. In Adams, G., Gullotta, T., Montemayor, R. (eds) *Adolescent identity formation*. London: Sage, pp. 145–72.

Phoenix, A. 1992. *Young mothers?* London: Polity.

Phoenix, A. 1997. The place of 'race' and ethnicity in the lives of children and young people. *Journal of Educational and Child Psychology* **14**, 5–24.

Phoenix, A. 1998. Representing new identities: whiteness as contested identity in young people's accounts. In Koser, K., Lutz, L. (eds) *New migration in Europe: social constructions and social realities.* London: Macmillan, pp. 109–23.

Phoenix, A., Woollett, A. 1991. Motherhood: social construction, politics and psychology. In Phoenix, A. Woollett, A., Lloyd, E. (eds) *Motherhood: meanings, practices and ideologies.* London: Sage, pp 13–27.

Piaget, J. 1932. *Le judgement moral chez l'enfant.* Paris: Presses Universitaires de France.

Piaget, J. 1952. *The origins of intelligence* (trans. M. Cook). New York: Basic Books (first published in French, 1936).

Piaget, J. 1954. *The construction of reality in the child* (trans M. Cook) New York: Basic Books (originally published in French, 1936).

Piaget, J. (1981). *Intelligence and affectivity. Their relationship during child development.* Palo Alto: Annual Rev. Inc.

Piaget, J., Inhelder, B. 1956. *The child's conception of space.* London: Routledge and Kegan Paul. (Original work published 1948.)

Piaget, J., Inhelder, B., Szeminska, A. 1960. *The child's conception of geometry.* London: Routledge and Kegan Paul.

Pikas, A. 1989. A pure conception of mobbing gives the best for treatment. *School Psychology International* **10**, 95–104.

Pike, A., McGuire, S., Hetherington, E.M., Reiss, D., Plomin, R. 1996. Family environment and adolescent depression and antisocial behaviour: a multivariate genetic analysis. *Developmental Psychology* **32**, 590–603.

Pine, F. 1985. *Developmental theory and clinical process.* New York: Yale University Press.

Pine, J., Lieven, E. 1993. Re-analyzing rote learned phrases: individual differences in the transition to multi-word speech. *Journal of Child Language* **20**, 551–74.

Pine, J.M. 1992. The functional basis of referentiality: evidence from children's spontaneous speech. *First Language* **12**, 39–56.

Pine, K.J., Messer, D.J. 1995. Children's changing representations of a balance beam task: a quasi-longitudinal study. Paper presented at the British Psychological Society London Conference, December, 1995.

Pinker, S. 1984. *Language learnability and language development.* Cambridge, MA: Harvard University Press.

Pinker, S. 1987. The bootstrapping problem in language acquisition. In MacWhinney, B. (ed.) *Mechanisms of language acquisition.* Hillsdale, NJ: Erlbaum.

Pinker, S. 1989. *Learnability and cognition: the acquistion of argument structure.* Cambridge, MA. MIT Press.

Pinker, S. 1991. Rules of language. *Science* **253**, 530–5.

Pinker, S. 1993. Interview with Jean A. Rondal: pieces of minds in psycholinguistics. *International Journal of Psychology* **28**, 459–80.

Pinker, S. 1994. *The language instinct.* New York: William Morrow.

Plaut, D.C., McClelland, J.L., Seifenberg, M.S., Patterson, K. 1996. Understanding normal and impaired word reading: computational principles in quasi-regular domains. *Psychological Review* **103**, 56–115.

Plomin, R. 1994. Nature, nurture, and social development. *Social Development* **3**, 37–76 [with commentaries and response to commentaries].

Plomin, R., Caspi, A. (1998). DNA and personality. *European Journal of Personality* **12**, 387–407.

Plomin, R., Chipuer, H., Neiderhiser, J. 1994. Behavioural genetic evidence for the importance of the non-shared environment. In Hetherington, E.M. Reiss, D., Plomin, R. (eds), *Separate social worlds of siblings: impact of non-shared environment on development*. Hillsdale, NJ: Erlbaum, 1–31.

Plomin, R., Daniels, D. 1987. Why are children in the same family so different from each other? *Behavioural and Brain Sciences* **10**, 1–16.

Plomin, R., DeFries, J.C. 1998. The genetics of cognitive abilities and disabilities. *Scientific American* May, 62–9.

Plomin, R., DeFries, J.C., Loehlin, J.C. 1977. Genotype-environment interaction and correlation in the analysis of human behavior. *Psychological Bulletin* **84**, 309–22.

Plomin, R., DeFries, J.C., McClearn, G.E., Rutter, M. 1997. *Behavioural genetics*. New York: W.H. Freeman & Co.

Plomin, R., Owen, M.J., McGuffin, P. 1994. The genetic basis of complex human behaviours. *Science* **264**, 1733–9.

Plomin, R., Rutter, M. 1998. Child development, molecular genetics, and what to do with genes once they are found. *Child Development* **69**, 1223–42.

Plowman, L. 1996. Narrative, linearity and interactivity – making sense of interactive multimedia. *British Journal of Educational Technology* **27**, 92–105.

Plunkett, K. 1995. Connectionist approaches to language acquisition. In Fletcher, P., MacWhinney, B. (eds) *Handbook of child language*. Oxford: Blackwell, 36–72.

Plunkett, K., Karmiloff-Smith, A., Bates, E., Elman, J., Johnson, M.H. 1997. Connectionism and developmental psychology. *Journal of Child Psychology and Psychiatry* **38**, 53–80.

Porter, R.H., Laney, M.D. 1980. Attachment theory and the concept of inclusive fitness. *Merrill-Palmer Quarterly* **26**, 35–51.

Postman, N. 1982. *The disappearance of childhood*. New York: Random House.

Potter, J., Wetherell, M. 1987. *Discourse and social psychology*. London: Sage.

Prather, P., Spelke, E.S. 1982. Three-month-old infants' perception of adjacent and partly occluded objects. Paper presented to the International Conference on Infant Studies, Austin, Texas.

Preisler, G. 1997. Social and emotional development of blind children: a longitudinal study. In Lewis V., Collis, G. (eds) *Blindness and psychological development in young children*. Leicester: BPS Books, 69–85.

Preisler, G., Ahlstrom, M., Tvingstedt, A. 1997. The development of communication and language in deaf preschool children with cochlear implants. *International Journal of Pediatric Otorhinolaryngology* **41**, 263–72.

Provenzo, E.F. 1991. *Video kids: making sense of Nintendo*. Cambridge, MA: Harvard University Press.

Pulkkinen, L., Tremblay, R.E. 1992. Patterns of boys' social adjustment in two cultures and at different ages: a longitudinal perspective. *International Journal of Behavioral Development* **15**, 527–53.

Quartz, S.R., Sejnowski, T.J. (1997). A neural basis of cognitive development: a constructivist manifesto. *Behavioural and Brain Sciences* 20, 537.

Quiggle, N.L., Garber, J., Panak, W.F., Dodge, K.A. 1992. Social information processing in aggressive and depressed children. *Child Development* **62**, 1305–20.

Quigley, S.P., Paul, P.V. 1984. *Language and deafness*. San Diego, CA: College Hill Press.

Quine, W.V.O. 1960. *Word and object*. Cambridge, MA: MIT Press.

Quine, W.V.O. 1969. *Ontological relativity and other essays*. New York: Columbia, University Press.

Quinton, D., Rutter, M. 1988. *Parenting breakdown*. Aldershot: Avebury.

Qureshi, H., Alborz, A. 1992. The epidemiology of challenging behaviour. *Mental Handicap Research* **5** 130–45.

Qvortrup, J. 1994. Childhood matters. In Qvortrup, J., Bardy, M., Sgritta, G., Wintersberger, H. (eds) *Childhood matters*. Avebury: Aldershot.

Qvortrup, J., Christoffersen, M.N. 1991. *Childhood as a social phenomenon*. Wien: European Centre.

Rabain-Jamin, J., Sabeau-Jouannet, E. 1989. Playing with pronouns in French maternal speech to prelingual infants. *Journal of Child Language* **16**, 217–38.

Rader, N., Spiro, D.J., Firestone, P.B. 1979. Performance on a stage IV object-permanence task with standard and nonstandard covers. *Child Development* **50**, 908–10.

Radford, A. 1995. Phrase structure and functional categories. In Fletcher, P., MacWhinney, B. (eds) *Handbook of child language*. Oxford: Blackwell, 483–507.

Rakic, P. 1987. Intrinsic and extrinsic determinants of neocortical parcellation: a radial unit model. In Rakic, P., Singer, W. (eds), *Neurobiology of neocortex*. Chichester: John Wiley and Sons, 5–27.

Rakic, P. 1988. Specification of cerebral cortical areas. *Science* **241**, 170–6.

Randall, P. 1997. *Adult bullying: perpetrators and victims*. London: Routledge.

Rao, J.M. 1990. A population-based study of mild mental handicap in children: preliminary analysis of obstetric associations. *Journal of Mental Deficiency Research* **34**, 59–65.

Rattansi, A., Phoenix, A. 1998. Rethinking youth identities: modernist and postmodernist frameworks. In Bynner, J., Chisholm, L., Furlong, A. (eds) *Youth, citizenship and social change in a European context*. Aldershot: Ashgate, pp. 121–50.

Rayner, K., Pollatsek, A. 1989. *The psychology of reading*. London: Prentice-Hall.

Reason, R., Boote, R. 1994. *Helping children with reading and spelling: a special needs manual*. London: Routledge.

Reicher, S. 1987. Crowd behaviour as social action. In Turner, J., with Hogg, M.,. Oakes, P, Reicher, S., Wetherell, M. *Rediscovering the social group: a self-categorization theory*. Oxford: Basil Blackwell, pp. 171–202.

Reilly, J., Klima, E., Bellugi, U. 1990. Once more with feeling: affect and language in atypical populations. *Development and Psychopathology* **2**, 367–91.

Reiss, D., Plomin, R., Hetherington, M., Howe, G., Rovine, M., Tryon, A. et al. 1994. The separate worlds of teenage siblings: an introduction to the study of the non-shared environment and adolescent development. In Hetherington, E.M., Reiss, D., Plomin, R. (eds), *Separate social worlds of siblings: impact of non-shared environment on development*. Hillsdale, NJ: Erlbaum, 63–109.

Remick, H. 1976. Maternal speech to children during language acquisition. In von Raffler-Engel, W., Lebran, Y. (eds) *Baby talk and infant speech*, Amsterdam: Swets and Zeitlinger, 346–52.

Remington, B. 1996. Assessing the occurrence of learning in children with profound intellectual disability: a conditioning approach. *International Journal of Disability, Development and Education* **43**, 101–18.

Ribbens, J. 1994. *Mothers and their children: a feminist sociology of childrearing*. London: Sage.

Ricci, C. 1887. *L'arte dei bambini*. Bologna: N. Zanichelli.

Rice, M.L., Huston, A.C., Truglio, R., Wright, J.C. 1990. Words from Sesame Sreet: learning vocabulary while viewing. *Developmental Psychology* **26**, 421–28.

Richards, M., Light, P. (eds) 1986. *Children of social worlds*. Cambridge: Polity Press.

Richardson, A., Ritchie, J. 1989. *Developing friendships: enabling people with learning difficulties to make and maintain friends*. London: Policy Studies Institute.

Rieber, R.W., Carton, A.S. 1993. *The fundamentals of defectology, Vol 2. The collected works of L.S. Vygotsky* (J. Knox and C.B. Stephens, trans.). New York: Plenum.

Rigby, K. 1993. School children's perceptions of their families and parents as a function of peer relations. *Journal of Genetic Psychology* **154**, 501–13.

Rigby, K. 1994. Psychosocial functioning in families of Australian adolescent school children involved in bully/victim problems. *Journal of Family Therapy* **16**, 173–87.

Rigby, K., Slee, P.T. 1991. Dimensions of interpersonal relations among Australian children and implications for psychological well-being. *Journal of Social Psychology* **133**, 33–42.

Rivers, I., Soutter, A. 1996. Bullying and the Steiner schools ethos: a case study analysis of a group centred educational philosophy. *School Psychology International* **17**, 359–79.

Roberts, K., Parsell, G. 1990. Young people's routes into UK labour markets in the late 1980s. ESCR 16-19 Initiative. London: City University.

Rodda, M., Cumming, C., Fewer, D. 1993. Memory, learning and language: implications for deaf education. In Marschark, M., Clark M.D. (eds) *Psychological perspectives on deafness*. Hillsdale: NJ: Lawrence Erlbaum.

Roe, K., Bjurström, E., Fornäs, J. 1994. Sweden. In Hurrelmann, K. (ed.) *International handbook of adolescence*. Greenwood: Westport, 374–85.

Rogers, C. 1942. *Counselling and psychotherapy: newer concepts in practice*. Boston, MA: Houghton Mifflin.

Rogers, C. 1951. *Client-centred therapy: its current practice, implications and theory*. Boston, MA: Houghton Mifflin.

Rogers, C. 1961. *On becoming a person*. London: Constable.

Rogers, S.J. 1996. Early intervention in autism. *Journal of Autism and Developmental Disorders* **26**, 243–6.

Rogoff, B. 1990. *Apprenticeship in thinking: cognitive development in a social context*. New York: Oxford University Press.

Roland, E. 1993. Bullying: a developing tradition of research and management. In Tattum, D.E. (ed.) *Understanding and managing bullying*. Oxford: Heinemann Educational Books, 15–30.

Romans, S., Roeltgen, D., Kushner, H., Ross, J. 1997. Executive function in girls with Turner's syndrome. *Developmental Neuropsychology* **13**, 23–40.

Rondal, J., Edwards, S. 1997. *Language in mental retardation*. London: Whurr Publishers.

Rosch, E., Mervis, C.B. 1975. Family resemblance: studies in the internal structure of categories. *Cognitive Psychology* **8**, 382–439.

Rose, D., Slater, A., Perry, H. 1986. Prediction of childhood intelligence from habituation in early infancy. *Intelligence* **10**, 251–63.

Rosenberg, S., Abbeduto, L. 1993. *Language and communication in mental retardation: development, processes and intervention*. Hillsdale, NJ: Lawrence Erlbaum Associates.

Rosson, M.B. 1983. From SOFA to LOUCH: lexical contributions to pseudoword pronunciation. *Memory and Cognition* **11**, 152–60.

Rothbaum, F., Weisz, J.R., Snyder, S.S. 1982. Changing the world and changing the self: a two-process model of perceived control. *Journal of Personality and Social Psychology* **42**, 5–37.

Rubenstein, H., Lewis, S.S., Rubenstein, M.A. 1971. Evidence for phonemic recoding in visual word recognition. *Journal of Verbal Learning and Verbal Behavior* **10**, 645–58.

Rumelhart, D.E., McClelland, J.L. 1986. On learning the past tenses of English verbs. In McClelland, J.L., Rumelhart, D.E. (eds) *Parallel distributed processing: explorations in the microstructure of cognition. Vol. 2*. Cambridge MA: MIT Press, 216–71.

Rumsey, J.M., Hamburger, S.D. 1988. Neuropsychological findings in high-functioning men with infantile autism, residual state. *Journal of Clinical and Experimental Neuropsychology* **10**, 201–21.

Russell, G., Russell, A. 1987. Mother–child and Father–child relationships in middle childhood. *Child Development* **58**, 1573–85.

Rutter, D.R., Durkin, K. 1987. Turn-taking in mother–infant interation: an examination of vocalizations and gaze. *Developmental Psychology* **23**, 54–61.

Rutter, M. 1970. Autistic children: infancy to adulthood. *Seminars in Psychiatry* **2**, 435–50.

Rutter, M. 1987. Psychosocial resilience and protective mechanisms. *American Journal of Orthopsychiatry* **57**, 350–63.

Rutter, M. 1991. Nature, nurture and psychopathology: a new look at an old topic. *Development and Psycholpathology* **3**, 125–36.

Rutter, M. 1996a. Psychosocial adversity. In Verhofstadt-Denève, L., Kienhorst, I., Braet, C. (eds) *Conflict and development in adolescence*. Leiden: DSWO Press, 21–34.

Rutter, M. 1996b. Stress research. In: Haggerty, R.J., Sherrod, L.R., Garmezy, N., Rutter, M. (eds) *Stress, risk and resilience in children and adolescents*. Cambridge: Cambridge University Press, 354–85.

Rutter, M., Bailey, A., Bolton, P., Le Couteur, A. 1993. Autism: syndrome definition and possible genetic mechanisms. In Plomin, R., McClearn, G.E. (eds), *Nature, Nurture, and Psychology*. Washington DC: American Psychological Association, 269–84.

Rutter, M., Plomin, R. 1997. Opportunities for psychiatry from genetic findings. *British Journal of Psychiatry* **171**, 209–19.

Saarni, C. 1979. Children's understanding of display rules for expressive behaviour. *Developmental Psychology* **15**, 424–9.

Saarni, C. 1984. Observing children's use of display rules: Age and sex differences. *Child Development* **55**, 1504–13.

Saarni, C. 1989. Children's understanding of strategic control of emotional expressions in social transactions. In Saarni, C., Harris, P.L. (eds) *The child's understanding of emotion*. New York: Cambridge University Press, 181–208.

Sachs, J., Johnson, M.L. 1976. Language development in a hearing child of deaf parents. In von Raffler-Engel, W., Lebrun, Y. (eds) *Baby talk and infant speech*. Lisse, Netherlands: Swets and Zeitlinger, 223–33.

Sachs, J.S. 1967. Recognition memory for syntactic and semantic aspects of connected discourse. *Perception and Psychophysics* **2**, 437–42.

Saenger, P. 1996. Turner's syndrome. *Current Concepts* **335**, 1749–54.

Sakamoto, A. 1994. Video game use and the development of sociocognitive abilties in children: three surveys of elementary school students. *Journal of Applied Social Psychology* **24**, 21–42.

Salmivalli, C., Lagerspetz, K., Björkqvist, K., Österman, K., Kaukiainen, A. 1996. Bullying as a group process: participant roles and their relations to social status within the group. *Aggressive Behavior* **22**, 1–15.

Salmon, P. 1998. *Life at school: education and psychology*. London: Constable.

Salthouse, T.A. 1985. *A theory of cognitive ageing*. Amsterdam: North Holland.

Sameroff, A.J. 1975. Early influences on development: fact or fancy? *Merrill Palmer Quarterly* **21**, 267–93.

Sameroff, A.J. 1990. Neo-environmental perspectives on developmental theory. In Hodapp, R.M. Burack, J.A., Zigler, E. (eds) *Issues in the developmental approach to mental retardation*. New York: Cambridge University Press, 93–113.

Sandler, J., Dare, C., Holder, A. 1972. Frames of reference in psychoanalytic psychology. II. The historical context and phases in the development of psychoanalysis. *British Journal of Medical Psychology* **45**, 143–7.

Sandler, J., Sandler, A.M. 1998. *Internal object revisited*. London: Karnac Books.

Sanson, A., Smart, D., Prior, M., Oberklaid, F. 1993. Precursors of hyperactivity and aggression. *Journal of Academic Child and Adolescent Psychiatry* **32**, 1207–16.

Savin-Williams, R.C., Berndt, T.J. 1990. Friendship and peer relations. In Feldman, S.S., Elliott, G.R. (eds), *At the threshold: the developing adolescent.* Cambridge, MA: Harvard University Press, 277–307.

Saxton, M. 1997. The contrast theory of negative input. *Journal of Child Language* **24**, 139–61.

Scarborough, H., Wyckoff, J. 1986. Mother, I'd still rather do it myself: some further non-effects of 'motherese' *Journal of Child Language 13*, 431–8.

Scarr, S. 1992. Developmental theories for the 1990s: development and individual differences. *Child Development* **63**, 1–19.

Schachar, R. 1991. Childhood hyperactivity. *Journal of Child Psychology and Psychiatry* **32**, 155–91.

Schäfer, M., Wellman, N.E., Crick, N.R. submitted. Relational aggression, physical aggression and bullying among German school children: relations among constructs, gender differences and links with adjustment.

Schaffer, H.R. 1996. *Social Development.* Oxford: Blackwell.

Schlesinger, H.S., Meadow, K.P. 1972. *Sound and sign: childhood deafness and mental health.* Berkeley, CA: University of California Press.

Schroeder, S.R., LeBlanc, J.M, Mayo, L. 1996. A life-span perspective on the development of individuals with autism. *Journal of Autism and Developmental Disorders* **26**, 155–7.

Schuster, B. 1997. Rejection, exclusion and harrassment at work and in schools: an intergration of results from research on mobbing, bullying and peer rejection. *European Psychologist* **1**, 293–317.

Schwartz, D., Dodge, K.A., Pettit, G.S., and Bates, J.E. 1997. The early socialization of aggressive victims of bullying. *Child Development* **68**, 665–75.

Schwartz, R., and Camarata, S. 1985. Examining relationships between input and language development: some statistical issues. *Journal of Child Language* **12**, 199–209.

Seidenberg, M.S., McClelland, J.L. 1989. A distributed developmental model of word recognition. *Psychological Review* **96**, 523–68.

Selfe, L. 1977. *Nadia: a case of extraordinary drawing ability in an autistic child.* London: Academic Press.

Selfe, L. 1995. Nadia reconsidered. In Golomb, C. (ed.) *The development of artistically gifted children: selected case studies.* Hillsdale, NJ: Lawrence Erlbaum Associates, 197–236.

Seligman, M.E.P. 1975. *Helplessness: on depression, development and death.* San Francisco: Freeman.

Setiono, K. 1994. Morality from the viewpoint of Javanese tradition. Paper presented at the Symposium 'Eco-Ethical Thinking From A Cross-Cultural Perspective'. Kirkel, Germany, July.

Sewell, T. 1997. *Black masculinities and schooling.* Stoke on Trent: Trentham Books.

Shah, A., Frith, U. 1983. An islet of ability in autistic children: a research note. *Journal of Child Psychology and Psychiatry* **24**, 613–20.

Sharp, S., Smith, P.K. 1995. *Tackling bullying in your school. A practical guide for teachers.* London: Routledge.

Sharp, S., Smith, P.K. 1991. Bullying in UK schools: the DES Sheffield bullying project. *Early Child Development and Care* **77**, 47–55.

Shatz, M., Gelman, R. 1973. *The development of communication skills: modification in the speech of young children as a function of the listener.* Monographs of the Society for Research in Child Development, 38. The Society, Chicago.

Shea, J.B., Morgan, R.L. 1979. Contextual interference effects on the acquisition, retention and transfer of a motor skill. *Journal of Experimental Psychology: Human Learning and Memory* **5**, 179–87.

Shucksmith, J., Hendry, L.B. 1998. *Health issues and young people.* London: Routledge.

Shucksmith, J., Hendry, L.B., Glendinning, A. 1995. Models of parenting. *Journal of Adolescence* **18**, 253–70.

Shweder, R.A., Sullivan, W.M. 1993. Cultural psychology: who needs it? *Annual Review of Psychology* **44**, 497–523.

Siegler, R.S. 1976. Three aspects of cognitive development. *Cognitive Psychology* **4**, 481–520.

Siegler, R.S. 1984. Mechanisms of cognitive growth. In Sternberg, R. (ed.) *Mechanisms of cognitive development.* New York: W.H. Freeman & Co, 141–62.

Siegler, R.S. 1989. How domain-general and domain-specific knowledge interact to produce strategy choices. *Merrill-Palmer Quarterly* **35**, 1–26.

Siegler, R.S., Richards, D. 1982. The development of intelligence. In Sternberg, R.J. (ed.) *Handbook of human intelligence.* Cambridge: Cambridge University Press.

Silbereisen, R.K., Walper, S., Albrecht, H.T. 1990. Family income loss and economic hardship. *New Directions in Child Development* **46**, 27–47.

Silk, A.M.J., Thomas, G.V. 1988. The development of size scaling in children's figure drawings. *British Journal of Developmental Psychology* **6**, 285–99.

Sillars, A.L. 1995. Communication and family culture. In Fitzpatrick M.A., Vangelisti, A.L. (eds) *Explaining family interactions.* London: Sage, pp 375–99.

Simon, E.W., Rappaport, D.A., Papka, M., Woodruffpak, D.S. 1995. Fragile X and Down's syndrome – are there syndrome specific cognitive profiles at low IQ scores. *Journal of Intellectual Disability Research* **39**, 326–30.

Simon, H.A. 1976. Identifying basic abilities underlying intelligent performance of complex tasks. In Resnick, L. (ed.) *The nature of intelligence.* Hillsdale, NJ: Erlbaum.

Simonoff, E., Bolton, P., Rutter, M. 1996. Mental retardation: genetic findings, clinical implications and research agenda. *Journal of Child Psychology and Psychiatry* **37**, 259–80.

Singer, J.L., Singer, D.G. 1981. *Television, imagination and aggression: a study of preschoolers.* Hillsdale, NJ: Lawrence Erlbaum Associates.

Siperstein, G., Leffert, J., Widaman, K. 1996. Social behaviour and the social acceptance and rejection of children with mental retardation. *Education and Training in Mental Retardation and Developmental Disabilities* **41**, 271–81.

Sitton, R., Light, P. 1992. Drawing to differentiate: flexibility in young children's human figure drawing. *British Journal of Developmental Psychology* **10**, 25–33.

Skinner, B.F. 1953. *Science and human behavior*. Toronto: Macmillan.

Skoe, E. 1998. The ethic of care: issues in moral development. In Skoe, E., von der Lippe, A. (eds) *Personality development in adolescence: a cross national and life span perspective*. London: Routledge, pp. 143–71.

Skuse, D.H., James, R.S., Bishop, D.V.M., Coppin, B. Dalton, Aaamodt-Leeper, G., Bacarese-Hamilton, M., Creswell, C., McGurk, R., Jacobs, P.A. 1997. Evidence from Turner's syndrome of an imprinted X-link locus affecting cognitive function. *Nature* **387**, 705–08.

Slater, A., Mattock, A., Brown, E. 1990. Size constancy at birth: newborn infants' responses to retinal and real sizes. *Journal of Experimental Child Psychology* **49**, 314–22.

Slater, A., Morison, V., Rose, D. 1983. Perception of shape by the newborn baby. *British Journal of Developmental Psychology* **1**, 135–42.

Slater, A., Morison, V. 1985. Shape constancy and slant perception at birth. *Perception* **14**, 337–44.

Slee, P.T., Rigby, K. 1993. Australian school children's self appraisal of interpersonal relations: the bullying experience. *Child Psychiatry and Human Development* **23**, 273–87.

Slobin, D.I. 1985. *The cross-linguistic study of language acquisition, Vol. 1: The data*. Hillsdale, NJ: Erlbaum.

Sloboda, J.A., Hermelin, B., O'Connor, N. 1985. An exceptional musical memory. *Music Perception* **3**, 155–70.

Smalley, S.L., Asarnow, R.F., Spence, M.A. 1988. Autism and genetics: a decade of research. *Archives of General Psychiatry* **45**, 953–61.

Smalley, S.L., Collins, F. 1996. Brief report: genetic, prenatal and immunologic factors. *Journal of Autism and Developmental Disorders* **26**, 155–7.

Smiley, P., Huttenlocher, J. 1989. Young children's acquisition of emotion concepts. In Saarni, C., Harris, P.L. (eds) *The child's understanding of emotion*. New York, Cambridge University Press, 27–49.

Smith L., von Tetzchner, S. 1986. Communicative, sensorimotor and language skills of young children with Down syndrome. *American Journal of Mental Deficiency* **91**, 57–66.

Smith, L.B., Thelen, E., Titzer, B., and McLin, D., 1995. The task dynamics of the A-not-B error.

Smith, N., Tsimpli, I. 1995. *The mind of a savant: language learning and modularity*. Oxford: Blackwell.

Smith, P.K. 1991. The silent nightmare: bullying and victimisation in school peer groups. *Psychologist* **4**, 243–48.

Smith, P.K., Levan, S. 1995. Perceptions and experiences of bullying in younger pupils. *British Journal of Educational Psychology* **65**, 489–500.

Smith, P.K., Myron-Wilson, R. in press. Parenting and bullying. *Clinical Child Psychology and Psychiatry*.

Smith, P.K., Sharp, S. (eds) 1994. *School bullying: insights and perspectives*. London: Routledge.

Smith, P.K., Thompson, D. 1991. *Practical approaches to bullying*. London: David Fulton.

Smith, P.M. 1993. Young children's depiction of contrast in human figure drawing: standing and walking. *Educational Psychology* **13**, 107–18.

Snarey, J.R. 1985. Cross-cultural universality of socio-moral development: a critical review of Kohlbergian research. *Psychological Bulletin* **97**, 202–32.

Snow, C. 1973. Mothers' speech to children learning language. *Child Development* **43**, 549–65.

Snow, C.E. 1977. Mothers' speech research: from input to interaction. In Snow, C.E., Ferguson, C.A. (eds), *Talking to children*. Cambridge: Cambridge University Press.

Snow, C. 1995. Issues in the study of Input. In Fletcher, P., MacWhinney, B. (eds) *Handbook of child language*. Oxford: Blackwell, 180–93.

Snowling, M. 1987. *Dyslexia: A cognitive perspective*. Oxford: Blackwell.

Sorce, J.F., Emde, R.N., Campos, J.J., Klinnert, M.D. 1985. Maternal emotional signalling: its effects on the visual cliff behaviour of 1-year-olds. *Developmental Psychology* **21**, 195–200.

Spangler, G., Grossmann, K.E. 1993. Biobehavioral organization in securely and insecurely attached infants. *Child Development* **64**, 1439–50.

Spearman, C. 1904. 'General Intelligence' objectively determined and measured. *American Journal of Psychology* **15**, 201–93.

Spelke, E., Cortelyou, A. 1981. Perceptual aspects of social knowing: looking and listening in infancy. In Lamb, M.E., Sherrod, L.R. (eds) *Infant social cognition: empirical and theoretical considerations*. Hillsdale NJ: Lawrence Erlbaum.

Spelke, E.S. 1991. Physical knowledge in infancy: reflections on Piaget's theory. In Carey, S., Gelman, R. (eds) *Epigenesis of the mind: essays in biology and knowledge*. New Jersey: Erlbaum, 133–69.

Spelke, E.S. 1994. Initial knowledge: six suggestions. *Cognition* **50**, 431–45.

Spelke, E.S., Breinlinger, K., Macomber, J., Jacobson, K. 1992. Origins of knowledge. *Psychological Review* **99**, 605–32.

Spencer, P.E., Deyo, D.A. 1993. Cognitive and social aspects of deaf children's play. In Marschark, M., Clark, D. (eds) *Psychological perspectives of deafness*. Hillsdale NJ: Lawrence Erlbaum, 65–91.

Spielthenner, G. 1996. *Psychologische Beiträge zur Ethik. Band 2: L. Kohlbergs Theorie des moralischen Begründens*. Frankfurt: Peter Lang GmbH.

Spigel, L. 1992. *Make room for TV. Television and the family ideal in postwar America*. Chicago: Chicago University Press.

Spitz, H.H. 1982. Intellectual extremes, mental age and the nature of human intelligence. *Merrill-Palmer Quarterly* **28**, 167–92.

Spradlin, J. 1963. Language and communication of mental defectives. In Ellis, N. (ed.) *Handbook of mental deficiency: psychological theory and research*. New York: McGraw-Hill, 512–55.

Spurgin, M., and Zentall, S.S. 1995. Contributing factors in the manifestation of aggression in preschoolers with hyperactivity. *Journal of Child Psychology and Psychiatry* **36**, 491–509.

Sroufe, L.A. 1986. Bowlby's contribution to psychoanalytic theory and developmental psychology. *Journal of Child Psychology and Psychiatry* **27**, 841–9.

Sroufe, L.A., Rutter, M. 1984. The domain of developmental psychopathology. *Child Development* **55**, 17–29.

St Peters, M., Fitch, M., Huston, A.C., Wright, J.C., Eakins, D.J. 1991. Television and families: what do young children watch with their parents. *Child Development* **62**, 1409–23.

St. Pierre, E. 1997. Guest editorial: an introduction to figurations – a post-structural practice of inquiry. *International Journal of Qualitative Studies in Education* **10**, 279–84.

Stanovich, K.E. 1988. Explaining the differences between the dyslexic and the garden-variety poor reader: the phonological-core variable-difference model. *Journal of Learning Disabilities* **21**, 590–612.

Stattin, H., Klackenberg, G. 1991. Family discord in adolescence in the light of family discord in childhood. Paper presented at the Conference Youth-TM. Utrecht.

Steele, H., Steele, M. 1998. Psychoanalysis and attachment: time for a reunion. *Social Development* **7**, 92–119.

Stegge, H. 1995. Mood dependent social judgements in children. Unpublished dissertation. Amsterdam: Free University.

Stephens, B., Grube, C. 1982. Development of Piagetian reasoning in congenitally blind children. *Journal of Visual Impairment and Blindness* **76**, 133–43.

Stephenson, P., Smith, D. 1989. Bullying in the junior school. In Tattum, D.P., Lane, D.A. (eds) *Bullying in schools*. Stoke-on-Trent: Trentham Books, 45–57.

Stern, D.N. 1974. Mother and infant at play: the dyadic interaction involving facial, vocal and gaze behaviours. In Lewis, M., Rosenblum, L.A. (eds) *The effect of the infant on its caregiver*. New York: Wiley,

Stern, D.N. 1985. *The interpersonal world of the infant: a view from psycho-analysis and developmental psychology*. New York: Basic Books.

Stern, D.N., Spieker, S., MacKain, K. 1982. Intonation contours as signals in maternal speech to prelinguistic infants. *Developmental Psychology* **18**, 727–35.

Stern, W. 1912. *Die psychologische methoden der intelligenzprufung*. Leipzig:

Sternberg, J.D. 1988. *The triarchic mind: a new psychology of human intelligence*. New York: Viking.

Sternberg, R.J. 1983. Components of human intelligence. *Cognition* **15**, 1–48.

Stevens, R. 1996. A humanistic approach to relationships. In Miell, D., Dallos, R. (eds) *Social interaction and personal relationships*. London: Sage, pp. 357–66.

Sticht, T.G. 1972. Learning by listening. In Freedle, R.O., Carroll, J.B. (eds) *Language comprehension and the acquisition of knowledge*. Washington, DC: Winston.

Stiles, J., Thal, D. 1993. Linguistic and spatial cognitive development following early focal brain injury: patterns of deficit and recovery. In Johnson, M.H. (ed.), *Brain development and cognition: a reader*, Oxford: Blackwell, 643–64.

Stormshak, E.A., Bellanti, C.J., Bierman, K.L. 1996. The quality of sibling relationships and the development of social competence and behavioral control in aggressvie children. *Developmental Psychology* **32**, 79–89.

Suchman, L.A. 1987. *Plans and situated actions*. Cambridge: Cambridge University Press.

Sunohara, G., Barr, C.L., Jin, U., Schachar, R., Roberts, W., Tannock, R. et al. 1997. Is the dopamine D4 receptor gene associated with children and adults with attention-deficit/hyperactivity disorder? *American Journal of Medical Genetics (Neuropsychiatric Genetics)* **74**, 629.

Suomi, S.J. 1995. Influence of attachment theory on ethological studies of biobehavioral development in nonhuman primates. In Goldberg, S., Muir, R., Kerr, J. (eds) *Attachment theory: historical, developmental and clinical significance*. Hillsdale, NJ: Analytic Press, 185–202.

Surgeon General's Report 1972. *Television and growing up: the impact of televised violence*. Washington, DC: United States Government Printing Office.

Sutton, J., Smith, P.K., Swettenham, J. 1997. *'Cold cognition' in bullying*. Paper presented at the British Psychological Society Developmental Section Annual Conference, Loughborough University. September, 12–15.

Sutton, J., Smith, P.K., Swettenham, J. in press. Bullying and 'theory of mind': a critique of the 'social skills deficit' view of anti-social behaviour. *Social Development*.

Sutton, J., and Smith, P.K. in press. Bullying as a group process: an adaptation of the participant role approach. *Aggressive Behaviour*.

Swisher, M.V. 1984. Signed input of hearing mothers to deaf children. *Language Learning* **34**, 69–85.

Sylvester-Bradley, B., Trearthen, C.B. 1978. Baby-talk as an adaptation to the infant's communication. In Waterson, N., Snow, C.E. (eds) *The development of communication*, New York: Wiley, 75–92.

Tager-Flusberg, H. 1985. The conceptual basis for referential word meaning in children with autism. *Child Development* **56**, 1167–78.

Tager-Flusberg, H. 1991. Semantic processing in the free recall of autistic children: further evidence for a cognitive deficit. *British Journal of Developmental Psychology* **9**, 417–30.

Tager-Flusberg, H., Sullivan, K. 1995. Attributing mental states to story characters: a comparison of narratives produced by autistic and mentally retarded individuals. *Applied Psycholinguistics* **16**, 241–56.

Tajfel, H. 1978. *Differentiation between social groups*. London: Academic Press.

Tajfel, H. 1981. *Human groups and social categories*. Cambridge: Cambridge University Press.

Takahashi, K. 1990. Are the key assumptions of the 'Strange Situation' procedure universal? A view from Japanese research. *Human Development* **33**, 23–30.

Tallal, P., Miller, S.L., Bedi, G., Byma, G., Wang, X., Nagarajan, S.J. et al. 1996. Language comprehension in language-learning impaired children improved with acoustically modified speech. *Science* **271**. 81–4.

Tantam, D. 1991. Asperger syndrome in adulthood. In Frith, U. (ed.) *Autism and Asperger syndrome.* Cambridge: Cambridge University Press, 147–83.

Tattum, D. 1993. *Understanding and managing bullying.* Heinemann.

Taylor, J., Laurillard, D. 1995. Supporting resource based learning. In Heap, N., Thomas, R., Einon, G., Mason, R., Mackay, H. (eds) *Information technology and society.* London: Sage.

Taylor, M., Bacharach, V. 1982. Constraints on the visual accuracy of drawings produced by young children. *Journal of Experimental Child Psychology* **34**, 311–29.

Temple, C., Carney, R., Mullarkey, S. 1996. Frontal-lobe function and executive skills in children with Turner's syndrome. *Developmental Neuropsychology* **12**, 343–63.

Teo, T., Becker, G., Edelstein, W. 1995. *Variability in structured wholeness: context factors in L. Kohlberg's data on the development of moral judgment.* Manuscript submitted for publication.

Thapar, A., Hervas, A., McGuffin, P. 1995. Childhood hyperactivity scores are highly heritable and show sibling competition effects: twin study evidence. *Behaviour Genetics* **25**, 537–44.

Thomas, E.L., Robinson, H.A. 1972. *Improving reading in every class: a sourcebook for teachers.* Boston, MA: Allyn and Bacon.

Thomas, G.V., Silk, A.M.J. 1990. *An introduction to the psychology of children's drawings.* New York: Harvester Wheatsheaf.

Thurstone, L.L. 1938. *Primary mental abilities.* Chicago, IL: University of Chicago Press.

Tiffin, J., Rajasingham, L. 1995. *In search of the virtual class.* London: Routledge.

Timme, S.G., Eccles, J., O'Brien, K. 1985. How children use time. In Juster, F.T., Stafford, F.P, (eds), *Time, goods and well-being.* Ann Arbor: Institute for Social Research, University of Michigan.

Tizard, B., Hughes, M. 1984. *Young children learning: talking and thinking at home and school.* London: Fontana.

Tizard, B., Phoenix, A. 1993. *Black, white or mixed race? Race and racism in the lives of young people of mixed-parentage.* London: Routledge.

Todman, J. and Seedhouse, E. 1994. Visual-action code processing by deaf and hearing children. *Language and Cognitive Processes* **9**, 129–41.

Tomasello, M., Kruger, A.C., Ratner, H.H. 1993. Cultural learning. *Behavior and Brain Sciences* **16**, 495–552.

Tomasello, M., Farrar, J. 1986. Joint attention and early language. *Child Development,* **57**, 1454–63.

Tomasello, M., Kruger, A.C. 1992. Joint attention on actions: acquiring verbs in ostensive and non-ostensive contexts. *Journal of Child Language* **19**, 311–33.

Toogood, S., Timlin, K. 1996. The functional assessment of challenging behaviour; a comparison of informant based, experimental and descriptive methods. *Journal of Applied Research in Intellectual Disabilities* **9**, 206–22.

Trevarthen, C. 1979. Communication and co-operation in early infancy: a description of primary inter subjectivity. In Bullowa, M. (ed.) Before Speech Cambridge: Cambridge University Press, 321–49.

Trevarthen, C. 1993. The function of emotions in early infant communication and development. In Nadel, J., Camaioni, L. (eds) *New perspectives in early communicative development*. London: Routledge,

Trivers, R.L. 1974. Parent-offspring conflict. *American Zoologist* **14**, 249–64.

Tronick, E.Z., Giannino, A.F. 1987. The transmission of maternal disturbance to the infant. In Tronick, E.Z., Field, T. (eds) *Maternal depression and infant disturbance*. San Francisco: Jossey-Bass.

Troster, H., Brambring, M. 1994. The play behavior and play materials of blind and sighted infants and preschoolers. *Journal of Visual Impairment & Blindness* **88**, 421–82.

Troyna, B., Hatcher, R. 1992. *Racism in children's lives: a study of mainly-white primary schools*. London: Routledge.

Turiel, E. 1983. *The development of social knowledge: morality and convention*. Cambridge: Cambridge University Press.

Turkle, S. 1994. Paradoxical reactions and powerful ideas: Educational computing in a Department of Physics. In Barrett, R. (ed.) *Sociomedia*. Cambridge, MA: MIT Press.

Turkle, S. 1996. *Life on the screen*. London: Weidenfield and Nicolson.

Tyson, P., Tyson, R.L. 1990. *Psychoanalytic theories of development: an integration*. New Haven: Yale University Press.

Udwin, O., Martin, N. 1987. Cognitive abilities and behavioural characteristics of children with idiopathic infantile, hypercalcaemia. *Journal of Child Psychology and Psychiatry* **28**, 297–309.

Ullah, P. 1985. Second generation Irish youth; identity and ethnicity. *New Community* **12**, 310–20.

Ullah, P. 1990. Rhetoric and ideology in social identification: the case of second generation Irish youths. *Discourse and Society* **1**, 167–88.

Underwood, G., Batt, V. 1996. *Reading and Understanding*. An introduction to the psychology of reading. Oxford: Blackwell.

Underwood, G., Everatt, J. 1992. The role of eye movements in reading: some limitations of the eye-mind assumption. In Chekaluk, E., Llewellyn, K.R. (eds) *The role of eye movements in perceptual processes*. Amsterdam: Elsevier.

Underwood, M.K., Cole, J.D., Herbsman, C.R. 1992. Display rules for anger and aggression in school-age children. *Child Development*, **63**, 366–80.

Valian, V. 1990. Null subjects: a problem for parameter-setting models of language acquisition. *Cognition* **35**, 105–22.

Valian, V. 1993. Parser failure and grammar change. *Cognition* **46**, 195–202.

van Bourgondien, M.E., Mesibov, G.B. 1989. Diagnosis and treatment of adoloscents and adults with autism. In Dawson, G. (ed.) *Autism: nature diagnosis and treatment*. New York: Guilford Press, 367–85.

van Dijk, T. 1987. *Communicating racism: ethnic prejudice in thought and talk*. London: Sage.

van Dijk, T. 1993. *Elite discourse and racism*. London: Sage.

van IJzendoorn , M.H., De Wolff, M.S. 1997. In search of the absent father: meta analyses of infant father attachment: a rejoinder to our discussants. *Child Development* **68**, 604–9.

van IJzendoorn , M.H., Goldberg, S., Kroonenberg, P.M., Frenkel, O.J. 1992. The relative effects of maternal and child problems on the quality of attachment: A meta-analysis of attachment in clinical-samples. *Child Development* **63**, 840–58.

van IJzendoorn , M.H., Juffer, F., Duyvesteyn, M.G.C. 1995. Breaking the intergenerational cycle of insecure attachment: a review of the effects of attachment-based interventions on maternal sensitivity and infant security. *Journal of Child Psychology, Psychiatry and Allied Disciplines* **36**, 225–48.

van IJzendoorn , M.H., Kroonenberg, P.M. 1988. Cross-cultural patterns of attachment: a meta-analysis of the strange situation. *Child Development* **59**, 147–56.

van Sommers, P. 1984. *Drawing and cognition: descriptive and experimental studies of graphic production processes*. Cambridge: Cambridge University Press.

Varnhagen, C.K., Das, J.P., Varnhagen, S. 1987. Auditory and visual memory span: cognitive processing by TMR individuals with Down syndrome or other etiologies. *American Journal of Mental Deficiency* **91**, 398–405.

Vereijken, C.M. 1996. *The mother–infant relationship in Japan: attachment, dependency and amae*. Capelle a/d IJssel: Labyrint Publication.

Vitaro, F., Gendreau, P.L., Tremblay, R.E., and Oligny, P. 1998. Reactive and proactive aggression differentially predict later conduct problems. *Journal of Child Psychology and Psychiatry* **39**, 377–85.

Volkmar, F.R. 1996. Brief report: diagnostic issues in autism: results of the DSM-IV field trial. *Journal of Autism and Developmental Disorders* **26**, 155–7.

Volterra, V., Erting, C.J. 1990. *From gesture to spoken language in hearing and deaf children*. Berlin: Springer-Verlag.

von Tetzchner, S., Martinsen, H. 1992. *An introduction to sign teaching and the use of communication aids*. London: Whurr.

von Tetzchner, S., Rogne, S.O., Lilleng, M.K. 1997. Literacy intervention for a deaf child with severe reading disorder. *Journal of Literacy Research* **29**, 25–46.

Vostanis, P., Hayes, M., DuFeu, M., Warren, J. 1997. Detection of behavioural and emotional problems in deaf children and adolescents: comparison of two rating scales. *Child Care Health and Development* **23**, 233–46.

Vygotsky, L.S. 1978. *Mind and society*. Cambridge: Harvard University Press.

Wagenaar, W.A. 1986. My memory: a study of autobiographical memory over six years. *Cognitive Psychology* **18**, 225–52.

Walker, L.J. 1984. Sex differences in the development of moral reasoning: a critical review. *Child Development* **55**, 667–91.

Walker, L.J., de Vries, B. 1985. Moral stages/moral orientations: do the sexes really differ? In Blake, C. (Chair) *Gender difference research in moral development*. Symposium conducted at the meeting of the American Psychological Association, Los Angeles. In Walker, L.J. 1986a. Sex differences in the development of moral reasoning. A rejoinder to Baumrind. *Child Development* **57**, 511–21.

Walkerdine, V. 1993. 'Daddy's gonna buy you a dream to cling to and mummy's gonna love you just as much as she can': young girls and popular television. In Buckingham, D. (ed.) *Reading audience*. Manchester: Manchester University Press.

Wallace, I.F., Gravel, J.S., Schwartz, R.G., Ruben, R.G. 1996. Otitis media, communication style of primary caregivers and language skills of two year olds, preliminary report. *Journal of Developmental and Behavioural Pediatrics* **17**, 29–35.

Warren, D. 1994. *Blindness and children: an individual differences approach*. Cambridge: Cambridge University Press.

Waterhouse, L., Morris, R., Allen, D., Dunn, M., Fein, D., Feinstein, C., Rapin, I., Wing, L. 1996. Diagnosis and classification in autism. *Journal of Autism and Developmental Disorders* **26**, 59–86.

Waters, E., Merrick, S.K., Albersheim, L., Treboux, D. 1995. From the Strange Situation to the Adult Attachment Interview: a 20-year longitudinal study of attachment security in infancy and early childhood. In Crowell, J.A., Waters, E. (Chairs) *Is the parent-child relationship a prototype of later love relationships? Studies of attachment and working models of attachment*. Symposium conducted at the biennial meeting of the Society for Research in Child Development, Indianapolis, Indiana, April.

Watson, J.B., Rayner, R. 1920. Conditioned emotional reactions. *Journal of Experimental Psychology* **3**, 1–14.

Webster, A. 1986. Deafness, development and literacy. Methuen: London.

Webster, A., Roe, J. 1998. *Children with visual impairments: social interaction, language and learning*. London: Routledge.

Weekes, D. 1997. Understanding young Black female subjectivity. Unpublished Ph.D. thesis: Department of Social Sciences, Nottingham Trent University.

Weinreich-Haste, H. 1982. Piaget on morality: a critical perspective. In Modgil, S., Modgil, C. (eds) *Jean Piaget. Consensus and controversy*. London: Holt, Rinehart and Winston, 181–206.

Weisman, J., Brosgole, L. 1994. Facial affect recognition in singly diagnosed mentally retarded people and normal young children: a methodological comparison. *International Journal of Neuroscience* **75**, 45–55.

Weiss, B., Weisz, J.R., Bromfield, R. 1986. Performance of retarded and non-retarded persons on information processing tasks: further tests of the similar structure hypothesis. *Psychological Bulletin* **100**, 157–75.

Weiss, P. 1982. *Psychogenetik: humangenetik in psychologie and psychiatrie*. Jena: Fischer.

Weisz, J. 1978. Transcontextual validity in developmental research. *Child Development* **49**, 1–12.

Weisz, J., Yeates, K.O. 1981. Cognitive development in retarded and non-retarded persons: Piagetian test of the similar structure hypothesis. *Psychological Bulletin* **90**, 153–78.

Weisz, J., Yeates, K.O., Zigler, E. 1982. Piagetian evidence and the developmental-difference controversy. In Zigler, E., Balla, D. (eds) *Mental retardation: the developmental–difference controversy*. Hillsdale, NJ: Erlbaum.

Weisz, J., Zigler, E. 1979. Cognitive development in retarded and nonretarded persons: Piagetian tests of the similar structure hypothesis. *Psychological Bulletin* **86**, 831–51.

Wellman, H. 1990. *The child's theory of mind*. Cambridge MA: MIT Press.

Werker, J.F., Tees, R.C. 1984. Cross-language speech perception: evidence for perceptual reorganization during the first year of life. *Infant Behaviour and Development* **7**, 49–63.

Werner, E.E., Smith, R.S. 1981. *Vulnerable, but invincible*. New York: MacGraw-Hill.

Wertsch, J.V. 1991. *Voices of the mind: a sociocultural approach to mediated action*. Cambridge, MA : Harvard University Press.

Westwood, S. 1990. Racism, Black masculinity and the politics of space. In Hearn, J., Morgan, D. (eds) *Men, masculinities and social theory*. London: Unwin Hyman, pp. 55–71.

Wetherell, M. 1995. Social structure, ideology and family dynamics: the case of parenting. In Muncie, J., Wetherell, M., Dallos, R., Cochrane, A. (eds) *Understanding the family*. London: Sage/Open University Press, pp 257–94.

Wetherell, M. 1996. Life histories/social histories. In Wetherell, M. (ed.) *Identities, groups and social issues*. London: Sage/Open University, pp. 299–361.

Wetherell, M., Potter, J. 1992. *Mapping the language of racism: discourse and the legitimation of exploitation*. London: Harvester Wheatsheaf.

White, D., Woollett, A. 1992. *Families: a context for development*. London: Falmer.

Whitney, I., Smith, P.K. 1993. A survey of the nature and extent of bullying in junior/middle and secondary schools. *Educational Research* **35**, 3–25.

Whitney, I., Smith, P.K., Thompson, P. 1994. Bullying and children with special educational needs. In Smith, P.K. and Sharp, S. (eds) *School bullying: insights and perspectives*. London: Routledge,

Wight, D. 1992. Impediments to safer heterosexual sex: a review of research with young people. *AIDSCARE* **4**, 1, 11–25.

Wilcox, T., Nadel, L., Rosser, R. 1996. Location memory in healthy preterm and full-term infants. *Infant Behavior and Development* **19**, 309–24.

Willats, J. 1997. *Art and representation: new principles in the analysis of pictures*. Princeton, NJ: Princeton University Press.

Williams, K., Chambers, M., Logan, S., Robinson, D. 1996. Association of common health symptoms with bullying in primary school children. *British Medical Journal* **313**, 17–19.

Williams, P. 1997. The emperor's new clothes. Lecture 1 in the 1997 Reith Lectures 'The genealogy of race: towards a theory of grace'. BBC Radio 4. Reprinted in *Seeing a color-blind future: the paradox of race*. London: Virago.

Williams, T.M., Handford, A.G. 1986. Television and other leisure activities. In Williams, T. (ed.) *The impact of television: a natural experiment in three communities*. London: Academic Press.

Wilson, B. 1984. The artistic tower of Babel: inextricable links between culture and graphic development. *Visual Arts Research* **11**, 90–104.

Wilson, R.S. 1983. The Louisville twin study: developmental synchronies in behaviour. *Child Development* **54**, 298–316.

Wing, L. 1988. The continuum of autistic characteristics. In Schopler, E., Mesibov, G. (eds) *Diagnosis and assessment in autism*. New York: Plenum Press, 91–107.

Wing, L. 1997. The history of ideas on autism: legends, myths and reality. *Autism: The International Journal of Research and Practice* **1**, 13–23.

Wing, L., Gould, J. 1979. Severe impairments of social interaction and associated abnormalities in children: epidemiology and classification. *Journal of Autism and Developmental Disorders* **9**, 11–29.

Winner, E. 1996. The rage to master: the decisive role of talent in the visual arts. In Ericsson, K.A. (ed.) *The road to excellence*. Hillsdale, NJ: Lawrence Erlbaum Associates.

Winnicott, D.W. 1965. *The maturational processes and the facilitating environment*. London: Hogarth Press.

Winnicott, D.W. 1967. Mirror role of mother and family in child development. In Lomas, P. (ed.) *The predicament of the family*. London: Hogarth Press,

Wishart, J. 1993. The development of learning difficulties in children with Down's syndrome. *Journal of Intellectual Disabilities Research* **37**, 389–403.

Wissler, C. 1901. The correlation of mental and physical tests. *Psychological*

Witkin, H. 1964. Heinz Werner: 1890–1964. *Human Development* **30**, 307–28.

Wolff, P. 1987. *The development of behavioral states and the expression of emotions in early infancy*. Chicago, IL: University of Chicago Press.

Wolff, P.H., Matsumiya, Y., Abroms, I.F., Van Velzar, C., Lombroso, C.T. 1974. The effect of white noise on the somatosensory evoked response in sleeping newborn infants. *Electroencephalography and Clinical Neurophysiology* **37**, 269–74.

Wolke, D., Schulz, H. 1997. Bullying bei Grundschulkindern: Prävalenz, Schulfaktoren und Täter-Opfer Charakteristiken. In Glück, J. (ed.) *13. Tagung Entwicklungspsychologie: Kurzfassungen*. Wien: Abtlg. fuer Entwicklungspsychologie und Pädagogische Psychologie, Institut für Psychologie, 320.

Wolffe, K., Sacks, S. 1997. The lifestyles of blind, low vision and sighted youths: a quantitative comparison. *Journal of Visual Impairment and Blindness* **91**, 245–57.

Wood, D., Wood, H., Griffiths, A., Howarth, I. 1986. *Teaching and talking with deaf children*. London: Wiley.

Wood, D.J., Bruner, J.S., Ross, G. 1978. The role of tutoring in problem solving. *Journal of Child Psychology and Psychiatry* **17**, 89–100.

Wood, W., Wong, F.Y., Chachere, J.G. 1991. Effects of media violence on viewers' aggression in unconstrained social interaction. *Psychological Bulletin* **109**, 371–83.

Woollett, A., Phoenix, A. 1991. Psychological views of mothering. In Phoenix, A., Woollett, A., Lloyd, E. (eds) *Motherhood: meanings, practices and ideologies*. London: Sage, pp 28–46.

Woollett, A., Phoenix, A. 1996. Motherhood as pedagogy: developmental psychology and the accounts of mothers of young children. In Luke, C. (ed.) *Feminisms and pedagogies of everyday life*. NY: State University of New York Press, pp 80–102.

World Federation of Neurology. 1968. *Report of research group on dyslexia and world illiteracy*. Dallas, TX: WFN.

World Health Organization 1990. *Mental disorders: a glossary and guide to their classification in accordance with the 10th revision of the International Classification of Diseases (ICD -10)*. Geneva: World Health Organization.

Wright, D.S. 1982. 'The Moral Judgment of the Child' revisited. In Locke, D., Weinreich-Haste, H. (eds) *Moral judgment and moral action*. London: Wiley.

Wyness, M. 1994. Keeping tabs on an uncivil society. *Sociology* **28**, 193–209.

Yates, C., Smith, P.K. 1989. Bullying in two English comprehensive schools. In Roland, E., Munthe, E. (eds) *Bullying: an international perspective*. London: David Fulton, 22–34.

Young, R.L., Nettelbeck, T. 1994. The 'intelligence' of calendrical calculators. *American Journal of Intellectual Disabilities* **99**, 186–200.

Zeaman, D., House, B.J. 1963. The role of attention and retardate discriminate learning. In Ellis, N.R. (ed.) *Handbook of Mental Deficiency*. New York: McGraw Hill.

Zeaman, D., House, B.J. 1979. A review of attention theory. In Ellis, N.R. (ed.) *Handbook of Mental Deficiency, Psychological Theory and Research*. Hillsdale, NJ: Erlbaum.

Zhi, Z., Thomas, G.V., Robinson, E.J. 1997. Contraints on representational change: drawing a man with two heads. *British Journal of Developmental Psychology* **15**, 275–90.

Zigler, E. 1969. Developmental versus difference theories of retardation and the problem of motivation. *American Journal of Mental Deficiency* **73**, 536–56.

Zigler, E. 1984. A developmental theory on mental retardation. In Blatt, B. Morris, R. (eds) *Perspectives in special education: personal orientations*. Santa Monica, CA: Scott, Foresman.

Zimmermann, P., Fremmer-Bombik, E., Spangler, G., Grossmann, K.E. 1995. Attachment in adolescence: a longitudinal perspective. Poster presented at the biennial meeting of the Society for Research in Child Development, Indianapolis, Indiana.

Zinnecker, J. 1991. Jugend als Bildungsmoratorium. In Melzer, W., Heitmeyer, W., Liegle, L. Zinnecker, J. (eds) *Osteuropäische Jugend im Wandel*. Weinheim: Juventa 1991.

Zinnecker, J. 1992. Deutsche Jugend heute. In Jugendwerk der Deutschen Shell (ed.) *Jugend '92*. Vol. 3. Opladen: Leske + Budrich.

Zweibel, A. 1987. More on the effects of early manual communication on the cognitive development of deaf children. *American Annals of the Deaf*, **132**, 16–20.

Subject index

Author index